AF794451

Fuzzy Logic in Computational Intelligence

Scrivener Publishing
100 Cummings Center, Suite 541J
Beverly, MA 01915-6106

Advances in Learning Analytics for Intelligent Cloud-IoT Systems

Series Editors: Dr. Souvik Pal (souvikpal22@gmail.com) and
Dr. Dac-Nhuong Le (nhuongld@hus.edu.vn)

The role of adaptation, learning analytics, computational Intelligence, and data analytics in the field of Cloud-IoT Systems is becoming increasingly essential and intertwined. The capability of an intelligent system depends on various self-decision making algorithms in IoT Devices. IoT based smart systems generate a large amount of data (big data) that cannot be processed by traditional data processing algorithms and applications. Hence, this book series involves different computational methods incorporated within the system with the help of Analytics Reasoning and Sense-making in Big Data, which is centered in the Cloud and IoT-enabled environments.

Publishers at Scrivener
Martin Scrivener (martin@scrivenerpublishing.com)
Phillip Carmical (pcarmical@scrivenerpublishing.com)

Fuzzy Logic in Computational Intelligence

Applications and Case Studies

Edited by

Rahul Kar

Faculty of Mathematics, Kalyani Mahavidyalaya, Kalyani, West Bengal, India

Gunjan Mukherjee

Department of Computational Sciences, Brainware University, Kolkata, India

Biswadip Basu Mallik

Department of Basic Science and Humanities, Institute of Engineering & Management, University of Engineering and Management, Kolkata, India

and

Ashok Kumar Shaw

Budge Budge Institute of Technology, Kolkata, India

Scrivener Publishing

WILEY

This edition first published 2026 by John Wiley & Sons, Inc., 111 River Street, Hoboken, NJ 07030, USA and Scrivener Publishing LLC, 100 Cummings Center, Suite 541J, Beverly, MA 01915, USA
© 2026 Scrivener Publishing LLC
For more information about Scrivener publications please visit www.scrivenerpublishing.com.

All rights reserved. No part of this publication may be reproduced, stored in a retrieval system, or transmitted, in any form or by any means, electronic, mechanical, photocopying, recording, or otherwise, except as permitted by law. Advice on how to obtain permission to reuse material from this title is available at http://www.wiley.com/go/permissions.

Wiley Global Headquarters
111 River Street, Hoboken, NJ 07030, USA

For details of our global editorial offices, customer services, and more information about Wiley products visit us at www.wiley.com.

The manufacturer' s authorized representative according to the EU General Product Safety Regulation is Wiley-VCH GmbH, Boschstr. 12, 69469 Weinheim, Germany, e-mail: Product_Safety@wiley.com

Limit of Liability/Disclaimer of Warranty
While the publisher and authors have used their best efforts in preparing this work, they make no representations or warranties with respect to the accuracy or completeness of the contents of this work and specifically disclaim all warranties, including without limitation any implied warranties of merchantability or fitness for a particular purpose. No warranty may be created or extended by sales representatives, written sales materials, or promotional statements for this work. The fact that an organization, website, or product is referred to in this work as a citation and/or potential source of further information does not mean that the publisher and authors endorse the information or services the organization, website, or product may provide or recommendations it may make. This work is sold with the understanding that the publisher is not engaged in rendering professional services. The advice and strategies contained herein may not be suitable for your situation. You should consult with a specialist where appropriate. Neither the publisher nor authors shall be liable for any loss of profit or any other commercial damages, including but not limited to special, incidental, consequential, or other damages. Further, readers should be aware that websites listed in this work may have changed or disappeared between when this work was written and when it is read.

Library of Congress Cataloging-in-Publication Data

ISBN 978-1-394-34566-3

Cover image: Generated with AI using Adobe Firefly
Cover design by Russell Richardson

Set in size of 11pt and Minion Pro by Manila Typesetting Company, Makati, Philippines

Printed in the USA

10 9 8 7 6 5 4 3 2 1

Contents

Part 4: Fuzzy Optimization 231

Preface

This book is a comprehensive exploration of the principles, applications, and advancements of fuzzy logic within the domain of computational intelligence. It has been meticulously compiled through the inclusion of high-quality chapters based on pioneering research conducted by eminent scholars. The volume examines both the theoretical foundations and practical implementations of fuzzy logic, highlighting its unique ability to address uncertainty and imprecision in computational systems.

Designed to serve as a resource for a diverse audience, including students, researchers, and industry professionals, this book offers a systematic understanding of fuzzy logic's role in enhancing computational intelligence. By bridging the gap between theoretical constructs and practical applications, it provides invaluable insights into how fuzzy logic facilitates problem-solving in real-world scenarios.

Fuzzy logic is based on the principles of uncertainty and has applications across a wide range of predictive and probabilistic environments. From agriculture to healthcare and numerous other sectors, fuzzy logic can be utilized to develop innovative and effective solutions.

The book starts with a solid introduction to fuzzy logic, focusing on its foundational concepts and theories. Readers will gain a clear understanding of how fuzzy logic mimics human reasoning, enabling computational systems to process vagueness and ambiguity effectively. The discussion then transitions into real-world applications, demonstrating the integration of fuzzy logic into various computational intelligence domains, including decision-making, pattern recognition, and control systems.

Throughout its chapters, the book highlights the versatility of fuzzy logic in addressing complex problems across diverse industries. It provides in-depth analyses of fuzzy logic–based applications and demonstrates how these approaches can contribute to the development of robust predictive models with improved inference capabilities.

Machine learning has emerged as a transformative force in modern research, and the integration of fuzzy logic with machine learning techniques has shown significant promise in improving accuracy and precision. This synergy is explored extensively throughout the book.

In later sections, the book examines advanced topics, including Type-2 fuzzy logic and intuitionistic fuzzy logic, which address the limitations of traditional fuzzy systems. These enhanced models demonstrate strong adaptability and performance in classification, prediction, and optimization tasks. Readers are introduced to cutting-edge research and applications ranging from stock market analysis and information retrieval to metaheuristic techniques and ensemble learning models.

The book also explores fuzzy logic applications in image processing, emphasizing algorithmic approaches and practical implementations within this important domain.

The preface concludes with a forward-looking perspective, exploring future directions at the intersection of fuzzy logic and computational intelligence. By presenting case studies drawn from social, economic, and technical domains, the book highlights the practical implications of fuzzy logic and its potential to inspire innovative solutions to contemporary challenges in image processing, machine learning, and artificial intelligence.

The volume has been carefully structured to serve readers from diverse backgrounds, offering clear explanations for beginners alongside in-depth discussions for experienced professionals. By combining theoretical depth with practical insights, it serves as both a valuable reference and a catalyst for further research and innovation in this dynamic field.

We invite readers to embark on this journey into the fascinating world of fuzzy logic and discover its transformative impact on computational intelligence. We are indebted to all the contributors for their invaluable contribution with qualitative research inputs. Finally, we extend our gratitude to Martin Scrivener and the team at Scrivener Publishing for their effort and guidance in bringing this work to publication.

The Editors

Part 1

INTRODUCTION TO FUZZY LOGIC

1

Flood Prediction Using Fuzzy Logic in Computational Intelligence: Applications and Insights

Jyotirmoy Sau[1], Anwesha Das[2] and Gunjan Mukherjee[3]*

[1]*Department of Condensed Matter Physics and Material Science, S. N. Bose National Centre for Basic Sciences, Salt Lake, Kolkata, India*
[2]*Department of Information Technology, RCC Institute of Information Technology, Canal S Rd, Beleghata, West Bengal, Kolkata, India*
[3]*Department of Computational Sciences, Brainware University, Kolkata, India*

Abstract

Flood prediction plays a crucial role in agricultural planning and disaster management, particularly in regions where crop irrigation heavily relies on rainwater. Traditional approaches to prediction, based on classical logic, often struggle to effectively handle the inherent uncertainties in weather forecasting or prediction with considerable amount of error. This paper advocates for the adoption of soft computing approach based on the fuzzy logic—a logical system that extends beyond binary outcomes to accommodate degrees of truth—as a promising alternative for rainfall prediction. By leveraging linguistic rules and fuzzy membership functions coupled with the inference laws, an expert system model has been developed to map input variables, such as temperature, humidity, air pressure and wind speed to the production of the output variables representing likelihood of rainfall. The study emphasizes the importance of effective planning in mitigating impact of natural disasters, such as flood and drought, underscoring the value of accurate rainfall forecasts in decision-making. Employing of the Mamdani method, the research provides a methodological framework for processing input variables and generating actionable insights for stakeholders in agriculture, meteorology, and disaster management. In our model, we initially considered four fuzzy variables: Temperature, Wind Speed, Atmospheric Pressure, and Humidity. Our findings indicated that the amount of rainfall is most influenced by temperature, humidity,

**Corresponding author*: mukherjee.gunjan@gmail.com

Rahul Kar, Gunjan Mukherjee, Biswadip Basu Mallik and Ashok Kumar Shaw (eds.) Fuzzy Logic in Computational Intelligence: Applications and Case Studies, (3–20) © 2026 Scrivener Publishing LLC

and wind speed. Our results match well with real-world data. It has been observed that the improvement for accuracy of any classification model depends on some tunable hyper parameters. In this paper the PSO based optimization approach has been utilized for scaling up the accuracy of fuzzy model to potentially high value. Ultimately, this paper highlights the transformative potential of fuzzy logic in enhancing the accuracy and reliability of rainfall prediction, enabling proactive planning in the face of increasingly erratic weather patterns.

Keywords: Fuzzy logic, rain prediction using artificial intelligence

1.1 Introduction

One of the most significant and difficult operational duties performed by meteorological services globally is weather forecasting. It's an intricate process involving many different specialized technological domains since all judgments in the field of meteorology are made in the face of ambiguity surrounding weather systems, the task is difficult. Rainfall is the weather phenomenon that is most essential to human life. The primary driver of daily precipitation events [1] will be the variability of the weather and other climatic elements, particularly those atmospheric parameters. Daily rainfall prediction is very much possible if the variability pattern [2] could be identified and used for future trajectory. Temperature and rainfall are significant climatic inputs in the context of climate variability, according to Nasher [3]. More research is currently being done on climate indices like rainfall, temperature, and so forth because of a rapid climatic oscillation. Since neglecting to plan is equivalent to planning for failure, planning has been highlighted as a roadmap to success. Future event information is essential for effective and efficient planning leading to the avoidance of a natural disaster, such as flooding, drought, etc. Predicting future events is essential in this context [10]. Predicting rainfall over an extended period of time is crucial for nations that depend heavily on agriculture. In an effort to find novel approaches for forecasting significant meteorological variables, scientists have created and refined strategies like intelligent methods—practical and adaptable approaches that are not dependent on system dynamic models. One of the meteorological processes that meteorologists are trying to forecast more precisely is rainfall which can happen abruptly.

Although a variety of models, including statistical models, have been used for years to predict rainfall, they have numerous shortcomings [4]. One of the disadvantages of statistical modeling is that it typically relies on a number of implicit assumptions about the system. Given how quickly meteorology technology is developing, it would be ideal to combine the knowledge of numerous forecasters with algorithms that could help in challenging predicting scenarios. According to Jang *et al.* [28], cognitive computing is an emerging class of problem solving algorithms that aims to mimic natural problem solving strategies. Fuzzy logic is one of the examples of this. Fuzzy logic [5, 6] is a straightforward but effective method for solving problems with a wide range of applications. Christian *et al.* [29] demonstrated the accuracy and amenability to fuzzy logic of the culturally constructed indigenous climate knowledge of extreme climatic events. In contrast to a fuzzy image in intermediate climatic conditions, farmers clearly associate extreme rainfall values with drought or heavy rainfall episodes. This demonstrates the fuzzy logic nature of indigenous climatic knowledge. A technique for simulating the type of uncertainty related to impression, vagueness, and/or lack of knowledge on a specific aspect of the issue at hand is fuzzy set theory [7]. The fuzzy logic model created by Agboola *et al.* [30] consists of two functional components: the fuzzy reasoning or decision making unit and the knowledge base. The fuzzy logic model underwent two chief processes: the fuzzification and defuzzification processes. Data on rainfall was compared with the outputs of the model that was predicted. According to Hasan and Rahman [31], a rainfall prediction approach based on fuzzy logic and the Mamdani fuzzy inference system [8] can be applied successively for the assessment of various environmental problems. in order to avoid unforeseen meteorological problems. Factors that are ambiguous or confusing in the antecedent and consequent aspects of the weather prediction are handled logically and using reliable algorithms [9]. Scientists have demonstrated that fuzzy set theory can be used to explain qualitative, ambiguous, and uncertain system expressions. Fuzzy set theory was developed to address issues with classical binary logic, which assumes that propositions can either be true or false [4]. Fuzzy logic addresses overlooked quantities in binary logic by allowing something to be partially true and partially false [10]. In order to obtain more precise forecasts for the area, the study is predicated on the application of fuzzy logic to one of the meteorological processes, namely rainfall. Thus, the purpose of this research is to investigate the application of fuzzy logic in rainfall forecasting and to create a fuzzified model for rainfall forecasting. The next steps, which call for the implementation of real-time applications employing fuzzy logic approaches [11].

1. Fuzzification: The process of transforming crisp or classical data into fuzzy membership functions (MFs) or data.

2. Fuzzy Inference Process: To communicate the fuzzy productivity, membership functions and control rules are integrated.
3. Defuzzification: Compute each related outcome separately using different methods.

Here is how the rest of the paper is set out in advance. The Section 1.2 discusses the use of fuzzy logic modeling to forecast rainfall. The application will be covered in Section 1.3, and the results are described in Section 1.4. Finally, Section 1.5 provides a conclusion.

1.2 Methodology

Objects with identical qualities form fuzzy sets [12], whereas objects in crisp sets are either part of the set or not. In actuality, the characteristic value of an object that is a part of the set under consideration is coded as 1, whereas the code for an object outside the set is 0. Crisp sets are devoid of any doubt or uncertainty regarding which object belongs in the set under consideration. Otherwise, people often encounter things in their daily lives that may seem identical yet have totally different characteristics. Thus, there is always some degree of uncertainty when determining whether a membership value is 0 or 1. Naturally, it makes sense that some identical items might only partially belong to the same set; as a result, it becomes unclear if an object belongs or not. To mitigate these circumstances [13], expanded the definition of the crisp set membership [14] degree to include any continuous value between 0 and 1. A generalization of traditional set theory is fuzzy sets. Fuzzy sets' fundamental concept is simple to understand. Items having a membership function of 1 are unquestionably part of the set, and those with a membership function of 0 are similarly unquestionably not; nevertheless, objects with intermediate membership functions are partially part of the same set. An object's degree of membership in the set increases with its membership function [15]. Hydrological modeling, including rainfall forecasting, inflow prediction, and reservoir operation, has also looked at fuzzy set theory. Along with the application of genetic algorithms, several fuzzy system and fuzzy control system based reservoir operation strategies are available in the literature. These models include hybrid fuzzy systems [16], fuzzy rule-based systems, and fuzzy optimization techniques [17]. Fuzzy rules were constructed in these models based on observed data or expert knowledge. It appears that fuzzy models and neural networks are better options than conventional modeling techniques for simulating nonlinear and non-stationary problems in water resources engineering, particularly when the problem's definition is ambiguous, as in the case of predicted rainfall and droughts.

A. Fuzzy Set
Let X be a set of all values. If A is a set of ordered pairs, it is referred to as a (fuzzy) subset of

$$X.\ A = \{(x, \mu(1.x)) : x \in X, \mu(1.x) \in [0, 1]\} \tag{1.1}$$

where μA denotes A's membership function and μA(x) denotes x's membership grade within A. A lower limit, an upper limit, and a value, m, where a ≤ m ≤ b, define the linguistic expression for the variables and their membership functions, which are evaluated from the following triangular membership functions. As illustrated in Figure 1.1, the membership function μA(x) has a value between 0 and 1, where 0 indicates no membership, 1 indicates full membership, and values in between indicate partial membership.

B. Fuzzy Systems
Mapping a given set of input and output *via* a set of fuzzy systems is the real process of fuzzy inference. There are four input variables and one output variable for this study. The amount of predictable rainfall is the output variable, whereas the input variables at any given time are temperature, wind speed, humidity, and atmospheric pressure. To create the equations that translate an input value to its matching membership value, all the membership values for a given input variable must be determined.

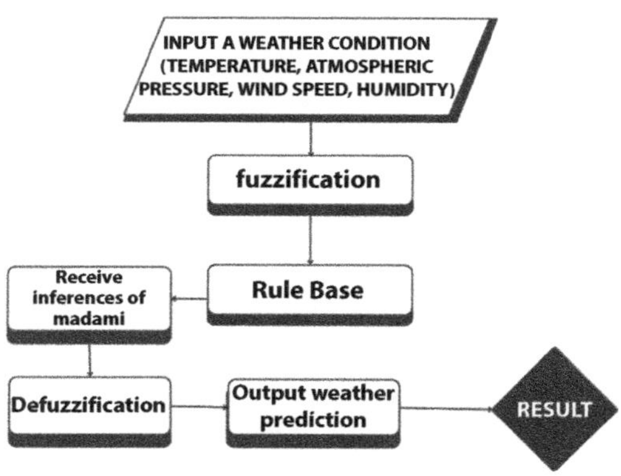

Figure 1.1 Weather prediction flowchart.

C. Temperature Equations

The following formulas provide the membership values for various ranges for every given temperature. As a result, five equations are created to implement the graph using the five lines in the graph's design, which is displayed below. Five equations for the temperature ranges of 10°C to 40°C must be developed for this investigation. Even if the linguistic variables—very low, low, normal, high, and very high—have the same temperature range, their equations will undoubtedly change. The graph is implemented using five equations, in the graph diagram displayed in Figure 1.2(a).

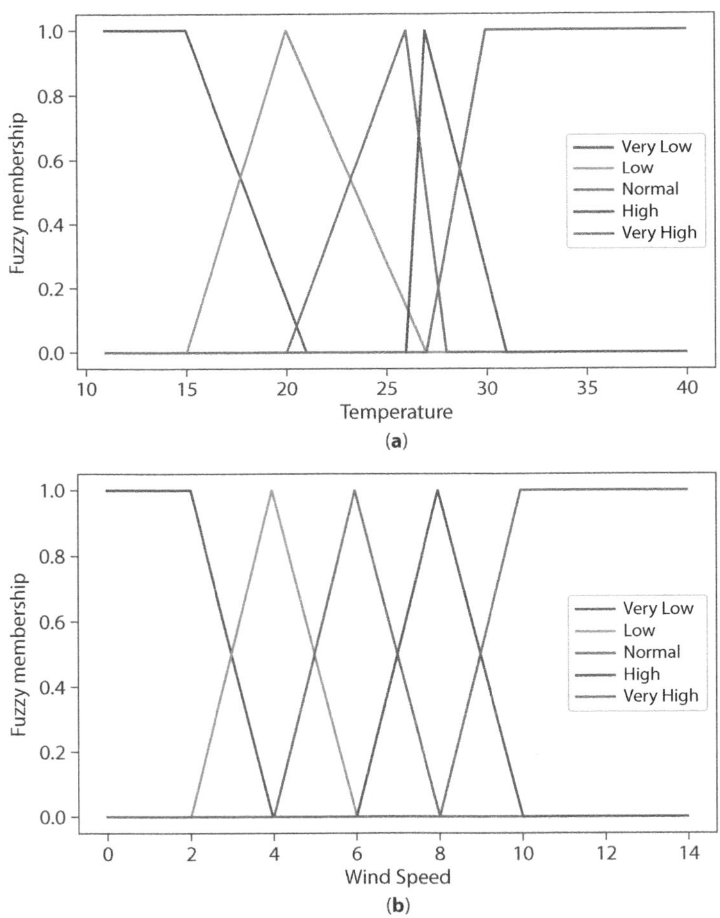

Figure 1.2 (a) Membership function for temperature along with its associated fuzzy levels. (b) Fuzzy levels associated with the wind speed mem bership function. *(Continued)*

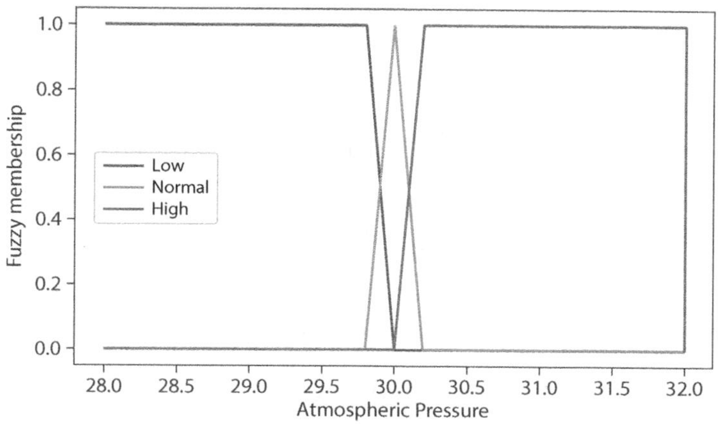

(c)

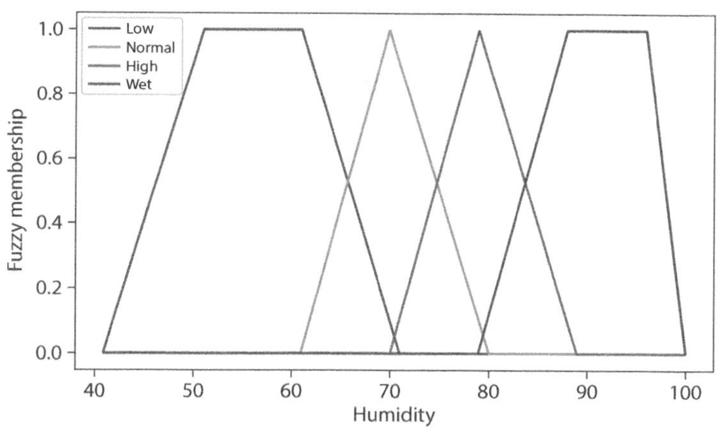

(d)

Figure 1.2 (Continued) (c) Fuzzy levels tied to the atmospheric pressure membership function. (d) Membership function of humidity and corresponding fuzzy levels.

1. Very Low Temperature (μtemp vl(x)) =

$$
\begin{array}{l}
1 \text{ if } x < 11 \\
\dfrac{x-11}{15-11} \text{ if } 11 \leq x < 15 \\
\dfrac{21-x}{21-15} \text{ if } 15 \leq x < 21 \\
0 \text{ otherwise}
\end{array}
$$

2. Low Temperature (μtemp l(x)) =

$$0 \text{ if } x \leq 15 \text{ or } x \geq 27$$
$$\frac{x-15}{20-15} \text{ if } 15 \leq x < 20$$
$$\frac{27-x}{27-20} \text{ if } 20 \leq x < 27$$

3. Normal Temperature (μtemp n(x)) =

$$0 \text{ if } x \leq 20 \text{ or } x \geq 28$$
$$\frac{x-20}{26-20} \text{ if } 20 \leq x < 26$$
$$\frac{28-x}{28-26} \text{ if } 26 \leq x < 28$$

4. High Temperature (μtemp h(x)) =

$$0 \text{ if } x \leq 26 \text{ or } x \geq 31$$
$$\frac{x-26}{27-26} \text{ if } 26 \leq x < 27$$
$$\frac{31-x}{31-27} \text{ if } 27 \leq x < 31$$

5. Very High Temperature (μtemp vh(x)) =

$$0 \text{ if } x < 27$$
$$\frac{x-27}{30-27} \text{ if } 27 \leq x < 30$$
$$1 \text{ if } 30 \leq x \leq 40$$

D. Wind Speed Equations

Membership functions for wind speed values ranging from 0 to 14 km/hr are defined using five distinct equations, each corresponding to a linguistic variable: very low, low, normal, high, and very high. Although the wind speed range remains consistent across these linguistic categories, the equations differ to accurately represent each category's characteristics. These five equations are used to generate the graph illustrated in Figure 1.2(b).

1. Very Low Wind (μwind vl(x)) =

$$1 \text{ if } 0 \le x \le 2$$

$$\frac{x-0}{2-0} \quad \text{if } 0 \le x < 2$$

$$\frac{4-x}{4-2} \quad \text{if } 2 \le x < 4$$

$$0 \text{ otherwise}$$

2. Low Wind (μwind l(x)) =

$$0 \text{ if } x \le 2 \text{ or } x \ge 6$$

$$\frac{x-2}{4-2} \text{ if } 2 \le x < 4$$

$$\frac{6-x}{6-4} \text{ if} 4 \le x < 6$$

3. Normal Wind (μwind n(x)) =

$$0 \text{ if } x \le 4 \text{ or } x \ge 8$$

$$\frac{x-4}{6-4} \quad \text{if } 4 \le x < 6$$

$$\frac{8-x}{8-6} \quad \text{if } 6 \le x < 8$$

4. High Wind (μwind h(x)) =

$$0 \text{ if } x \le 6 \text{ or } x \ge 10$$

$$\frac{x-6}{8-6} \quad \text{if } 6 \le x < 8$$

$$\frac{10-x}{10-8} \quad \text{if } 8 \le x < 10$$

5. Very High Wind (μwind vh(x)) =

$$0 \text{ if } x < 8$$

$$\frac{x-8}{10-8} \quad \text{if } 8 \leq x < 10$$

$$1 \text{ if } 10 \leq x \leq 14$$

E. Atmospheric Pressure Equations

The membership values are constructed for any wind speed value using the following equations. utilizing the 28–32 Hg atmospheric pressure ranges to create three equations for these ranges. Even while the range of atmospheric pressure for the linguistic variables (low, normal, and high) may be the same, their equations will undoubtedly change. Three equations, where AP stands for wind speed and m for membership value, respectively, implement the graph and are followed in the diagram of the graph displayed in Figure 1.2(c).

1. Low Atmospheric Pressure (μatm l(x)) =

$$1 \text{ if } x < 8$$

$$\frac{x-28}{29.8-28}$$
$$\text{if } 28 \leq x < 29.8$$

$$\frac{30.-x}{30-29.8}$$
$$\text{if } 29.8 \leq x < 30$$

$$0 \text{ otherwise}$$

2. Normal Atmospheric Pressure (μatm n(x)) =

$$0 \text{ if } x \leq 29.8 \text{ or } x \geq 30.2$$

$$\frac{x-29.8}{30-29.8}$$
$$\text{if } 29.8 \leq x < 30$$

$$\frac{30.2.-x}{30.2-30}$$
$$\text{if } 30 \leq x < 30.2$$

3. High Atmospheric Pressure (μatm h(x)) =

$$0 \text{ if } x < 30$$
$$\frac{x-30}{30.2-30} \text{ if } 30 \leq x < 30.2$$
$$1 \text{ if } 30.2 \leq x \leq 32$$

F. Humidity

The membership values for any humidity value are constructed using the equations below to create four equations for the humidity ranges of 40 to 100%. Even though the four linguistic variables—low, normal, high, and wet—have the same range of humidity, their equations will undoubtedly change. The graph in Figure 1.2(d) is implemented using three equations:

1. Low Humidity (μhumid l(x)) =

$$0 \text{ if } x < 41$$
$$\frac{x-41}{51-41} \text{ if } 41 \leq x < 51$$
$$1 \text{ if } 51 \leq x \leq 61$$
$$\frac{71.-x}{71-61} \text{ if } 61 \leq x < 71$$
$$0 \text{ if } x \geq 71$$

2. Medium Humidity (μhumid m(x)) =

$$0 \text{ if } x \leq 61 \text{ or } x \geq 80$$
$$\frac{x-61}{70-61} \text{ if } 61 \leq x < 70$$
$$\frac{80.-x}{80-70} \text{ if } 70 \leq x < 80$$

3. High Humidity (μhumid h(x)) =

$$0 \text{ if } x \leq 70 \text{ or } x \geq 89$$

$$\frac{x-70}{79-70} \text{ if } 70 \leq x < 79$$

$$\frac{89.-x}{89-79} \text{ if } 79 \leq x < 89$$

4. Wet Humidity (μhumid wet(x)) =

$$0 \text{ if } x < 79$$

$$\frac{x-79}{88-79} \text{ if } 79 \leq x < 88$$

$$1 \text{ if } 88 \leq x \leq 96$$

$$\frac{100.-x}{100-96} \text{ if } 96 \leq x \leq 100$$

G. Rainfall Equations

The category of temperature, atmospheric pressure, humidity, and wind speed all affect the output variable rainfall extremely low, low, normal, high, and extremely high are the possible outcomes. Five equations must be created for these categories in this investigation. The amount of rainfall (RF) in each category can be found using the following five equations, which correspond to the graph's diagram in Figure 1.3.

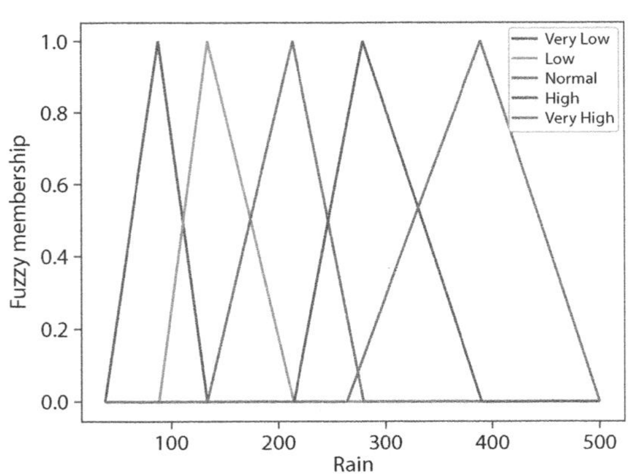

Figure 1.3 Amount rainfall for different categories.

1. Very Low Rainfall (μrain vl(x)) =

$$0 \text{ if } x \leq 40 \text{ or } x \geq 135$$

$$\frac{x-40}{90-40} \text{ if } 40 \leq x < 90$$

$$\frac{135.-x}{135-99} \text{ if } 90 \leq x < 135$$

2. Low Rainfall (μrain l(x)) =

$$0 \text{ if } x \leq 90 \text{ or } x \geq 215$$

$$\frac{x-90}{135-90} \text{ if } 90 \leq x < 135$$

$$\frac{215.-x}{215-135} \text{ if } 135 \leq x < 215$$

3. Normal Rainfall (μrain n(x)) =

$$0 \text{ if } x \leq 135 \text{ or } x \geq 280$$

$$\frac{x-135}{215-135} \text{ if } 135 \leq x < 215$$

$$\frac{280.-x}{280-215} \text{ if } 215 \leq x < 280$$

4. High Rainfall (μrain h(x)) =

$$0 \text{ if } x \leq 215 \text{ or } x \geq 390$$

$$\frac{x-215}{280-215} \text{ if } 215 \leq x < 280$$

$$\frac{390.-x}{390-280} \text{ if } 280 \leq x < 390$$

5. Very High Rainfall (μrain vh(x)) =

$$0 \text{ if } x \leq 265 \text{ or } x \geq 500$$

$$\frac{x-265}{390-265} \text{ if } 265 \leq x < 390$$

$$\frac{500.-x}{500-390} \text{ if } 390 \leq x < 500$$

1.3 Application

The inference stage [18, 19] is the next step in the fuzzy calculation process. This procedure is used to convert fuzzy input into a fuzzy output value. This is the procedure: an input value from the fuzzification process is fed into a rule that is designed to produce a fuzzy output [20–23]. The four fuzzy inputs will be used to establish the rules that need to be set. Depending on the data values for the input size, which include temperature, atmospheric pressure, wind speed, humidity, and the output, which includes decision variables. Calculate the monthly rainfall, while the annual measurements of temperature, air pressure, humidity, and wind speed are taken. Table 1.1 illustrates the relationship between the output value and the four input variables. We utilized five rules for that. However, in previous studies [24–27], not all fuzzy membership functions were considered, leading to predicted values that deviated significantly from the actual system. Our analysis shows that three out of the four fuzzy membership values are more influential in predicting rainfall, and these predictions closely align with the actual values. Figures 1.4(a),(b) illustrates how these four fuzzy membership values contribute to the likelihood of flooding. In Figures 1.4(a),(b), the red color on the color bar indicates a flood risk. The temperature, air pressure, humidity, wind speed, and predicted amount of rainfall for a specific year were all taken into account when creating the table. We have illustrated the variation between the actual and predicted rainfall values in Figure 1.5.

Table 1.1 Fuzzy logic rules for rain prediction.

Rule no.	Condition	Action	Output
1	If (temp is very low or low) and (wind is very low or low)	Rain is very low	*r1_out* = min(fire_rule1, rain_vl)
2	If ((temp is very low) and (wind is normal or high)) or ((temp is low) and (wind is normal)) or ((temp is normal) and (wind is very low or low)) or ((temp is high) and (wind is very low))	Rain is low	*r2_out* = min(fire_rule2, rain_l)
3	If ((temp is very high) and (wind is very low)) or ((temp is high or very high) and (wind is low)) or ((temp is normal or high) and (wind is normal)) or ((temp is low or normal) and (wind is high)) or ((temp is very low or low) and (wind is very high))	Rain is normal	*r3_out* = min(fire_rule3, rain_n)
4	If ((temp is very high) and (wind is normal)) or ((temp is high or very high) and (wind is high)) or ((temp is normal or high) and (wind is very high))	Rain is high	*r4_out* = min(fire_rule4, rain_h)
5	If (temp is very high) and (wind is very high)	Rain is very high	*r5_out* = min(fire_rule5, rain_vh)

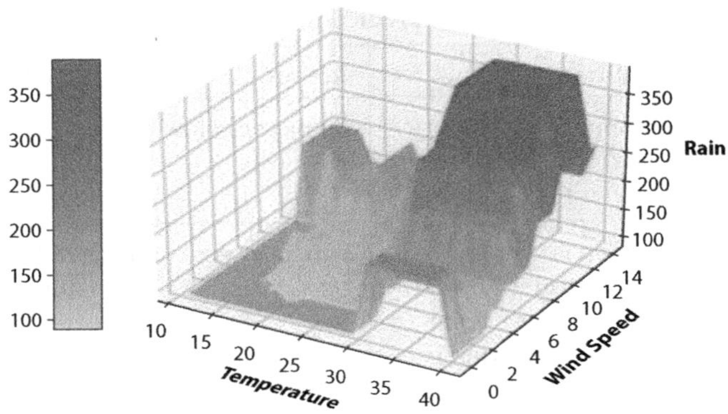

(a)

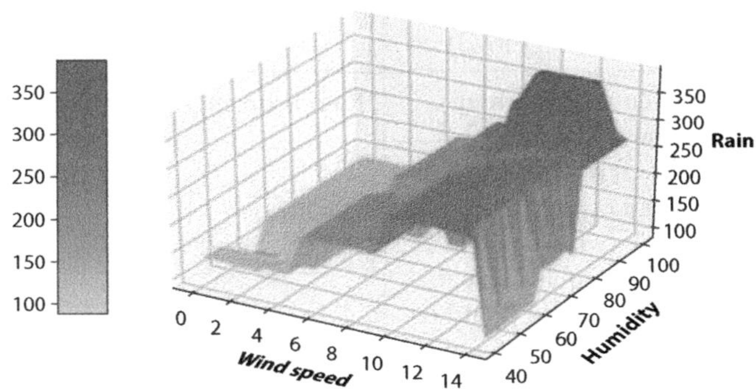

(b)

Figure 1.4 (a, b) The likelihood of flooding is analyzed based on the variation in temperature, wind speed, and humidity.

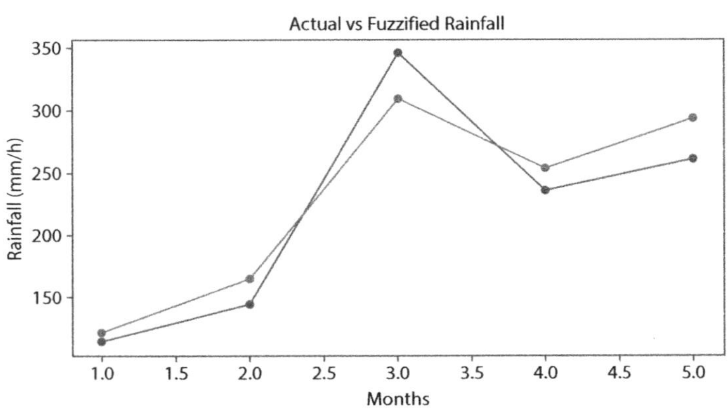

Figure 1.5 The variation between actual and fuzzified rainfall.

1.4 Conclusion

The amount of predictable rainfall is the output variable in this study, while the four input variables are temperature, wind speed, humidity, and atmospheric pressure at a specific day. The selection of temperature and wind speed is based on their primary influence on the frequency of rainfall. Five equations related to temperature and wind speed are created, and they implement the graph's diagram and fall within the membership values. Rainfall similarly creates five equations for various groups. These five equations calculate the amount of rainfall and display the graph's diagram. Table 1.1 illustrates the relationship between the two input variables and the output value. The rainfall patterns for a given year are shown in the table together with the temperature, wind speed, humidity, and air pressure readings. As the climatic conditions that boost the occurrence of rainfall, temperature and wind speed were fuzzified, and the fuzzy levels and membership functions that were obtained after the minimum composition of the inference section were taken into consideration. The product of wind speed and temperature seems to be a reasonable attempt to make the model resemble the real rainfall events, which are necessary for agricultural productivity. Lastly, the current study attempts to use fuzzy logic to predict rainfall depending on temperature and wind speed.

Acknowledgment

J.S thanks University Grant Commission (UGC) for Ph.D. fellowship.

References

1. Leclerc, C., Mwongera, C., Camberlin, P., Boyard Micheau, J., *Ecol. Soc.*, 18, 2013.
2. Edvin, E. and Djamil, Y.D., *Makara J. Sci.*, 12, 5, 2008.
3. Nasher, N., *Eur. J. Clim. Change*, 11, 5, 2013.
4. Cirstea, M., Dinu, A., McCormick, M., Khor, J.G., *Neural and fuzzy logic control of drives and power systems*, Elsevier, 2002.
5. Singh, H., Gupta, M.M., Meitzler, T., Hou, Z.-G., Garg, K.K., Solo, A.M., Zadeh, L.A., *Adv. Fuzzy Syst.*, 2013, 3, 2013.
6. Gupta, P., *Int. J. Adv. Res. Comput. Sci.*, 8, 2017.
7. Ross, J., Mason, D., Linkens, D., Edwards, N., *Br. J. Anaesth.*, 78, 412, 1997.
8. Chai, Y., Jia, L., Zhang, Z., *Int. J. Comput. Inf. Eng.*, 3, 663, 2009.
9. Tatli, H. and Sen, Z., *J. Eng. Environ. Sci.*, 23, 173, 1999.

10. Jimoh, R., Olagunju, M., Folorunso, I., Asiribo, M., *Int. J. Innovative Res. Compute Commun. Eng.*, 1, 929, 2013.
11. Bai, Y., Ma, X., Ding, L., *Atmosphere*, 11, 1055, 2020.
12. Mohan, C., *An introduction to fuzzy set theory and fuzzy logic*, MV Learning, 2015.
13. Zadeh, L.A., *Inf. Control*, 8, 338, 1965.
14. Ragin, C.C., Comparative Methods for the Advancement of Systematic cross-case analysis and Small-N studies (COMPASS), 2005.
15. Hasan, M., Tsegaye, T., Shi, X., Schaefer, G., Taylor, G., *Agric. Water Manage.*, 95, 1350, 2008.
16. Sun, Y.L. and Er, M.J., *IEEE Trans. Fuzzy Syst.*, 12, 755, 2004.
17. Precup, R.-E. and Preitl, S., *Eng. Appl. Artif. Intell.*, 17, 661, 2004.
18. Janarthanan, R., Konar, A., Chakraborty, A., *Int. J. Approximate Reasoning*, 82, 138, 2017.
19. Konar, A., *Artificial intelligence and soft computing: behavioral and cognitive modeling of the human brain*, CRC press, 2018.
20. van der Wal, A.J., *Fuzzy Sets Syst.*, 74, 33, 1995.
21. Srivastava, P.K. and Bisht, D.C., *Advanced fuzzy logic approaches in engineering science*, pp. 327–340, IGI Global, 2019.
22. Rau, G., Becker, K., Kaufmann, R., Zimmermann, H.-J., *Artif. Organs*, 19, 105, 1995.
23. ROSS, T.J., Fuzzy logic with engineering applications, 1997.
24. Setyanugraha, N., Al Aziz, S., Harmoko, I.W., Fianti, F., *Phys. Commun.*, 6, 61, 2022.
25. Jimoh, R., Olagunju, M., Folorunso, I., Asiribo, M., *Int. J. Innovative Res. Comput. Commun. Eng.*, 1, 929, 2013.
26. Santha, S. and Devi, M.B., *Journal of Physics: Conference Series*, vol. 1947, IOP Publishing, p. 012005, 2021.
27. Utnasari, I. and Putria, N.E., *IJISTECH (International J. Inf. Syst. Technol.*, 5, 518, 2021.
28. Musslick, S., Jang, S.J., Shvartsman, M., Shenhav, A., Cohen, J.D., Constraints associated with cognitive control and the stability-flexibility dilemma, in: *Proceedings of the Annual Meeting of the Cognitive Science Society*, vol. 40, 2018.
29. Patel, D.A. and Christian, R.A., Proposed framework of temperature prediction using clustering based fuzzy logic. *Glob. J. Eng. Appl. Sci.*, 1, 1–3, 2013.
30. Agboola, A.H., Gabriel, A.J., Aliyu, E.O., Alese, B.K., Development of a fuzzy logic based rainfall prediction model. *Int. J. Eng. Technol.*, 3, 4, 427–435, 2013.
31. Hasan, A. and Rahman, M.A., A Study on Rainfall Calibration and Estimation at the Northern Part of Bangladesh by Using Mamdani Fuzzy Inference System. *JEPSD*, 5, 2, 58–69, 2019.

2

Fuzzy Promethee Analysis on Attributes in Procuring Gold

Kala Raja Mohan[1*], **Regan Murugesan**[2], **R. Narmada Devi**[2] **and Sathish Kumar Kumaravel**[2]

[1]*Department of Mathematics, Panimalar Engineering College, Poonamallee, Chennai, Tamil Nadu, India*
[2]*Department of Mathematics, Vel Tech Rangarajan Dr. Sagunthala R&D Institute of Science and Technology, Avadi, Chennai, Tamil Nadu, India*

Abstract
One of the precious metals that is bought by all category of people with more enthusiasm is gold. Gold is often considered to be a metal of wealth and financial investment. It is worn as an ornament in various forms to add beauty to a person. It is a precious metal gaining attraction from all ages of people. Despite being the costliest metal, people buy it for various reasons. It is also considered to be a holy metal acquiring importance in all marriages in the form of mangalyam. This chapter aims to analyze various factors involved in the purchase of gold. The analysis has been performed with fuzzy set by using outranking method as a working process.

Keywords: Fuzzy numbers, gold, procure, promethee, statistical analysis

2.1 Introduction

The only metal which gives happiness when the amount of purchase remains high is gold. A naturally occurring metal with the property of being less reactive to other metals. It does not react with oxygen which helps to maintain the originality of the metal. It has attracted people of all age groups from ancient times to the modern age. The metal when worn gives happiness and

**Corresponding author*: kalamohan24@yahoo.co.in

Rahul Kar, Gunjan Mukherjee, Biswadip Basu Mallik and Ashok Kumar Shaw (eds.) Fuzzy Logic in Computational Intelligence: Applications and Case Studies, (21–38) © 2026 Scrivener Publishing LLC

pride. It remains as a metal to show the level of economy and prestige in society. Few people also buy it as metal to give confidence to them, when they are in a difficult financial crisis. Wearing the metal also helps in reducing the temperature of our body.

Gold is worn by all people in various forms of ornament. It decorates the person starting from the head to toe. In ancient times, jewelry was made with the help of shells and beads. Due to the less sustainability of the ornaments, there was a necessity to switch over to some other alternative. Jewels designed from metals were first introduced by the Indus Valley people. It is a metal that is used in making Mangalya sutra which is tied as a mangal knot in marriages. Later gold jewelry got more attraction by gems, colored stones engraved in them. Diamond is one of the costliest stones engraved in gold jewels to add more beauty to the jewels.

Gold in its pure state is not used for making jewels. Few other metals are mixed with gold to maintain the sustainability of the jewels made. Initially, the accessories made of gold were man-made. The set of people who make jewels is termed as goldsmith. They used to sit for hours together in making them. The process also involved the wastage of gold in the process. Technology has brought a solution to overcome their difficulty by introducing machines that make gold ornaments. Molds are used to design the jewels and have made the gold smith finish their work at ease. Designing the jewels as required by the drawing is also done with ease with the help of the technology available.

The purchase of gold brings happiness in all aspects whether they bought in the form of gold coins or gold bonds or gold any related form. Being the costliest metal, many factors such as design, cost, quality, luck, and many more factors are considered in the process of the purchase. This paper aims to analyze the factors involved in the purchase of gold.

The method of Multi Criteria Decision Making method has attracted most researchers, since it serves as an efficient method in identifying the selection of finalists. This decision identifying method comes with different forms of analysis. A few of them are AHP, ANP, TOPSIS, CBA, ranking and correlation. The major focus of this paper is to identify the factors involved in the purchase of gold making use of MCDM method based on the promethee method in fuzzy numbers.

Many researchers have made use of MCDM methods in finding decisions to various real-life situations. A few of them are narrated here for reference.

N. Halouani *et al.* in the year 2009, made use of promethee method for identifying a suitable project [25]. Vijay Manikrao Athawale *et al.* has made their selection of location as per required facilities applying promethee method in the year 2010 [32]. Laurence Turcksina in the year 2011 used AHP promethee method in identifying a suitable policy for energizing vehicle fleet [16]. Mark Velasquez *et al.* in the year 2013 have made a study on various multi criteria decision making models [19]. M. Khalid *et al.* made a study on the gold rate at the Pakistan market in forecasting its price in the year 2014 [18].

Danielle Costa Morais *et al.* in the year 2015 made their work in energy generation with the help of promethee method in the assessment of technology [5]. Reverse logistics has been made as a study in the work done by Jafar Rezaei in the year 2015 with the help of multi criteria decision making [12]. Dilber Uzun Ozsahi *et al.* in the year 2017 made an analysis in cancer treatment applying the fuzzy promethee method. In the year 2017 [6]. Riska Hanifah *et al.* presented their decision making work on the banking sector [29]. Iftikhar Ul Sami *et al.* in the year 2017 applied a machine learning approach in predicting the future rate of gold [10].

Ade Parlaungan Nasution *et al.* in the year 2019 various applications of promethee method in decision making [1]. Lazim Abdullah *et al.* in the same year made a comparative analysis on green supplier selection making use of the preference function [17]. Akmaludin, Erene Gernaria Sihombing *et al.* in the year 2020 made selection of credit loan during the COVID pandemic period using multi criteria decision making method [2]. Bettina Zargini in the same year applied alternative preference functions in decision making problems [3]. In the same year, Chao Tian *et al.* applied AHP and fuzzy picture method to identify a suitable tourism environment [4]. Ikuobase Emovon and Okpako Stephen Oghenenyerovwho in the year 2020 applied multi criteria decision making model in selecting material that gives optimal output [11]. Qiang Zhang, Junhua Hu *et al.* in the year 2020 applied multi criteria decision making method in the selection of material for GGPFWA operator [27].

Fernando Castro Sánchez *et al.* in the year 2021 performed an analysis of statistics in the development of education [7]. Laila Oubahman *et al.* in the year 2021 made a review on transportation using promethee method [14]. Selection of suppliers using AHP promethee method has been done by Muhammad Akmal Md Isa in the year 2021 [23]. Laor Boongasame *et al.* analyzed to forecast on the price of gold using the association rule in the year 2022 [15].

The selection of elective courses making use of promethee method has been done by Haryono Setiadi in the year 2022 [9]. Said Broumi *et al.* in the year 2022 performed medical diagnosis problems using neutrosophic seta with their hybrid structure [31].

Martina Bertoncini *et al.* in the year 2022 made a comparative study on energy requalification applying the promethee method [20]. Fuzzy promethee method in the selection of media platform has been done by Melike Kubra Ekiz Bozdemir *et al.* in the year 2022 [22]. Musavarah Sarwar *et al.* in the year 2022 made use of fuzzy promethee method in selecting an optimal supplier for industrial management [24]. Ömer Ramadan *et al.* in the year 2022 [26] performed fuzzy promethee method in the selection of rail projects which involves priority. Rushikesh Ghule and Abhijeet Gadhave have predicted the price of gold applying machine learning in the year 2022 [30].

Hamed Taherdoost and Mitra Madanchian applied multi criteria decision making method in applications together with its procedures in the year 2023 [8]. Kala Raja Mohan *et al.* in the year 2023 analyzed gold rate using neutrosophic statistics [13]. Mayang Sari *et al.* in the year 2023 made use of promethee method in identifying the priority in the road improvement system [21]. Regan Murugesan *et al.* have done an analysis on FCM and NCM for COVID variants in the year 2023 [28].

2.2 Standard Definitions

Various definitions involved in the decision-making algorithm are listed below for references.

2.2.1 Attributes

Attributes refer to the objective responsible for the selection of the decision. The criteria are fixed based on the requirement of the solution required. The important objectives which are required for the decision are termed as beneficial attributes. The attribute that requires very little weightage are termed as non-beneficial attributes.

2.2.2 Sub-Attributes

The attributes defined for the study are further split into sub-attributes to fine tune the decision to be obtained. This helps to bring about more accurate results.

2.2.3 Criteria

In providing a fair selection of decisions, factors related to the decision problem are termed as criteria. Various rules, values, and conditions are represented as criteria. This helps to improve the fairness of the selection.

2.2.4 Decision Matrix

A matrix of dimension $m \times n$ in which the values are fixed based on the relationship between the attributes and criteria is a decision matrix. Here m represents the number of attributes and n is the number of criteria.

2.2.5 Normalized Decision Matrix

The matrix obtained from the decision matrix by dividing the elements by its Euclidian norm is termed a normalized Norm. Euclidian norm is found by taking the square root of the sum of squares of the elements.

2.2.6 Weights

Weights are numerical values assigned in criteria evaluation in the process of decision making. The values depend on the level of importance of the criteria chosen.

2.2.7 Weighted Normalized Matrix

The measure of preference given for each attribute is termed as weights. The matrix obtained from the product of normalized decision matrix and a weighted matrix is termed as weighted normalized matrix.

2.2.8 Preference Function

A preference function is takes values from 0 to 1, which helps to know the variations between two criteria. It is assessed according to the criteria chosen related to the decision which is to be made. Various combinations of the decision makers are taken into consideration while forming this function.

2.2.9 Aggregate Preference Function

The aggregate preference function depends on the preference function taking into consideration the weights allotted for each criteria.

2.2.10 Leaving and Entering Flow

The term used to determine how an attribute shows positive outranking related to all other attributes is termed as leaving flow. This helps to find the net value which helps in finalizing the decision.

2.2.11 Net Out Ranking Flow

The term used to determine how an attribute shows positive outranking related to all other attributes is termed as entering flow.

2.2.12 Rank

The order of the values which are arranged either in ascending or descending order of preference is termed as rank. This rank helps to finalize the decision involved with the problem.

2.3 Promethee Algorithm

Promethee method refers to "Preference Ranking Organization Method for Enrichment Evaluation". The method makes use of weights and ranks in identifying the decision in real time problems. The method is flexible, transparent and provides reliable results related to the identified problem. The method also involves in sensitivity analysis. The various steps involved in the process of promethee outranking algorithm are given below in Figure 2.1.

2.4 Gold as a Metal

Gold in the form of a chemical has a symbolic representation as Au and it occupies the 79th position in the Periodic table. The symbol Au originated from Latin word 'Aurum'. It is a yellow-colored metal with a property of being soft, ductile, and malleable. The color of the metals takes different shades starting from silverish white to reddish yellow. The metal is extracted from mines where alluvial deposits are found. Various methods of mining are taking place in the extraction of gold. Hard rock mining and placer mining are a few of them. It is considered to be an immovable asset. It is used as a money investment metal as the rate of it keeps on increasing.

2.4.1 Various Forms

Gold is available in various forms. Based on the color and properties they are assigned various names. A few of them are listed below.

- Yellow Gold: It is a metal that occurs naturally in golden color. With a motive to make jewels from it, copper, silver and zinc

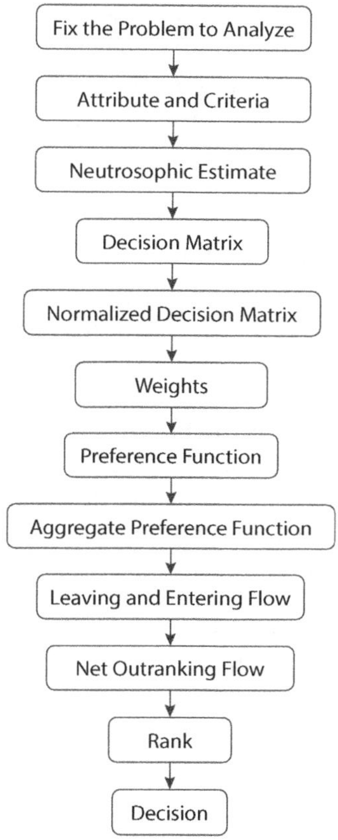

Figure 2.1 Flow diagram of the described work.

are mixed into it. This gives strength to the metal while forming jewelry. Gold usually refers to this yellow-colored gold.

- White Gold: Yellow gold when mixed with zinc, nickel, palladium, white gold is formed. Rhodium plating helps to bring about a silverish shade of the metal.
- Rose Gold: When pure gold gets mixed with copper alloy, it comes up with a signature pink color. Hence it is termed as rose gold. Based on the various percentage of alloy mixed, it comes up with various color pink color shades of gold, hence also called red gold.
- Black Gold: Black-colored gold is obtained when pure gold undergoes a couple of methods. One way of it is the oxidation process which applies sulphur-oxygen for the process.

Another method is the process of controlled oxidation which contains chromium or cobalt. Various shades of colors from brown to black is obtained when copper-rich alloys are treated with potassium sulphide.

2.4.2 Measure of Gold

The jewelry of gold are made by adding other valuable metals to obtain sustainability of the material. Based on the percentage of other metals added, gold is split into various categories. The purity of the gold is measured in Karat. The various Karats of gold are given below.

- 24 Karat Gold: This is the Purest form of gold that occurs in nature. It is the costliest type of gold.
- 22 Karat Gold: This is a mixture of 92% of gold with 8% of other metals. It is the softest alloy of metals which requires caution while handling it.
- 18 Karat Gold: This is a mixture of 75% of gold with 25% of other metals. Vowing to the cost, it is preferred as budget-friendly gold jewelry.
- 14 Karat Gold: This is a mixture of 58% of gold with 42% of other metals. This type of gold is preferred mostly for day-to-day usage.

2.4.3 Jewelry Making Procedure

Goldsmith is the group of people involved in jewelry making. Every jewel worn undergoes a long process to get an end product. The model of the jewel is first designed. The required model is converted into a wax model. The molten metal of the gold is poured into the wax mold. The product removed from the mold is refined to form a good structure of it. To add beauty of the jewel, additional decorative stones are fixed to it. The jewel is then polished to get an end product. The process involved hand-made jewel is given in Figure 2.2 and that of machine-made jewel is given as Figure 2.3.

2.4.4 Methods of Jewelry Making

Initially, jewels were made of hand. It is a long-term process. Wastage of gold was a little high concerning these type of jewels. The wastage inquired

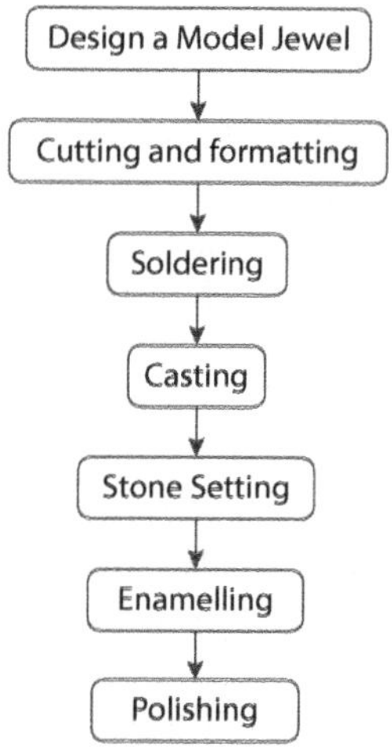

Figure 2.2 Hand-made jewelry making process.

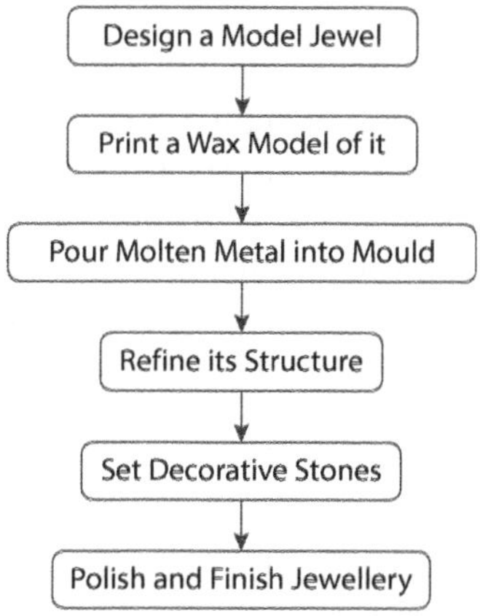

Figure 2.3 Machine-made jewelry making process.

is added to the cost of the jewels in billing. As a result, the cost of the jewel also gets increased. Technology has brought about various developments in all fields. Machine-made jewels occupy the next methodology, which overcomes the difficulty of wastage and over cost. Casting jewels was introduced to make jewels of desired design.

2.5 Gold Procure

Gold is considered to be a metal of investment. Being the costliest metal, many factors are considered into account while purchasing the metal. More than a metal it is seen as an asset. The budget decides the weightage of the purchase. Few people purchase it when the price becomes low. Few people get simulated to purchase gold, when they feel that the design and the quality of a third person attracts them. Offers and compliments announced by the jewel shop also attract people to purchase gold. The festive occasion also remains a reason behind jewel purchases. The benefit of pledging the jewel during an emergency also creates interest among people to purchase gold. The aim of this article is to analyze the various factors involved in the purchase of gold.

Fuzzy numbers in promethee method has been adopted to bring about the results. The outcome of the work helps to identify the major factors involved in the procurement of gold. This would give a guideline for Entrepreneurs who have the idea to invest in gold business. To make an analysis four respondents are considered, who are termed as P1, P2, P3, P4, P5, P6, P7, P8. Seven different attributes are identified for the study. To each of these attributes, criteria are identified. The assigned score function related to attributes and criteria is given in Table 2.1.

The data related to each of the eight alternatives are given in Table 2.2. Each of the attributes is assigned criteria as fuzzy values.

Corresponding to the data obtained from eight alternatives, the decision matrix is obtained relating a score function as given in Table 2.1. Table 2.2 represents the data set involved in the process of decision making. The decision matrix obtained is shown in Table 2.3.

The normalized decision matrix is obtained using the relation concerning beneficial criteria.

$$R_{ij} = [X_{ij} - \min(X_{ij})] / [\max(X_{ij}) - \min(X_{ij})]$$

For non-beneficial criteria, it is found using the relation

$$R_{ij} = [\max(X_{ij}) - X_{ij}] / [\max(X_{ij}) - \min(X_{ij})]$$

The purchase of gold based on simulation by others and gifts is considered a non-beneficial attribute, since it involves a process of purchase for

Table 2.1 Attribute and criteria with fuzzy estimate.

S. no.	Attribute	Criteria	Symbol	Score
1	Savings	Budget	A1	0.6
		Requirement	A2	0.5
		Price Slash	A3	0.4
2	Simulation by others	Quality	B1	0.2
		Design	B2	0.4
		Luckiness	B3	0.1
3	Offers	Price of Gold	C1	0.7
		Other Compliments	C2	0.5
		Silver offer	C3	0.4
4	Gift	Friends/Relative	D1	0.6
		Family Members	D2	0.7
		Prizes for Competition	D3	0.3
5	Festive Occasion	Birthday/Relatives function	E1	0.5
		Akshaya Trithi	E2	0.6
		Aadi Peruku	E3	0.4
6	Benefits of Purchase	Resale value	F1	0.8
		Gold Exchange	F2	0.4
		Lending Purpose	F3	0.6
7	Method of Purchase	Gold Exchange	G1	0.4
		Buy Newly	G2	0.5
		Resale Ornament and Pay Extra Amount for Purchase	G3	0.7

gifting others. The normalized decision matrix is calculated and the results are shown in Table 2.4.

All couple combinations of alternatives are formed and each of the combination preference functions is calculated. The values are obtained using

Table 2.2 Data set for decision making.

	1	2	3	4	5	6	7
P1	A1	B1	C1	D1	E2	F3	G3
P2	A1	B2	C2	D2	E3	F3	G3
P3	A3	B1	C2	D1	E2	F1	G2
P4	A3	B2	C2	D1	E2	F2	G2
P5	A2	B3	C3	D3	E1	F3	G1
P6	A3	B1	C2	D2	E2	F1	G3
P7	A3	B2	C1	D1	E3	F2	G3
P8	A1	B1	C1	D1	E3	F3	G2

Table 2.3 Decision matrix.

	1	2	3	4	5	6	7
P1	0.6	0.2	0.7	0.6	0.6	0.6	0.7
P2	0.6	0.4	0.5	0.7	0.4	0.6	0.7
P3	0.4	0.2	0.5	0.6	0.6	0.8	0.5
P4	0.4	0.4	0.5	0.6	0.6	0.4	0.5
P5	0.5	0.1	0.4	0.3	0.5	0.6	0.4
P6	0.4	0.2	0.5	0.7	0.6	0.8	0.7
P7	0.4	0.4	0.7	0.6	0.4	0.4	0.7
P8	0.6	0.2	0.7	0.6	0.4	0.6	0.5

the relation given below. A total of 56 combinations are carried out. As a sample, first seven combinations are presented below.

$$P_n(i,k) = 0 \text{ } if \, R_{ij} \leq R_{kj} \text{ and}$$
$$P(i,k) = R_{ij} - R_{kj} \text{ } if \, R_{ij} > R_{kj}$$

The values are calculated corresponding to each row and the values are listed in Table 2.5.

Table 2.4 Normalized decision matrix.

	1	2	3	4	5	6	7
P1	1	0.667	1	0.033	1	0.5	1
P2	1	0	0.33	0	0	0.5	1
P3	0	0.667	0.33	0.033	1	1	0.33
P4	0	0	0.33	0.033	1	0	0.33
P5	0.25	1	0	1	0.5	0.5	0
P6	0	0.667	0.33	0	1	1	1
P7	0	0	1	0.033	0	0	1
P8	1	0.667	1	0.033	0	0.5	0.33

Table 2.5 Preference function.

	1	2	3	4	5	6	7
P1, P2	0	0.667	0.67	0.033	1	0	0
P1, P3	1	0	0.67	0	0	0	0.67
P1, P4	1	0.667	0.67	0	0	0.5	0.67
P1, P5	0.75	0	1	0	0.5	0	1
P1, P6	1	0	0.67	0.033	0	0	0
P1, P7	1	0.667	0	0	1	0.5	0
P1, P8	0	0	0	0	1	0	0.67

The weights are calculated based on the importance of each of the attribute. The weights are assigned to be 0.3, 0.1, 0.1, 0.1, 0.1, 0.2, and 0.1 corresponding to each of the attribute. The aggregate preference function given in Table 2.6 is calculated using the relation

$$\pi(i,k) = \sum [w_j \ P(j,k)] / \sum w_j$$

Table 2.6 Aggregate preference function.

	P1	P2	P3	P4	P5	P6	P7	P8
P1	--	0.237	0.434	0.6007	0.475	0.3703	0.5667	0.167
P2	0	---	0.367	0.467	0.358	0.3	0.4	0.067
P3	0.1	0.27	---	0.2667	0.216	0.0033	0.1667	0.2
P4	0	0.1033	0	---	0.083	0.0033	0.1	0.1
P5	0.13	0.25	0.205	0.3717	---	0.2083	0.4217	0.28
P6	0.1	0.2667	0.067	0.337	0.283	---	0.3667	0.267
P7	0	0.0703	0.134	0.134	0.2	0.3707	---	0.067
P8	0	0.204	0.367	0.5337	0.358	0.3707	0.4667	---

Leaving flow also known as positive flow is calculated using the relation

$$\varnothing_i^+ = \frac{1}{n-1}\sum \pi(i,k) \; when \; i \neq k$$

Entering flow also known as negative flow is calculated using the relation

$$\varnothing_i^+ = \frac{1}{n-1}\sum \pi(k,i) \; when \; i \neq k$$

Net outranking flow $\varnothing$ is calculated by subtracting negative flow from positive flow related to each of the alternatives. From the net outranking values, the ranks are assigned which is used to determine the decision on the purchase of gold. All these values are listed in Table 2.7.

The outcome received from the rank is written as $P1 > P8 > P2 > P6 > P3 > P5 > P7 > P4$. The ranks obtained show that the person with the first response occupies first place, the eighth response occupies second place, the second response occupies third place, the sixth response occupies the fourth place, the third response occupies the fifth place, the fifth response occupies the sixth place, the seventh response occupies the seventh place and the fourth response occupies eighth place.

Table 2.7 Leaving, entering, net outranking flow, rank.

	$\varnothing_i^+$	$\varnothing_i^+$	$\varnothing$	**Rank**
P1	0.409	0.047	0.362	1
P2	0.279	0.200	0.079	3
P3	0.175	0.225	-0.05	5
P4	0.056	0.387	-0.331	8
P5	0.267	0.282	-0.015	6
P6	0.241	0.232	0.009	4
P7	0.139	0.356	-0.217	7
P8	0.029	0.164	0.165	2

2.6 Conclusion

Multi Criteria Decision Making methods find their applications in various daily life situations. The selection process provides an eminent solution. Among various MCDM methods, promethee method are applied to identify the factors involved in the purchase of gold. The various criteria and attributes related to the study on the purchase of gold have been identified. The scoring system based on fuzzy data has been generated. The identification of various factors involved in the procurement of gold has been done by applying promethee method and the decision based on the algorithm is identified. The analysis is done with the help of fuzzy numbers in promethee method. New entrepreneurs involved in the gold business can make use of these factors while starting their business.

References

1. Nasution, A.P., Harahap, D.A., Watrianthos, R., Application Decision Support System using PROMETHEE Method. *J. Adv. Res. Dyn. Control Syst.*, 11, 506–511, 2019.
2. Akmaludin, E.G.S., Dewi, L.S., Rinawati, E.A., Credit Loan Selection During the Pandemic Recommendation MCDM-Promethee Method. *Sinkron*, 5, 1, 122–128, 2020.

3. Zargini, B., Multicriteria Decision Making Problems Using Variable Weights of Criteria Based on Alternative Preferences. *Am. Sci. Res. J. Engineering Technol.*, 74, 1, 1–14, 2020.
4. Tian, C., Peng, J., Zhang, W., Zhang, S., Wang, J., Tourism Environmental Impact Assessment Based On Improved AHP and Picture Fuzzy Promethee II Methods. *Technol. Econ. Dev. Econ.*, 26, 2, 355–378, 2020.
5. Costa Morais, D., Teixeira de Almeida, A., Alencar, L.H., Negreiros Clemente, T.R., Barbosa Cavalcanti, C.Z., PROMETHEE-ROC Model for Assessing the Readiness of Technology for Generating Energy. *Math. Probl. Eng.*, Article ID 530615, 1–11, 2015.
6. Ozsahin, D.U., Uzun, B., Musa, M.S., Helwan, A., Wilson, C.N., Nurcin, F.V., Şenturk, N., Ozsahin, I., Evaluating Cancer Treatment Alternatives using Fuzzy PROMETHEE Method. *Int. J. Adv. Comput. Sci. Appl.*, 8, 10, 177–182, 2017.
7. Sánchez, F.C., Almeida Blacio, J.H., Flores Bracho, M.G., Andrade Santamaria, D.R., Casanova, R.S., Neutrosophic and Plithogenic Statistical Analysis in Educational Development. *Neutrosophic Sets Syst.*, 44, 223–234, 2021.
8. Taherdoost, H. and Madanchian, M., Using PROMETHEE Method for Multi-Criteria Decision Making: Applications and Procedures. *Iris J. Econ. Bus. Manage.*, 1–7, 2023.
9. Setiadi, H., Mosaik Suni, N.A., Wardani, D.W., Decision Support System to Select Elective Courses Using Hybrid AHP-PROMETHEE Method. *Performa Media Ilmiah Teknik Industri*, 21, 1, 105–112, 2022.
10. Sami, I. and Junejo, K.N., Predicting Future Gold Rates using Machine Learning Approach. *Int. J. Adv. Comput. Sci. Appl.*, 8, 12, 92–9, 2017.
11. Emovon, I. and Oghenenyerovwho, O.S., Application of MCDM method in material selection for optimal design: A review. *Results Mater.*, 7, 1–21, 2020.
12. Rezaei, J., A systematic review of multi-criteria decision-making applications in reverse logistics. *Transp. Res. Procedia*, 10, 766 – 776, 2015.
13. Kala Raja Mohan, R., Devi, N., Nagaram, N.B., Bharathi, T., Rasappan, S., Neutrosophic Statistical Analysis on Gold Rate. *Neutrosophic Sets Syst.*, 60, 113–123, 2023.
14. Oubahman, L. and Duleba, S., Review of PROMETHEE method in transportation. *Prod. Eng. Arch.*, 27, 1, 69–74, 2021.
15. Boongasame, L., Viriyaphol, P., Tassanavipas, K., Temdee, P., Gold-Price Forcasting Method Using Long Short-Term Memory and the Association Rule. *J. Mob. Multimedia*, 19_1, 165–186, 2022.
16. Turcksina, L., Bernardini, A., Macharis, C., A combined AHP-PROMETHEE approach for selecting the most appropriate policy scenario to stimulate a clean vehicle fleet. *Procedia Social Behav. Sci.*, 20, 954–965, 2011.
17. Abdullah, L., Chan, W., Afshari, A., Application of PROMETHEE method for green supplier selection: a comparative result based on preference functions. *J. Ind. Eng. Int.*, 15, 271–285, 2019.

18. Khalid, M., Sultana, M., Zaidi, F., Forcating Gold Price: Evidence from Pakistan Market. *Res. J. Finanace Accounting*, 5, 3, 70–74, 2014.
19. Velasquez, M. and Hester, P.T., An Analysis of Multi-Criteria Decision Making Methods. *Int. J. Oper. Res.*, 10, 2, 5666, 2013.
20. Bertoncini, M., Boggio, A., Dell'Anna, F., Becchio, C., Bottero, M., An application of the PROMETHEE II method for the comparison of energy requalification strategies to design Post-Carbon Cities. *AIMS Energy*, 10, 4, 553–581, 2022.
21. Sari, M., Kosim, K., Saputra, A., Application of the Promethee II Method for Determining Road Improvement Priorities. *J. Math. Instruction Social Res. Opin.*, 2, 1, 11–22, 2023.
22. Bozdemir, M.K.E. and Alkan, A., Selection of Social Media Platforms Using Fuzzy PROMETHEE Method With Different Scenario Types. *J. Eng. Stud. Res.*, 28, 4, 41–50, 2022.
23. Akmal Isa, M., Saharudin, N.S., Anuar, N.B., Mahad, N.F., The application of AHP-PROMETHEE II for supplier selection. *J. Phys. Conf. Ser.*, 1988, 1–16, 2021.
24. Sarwar, M., Zafar, F., Majeed, I.A., Javed, S., Selection of Suppliers in IndustrialManufacturing: A Fuzzy Rough PROMETHEE Approach. *Math. Probl. Eng.*, Article ID 6141225, 1–19, 2022.
25. Halouani, N., Chabchoub, H., Martel, J.-M., PROMETHEE-MD-2T method for project selection. *Eur. J. Oper. Res.*, 195, 841–849, 2009.
26. Ramadan, O. and Ozdemir, Y.S., Prioritization of rail system projects by using FUZZY AHP and PROMETHEE. *J. Optim. Decis. Making*, 1, 2, 114–122, 2022.
27. Zhang, Q., Hu, J., Feng, J., Liu, A., A novel multiple criteria decision making method for material selection based on GGPFWA operator. *Mater. Des.*, 195, 1–14, 2020.
28. Murugesam, R., Parthiban, Y., Narmada Devi, R., Mohan, K.R., Kumaravel, S.K., A Comparative Study of Fuzzy Cognitive Maps and Neutrosophic Cognitive Maps on Covid Variants. *Neutrosophic Sets Syst.*, 55, 329–343, 2023.
29. Hanifah, R., Multi Criteria Decision Making for Bank Rating Based on Health Level of Bank. *Int. J. Progressive Sci. Technol.*, 5, 2, 53–62, 2017.
30. Ghule, R. and Gadhave, A., Gold Price Prediction using Machine Learning. *Int. J. Sci. Res. Eng. Manage.*, 6, 6, 1–9, 2022.
31. Broumi, S., Dhar, M., Bakhouyi, A., Bakali, A., Talea, M., Medical Diagnosis Problems Based on Neutrosophic Sets and Their Hybrid Structures: A Survey. *Neutrosophic Sets Systems*, 49, 1–18, 2022.
32. Athawale, V.M. and Chakraborty, S., Facility Location Selection using PROMETHEE II Method. *Proceedings of the 2010 International Conference on Industrial Engineering and Operations Management Dhaka, Bangladesh, January 9 – 10*, pp. 59–64, 2010.

3

Fuzzy-Based Model for the Study of Crop Production Optimization

Soumen Santra[1], Sudip Barik[1], Subrata Jana[2,3]* and Anirban Sarkar[4]

[1]Department of Master of Computer Application, Techno International New Town, Kolkata, West Bengal, India
[2]Department of Mathematics, Jadavpur University, Kolkata, West Bengal, India
[3]Department of Basic Science and Humanities, Techno International New Town, Kolkata, West Bengal, India
[4]Department of Management and Marketing, West Bengal State University, Barasat, West Bengal, India

Abstract

This research work involves developing a Python script that is designed to make yield forecasts using different inputs and their member functions that come with them. The member functions represent expert knowledge or the relationship between inputs and outputs. It will use libraries like Pandas for data processing, NumPy for numerical calculations, and Matplotlib for visualization. Moreover, it will do the Gaussian mixture modeling and fuzzy logic operations using the Scikit-learn Gaussian mixture and the Scikit-Fuzzy libraries, respectively. The prediction data will be in a dictionary form containing dates, data sets 1 and 2, and more. Using Scikit-learning ctrl.Alpha/ctrl, the script will define the intended yield (yield) and the fuzzy logic variables (date, data1, data2), category of deductions. It will be used to automatically generate the fuzzy rules. Every data point will have a control system built for it, and Matplotlib will be used to visualize the expected yield. This Study provides some background in the principles of fuzzy logic, including how uncertainty is represented and imperfect data interpreted, along with technical application. It also illustrates how fuzzy logic can be applied to modeling complex agricultural systems involving subjective or imperfect data. It supports this discussion with illustrated graphs demonstrating the relations between crop quality and production as well as a pyramid chart that depicts the distribution of yield forecasts across categories. This research aims to develop and

**Corresponding author*: 87subratajana87@gmail.com

Rahul Kar, Gunjan Mukherjee, Biswadip Basu Mallik and Ashok Kumar Shaw (eds.) Fuzzy Logic in Computational Intelligence: Applications and Case Studies, (39–54) © 2026 Scrivener Publishing LLC

implement an optimized fuzzy model based on fuzzy logic for agricultural optimization issues.

Keywords: Crop production, fuzzy inference engine, classification, machine algorithm, optimization

3.1 Introduction

A fuzzy-based model is a mathematical framework representing and controlling the degree of ambiguity and uncertainty in a system with the help of fuzzy logic [1, 2]. Unlike standard models, which work with discrete values, fuzzy models can have the possibility of inclusion of membership or truth degrees between 0 and 1 [3, 4]. Fuzzy logic is utilized within the scope of artificial intelligence in handling imprecise and uncertain input. It is a method of description and drawing conclusions from incomplete and vague knowledge [5]. With degrees of truth, it may be able to approximate the vagueness and ambiguity that characterizes most real-world problems [6]. Fuzzy models use linguistic rules in capturing relationships among data. These rules are represented in fuzzy sets with membership functions like "If the temperature is hot, then the fan speed is high." The model applies fuzzy inference to process these rules and produces an output depending upon the input data and membership in fuzzy sets [7–9].

Fuzzy logic provides a strict framework in the treatment of imprecise and uncertain information. Moreover, it also facilitates more intricate reasoning and decision making through the notion of degrees of truth [10]. Fuzzy control systems find successful applications based on fuzzy logic in control theory and artificial intelligence. In contrast, the ant colony optimization algorithm uses a probabilistic methodology for modeling the foraging activity of ants with the aim of solving computing issues. Both concepts make unique contributions to the study of optimization and have found many practical applications in a wide variety of fields [12, 13].

3.2 Fuzzy-Based Model for the Study of Optimization

In fact, because fuzzy models can handle ambiguity and uncertainty, they offer something new to the optimization community. For example, it is very useful in dealing with complexity in the actual world, which happens to be a problem for traditional optimization methods [2–5, 11]. Fuzzy models are very good at incorporating imprecise data or subjective factors because of their fuzzy logic and fuzzy rules. Fuzzy logic can be used for expressing the degrees of truth, which makes it possible to allow for ambiguity in criteria or data by the model [1, 13, 14].

This flexibility allows decisions to be made that involve a combination of "shades of grey" instead of simple binary choices [15]. The fact that fuzzy rules can account for complexities and uncertainties associated with the real world is another aspect that makes them akin to human decision-making process [4, 16]. The fact that fuzzy models incorporate several factors along with their relative importance makes it possible to provide more adaptive and reliable answers. One of the important advantages of fuzzy models is that they are adaptive [17]. They can be forced to learn new knowledge and changing conditions without requiring complete reorganization. This is achieved by updating membership features and policies according to expert opinion or up-to-date information [11–13, 18].

The model adaptability allows it to always be relevant and effective for a given scenario, which is the nature of all scenarios-exploding with new twists and turns. In cases of conflicting goals in multi-objective optimization scenarios, fuzzy models work best. It is possible to find solutions partially satisfying objectives by assigning varied degrees of relevance to different objectives [19]. The ability to handle conflicting goals is one major advantage in complicated optimization problems. In a nutshell, the fuzzy models allow the realm of optimization through effective management of ambiguity and unpredictability [5–8, 20].

Their strong characteristics include their ability to handle multi-objective optimization problems, fuzzy logic and rules, adaptability toward changed conditions, and dealing with complexity found in the real world. The process of optimization involves several key steps [19, 21]. To model the problem, input variables and the desired result must first be specified. Fuzzy sets are then constructed to represent different degrees or categories of these variables [22, 23].

Then the input and output variables are defined by a set of fuzzy rules created ivia/i fuzzy logic. To find the best possible solution, the fuzzy model then accretes the input data, determines membership in fuzzy sets, and imposes fuzzy rules [24, 25]. This best solution may be a specific value or a set of values depending on the situation. The optimization process is now complete. Some of the applications of optimization include control systems, scheduling, resource allocation, and portfolio optimization. Applications that are related to the optimization of resource distribution, scheduling, control parameters under uncertain conditions, and portfolio asset selection with proper allocation include those above.

3.3 Literature Study on Agricultural Problems

There will always be more mouths to feed, and it is the agricultural sector that has to produce under the double constraint of resources and the environment. Recently, fuzzy logic combined with mathematical models has been used in new ways to enhance many aspects of farming. Three potential theses of this nature are discussed here, discussing their methods, applications, and implications. From the review of these experiments and relevant literature, we detail the role that fuzzy-based model-based optimization plays in solving complex agricultural problems. Li, Ming proposed in 2020 the precision Agriculture's Fuzzy Optimization of Irrigation Scheduling for Water Management. Among important scheduling activities in agricultural management, the irrigation scheduling has a direct impact on crop growth, effective water use, and the total productivity of the farm. Most of the traditional irrigation processes largely rely on manual interventions or pre-programmed schedules that have no regard for crop water needs or other prevailing environmental conditions. Data-driven paradigms in precision agriculture will overcome such limitations by optimizing irrigation processes. In that connection, since Li's thesis examines the development of fuzzy logic to improve irrigation scheduling efficiency and accuracy, it becomes quite a significant contribution to the area. The work of Li contributes to the improvement in the water management in precision agriculture by developing a fuzzy optimization framework for irrigation scheduling. This is possible using the integration of fuzzy logic, which facilitates the inclusion of complicated linkages between many parameters that impact irrigation decisions and uncertain inputs. The fuzzy model presents optimal irrigation strategies tailored to specific farming conditions with regard to numerous data such as soil moisture, weather forecast, crop water requirement, and irrigation systems. In 2022, Wang, Xiaohui, introduced a Fuzzy-Based Model for Optimizing Crop Yield under Fertilizer Management Constraints. Particularly, Wang's thesis in "A Fuzzy-Based Model for Optimizing Crop Yield under Fertilizer Management Constraints" is an important contribution to the optimization domain in agronomy, particularly fertilizer management. Fertilizers are significant inputs into modern agriculture to raise crop productivity. However, overuse or inappropriate application of fertilizers result in soil erosion, water pollution, and other associated greenhouse gas emissions. It tries to overcome those tough challenges by attempting to build a holistic fuzzy-based model. The fertilizer utilization technique, on the other hand, should adhere to the restrictions of fertilizer usage and simultaneously maximize crop productivity. Fertilizer management is challenging because it involves simultaneously managing multiple goals: maximizing productivity, optimizing resources, and minimizing environmental effect. Luis Garcia, 2021: Multidirectional Fuzzy Approach for Optimal Pest and Disease Management in Sustainable Agriculture Pest and disease management is one of the most critical tasks in agriculture with a larger impact on environmental sustainability, food safety, and productivity. Traditional methods of pest management often hinge on reactive actions, such as inconsiderate use of chemical pesticides, which may lead to adverse ecological responses, the development of resistance in pests, as well as health risks to humans. An increased awareness of a need for more sustainable IPM solutions that take into account socioeconomic and environmental issues in addition to efficacy has responded to these challenges.

3.4 Objectives

By our study, we will be coming up with innovative approaches to solve the challenging agricultural problems, though it makes a huge contribution in the field of fuzzy-based optimization research. What we are trying to achieve here includes the study of new methods that can possibly improve the efficacy and efficiency of fuzzy-based models in agriculture system optimization, taking cues from the dynamic field of fuzzy-based evolutionary algorithms. Our project dealt with investigation of the application of fuzzy-based optimization models for solving crop rotation planning agricultural problem identified to be a research gap in the literature analysis. Our approach will help farmers and agronomists design adaptable and sustainable crop rotation plans, maximize yields, reduce adverse impacts on the environment, and enhance resistance and longevity of soil through their use of fuzzy logic techniques.

Our objective is to optimize the crop production is to be followed by those steps:

- Analyze how genetic algorithms and programming can be used in optimizing fuzzy systems for crop rotation planning and other agricultural decision-making methods.
- Investigate fuzzy systems using differential evolution algorithms to better improve the convergence and robustness of optimization solutions to dynamic situations in agriculture.

- Develop optimization methods inspired by nature suitable for deep neuro-fuzzy systems so that fuzzy-based models for agricultural optimization are flexible and scalable.
- Enlarge the scope of our work in terms of considering many-objective optimization of fuzzy systems by means of optimization methods inspired by nature, such as optimizing competing objectives like maximization of agricultural output, reduction in the consumption of resources, and enhancement of environmental sustainability.
- Evaluate swarm intelligence algorithms in their use for fuzzy systems to resolve complex problems of optimization in agricultural fields; more attention should be given to possible uses of collective behaviors for solving the optimal solution of complex large-scale agricultural systems.
- In order to demonstrate the actual relevance and applicability of fuzzy-based models in agricultural engineering, apply a variety of objective optimization techniques to engineering design problems in agriculture, such as the optimal design of irrigation systems, crop rotation schedules, or precision farming strategies.

3.5 Input Datasets with Case Study

Crop rotation refers to cultivating several crops in one location over some seasons or years. Crop rotation is an essential agriculture practice essential for improving the general production of crop yields, controlling pests and diseases, and maintaining soil fertility. However, crop rotation programs described in Table 3.1 can be difficult to design. It is not easy to find a suitable balance between several objectives such as increased output, reduced environmental impact, and maintaining soil health. In this context, we see crop rotation planning as an agricultural problem which can also be solved through fuzzy-based optimization models.

A real-practical approach towards the optimization of various problems of agriculture can be obtained using fuzzy-based model-based optimization; specifically, problems concerning farming include the mode of water, fertilizer, and pesticide distribution to crops in such a manner that tries to maximize production while minimizing expenditure and negative environmental impacts. It can also be applied in irrigation scheduling in order to ensure that at the right time, crops get the right quantity of water in addition to helping establish the best periods to plant and harvest crops.

Table 3.1 Year wise crop and others necessary productions in India.

Crop	2004–05	2005–06	2006–07	2007–08	2008–09	2009–10	2010–11	2011–12
Rice	100	101	99	105	112	121	117	110
Wheat	100	101	112	115	117	127	120	108
Coarse cereals	100	107	110	115	113	123	122	136
Pulses	100	108	134	124	124	146	137	129
Vegetables	100	109	103	118	113	124	128	115
Fruits	100	99	99	98	102	104	114	119
Milk	100	97	98	98	98	112	123	124
Eggs, fish and meat	100	102	101	100	99	116	133	137
Oilseeds	100	86	85	97	104	103	99	102
Sugarcane	100	96	91	87	80	81	109	107
Fibers	100	92	91	96	109	107	138	140
All agriculture	100	99	101	104	106	115	123	122

The picture portrays the dataset - in other words, a table that shows the production level of eight years of agricultural products. This dataset may, therefore, be used as the basis upon which to construct a fuzzy logic model so that maximum yield is reaped from agriculture. For example, it could decide which crops, considering the type of environment expected as well as market pricing, are likely to be profitable in a particular year. Some of the few relevant variables that the model would consider include crop yield, market prices, the weather, and soil conditions. The model's findings on the variables above may be of great benefit to the farmers in improving their production methods in agriculture.

3.6 Methodology

- Step 1: Identify the problem for which the fuzzy model shall be applied. Identify input variables, output variables, and their interactions.

- Step 2: Acquire data to train and test the fuzzy model. Verify that the information acquired is accurate and preprocess appropriately: for example, to deal with missing values, normalization.
- Step 3: FIS design: Determine the appropriateness of membership functions for input and output variables.
- Step 4: Construct fuzzy rules based on data-driven methods or domain knowledge. Choose an inference method according to the problem at hand. Decide if it's classification or regression problem.
- Step 5: Optimization Study in Action: Choose optimization method according to the nature of the problem. The problem may be a problem of minimization or maximization. Some popular optimization techniques are PSO: particle swarm optimization, and genetic algorithms.
- Step 6: Find the objective function for the optimization. Identify what constraints the optimization algorithm will face.
  Step 6.1: Fuzzy Model Integration with Optimization:
  Modify the fuzzy model to include optimization parameters. Select the parameters to be optimized-for example, rule weights, membership function parameters, etc. Establish a connection between the optimization algorithm and the fuzzy model.
- Step 7: Put Python Code into Practice:
  Setup the Python environment with libraries such as NumPy, SciPy, and scikit-fuzzy. Classify and define functions related to fuzzy inference, optimization, and membership functions. Develop modules for data preprocessing, fuzzy model development, optimization, and outcomes evaluation. Fuzzy Model Development Start-up: Initialize and prepare the FIS with optimized or preset parameters. Train the fuzzy model using the attained data. Test the trained model to make sure that it is accurate and generalizable.
- Step 8: Enhance the Fuzzy Model:
  Combine the fuzzy model with the optimization algorithm. Identify optimization parameters, such as the number of maximal iterations/generations, criterion of convergence, and size of population. In order to improve parameters of the fuzzy model, carry out the optimization process.
- Step 9: Assess the Performance of the Model:
  Assess the optimized fuzzy model's performance by utilizing validation data. Evaluate pertinent information.

3.7 Algorithms

i. Start by clearly stating the optimization problem to set things in motion. To solve a problem effectively, this means that the objective function to be maximized or minimized has to be clearly described along with any restrictions that have to be observed; identify which decision variables have to be changed, and select the most appropriate optimization technique.
ii. Having defined the optimization problem, the base of the fuzzy model is built next. This is done with the help of the linguistic variables that, in their very essence, are qualitative input and output variables. Along with it, he has to build fuzzy rules describing the links between the input and the output variables and build membership functions further more to qualify each linguistic variable with the degree of membership. Last but not the least, one should install the framework for the processing of the fuzzy input and the production of the fuzzy output or the fuzzy inference system.
iii. The next step, after establishing the framework of a fuzzy model, is to prepare all the input data. It means fetching relevant information about the problem from various sources and preparing it in a manner the fuzzy model may work with it. Data preprocessing includes some examples of cleaning, addressing missing values in data, scaling or normalization of data, and transforming it in a format that may be suitable for fuzzy inference.
iv. Proceed to the fuzzy inference process, applying the input data defined from the fuzzy model as well as the operations in accordance with fuzzy logic. To accomplish this, in this procedure, it employs defined linguistic variables, membership functions, and fuzzy rules to determine a fuzzy output describing how the system will react to incoming data.
v. After obtaining the fuzzy output, it requires defuzzification to convert this into an exact, useful value. Thus, mapping the fuzzy output on a clear value that would be easy enough to understand and apply in actual decision-making is called defuzzification.
vi. The clear output obtained ivia/i defuzzification can be used to find the best solution by using the optimization algorithm.

The crisp output is used as a guide by the optimization algorithm in order to scan the solution space and identify which configuration of choice variables maximizes the objective function within the imposed set of restrictions.

vii. Finally, evaluate the results of the optimization process. Compare the optimized result with some predefined benchmarks or objectives in order to measure the fuzzy model's performance. Evaluate the fuzzy model's ability to solve the optimization problem and point out areas where the strategy of the modeler must be upgraded.

3.8 Results and Discussion

This Python script later describes how a fuzzy logic system can predict an output variable given two groups of data, and date-related input variables. A detailed explanation of the components of the code and their results will follow. First is to import all the libraries, which shall include the functionalities for fuzzification, data processing, numerical operations, plotting, and

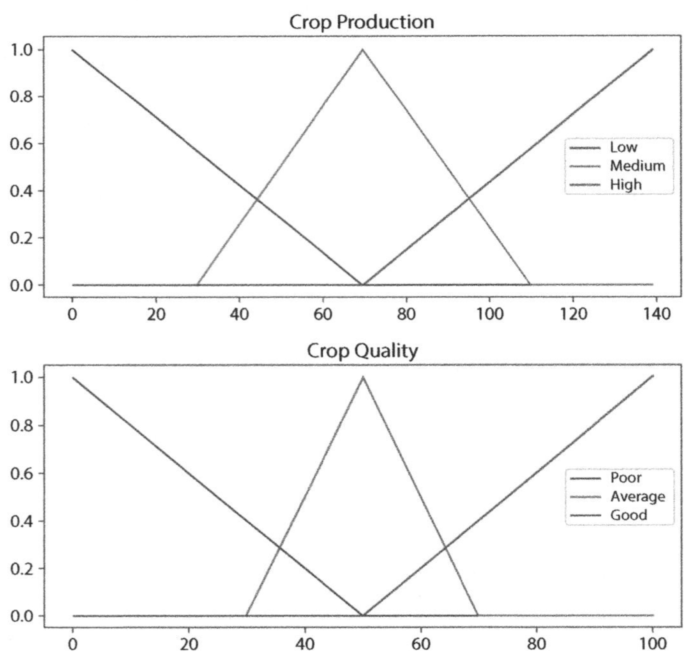

Figure 3.1 Comparison of crop production and crop quality.

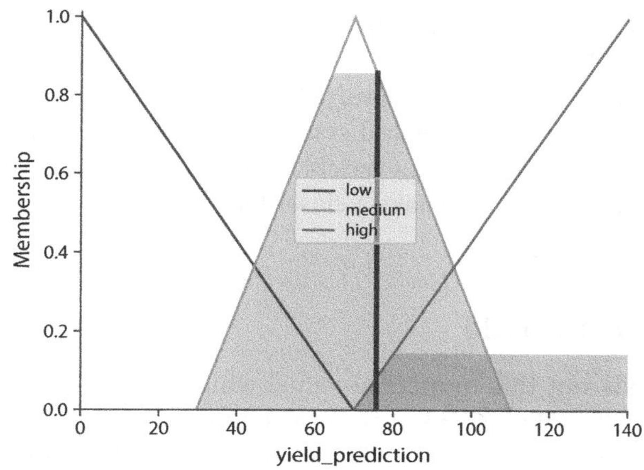

Figure 3.2 Comparison graph of membership vs. yield prediction of crops as per low, medium, and high.

Gaussian mixture model. Libraries needed for this application are Pandas and NumPy for efficient data manipulation, Matplotlib for graphical plots, while GaussianMixture comes from sklearn. The line of the import statement of Matplotlib is wrong and should read as import matplotlib. pyplot as plt. The dates, data1 and data2, are in dictionary format with dates as 'dd-mm-yy' and corresponding numerical data for data1 and data2. Define the Antecedents date, data1, data2 along with Ctrl, and Consequents (output) within the fuzzy logic system. Controller and antecedent. Classes derived from scikit-fuzzy. Using the automf() technique, membership functions are automatically built for each variable with three categories: bad, average, and good. Using input variables combined, their corresponding membership functions are used to create fuzzy rules. For example, rule 1 states that the output will be 'poor' if any of the input variables were 'poor'. Established rules determine the design of a control system, which then gets simulated based on every single input piece of data.

Set the inputs of the fuzzy system and calculate the output based on fuzzy logic; this output is then printed in each iteration of every date. Finally, Matplotlib is used to visualize the output and provide an illustrative view of the expected outcomes. Fuzzy logic is applied to the modeling and interpretation of imprecision and uncertainty in data with a strong computing framework. Since in traditional logic the variables are assigned binary values true/false or 0/1, the latter being too strict for the handling of real data that doesn't easily categorize into set categories, fuzzy logic offers a way to represent variables as fuzzy sets. In the former, the degree of membership of any element in a set can be given to be any value lying between 0 and 1.

The flexibility of fuzzy logic captures the complex linkages and uncertainties often seen in many real-world systems. Here's a code applying a fuzzy logic system to predict an output variable called "yield" given two sets of data and date-related inputs. Let's take a closer look at how one should interpret the code's output.

3.8.1 Predicted Yield

The code spits out this numerical value, which is the expected yield, in this case 75.72813596108733. It is the absolute outcome of the fuzzy logic system's computation for the given inputs. It's essential to note that this prediction is a fuzzy number representing the inherent uncertainty within the system rather than an exact point estimate. Figure 3.1 depicts the relationship between crop production and crop quality. The graph utilizes a scale ranging from 0 to 1 for both crop production and quality.

Here's a breakdown of the information displayed in the graph:

- Positive correlation: The graph indicates a positive correlation between crop quality and productivity. Thus, crop quality goes hand in hand with crop production whereby crop quality tends to increase when crop production increases. This is quite evident due to the slope of the increasing line.
- Non-linear relationship: Quality improvements in crops might be seen more on their production levels when at a low rate due to the steeper slope of the line on low crop production levels. With increases in output, the line tends to flatten out showing that quality gains are less observable.

It should be recalled that the graph probably represents a very much oversimplified model and, therefore cannot give the full impression of the complexity of the relationship which in reality exists between crop yield and quality. Crop quality is sensitive to several variables including both climatic conditions and soil qualities as well as specific crop varieties.

Figure 3.2 suggests a pyramid chart titled "Membership". The chart shows the distribution of yield prediction across three categories: low, medium, and high.

Here's a breakdown of the data shown in the chart:

The base of the pyramid represents a poor yield projection. It contains the most number of members; therefore, a bigger percentage of forecasts fall into this category. The peak value in this region is about 0.6. The center half of the pyramid indicates a middle yield. It contains fewer members than Low. The peak value in this region is about 0.4. This top category of the pyramid has a high yield projection. It possesses the smallest membership out of the three divisions. The peak value in this area is approximately 0.2.

Recall that a pyramid chart only indicates the distribution of yield predictions in these classes. Such a pyramid doesn't indicate the true yield or if yield was to occur.

3.9 Limitations and Conclusions

FLSs are a paradigm of great utility in predictive modeling when a dataset contains imprecise or uncertain input, but their practical applicability is subject to overcoming several limitations that can compromise the accuracy, robustness, and generalizability of the model. Model-based optimization, based on fuzzy theory, may be one possible way to apply agricultural engineering optimization to farmers to successfully handle a range of issues, including greater allocation of available resources, yield improvement, cost reduction, and environmental impact reduction.

Fuzzy logic systems may, therefore, help an agricultural practitioner to simplify the decision-making processes involved in, among others, allotment of water, fertilizers, and pesticides, or even calculation of optimal periods for planting and harvesting. The dataset presented above can thus provide a beginning point for the construction of a fuzzy logic model in optimizing agricultural productivity. It covers eight years, from which production data regarding numerous agricultural products may be obtained to provide insight into past trends. However, several limitations have to be noted first. First, the time span of the dataset may not be very large or sufficient enough to model a robust fuzzy logic, because the agricultural dynamics have been affected by long-term trends as well as cyclical patterns.

Moreover, it has lacked crucial information regarding market pricing, climate conditions, and properties of soil which make building a complete model quite challenging.

Still, the dataset remains useful as a starting point for modeling efforts. The Python script appearing in the interpretation is a real-world illustration of how a single person can implement a fuzzy logic system to predict the output of agriculture based on date-related input variables and two data sets. Specifying linguistic variables and fuzzy rules enables the model to start reasoning about yield predictions by inferred properties of input data. The output, expressed in value as an integer, is an expression of the vagueness involved in agricultural systems that gives an expression of the overall output or result of the process of fuzzy inference.

Interpreting the output of the fuzzy logic system gives critical information about how input variables and expected yield are interrelated. This system would be suitable to simulate the actual conditions of agriculture wherein data has a tendency to be incomplete or confusing. It can handle the impreciseness and vagueness nature of the data that occurs within real-world problems of agriculture. The understanding that becomes available about possible yield results-through graphical representation of anticipated yield distribution into low, medium, and high categories-informs decision-making. The interpretation of the graphs comes with the explanations which help in understanding the relationships portrayed. The crop output and quality indicate that higher levels of production may not result in as great a return on investment concerning quality improvements as lower levels of production would. A yield prediction distribution like the pyramid figure illustrates the possible classifications that the model might make for yield outcomes, which serves towards decision-making as it offers a probabilistic appraisal of the possible outcome. In a nutshell, application of fuzzy logic system in agriculture offers a strong tool to enhance the decision-making process, rationalize the process, and eliminate risks.

The model and the dataset have inherent drawbacks; however, they helped serve the purpose of demonstrating how one might apply fuzzy logic to such difficult agricultural issues.

Future potential developments in data that measure variables with more variability will produce further research using the concept of developing fuzzy logic models, thereby making predictions for effective and sustainable agriculture methods to be more accurate and less likely.

References

1. Xiao, C., Zou, H., Fan, J., Zhang, F., Li, Y., Sun, S., Pulatov, A., Optimizing irrigation amount and fertilization rate of drip-fertigated spring maize in northwest China based on multi-level fuzzy comprehensive evaluation model. *Agric. Water Manage.*, 257, 107157, 2021, https://doi.org/10.1016/j.agwat.2021.107157.
2. Fan, J., Yue, W., Wu, L., Zhang, F., Cai, H., Wang, X., Lu, X., Xiang, Y., Evaluation of SVM, ELM and four tree-based ensemble models for predicting daily reference evapotranspiration using limited meteorological data in different climates of China. *Agric. For. Meteorol.*, 263, 225–241, 2018, https://doi.org/10.1016/j.agrformet.2018.08.019.

3. Santos, F., Multi-objective models for optimizing olive crop management for olive oil production, 2023, Retrieved from https://doi.org/10.11606/d.18.2023.tde-26092023-105100.
4. Ly, Q.V., Truong, V.H., Ji, B., Nguyen, X.C., Cho, K.H., Ngo, H.H., Zhang, Z., Exploring potential machine learning application based on big data for prediction of wastewater quality from different full-scale wastewater treatment plants. *Sci. Total Environ.*, 832, 154930, 2022, https://doi.org/10.1016/j.scitotenv.2022.154930.
5. Agriculture crop production in India. *Kaggle*, 2017, August 13, Retrieved from https://www.kaggle.com/datasets/srinivas1/agricuture-crops-production-in-india/data.
6. Satishgunjal, Fuzzy Record Matching using Machine Learning. *Kaggle*, 2021, December 25, https://www.kaggle.com/code/satishgunjal/fuzzy-record-matching-using-machine-learning.
7. Li, F. and Jin, C., Study on fuzzy optimization methods based on principal operation and inequity degree. *Comput. Math. Appl.*, 56, 6, 1545–1555, 2008, https://doi.org/10.1016/j.camwa.2008.02.042.
8. Agronomy, *MDPI*, n.d, Retrieved from https://www.mdpi.com/2073-4395/12/5.
9. Zhang, C., Bai, M., Zheng, Y., Li, Y., Ma, W., Xie, X., Liu, Y., Understanding large language model based fuzz driver generation. arXiv e-prints, 2023, arXiv-2307.
10. Miller, B.P., Fredriksen, L., So, B., An Empirical Study of the Reliability of UNIX Utilities. *Commun. ACM*, 33, 11, 32–44, December 1990, https://doi.org/10.1145/96267.96279.
11. Novák, V., Perfilieva, I., Mockor, J., *Mathematical principles of fuzzy logic*, vol. 517, Springer Science & Business Media, 2012.
12. Fuzzy Logic, in: *Stanford Encyclopedia of Philosophy*, Bryant University, 2006, July 23, Retrieved September 30, 2008.
13. Zadeh, L.A., Fuzzy sets. *Inf. Control*, 8, 3, 338–353, 1965.
14. What is Fuzzy Logic? *Mechanical Engineering Discussion Forum*, mechanicalsite.com, Retrieved November 11, 2018.
15. Babuška, R., *Fuzzy Modeling for Control*, Springer Science & Business Media, 1998, ISBN 978-94-011-4868-9. Fuzzy Logic. YouTube, Retrieved May 11, 2020.
16. K. H., Asli, S.A.O., Aliyev, S., Thomas, D.A. Gopakumar, (Eds.), *Handbook of research for fluid and solid mechanics: theory, simulation, and experiment*, CRC Press, 2017.
17. Chaudhuri, A., Mandaviya, K., Badelia, P., K Ghosh, S., Chaudhuri, A., Mandaviya, K., Ghosh, S.K., *Optical character recognition systems*, pp. 9–41, Springer International Publishing, 2017.
18. Zadeh, L.A., Klir, G.J., Yuan, B., *Fuzzy sets, fuzzy logic, and fuzzy systems: selected papers*, vol. 6, World scientific, 1996.
19. Xiao, Z., Xia, S., Gong, K., Li, D., The trapezoidal fuzzy soft set and its application in MCDM. *Appl. Math. Modell.*, 36, 12, 5846–5847, 2012, December 1, doi: 10.1016/j.apm.2012.01.036.

20. Wierman, M.J., *An Introduction to the Mathematics of Uncertainty: including Set Theory, Logic, Probability, Fuzzy Sets, Rough Sets, and Evidence Theory*, Creighton University, Retrieved July 16, 2016.
21. Zadeh, L.A., A fuzzy-set-theoretic interpretation of linguistic hedges, 1972.
22. Sousa, J.M., Babuška, R., Verbruggen, H.B., Fuzzy predictive control applied to an air-conditioning system. *Control Eng. Pract.*, *5*, 10, 1395–1406, 1997.
23. Haruki, T. and Kikuchi, K., Video camera system using fuzzy logic. *IEEE Trans. Consum. Electron.*, *38*, 3, 624–634, 1992.
24. Lucas, C., Milasi, R.M., Araabi, B.N., Intelligent modeling and control of washing machine using locally linear neuro-fuzzy (llnf) modeling and modified brain emotional learning based intelligent controller (BELBIC). *Asian J. Control*, *8*, 4, 393–400, 2006.
25. Godoy, J., Pérez, J., Onieva, E., Villagrá, J., Milanés, V., Haber, R., A driverless vehicle demonstration on motorways and in urban environments. *Transport*, *30*, 3, 253–263, 2015.

4

Application of Neutrosophic Over Hypersoft Sets in the Selection of Food Shop Locations

R. Narmada Devi* **and Yamini Parthiban**

Department of Mathematics, Vel Tech Rangarajan Dr. Sagunthala R&D Institute of Science and Technology, Avadi, Chennai, Tamil Nadu, India

Abstract

Risk is always with us in our day-to-day activities, right from throwing a dice or flipping a coin and having it to land on a quilt. In making decisions for instance when deciding where to locate a grocery store, then there is need to use complex mathematical concepts as a way of dealing with uncertainty and vagueness that is inherent in real life data. This paper presents a new solution that is developed by integrating Neutrosophic Set Theory with Hypersoft Set Theory to explain how one can solve a problem of choosing the right place to open a food shop. Neutrosophic Set Theory is introduced to depict the uncertainty of location factors including population density, competition, and consumers' preference as such factors are imprecise. Hypersoft Set Theory on the contrary is an extension of the classical soft set theory that provides a mechanism for incorporating the idea of a soft set whose members have real degrees of being a part of the set, thus providing for a more accurate description of the impacts of location parameters. These theoretical constructs are used in this study to offer a sound foundation for decision-making in relation to the placement of a food store, with regard to many variables and correlations and assisted uncertainties. By means of an analytic case study and comparison, the adaption and utility of the suggested approach as a tool for a decision-making process in the field of business location choosing is substantiated by using correlation method.

Keywords: Neutrosophic over hypersoft sets, neutrosophic over hypersoft topological space, neutrosophic over hypersoft function

**Corresponding author*: narmadadevi23@gmail.com

Rahul Kar, Gunjan Mukherjee, Biswadip Basu Mallik and Ashok Kumar Shaw (eds.) Fuzzy Logic in Computational Intelligence: Applications and Case Studies, (55–66) © 2026 Scrivener Publishing LLC

4.1 Introduction

[23] Zadeh in 1965 introduced fuzzy sets, laying the groundwork for handling vagueness in data through membership functions, initiating a major shift in uncertainty modeling. [3] Bellman and Zadeh in 1970 applied fuzzy set theory to decision-making under uncertainty, providing the first model for fuzzy decision environments in management science. [24] Zadeh in 1978 further extended fuzzy set theory by proposing the possibility theory, presenting an alternative framework to probability for modeling imprecise information. [13] Molodtsov in 1999 proposed soft set theory as a new mathematical tool to address uncertainties without the need for parameterization, significantly influencing decision sciences. [18] Smarandache in 1999 introduced neutrosophic logic, generalizing fuzzy and intuitionistic logic to model indeterminacy explicitly, leading to neutrosophic set theory. [12] Maji *et al.* in 2003 developed foundational operations for soft set theory, enhancing its utility in decision-making and establishing a basis for further theoretical growth. [1] Ali *et al.* in 2009 investigated new operations within soft set theory, offering innovative algebraic structures and properties to facilitate complex applications. [2] Atanassov in 2012 comprehensively explored intuitionistic fuzzy sets, extending fuzzy logic with degrees of membership and non-membership to improve modeling precision.

Broumi [4] in 2013 introduced the generalized neutrosophic soft set, merging neutrosophic and soft set theories to better handle data ambiguity and vagueness. [16] Saeed *et al.* in 2020 laid down the foundational theory of hypersoft sets, generalizing soft sets to allow multi-parameterized data structures for flexible modeling. [17] Saqlain *et al.* in 2020 proposed single and multi-valued neutrosophic hypersoft sets with similarity measures, contributing novel tools for complex decision-making scenarios. [19] Smarandache in 2016 introduced the neutrosophic overset, underset, and offset, which allow modeling beyond classical boundaries in logic and uncertainty quantification. [20] Smarandache in 2017 developed the theory of plithogeny and plithogenic sets, enabling multidimensional decision-making through aggregation of contradictory attributes.

[21] Smarandache in 2018a extended soft sets to hypersoft sets and plithogenic hypersoft sets, broadening the framework for uncertainty modeling in multiple domains. [22] Smarandache in 2018b revisited the plithogenic set, further refining its theoretical construction as an encompassing model over crisp, fuzzy, and neutrosophic sets. [5] Feng and Guo in 2018 proposed a fuzzy soft set-based group decision-making method, integrating fuzzy logic with soft set parameters for enhanced consensus modeling. [6] Devi and Parthiban in 2023 introduced a correlation-based decision model

using neutrosophic pythagorean soft sets, improving selection accuracy in multi-criteria problems. [11] Kumaravel *et al.* in 2023 applied fuzzy and neutrosophic cognitive maps to analyze the spread and impact of dengue, showcasing the fusion of medical and computational intelligence.

[14] Murugesan *et al.* in 2023 conducted a comparative analysis of fuzzy and neutrosophic cognitive maps to understand COVID-19 variants, advancing disease modeling frameworks. Devi and Parthiban have made significant contributions to the development and application of neutrosophic and soft topological frameworks in decision-making across various domains. In 2024, they introduced decision-making methodologies using neutrosophic over soft topological spaces [7], and extended this approach by integrating plithogenic hypersoft sets with the TOPSIS method for school selection problems [8]. That same year, they explored neutrosophic over supra exterior modal topological structures for healthcare applications [9], and utilized neutrosophic over soft hyperconnected spaces for analyzing pharmaceutical compounds [10]. In 2025, they applied neutrosophic pythagorean supra topological spaces in attribute-based decision-making, enhancing analytical depth in management sciences [15].

4.2 Preliminary

Definition 4.2.1 Let $^{\circ}\mathrm{F}$ be a universal set and $\mathcal{Q}$ is said to be a neutrosophic set (NS). Then

$$\mathcal{Q}=\left\{\left\langle \mathfrak{w},\aleph_Q(\mathfrak{w}),\mathfrak{Z}_Q,(\mathfrak{w})\Upsilon_Q(\mathfrak{w})\right\rangle:\mathfrak{w}\in {}^{\circ}\mathrm{F}\right\}$$

where $0\leq\aleph_Q(\mathfrak{w})+\mathfrak{Z}_Q(\mathfrak{w})+\Upsilon_Q(\mathfrak{w})\leq 3$, for all $\mathfrak{w}\in {}^{\circ}\mathrm{F},\aleph_Q,\mathfrak{Z}_Q,\Upsilon_Q\in[0,1]$. Here $\aleph_Q(\mathfrak{w})$ be a degree of true membership, $\mathfrak{Z}_Q(\mathfrak{w})$ be a degree of indeterminacy and $\Upsilon_Q(\mathfrak{w})$ be a degree of falsity.

Definition 4.2.2 Let $^{\circ}\mathrm{F}$ be a universal set and NS $\mathcal{Q}$ is said to be a neutrosophic over set (NO-set). If it is characterized as having at least one neutrosophic component that is >1 and no other components that are <0,

$$\mathcal{Q}=\left\{\left\langle \mathfrak{w},\aleph_Q(\mathfrak{w}),\mathfrak{Z}_Q(\mathfrak{w}),\Upsilon_Q(\mathfrak{w})\right\rangle:\mathfrak{w}\in {}^{\circ}\mathrm{F}\right\}$$

where $0\leq\aleph_Q(\mathfrak{w})+\mathfrak{Z}_Q(\mathfrak{w})+\Upsilon_Q(\mathfrak{w})\leq 3$, for all $\mathfrak{w}\in {}^{\circ}\mathrm{F},\aleph_Q,\mathfrak{Z}_Q,\Upsilon_Q\in[0,\Omega]$, ' is called as over limit. Here $\aleph_Q(\mathfrak{w})$ be a degree of true membership, $\mathfrak{Z}_Q(\mathfrak{w})$ be a degree of indeterminacy and $\Upsilon_Q(\mathfrak{w})$ be a degree of falsity.

Definition 4.2.3 Let °F be a universal set and NO-set Q is said to be an NO-universal set and NO- null set are denoted as $\Delta = \{\langle \mathfrak{w}, \Omega, \Omega, 0\rangle : \mathfrak{w} \in °\mathrm{F}\}$ and $\nabla = \{\langle \mathfrak{w}, 0, 0, \Omega\rangle : \mathfrak{w} \in °\mathrm{F}\}$.

Remark 4.2.4

(i). Δ^C=∇

(ii). ∇^C=Δ

Definition 4.2.5 Let $°\mathrm{F}^{p}$ be a power set of °F and $n \geq 1$, there are n distinct attributes such as $\mathfrak{K}_1, \mathfrak{K}_2, \mathfrak{K}_3 \ldots \mathfrak{K}_n$ with the intersection of any two attributes is ∇. Pair (F,Q) is said to be NHS-set on °F. If there exists a relation $\mathfrak{K}_1 \times \mathfrak{K}_2 \times \mathfrak{K}_3 \times \ldots \times \mathfrak{K}_n = Q$. Where $F: \mathfrak{K}_1 \times \mathfrak{K}_2 \times \mathfrak{K}_3 \times \ldots \times \mathfrak{K}_n \rightarrow °\mathrm{F}^{p}$ and $F_Q(\mathfrak{K}_1 \times \mathfrak{K}_2 \times \mathfrak{K}_3 \times \ldots \times \mathfrak{K}_n) = \{\langle \mathfrak{w}, \aleph_Q(\mathfrak{w}), \mathfrak{Z}_Q(\mathfrak{w}), \Upsilon_Q(\mathfrak{w})\rangle : \mathfrak{w} \in °\mathrm{F}\}$.

4.3 Neutrosophic Over Hypersoft Topological Space and Tangent Similarity Measure

Definition 4.3.1 Let °F be a universal set and $°\mathrm{F}^{p}$ be a power set of °F and $n \geq 1$, there are n distinct attributes such as $\mathfrak{K}_1, \mathfrak{K}_2, \mathfrak{K}_3 \ldots \mathfrak{K}_n$ with the intersection of any two attributes is ∇. Then the pair (F, Q) is said to be NOHS-set on °F. If there exists a relation $\mathfrak{K}_1 \times \mathfrak{K}_2 \times \mathfrak{K}_3 \times \ldots \times \mathfrak{K}_n = Q$. Where $F: \mathfrak{K}_1 \times \mathfrak{K}_2 \times \mathfrak{K}_3 \times \ldots \times \mathfrak{K}_n \rightarrow °\mathrm{F}^{p}$ and $F_Q(\mathfrak{K}_1 \times \mathfrak{K}_2 \times \mathfrak{K}_3 \times \ldots \times \mathfrak{K}_n) = \{\langle \mathfrak{w}, \aleph_Q(\mathfrak{w}), \mathfrak{Z}_Q(\mathfrak{w}), \Upsilon_Q(\mathfrak{w})\rangle : \mathfrak{w} \in °\mathrm{F}\}$.

Definition 4.3.2 Let (F, Q) and (F, R) be any two NOHS-sets then union, intersection and compliment and other properties are defined as

(i) $$(F, Q \cup R) = \Big\{\Big\langle \mathfrak{w}, \max(\aleph_Q(\mathfrak{w}), \aleph_R(\mathfrak{w})), \max(\mathfrak{Z}_Q(\mathfrak{w}), \mathfrak{Z}_R(\mathfrak{w})), \min(\Upsilon_Q(\mathfrak{w}), \Upsilon_Q(\mathfrak{w}))\Big\rangle : \mathfrak{w} \in °\mathrm{F}\Big\}$$

(ii) $$(F, Q \cap R) = \Big\{\Big\langle \mathfrak{w}, \min(\aleph_Q(\mathfrak{w}), \aleph_R(\mathfrak{w})), \min(\mathfrak{Z}_Q(\mathfrak{w}), \mathfrak{Z}_R(\mathfrak{w})), \max(\Upsilon_Q(\mathfrak{w}), \Upsilon_Q(\mathfrak{w}))\Big\rangle : \mathfrak{w} \in °\mathrm{F}\Big\}$$

(iii) $(F, Q^c) = \{\langle \mathfrak{w}, \Upsilon_Q(\mathfrak{w}), \Omega - \mathfrak{Z}_Q(\aleph), \mathfrak{w}_Q(\mathfrak{w})\rangle : \mathfrak{w} \in °\mathrm{F}\}$

(iv) $\nabla \cup Q = Q$

(v) $\boxplus \cup Q = \boxplus$

(vi) $Q \cap \nabla = \nabla$

(vii) $\boxplus \cap Q = Q$

(viii) $Q \cup R = R \cup Q$

(ix) $R \cap Q = Q \cap R$
(x) $(Q^c)^c = Q$

Definition 4.3.3 A NOHS-Topology τ is an assortment of subgroups of °F then it satisfies the following condition,

(i) Δ, ∇∈τ
(ii) Union of the sets of any sub-collection of τ is in τ
(iii) Intersection of the elements of any finite sub-collection τ is in τ

Then (°F,τ) pair is known as NOHS-topological space. Where a collection of τ is called a NOHS open set. Compliment of τ is known as NOHS closed set.

Definition 4.3.4
Let Q be NOHS-set then NOHS-topological interior and closure are defined as

$$int(Q) = \cup\{L: L \subseteq {}^{\circ}\mathrm{F} \text{ and } L \in \tau\}$$

$$cl(Q) = \cap\{M: M \supseteq {}^{\circ}\mathrm{F} \text{ and } M^C \in \tau\}$$

Proposition 4.3.5
Let (°F,τ) is an NOHS-topological space and Q be an NOHS-set then

(i) $int(Q)$ is the largest NOHS open set
(ii) $cl(Q)$ is the smallest NOHS closed set

Proof: The proof is obvious.

Definition 4.3.6 Let two NOHS-set as $= \{\langle \mathfrak{w}, \aleph_Q(\mathfrak{w}), \mathfrak{Z}_Q(\mathfrak{w}), \Upsilon_Q(\mathfrak{w})\rangle : \mathfrak{w} \in {}^{\circ}\mathrm{F}\}$ and $R = \{\langle y, \aleph_R(y), \mathfrak{Z}_R(y), \Upsilon_R(y)\rangle : y \in \mathfrak{Y}\}$ and $\mathfrak{f}^{\rightarrow} : {}^{\circ}\mathrm{F} \rightarrow \mathfrak{Y}$ be a function,

(i) $\mathfrak{f}^{\rightarrow}(Q) = \left\{\left\langle y, \mathfrak{f}^{\rightarrow}(\aleph_Q)(y), \mathfrak{f}^{\rightarrow}(\mathfrak{Z}_Q)(y), \left(1 - \mathfrak{f}^{\rightarrow}(1 - \Upsilon_Q)\right)(y)\right\rangle : y \in \mathfrak{Y}\right\}$
is a NOHS-set on Q called the image of Q under $\mathfrak{f}^{\rightarrow}$

(ii) $\mathfrak{f}^{\leftarrow}(R) = \{\langle \mathfrak{w}, \mathfrak{f}^{\leftarrow}(\aleph_S)(\mathfrak{w}), \mathfrak{f}^{\leftarrow}(\mathfrak{Z}_R)(\mathfrak{w}), \mathfrak{f}^{\leftarrow}(\Upsilon_R)(\mathfrak{w})\rangle : \mathfrak{w} \in {}^{\circ}\mathrm{F}\}$ is a NOHS-set on $\mathfrak{Y}$ is called the pre-image of R under $\mathfrak{f}^{\rightarrow}$

where,

$$\mathfrak{f}^{\rightarrow}(\aleph_Q)(y)=\begin{cases}\sup\limits_{\mathfrak{w}\in\mathfrak{f}^{\leftarrow}}(y)\aleph_Q(\mathfrak{w}), & \text{if } \mathfrak{f}^{\leftarrow}(y)\neq\varnothing\\ 0, & \text{otherwise}\end{cases}$$

$$\mathfrak{f}^{\rightarrow}(\mathfrak{Z}_Q)(y)=\begin{cases}\sup\limits_{\mathfrak{w}\in\mathfrak{f}^{\leftarrow}}(y)\mathfrak{Z}_Q(\mathfrak{w}), & \text{if } \mathfrak{f}^{\leftarrow}(y)\neq\varnothing\\ 0, & \text{otherwise}\end{cases}$$

$$\left(1-\mathfrak{f}^{\rightarrow}(1-\Upsilon_Q)\right)(y)=\begin{cases}\mathop{inf}\limits_{\mathfrak{w}\in\mathfrak{f}^{\leftarrow}}(y)\Upsilon_Q(\mathfrak{w}), & \text{if and only if } \mathfrak{f}^{\leftarrow}(y)\neq\varnothing\\ 1, & \text{otherwise}\end{cases}$$

Let us introduce the symbol $\mathfrak{f}^{\rightarrow}_{-}(\Upsilon_Q)$ for $\left(1-\mathfrak{f}^{\rightarrow}(1-\Upsilon_Q)\right)$

Definition 4.3.7

Consider two NOHS-sets $\mathcal{Q}$ and $\mathcal{S}$ over °F. Then develop a tangent similarity metric that measures how well two sets align with each other, ignoring any differences in their separation.

Tangent Similarity Measure

$\rho(\mathcal{Q},\mathcal{S})=$

$$\frac{1}{n}\left(\sum_{i=1}^{n}1-\tan\left[\frac{\pi\left[\left|\aleph_Q(\mathfrak{w})-\aleph_S(\mathfrak{w})\right|+\left|\mathfrak{Z}_Q(\mathfrak{w})-\mathfrak{Z}_S(\mathfrak{w})\right|+\left|\Upsilon_Q(\mathfrak{w})-\Upsilon_S(\mathfrak{w})\right|\right]}{12}\right]\right)$$

Proposition 4.3.8 The defined tangent similarity ($\rho(\mathcal{Q},\mathcal{S})$) for the two NOHS-sets $\mathcal{Q}$ and $\mathcal{S}$ over a universal set °F. Then,

(i) $0\leq\rho(\mathcal{Q},\mathcal{S})\leq 1$
(ii) $\rho(\mathcal{Q},\mathcal{S})=1$ iff $\mathcal{Q}=\mathcal{S}$
(iii) $\rho(\mathcal{Q},\mathcal{S})=\rho(\mathcal{S},\mathcal{Q})$

Proof: (i) Since $\aleph_Q, \mathfrak{Z}_Q, \Upsilon_Q$ of the NOHS-sets fall within the interval [0, Ω], and resulting correlation measure based on the tangent function will likewise yield values within [0,1].

Hence $0\leq\rho(\mathcal{Q},\mathcal{S})\leq 1$

(ii) Any two NOHS-sets $\mathcal{Q}$ and $\mathcal{S}$

if $\mathcal{Q}=\mathcal{S}$ then

$$\Rightarrow \aleph_Q(\mathfrak{w}) = \aleph_S(\mathfrak{w}),\ \mathfrak{Z}_Q(\mathfrak{w}) = \mathfrak{Z}_S(\mathfrak{w}),\ \Upsilon_Q(\mathfrak{w}) = \Upsilon_S(\mathfrak{w})$$

Then $|\aleph_Q(\mathfrak{w}) - \aleph_S(\mathfrak{w})| = 0, |\mathfrak{Z}_Q(\mathfrak{w}) - \mathfrak{Z}_S(\mathfrak{w})| = 0, |\Upsilon_Q(\mathfrak{w}) - \Upsilon_S(\mathfrak{w})| = 0$
Thus $\rho(\mathcal{Q},\mathcal{S}) = 1$
Conversely, $\rho(\mathcal{Q},\mathcal{S}) = 1$
Then $|\aleph_Q(\mathfrak{w}) - \aleph_S(\mathfrak{w})| = 0, |\mathfrak{Z}_Q(\mathfrak{w}) - \mathfrak{Z}_S(\mathfrak{w})| = 0, |\Upsilon_Q(\mathfrak{w}) - \Upsilon_S(\mathfrak{w})| = 0$

$$\Rightarrow |\aleph_Q(\mathfrak{w}) - \aleph_S(\mathfrak{w})| = 0, |\mathfrak{Z}_Q(\mathfrak{w}) - \mathfrak{Z}_S(\mathfrak{w})| = 0, |\Upsilon_Q(\mathfrak{w}) - \Upsilon_S(\mathfrak{w})| = 0$$
$$\Rightarrow \mathcal{Q} = \mathcal{S}$$

(iii) From the definition we know that,

$$\rho(\mathcal{Q},\mathcal{S}) = \frac{1}{n}\left(\sum_{i=1}^{n} 1 - \tan\left[\frac{\pi\left[|\aleph_Q(\mathfrak{w}) - \aleph_S(\mathfrak{w})| + |\mathfrak{Z}_Q(\mathfrak{w}) - \mathfrak{Z}_S(\mathfrak{w})| + |\Upsilon_Q(\mathfrak{w}) - \Upsilon_S(\mathfrak{w})|\right]}{12}\right]\right)$$
$$= \frac{1}{n}\left(\sum_{i=1}^{n} 1 - \tan\left[\frac{\pi\left[|\aleph_S(\mathfrak{w}) - \aleph_Q(\mathfrak{w})| + |\mathfrak{Z}_S(\mathfrak{w}) - \mathfrak{Z}_Q(\mathfrak{w})| + |\Upsilon_S(\mathfrak{w}) - \Upsilon_Q(\mathfrak{w})|\right]}{12}\right]\right)$$
$$= \rho(\mathcal{Q},\mathcal{S})$$
$$\Rightarrow \rho(\mathcal{Q},\mathcal{S}) = \rho(\mathcal{S},\mathcal{Q})$$

4.4 Algorithm

Step 1: Collection of Data

Consider $\mathfrak{m}$ attributes $\mathcal{A}_1,\mathcal{A}_2,\mathcal{A}_3,\ldots,\mathcal{A}_\mathfrak{m},\mathcal{A}$ replacement $\mathcal{C}_1,\mathcal{C}_2,\mathcal{C}_3,\ldots,\mathcal{C}_\mathfrak{n}$ and $\mathfrak{p}$ replacement $\mathcal{D}_1,\mathcal{D}_2,\mathcal{D}_3,\ldots,\mathcal{D}_\mathfrak{p}$. Here $(\mathfrak{n} \le \mathfrak{p})$ for multi-attributes decision making problem (MADMP).

$\mathcal{D}_\mathfrak{p} \setminus \mathcal{A}$	$\mathcal{A}_1$	$\mathcal{A}_2$	...	$\mathcal{A}_m$
$\mathcal{D}_1$	$\mathfrak{d}_{11}$	$\mathfrak{d}_{12}$	...	$\mathfrak{d}_{1m}$
$\mathcal{D}_2$	$\mathfrak{d}_{21}$	$\mathfrak{d}_{12}$	...	$\mathfrak{d}_{2m}$
.	.	.	.	.
.	.	.	.	.
.	.	.	.	.
$\mathcal{D}_p$	$\mathfrak{d}_{p1}$	$\mathfrak{d}_{p2}$	...	$\mathfrak{d}_{pm}$

$\daleth_i \setminus \mathcal{C}_j$	$\mathcal{C}_1$	$\mathcal{C}_2$	...	$\mathcal{C}_n$
$\daleth_1$	λ_{11}	λ_{12}	...	λ_{1n}
$\daleth_2$	λ_{21}	λ_{22}	...	λ_{2n}
.	.	.	.	.
.	.	.	.	.
.	.	.	.	.
$\daleth_m$	$\daleth_{m1}$	λ_{m2}	...	λ_{mn}

Step 2: Calculation
Calculating the tangent similarity measure with collected data.

Step 3: Final Decision
Pick the highest tangent measure from each row.

4.5 Flow Chart

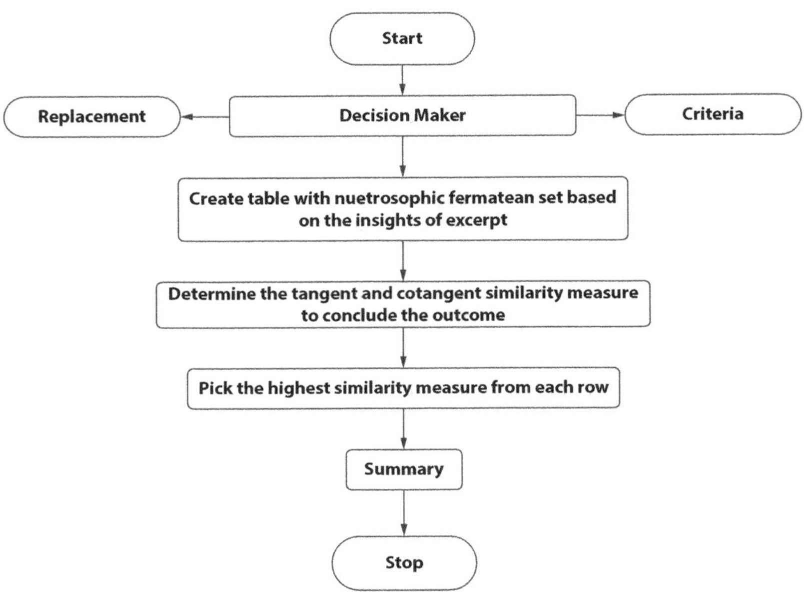

4.6 Numerical Illustrations

Location plays a crucial role in the decision-making process when setting up a food shop, as it influences visibility, accessibility, and customer traffic flow. A good location contributes to brand familiarity since it will attract more people; this is because visibility and traffic hand the word-of-mouth advantage to a business. Another factor is relative accessibility; a store that can be accessed by different means of transport and has sufficient parking space increases the customers' ease and frequency of visitation. Conforming to zoning and health laws is instrumental in making operations to run smoothly while reviewing the cost of rent and possibility of expansion provides the means of assessing the financial viability and expansion of the business. Therefore, the choice of a location is never good for the operational performance of the shop only, but also for its sustained success and profitability.

Let S be a shop spots in different location given as $S = \{s_1, s_2, s_3\}$

Let ε be the set of result category under consideration given as

$$\varepsilon = \{Selected(\varepsilon_1), Not-selected(\varepsilon_2)\}$$

The set of attributes related to S and ε is

$$\beth = \{Budget(\beth_1), Neighborhood(\beth_2), Accessibility(\beth_3)\}$$

Here,

$$\beth_1 = \{Base\ rent(\beth_{11}),\ Moderate\ rent(\beth_{12}),\ High\ rent(\beth_{13})\}$$

$$\beth_2 = \{Safe(\beth_{21}), Unsafe(\beth_{22})\}$$

$$\beth_3 = \{Minimum(\beth_{31}), Desired(\beth_{32}), Excellent(\beth_{33})\}$$

Then NOHS-set are given as

$$F_S(\beth_{12} \times \beth_{21} \times \beth_{33}) = \{s_1, s_2, s_3\}$$

$$F_\varepsilon(\beth_{12} \times \beth_{21} \times \beth_{33}) = \{\varepsilon_1, \varepsilon_2, \varepsilon_3\}$$

Table 4.6.1 presents the relationship between the set of attributes and shop spots in different location, displaying their corresponding neutrosophic values. Table 4.6.2 presents the relationship between the set of result category under consideration and set of attributes. Table 4.6.3 provides the computed association between the evaluation criteria and each shop spot, helping to quantify their suitability. Finally, Table 4.6.4 summarizes the decision outcome, clearly indicating which shop spot has been selected based on the neutrosophic analysis.

Table 4.6.1 Relation between $\beth$ and S.

	$\beth_{12}$	$\beth_{21}$	$\beth_{33}$
s_1	(1.8,0.3,0.1)	(1.5,0.4,0.1)	(1.6,0.4,0.1)
s_2	(0.8,1.02,1.02)	(0.9,1.1,0.1)	(0.9,0.1,1.2)
s_3	(1.7,0.3,0.2)	(0.7,1.4,0.0)	(0.7,0.3,1.2)

Table 4.6.2 Relation between $\beth$ and ε.

	ε_1	ε_2
$\beth_{12}$	(0.5,0.3,1.3)	(1.7,0.1,0.3)
$\beth_{21}$	(0.6,0.3,1.2)	(1.6,0.3,0.2)
$\beth_{33}$	(0.7,1.3,0.1)	(0.7,1.2,0.1)

Table 4.6.3 Relation between ε and S.

	ε_1	ε_2
s_1	0.9903	**0.9963**
s_2	**0.9909**	0.9902
s_3	0.9898	**0.9933**

Table 4.6.4 Relation between ε and S.

Shop spots	**Decision**
s_1	Not selected
s_2	Selected
s_3	Not selected

4.7 Conclusion

Location is one of the most critical factors in the performance of any food shop since it affects observation by customers, ease of access and traffic. A good selection of sites can thus help place the brand in very conspicuous areas with high human traffic which is crucial in creating awareness, and encouraging people to visit the premise unknown to them that they actually want to go there as well as getting people to revisit the place. Transportation is an important factor; if a store is easy to get to by a number of means of transport and has enough parking spaces, then customers and visitors would be frequenting the place more often. Demographic knowledge of the particular area is also essential so as not to attract competitors' audiences and offer appropriate products and advertisements. The restriction in accordance to zoning and health issues is of paramount concern and assessment of rent expenses and growth assists to approach the organization's financial wellbeing. This paper shows how these factors led to the choice of location s_2 to underscore the criticality of a proper site choice to achieving optimal operation and sustainable profitability of the company.

References

1. Ali, M.I., Feng, F., Liu, X., Min, W.K., Shabir, M., On some new operations in soft set theory. *Comput. Math. Appl.*, 57, 9, 1547–1553, 2009.
2. Atanassov, K.T., *On intuitionistic fuzzy sets theory*, vol. 283, Springer, 2012.
3. Bellman, R.E. and Zadeh, L.A., Decision-making in a fuzzy environment. *Manage. Sci.*, 17, 4, B–141, 1970.
4. Broumi, S., *Generalized neutrosophic soft set*, Infinite Study, 2013.
5. Feng, Q. and Guo, X., A novel approach to fuzzy soft set-based group decision-making. *Complexity*, 2018.
6. Christianto, V., Boyd, R.N., Smarandache, F., *Three possible applications of neutrosophic logic in fundamental and applied sciences*, Infinite Study, 2020.
7. Devi, R.N. and Parthiban, Y., Decision making process over neutrosophic pythagorean soft sets using measure of correlation. *Southeast Eur. J. Soft Comput.*, 12, 2, 06–09, 2023.
8. Devi, R.N. and Parthiban, Y., Enhancing Decision-Making for Parents: A Neutrosophic Pythagorean Plithogenic Hypersoft Set Approach to School Selection With TOPSIS Method, in: *MultiCriteria Decision Making Models and Techniques: Neutrosophic Approaches*, pp. 01–20, IGI Global, 2024.

9. Devi, R.N. and Parthiban, Y., Exploring neutrosophic over supra exterior modal topological structure: Theory and application in healthcare decision-making. *Neutrosophic Sets Syst.*, 72, 272–285, 2024.
10. Devi, R.N. and Parthiban, Y., Analyzing pharmaceutical compounds through neutrosophic over soft hyperconnected spaces. *Orient. J. Chem.*, 40, 6, 1627–1633, 2024.
11. Kumaravel, S.K., Murugesan, R., Nagaram, N.B., Rasappan, S., Yamini, G., Applications of fuzzy cognitive maps and neutrosophic cognitive maps on analysis of dengue fever, in: *Fuzzy Logic Applications in Computer Science and Mathematics*, pp. 249–265, 2023.
12. Maji, P.K., Biswas, R., Roy, A.R., Soft set theory. *Comput. Math. Appl.*, 45, 4–5, 555–562, 2003.
13. Molodtsov, D., Soft set theory first results. *Comput. Math. Appl.*, 37, 4–5, 19–31, 1999.
14. Murugesan, R., Parthiban, Y., Devi, R., Mohan, K.R., Kumarave, S.K., A Comparative Study of Fuzzy Cognitive Maps and Neutrosophic Cognitive Maps on Covid Variants. *Neutrosophic Sets Syst.*, 55, 1, 20, 2023.
15. Devi, R.N. and Parthiban, Y., Application of Neutrosophic Pythagorean Supra Topological Spaces in Attribute Decision-Making, in: *Applications of Fuzzy Logic in Decision Making and Management Science*. Information Systems Engineering and Management, vol. 29, Springer, Cham, 2025.
16. Saeed, M., Ahsan, M., Siddique, M.K., Ahmad, M.R., *A study of the fundamentals of hypersoft set theory*, Infinite Study, 2020.
17. Saqlain, M., Jafar, N., Moin, S., Saeed, M., Broumi, S., Single and multi-valued neutrosophic hypersoft set and tangent similarity measure of single valued neutrosophic hypersoft sets. *Neutrosophic Sets Syst.*, 32, 1, 317–329, 2020.
18. Smarandache, F., A unifying field in Logics: Neutrosophic Logic, in: *Philosophy*, pp. 1–141, American Research Press, 1999.
19. Smarandache, F., *Neutrosophic Overset, Neutrosophic Underset, and Neutrosophic Offset. Similarly for Neutrosophic Over-/Under-/Off-Logic, Probability, and Statistics*, Infinite Study, 2016.
20. Smarandache, F., *Plithogeny, plithogenic set, logic, probability, and statistics*, Infinite Study, 2017.
21. Smarandache, F., Extension of soft set to hypersoft set, and then to plithogenic hypersoft set. *Neutrosophic Sets Syst.*, 22, 1, 168–170, 2018.
22. Smarandache, F., *Plithogenic set, an extension of crisp, fuzzy, intuitionistic fuzzy, and neutrosophic sets-revisited*, Infinite Study, 2018.
23. Zadeh, L.A., Fuzzy sets. *Inf. Control*, 8, 3, 338–353, 1965.
24. Zadeh, L.A., Fuzzy sets as a basis for a theory of possibility. *Fuzzy Sets Syst.*, 1, 1, 3–28, 1978.

Part 2

FUZZY APPLICATION WITH AI AND ML CONCEPT

5

Application of Fuzzy Set Theory to AI and Machine Learning Domain

Gourab Dutta, Rahul Kumar Ghosh and Gunjan Mukherjee*

Department of Computational Sciences, Brainware University, Kolkata, India

Abstract

Fuzzy set theory has emerged as a significant technique in artificial intelligence (AI) and machine learning (ML) for effectively handling the inherent uncertainty and imprecision in real-world data. This abstract explores the significant impact of fuzzy set theory on artificial intelligence (AI) and machine learning (ML) methodologies, offering a comprehensive overview of its applications and benefits. The incorporation of fuzzy set theory into AI and ML systems improves their efficacy by including the concept of partial membership and granular boundaries. This enables them to precisely describe and analyze information that is confusing, ambiguous, and uncertain. AI systems can employ fuzzy logic-based inference mechanisms, such as fuzzy rule-based systems and fuzzy clustering algorithms, to improve decision-making and extract important insights from complex and ambiguous datasets with increased accuracy and robustness. Moreover, the integration of fuzzy set theory with deep learning frameworks has led to the development of hybrid models that can proficiently handle both structured and unstructured data effortlessly. This abstract also explores the challenges and future directions in applying fuzzy set theory in machine learning (ML) and artificial intelligence (AI) domains, including the need for algorithms capable of handling large-scale problems, the ability to interpret the outcomes, and the resilience against adversarial attacks. Generally, the integration of fuzzy set theory represents a fundamental shift in how machine learning (ML) and artificial intelligence (AI) systems comprehend and examine ambiguity. This modification creates opportunities for the advancement of intelligence that is flexible enough, resilient, and capable of imitating human-like behavior.

**Corresponding author*: mukherjee.gunjan@gmail.com

Rahul Kar, Gunjan Mukherjee, Biswadip Basu Mallik and Ashok Kumar Shaw (eds.) Fuzzy Logic in Computational Intelligence: Applications and Case Studies, (69–86) © 2026 Scrivener Publishing LLC

Keywords: Fuzzy set, AIML, fuzzy rule-base, fuzzy logic-base, fuzzy clustering algorithms

5.1 Introduction of Fuzzy Set Theory

The initial works on fuzzy theory by Zadeh [1965] and Goguen [1967, 1969] demonstrate extending the traditional idea of a set and allied proposition to incorporate the idea of fuzziness, as explained in section 1.1. Zadeh (1965, p. 339) states, "The notion of a fuzzy set provides a convenient point of departure for the construction of a conceptual framework which parallels in many respects the framework used in the case of ordinary sets but is more general than the latter and, potentially, may prove to have a much wider scope of applicability, particularly in the fields of pattern classification and information processing. Essentially, such a framework provides a natural way of dealing with problems in which the source of imprecision is the absence of sharply defined criteria for class membership rather than the presence of random variables. In this context "meant" refers to the concept of ambiguity instead of the absence of information regarding the parametric values, as seen in tolerance analysis [37, 38].

The fuzzy theory offers a rigorous mathematics framework for the detailed study of hazy conceptual phenomena. It may also be seen as a modeling language suitable for situations with fuzzy linkages, criteria, and phenomena [19]. The semantic definition of fuzziness has not yet been established definitively and is unlikely ever to be. The interpretation of its meaning will vary based on the specific field of application and the measurement method. Meanwhile, a multitude of authors have made significant contributions to this idea [28]. By 1984, there were already up to 4,000 publications, and by 2000, the number had increased to almost 30,000. The proliferation of these publications potentially intensifies, rendering it increasingly challenging for novices in this field to locate a suitable introduction and comprehend and value the philosophy, formalism, and practicality of the concerned theory. In broad view, the fuzzy theory has evolved in dual and distinct directions during the past twenty years:

1. As a formal theory, it has evolved to become more complex and precise over time. It has incorporated conceptual novelty, and expanded by including traditional fields of mathematics such as algebra, graph theory, topology, and others, using the generic concept and making them less precise (fuzzifying).

2. As a practical and versatile technology, fuzzy logic serves as a valuable for modeling, problem-solving, and data mining. It has demonstrated its superiority over current methods in some circumstances and is also a beneficial addition to traditional approaches in other scenarios.

5.2 Fuzzy Basic Definitions

A classical concept of set is typically described as a collection consisting of different elements or objects x belonging to X, which might possess the finiteness or uncountable, or uncountable. Every individual element can be classified as either a member or a non-member of a set A, denoted as $A \subseteq X$. In the first scenario, the statement "x is a member of A" is accurate, but in the second case, this assertion is incorrect. A classical set is defined in various ways. One approach is to make enumeration of the elements that belong to the set. Another option is to describe the set analytically by membership conditions, such as $A = \{x \mid x \leq 5\}$. Alternatively, the member elements can be defined using the characteristic function, where I indicate membership and 0 indicates non-membership. The characteristic function of a fuzzy set enables the assignment of different degrees of membership to the components of a certain set.

5.2.1 Definition

If X is a group of things referred to generally as x, then e is a fuzzy set. Ain X is a collection of pairs of elements that are arranged in a certain order:

A is defined as the set of all pairs (x, J.!A (x)), where x is found in the set E. The function J.!A(X) is referred to as the membership function or grade of membership, which represents the degree of compatibility or truth of x belonging to A. This function maps X to the membership space M. When the set M consists of only two points, ° and 1, A is a non-fuzzy set and J.!A(X) is equivalent to the characteristic function of a non-fuzzy set. The membership function's range is a subset of the real numbers with nonnegativity with a finite supremum. Elements that have a membership degree of 0 are typically excluded from the list.

Example 1:

A real estate agent seeks to categorize the properties he presents to his clients. An indicator of the level of comfort in these residences may be determined by bedroom numbers they have. Consider the set X = {I, 2, 3, 4, . . ., 10}, which represents the many types of homes accessible. In this set, x represents the number of bedrooms in a house. The fuzzy set representing the "comfortable type of house for a four-person family" may be defined as A= {(l, .2), (2, .5), (3, .8), (4, 1), (5, .7), (6, .3)} Various methods of indicating fuzzy sets may be found in the literature. A fuzzy set is represented as an ordered collection of pairs, where the first element indicates the element itself and the second element represents the degree of membership.

Example 2

A= "real numbers considerably larger than 10" A= {(x, J.!A (x))l XEX}

where,

{ O, x::; 10 J.! -(x) = A (l +(x -1O)-2r', x> 10

Example 2-1c
A "real number close to 10" see Figure 5.1. A fuzzy set is characterized by stating its membership function [for instance, Negoita and Ralescu 1975].

5.3 Applications of Fuzzy Set Theory

Fuzzy theory is already being applied in several domains. These applications can be classified as follows:

1. Applications of mathematics encompass several fields, including topology, graph theory, algebra, logic, and others, which extend beyond standard mathematical concepts.

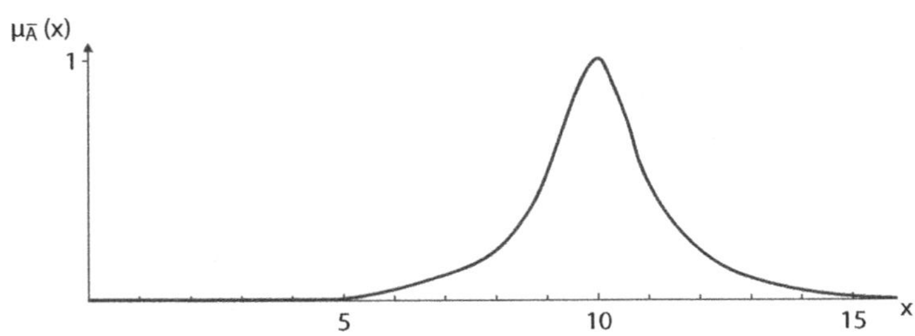

Figure 5.1 Real number close to 0.

2. Applications of algorithms include clustering approaches, control algorithms, mathematical programming, and other similar areas.
3. Applications to conventional models such as "the transportation model," "inventory control models," "maintenance models," and similar ones.
4. Ultimately, the use of various types of applications to address practical issues in the actual world.

5.4 Artificial Intelligence Methods

Artificial intelligence applications are becoming more and more common nowadays. There are artificial intelligence technologies under many applications that most people are not aware of but that we use widely today. The most straightforward implementation is the algorithm used for the classification of e-mails. An algorithm decides whether an e-mail should be in the spam box or not, whether it contains advertisements or not, and then it forwards the e-mail to the corresponding folder. Moreover, machines or computers, including software or hardware, can imitate many human-specific and intelligence-expressing features such as voice recognition, speech, inference, and problem-solving. Devices can perform these operations based on advancements in the field of artificial intelligence, such as inference and automated reasoning, multi-agent systems and autonomous agents, artificial consciousness, machine learning, case-based reasoning, deep learning, representation and knowledge reasoning [35], neuro-inspired computing, natural language processing, and robotic process automation. This is a structure that extends from data collection to creating artificial consciousness. Indeed, the main objective is to figure out correlations and patterns to reveal tacit knowledge and make predictions about future situations by analyzing data collected from current and past experiences. An AI-based system should receive different stimuli from its environment to achieve certain targets and decide by itself how to respond to the stimulus based on the relationship between the target and the stimulus. This component of AI is called an autonomous agent. Autonomous agents have been designed to independently accomplish assigned tasks in a distributed system. They utilize multiple agents and encompass capabilities like coordination, cooperation, self-analysis, and self-learning. One of the agent-based applications of AI that have become widespread recently is robotic process automation. Robotic process automation is another application area of AI. The main objective of robotic process automation is to construct software robots that implement and control real-world operations by emulating human actions. These robots perform a wide range of defined actions regarding simple human tasks such as Determining what is displayed on a screen, executing the correct keystrokes, navigating through systems, and identifying and extracting data. Moreover, they can perform these tasks more consistently and rapidly than humans. To achieve common goals, the features, including learning from experience, dynamically evolving, and cooperation among agents, are vital in the development of agent-based systems [22]. Therefore, developing an AI-based system requires addressing four fundamental cognitive skills: knowledge representation, learning, reasoning, and self-correction. To effectively solve complex real-world problems, the information and constraints related to the problem must be clearly defined. Knowledge representation plays a crucial role in this process by accurately depicting the real world in a manner that a computer can comprehend and use. In other words, knowledge representation is interested in the symbolic representation of knowledge and the automated manipulation of knowledge [7]. There are five key factors for knowledge representation. These are (i) the ability of a generic representation, (ii) the ability to recognize, (iii) the ability of the combination of representations, (iv) the ability to extensive view, and (v) the ability to capture the real-world complexity [13]. For this reason, natural language processing [9] is widely used to develop AI applications. Natural language processing refers to the ability of computer systems to understand written and spoken words as successfully as humans. So, natural language processing is related to machine-based technologies, including understanding, analyzing, manipulating, and interpreting human languages, and it consists of five steps: (i) lexical and morphological analysis, (ii) pragmatic analysis, (iii) discourse integration, (iv) semantic analysis, and (v) syntactic analysis. Based on these technologies, human tasks such as speech recognition, machine translation, and machine text reading can be quickly succeeded by computers. Learning, which is the second issue, focuses on collecting data, revealing knowledge, and creating rules to turn data into action. For the learning process, machine learning and deep learning are the most commonly used AI techniques. They explore and analyze data, learn from it, and apply these learnings to new data sets to make decisions. Unlike machine learning, deep learning is a subset that can independently learn and make intelligent decisions. The third fundamental skill is reasoning, which involves the ability to draw inferences. This process, when automated using information processing systems to establish relationships among system variables, is known as automatic reasoning [14]. It aims to enable computers to define problems, represent them in a suitable language, and find solutions through analogy and experience.

The goal is to create deep learning systems capable of human-like inference without human intervention [31]. Understanding how humans make precise decisions despite incomplete and imprecise information is crucial for developing effective automatic reasoning systems.

To develop machine inference, researchers often draw inspiration from biological systems. Bio-inspired computing uses algorithms based on nature and biology (such as animals or plants) to tackle complex optimization problems that deterministic algorithms struggle with. These strategies emulate the cognitive processes observed in living beings. Algorithms like genetic algorithms, neural networks, ant colonies, bee algorithms, and swarm optimization are extensively used due to their effectiveness in complex scenarios, outperforming traditional methods. Another inference method, case-based reasoning, involves using previously stored cases to solve new problems. These cases represent past problem-solving episodes similar to the current situation, and their solutions are adapted to meet the current problem's specific needs. Case-based reasoning relies on principles of knowledge representation, reasoning, and learning from experience. Its primary goal is to understand how humans generate hypotheses about new situations based on past experiences [27].

The last cognitive skill is self-correction, related to consciousness. Artificial consciousness refers to non-biological systems aware of their existence. This is the most challenging aspect of AI, as human consciousness is profoundly complex and elusive. As a result, achieving synthetic consciousness seems unlikely shortly due to the many unresolved questions in this field [32].

5.5 Fuzzy Sets Theory and Its Extensions

Starting with binary logic, multivalued logic has evolved to its current peak with L. A. Zadeh's continuous fuzzy logic. Zadeh's concept of ordinary fuzzy sets (OFS) [36] is represented by singletons, which consist of one element and its associated degree of membership to the set. The absence of an element's membership is the inverse of the degree of membership, equating to 1. This aspect of traditional fuzzy sets has faced criticism in numerous studies [33].

These scholars argue that the complementary element of OFS is unnecessary. As a result, removing this characteristic has enabled the expansion of OFS to include various extensions that offer a more detailed description of membership functions. These new extensions are historically depicted in Figure 5.2. A crisp membership value for any x value led to criticisms of type-1 membership functions, prompting the development of type-2 fuzzy sets and interval-valued fuzzy sets, which introduced fuzziness to the membership functions [21, 23].

Later, Atanassov [3] introduced intuitionistic fuzzy sets (IFSs), which include x values with degrees of membership and non-membership, with their sum being at most equal to 1. The complement of the membership and non-membership degrees to one is referred to as the hesitancy or indeterminacy degree of the decision-maker. Torra [30] introduced hesitant fuzzy sets (HFSs) to handle a set of potential membership values of an element in a fuzzy set. Atanassov [4] also introduced intuitionistic type-2 fuzzy sets (IFS2) in his book, allowing the squared sum of membership and non-membership degrees to be at most equal to one. Yager [34] later referred to IFS2 as Pythagorean fuzzy sets (PFSs) and introduced q-rung orthopedic fuzzy sets (Q-ROFSs) as a generalization of IFSs. In Q-ROFSs, the sum of the qth powers of membership and non-membership is limited to a maximum of one.

Smarandache [29] proposed the concept of neutrosophic sets, where the degrees of truth, indeterminacy, and falsehood for each element in the universe are limited to a maximum of one, and their combined value cannot exceed 3. Coung [12] introduced the concept of picture fuzzy sets, characterized by three parameters: yes, no, and abstention, with the complement of these factors, referred to as the refusal degree. Kahraman and KutluGündodu [18] proposed spherical fuzzy sets, characterized by the squared sum of the same parameters as picture fuzzy sets being limited to a maximum value of one. Figure 5.2 illustrates the chronological development of fuzzy sets in the literature [20].

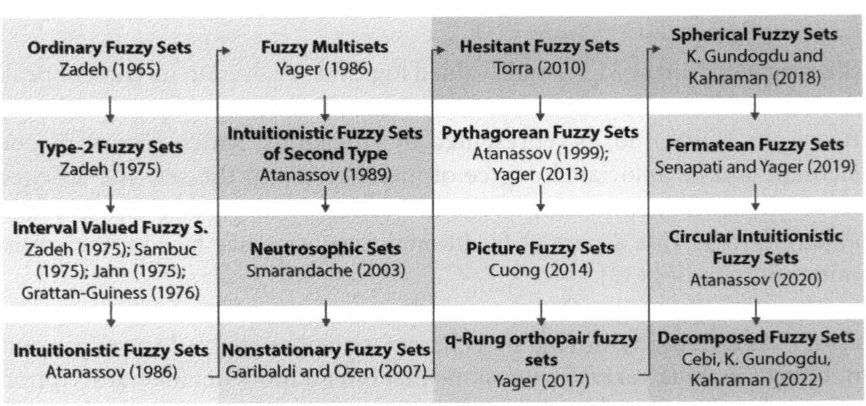

Figure 5.2 Chronological literature review.

The purpose of these modifications is to elucidate the inclusion of an element inside a fuzzy set by including more criteria and providing more comprehensive information.

5.6 Intelligent Systems Integrated with Fuzzy Sets: A Literature Review

This study performed an extensive literature review to investigate recent advancements in intelligent approaches incorporating fuzzy sets. We analyzed nine intelligent systems: automated reasoning, multi-agent systems and autonomous agents, machine learning, deep learning, case-based reasoning, knowledge reasoning and representation, natural language processing, neural networks, and symbolic reasoning and regulation. Additionally, we examined how these systems have been enhanced through the use of fuzzy sets. Our investigation utilized the Scopus database. Figure 5.3 displays the total number of research studies that have integrated fuzzy logic with intelligent approaches. Neural networks and machine learning algorithms are frequently used in intelligent systems combined with fuzzy sets.

5.7 Automated Reasoning and Inference

In this study, we used the Scopus database to search for "Automated reasoning" and "fuzzy" terms. This research revealed a total of 104 studies that apply fuzzy logic in automated reasoning. The number of studies conducted over the years is shown in Figure 5.3. The earliest studies date back

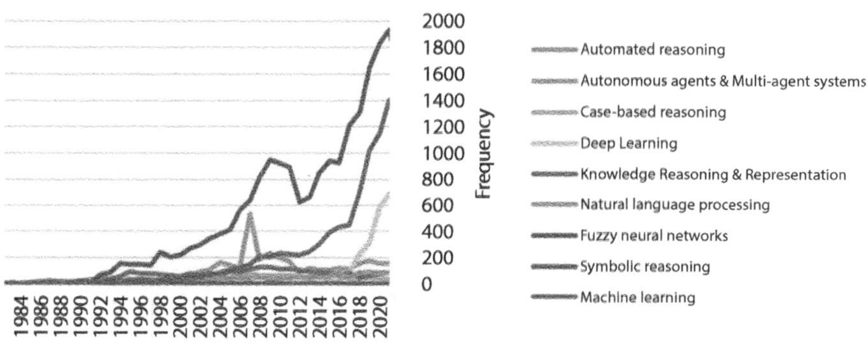

Figure 5.3 Intelligent techniques integrated with fuzzy sets (Scopus database).

to 1986, with the most recent ones from 2022. Ross *et al.* [26] developed an automated reasoning system for the damage assessment of protective structures within the Air Force. This new system uses fuzzy logic for representing uncertain knowledge and combines this data with data represented with crisp values. Zhu and Wang [39] developed a fuzzy comprehensive evaluation-based artificial consciousness model [8]. In a newer study, Cordero *et al.* [11] developed a coding package that extends formal concept analysis by fuzzy sets in developing automated reasoning tools.

5.7.1 Autonomous Agents and Multi-Agent Systems

In this section, we used the Scopus database to search for "Autonomous agents" or "multi-agent systems" combined with "fuzzy" terms. Our research identified a total of 972 studies that apply fuzzy logic to autonomous agents and multi-agent systems [16]. Figure 5.4 shows the number of studies conducted over the years, with the earliest dating back to 1994 and the most recent ones from 2022. Bonarini [5] applied evolutionary learning of fuzzy rules for creating autonomous agents. This novel approach overcomes the problems such as evaluation function biases. Alcantud [2] uses hesitant fuzzy sets for developing a multi-agent decision process.

5.7.2 Case-Based Reasoning

In this section, we used the Scopus database to search for "case-based reasoning" and "fuzzy" terms. Our research identified a total of 1,084 studies that incorporate fuzzy logic in case-based reasoning. Figure 5.5 shows the number of studies conducted over the years, with the earliest dating back to 1989 and the most recent ones from 2022. Notably, Bonnie and Maryanski [6] developed a knowledge system that integrates fuzzy logic into case-based

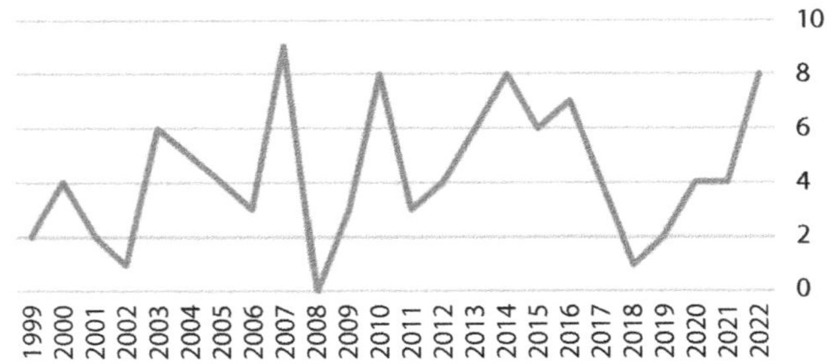

Figure 5.4 Fuzzy automated reasoning (Scopus database).

[10] reasoning, and Gao *et al.* [15] created an intuitionistic fuzzy entropy formula for constructing a case-based reasoning decision matrix.

5.7.3 Machine Learning

In this section, we employed the Scopus database to search for "machine learning" combined with "fuzzy" terms. Our investigation revealed a total of 9,174 studies integrating fuzzy logic into machine learning. Figure 5.6 displays the number of studies conducted over the years. Notably, Adlassnig and Kolarz [1] developed a machine learning program, which is part of a computer-aided medical expert system. The program uses 3530 rheumatologically patient records to create inductive learning. In a recent study, Pascual *et al.* [25] utilized fuzzy random forests as a machine-learning classification method in which the linguistic scales can be represented with fuzzy sets. The fuzzy decision tree-based fuzzy random forests are claimed to be beneficial while dealing with imbalanced data between classes. The authors introduced a new fuzzy random forest method and applied it to forecast the risk of developing diabetic retinopathy.

5.7.4 Deep Learning

In this section, we utilized the Scopus database to search for "deep learning" along with "fuzzy" terms. Our investigation identified a total of 2,734 studies integrating fuzzy logic into deep learning. The distribution of studies over the years is presented in Figure 5.7. Pioneer studies combining deep learning and fuzzy sets are relatively recent compared to other intelligent techniques. In one of the earlier studies, Hu *et al.* [17] introduced granular deep learning, where the granular system is defined by fuzzy logic. Additionally, Parveen [24] developed a deep learning algorithm enhanced with fuzzy sets for disease risk prediction using extensive healthcare information.

5.8 Real Applications and Patents on Artificial Intelligence Techniques and Fuzzy Sets

Many products have been and can be improved by integrating fuzzy sets with artificial intelligence. Self-driving cars are an example of fuzzy logic-based artificial intelligence. Self-driving cars use a variety of sensors and machine learning algorithms to perceive and understand their environment, and to make decisions about how to navigate and move safely. Fuzzy logic is often used to handle the uncertainty and imprecision that can arise in this complex and dynamic environment. For instance, fuzzy logic can be applied to interpret sensor data and determine responses to factors like other vehicles, pedestrians, or road conditions. It's also useful for assessing multiple criteria and deciding the most suitable action in a given scenario. Application domains for fuzzy logic include Automotive Systems (e.g., four-wheel steering, automatic gearboxes, vehicle environment control), Domestic Goods (e.g., refrigerators, microwave ovens, toasters, washing machines, vacuum cleaners), Consumer Electronic Goods (e.g., hi-fi systems, photocopiers, cameras, dishwashers, televisions), Environment Control (e.g., air conditioners, dryers, heaters, humidifiers), Elevators, Language filters, Pattern recognition, and Video games. Japanese companies such as Matsushita, Toshiba, Sanyo, Hitachi, Yamaichi, Sony, Canon, Nippon, Subaru, Minolta, Ricoh, Panasonic, and Nissan have extensively used fuzzy logic in their products. Several technologies employing fuzzy control are illustrated in Figure 5.5 rice cookers, for instance, incorporate computer chips to adjust cooking time and temperature accurately. Fuzzy logic-based automatic control in Sendai subway trains ensures smoother, more efficient rides with improved stopping precision. Washing machines with fuzzy logic control feature multiple sensors that manage the washing process, adjusting water intake, wash duration, rinse performance, and spin speed based on factors like load weight, fabric type, water amount and temperature, detergent amount, and spin cycle speed and duration. Fuzzy logic-controlled cameras have automatic exposure, automatic focus, and automatic white balance controls on them. In this section, we also try to outline the role of fuzzy sets in artificial intelligence from the patent perspective. A patent is a legal

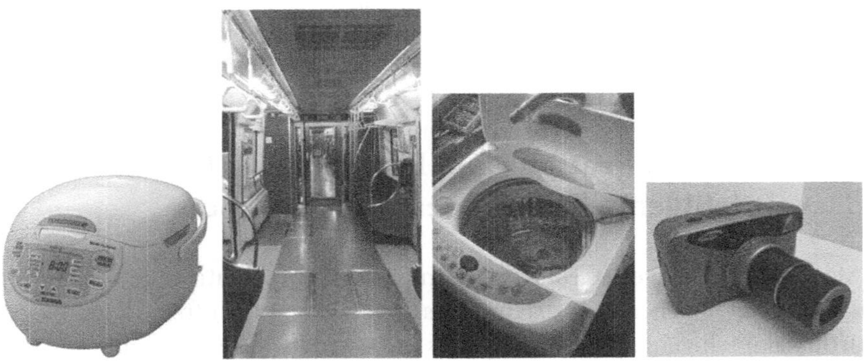

(a) Rice cooker (b) Sendai Metro (c) Washing machine (d) Camera

Figure 5.5 Fuzzy logic controlled technologies.

privilege given to an inventor, allowing them exclusive rights to their creation. An invention can be a product or a process that introduces a novel method of accomplishing something or presents a fresh technological resolution to a problem. To assess the present status and patterns of patents, a yearly search was conducted on Google Patents using appropriate keywords to determine the number of patents acquired.

The research includes the following keywords: Fuzzy automated reasoning inference, Fuzzy autonomous agents and multi-agent systems, Fuzzy artificial consciousness, Fuzzy case-based reasoning, Fuzzy machine learning, Fuzzy deep learning, Fuzzy knowledge reasoning representation, Fuzzy natural language processing, Fuzzy neuro-inspired computing, Fuzzy robotic process automation, and Fuzzy symbolic reasoning regulation. Analysis of patents containing these keywords over the last decade reveals that the most prevalent term is "Fuzzy Machine Learning," as depicted in Figure 5.6. Following this, "Fuzzy Deep Learning" and "Fuzzy Case-Based Reasoning" are the next most common keywords. These top three keywords collectively account for 70% of the total patents examined.

The annual numbers of total patents containing the keywords we mentioned before are given in Figure 5.7. There is a stable trend in this area

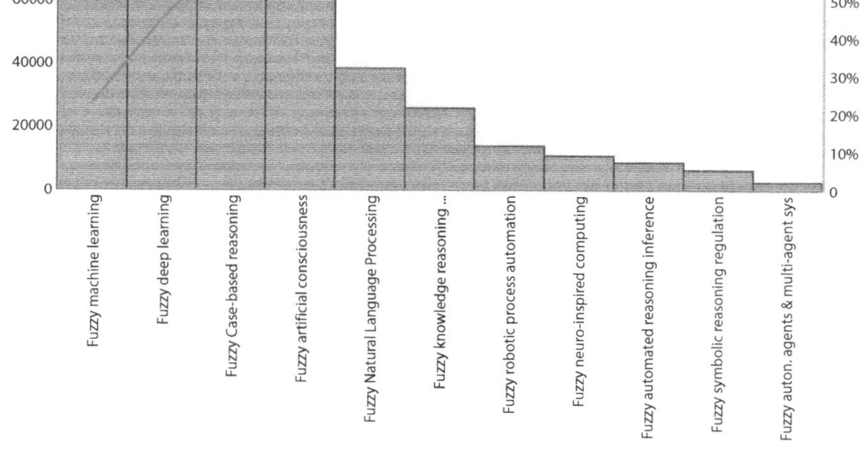

Figure 5.6 Patent numbers by fuzzy intelligent techniques.

until 2018. However, after 2019, a decrease in the number of patents in this field is noteworthy. It can be thought that the reason for this decrease is the pandemic that has taken over the world.

Changes in the frequency of patents containing the examined keywords have been noted over the years. To mitigate this effect, the number of patents containing these keywords was normalized against the total number of patents for each respective year, yielding relative patent numbers. The outcomes are depicted in Figure 5.8.

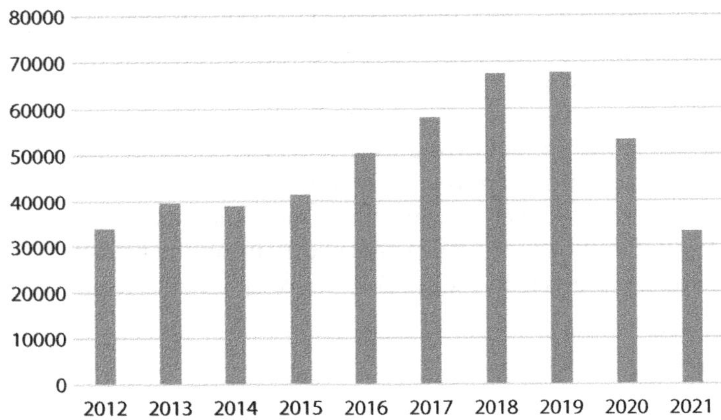

Figure 5.7 Annual patent numbers.

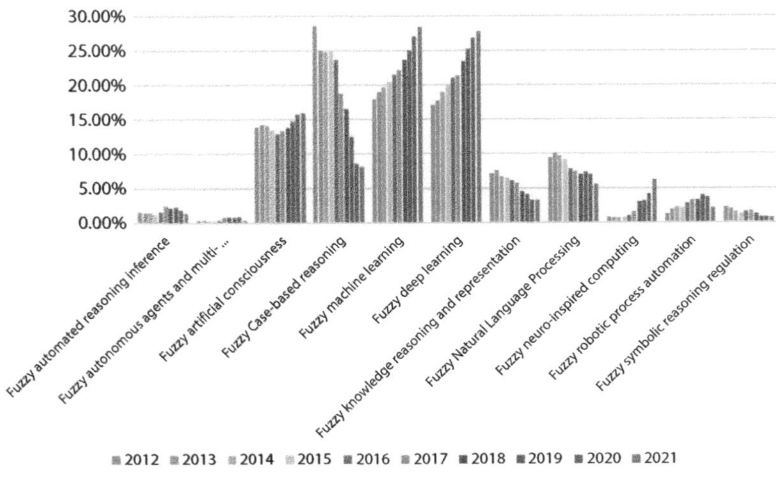

Figure 5.8 Yearly trends concerning relative patent numbers.

When Figure 5.8 is examined carefully, it is seen that the most important trend changes are in the fields of "Fuzzy machine learning" and "Fuzzy deal learning". These two keywords have been increasing their rate among all patents in the field of study over the years. While the keyword "Fuzzy Case-based reasoning" had close to 30% of all patents in 2012, it is seen that this ratio has steadily decreased and fallen below 10%. Conversely, there has been a consistent rise in patents related to "Fuzzy Artificial Consciousness," surpassing 15%. Likewise, an upward trend is observed in patents associated with "Fuzzy Neuro-inspired Computing" and "Fuzzy Robotic Process Automation." Additionally, Figure 5.8 illustrates a declining trend in the relative number of patents for "Fuzzy Knowledge Reasoning and Representation" and "Fuzzy Natural Language Processing."

5.9 Conclusion

Fuzzy Logic mirrors human reasoning and is integral to artificial intelligence, a field heavily reliant on human-like reasoning. Within artificial intelligence, various techniques and methods are employed to address diverse problems and complex systems. Fuzzy sets provide us with mathematical concepts to model human reasoning. Thus, fuzzy sets are quite important in human reasoning-based artificial intelligence applications such as humanoid robots and human decision-making. Besides, intelligent machines of manufacturing and service sectors such as televisions, washing machines, refrigerators, photocopy machines, cameras, and search engines use fuzzy logic. The literature review shows that Intelligent techniques integrated with fuzzy sets are used more and more each year. Fuzzy automated reasoning shows a highly fluctuating usage frequency distribution, with the annual average frequency remaining constant. Fuzzy autonomous agents and multi-agent systems maintain their popularity with a usage frequency of 100-200 annually. The frequency of use of fuzzy case-based reasoning seems to be on a downtrend. The frequencies of fuzzy machine learning and fuzzy deep learning exhibit significant growth, although they seem to have experienced a decline after 2008, coinciding with the peak frequency of fuzzy knowledge reasoning. Fuzzy natural language processing and fuzzy neural networks demonstrate notable acceleration, characterized by minor fluctuations in frequency of use.

The annual usage frequency of fuzzy symbolic reasoning and regulation fluctuates between 1 and 2 years post-2018. Patent search results indicate that fuzzy machine learning, fuzzy deep learning, and fuzzy case-based reasoning are the leading patented intelligent techniques. When examining these techniques annually, an increasing number of patents are observed for fuzzy machine learning and fuzzy deep learning, while a decrease is noted in patents for fuzzy case-based reasoning over time.

There is a decrease in the number of patents received for fuzzy intelligence techniques after 2019. Although Fuzzy Artificial Consciousness has received fewer patents compared to these three techniques in total, the number of patents has increased over the years. For further research, we suggest a closer look at the artificial intelligence applications using the fuzzy set theory and present some of their fuzzy control mechanisms with illustrations.

References

1. Adlassnig, K.P. and Kolarz, G., Representation and semiautomatic acquisition of medical knowledge in CADIAG-1 and CADIAG-2. *Comput. Biomed. Res.*, 19, 1, 63–79, 1986.
2. Alcantud, J.C.R., Ranked hesitant fuzzy sets for multi-criteria multi-agent decisions. *Expert Syst. Appl.*, 209, 118276, 2022.
3. Atanassov, K., Intuitionistic fuzzy sets. *Fuzzy Sets Syst.*, 20, 1, 8796, 1986.
4. Atanassov, K., *Intuitionistic fuzzy sets, theory and applications*, Heidelberg: Physica-Verlag, Newyork, 1999.
5. Bonarini, A., Evolutionary learning of general fuzzy rules with biased evaluation functions: Competition and cooperation. *IEEE Conference on Evolutionary Computation - Proceedings*, vol. 1, pp. 51–56, 1994.
6. Bonnie, M. and Maryanski, F., Knowledge base for code reuse by similarity. *Proceedings - IEEE Computer Society's International Computer Software & Applications Conference*, pp. 634–641, 1989.
7. Brachman, R. and Levesque, H., *Knowledge Representation and Reasoning*, Morgan Kaufmann, 2004, ISBN: 9780080489322.
8. Cerutti, S. and TimPieri, C., A method for the quantification of the decision-making process in a computer oriented medical world. *Int. J. Bio-Med. Comput.*, 12, 1, 29–57, 1981.
9. Chen, X., Zhang, W., Xu, X., Cao, W., Managing Group Confidence and Consensus in Intuitionistic Fuzzy Large Group Decision-Making Based on Social Media Data Mining. *Group Decis. Negotiation*, 31, 5, 995–1023, 2022.
10. Chiu, C., Hsu, P.-L., Norcio, A.F., Fuzzy reasoning approach to support knowledge acquisition. *Int. J. Gen. Syst.*, 28, 2, 227–241, 1999.
11. Cordero, P., Enciso, M., López-Rodríguez, D., Mora, D., Formal Concept Analysis with R. *R J.*, 14, 1, 341–360, 2022.
12. Coung, B., Picture fuzzy sets. *J. Comput. Sci. Cybern.*, 30, 4, 409420, 2014.
13. Davis, R., Shrobe, H., Szolovits, P., What is a Knowledge Representation? *AI Mag.*, 14, 1, 17–33, 1993.

14. Frederic, P., Automated Reasoning, in: *The Stanford Encyclopedia of Philosophy (Fall 2021 Edition)*, Zalta, E.N. (Ed.), URL = ¡https://plato.stanford.edu/archives/fall2021/entries/reasoning-automated/¿.
15. Gao, Y., Bao, R., Pan, Z., Ma, G., Li, J., Cai, X., Peng, Q., Mechanical equipment health management method based on improved intuitionistic fuzzy entropy and case reasoning technology. *Eng. Appl. Artif. Intell.*, 116, 105372, 2022.
16. Hoitsma, F., Knoben, A., Espinosa, M.L., Npoles, G., Symbolic explanation module for fuzzy cognitive map-based reasoning models. *Lecture Notes in Computer Science (including subseries Lecture Notes in Artificial Intelligence and Lecture Notes in Bioinformatics)*, vol. 12498 LNAI, pp. 21–34, 2020.
17. Hu, H., Pang, L., Shi, Z., Image matting in the perception granular deep learning. *Knowledge-Based Syst.*, 102, 51–63, 2016.
18. Kahraman, C. and KutluGndogdu, F., From 1D to 3D membership: spherical fuzzy sets, BOS/SOR 2018. *Polish Operational and Systems Research Society*, September 24th 26th 2018.
19. Kandel, A. and Schneider, M., Fuzzy Sets and Their Applications to Artificial Intelligence, in: *Advances in Computers*, vol. 28, M.C. Yovits (Ed.), pp. 69–105, Elsevier, 1989, ISBN 9780120121281.
20. KutluGndodu, F. and Kahraman, C., Spherical fuzzy sets and spherical fuzzy TOPSIS method. *J. Intell. Fuzzy Syst.*, 36, 1, 337–352, 2019.
21. Lee, S.C. and Lee, E.T., Fuzzy sets and neural networks. *J. Cybern.*, 4, 2, 83–10, 1974.
22. Liu, J., *Autonomous Agents and Multi-Agent Systems: Explorations in Learning, Self-Organization and Adaptive Computation*, World Scientific Publishing Company, 2001, ISBN: 9810242824.
23. Liu, Y., Zhao, J., Wang, L., Wang, W., Unified Modeling for Multiple-Energy Coupling Device of Industrial Integrated Energy System. *IEEE Trans. Ind. Electron.*, 70, 1, 1005–1015, 2023.
24. Parveen, H., Rizvi, S.W.A., Shukla, P.K., Disease risk level prediction based on knowledge driven optimized deep ensemble framework. *Biomed. Signal Process. Control*, 79, 103991, 2023.
25. Pascual-Fontanilles, J., Valls, A., Moreno, A., Romero-Aroca, P., Continuous Dynamic Update of Fuzzy Random Forests. *Int. J. Comput. Intell. Syst.*, 15, 174, 2022.
26. Ross, T.J., Wong, F.S., Savage, S.J., Sorensen, H.C., *Daps: An Expert System for Damage Assessment of Protective Structures*, pp. 109–120, 1986.
27. Shiu, S. and Pal, S.K., *Foundations of Soft Case-Based Reasoning*, John Wiley & Sons, 2004, ISBN: 9780471086352.
28. Singh, H., Gupta, M.M., Meitzler, T., Hou, Z.G., Garg, K.K., Solo, A.M.G., Zadeh, L.A., Real-Life Applications of Fuzzy Logic, in: *Advances in Fuzzy Systems*, 2013.
29. Smarandache, F., *Neutrosophy: neutrosophic probability, set, and logic: analytic synthesis & synthetic analysis*, American Research Press, 1998.

30. Torra, V., Hesitant fuzzy sets. *Int. J. Intell. Syst.*, 25, 6, 529–539, 2010.
31. Valdez, F., Castillo, O., Melin, P., Bio-Inspired Algorithms and Its Applications for Optimization in Fuzzy Clustering. *Algorithms*, 14, 122, 2021.
32. Watanabe, M., *From Biological to Artificial Consciousness: Neuroscientific Insights and Progress*, Springer International Publishing, 2022, ISBN: 9783030911386.
33. Yager, R., Pythagorean fuzzy subsets, in: *Proceedings of the 2013 Joint IFSA World Congress and NAFIPS Annual Meeting, IFSA/NAFIPS 2013*, 2013.
34. Yager, R., Generalized orthopair fuzzy sets. *IEEE Trans. Fuzzy Syst.*, 25, 5, 1222–1230, 2017.
35. Yue, W., Wan, X., Li, S., Ren, H., He, H., Simplified Neutrosophic Petri Nets Used for Identification of Superheat Degree. *Int. J. Fuzzy Syst.*, 2022.
36. Zadeh, L.A., Fuzzy set. *Inf. Control*, 8, 3, 338–353, 1965.
37. Zadeh, L.A., The concept of a linguistic variable and its application. *Inf. Sci.*, 8, 3, 199–249, 1975.
38. Zadeh, L.A., Fuzzy sets as a basis for a theory of possibility, fuzzy sets and systems. 1, 1, 3–28, 1978.
39. Zhu, C. and Wang, Z., Fuzzy comprehensive evaluation-based artificial consciousness model, in: *Proceedings of the World Congress on Intelligent Control and Automation (WCICA)*, art. no. 5554447, 15941598, 2010.

6

Fuzzy Logic in Machine Learning and AI Applications

Ravi Sheth* **and Chandresh Parekha**

School of IT, AI and Cyber Security, Rashtriya Raksha University, Lavad, Dahegam, Gandhinagar, Gujarat, India

Abstract

Fuzzy logic dances gracefully in the realm of mathematics, its versatile framework embraced by machine learning and Artificial Intelligence (AI). In the land of machine learning, fuzzy logic wields its power to confront scenarios where traditional binary logic falters. Fuzzy controllers reign supreme in control systems, masterfully navigating dynamic environments that defy precise mathematical models. Within the realm of game AI, fuzzy logic empowers the creation of intelligent, adaptive non-player characters (NPCs) that react authentically to player actions and ever-evolving in-game landscapes. In essence, fuzzy logic's dexterity in handling uncertainty and imprecision positions it as a vital asset in the arsenal of machine learning and AI applications. It bridges the chasm left by conventional binary logic, providing answers for intricate, real-world challenges across a myriad of domains. Its adaptability and effectiveness in wrangling uncertain data underscore its role in propelling the capabilities of AI and machine learning systems. This chapter offers a concise panoramic view of how fuzzy logic is harnessed within these domains, highlighting its capacity to confront real-world problems teeming with ambiguity and imprecision.

Keywords: Fuzzy logic, machine learning, artificial intelligence, mathematics

6.1 Introduction

Machine learning (ML) and artificial intelligence (AI) have made incredible progress in recent years, but the challenges of dealing with uncertainty,

**Corresponding author*: raviesheth@gmail.com

Rahul Kar, Gunjan Mukherjee, Biswadip Basu Mallik and Ashok Kumar Shaw (eds.) Fuzzy Logic in Computational Intelligence: Applications and Case Studies, (87–108) © 2026 Scrivener Publishing LLC

ambiguity, and imprecise decision making are a factor which continues to worry in the 1960s, Drs. Fuzzy logic introduced by Lotfi Zadeh provides an elegant solution to these challenges by allowing fuzzy representations and enabling the system to make decisions based on degrees of truth. This chapter explores the integration of Fuzzy Logic in ML and AI applications, and its ability to multi-facet handle complex, real-world problems emphasize its effectiveness [11]. Traditional binary logic operates on the values: 0 or 1, true or false [11] is a sentence that has been rephrased to make it appear better in a better possible way. Even though it is appropriate for many uses, it usually fails in dealing with the real-life issues where the vagueness and the ambiguity are so common. Unlike in Yes-No Logic, the Fuzzy Logic is based on the idea of "fuzzy sets" and degrees of truth. It enables the symbolization of uncertain data through the use of linguistic variables, for example, "very hot" or "somewhat cold", instead of the strictly binary terms. This would mean that the complex evaluation of the given issue is similar to the way human cognition works; therefore, it is the right thing for AI and Machine Learning applications [2, 3]. One of the most striking features that Fuzzy Logic offers is the possibility of dealing with complex, non-linear dependencies and making decisions with incomplete and uncertain data [6].

The combination of fuzzy logic with AI/ML allows using of fuzzy logic principles and methods to improve AI-ML regardless of the data unspecific, underspecified, and qualitative nature [5].

Fuzzy logic derived from fuzzy set theory provides a framework for reasoning and decision making under uncertainty. Unlike traditional binary arguments, which function as explicit, true/false, implicit arguments allow for multiple truths, enabling a more flexible representation of knowledge. This variation is particularly useful in areas where data can be ambiguous or where uncertainty lies, such as natural language processing, image recognition, and expert systems [16, 17].

Fuzzy Logic can be greatly used in the context of problems related to uncertainty and imprecision in AI-ML applications. One of the techniques very well-known is fuzzy input-output relationships using fuzzy logic rules. These rules can bypass vague, subjective human judgment and allow the system to make decisions with incomplete or uncertain information. Moreover, Fuzzy Logic can be combined with other AI and ML techniques such as neural networks, genetic algorithms, and expert algorithms, and hence, their capabilities can be enhanced. For example, neuro-fuzzy systems are a combination of learning and adaptive abilities of neural networks with reasoning skills of Fuzzy Logic used to form hybrid intelligent systems that can process complex, uncertain data. Moreover, Fuzzy Logic applies in pattern recognition, control systems, decision support systems, and data mining, among other areas, where its capacity to treat uncertainty and imprecision is of unique value. Researchers and practitioners look for methods to integrate Fuzzy Logic into AI-ML systems in order to enhance the robustness, flexibility, and interpretability of intelligent systems with the final goal of improving their performance in real-world applications.

6.2 Foundation of Artificial Intelligence (AI) and Machine Learning

AI or artificial intelligence refers to how machines, especially computer systems, simulate human mental processes. It involves developing algorithms, software, and hardware that enable computers to perform tasks that typically require human intelligence, such as understanding natural language, recognizing patterns, making decisions, and learning from experience [7]. Although, ML, which is a branch of AI, is a subfield of the artificial intelligence that concentrates on the creation of algorithms and statistical models that will allow the computer systems to enhance their performance on a special task through the learning from data. In a nutshell, machine learning systems learn from examples and experiences rather than being directly programmed to do the task [8].

The artificial intelligence (AI) and machine learning (ML) foundations detail the concepts, methods and principles that drive the development and implementation of these areas Here are the foundational elements of AI and ML [1, 8]:

Computational Mathematics: Mathematics is the pillar of AI and ML. Concepts of linear algebra, statistics, probability theory, and statistics are important for modeling, optimization, and data understanding.

Data and Data Preprocessing: Data is the essence of AI and ML. Data collection, cleaning, and construction are important steps in an effective model. Data preprocessing techniques include normalization, feature engineering, and missing data handling.

Algorithms and Models: AI and ML depend on different algorithmic models, such as decision trees, support vector machines, neural networks, and so on. These algorithms are used for tasks such as classification, regression, clustering, and reinforcement learning.

Supervised and Unsupervised Learning: Supervised learning is learning from labeled data, unsupervised learning deals with unlabeled data and search patterns, and reinforcement learning focuses on decision making in dynamic areas Neural networks and in-depth study: M.L. Convolutional neural networks (CNNs) are used for image analysis, and recurrent neural networks (RNNs) process sequential data.

Natural Language Processing (NLP): Machine language an interaction between computer and human language is the province of NLP. Methods such as tokenization, sentiment analysis, and named entity recognition are vital activities of NLP.

Computer Vision: Computer vision allows machines to interpret and understand visual information from images or video. Object recognition, image segmentation, and facial recognition are common features.

Reinforcement Learning and Autonomous Agents: Reinforcement learning is used to make choices, through interaction with surroundings, is done by automated creatures using reinforcement learning. This is found in self-operating machines and games.

Probability and Statistics: AI and ML both use numbers and data to figure out uncertainty, guess new ideas, and find patterns.

Optimization Algorithms: Optimization is taken to efficiently train the model with proper parameterization. Gradient descent is the optimization algorithm for machine learning, and the one that has received much attention in ML.

Ethics and Fairness: The ethical considerations in AI and ML are starting to increase. Subjects such as bias in algorithms, transparency, and responsible AI are central to discussions nowadays.

Big Data and Distributed Computing: AI and ML often work with big data, requiring distributed computing systems like Hadoop and Spark to efficiently handle and analyze data from.

Interpretability and Explainability: The indispensable aspect in ML is that how the AI and ML models make decisions. Interpreting and explainability methods assume to make models intuitive by producing visual evidence.

Robotics and Autonomous Systems: In robotics, AI is used for tasks such as navigation, maneuvering, and sensing. Autonomous systems, such as self-driving cars, rely on AI to make decisions.

Human-Machine Interaction: The human-computer interaction (HCI) sciences represent a set of principles for creating intelligent systems that are user-oriented, i.e. voice assistants and virtual dictators.

These foundational elements interact and complement each other, and AI and ML practitioners continue to expand the boundaries of what AI and ML can achieve by drawing on these principles to design AI frameworks and solutions on the many varieties.

6.3 Foundation of Fuzzy Logic

Fundamentals of fuzzy logic form the basis of this accounting system for dealing with uncertainty and inaccuracies in decision making. Here are the key foundational concepts of Fuzzy Logic explained in Figure 6.1 [2, 4, 11]:

Fuzzy Sets: Fuzzy Sets is an important concept that has a role is Fuzzy Logic. Contrary to classical sets (crisp sets), which consist of objects, either being members or not, in fuzzy sets elements have different degrees of membership (may be equal to 0 or 1), which in turn disallow division into typical groups. Membership functions are the parameters of fuzzy sets that can assign membership grades to elements [11].

Membership Functions: Membership functions are mathematical functions that describe the degree of membership of elements in a fuzzy set [1, 3].

In Figure 6.2 we can see the various membership functions and its working mechanism. This function maps input values to membership degrees in the range [0,1] different shapes, such as rectangular, rectangular, and Gaussian, can be adopted depending on the type of fuzzy set.

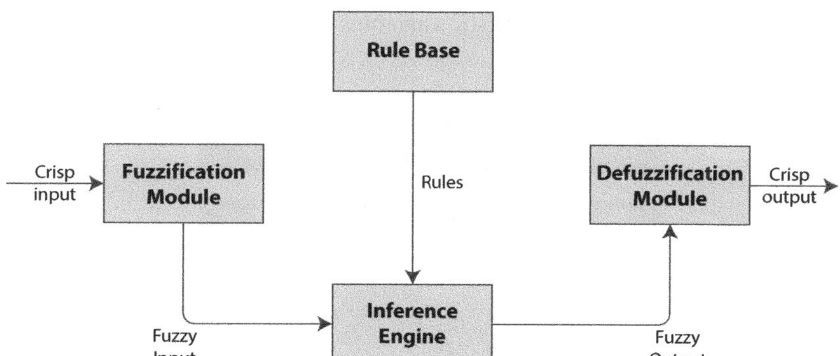

Figure 6.1 Basics of fuzzy logic.

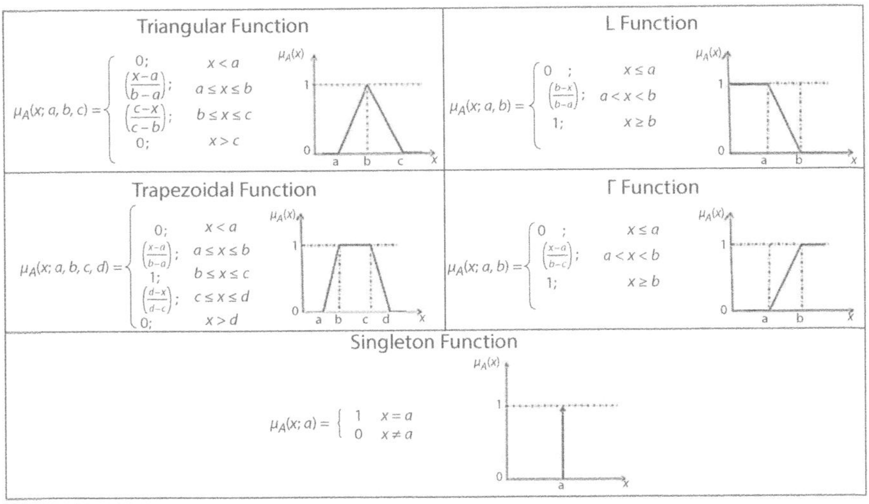

Figure 6.2 Membership functions.

Linguistic Variables: Fuzzy logic brings in the concept of linguistic variables, which deal with attributes or linguistic terms rather than absolute mathematical values. Terms such as "very hot," "hot," or "cold" could be used to describe the temperature, hence representing the data in a more human-like way. Figure 6.3 gives the basic idea about how fuzzy logic is differs from normal Boolean expression.

Fuzzy Rules: Fuzzification Rules are statements that relate words and fuzzy sets to be used in decisions or to perform an action. This is usually in the form of the logical sentence "IF [antecedent], THEN [consequent]}, where antecedents and consequents consist of linguistic variables and fuzzy set operations.

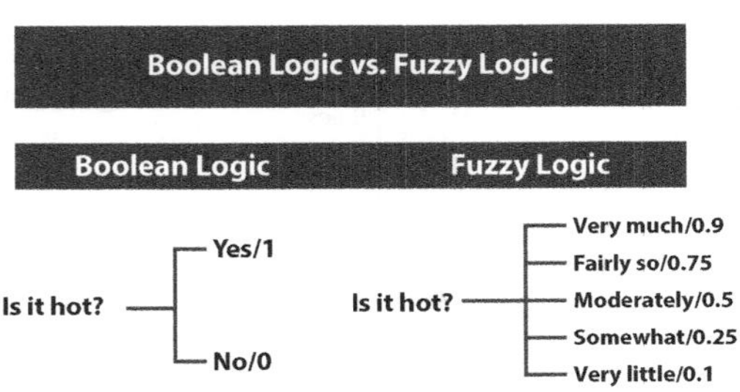

Figure 6.3 Boolean logic vs. fuzzy logic.

A typical Zadeh-Mamdani type fuzzy rule-based system is composed of fuzzy rules in Equation 6.1.

$$X_i : if\ (a_1\ is\ Y_{i,1})\ AND\ if\ (a_2\ is\ Y_{i,2})\ AND \ldots.$$
$$AND\ if\ (a_N\ is\ Y_{i,N})\ \text{THEN}\ (z_i\ is\ Y_{i,out}) \tag{6.1}$$

Where X_i is the ith fuzzy rule; $a = [a_1, a_2, \ldots a_N]^T$ is the N × 1 dimensional system input; a_n is the nth input variable; $Y_{i,1}$ is the linguistic term of the nth premise fuzzy set of X_i; $Y_{i,out}$ is the linguistic term of the output; z_i is the output of X_i.

In contrast, a typical Takagi-Sugeno-Kang type fuzzy rule-based system consists of fuzzy rules in the following form:

$$X_i : if\ (a_1\ is\ Y_{i,1})\ AND\ if\ (a_2\ is\ Y_{i,2})\ AND \ldots.$$
$$AND\ if\ (a_N\ is\ Y_{i,N})\ \text{THEN}\ (z_i = b_i^T \bar{a}) \tag{6.2}$$

Where $\bar{a} = [1, a^T]^T$; $a = [a_1, a_2, \ldots a_N]^T$; is the (N+1) × 1 dimensional consequent parameter vector of X_i.

Angelov and yager proposed a new kind of fuzzy rules in 2012 [22] in their research based on $Y_n z_i$. These rules simplify the foreparts of each rule by means of numerically based prototypes that are abstracted from data. Additionally, these same fuzzy rules help eliminate the need for membership functions of every variable. A zero-order $Y_n z_i$ type fuzzy rule can be formulated as follows:

$$X_i : if\ (a \sim b_i)\ THEN\ (z_i\ \text{is}\ Y_{i,\text{out}}) \tag{6.3}$$

and a first-order $Y_n z_i$ type fuzzy rule is expressed as:

$$X_i : if\ (a \sim b_i)\ THEN\ (z_i = b_i^T \bar{a}) \tag{6.4}$$

where b_i is the prototype of X_i "~" denotes similarity. One can see from Equations (6.3) and (6.4) that $Y_n z_i$ type fuzzy rules have the same consequent parts as the Zadeh-Mamdani type and Takagi–Sugeno-Kang type fuzzy rules. $Y_n z_i$ fuzzy rule-based systems also follow the same standard fuzzy inference procedure.

Fuzzy Inference: Fuzzy inference can be described as a system which basically utilizes simple rules and data input to come out with some conclusions. Fuzzy inference engines are based on fuzzy rules and are fed by the non-crisp input data.

They produce fuzzy outputs as fuzzy sets with the number of ones between the rules and input value.

Defuzzification: Defuzzification is a process by which the fuzzy output is converted to a crisp value for being used practically or in any decision-making scenario. This could be based on the centroid deflection or maximum membership inflation to arrive at a single output value.

Fuzzy Logic Control (FLC): Fuzzy logic is a control system with fuzzy logic used as the weight of the application. FCL systems mentioned in Figure 6.4 use fuzzy logic rules and membership functions to manage dynamic systems: for example, industrial automation, robotics, and driverless cars FLC allows the system to self-notify when it receives excessive energy and uncertainty.

Fuzzy Mathematics: Fuzzy Logic is based on mathematical theory (known as fuzzy set theory) which also includes operations on fuzzy sets and fuzzy relations. This mathematics of fuzzy logic provides the foundation and root for construction and evaluation of fuzzy modeling.

Uncertainty and Imprecision: Fuzzy Logic is primarily designed to handle uncertainty and imprecision in data and decision-making. It provides a way to model and reason with information that is not strictly true or false.

Applications: Fuzzy Logic can be used in a variety of fields, such as control systems, natural language processing, expert systems, image processing, and decision support systems. Due to the great number of applications, it is a useful tool

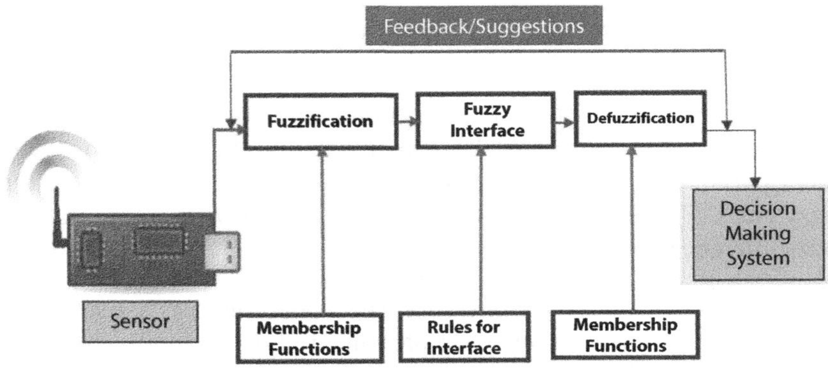

Figure 6.4 Fuzzy logic control (FLC).

in searching through complex and practical gaps that we meet in life. Fuzziness is the key to the application of Fuzzy Logic, which allows its usage for modeling and processing of vague and unreliable data, usually out of the crisp logic scope. By pasting in and using linguistic variables and fuzzy sets for making it look human, representation of knowledge and decision making enables relevancy of it to AI, machine learning, and control systems.

6.4 Need of Fuzzy Logic in AI and ML

Fuzzy Logic is required in AI and ML for several important reasons, particularly when dealing with real-world problems that involve uncertainty, imprecision, and qualitative information. Here's why Fuzzy Logic is valuable in AI and ML [5–7]:

Handling Uncertainty: Most problems in the real world are filled with uncertainty or imprecision. Fuzzy logic lets this uncertainty be represented by assigning true or membership rates to data points. This is mainly useful when the data is not strictly true or false. In many AI applications, such as natural language processing, image recognition, or expert systems, uncertainty is often a characteristic of the data itself. For instance, when analyzing human speech or recognizing things in images, data input can have imprecision and uncertainty. Fuzzy logic provides a framework to represent this uncertainty. With a sequence of truth values from 0 to 1, fuzzy logic allows AIs to reason with vaguely incomplete information in more human-like ways. Instead of making rigorous decisions based on rigorous information, which is dual, vague understanding serves the ability of AIs to make informed decisions about input data or evidence value under conditions where accurate decision-making is difficult with incomplete or imprecise data.

Rule-Based System: Rule-based systems are considered as the understanding of the AI model that operates on the basis of rules, each rule being an if-then statement which is being followed by the corresponding actions or the conclusions. These turfs are mainly popular in many areas for problem-solving, decision-making, and expertise. Fuzzy logic makes the rule-based systems more powerful by repeatedly using the idea of fuzzy rules. In the case of the traditional rule-based systems, the rules are articulated through crisp Boolean logic that provides only for the binary true/false decisions. On the contrary, fuzzy rules enable imprecision and uncertainty by enabling conditions to be represented in terms of auditory modalities and linguistic variables. This reflects not the two-value principles true or false, but many truth degrees and thus fits to both simple and complex decisions demands Fuzzy rules are quite a natural modeling of an expert's knowledge or experience. In this case, the field of experts is based on linguistic flavors and imprecise to quantitative speculations instead of accurate numerical measurements. The ability of fuzzy rules to imitate human reasoning processes more accurately is one of their most important advantages. Human-based decision-making approaches and fuzzy knowledge get incorporated into their reasoning processes through fuzzy rules.

Fuzzy Inference Systems (FIS): Fuzzy inference is an AI paradigm that takes inspiration from human decision-making processes, especially in situations where decisions are based on uncertain or uncertain information FIS is a fuzzy logic rule, a way of combining these rules so that predictions can make decisions [1, 2].

Figure 6.5 shows the basic structure of the FIS. It comprising of four major components namely: fuzzification, defuzzification, fuzzy rules and decision system. FIS is additionally used when (in cases) where formal mathematical models are found to be hard (almost impossible) to define or between inputs and outcomes there is a complicated relation (connections). Therefore, simple theoretical frameworks play the role of offering an understanding of a decision-making process that can be used in AI models or might be interpreted as a human-like decision-making process. Thru the implementation of uncertainty and uncertainty in their judgment mechanism, Fuer learn to adjust more complex relations of the inputs and the outputs and therefore should be well suited to use in those fields where conventionally used common mathematical models might be quite under fitting.

Control Systems: The use of fuzzy logic is boundless and is prominent in most fields, which may include control systems, industrial automation, and robotics. Fuzzy controllers

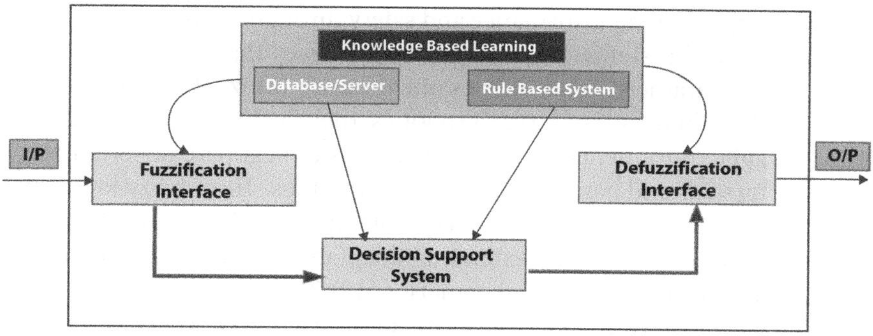

Figure 6.5 Fuzzy interface system.

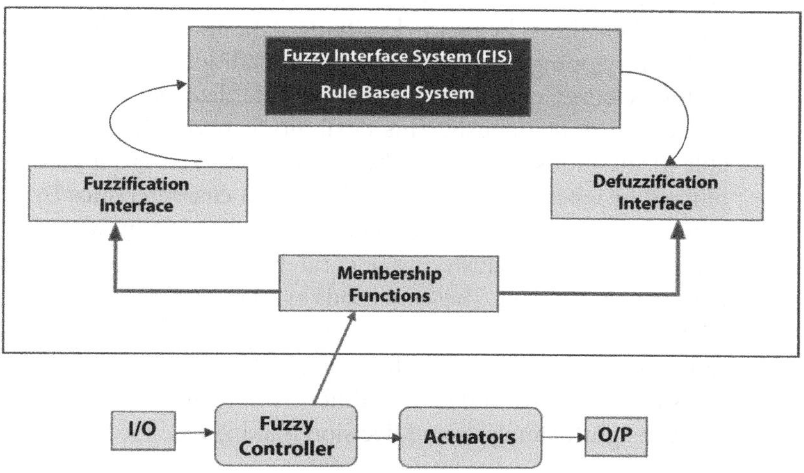

Figure 6.6 Fuzzy interface and control system.

stand out when dealing with complex and nonlinear dynamics, especially when there is fuzzy or imprecise information. They provide a structured basis in taking into consideration the issues mentioned above. They serve as an imperative for depicting and inferring uncertainty, thus enabling the algorithm to become self-adaptive and may even resist unforeseen circumstances. Figure 6.6 gives the basic architecture of Fuzzy interface and Control system. Such systems dynamically adjust the control actions by using fuzzy rules and real-time feedback for optimum performance, even in unpredictable environments. Industrial settings are improved in performance and safety through the use of fuzzy control systems, which regulate processes that have changing parameters and, at the same time, minimize the effects of disturbances [3, 4, 10]. In robotics, they facilitate precise and agile movements, enabling the robots to negotiate uncertain terrains and handle dynamic surroundings. Thus, fuzzy logic allows control systems to make intelligent decisions based on fuzzy rules, thereby extending adaptability and reliability in all possible operational scenarios [19–21].

Fuzzy Clustering and Pattern Recognition: Fuzzy logic methods play an important role in pattern recognition tasks in AI, providing solutions to the challenges posed by complex and uncertain data Fuzzy c-means clustering like fuzzy clustering algorithms, helps in classifying data points to clusters with overlapping boundaries. Unlike traditional clustering methods, fuzzy clustering allows multiple data points to be clustered simultaneously. This flexibility is particularly valuable in situations where clear boundaries between groups are blurred or when data points exhibit mixed characteristics By allowing for sequential assignment of membership in. within each group, fuzzy clustering accurately captures the subtle relationships in data. These methods excel in situations where traditional pattern recognition methods struggle to produce satisfactory results. By using fuzzy logic, AI systems can identify subtle patterns in data that differ from reality, facilitating more insightful analysis and decision making [12, 13, 15].

It can be clearly seen that Fuzzy Logic can be integrated with other AI and ML techniques to combine the strengths of different approaches. Hybrid models often perform better in certain scenarios. Fuzzy Logic is required in AI and ML because it provides a powerful framework for handling uncertainty, imprecision, and qualitative information. It enhances the versatility and adaptability of AI systems, making them more robust, interpretable, and suitable for real-world applications where data is not always crisp and clear-cut.

6.4.1 Application of Fuzzy Logic in AI and ML

Fuzzy logic can be used in various areas of Artificial Intelligence and Machine Learning such as described below:

Control Systems and Robotics: FLC has brought revolutionizing change in the domain of robotics and automation by making robots capable of taking decisions at runtime in dynamic environments. Applications include autonomous vehicles, industrial automation, and household robots. Figure 6.7 explains how the fuzzy logic intersect with the AI and navigate the path for the vehicles. When the fuzzy logic method is employed, it first simplifies the business question by making it a series of constant yes and no questions to which a consumer can respond accordingly. The neural networks, on the other hand, use machine learning to teach the algorithm to recognize patterns and learn from its mistakes. The hybridization of fuzzy reasoning of Fuzzy Logic with neural networks unique learning and adaptive features improves the system's performance to be more robust and flexible. A Neuro-Fuzzy system is yielded setting to the fuzzy rules and membership functions with the help of neural network training algorithms based on data. It provides the system with of the possibility to self-improve as well as to react rapidly on feedback. It could save time and resources while working out the most appropriate course of action amongst many possible routes [18, 19].

Natural Language Processing (NLP): Fuzzy Logic allows NLP models to deal with the ambiguity and vagueness of human language. It helps in sentiment analysis, text classification, and machine translation. In the domain of natural language

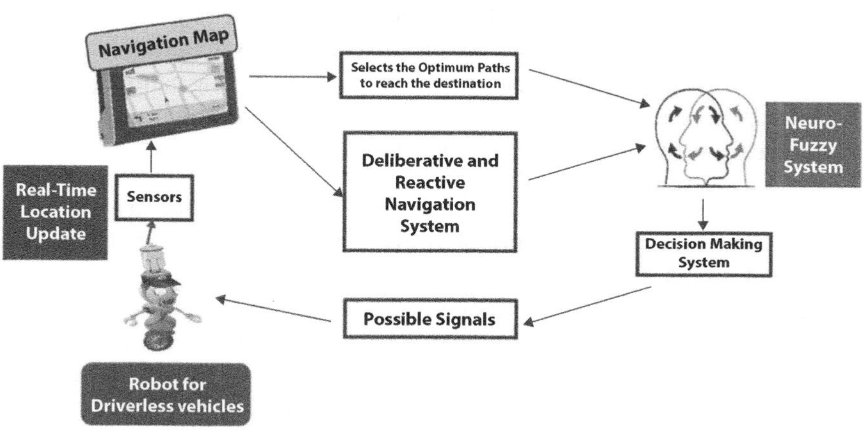

Figure 6.7 Fuzzy logic application in robotics.

processing, though computers have made significant strides in translation, they lack the finesse to proofread effectively. This is a result of the fact that out of the three cognitive faculties, namely computation, memory, and common sense, humans utilize all three efficiently, while computers, by default, excel at computation and memory. Fuzzy logic fills this gap by providing a framework imbued with logical reasoning, offering valid and logical solutions to questions that require complex logic [15, 20]. Today, Fuzzy Systems are a top tech achievement, especially in advanced control and thinking systems. They work like human decision-making, which makes them excellent at solving problems and giving accurate solutions like a human mind. While current translation and retrieval mainly use rules, there's a need to add common sense into language systems. Figure 6.8 shows how fuzzy logic and natural language processing combine. It gives more accurate results when finding similarities between articles. The semantic Rule based learning is being given to the FIS which has a capability to extract the important features and based on that it shall give the similarity detection [15].

The growth of transparent and flexible fuzzy models is essential. These are able to provide almost good solutions for different variables, therefore lower the computational complexity of such systems as compared to traditional systems. In addition, fuzzy approaches utilize sub-symbolic information within the universe of discourse which imparts contextual relevance into the model and its solutions—a clear edge over other methods. Combining natural language processing with fuzzy logic seems to be a very promising way how to make scientific output better measured. These systems use fuzzy logic to help with big issues for people and make life better. Using natural language with fuzzy logic can make AI a force for good in the world. This teamwork can solve problems and make life better for everyone [14, 15].

Image and Pattern Recognition: Fuzzy Logic can be used to interpret and recognize objects from an image by computer vision systems, even when images are noisy or imprecise. Figure 6.9 shows how the face recognition system can be created with the help of fuzzy logic and AI. The extracted features are undergone the process of fuzzification with the membership functions, which enables the most prominent features to be extracted and which shall be applied to the FIS along with the fuzzy rules mentioned in the earlier section [13, 19].

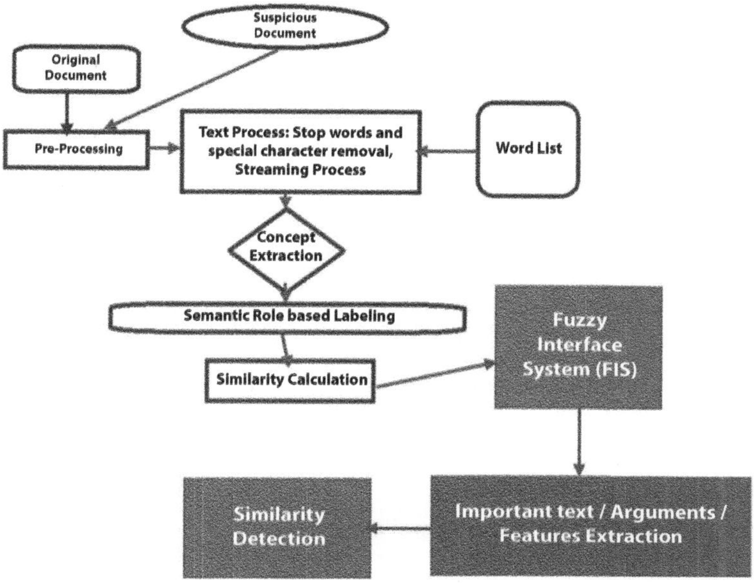

Figure 6.8 Fuzzy logic application in NLP.

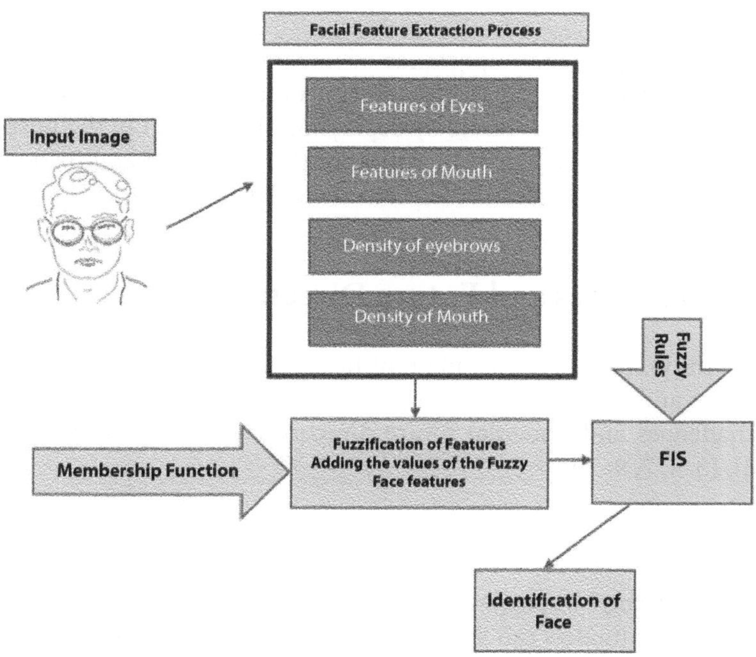

Figure 6.9 Fuzzy logic application in image processing.

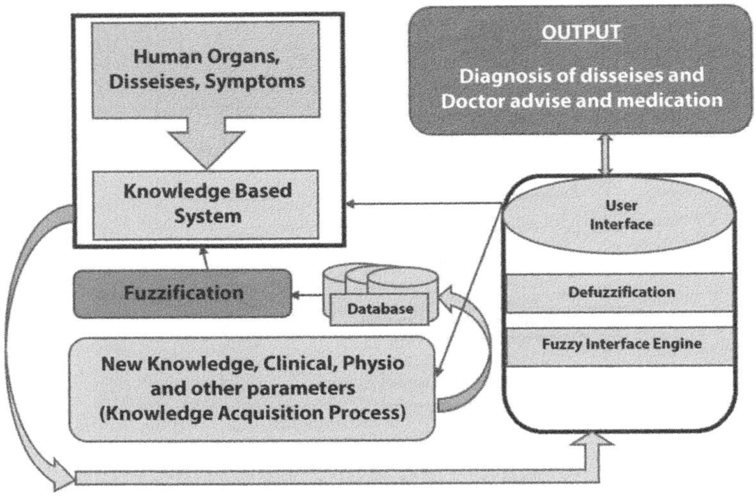

Figure 6.10 Fuzzy logic application in medical science.

Medical Diagnoses: Fuzzy Logic helps doctors to decide on sickness using many signs and expert views. It is used to find cause of diseases and recommend the prescription based on the rules.

Figure 6.10 gives the importance of integration of fuzzy logic and AI in medical science. The diagnosis and recommendation for the doctors become very easy and accurate by deploying such system in the hospitals. This will also decrease the death ration in the real world and patients get proper and effective treatment without any delay [14].

6.5 Challenges and Future Direction

While Fuzzy Logic is a valuable tool in AI and ML, it also faces several challenges and presents opportunities for future directions. Here are some key challenges and potential future directions for using Fuzzy Logic in AI-ML [3, 4, 7, 9, 10]:

6.5.1 Challenges

Model Complexity: Managing large numbers of variables and fuzzy rules in Fuzzy Logic models can get really complicated. The more variables and rules that are added, the harder it is to keep everything running smoothly. It takes so much careful attention to make things work nicely. In addition, the more complex it is, the harder it gets to fine-tune the model. You really need tons of expertise and computer power to handle it all. And as the model grows, figuring out how all the variables relate to each other becomes a real puzzle. It's hard to get and make better the model. Handling these problems needs using good plans and cool computer ways. But even with the troubles, learning these hard things is really needed for getting the best from Fuzzy Logic models. They're really helpful in many areas, like controlling systems and making choices, especially when things aren't very clear.

Integration with Deep Learning: A persistent obstacle to integrate Fuzzy Logic with deep learning models is the implementation. The combination of this synergy in Fuzzy Logic that interprets with deep learning that has huge computational powers presents a promising field to explore. Scientists anticipate a harmonious teaming up between these two methodologies and are therefore optimistic about enhancing comprehension of complex systems as well as the feasible applications of these approaches. While achieving the integration that is seamless, it may become highly possibly that technical difficulties, which are difficult to resolve, such as how to harmonize diverging paradigms, and how to optimize hybrid design can lead to the modification or partial re-design of the existing system. However, the idea that blending the convergent advantages of Fuzzy Logic and deep learning will facilitate forward-looking innovative research remains to be a dynamic reality that will surely yield the necessity of critical breakthroughs in varied fields of the study and industry application.

Scalability: Making fuzzy logic work with big data is costly. We need smart algorithms and parallel processing to deal with it better. Doing that enables the Fuzzy Logic models to handle vast datasets much more quickly and cost-effectively. This makes it very important to apply Fuzzy Logic in real life, especially when dealing with large volumes of data.

Data Interpretability: Fuzzy logic makes it easy to understand patterns, but difficult to interpret decisions in the face of complex and highly dimensional data. With so many variables, it's hard to know the reasoning behind decisions. Thus, while Fuzzy Logic is great for clarity, it can struggle to explain decisions with complex data, and requires great care to understand and analyze.

Handling High-Dimensional Data: The Fuzzy Logic becomes also very complex when there are a lot of dimensions involved. This is caused by the so-called curse of dimensionality phenomenon. The data is due to sparsity which in turn complicates Fuzzy logic to yield optimum results. Consequently, it might be the case that fuzzy models will handle the high dimension but will have lower accuracy and can be difficult to comprehend. It is difficult to find patterns and to make concrete conclusions from such data.

Benchmark Datasets: One major problem is that without standard benchmark datasets for Fuzzy Logic in AI and machine learning, a comparison of different methods cannot be properly made. Every dataset is unique, which does not let the effectiveness of Fuzzy Logic be seen across many different situations. This makes it tricky for researchers and practitioners to measure the performance and usefulness of Fuzzy Logic models, and therefore progress in AI and machine learning slows down.

Hybrid Approaches: Mixing Fuzzy Logic with other AI and machine learning is hard but important. We must find the right blend of methods and ensure they work well in various situations. Testing and adjusting are crucial to make sure they work effectively. Researchers and experts always strive to enhance the integration and dependability of Fuzzy Logic in these hybrid AI and machine learning systems.

Ethical Considerations: Using Fuzzy Logic requires the same care as any other AI approach to ensure that AI and machine learning models are fair and unbiased. This means scrutinizing data and algorithms to identify and eliminate any biases that could lead to abnormal results. It is also important to use data types and techniques to reduce bias. By focusing on fairness, researchers and practitioners can make people feel more confident in applying fuzzy logic to AI and machine learning algorithms.

6.5.2 Future Directions

Hybrid Models: This leads to the investigation of hybrid models that combine Fuzzy Logic with deep learning, reinforcement learning, or other AI techniques, resulting in more potent and interpretable systems.

Explainable AI: Making feasible Fuzzy Logic models AI that can explain itself, especially when handling complex data, will be an important task needed for wider acceptance.

Big Data and Scalability: Research efforts focus on making Fuzzy Logic more flexible for big data applications. Distributed computing and parallelization can be explored.

Interdisciplinary Collaboration: Innovative solutions can be found to complex problems through the interaction of Fuzzy Logic experts, AI researchers, and domain specialists in collaborative effort.

Human-AI Collaboration: Discovering ways in which Fuzzy Logic models can work together with human experts in decision-making processes can have substantial applications in various fields.

Ethical Frameworks: Evolving ethical frameworks and guidelines for using Fuzzy Logic in AI-ML to address fairness, transparency, and accountability concerns is essential.

Quantum Fuzzy Logic: The other area of research will involve the investigation of the application of principles in Fuzzy Logic in quantum computing and quantum machine learning, as this field is in its infancy but could give huge advantages in the processing of quantum data.

Edge and IoT Devices: Fuzzy logic can be integrated with the emerging technologies such as Internet of Things (IoT) can enable real-time decision-making in IoT applications.

Robotic Autonomy: With the constant effort Fuzzy Logic Control (FLC) for robotics and autonomous systems shall capable to enhance their adaptability and robustness in complex environments.

6.6 Conclusion

Fuzzy Logic has etched a niche in the world of ML and AI, providing a robust framework for dealing with uncertainty and imprecision. It is being applied in a variety of fields, from robotics to natural language processing, assisting in making systems more intelligent, adaptive, and human-friendly. And with the development of AI and ML, Fuzzy Logic remains a valuable tool to address the complex challenges that occur in this real-world scenario. In conclusion, improvement of uncertainty and interpretability in AI-ML using Fuzzy Logic is a great function but optimizations of challenges and the direction of the future will also be instrumental in creating a greater impact of this on different fields. Shared work between researchers, specialists and bioethicists will become important in driving Fuzzy Logic in AI and ML in future.

References

1. Chrysafiadi, K., The Role of Fuzzy Logic in Artificial Intelligence and Smart Applications, in: *Fuzzy Logic-Based Software Systems. Learning and Analytics in Intelligent Systems*, vol. 34, Springer, Cham, 2023, https://doi.org/10.1007/978-3-031-44457-9_2.
2. Guidara, A., Artificial Intelligence and Fuzzy Logic, in: *Policy Decision Modeling with Fuzzy Logic. Studies in Fuzziness and Soft Computing*, vol. 405, Springer, Cham, 2021, https://doi.org/10.1007/978-3-030-62628-0_5.

3. Chan, S., Reddy, V., Myers, B., *et al.*, Machine Learning in Dermatology: Current Applications, Opportunities, and Limitations. *Dermatol. Ther. (Heidelb)*, 10, 365–386, 2020. https://doi.org/10.1007/s13555-020-00372-0.
4. Lucci, S. and Kopec, D., *Artificial intelligence in the 21st century: A living introduction 2/E*, Mercury Learning and Information, Dulles, VA, 2016.
5. Pratama, M., Dimla, E., Tjahjowidodo, T., Pedrycz, W., Lughofer, E., Online tool condition monitoring based on parsimonious ensemble+. *IEEE Trans. Cybern.*, 50, 2, 664–677, 2020a.
6. Cabrera, I.P., Cordero, P., Ojeda-Aciego, M., Fuzzy Logic, Soft Computing, and Applications, in: *Bio-Inspired Systems: Computational and Ambient Intelligence. IWANN 2009. Lecture Notes in Computer Science*, vol. 5517, J. Cabestany, F. Sandoval, A. Prieto, J.M. Corchado (Eds.), Springer, Berlin, Heidelberg, 2009, https://doi.org/10.1007/978-3-642-02478-8_30.
7. Alfaverh, F., Denai, M., Sun, Y., Demand response strategy based on reinforcement learning and fuzzy reasoning for home energy management. *IEEE Access*, 8, 39310–39321, 2020.
8. Gu, X., Han, J., Shen, Q., *et al.*, Autonomous learning for fuzzy systems: A review. *Artif. Intell. Rev.*, 56, 7549–7595, 2023. https://doi.org/10.1007/s10462-022-10355-6.
9. Varshney, A.K. and Torra, V., Literature Review of the Recent Trends and Applications in Various Fuzzy Rule-Based Systems. *Int. J. Fuzzy Syst.*, 25, 6, 2163–2186, 2023, May 24. https://doi.org/10.1007/s40815-023-01534-w.
10. Editorial: Fuzzy Logic and Artificial Intelligence: A Special Issue on Emerging Techniques and Their Applications, in: *IEEE Transactions on Fuzzy Systems*, vol. 28, pp. 3063–3064, Dec. 2020.
11. Paja, W., Pancerz, K., Pękala, B., Sarzyński, J., Application of the Fuzzy Logic to Evaluation and Selection of Attribute Ranges in Machine Learning. *2021 IEEE International Conference on Fuzzy Systems (FUZZ-IEEE)*, pp. 1–6, 2021, doi: 10.1109/FUZZ45933.2021.9494515.
12. Mittal, K., Jain, A., Vaisla, K.S., Castillo, O., Kacprzyk, J., A comprehensive review on type 2 fuzzy logic applications: Past, present and future. *Eng. Appl. Artif. Intell.*, 95, 103916, 2020, October. https://doi.org/10.1016/j.engappai.2020.103916.
13. Rajawat, A.S., Bedi, P., Goyal, S.B., Bhaladhare, P., Aggarwal, A., Singhal, R.S., Fusion fuzzy logic and deep learning for depression detection using facial expressions. *Procedia Comput. Sci.*, 218, 2795–2805, 2023. https://doi.org/10.1016/j.imu.2019.100288.
14. Brownlee, J., *Stacking Ensemble Machine Learning With Python*, 2021, April 26, MachineLearningMastery.com. https://machinelearningmastery.com/stacking-ensemble-machine-learning-with-python/ (Accessed on 18th September 2023).
15. Sobowale, A., Esan, A., Tomilayo, A., Jooda, B., Bolajoko, A., Automatic plagiarism detection using fuzzy-logic. *Dutse J. Pure Appl. Sci.*, 9, 3a, 312–318, 2023. https://doi.org/10.4314/dujopas.v9i3a.31.

16. Yen, J., Fuzzy logic-a modern perspective, in: *IEEE Transactions on Knowledge and Data Engineering*, vol. 11, pp. 153–165, Jan.-Feb. 1999.
17. Soares, C.V., *Improving Prediction Accuracy Using Class-specific Ensemble Feature Selection*, 2010, December 13, A dissertation submitted to the Graduate Faculty of Auburn University in partial fulfilment of the requirements for the Degree of Doctor of Philosophy Auburn, Alabama.
18. Sangiovanni, G., Definition of fuzzy logic rules representing finite element method experts' reasoning. *Fuzzy Sets Syst.*, 160, 10, 1444–1456, 2009, May. https://doi.org/10.1016/j.fss.2008.11.015.
19. Singh, N.H. and Thongam, K., Mobile robot navigation using fuzzy logic in static environments. *Procedia Comput. Sci.*, 125, 11–17, 2018. https://doi.org/10.1016/j.procs.2017.12.004.
20. Silva, S., Costa, P., Santana, M., Leite, D., Evolving neuro-fuzzy network for real-time high impedance fault detection and classification. *Neural Comput. Appl.*, 32, 12, 7597–7610, 2020.
21. Rong, H.J., Angelov, P., Gu, X., Bai, J.-M., Stability of evolving fuzzy systems based on data clouds. *IEEE Trans. Fuzzy Syst.*, 26, 5, 2774–2784, 2018.
22. Angelov, P. and Yager, R.R., A new type of simplified fuzzy rule-based system. *Int. J. Gen. Syst.*, 41, 2, 163–185, 2012. https://doi.org/10.1080/03081079.2011.634807

7

Enhancing Machine Learning Models through Adaptive Fuzzy Logic-Based Hyperparameter Tuning

M. Robinson Joel[1], V. Ebenezer[2*], K. Martin Sagayam[3], E. Bijolin Edwin[4], M. Roshni Thanka[2] and S. Stewart Kirubakaran[5]

[1]Department of Computer Science and Engineering, KCG College of Technology, Chennai, Tamil Nadu, India
[2]Division of Data Science and Cyber Security, Karunya Institute of Technology and Sciences, Coimbatore, Tamil Nadu, India
[3]Department of ECE, SRM Institute TRP Engineering College, Trichy, India
[4]Division of Computer Science and Engineering, Karunya Institute of Technology and Sciences, Coimbatore, Tamil Nadu, India
[5]Division of Computer Science and Engineering, Karunya Institute of Technology and Sciences, Coimbatore, Tamil Nadu, India

Abstract

Optimizing the performance and generalization of machine learning (ML) models requires hyperparameter adjustment. This paper examines the crucial role that hyperparameter tuning plays in machine learning, outlining its significance, uses, and different optimization strategies. Along with the effects of hyperparameters like learning rate and batch size on model training, important ML performance determinants are covered, including data quality, method selection, and model complexity. Numerous tuning techniques, such as Bayesian optimization, grid search, random search, and meta-learning, are investigated. In deep learning, particular attention is paid to the learning rate, emphasizing methods for maximizing it. Additionally covered are trade-offs in hyperparameter optimization, such as weighing performance gain against computational cost. The importance of hyperparameter tweaking in machine learning is examined in this work, along with its applications, significance, and various optimization techniques. Important ML performance factors are discussed, such as data quality, method selection, and

**Corresponding author*: ebenezerv@karunya.edu

Rahul Kar, Gunjan Mukherjee, Biswadip Basu Mallik and Ashok Kumar Shaw (eds.) Fuzzy Logic in Computational Intelligence: Applications and Case Studies, (109–128) © 2026 Scrivener Publishing LLC

model complexity, in addition to the implications of hyperparameters like learning rate and batch size on model training. Instead of only using the conventional true or false values, fuzzy logic allows variables' truth values to be any real number between 0 and 1. It is a mathematical approach to modeling ambiguity and uncertainty in decision-making and is used to deal with imprecise or uncertain information. The foundation of fuzzy logic is the notion that there are numerous shades of gray in between true and false, and that the binary distinction is frequently overly restrictive. Partial truths are permitted, meaning that a proposition may be somewhat true or untrue instead of entirely true or false.

Keywords: Machine learning, fuzzy logic, hyperparameter tuning, model optimization, adaptive systems, interpretability, predictive accuracy

7.1 Introduction

Natural language processing, computer vision, recommendation systems, advertising, and user behavior analytics are just a few of the application domains where machine learning (ML) [1] techniques have found widespread use. This is due to their overall character and their remarkable performance in data analytics issues. Some datasets or problem categories are better suited for different machine learning techniques. Developing a successful machine learning model is often a difficult and time-consuming process that includes choosing the best algorithm and fine-tuning the model's hyper-parameters (HPs) [2] to create the best model architecture. hyperparameter modification. The importance of hyperparameter tweaking in machine learning is examined in this work, along with its applications, significance, and various optimization techniques. Important ML performance factors are discussed, including data quality, technique selection, and model complexity, in addition to the implications of hyperparameters like learning rate and batch size on model training. Trade-offs in hyperparameter optimization, such as balancing computational cost and performance benefit, are also discussed. One of the most important steps in creating machine learning models is hyperparameter tweaking. Finding the ideal set of hyperparameters that control how a machine learning algorithm behaves is both an art and a science. Hyperparameters are predetermined settings that are not discovered through the use of actual data. They have a big influence on how well a model performs, and selecting the appropriate hyperparameters can mean the difference between a model that performs poorly and one that produces cutting-edge outcomes. Grid search is a systematic approach that involves specifying a range of values for each hyperparameter and exhaustively testing all possible combinations. While it can be computationally expensive, it ensures that no optimal configuration is missed.

7.2 Fuzzy Logic

Hyperparameters are the parameters that are set before the learning process begins, and they can significantly affect how well the model learns from the data. Proper tuning can lead to better generalization, reduced overfitting, and ultimately a more accurate model. Things that are unclear or ambiguous are said to as fuzzy. Their fuzzy logic offers a great deal of flexibility for thinking in situations where we frequently find ourselves unable to decide whether a state is true or false in the real world. This allows us to take into account the uncertainties and inaccuracies of any given circumstance. Control systems, image processing, natural language processing, medical diagnostics, and artificial intelligence are just a few of the many fields that use fuzzy logic [3]. The membership function, which establishes the extent to which an input value belongs to a certain set or category, is the core idea of fuzzy logic. A mapping from an input value to a membership degree between 0 and 1, where 0 denotes non-membership and 1 denotes full membership, is known as the membership function. The below Figure 7.1 explain about the adaptive fuzzy logic-based hyperparameter tuning.

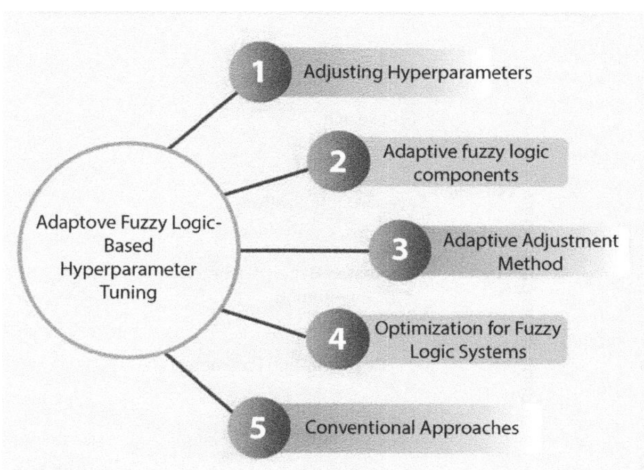

Figure 7.1 Fuzzy logic.

7.3 Adjusting Hyperparameters

Mathematical model having multiple parameters that must be learned from the data is called a machine learning model. We can fit the model parameters by using the data that already exists to train the model. Hyperparameters, [4] on the other hand, are a different class of parameter that cannot be directly learned through standard training. Usually, they are addressed prior to the start of the training procedure. Important characteristics of the model, including its complexity or learning speed, are expressed by these parameters.

7.3.1 Grid Search

We look at grid search [5] and meta-learning random search. In deep learning, the learning rate is specifically taken into account, with a focus on methods for maximizing it. Additionally covered are trade-offs in hyperparameter tuning, such as weighing the benefits of performance against computational cost. Grid search is a thorough and all-encompassing approach to hyperparameter optimization. A grid search builds models for every possible combination of those discrete hyperparameter values once data scientists have determined every potential value for each hyperparameter.

Grid search is a hyperparameter optimization technique that entails training a model for every possible combination of values after you supply a list of values for each hyperparameter you wish to optimize [6]. For instance, you would supply a list of values for alpha and a different list of values for beta if you wanted to use grid search to optimize two

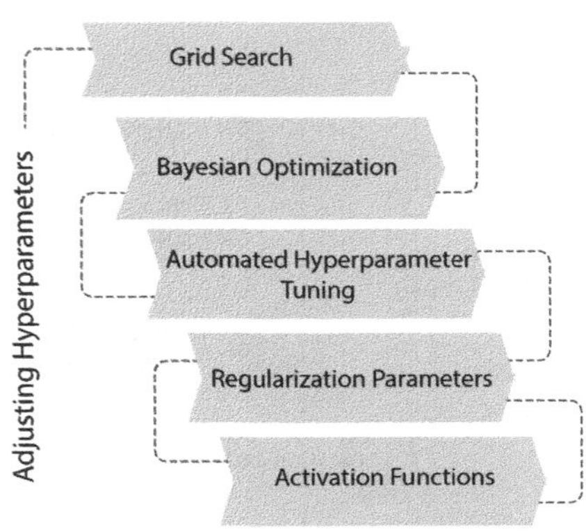

Figure 7.2 Adjusting hyperparameters.

hyperparameters, alpha and beta. After that, the grid search algorithm would train a model with each of these value combinations and assess each model's performance. The models' performance is then used to determine the ideal values for the hyperparameters. The Figure 7.2 explains the adjusting hyperparameters in details.

7.3.2 Bayesian Optimization

In statistical analysis, a-priori information is the focus of Bayesian inference. However, Bayesians typically assume that probability may be used to model any type of uncertainty. Unfortunately, depending on how uncertainties are defined, this isn't necessarily the case. Probabilistic uncertainty is not the same as the uncertainty of continuous quantity measurement findings. Fuzziness is another type of uncertainty present in individual measurement data. The sequential model-based optimization (SMBO) [7] approach known as Bayesian optimization enhances the sampling technique of subsequent testing iterations.

Although grid and random searches can be run simultaneously, each test is run separately, and data scientists are unable to apply their knowledge to guide future testing. Bayesian optimization probabilistically chooses a fresh set of hyperparameter values that are likely to produce superior outcomes based on previous experiments. The term "surrogate of the original objective function" [8] refers to the probabilistic model. Every time the objective function is performed, surrogate models are typically updated and enhanced due to their computational efficiency.

7.3.3 Automated Hyperparameter Tuning

The good news is that hyperparameter adjustment can be done automatically. You may quickly identify the ideal hyperparameters by experimenting with a number of combinations and terminating the least promising ones early. The goal of hyperparameter tuning is to experiment with a variety of configurations "n" on a particular problem. You may choose to continue or finish each trial early based on how it goes. You have to choose between having an endless budget (B) and trying as many configurations (also known as sets of hyperparameters) as you can. As a result, you must carefully divide the budget you allot to each configuration (B/n, budget per configuration). Hyperparameter tweaking can be automated with tools like AutoML and platforms like H2O.ai and Google's Cloud AutoML [9]. These platforms minimize the need for manual involvement and streamline the process.

7.3.4 Regularization Parameters

One of the key ideas in machine learning is regularization. It is a method of supplying more data to the model to keep it from overfitting. On occasion, a machine learning model may perform well on training data but poorly on test data. The model is referred to as overfitted since it is unable to forecast the outcome when dealing with unseen data by adding noise to the output [10]. A regularization technique can be used to address this issue. A learning machine's reasoning and inference can be directly enhanced by the application of fuzzy logic. Fuzzy logic can be used to model qualitative knowledge, even if it is imprecise, so that machine learning outcomes can be expressed symbolically. By using neural networks, the system gains huge parallelism, resilience, and learning capabilities. When creating machine learning models, you have probably come across instances when the model's training accuracy is great but its validation or testing accuracy is low. This is how a basic linear regression relation appears. In this case, β stands [11] for the coefficient estimates for various variables or predictors (X), and Y for the learnt relation.

7.3.5 Activation Functions

The output of a neural network node given an input or group of inputs is determined by mathematical equations known as activation functions. They are essential in giving the model non-linearity so that it can recognize intricate patterns and render judgments based on the information. Before transmitting the input to the subsequent layer of neurons or completing it as an output, we apply a non-linear alteration known as the activation function [12]. One of the simplest kinds of activation functions is the step function. Here, a threshold value is examined, and the neuron is activated if the net input value, let's say y, exceeds the threshold. Through gradient descent, our model can learn a variety of logical operations thanks to a novel, parameterized, differentiable activation function. A neural network can ascertain the connections between its input variables thanks to this activation function, which also sheds light on the logical meaning of learning network parameters.

7.4 Adaptive Fuzzy Logic Components

FLC finds application in anything from biomedical equipment and security to industrial process control. Compared to typical control systems, FLC [13] has shown the best results when applied to complicated, poorly defined issues that can be managed by a skilled human operator who is unaware of the underlying dynamics. A control system is a configuration of physical components designed to change another physical system such that it exhibits particular desired characteristics.

These systems draw conclusions from input data using fuzzy logic. They include fuzzification and defuzzification techniques, an inference engine, and a rule base. Fuzzy logic is incorporated into machine learning models by a fuzzy inference system (FIS) to improve decision-making. The purpose of adaptive fuzzy logic systems (AFLS) [14] is to manage uncertainty and adjust to shifting conditions. Through the addition of learning mechanisms that enable them to modify their parameters in response to fresh data, they expand on conventional fuzzy logic systems. In real-world applications, where circumstances might change dramatically, this flexibility is essential.

7.4.1 Fuzzification

The technique of employing membership functions to transform precise inputs into fuzzy values. Real-world data is transformed into a format that the fuzzy logic system can process in this step. This can be accomplished by recognizing that the different known deterministic and crisp quantities are actually highly uncertain and entirely nondeterministic. 'Fuzzy' [15] refers to things that are unclear or ambiguous. In real life, we are occasionally unable to determine if a certain issue or assertion is accurate or untrue. This idea at the time offers a wide range of values between true and false, allowing for flexibility in determining the optimal solution to the issue at hand.

7.4.2 Fuzzy Rule Base

The Figure 7.3 shows the different components of adaptive fuzzy logic in detail. Rule-based reasoning is a widely used technique in artificial intelligence that builds decision support systems that let practitioners acquire

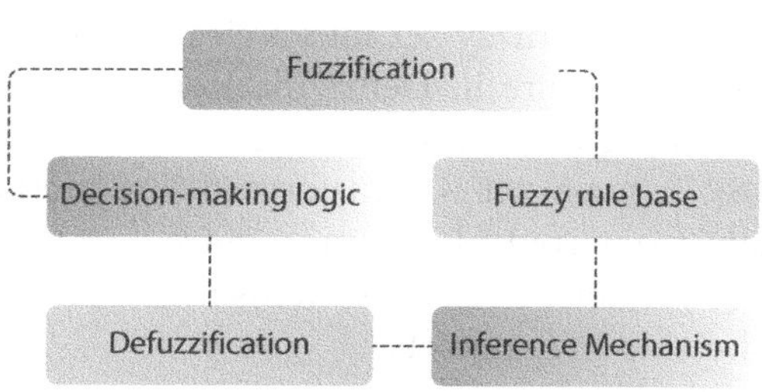

Figure 7.3 Adaptive fuzzy logic components.

outcomes fast by just providing the required inputs. Fuzzy inference techniques introduce subjectivity, ambiguity, uncertainty, and inaccurate information into the knowledge domain to show the relationships and interactions between the variables. For this reason, fuzzy rule-based systems (FRBS) [16] are essential for modeling human cognitive processes.

Fuzzy systems have been widely used in many situations and have proven to be effective in solving a variety of real-world problems. However, the realization of such systems requires a thorough understanding of key theoretical underpinnings by scientists and technologists.

7.4.3 Inference Mechanism

"Inference" often overlooked during the training and model-building processes. Nonetheless, it is significant because it bridges the gap between trained models and real-world applications. This article will discuss inference in machine learning, including its definition, different methods, and practical uses in a range of learning paradigms. Our understanding of the inference concept may be useful in a number of machine learning domains.

Since it permits the deployment and application of trained models in practical contexts, inference is an essential part of the machine learning workflow. [17] Making predictions or classifications on fresh data during the inference phase is the main function of a model after it has been trained on historical data. Applications such as recommendation systems, picture recognition, and natural language processing, among others, depend on this stage. Deploying machine learning models successfully and attaining desired results in real-world scenarios depend on accurate and efficient inference.

7.4.4 Defuzzification

The method of defuzzification involves taking fuzzy sets and their related membership degrees and using crisp logic to get a measurable outcome. This procedure converts a fuzzy set into a clear set. Generally speaking, fuzzy control systems require it. Defuzzification is the practice of using fuzzy sets and matching membership degrees to logically get a quantitative outcome [18]. A fuzzy set is transformed into a crisp set ivia/i this technique. Usually, fuzzy control systems require it. A variety of rules will convert a range of variables in these systems into a fuzzy result, which is defined by membership in fuzzy sets.

Here, the mapping is done to turn the fuzzy results into crisp ones, whereas the former was used to turn the crisp results into fuzzy ones.

This procedure can produce a non-fuzzy control action that shows the distribution of possibilities for an inferred fuzzy control action.

7.4.5 Logic in Decisions

The decision-making task is specified in the first phase, which involves identifying the variables, criteria, and options. Real variables are changed to linguistic ones throughout the fuzzification process. The variables that the user wishes to add to the knowledge base are chosen by them. The universe, or all potential values that the parameter can take, is first defined for each indicator. Fuzzy sets, together with their numbers and names, are then identified within the universe. When discussing variable reliability, for example, the following attributes might be chosen: absolute, very high, high, medium, low, extremely low, no, or zero dependability. The definition of linguistic variables is dependent on the fundamental linguistic variable. The more qualities (fuzzy sets) [19] there are, the more detailed the variable (the universe) can be defined, but the work will become computationally challenging.

Since it is essentially a simulation of the semantics of natural language terms, the most popular and straightforward membership function is built using experimental estimations of one or more of those questioned. The procedure's validity is further supported by the fact that everyone understands the essential words to a certain extent. The most widely used membership functions come in a variety of ways.

7.5 Adaptive Adjustment Method

A dynamic and iterative method of optimizing machine learning model parameters is used in the adaptive tuning process of a fuzzy logic-based hyperparameter tuning system. This procedure allows the system to adapt to changes and get better over time by continuously updating hyperparameters. A neuro-fuzzy network with three different subnet types for pattern recognition, fuzzy reasoning, and control synthesis is the result of an FLCS's decision-making process [20]. This structured network's special knowledge structure allows it to perform adaptive modifications of fuzzy reasoning techniques and membership functions for input signal patterns and output control actions. The Figure 7.4 shows the adaptive adjustment method in detail.

These modifications can then be recovered separately and fully from its subnets at a later time. Offline training rules and online learning algorithms for the structured neuro-fuzzy network have been derived using

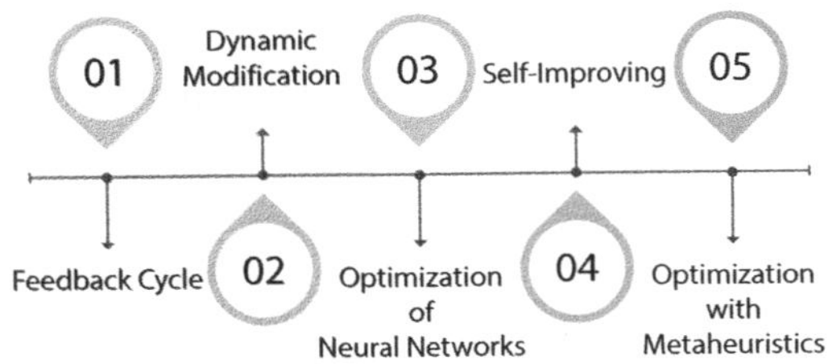

Figure 7.4 Adaptive adjustment method.

gradient optimization techniques. The control loop is finished when the fuzzy control output is translated into tangible changes, such changing the length of the rod. This complex interaction between mechanical adaptation, fuzzy inference, and real-time parameter [21] evaluation highlights the system's ability to dynamically adjust its stiffness, guaranteeing peak performance in a wide range of operational conditions.

7.5.1 Feedback Cycle

Remember that homeostasis refers to the preservation of a relatively constant internal environment. In order to keep systems functioning near a predetermined point, or optimal level, feedback loops respond to external stimuli. Feedback occurs when the input or stimulus is impacted or influenced by the loop's output or reaction [22]. The overall feedback loop. A variable changes as a result of a stimulus or initiating event. The receptor notices a change in the variable. The control center compares this number to a reference value, also known as a set point.

The variable is modified by effectors. When a system's outputs are redirected as inputs as part of a sequence of cause-and-effect events that form a circuit, the system is said to feed back into itself loop. When it comes to feedback systems, the idea of cause-and-effect needs to be handled carefully.

7.5.2 Dynamic Modification

In the Quality Inspection Engine (QIE) [23], there are various methods for figuring out how frequently a process should be inspected. For instance, you can determine the current inspection scope using the information from previous inspection values. The scope of the examination can be dynamically changed to allow for flexible responses to this data. Dynamic modification rules and sampling techniques can be used to accomplish this.

In order to accomplish a predetermined quality target with a high degree of certainty, dynamic modification enables you to regulate the inspection scope for a series of inspection documents with respect to sample sizes and inspection likelihood. You can make dynamic changes at the inspection document level in the QIE.

7.5.3 Optimization of Neural Networks

In the realm of optimization, where uncertainty frequently complicates and taints decision-making processes [24], fuzzy optimization strategies have proven helpful. These techniques use fuzzy logic concepts to address ambiguity and vagueness, making them useful to a wide range of domains, including engineering, economics, healthcare, and environmental management. In many different industries, optimization strategies are essential for improving performance and efficiency. Among these methods, fuzzy logic provides a strong approach by managing the imprecision and uncertainties that are common in real-world situations.

The mathematical field of optimization is concerned with selecting the optimal option from a range of workable options. Techniques range from straightforward linear programming to intricate evolutionary algorithms, and each is appropriate for a particular kind of issue. The optimizer contributes to model improvement by altering the model's parameters to lower the loss function value. The optimizers include RMSProp, Newton's method, SGD, and ADAM [25]. Identifying the ideal neural network parameters (weights and biases) that allow for accurate prediction is the optimizer's responsibility.

7.5.4 Self-Improving

Optimization is the process of selecting the best option among the numerous feasible options. In other words, optimization is the process of finding the function's optimal or least value. Adaptive tuning allows loops to be adjusted without affecting the process. Should you consider integrating this technology into your plant? This work examines some of the advantages and disadvantages of adaptive tuning.

It is commonly known that forecasts generated by fuzzy systems are both accurate and understandable. However, the explainability of linguistic notions may be jeopardized if they are not semantically anchored. Additional non-trivial challenges would arise if a prediction were to be explained counterfactually, that is, in terms of hypothetical, non-predicted outputs. how the output of fuzzy rule-based classifiers [26] could be supported by automated explanations, both factual and counterfactual, so enhancing their credibility.

7.5.5 Optimization with Metaheuristics

Because metaheuristic optimization techniques are sophisticated algorithms that effectively search and exploit huge and complex search spaces, they are perfect for hyperparameter tuning in machine learning. Genetic techniques (GA) [27], Particle Swarm Optimization (PSO), Simulated Annealing (SA), Differential Evolution (DE), and Ant Colony Optimization (ACO) are some of the methods used to obtain the optimum responses that draw inspiration from annealing, swarm intelligence, and evolution, among other natural phenomena. GAs are used to generate the optimal set of rules for a fuzzy inference engine. The use of GAs optimizes the choice of membership functions. A fuzzy GA is a directed random search over all discrete fuzzy subsets. It can mimic human decision-making.

7.6 Optimization for Fuzzy Systems

These methods can be very helpful when fuzzy logic systems are applied in machine learning, control systems, and decision-making applications. The main objective is to increase efficiency, robustness, and accuracy. The following are some of the most popular methods for optimizing fuzzy logic systems. Combining fuzzy set theory with traditional optimization methods is known as fuzzy system optimization. It is employed when uncertainty makes it impossible to ascertain the precision of a system's performance criteria and decision variables. The goal of fuzzy optimization is to solve fuzzy models as efficiently as possible by applying optimization strategies based on possibility distribution functions or membership functions. The Figure 7.5 explains the different optimization for fuzzy logic system.

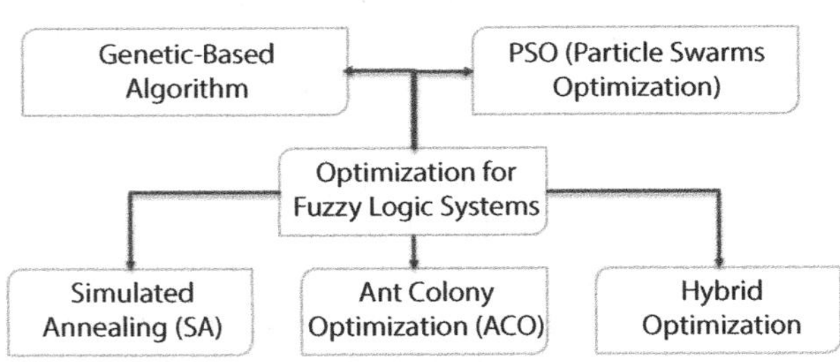

Figure 7.5 Optimization fuzzy logic system.

7.6.1 Genetic-Based Algorithm

Genetic algorithms, sometimes known as GAs, are adaptive heuristic search techniques that fall under the larger category of evolutionary algorithms. Genetic algorithms are based on genetics and natural selection. These are ingenious applications of random searches that concentrate the search on the region of the solution space with the best performance by utilizing past data [28]. Fuzzy logic and genetic algorithms have advanced quickly in the industrial sector to efficiently tackle real-world challenges. Genetic algorithms are evolutionary algorithms that make use of methods like inheritance, mutation, selection, and crossover that are influenced by evolutionary biology.

The following algorithmic iteration then makes use of the newly generated population. The algorithm typically stops when the population reaches a certain level of fitness or when a limit number of generations has been produced. If the algorithm Higher fitness rating individuals are chosen to mate and create superior children by fusing their parents' chromosomes. The population size stays the same, thus there must be room for new arrivals.

7.6.2 PSO (Particle Swarms Optimization)

They simulate "survival of the fittest" among individuals from multiple generations in order to solve an issue. greater fitness ratings are associated with a greater more likely to have children than others. Those with higher fitness ratings are selected to mate and produce superior offspring by combining the chromosomes of their parents. FHPSO, a fuzzy logic and hierarchical learning mechanism-based PSO, is proposed to improve optimization capabilities. However, PSO [29] suffers from the loss of population variety and is prone to local optimum due to limitations like a single learning sample. A PSO based on fuzzy logic and hierarchical learning mechanism (FHPSO) is suggested in order to improve optimization capability.

Fuzzy logic is used in FHPSO to dynamically modify the parameters. The fuzzy system's goal is to better balance exploration and exploitation capabilities by generating suitable parameters depending on performance measurements at each iteration. After that, particles are categorized according to their fitness into various layers, and the particles in these layers use various learning strategies. The particles are separated into high-energy and low-energy particles by each layer. The low-energy particles in each layer learn from the high-energy particles in their layer, and the high-energy particles in each layer are qualified to learn from the particles in the top layer.

7.6.3 Simulated Annealing (SA)

Numerous combinatorial optimization issues have been successfully solved using the simulated annealing method. Simple methods with a larger transition probability at the start of the search and a lower probability at the end of the search determine temperature and local search repetition in the traditional simulated annealing. However, these straightforward techniques may result in an ineffective search procedure. This study presents a fuzzy logic controller (FLC) [30] adaptive simulated annealing approach to address this shortcoming. The simulated annealing search process can be made more efficient by using FLC to regulate the temperature and the local search repetition.

According to the description given above, the objective function is a formula or any other logical expression that establishes a relationship between the affected factors and the desired result or outputs. Depending on the particular situation, algorithms might be closed form, numerical, discrete, or involve local and global minima, among other types. For determining the proper optimum value, traditional optimization techniques like the Newton or Conjugate Gradient Method are appropriate.

7.6.4 Ant Colony Optimization

The Figure 7.6 shows the algorithm used by the ant colony optimization. There are ants in the actual world that can make a road from their nest to the food using a trail substance or pheromone, and they can somehow make this path as efficient as possible. Each artificial ant used in this instance by ACO symbolizes a solution to the issue being addressed (the issue must be represented as a graph). Equations define the dynamics of the ACO [31]. Because in many real-world applications, the element of uncertainty not only exists but also has a major impact on system performance. Therefore, developing effective strategies to deal with such circumstances is necessary.

By measuring the pheromone concentration, Ant Colony Optimization (ACO), a meta-heuristic method created and popularized by Dorigo, enables ants to ascertain the path of their travel. The likelihood that they will follow and

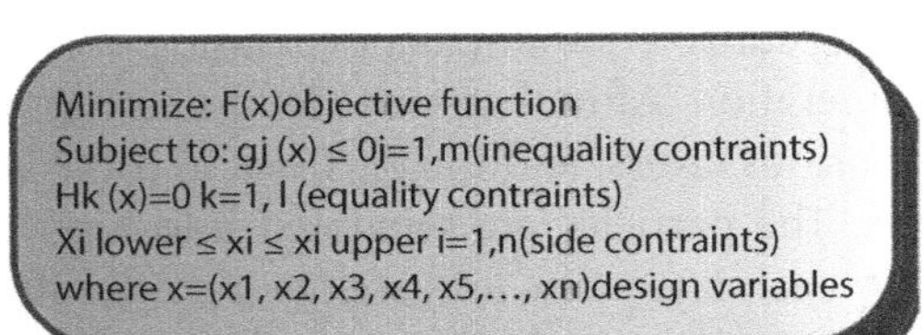

Figure 7.6 Simulated annealing.

crawl the trail increases with pheromone concentration. As a result, the pheromone concentration is highest along the most effective path. Node selection and pheromone updating are crucial components of the ACO technique. In fact, algorithms that follow natural norms produce intriguing outcomes. These algorithms include a subtype known as evolutionary algorithms.

7.6.5 Hybrid Optimization

A hybrid algorithm that blends optimization and machine learning techniques is an effective strategy that makes use of the advantages of both methods to provide a solid basis for resolving difficult problems. By incorporating optimization methods into the machine learning process and vice versa, this fusion enables improved decision-making capabilities.

Thus, a hybrid algorithm [32] can use optimization capabilities to direct learning and improve decision-making efficiency and accuracy. Because of this integration, the algorithm can make use of data- driven learning capabilities and explicit mathematical optimization techniques, which results in more effective and efficient decision-making. Although there are many different approaches and algorithms available today to address optimization challenges, none of them are all- inclusive or flawless enough to address every one of these issues.

7.7 Conventional Approaches

The main focus of hyperparameter tuning is the objective function, which assesses a tuple of hyperparameters and calculates the predicted loss. Optimal hyperparameter [33] adjustment is used to reduce loss depending on the metrics that have been chosen. The results are validated using cross-validation, which measures how well the conclusions apply to datasets other than the specific training instance.

7.7.1 Gradient Descent-Based Optimization

When the dynamics of a system are too complex and imprecise, the fuzzy logic method can offer a flexible and intuitive way to depict ambiguous results. Better answers could be obtained by updating the control schemes' coefficients by combining them with fuzzy systems. It is just the first derivative at a certain place when dealing with a univariate function. A multivariate function is a vector of derivatives [34] along the variable axes in each main direction. These derivatives are referred to as partial derivatives as we are only interested in a slope along one axis and not the other.

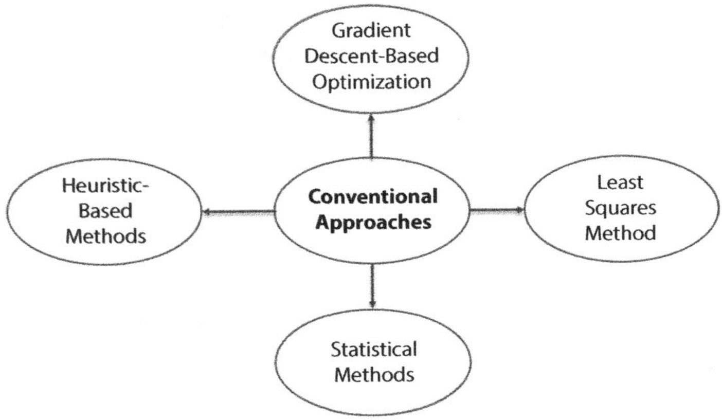

Figure 7.7 Over view conventional approaches.

The Figure 7.7 shows the over view conventional approaches and its methods. The gradient descent method is used to propose an enhanced self-tuning mechanism for fuzzy control. Using the steepest gradient descent approach, the parameters of the membership function are adjusted by minimizing a criterion that is set on the control output. A collection of fuzzy rules is used to continuously adjust the factor that determines how much the fuzzy controller settings are changed. The values of the objective function and its change are taken into consideration when determining this variable.

7.7.2 Least Squares Method

Scatter data is described in statistics as data that may be represented using the independent and dependent variables as the x and y coordinates on a Cartesian plane. This information might not help with data interpretation or forecasting dependent variable values for independent variables. A line's equation that best fits the given data points is then attempted to be found using the Least Square Method [35].

Traders and statisticians who wish to spot patterns and trading opportunities frequently employ this technique. Many interconnected variables are encountered in time series analysis. Establishing a relationship between two or more variables is frequently necessary.

7.7.3 Statistical Methods

A straightforward method for drawing a firm conclusion from unclear, imprecise, noisy, or missing input data is fuzzy logic. The fundamentals of fuzzy logic and the application of statistical techniques to fuzzy data sets are skill fully explained in Statistical Methods for Fuzzy Data. Subjects are precisely classified as either belonging to a set or not. The subject near the edge, on the other hand, simultaneously belongs to and does not belong to a set according to fuzzy sets theory.

As a mathematical representation, in classical set theory, an object takes on the membership value of 1 if it is a member of the set and 0 otherwise utilizing non-fuzzy data to solve conventional statistical problems. Even though there is a growing body of research on the creation and use of fuzzy techniques in statistical analysis, a more thorough understanding of the possibilities for cross-fertilization between fuzzy logic and statistics is still needed.

7.7.4 Heuristic-Based Methods

Heuristics utilize systematic methods to search the problem's search space for the best or closest-to-optimal solution. Unlike a brute-force strategy, which thoroughly examines every potential answer, a heuristic search method makes use of heuristic information to identify a path that appears more likely than the others. In this context, heuristics refer to a collection of standards or guidelines that provide an approximation of a company's profitability.

A heuristic is a method that solves a problem more quickly than traditional approaches. When traditional methods fail to provide an approximate solution to a problem, these techniques are employed. Heuristics are described as the methods of problem-solving that produce rapid and useful answers. Heuristics are methods based on prior experience with related issues. Heuristics employ workable techniques and that might not be ideal but are adequate in a specific amount of time.

7.8 Conclusion

A hyperparameter tweaking approach for Bayesian optimization-based machine learning models was proposed in this study. In Bayesian optimization, the posterior of a function was obtained by combining sample information (evidence) and the function's prior distribution. The posterior information was then used to determine the function's maximum according to a criterion. Standard datasets were used for a number of tests. According to experimental findings, the Gaussian process-based Bayesian optimization technique can get high accuracy in a small number of samples. In addition, the runtime is substantially less than with manual search. The application of fuzzy optimization techniques offers a solid basis for handling complex decision-making problems characterized by uncertainty and imprecision. Fuzzy logic combined with traditional optimization techniques provides flexible and useful solutions for a wide range of applications. As the world attempts to find adaptable and practical answers to increasingly complex issues, the importance of fuzzy optimization cannot be overstated.

References

1. Rahmani, A.M., Yousefpoor, E., Yousefpoor, M.S., Mehmood, Z., Haider, A., Hosseinzadeh, M., Ali Naqvi, R., Machine learning (ML) in medicine: Review, applications, and challenges. *Mathematics*, 9, 22, 2970, 2021, https://doi.org/10.3390/math9222970.
2. Mariana, M., HPS, A.K., Mistar, E.M., Yahya, E.B., Alfatah, T., Danish, M., Amayreh, M., Recent advances in activated carbon modification techniques for enhanced heavy metal adsorption. *J. Water Process Eng.*, 43, 102221, 2021, https://doi.org/10.1016/j.jwpe.2021.102221.
3. Weerts, H.J., Mueller, A.C., Vanschoren, J., Importance of tuning hyperparameters of machine learning algorithms, 2020, arXiv preprint arXiv:2007.07588, https://doi.org/10.48550/arXiv.2007.07588.
4. Toubes, D.R., Araújo-Vila, N., Fraiz-Brea, J.A., Organizational learning capacity and sustainability challenges in times of crisis: A study on tourism SMEs in Galicia (Spain). *Sustainability*, 13, 21, 11764, 2021, https://doi.org/10.3390/su132111764.
5. Liashchynskyi, P. and Liashchynskyi, P., Grid search, random search, genetic algorithm: a big comparison for NAS, 2019, arXiv preprint arXiv:1912.06059, https://doi.org/10.48550/arXiv.1912.06059.
6. Thammano, A. and Poolsamran, P., SMBO: A self-organizing model of marriage in honey-bee optimization. *Expert Syst. Appl.*, 39, 5, 5576–5583, 2012, https://doi.org/10.1016/j.eswa.2011.12.078.
7. Zeng, Y. and Zhang, J., A machine learning model for detecting invasive ductal carcinoma with Google Cloud AutoML Vision. *Comput. Biol. Med.*, 122, 103861, 2020, https://doi.org/10.1016/j.compbiomed.2020.103861.
8. Palahí, M., Pukkala, T., Blasco, E., Trasobares, A., Comparison of beta, Johnson's SB, Weibull and truncated Weibull functions for modeling the diameter distribution of forest stands in Catalonia (north-east of Spain). *Eur. J. For. Res.*, 126, 563–571, 2007, https://doi.org/10.1007/s10342-007-0163-2.
9. Ramachandran, P., Zoph, B., Le, Q.V., Searching for activation functions, 2017, arXiv preprint arXiv:1710.05941, https://doi.org/10.48550/arXiv.1710.05941.
10. Deng, W., Ying, H., Helliwell, C.A., Taylor, J.M., Peacock, W.J., Dennis, E.S., FLOWERING LOCUS C (FLC) regulates development pathways throughout

the life cycle of Arabidopsis. *Proc. Natl. Acad. Sci.*, 108, 16, 6680–6685, 2011, https://doi.org/10.1073/pnas.1019637108.
11. Roshan, S.P., Edwin, E.B., Thanka, M.R., Ebenezer, V., Priscilla Joy, R., XGBoost Based Machine Learning Techniques for Water Quality Prediction, in: *2023 International Conference on Circuit Power and Computing Technologies (ICCPCT)*, IEEE, pp. 364–369, 2023, https://doi.org/10.1109/ICCPCT58313.2023.10244964.
12. Waxman, E., On the origin of fast radio bursts (FRBs), 2017, arXiv preprint arXiv:1703.06723, https://doi.org/10.48550/arXiv.1703.06723.
13. Herbst, J., A machine learning approach to workflow management, in: *European conference on machine learning*, Springer Berlin Heidelberg, Berlin, Heidelberg, 2000, May, https://doi.org/10.1007/3-540-45516-3_18.
14. Chakraverty, S., Sahoo, D.M., Mahato, N.R., Chakraverty, S., Sahoo, D.M., Mahato, N.R., Defuzzification. *Concepts of soft computing: Fuzzy and ANN with programming*, vol. 117–127, 2019.
15. Pillai, V., Enhancing Transparency and Understanding in AI Decision-Making Processes. *Iconic Res. Eng. J.*, 8, 1, 168–172, 2024.
16. Tsiakmaki, M., Kostopoulos, G., Kotsiantis, S., Ragos, O., Fuzzy-based active learning for predicting student academic performance using autoML: a step-wise approach. *J. Comput. Higher Educ.*, 33, 3, 635–667, 2021, https://doi.org/10.1007/s12528-021-09265-3.
17. Thanka, M.R., Sri Ram, K., Gandu, S.P., Bijolin Edwin, E., Ebenezer, V., P.J., Comparing Resampling Techniques in Stroke Prediction with Machine and Deep Learning, in: *2023 International Conference on Sustainable Computing and Smart Systems (ICSCSS)*, IEEE, pp. 1415–1420, 2023, https://doi.org/10.1109/ICSCSS57650.2023.10169237.
18. Qie, S. and Diehl, J.A., Cyclin D1, cancer progression, and opportunities in cancer treatment. *J. Mol. Med.*, 94, 1313–1326, 2016, https://doi.org/10.1007/s00109-016-1483-7.
19. Gower, R.M., Loizou, N., Qian, X., Sailanbayev, A., Shulgin, E., Richtárik, P., SGD: General analysis and improved rates, in: *International conference on machine learning*, PMLR, pp. 5200–5209, 2019, May.
20. Kingma, D.P., Adam: A method for stochastic optimization, 2014, arXiv preprint arXiv:1412.6980, https://doi.org/10.48550/arXiv.1412.6980.
21. Zou, F., Shen, L., Jie, Z., Zhang, W., Liu, W., A sufficient condition for convergences of adam and rmsprop, in: *Proceedings of the IEEE/CVF Conference on Computer Vision and Pattern Recognition*, pp. 11127–11135, 2019, https://doi.org/10.1109/CVPR.2019.01134.
22. Jones, D.R. and Smith, M.J., Implementing new technology, in: *Proceedings of the Human Factors and Ergonomics Society Annual Meeting*, vol. 48, SAGE Publications, Sage CA: Los Angeles, CA, pp. 1601–1604, 2004, September, https://doi.org/10.1177/154193120404801409.
23. Ebenezer, V., Bijolin, E., Sharan, D., Thanka, R., Pose Estimation Approach for Gait Analysis using Machine Learning, in: *2023 Second International*

Conference on Electronics and Renewable Systems (ICEARS)2023, IEEE, pp. 1071–1075, https://doi.org/ 10.1109/ICEARS56392.2023.10085311.
24. Marini, F. and Walczak, B., Particle swarm optimization (PSO). A tutorial. *Chemom. Intell. Lab. Syst.*, 149, 153–165, 2015, https://doi.org/10.1016/j.chemolab.2015.05.005.
25. Eysenbach, G., Powell, J., Kuss, O., Sa, E.R., Empirical studies assessing the quality of health information for consumers on the world wide web: a systematic review. *JAMA*, 287, 20, 2691–2700, 2002, https://doi.org/10.1001/jama.287.20.2691.
26. Picton, T.W., John, M.S., Dimitrijevic, A., Purcell, D., Human auditory steady-state responses: Respuestas auditivas de estado estable en humanos. *Int. J. Audiol.*, 42, 4, 177–219, 2003, https://doi.org/10.3109/14992020309074635.
27. Hamza, M.F., Yap, H.J., Choudhury, I.A., Recent advances on the use of meta-heuristic optimization algorithms to optimize the type-2 fuzzy logic systems in intelligent control. *Neural Comput. Appl.*, 28, 979–999, 2017, https://doi.org/10.1007/s00500-016-2252-8.
28. Thanka, M.R., Bijolin Edwin, E., Ebenezer, V., Martin Sagayam, K., Jayakeshav Reddy, B., Günerhan, H., Emadifar, H., A hybrid approach for melanoma classification using ensemble machine learning techniques with deep transfer learning. *Comput. Methods Programs Biomed. Update*, 3, 100–103, 2023, https://doi.org/10.1016/j.cmpbup.2023.100103.
29. Qian, M.W., Tan, G.J., Li, Y.Z., Liu, S.J., Wang, L., A multi-objective optimization method for scheduling of hybrid renewable energy system. *Sustainable Energy Technol. Assess.*, 39, 100732, 2020, https://doi.org/10.1016/j.seta.2020.100732.
30. Cruz, J.D., Peixoto, M., Lopes, M.M., Marques, M., Machine learning in life sciences: Current challenges and future perspectives. *Biotechnol. Adv.*, 49, 107700, 2021, https://doi.org/10.1016/j.biotechadv.2021.107700.
31. Mallqui-Bonnet, J., Echeverría, F.A., Zubair, S.M., Solving constrained optimization problems with heuristic algorithms. *Comput. Appl. Math.*, 40, 1, 1–12, 2020, https://doi.org/10.1007/s40314-020-01361-0.
32. Santos, P.A. and Porrata, D., Patient's preference on the use of artificial intelligence in the healthcare. *Artif. Intell. Med.*, 109, 101968, 2020, https://doi.org/10.1016/j.artmed.2020.101968.
33. Hasanzadeh, F. and Sadeghzadeh, K., A comprehensive review of meta-heuristic optimization algorithms in the last decade. *Comput. Ind. Eng.*, 155, 107093, 2021, https://doi.org/10.1016/j.cie.2021.107093.
34. Mehdizadeh, A. and Babajani, A., Role of deep learning in intelligent transportation systems: A review. *Comput. Environ. Urban Syst.*, 69, 23–36, 2018, https://doi.org/10.1016/j.compenvurbsys.2018.04.004.
35. Widyanto, R.R. and Hardiyanto, B., A study of several meta-heuristic algorithms on the knapsack problem. *IOP Conf. Ser.: Mater. Sci. Eng.*, 1092, 012067, 2022, https://doi.org/10.1088/1757-899X/1092/1/012067.

8

Machine Learning Models with Fuzzy Logic-Based Tuning

Bhanu Pratap Singh[1]*, Arun Kumar[2], Ankit[2], Vikanksha[2] and Jatinder Singh[2]

[1]*School of Computer Science, Lovely Professional University, Phagwara, Punjab, India*
[2]*School of Agriculture, Lovely Professional University, Phagwara, Punjab, India*

Abstract

Such integration of machine learning models enhanced with fuzzy logic-based calibration constitutes a huge leap in AI research, on two main fronts: accuracy and adaptability. While its primary strength lies in harnessed machine learning algorithms that efficiently handle big data and complex patterns, it leverages fuzzy logic to deal with the uncertainties and vagueness related with the data. One can fine-tune such machine learning models through fuzzy logic to go beyond their performance in variable and unpredictable contexts. Based on this work, the book discusses several approaches towards the integration of fuzzy logic-based tuning into machine learning. Its implementation domain includes robotics, healthcare, finance, environmental monitoring. The inclusion of machine learning with fuzzy logic improves the resilience, interpretability, and decision-making capacity of models. Important case studies deliver considerable evidence for the practical advantages and enhanced performance based on this integrated strategy. The chapter will close with an overview of possible research avenues, elaborating on progress and challenges towards developing machine learning models enriched by fuzzy logic-inspired adjustments.

***Keywords*:** Machine learning, fuzzy logic, model tuning, artificial intelligence

8.1 Introduction

From an abstract concept, machine learning has grown into tangible technology, pushing change forward in fields as diverse as it is vast. This range

**Corresponding author*: thakurbhanu2924@gmail.com

Rahul Kar, Gunjan Mukherjee, Biswadip Basu Mallik and Ashok Kumar Shaw (eds.) Fuzzy Logic in Computational Intelligence: Applications and Case Studies, (129–156) © 2026 Scrivener Publishing LLC

of capabilities-the processing of large amounts of data in a way to produce meaningful insight-based change has significantly changed the process by allowing organizations to optimize operations, enhance customer experience, and develop new fields for growth [1]. At the core of machine learning, it involves predictive modeling that observes data in order to acquire good predictive and or estimation performance by exploring patterns. However, such mathematical constructs proved not to be effective without taking into account various other configurations, often referred to as hyperparameters, decided carefully in advance of their execution for optimal performance.

Hyperparameter tuning, commonly referred to as the optimization of machine learning models, constitutes a crucial component of the model development procedure. This process involves the meticulous adjustment of hyperparameters to achieve optimal accuracy and generalization to unseen data. The challenge associated with hyperparameter tuning arises from the vast and frequently complex search space, where numerous combinations of hyperparameters can significantly affect the model's operational behavior and its predictive accuracy [2]. Historically, methods like grid search and random search had been used to find the way through this research field. These methods are useful in some way but are computationally inefficient and may miss optimal variations, especially in a high-dimensional parameter space.

8.1.1 Fuzzy Logic: A Paradigm Shift in Tuning

During the past few years, there has been a growing interest for employing fuzzy logic, which is specifically designed to manage uncertainty and imprecision, to overcome the challenges related to hyperparameter tuning. Unlike classical binary logic, fuzzy logic provides the means to articulate uncertainty through various levels of truth, rather than simple true/false statements [3]. Since such a methodology is inherently adaptive, it proves to be very appropriately representative of the complex, sometimes ambiguous relationships between hyperparameters and the performances of models. Fuzzy logic is based on the foundation of fuzzy sets in which elements can have partial memberships in a set. It assigns a value between 0 and 1 depending on the degree to which the element corresponds to the set, known as membership operation, which determines the degree of membership of an element. Fuzzy logic further develops this notion by integrating fuzzy rules and inference systems, thereby facilitating the formulation of rules that effectively capture the ambiguous relationships between input variables and expected outcomes [4]. Fuzzy logic, since it does involve vague reasoning and decision-making processes, closely mirrors the way humans' approach complex problems. This attribute makes it a potent tool to effectively handle the ambiguities involved in hyperparameter tuning. There are several noteworthy advantages of incorporating fuzzy logic into the hyperparameter tuning methodology. Fuzzy logic does reveal high effectiveness in uncertainty and errors resolution; thus, it allows for better exploration of the hyperparameter space. It permits continuous and subtle tuning of hyperparameter settings, not as discrete parameter values as other conventional methods [5]. Therefore, this approach supports more informed decision-making. For instance, fuzzy logic offers better flexibility in the description of complex interrelations among hyperparameters, making it sensitive to subtle features that might elude conventional approaches. Such flexibility makes the tuning process highly flexible and responsive, allowing the model to change hyperparameters based on conditions or inputs that vary. Conclusion in general, fuzzy logic provides a more intuitive approach to the hyperparameter tuning process such that it allows practitioners to use their experience, knowledge, and judgment as guides during the tuning process. Using fuzzy-logic-based tuning, hence, produces results that are qualitatively interpreted along with good quantitative metrics [6]. In turn, this approach enables operators to make better choices in configuring the model. As machine learning continues to advance, the significance of hyperparameter adjustment is sure to rise. Fuzzy logic provides an appealing methodology for improving the effectiveness as well as efficiency of the tuning process so that developers can explore the full potential of their machine learning models. Notwithstanding, there remain challenges that need to be solved like formulating effective membership functions, computational complexity management, and adapting the fuzzy logic-based tuning methodologies for large datasets and complex models. To overcome these, additional research and technological advancements are anticipated. Despite this, the potential benefits are significant. The application of fuzzy logic-based tuning enables practitioners to accelerate the development and deployment of high-performing machine learning models, thereby fostering progress and expansion across various domains.

8.2 Fundamentals of Fuzzy Logic

Consequently, fuzzy logic is a mathematical framework that accounts for predictability and imperfection; hence, it is an important tool for modeling complex systems that cannot be handled by the binary logic.

Fuzzy logic extends the classic set theory notions with the concept of fuzzy sets whereby the elements belonging to a set can come in various degrees [7]. This deviation from clear-cut, binary inclusion to a more adaptable and subtle portrayal of unpredictability ensures fuzzy logic that is especially appropriate for the execution of imprecise or unclear information tasks.

8.2.1 Definition and Concepts of Fuzzy Logic

Fuzzy logic is based on the concept of fuzzy sets, which were established by Lotfi Zadeh in the 1960s. Fuzzy sets, in contrast to conventional set theory, include the concept of partial affiliation, where items may have varying degrees of belongingness to a set, represented by values between 0 and 1. The degree of connection is established by a membership function that assigns a certain degree of belonging to each element. Fuzzy logic offers a more adaptable and articulate structure for thinking about ambiguity by measuring the extent within which a component relates to a group [8].

8.2.2 Fuzzy Sets and Membership Functions

Fuzzy sets are fundamental to fuzzy logic, providing a formal method for representing notions that are unclear or inaccurate. A fuzzy set is defined by its membership function, which assigns varying degrees of membership to components inside a certain realm of conversation. The inclusion of several membership operations, including triangular, trapezoidal, Gaussian, and sigmoidal shapes, allows for the representation of distinct aspects of doubt [9]. By defining fuzzy sets and their related membership functions, professionals may create models that encapsulate complex interactions and enable informed choices in the face of ambiguity.

8.2.3 Fuzzy Rules and Inference Systems

Fuzzy rules and inference algorithms (Figure 8.1) are essential components that enable the development of fuzzy logic-based models and reasoning processes, extending beyond the domain of fuzzy sets [10]. Fuzzy rules represent the connections underlying the input parameters and predicted results using language expressions, usually in the form of "if-then" expressions. These criteria include subjective observations and particular expertise, enabling professionals to use their skills in the process of developing the model. Inference algorithms are used to supplement fuzzy rules by

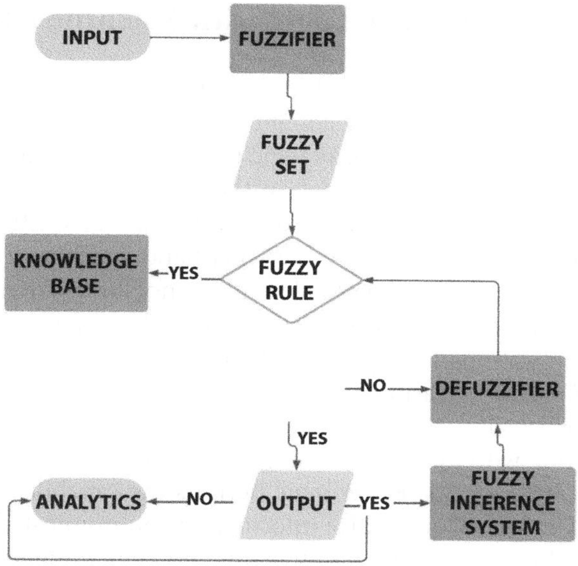

Figure 8.1 Schematic representation of fuzzy logic.

providing a formal way to combine them and provide precise output values. Inference systems use fuzzy rules to process incoming data and combine the outcomes, allowing for the implementation of fuzzy logic-based reasoning and choice-making in practical scenarios [11].

8.2.4 Defuzzification Methods

In the realm of fuzzy logic, the output of the fuzzy inference system may exist as a fuzzy set characterized by a membership function. However, several real-world applications require the conversion of these vague outcomes into specific usable values. Defuzzification is the process of mapping the fuzzy output set to a crisp outcome number with the help of some predecided criteria or rules of decision making. The centroid, maximal membership and weighted mean can be regarded as defuzzification techniques that are commonly applied [12]. As it has been observed, each method has its own characteristic way of how simple it is and how precise it can be. This way, employing defuzzification techniques, much important information can be received from the models based on the fuzzy logic and further decisions may be made in various practical cases.

8.3 Integrating Fuzzy Logic with Machine Learning

In integrating fuzzy logic with machine learning, both approaches combine the advantages in handling very complex issues described by uncertainty and imprecision (Table 8.1). Fuzzy logic takes its relation in the theory of fuzzy sets developed by Lotfi Zadeh in the 1960s; thus, it presents a systemic approach in managing data and making decisions with imprecision and uncertainty involved [13]. On the other hand, machine learning algorithms are known for their remarkable competence for discovering patterns and generating predictions from large datasets. These methodologies have integrated applications in improving the robustness, interpretability, and flexibility of machine learning models, which is challenging to compute accurately for specific domains. The main advantage of using this fuzzy logic integration with machine learning is its capability to handle linguistic variables and fuzzy rules. Fuzzy logic permits the capability to represent and manipulate logical qualitative information communicated using natural language phrases like "high," "low," "hot," or "cold." Linguistic flexibility yields a system that is much clearer and more intuitive, since it incorporates a specialist's knowledge and intuition [14]. However, when fuzzy logic-based inference processes are added to the machine learning algorithms, then we have the means of capturing inherent uncertainty attached to real-world data and draw more knowledgeable conclusions. Fuzzy logic may be applied to algorithms such as fuzzy clustering, fuzzy classification, or fuzzy regression in supervised learning applications to represent complex relationships between the inputs and outputs. The advantage that fuzzy clustering approaches, such as fuzzy c-means, have over traditional crisp clustering techniques is the flexible division of data points into clusters or groups, providing it with the ability to allow overlapping memberships and successfully manage noisy or uncertain data [15]. In like manner, fuzzy classification techniques, be it fuzzy decision trees or fuzzy inference systems, systematically approach ambiguity in class boundaries and decision boundaries and, hence, lead to more resilient and understandable models. Fuzzy logic can be adapted to unsupervised learning scenarios to support exploratory data analysis, feature selection, and anomaly detection. A flexible framework in expressing and reasoning over vague or incomplete information, fuzzy logic-based anomaly detection techniques can systematically identify outliers from expected patterns in data streams or time series with a gradual shift from normal towards abnormal behavior. It can, therefore, enhance flexible and understandable autonomous systems that operate under uncertainty or time-varying environments. Fuzzy logic

Table 8.1 Summary of integration of fuzzy logic with machine learning.

Integration aspect	Description	References
Fuzzy logic-based tuning	Optimizing machine learning model parameters using fuzzy logic principles to handle uncertainty and imprecision in data.	[17]
Fuzzy clustering	There is the use of fuzzy clustering algorithms with soft cluster assignments while considering partial membership of the data points to several clusters.	[18]
Fuzzy inference systems	Fuzzy Inference Systems were used for modeling complex input/ output relationships that are more interpretable and flexible.	[19]
Fuzzy rule-based systems	Fuzzy rule-based systems are put into effect while encoding the knowledge or heuristics of the experts in the learning machine, making it adaptive and reasonable.	[20]
Fuzzy neural networks	Incorporation of fuzzy logic principles to neural network architectures in enhancing the development of more robust and interpretable models that can solve uncertain or imprecise data.	[21]
Fuzzy ensemble learning	Application of fuzzy logic in ensemble learning techniques for combining models, thus improving predictive results mainly for environments that are ambiguous or uncertain.	[22]
Fuzzy reinforcement learning	The application of fuzzy logic to strengthen learning algorithms such that agents can make better decisions in difficult and uncertain environments.	[23]
Fuzzy evolutionary algorithms	Employing fuzzy logic-driven algorithmic evolution to enhance machine learning models, facilitating adaptable and resilient optimization in fluctuating contexts.	[24]

controllers, such as FLCs, are rule-based approaches at making decisions that elegantly handle imprecise sensor inputs and complex control objectives far better than the rather dated PID controllers [16]. Integration of techniques in fuzzy logic-based control with reinforcement learning algorithms could lead to the development of autonomous systems that adapt more robustly to change. These systems can learn from experience, thus adjusting to dynamic settings in real-time.

8.3.1 Concept and Benefits of Fuzzy Logic-Based Tuning

Fuzzy logic-based tuning, FLBT, is a method for adapting the tuning of complex systems, especially in control systems and machine learning algorithms [25]. It is based on principles drawn from fuzzy logic, thus allowing for uncertainty and imprecision that best characterizes real-world systems where direct, precise mathematical models are not readily available or cannot be constructed with any degree of confidence. FLBT works on defining the fuzzy sets representing the range of parameter values and the linguistic terms describing the significance of parameter values. Such fuzzy sets then form a set of fuzzy rules which map the system's performance metrics into changes of parameters. FLBT checks and examines the behavior of the system for various parameter configurations, updating fuzzy rules according to observed performance and, on following such an iterative procedure, enhancing the values of the parameters.

The benefits of FLBT include:

1. Robustness: FLBT can change the parameters flexibly toward resisting changes in the dynamics of the system or the situation in the environment, making it highly robust and reliable.
2. Interpretability: The employment of language concepts as well as fuzzy rules will facilitate increasing the interpretability of FLBT models to be undertaken by domain experts, with the opportunity to more deeply enhance the tuning procedure.
3. Efficiency: FLBT can potentially achieve optimal or very close-to-optimal parameter values efficiently compared to traditional methods of tuning. This is much more efficient when applied, and consequently human tuning time and effort reduces.
4. Adaptability: FLBT enables it to iteratively adjust the values of the parameters with the help of real-time input and hence sensitivity can be built in with respect to the changing operational conditions or requirement.

In simpler words, Fuzzy Logic-Based Tuning provides a systematic and flexible approach toward parameter optimization, especially in complex structures where modeling cannot be possible precisely or personal tuning is also not feasible [26].

8.3.2 Handling Uncertainty

It is very effective in many fields: decision-making, management systems, and machine learning. Many ways have surfaced dealing with uncertainty. Probabilistic approaches include Bayesian inference, which assigns probability to events and gives a structured basis for data-driven reasoning [27]. Fuzzy logic employs linguistic variables and fuzzy sets that can easily and smoothly change between true and false values; it is therefore very suitable for applications involving imprecise or vagueness in information. Interval analysis bounds uncertain numbers to intervals, which ensures that there is guaranteed analysis regardless of if one might not know the exact values. Monte Carlo simulation applies a large number of samples at random to provide a very detailed estimate of system behaviors. Evidence theory is an extension of probability theory and therefore provides a framework for adaptive understanding when data may be incomplete or vague and the values are best expressed using belief functions. Uncertainty in machine learning approaches-ensemble approaches and dropout periodicity are addressed by either aggregating the various forecasts or adding randomness [28]. Expert judgment, aided by expert elicitation procedures, supports quantitative data through specialized knowledge navigating through unclear circumstances. Uncertainty can be successfully handled by professionals using judicious application of many approaches, which in turn will allow for well-informed decision-making in a wide range of real-life situations.

8.3.3 Flexibility in Parameter Evaluation

Flexibility in parameter evaluation is essential for adapting to diverse scenarios and optimizing system performance. Several strategies enable this flexibility:

1. Dynamic Parameter Adjustment: Algorithms have the ability to adaptively modify variables in response to immediate information or fluctuations in their surroundings. Evolutionary algorithms watch the moves of a given thing without any disturbance and change the variables in such a

manner so that the best achievement is sustained, and there is always flexibility in situations [29].

2. Metaheuristic Optimization: Metaheuristic management techniques, which include genetic algorithms, particle swarm optimization, or simulated annealing, have the capability to search parameter space suitably to find systems that are near optimum. These methods provide flexibility in the form of the exploration of alternatives throughout a wide spectrum of value ranges and support various optimal aims and restrictions [30].
3. Multi-objective Optimization: Optimization for multiple objectives generally involves multiple consideration of several objectives that often tend to conflict with each other. This approach allows for the calculation of compromises among different indicators of success. Multi-objectify optimization heightens decision making and system flexibility in improving variables to attain equilibrium of competing goals [31].
4. Bayesian Optimization: Bayesian optimization applies probabilistic models so as to guide the exploration process for optimal parameter combinations. Bayesian optimization effectively searches the parameter space by combining previous information and changing assumptions according to observable results [32]. It automatically focuses on searching on areas of opportunity to enhance effectiveness.

8.3.4 Improved Model Robustness and Performance

Improvement of model resilience and efficiency is an extremely complex activity that holds a high relevance in different domains. A fundamental component is ensuring data integrity and sufficiency, making proper training and generalization possible. Strategic tweaking and selection enhance the capability of understanding and effective employment of the model by highlighting the most salient features of the data [33]. Methods of normalization appropriately reduce overfitting, and the constructed models generalize well to new and previously unseen data. Ensemble methods use knowledge gain from several models to reduce individual biases and noise, thereby strengthening robustness and the correctness of predictions. The overextension of cross-validation and evaluation procedures guarantees the correctness of the performance of the model on various datasets, which makes the built model trustworthy in real practice [34]. Besides, the process of hyperparameter tuning as well as the use of transferable learning leverages the known knowledge to enhance models that solve specific tasks or domains. Readable and interpretable designs not only increase trust but also robustness through the ability of the operator to identify and correct any potential bias or mistake. By adopting a holistic approach that comprises these strategies, professionals might manage to make models more effective and long-lasting, thereby allowing them to solve highly complex problems in a wide array of fields and contexts.

8.4 Fuzzy Logic-Based Tuning for Supervised Machine Learning Models

Fuzzy logic-based tuning (FLBT) is an approach that methodically tunes the parameters of supervised machine learning models depicted in Table 8.2. Hence, FLBT enhances the performance and adaptability of such models [35]. Compared to the conventional optimization approaches based on mathematical formulations which resort to using the exact mathematical derivation or exhaustive search strategies, FLBT makes use of fuzzy concepts pertaining to the resolution of the uncertainty and vagueness in the optimization process as presented in Figure 8.2.

FLBT's key idea is the expression of parameters with their corresponding values as fuzzy sets, which makes a smooth, progressive transition between different parameter settings. Linguistic variables and fuzzy rules incorporate the subject expertise with professional intuition into the tuning procedure, so the system is capable of well understanding and responding to qualitative input [36]. FLBT Algorithms model evaluation is based on various parameters where a model is assessed with several numerical and non-numerical values, such as understanding and sustainability.

8.4.1 Fuzzy Logic for Hyperparameter Tuning

A sophisticated alternative is the use of Fuzzy Logic in hyperparameter tuning; actually, it makes possible the enhancement of machine learning model parameters in a very sophisticated way. Traditionally, hyperparameter tuning approaches rely on deep research or heuristic-based strategies that typically find difficulties in handling complexities in modern models and datasets [43]. Fuzzy Logic provides birth to an interactive and flexible framework to best explore the parameter space. Fuzzy logic-based

Table 8.2 Fuzzy logic-based tuning approaches for supervised machine learning models.

Aspect	Description	Approach	References
Parameter optimization	FLBT optimizes hyperparameters of supervised learning models, such as support vector machines (SVMs) and decision trees, using fuzzy logic principles.	Grid search and fuzzy logic-based tuning are combined to explore hyperparameter space efficiently.	[37]
Uncertainty handling	Fuzzy logic handles uncertainty in model parameters and data, enabling more robust and interpretable predictions in supervised learning tasks.	Fuzzy sets are used to represent uncertainty, allowing for flexible and adaptive decision-making.	[38]
Rule-based model interpretability	FLBT incorporates fuzzy rule-based systems to enhance model interpretability by encoding expert knowledge or heuristics into the learning process.	Linguistic rules are defined based on domain expertise, improving model transparency and usability.	[39]
Data imbalance correction	Utilizing fuzzy logic to address class imbalance issues in supervised learning datasets, improving the model's ability to generalize across different classes.	Fuzzy undersampling and oversampling techniques are employed to balance class distributions effectively.	[40]

(*Continued*)

Table 8.2 Fuzzy logic-based tuning approaches for supervised machine learning models. (*Continued*)

Aspect	Description	Approach	References
Adaptive learning rates	FLBT dynamically adjusts learning rates and other optimization parameters based on fuzzy logic principles, optimizing model convergence and performance.	Fuzzy logic-based control mechanisms adapt learning rates in real-time, improving model stability and convergence.	[41]
Ensemble model optimization	Fuzzy logic guides the optimization of ensemble models, such as random forests and gradient boosting machines (GBMs), by fine-tuning individual model parameters.	Ensemble learning techniques are combined with fuzzy logic-based optimization to enhance model diversity and performance.	[42]

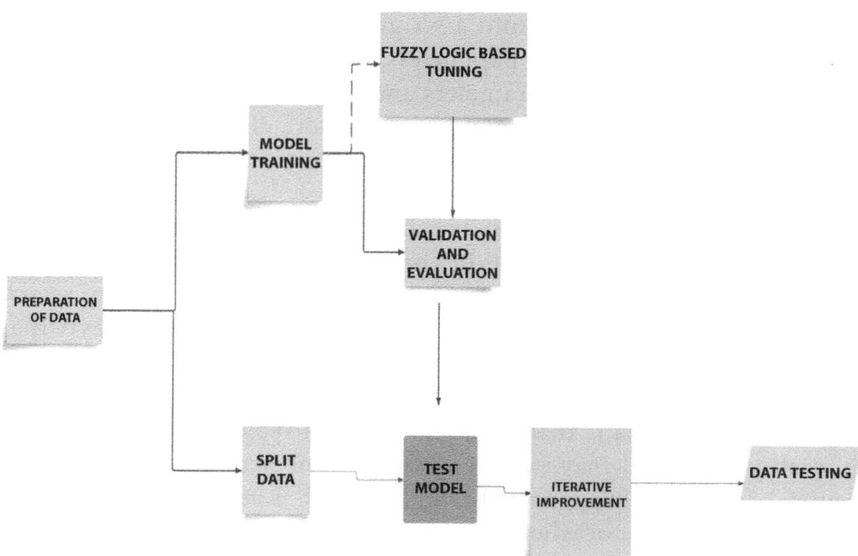

Figure 8.2 Introduction to supervised learning model with fuzzy logic base tuning model.

hyperparameter tuning applies fuzzy sets to express parameters with their values in such a way that it is easy to make a transition between different configurations. Linguistic variables and fuzzy rules explicitly introduce subject expert judgment into the process of tuning, thereby facilitating a proper interpretation by the algorithm of the qualitative input [44]. The system employs fuzzy inference procedures to test the performance of the model under varied settings of hyperparameters-both in terms of quantitative metrics and qualitative factors like interpretability and robustness. Fuzzy Logic excels at handling the uncertainties and imprecisions intrinsically generated in hyperparameter tuning procedures. By employing fuzzy reasoning, the system can make sound judgments even when perfect numerical data does not exist. In addition, the Fuzzy Logic-based frameworks will mainly comprise algorithms in handling shifting conditions and consumer preferences, creating an improved flexible and agile method of optimization.

8.4.2 Fuzzy Grid and Random Search

Two methods which are quite distinct from each other and whose respective advantages in use are as follows, are hyperparameter optimization using Fuzzy Grid Search and Random Search. Fuzzy Grid Search is a combination of the advantageous structure of grid search with the flexibility of fuzzy logic. With fuzzy grid search, rather than discretizing the whole parameter space into a set grid, the space is overlapped and transitions gradually among parameters. Fuzzy grid search applies fuzzy sets to denote ranges for parameters and linguistic phrases to represent their relevance [45]. Therefore, it provides more efficient exploration of the parameter space with emphasis on promising areas but still maintains understandability. Such a strategy is particularly handy in cases of intricate and non-linear relations between hyperparameters to permit even subtler optimization strategies. In contrast, Random Search is another, more probabilistic kind of hyperparameter tweaking. The random search is a technique that does not try all combinations of the set of hyperparameters exhaustively; it samples randomly from the parameter space and evaluates a few configurations [46]. This kind of approach may seem more superficially systematic than grid search, but it typically performs better in reality because it may explore a larger number of different hyperparameter settings. It happens that random search is very efficient when the search space is huge or when some hyperparameters greatly affect model performance. The Fuzzy Grid Search method gives a rather systematic and adaptive approach to hyperparameter optimization by leveraging fuzzy logic to examine intricate parameter spaces [47]. On the other hand, the Random Search gives a more probabilistic, exploratory approach by randomly picking from the area of parameters to discover potentially favorable combinations.

8.5 Fuzzy Logic-Based Tuning for Unsupervised Machine Learning Models

Fuzzy Logic-Based Tuning is a structured methodology for adjusting variables in unsupervised models of machine learning. These range from clustering techniques that involve unsupervised models to be achieved, such as the K-means model. Unlike other typical methods used in tuning, FLBT incorporates fuzzy set theory. Using this theory, one can prevent the non-determinism and imprecision seen when using unsupervised tasks [48]. Variables that involve tuning in FLBT include the number of clusters, K, used in a K-means algorithm. These variables are represented as fuzzy sets. This representation allows for smooth transitions among various configurations. Linguistic variables and fuzzy rules impart domain knowledge and sensibility into the tuner manager, thereby allowing the algorithm to interpret correctly the quantitative input [44]. FLBT algorithms examine the performance of the unsupervised model for various parameter settings both in terms of quantitative metrics and qualitative parameters such as cluster coherency and interpretability. FLBT makes use of an iteration procedure to fine-tune the rules and modify parameters, which facilitates the adaptive update of fuzzy rules and membership functions in the way that best enhances the model. It is in this regard that FLBT uses the expressive ability of fuzzy logic towards providing systematic and adaptive means for modification of parameters in unsupervised learning models. It would certainly probe into the intricacies of feature locations, making it possible to produce enhanced clustering results and, in turn, shed light upon the underlying structure of information.

8.5.1 Fuzzy Logic in Clustering

Fuzzy logic comes into the algorithm in such a way that the framework formed here can handle one point of uncertainty and flexible information assignments that represent a cluster. Classical approaches, like K-means, to clustering assign the data point strictly to one single cluster, which often leads to boundaries that are too rigid and, hence, not very efficient representations of the underlying structure. Fuzzy clustering techniques are able to progressively assign data points into different groups, corresponding to the inherent fuzziness or vagueness present in the data [50]. Among the fuzzy clustering algorithms, the most famous is Fuzzy C-Means (FCM) technique. The K-means algorithm is improved by FCM by implying membership values for each point of data, capable of computing the degree to which the data point belongs to each group. Membership figures may be manipulated a few times considering the gaps between data values and the centroids in the cluster. Algorithms of fuzzy membership determine how converged each cluster is with regard to other clusters.

Fuzzy clustering offers several advantages:

1. Robustness: Fuzzy clustering has superior efficacy in handling noisy data and groups that overlap compared to conventional approaches, resulting in more resilient and precise cluster allocations.
2. Flexibility: Fuzzy clustering enables the incorporation of flexible borders within clusters, supporting intricate spread of data and retaining nuanced interactions between data points.
3. Interpretability: The fuzzy membership values supplied to data points offer a sense of any uncertainty or contradiction in the clustering manipulation, facilitating improved understanding of findings.
4. Adaptability: Fuzzy clustering techniques provide the ability to adjust to changes in statistical distributions or cluster topologies as time progresses, therefore being well-suited for dynamic or developing datasets.

In general, fuzzy logic improves methods for clustering by including a more detailed description of the lack of clarity of the data, resulting in enhanced cluster assignments and a deeper understanding of the data organization [51].

8.5.2 Fuzzy C-Means Clustering

FCM is the most commonly used fuzzy partitioning algorithm that partitions the data into clusters of soft boundaries. Differing from the traditional hard-boundary-based algorithms such as K-means, where every data point belongs to a single cluster, in FCM, every data point gets membership values for every cluster, representing the degree of association with each. The soft assignment thus helps the better handling capabilities of FCM towards uncertainty and overlapping of clusters [52].

The FCM algorithm works as follows:

1. Initialization: Randomly initialize cluster centroids and specify a fuzziness parameter \(m \), which determines the degree of fuzziness in the cluster assignments.
2. Membership Calculation: For each data point, calculate membership values indicating its degree of belongingness to each cluster using the fuzzy membership function:

$$\mu ij = \sum k = 1c(||xi - vk||||xi - vj||)m - 121$$

   where:

   - \(\mu_{ij} \) is the membership of data point \(i \) to cluster \(j \).
   - \(x_i \) is the data point.
   - \(v_j \) is the centroid of cluster \(j \).
   - \(c \) is the number of clusters.
   - \(m \) is the fuzziness parameter.
3. Centroid Update: Update cluster centroids using the calculated membership values:

$$vj = \sum i = 1n(\mu ij)m \sum i = 1n(\mu ij)m \cdot xi$$

4. Iteration: Iterate steps 2 and 3 until convergence criteria are met (e.g., small changes in centroids or membership values).
5. Cluster Assignment: After convergence, assign each data point to the cluster with the highest membership value. FCM offers several advantages; it can deal with non-overlapping and non-spherical clusters, as well as noisy data and overlapping clusters with each other [53]. However, it is also very sensitive to the value of the fuzziness parameter m and is prone to establishing appropriate cluster centroids requiring careful initialization. Despite these challenges, FCM remains one of the most frequently used approaches to fuzzy clustering on a vast scale of applications, including image segmentation, pattern detection, and data extraction.

8.5.3 Tuning K-Means with Fuzzy Logic

An extension of the traditional K-means algorithm toward the use of fuzzy logic extends in using fuzzy categories to efficiently treat inconsistency and for producing softer clusters [54]. The technique allows for more elasticity and resistance in clustering, especially when points of information are going to be assigned to multiple clusters simultaneously. That's how the K-means algorithm can be fine-tuned with fuzzy logic:

1. Fuzzy Memberships: Instead of all statistics belonging to a particular group fuzzy logic assigns membership values that delineate the degree of how much they relate with each one of the groups. Membership values are continuous ranging from 0 to 1 and hence, can be assigned flexibly [55].
2. Fuzzy Partition Matrix: It is defined by U which stores the membership values of data points for each cluster. For this matrix U, every row represents data point and every column in the matrix actually represents a cluster. The values of the matrix U are iteratively updated in the course of the clustering process [56].
3. Fuzzy Centroids. While using hard-cluster centroids, fuzzy logic makes use of fuzzy centroids with a feature of the vector of participation numbers [57]. The membership values quantify how much or little to reflect elements of the information in each cluster whether the centroid should.
4. Fuzzy objective function. In fuzzy K-means, an objective function is changed to be used with fuzzy memberships [58]. Objective: minimize the sum of squared distances between data points and fuzzy centroids while distances are weighted by membership values.
5. Fuzzy Clustering Algorithm: The fuzzy K-means algorithm operates by iteratively updating the fuzzy affinities and fuzzy centroids until convergence is achieved [59]. Data points at each iteration obtain new membership values according to their distances to fuzzy centroids. The fuzzy centroids are updated through a weighted median of the data points along membership values. Implementation of fuzzy logic in K-means technique helps the practitioners to achieve more flexible and complex clustering results. This is especially useful in overlapping clusters or noisy data. However, for optimal result to be achieved using the fuzzy K-means

algorithm, the fuzziness coefficient and convergence conditions must be seriously considered.

8.6 Adaptive Tuning Parameters using Fuzzy Logic Towards Reinforcement Learning Models

Fuzzy logic-based tuning: This could very well be an effective reinforcement learning fine-tuning method by being used for fine-tuning several RL algorithm elements, from designing the reward function to adapting the learning rates. Introducing fuzzy logic allows models to dynamically update parameters regarding unclear or wrong input data, and it might augment the accuracy and robustness of RL models more in dynamic environments.

8.6.1 Reward Function Design Using Fuzzy Logic

Fuzzy Logic lies at the heart of proper reward-function creation in Reinforcement Learning (RL) since it captures mathematically the subtleties of the interplay between actions and results. Traditional RL schemes based on predefined rewards/penalties suffer from the lack of detailed representation of real world.

Fuzzy Logic enables the representation of fuzzy sets and linguistic variables to enable RL agents to reason with imprecise or qualitative information. Fuzzy Logic could be used in defining a reward function toward developing fuzzy rules associating state-action pairings with rewards that are conditioned by domain knowledge or historical records of a problem [60]. These heuristic principles enable reinforcement learning machines to make informed choices even in situations where the best course of action is vague or ambiguous. Additionally, Fuzzy Logic enables Reinforcement Learning agents to take account of many goals or preferences at once, leading to behavior that is much more adaptive and flexible.

8.6.2 Adaptive Learning Rates with Fuzzy Logic

Agents require adaptive learning rates because they must update the rate at which they change their actions according to what they see in the reward. Classical adaptation of the learning rate methods, especially the fixed schedule and heuristic modifications, do not perform too well under dynamic contexts where the optimal learning rate itself is time dependent. Fuzzy Logic provides an organized framework for adapting the learning rate based on reward fluctuation, vagueness of phase halt, and past experience of an agent [61]. It can set up fuzzy rules for adaptive adjustment of a learning rate along with a situation that the reinforcement learning agent learns knowledge efficiently while maintaining consistency and convergence properties. The inclusion of Fuzzy Logic in the design of the patterns of both reward functions' and learning rates' adjustment processes enables RL models to operate more efficiently and effectively in various tasks and scenarios [62]. FLBT thus allows an agent to have improved logical reasoning using uncertain or imprecise knowledge and thereby facilitates improved capacities for decision-making in complex real-world problems.

8.7 Advanced Applications of Fuzzy Logic-Based Tuning

It has wide applications from deep learning to aggregation approaches, optimization of the model, and enhancement of flexibility with fuzzy logic concepts. The FLBT is a technique for deep learning in which neural networks improve their resilience *via* dynamic hyperparameters adaptation like capacity for learning and components of periodicity [63]. This allows the networks to handle vagueness in inputs and to negotiate complexly constrained choices very effectively. This systematic method also applies in fine-tuning the structures and variables of DNNs, ensuring that the best possible outcomes are produced in a wide range of tasks-from image categorization to the analysis of natural language. FLBT, additionally, also improves better feature extraction, modeling of temporal patterns and sequence forecasting in CNNs and RNNs [64], thus offering more interpretable and robust models to efficiently manage complicated settings of data. FLBT improves ensemble approaches to dynamically change parameters and weight contributions of a base model, in order to enhance its contribution toward better performance and adaptability for classification and regression. The boosting and bagging algorithms proposed here are with fuzzy logic in order to improve overall performance adjustment with techniques for learning rates and sample weights for maximizing the contributions of each individual learner. FLBT adopts fuzzy logic principles, specifically regarding stacking and blending techniques in evaluating dependability and complementarity, which means their optimization in the process of selecting and fusing the models. In most real-world applications, the method yields robust performance for ensemble methods. FLBT or fuzzy logic-based machine learning frees up the models of machine learning from traditional constraints with the ability to include fuzzy logic principles [65]. This allows the innovation of new better abilities and flexibility in dealing with complicated problems.

8.7.1 Fuzzy Logic in Deep Learning

The deep integration of Fuzzy Logic deeply alters the optimization and training techniques. Fuzzy sets and rules augment the learning procedure by imbibing inherent ambiguities and imprecisions seen within large datasets. DNNs employ FLBT in a dynamic fashion that can modify self-tuning hyperparameters such as neural network learning rates and normalization factors [66]. This flexibility helps in improving the completion and efficiency of the model especially when concerned with hard and highly dimensional data sets. DNNs utilize fuzzy logic concepts to successfully navigate intricately limited decisions that build up reliable adaptation and resilience.

8.7.2 Tuning Deep Neural Networks

Application of Fuzzy Logic-Based Tuning to Deep Neural Networks It gives a systematic and flexible approach for optimizing model designs and hyperparameters to improve the performance of DNNs [67]. FLBT adjusts learning rates, failure rates, and layer arrangements based on different situations while it enhances the model's capacity to effectively learn knowledge from the data. Fuzzy logic principles utilize the strengths of deep neural networks in effectively handling the ambiguities and imprecisions that may be present within training data to develop stronger and more dependable models. Moreover, FLBT improves the interpretability of deep neural networks (DNNs) since it allows one to learn with a better understanding of how different hyperparameters influence the performance of the model [68]. Including FLBT in the tuning process will allow deep learning practitioners to attain superior and flexible performances in many deep learning tasks-from a good performance in image classification to a satisfactory performance in language recognition.

8.7.3 Fuzzy Logic in CNNs and RNNs

A large amount of Fuzzy Logic is applied to CNNs and RNNs in order to enhance their skills in image processing, sequence modeling, and other associated fields. Fuzzy rules applied to Convolutional Neural Networks (CNNs) act as guidelines for the feature extraction and selection process [69]. In this manner, a more detailed and sophisticated representation of complex visual input is created. In addition, the RNNs use fuzzy logic to express dependency on time and capture long-range relationships in sequential data.

8.8 Challenges and Limitations

The challenges and limitations of implementing Fuzzy Logic-Based Tuning (FLBT) are ongoing, primarily due to computational complexity and efficiency concerns, the scaling problem, and the ability to deal with high-dimensional data robustly.

Another crucial barrier is the computation complexity of, and the performance of the FLBT algorithm. Optimization algorithms founded on fuzzy logic tend to be repetitive procedures with complex computations in mathematics, making the entire process much more intensive in terms of computing [70]. The computational demands of FLBT could be quite intolerably high if the problem size becomes rather large and then too heavy to apply in practice, especially for online or real-time as well as resource-constrained applications, as the amount of data goes up in terms of number and complexity. So, FLBT suffers from a scalability problem. In terms of practical applicability on large databases, even if FLBT may be enough for datasets on small to medium-sized information, the problem indeed persists in using FLBT on big databases. With more points of information or dimensions, FLBT algorithms may experience the hassle of appropriately finding an optimal solution within the parameter space, thus entailing scalability problems and high computing load as well [71]. FLBT places strong emphasis on multidimensional data. The curse of dimensionality can actually increase the computational cost and even impair the performance of FLBT algorithms significantly at high dimensions. It also becomes difficult to extract interesting trends or to optimize variables due to increased sparsity and duplication in the high-dimensional data. This may tend to degrade speed and readability.

FLBT is motivated more by the need to ensure robustness and generalization particularly in cases of noisy or ambiguous datasets. Most optimization methods through fuzzy logic have limitations with respect to their inability to generalize well to unobserved data or adaptability to changing environments, which can, in some cases, degrade performance to suboptimal and hence limit applicability in real-world scenarios. Therefore, these challenges have to be addressed with better algorithms; computationally efficient procedures; and scalable methods in FLBT. Moreover, by integrating FLBT with other ancillary techniques [72] such as dimensionality reduction and optimization strategies which are of a robust nature, it would further improve the generalization capabilities as well as robustness of the technique. Once these bottlenecks are eliminated, FLBT can come to realize its full potential as an effective optimization tool in multiple machine learning applications.

8.9 Conclusion

A rather important opportunity for improving the efficiency, flexibility, and resilience of machine learning models in numerous contexts and situations is by the incorporation of Fuzzy Logic-Based Tuning into these models. FLBT uses fuzzy logic concepts for systematic and flexible optimization of the parameters and structures of a model. In effect, it decongests the difficulties relating to uncertainty, imprecision, and complexity that are typically very common with most real-world datasets. FLBT will combine the information of fuzzy sets, linguistic variables, and fuzzy rules within conventional machine learning approaches to represent information that is vague or blurry. The parameters in FLBT are adjusted qualitatively and quantitatively with input, making the models more interpretable and generalizable. Therefore, it gives way to more dependable results of applicability. It extends the traditional supervised learning environment to unsupervised learning, reinforcement learning, and ensemble approaches, helping to evolve the domains of deep learning, clustering, and ensemble modeling. In reality, complexity, scalability, and dimensionality are issues with computation; it still progresses machine learning and AI with continued innovation and research in FLBT. In fact, there is a tendency for machine learning models to use fuzzy logic-based tuning strategies as this will help them better cope with uncertainties while they may adapt to dynamic settings or yield more substantial responses on intricate problems.

References

1. Gupta, S., Leszkiewicz, A., Kumar, V., Bijmolt, T., Potapov, D., Digital analytics: Modeling for insights and new methods. *J. Interact. Marketing, 51*, 1, 26–43, 2020.
2. Yu, T. and Zhu, H., Hyper-parameter optimization: A review of algorithms and applications, 2020. arXiv preprint arXiv:2003.05689.
3. Bělohlávek, R., Dauben, J.W., Klir, G.J., *Fuzzy logic and mathematics: A historical perspective*, Oxford University Press, Oxford, U.K., 2017.

4. Williams, J.K., Introduction to fuzzy logic, in: *Artificial Intelligence Methods in the Environmental Sciences*, pp. 127–151, Springer Netherlands, Dordrecht, 2009.
5. Andonie, R., Hyperparameter optimization in learning systems. *J. Membr. Comput.*, *1*, 4, 279–291, 2019.
6. Iqbal, S., Qureshi, A.N., Aurangzeb, K., Alhussein, M., Wang, S., Anwar, M.S., Khan, F., Hybrid Parallel Fuzzy CNN Paradigm: Unmasking Intricacies for Accurate Brain MRI Insights. *IEEE Trans. Fuzzy Syst.*, 2024.
7. Gottwald, S., *Fuzzy sets and fuzzy logic: The foundations of application—from a mathematical point of view*, Springer-Verlag, Berlin, Germany, 2013.
8. Zarghami, S.A. and Dumrak, J., Reimaging stakeholder analysis in project management: network theory and fuzzy logic applications. *Eng. Constr. Archit. Manage.*, *28*, 9, 2426–2447, 2021.
9. Kayacan, E., Sarabakha, A., Coupland, S., John, R., Khanesar, M.A., Type-2 fuzzy elliptic membership functions for modeling uncertainty. *Eng. Appl. Artif. Intell.*, *70*, 170–183, 2018.
10. Mohd Adnan, M.R.H., Sarkheyli, A., Mohd Zain, A., Haron, H., Fuzzy logic for modeling machining process: a review. *Artif. Intell. Rev.*, *43*, 345–379, 2015.
11. Karthiga, R., Saravanan, V., Kumar, S., Rajakumar, S., Fuzzy Logic-Based Monitoring of Earth Observations, in: *Novel AI Applications for Advancing Earth Sciences*, pp. 151–164, IGI Global, PA, USA, 2024.
12. Pokorádi, L., Koçak, S., Tóth-Laufer, E., Fuzzy failure modes and effects analysis using summative defuzzification methods. *Acta Polytech. Hung.*, *18*, 9, 111–126, 2021.
13. Zadeh, L.A., Fuzzy logic—a personal perspective. *Fuzzy Sets Syst.*, *281*, 4–20, 2015.
14. Sugisaki, K. and Bleiker, A., Usability guidelines and evaluation criteria for conversational user interfaces: A heuristic and linguistic approach. In. *Proc. Mensch und Comput.*, *2020*, 309–319, 2020.
15. Ikotun, A.M., Ezugwu, A.E., Abualigah, L., Abuhaija, B., Heming, J., K-means clustering algorithms: A comprehensive review, variants analysis, and advances in the era of big data. *Inf. Sci.*, *622*, 178–210, 2023.
16. Jia, Y. and Wang, Z., Application of artificial intelligence based on the fuzzy control algorithm in enterprise innovation. *Heliyon*, *10*, 6, 2024.
17. Helmy, T., Rasheed, Z., Al-Mulhem, M., Adaptive fuzzy logic-based framework for handling imprecision and uncertainty in classification of bioinformatics datasets. *Int. J. Comput. Methods*, *8*, 03, 513–534, 2011.
18. Kashan, A.H., Rezaee, B., Karimiyan, S., An efficient approach for unsupervised fuzzy clustering based on grouping evolution strategies. *Pattern Recognit.*, *46*, 5, 1240–1254, 2013.
19. Padrón-Tristán, J.F., Cruz-Reyes, L., Espín-Andrade, R.A., Llorente-Peralta, C.E., A brief review of performance and interpretability in fuzzy inference systems. *New Perspect. Enterp. Decision-Making Applying Artif. Intell. Tech.*, 237–266, 2021.

20. Ravi, C. and Khare, N., Review of fuzzy rule based classification systems. *Res. J. Pharm. Technol.*, *9*, 8, 1299–1302, 2016.
21. Pezeshki, Z. and Mazinani, S.M., Comparison of artificial neural networks, fuzzy logic and neuro fuzzy for predicting optimization of building thermal consumption: a survey. *Artif. Intell. Rev.*, *52*, 1, 495–525, 2019.
22. Al Kailani, H., Sweis, G.J., Sammour, F., Maaitah, W.O., Sweis, R.J., Alkailani, M., Predicting construction cost index using fuzzy logic and machine learning in Jordan. *Constr. Innovation.*, 2024.
23. Alfaverh, F., Denai, M., Sun, Y., Demand response strategy based on reinforcement learning and fuzzy reasoning for home energy management. *IEEE Access*, *8*, 39310–39321, 2020.
24. Santiago, A., Dorronsoro, B., Nebro, A.J., Durillo, J.J., Castillo, O., Fraire, H.J., A novel multi-objective evolutionary algorithm with fuzzy logic based adaptive selection of operators: FAME. *Inf. Sci.*, *471*, 233–251, 2019.
25. Dumitrescu, C., Ciotirnae, P., Vizitiu, C., Fuzzy logic for intelligent control system using soft computing applications. *Sensors*, *21*, 8, 2617, 2021.
26. Joseph, S.B., Dada, E.G., Abidemi, A., Oyewola, D.O., Khammas, B.M., Metaheuristic algorithms for PID controller parameters tuning: Review, approaches and open problems. *Heliyon*, *8*, 5, 2022.
27. Kelly, D. and Smith, C., *Bayesian inference for probabilistic risk assessment: A practitioner's guidebook*, Springer Science & Business Media, Berlin, Germany, 2011.
28. Khaleghi, B., Khamis, A., Karray, F.O., Razavi, S.N., Multisensor data fusion: A review of the state-of-the-art. *Inf. Fusion*, *14*, 1, 28–44, 2013.
29. Nayyar, A., Garg, S., Gupta, D., Khanna, A., Evolutionary computation: theory and algorithms, in: *Advances in swarm intelligence for optimizing problems in computer science*, pp. 1–26, Chapman and Hall/CRC, Boca Raton, FL, USA, 2018.
30. Jahandideh-Tehrani, M., Bozorg-Haddad, O., Loáiciga, H.A., Application of particle swarm optimization to water management: an introduction and overview. *Environ. Monit. Assess.*, *192*, 5, 281, 2020.
31. Madoumier, M., Trystram, G., Sébastian, P., Collignan, A., Towards a holistic approach for multi-objective optimization of food processes: A critical review. *Trends Food Sci. Technol.*, *86*, 1–15, 2019.
32. Frazier, P., II, Bayesian optimization, in: *Recent advances in optimization and modeling of contemporary problems*, pp. 255–278, Informs, Catonsville, MD, USA, 2018.
33. Wang, Y., Kung, L., Byrd, T.A., Big data analytics: Understanding its capabilities and potential benefits for healthcare organizations. *Technol. Forecasting Social Change*, *126*, 3–13, 2018.
34. Ali, S., Abuhmed, T., El-Sappagh, S., Muhammad, K., Alonso-Moral, J.M., Confalonieri, R., Herrera, F., Explainable Artificial Intelligence (XAI): What we know and what is left to attain Trustworthy Artificial Intelligence. *Inf. Fusion*, *99*, 101805, 2023.

35. Muhammad, K., Obaidat, M.S., Hussain, T., Ser, J.D., Kumar, N., Tanveer, M., Doctor, F., Fuzzy logic in surveillance big video data analysis: Comprehensive review, challenges, and research directions. *ACM Computing Surveys (CSUR)*, *54*, 3, 1–33, 2021.
36. Leite, D., Costa, P., Gomide, F., Evolving granular neural networks from fuzzy data streams. *Neural Networks*, *38*, 1–16, 2013.
37. Tsiakmaki, M., Kostopoulos, G., Kotsiantis, S., Ragos, O., Fuzzy-based active learning for predicting student academic performance using autoML: A step-wise approach. *J. Comput. Higher Educ.*, *33*, 3, 635–667, 2021.
38. Wang, H., Xu, Z., Pedrycz, W., An overview on the roles of fuzzy set techniques in big data processing: Trends, challenges and opportunities. *Knowledge-Based Syst.*, *118*, 15–30, 2017.
39. Minutolo, A., Esposito, M., De Pietro, G., A fuzzy framework for encoding uncertainty in clinical decision-making. *Knowledge-Based Syst.*, *98*, 95–116, 2016.
40. Fan, Z., Wu, Y., Zhou, C., Zhang, X., Tao, Z., Class-imbalanced voice pathology detection and classification using fuzzy cluster oversampling method. *Appl. Sci.*, *11*, 8, 3450, 2021.
41. Kumar, R., Srivastava, S., Gupta, J.R.P., Mohindru, A., Diagonal recurrent neural network based identification of nonlinear dynamical systems with Lyapunov stability based adaptive learning rates. *Neurocomputing*, *287*, 102–117, 2018.
42. Btoush, E.A.L.M., Zhou, X., Gururajan, R., Chan, K.C., Genrich, R., Sankaran, P., A systematic review of literature on credit card cyber fraud detection using machine and deep learning. *PeerJ Comput. Sci.*, *9*, e1278, 2023.
43. Stoean, C., Zivkovic, M., Bozovic, A., Bacanin, N., Strulak-Wójcikiewicz, R., Antonijevic, M., Stoean, R., Metaheuristic-based hyperparameter tuning for recurrent deep learning: Application to the prediction of solar energy generation. *Axioms*, *12*, 3, 266, 2023.
44. Vahidnia, M.H., Alesheikh, A.A., Alimohammadi, A., Hosseinali, F., A GIS-based neuro-fuzzy procedure for integrating knowledge and data in landslide susceptibility mapping. *Comput. Geosci.*, *36*, 9, 1101–1114, 2010.
45. Burrough, P.A., Natural objects with indeterminate boundaries. *Geogr. Objects Indeterminate Boundaries*, 3–28, 2020.
46. Talaat, F.M. and Gamel, S.A., RL based hyper-parameters optimization algorithm (ROA) for convolutional neural network. *J. Ambient Intell. Hum. Comput.*, *14*, 10, 13349–13359, 2023.
47. Silva, P.C., Lucas, P.D.O., Sadaei, H.J., Guimaraes, F.G., Distributed evolutionary hyperparameter optimization for fuzzy time series. *IEEE Trans. Netw. Serv. Manage.*, *17*, 3, 1309–1321, 2020.
48. Seoni, S., Jahmunah, V., Salvi, M., Barua, P.D., Molinari, F., Acharya, U.R., Application of uncertainty quantification to artificial intelligence in healthcare: A review of last decade (2013–2023). *Comput. Biol. Med.*, 107441, 2023.

49. Vahidnia, M. H., Alesheikh, A. A., Alimohammadi, A., Hosseinali, F. A GIS-based neuro-fuzzy procedure for integrating knowledge and data in landslide susceptibility mapping. *Computers & Geosciences*, *36*, 9, 1101–1114, 2010.
50. Sirmen, R.T. and Üstündağ, B.B., Internal Validity Index for Fuzzy Clustering Based on Relative Uncertainty. *Computers Mater. Continua*, *72*, 2, 2022.
51. Baradaran, A.A. and Navi, K., HQCA-WSN: High-quality clustering algorithm and optimal cluster head selection using fuzzy logic in wireless sensor networks. *Fuzzy Sets Syst.*, *389*, 114–144, 2020.
52. Shao, P., Shi, W., He, P., Hao, M., Zhang, X., Novel approach to unsupervised change detection based on a robust semi-supervised FCM clustering algorithm. *Remote Sens.*, *8*, 3, 264, 2016.
53. Huang, H., Meng, F., Zhou, S., Jiang, F., Manogaran, G., Brain image segmentation based on FCM clustering algorithm and rough set. *IEEE Access*, *7*, 12386–12396, 2019.
54. Abikoye, O.C., Olajide, E.O., Babatunde, A.N., Akintola, A.G., K-means and fuzzy logic-based system for clinical diagnosis (staging) of cervical cancer. *Int. J. Telemed. Clin. Pract.*, *2*, 2, 168–196, 2017.
55. Urbano, E.M., Martinez-Viol, V., Kampouropoulos, K., Romeral, L., Quantitative and qualitative risk-informed energy investment for industrial companies. *Energy Rep.*, *9*, 3290–3304, 2023.
56. Li, Y., Yang, G., He, H., Jiao, L., Shang, R., A study of large-scale data clustering based on fuzzy clustering. *Soft Comput.*, *20*, 3231–3242, 2016.
57. Chauhan, K., Fuzzy Approach for Designing Security Framework. *Artif. Intell. Data Min. Approaches Secur. Frameworks*, 173–195, 2021.
58. Khan, I., Luo, Z., Huang, J.Z., Shahzad, W., Variable weighting in fuzzy k-means clustering to determine the number of clusters. *IEEE Trans. Knowl. Data Eng.*, *32*, 9, 1838–1853, 2019.
59. Li, D., Zhou, S., Pedrycz, W., Accelerated Fuzzy C-Means Clustering Based on New Affinity Filtering and Membership Scaling. *IEEE Trans. Knowl. Data Eng.*, 2023.
60. Lu, J., Yan, Z., Han, J., Zhang, G., Data-driven decision-making (d 3 m): Framework, methodology, and directions. *IEEE Trans. Emerging Top. Comput. Intell.*, *3*, 4, 286–296, 2019.
61. Imani, M. and Montazer, G.A., A survey of emotion recognition methods with emphasis on E-Learning environments. *J. Network Comput. Appl.*, *147*, 102423, 2019.
62. Chen, M., Lam, H.K., Shi, Q., Xiao, B., Reinforcement learning-based control of nonlinear systems using Lyapunov stability concept and fuzzy reward scheme. *IEEE Trans. Circuits Syst. II Express Briefs*, *67*, 10, 2059–2063, 2019.
63. Wazirali, R., Yaghoubi, E., Abujazar, M.S.S., Ahmad, R., Vakili, A.H., State-of-the-art review on energy and load forecasting in microgrids using artificial neural networks, machine learning, and deep learning techniques. *Electr. Power Syst. Res.*, *225*, 109792, 2023.

64. Lai, G., Chang, W.C., Yang, Y., Liu, H., Modeling long-and short-term temporal patterns with deep neural networks, in: *The 41st international ACM SIGIR conference on research & development in information retrieval*, pp. 95–104, 2018, June.
65. Singh, S.K., Abolghasemi, V., Anisi, M.H., Fuzzy logic with deep learning for detection of skin cancer. *Appl. Sci.*, *13*, 15, 8927, 2023.
66. Talpur, N., Abdulkadir, S.J., Alhussian, H., Hasan, M.H., Aziz, N., Bamhdi, A., Deep Neuro-Fuzzy System application trends, challenges, and future perspectives: A systematic survey. *Artif. Intell. Rev.*, *56*, 2, 865–913, 2023.
67. Ogundokun, R.O., Misra, S., Douglas, M., Damaševičius, R., Maskeliūnas, R., Medical internet-of-things based breast cancer diagnosis using hyperparameter-optimized neural networks. *Future Internet*, *14*, 5, 153, 2022.
68. Madhushani, C., Dananjaya, K., Ekanayake, I.U., Meddage, D.P.P., Kantamaneni, K., Rathnayake, U., Modeling streamflow in non-gauged watersheds with sparse data considering physiographic, dynamic climate, and anthropogenic factors using explainable soft computing techniques. *J. Hydrol.*, 130846, 2024.
69. Moustakidis, S. and Karlsson, P., A novel feature extraction methodology using Siamese convolutional neural networks for intrusion detection. *Cybersecurity*, *3*, 1, 16, 2020.
70. Alakhras, M., Oussalah, M., Hussein, M., A survey of fuzzy logic in wireless localization. *EURASIP J. Wireless Commun. Networking*, *2020*, 1–45, 2020.
71. Maraniello, S. and Palacios, R., Parametric reduced-order modeling of the unsteady vortex-lattice method. *AIAA J.*, *58*, 5, 2206–2220, 2020.
72. Beniwal, S.S., Lamo, P., Kaushik, A., Lorenzo-Villegas, D.L., Liu, Y., MohanaSundaram, A., Current Status and Emerging Trends in Colorectal Cancer Screening and Diagnostics. *Biosensors*, *13*, 10, 926, 2023.

9

A Tuning Perspective of Fuzzy Logic Enhanced Machine Learning Models and Its Applications

M. Jayanthi[1]*, S. T. Shenbagavalli[1], M. Sowmiya[2] and P. Kasthuri Rengan[3]

[1]*Department of Computer Science and Engineering, PSNA College of Engineering and Technology, Dindigul, Tamilnadu, India*
[2]*Department of Artificial Intelligence and Data Science, Sri Eshwar College of Engineering, Coimbatore, Tamilnadu, India*
[3]*Department of Computer Science and Engineering, K. Ramakrishnan College of Engineering, Samayapuram, Trichy, Tamilnadu, India*

Abstract

The fuzzy logic, which is capable of dealing with the uncertainty and imprecision, is a desirable approach to enhance different types of machine learning algorithms in different domains of applications. This chapter will seek to offer a detailed discussion on the use of fuzzy logic in machine learning model tuning. This chapter explores different aspects of integrating fuzzy logic and starts with a brief description of fundament principles of fuzzy logic and its applicability to machine learning algorithm. In the following chapters, the author presents a number of fuzzy logic based approaches including fuzzy inference systems, fuzzy clustering, and fuzzy rule based systems and how these can be used in tuning of machine learning models. This chapter devotes a significant amount of effort to providing the tuning strategies and methodologies for the fuzzy logic-integrated machine learning models. This includes optimization methods, parameter adjusting techniques, and integration models that consist of fuzzy logic and other optimization models as well as machine learning algorithms. Also, the chapter deals with issues and concerns arising from the tuning of fuzzy logic enhanced models, providing guidance on how to select appropriate tuning parameters, how to manage the computational intensity, and how to evaluate the performance of the developed models. Financial, health care, and engineering applications with real life problems

**Corresponding author*: jayantheemurugesan@gmail.com

Rahul Kar, Gunjan Mukherjee, Biswadip Basu Mallik and Ashok Kumar Shaw (eds.) Fuzzy Logic in Computational Intelligence: Applications and Case Studies, (157–186) © 2026 Scrivener Publishing LLC

demonstrate the actual implementation of fuzzy logic based tuning strategies and its ability to enhance model performance. This chapter is useful for the researchers, practitioners, and students who want to use the fuzzy logic to enhance the ML models and solve the real-world problems more efficiently.

***Keywords*:** Fuzzy logic, fuzzy inference systems, fuzzy clustering, fuzzy rule-based systems, machine learning models, optimization techniques

9.1 Introduction to Fuzzy Logic Integration in Machine Learning

Machine learning routinely deals with data processing and prediction of results by learning from existing data, it encounters challenges when facing such real-world uncertainties and imprecise data. Decision making that incorporates probabilities involves such uncertainties and fuzzy logic, a mathematical initiative that resolves such quandaries presents significant solutions to these puzzles [1]. This chapter examines the possibility of extending the use of fuzzy logic for reinforcement in the new machine learning and how this reinforcement can be used to improvise the model. This introduction shall explore a common ground to facilitate the knowledge of the interaction between fuzzy logic and machine learning. We start with the motor basics of Fuzzy systems and their operations such as fuzzy sets, fuzzy membership functions and fuzzy inference systems. These elements outlined below serve as a foundation for using fuzzy logic in the process of machine learning.

Fuzzy logic emerged from the hand of LotfiZadeh in the 1960's as an extension of classical Boolean logic which deals with degrees of truth, and not just true or false. Fuzzy sets are different from binary sets in that there are defined levels of membership where the elements can contain certain value between 0 level and 1 level. Fuzzy sets, thus, comprises of elements that may belong to a number of sets to varying extents. Membership Functions are functions that assign the extent of belonging to a fuzzy set of an element within a universal set. Linguistic variables are variables classified by words which are fuzzy in nature (e. g., high, medium low etc.). Fuzzy rule is the relationship between Fuzzy variables and can be defined as IF – THEN rule. The specific techniques that allow the integration of fuzzy logic with machine learning are: 1) Fuzzy Inference Systems (FIS): This method uses fuzzy logic to use the data to logically determine relationship between inputs that are even more fuzzy to arrive at the conclusion. 2) Fuzzy Clustering system: Fuzzy clustering is another type of clustering technique. It allows multiple clusters for a given data point with distinct membership degrees [2].

3) Fuzzy Rule-Based Systems: Fuzzy logic systems employ a collection of fuzzy rules to draw the conclusions, which can be easily supplemented with the expert's knowledge on a certain issue. Advantages of integrating fuzzy logic in machine learning include 1) Improved Interpretability: Fuzzy systems have unambiguous rules as they are explicit in identifying the relevant rules, which can only be considered an advantage when it comes to model interpretability. 2) Enhanced Robustness: Fuzzy logic techniques enables the system to deal with ambiguous, noisy, imprecise and uncertain data.3) Flexibility: The use of Fuzzy systems is still advantageous because may can quantify relationships that are hard to model through conventional means such as statistics [3]. Challenges and Considerations include 1) Computational Complexity: Auditing decisions made by the fuzzy logic systems may be problematic particularly if the system contains a large number of rules and variables 2) Parameter tuning: Selecting the optimal number of membership functions and fuzzy rules can be difficult, and more often than not may need the input of an expert.

Various attempts have also been made in the literature to propose and design the tuning strategies and methodologies specifically for the fuzzy logic incorporated machine learning models. Tuning is important in order to achieve the best results with the help of a model. In the context of adjusting the parameters of a fuzzy system, some more adequate techniques are genetic algorithms or particle swarm optimization, for example. Moreover, there are presented hybridization techniques where fuzzy logic is combined with other optimization and neural networks or other heuristic techniques to produce even better results. As a result, practical questions and difficulties such as tuning parameters' choice, computational burden, and model evaluation are also considered. It is crucial to comprehend these employed tangible aspects in order to effectively deploy fuzzy logic when it comes to applying to machine learning problems [4]. To illustrate this, examples of applications of the combination of fuzzy logic with machine learning in various areas such as finance, healthcare, and engineering is done. These examples show that the use of fuzzy logic will improve the models as well as reduce the margin of error to near zero which provides solid proof that the subject under discussion can be effectively solved.

9.2 Fuzzy Inference Systems: Principles and Applications

Fuzzy Inference Systems (FIS) is a kind of model that employs the fuzzy logics for establishing the relationship between inputs and outputs.

This system is most suitable for dealing with the uncertainties and for approximating complex nonlinear relationships. They take decisions with the help of a number of fuzzy rules incorporating imprecise or vague information. In this section, FIS and its multiple applications will be presented along with its fundamental concepts.

9.2.1 Principles of Fuzzy Inference Systems

A Fuzzy Inference System works on the processes of fuzzy logic that involves the use of fuzzy sets, membership functions and fuzzy rules to handle the input data then produce the output. There are several components of Fuzzy systems, of which Fuzzification is an important one; it is the process of transforming the crisp input data into the fuzzy domains using membership functions. The example of this process is taking a numeric value of 75 degrees Fahrenheit and converting it into the linguistic measures of 'warm' and 'hot'. Second is the Knowledge Base that is broken down into two parts; there is a database containing all the data and a rule base. Database holds information about a set which is fuzzy in nature and with the help of these memberships functions values of a set are defined. Rule Base consists of IF-THEN rules, which could be acquired from specialists or learned from the data. Third component is Inference Engine which is responsible for the usage of fuzzy rules to arrive at the resultant fuzzy outputs from the fuzzy inputs. Some of the techniques that can be used include the Mamdani and Sugeno techniques. Mamdani Method employs operation of min- and max- for rating and summing up the rules. Sugeno Method applies the weighted average in the calculation of output frequently coupled with linear or constant output functions. The Fourth component is defuzzification: It is the converting of fuzzy output into crisp values i.e. non- fuzzy values. Typically, such techniques are referred to as Centroid, Bisector, and Mean of Maximum. Centroid Method determines the final point at which the line going through the 'middle' of the curve of the fuzzy set intersects the curve. Using Bisector Method one gets to identify the vertical line, which has a capacity of partitioning the curvilinear area into two equal regions [5].

9.2.2 Applications of Fuzzy Inference Systems

Fuzzy Inference Systems are used in various fields to address problems involving uncertainty and imprecision. Figure 9.1 shows some key applications.

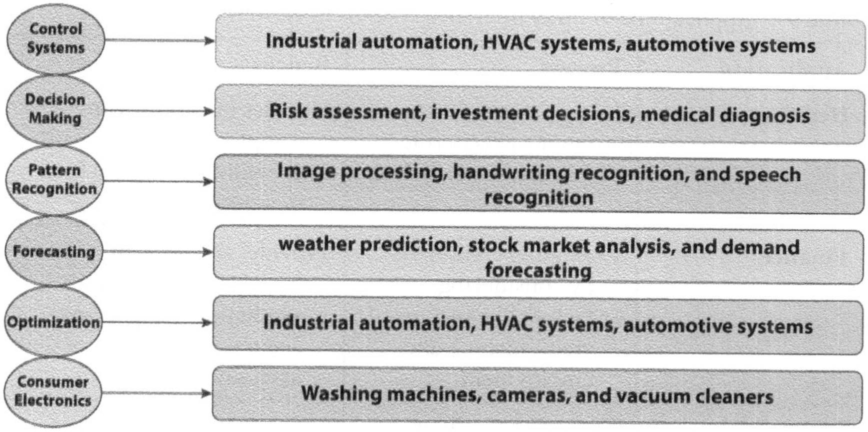

Figure 9.1 Applications of fuzzy inference systems.

9.2.3 Enhancing Machine Learning Models with Fuzzy Inference Systems

The usage of fuzzy inference systems (FIS) integrated with models based on the machine learning listed in Table 9.1 can be an efficient way to increase interpretability, robustness, and predictive accuracy of the models. The fuzzy systems relief theories of human reasoning in the machine learning process and enhance the efficiency of the models when it is faced with the aspect of uncertainties and imprecise information [6].

9.2.4 Case Study: Fuzzy Logic Controller in Washing Machines

Power management in many current washing machines is supported by fuzzy logic controllers to fine-tune washing conditions. It is however important to note that what is shown in Figure 9.2 is only a very simplified diagram that illustrates the basic procedure through which a fuzzy inference system is used. It makes washing effective through using appropriate amounts of water and energy, which also bid automatically to different conditions. Fuzzy controllers employ Fuzzy Inference Systems that allows the modeling and decision-making activities in settings with uncertainties and imprecision. Honey nets can learn expert knowledge through its fuzzy rules and hence they can be used in areas like industrial control to consumer electronics [7, 8].

Table 9.1 Applications of fuzzy inference systems in various domains.

Application	Process	Benefit
Healthcare	Using patient data as input to fuzzy rules for disease prediction.	Handles uncertainty in symptoms and test results, providing more reliable diagnoses.
Finance	Evaluating credit risk by considering factors like income, credit history, and employment.	Provides transparent, rule-based evaluations and predictions, improving accuracy in risk assessment.
Engineering	Controlling industrial processes like temperature and pressure using fuzzy logic.	Manages complex systems with imprecise data, enhancing system stability and performance.
Customer Relationship Management (CRM)	Segmenting customers based on purchasing behavior and predicting future actions.	Improves marketing strategies through better customer understanding, increasing customer satisfaction and retention.
Image processing	Transforming image data into fuzzy sets for better feature extraction.	Highlights important features and reduces noise, improving image analysis and interpretation.
Environmental monitoring	Using sensor data to monitor air quality, weather patterns, etc.	Effectively handles data variability and uncertainty, providing accurate and timely environmental assessments.
Smart Grids	Applying fuzzy logic to control and predict energy demands.	Optimizes energy usage and improves grid reliability, enhancing efficiency and sustainability of energy systems.

1. Fuzzification:
- Inputs: Dirt level, load size, and fabric type.
- Membership Functions: Define fuzzy sets for inputs, e.g., "light," "medium," "heavy" for dirt level.

2. Knowledge Base:
- Rule Base: Contains rules like "IF dirt level is heavy AND load size is large THEN wash time is long AND water level is high."

3. Inference Engine:
- Applies the rules to fuzzified inputs, determining fuzzy outputs for wash time and water level.

4. Defuzzification:
- Converts fuzzy outputs into crisp values to set the actual wash time and water level.

Figure 9.2 Case study: Fuzzy logic controller in washing machines.

As the fuzzy logic advances in to its next generation, there are great potentialities for the improvement of effects of the integration of this form of reasoning into intelligent systems than the way they currently handle the real life scenarios.

9.3 Fuzzy Clustering Techniques for Model Enhancement

Fuzzy clustering is a powerful technique used to partition data into clusters where each data point can belong to multiple clusters with varying degrees of membership. This approach is particularly beneficial for handling overlapping clusters and imprecise data, which are common in real-world scenarios. Fuzzy clustering techniques can significantly enhance machine learning models by providing better data insights, improving feature selection, and enabling more robust model training [9].

9.3.1 Key Fuzzy Clustering Techniques

Several fuzzy clustering methods have been developed, each with its own strengths and applications. Here are some of the most widely used techniques:

9.3.1.1 Fuzzy C-Means (FCM)

The algorithm is an extension of the k-means algorithm where each data point can belong to multiple clusters with a membership degree. Its process, minimizes an objective function that incorporates the membership degrees and distances to cluster centers [2]. The advantage is it handles overlapping clusters well, provides more informative clustering results. Applications are image segmentation, pattern recognition, bioinformatics.

1. Initialize cluster centers and membership matrix randomly.

$$X = x_1, x_2, \ldots, x_n$$

2. Update membership matrix based on the distance of each data point to cluster centers.

$$U_{ij} = \frac{1}{\sum_{k=1}^{c} \frac{|x_i - v_j|}{|x_i - v_k|}^{\frac{2}{m-1}}}$$

   where v_j is the center of cluster j. m is the fuzziness parameter.
3. Update cluster centers based on the weighted average of all data points.

$$v_j = \frac{\sum_{i=1}^{n} u_{ij}^{m} x_i}{\sum_{i=1}^{n} u_{ij}^{m}}$$

4. Iterate until convergence.

9.3.1.2 Gustafson-Kessel (GK) Algorithm

The algorithm is a variant of FCM that adapts the shape of the clusters by using an adaptive distance norm. The process uses covariance matrices of the clusters to update the distance measure dynamically. It can detect clusters with different shapes and orientations [10]. The applications of GK algorithm is medical imaging, market segmentation.

1. Define number of clusters and initialize membership matrix.

$$v_j = \frac{\sum_{i=1}^{n} u_{ij}^{m} x_i}{\sum_{i=1}^{n} u_{ij}^{m}}$$

2. Compute covariance matrices for each cluster.

$$F_j = \frac{\Sigma_{i=1}^{n} u_{ij}^{m} (x_i - v_j)(x_i - v_j)^T}{\Sigma_{i=1}^{n} u_{ij}^{m}}$$

3. Calculate mahalanobis distances using covariance matrices.

$$D_{ij}^2 = (x_i - v_j)^T F_j^{-1} (x_i - v_j)$$

4. Update membership values based on new distances.

$$u_{ij} = \frac{1}{\Sigma_{k=1}^{c} \frac{D_{ij}^{\frac{2}{m-1}}}{D_{ik}}}$$

5. Repeat the above steps until membership values stabilize. Optionally, assign each data point to the cluster with the highest membership.

9.3.1.3 *Fuzzy Subtractive Clustering*

The algorithm is a fast method that estimates the number and initial locations of clusters based on data density. It identifies cluster centers by evaluating the potential of each data point to be a cluster center. It is efficient for large datasets, no need to predefine the number of clusters [11]. Applications of fuzzy subtractive clustering include real-time systems and large-scale data analysis.

1. Calculate potential for each data point based on its density.

$$P_i = \Sigma_{j=1}^{n} \exp(-\alpha |x_i - x_j|^2)$$

2. Select the point with the highest potential P_i as the first cluster center.
3. Reduce the potential of neighboring points.

$$P_j = P_j - P_{ck} \exp(-\beta \left| x_j - c_k \right|^2)$$

4. Repeat until all cluster centers are identified.

9.3.2 Enhancing Machine Learning Models with Fuzzy Clustering

Fuzzy clustering can be integrated into machine learning workflows to enhance model performance and provide deeper insights into the data. Table 9.1 summarizes the integration of fuzzy clustering techniques in various stages of machine learning to enhance model performance and effectiveness [12]. Table 9.2 conveys some ways of how fuzzy clustering can be utilized.

Table 9.2 Applications and benefits of fuzzy clustering.

Application	Process	Benefit
Feature selection and extraction	-Use fuzzy clustering to identify relevant features or to extract new features based on cluster membership.	-Reduces dimensionality, removes redundant features, and improves model interpretability.
Data preprocessing	-Apply fuzzy clustering to preprocess the data, handling noise and identifying outliers.	-Leads to cleaner datasets, which can improve the accuracy of machine learning models.
Improving classification models	-Use cluster memberships as additional features in classification models.	-Provides more context and improves the model's ability to differentiate between classes, especially with overlapping class boundaries.
Model training	-Train models within each fuzzy cluster to handle local variations in the data.	-Enhances model robustness and accuracy by capturing local patterns and relationships.
Hybrid models	-Combine fuzzy clustering with other machine learning techniques (e.g., fuzzy rule-based systems or neural networks).	-Leverages the strengths of different approaches, resulting in more flexible and powerful models.

9.3.3 Case Study: Image Segmentation with Fuzzy C-Means

The objective of image segmentation with fuzzy C-Means is to segment an MRI image into different tissue types (e.g., white matter, gray matter, and cerebrospinal fluid). The outcome is improved segmentation accuracy by effectively handling the overlapping intensity ranges of different tissues [13].

Fuzzy clustering techniques offer a robust approach to handling data with overlapping clusters and imprecise boundaries. By integrating fuzzy clustering into machine learning workflows, practitioners can enhance model performance, improve data preprocessing, and gain deeper insights into the data structure. As the field of machine learning continues to evolve, the combination of fuzzy logic and clustering will likely play an increasingly important role in developing advanced and intelligent systems [14]. Figure 9.3 shows the case study of MRI.

9.4 Parameter Optimization Strategies for Fuzzy Logic Models

Parameter optimization in fuzzy logic models is crucial for enhancing their performance and accuracy. Fuzzy logic systems rely on various parameters, such as membership functions, fuzzy rules, and the inference mechanism. Here are some effective strategies for parameter optimization in fuzzy logic models:

9.4.1 Gradient-Based Methods

Gradient-based methods are optimization techniques that use the gradient (or approximate gradient) of an objective function to find the optimal

1. Data preparation:
- Collect MRI images and preprocess them (e.g., normalization, noise reduction).

2. Fuzzy C-Means Clustering:
- Initialize cluster centers corresponding to different tissue types.
- Apply FCM to assign membership values for each pixel to different clusters

3. Post-Processing:
- Use membership values to assign each pixel to the tissue type with the highest membership.
- Apply morphological operations to refine the segmentation.

4. Evaluation:
- Compare the segmentation results with ground truth using metrics like Dice coefficient and Jaccard index.

Figure 9.3 Case study: fuzzy c-means in MRI.

parameters that minimize or maximize this function. In the context of fuzzy logic models, gradient-based methods can be used to adjust parameters such as membership functions, fuzzy rules, and other related parameters to improve the system's performance [15].

9.4.1.1 *Gradient Descent*

Gradient Descent is the most common gradient-based optimization algorithm. It iteratively adjusts the parameters in the opposite direction of the gradient of the objective function to find the minimum value.

- Initialize Parameters: Start with initial values for the fuzzy logic parameters.
- Calculate the gradient of the objective function with respect to each parameter.
- Adjust the parameters using the formula:

$$\theta_{new} = \theta_{old} - \eta \cdot \nabla J(\theta)$$

where θ represents the parameters, η is the learning rate, and $\nabla J(\theta)$ is the gradient of the objective function J with respect to θ. Iterate the process until convergence, i.e., until the changes in the objective function value are below a predefined threshold [16].

9.4.1.2 *Stochastic Gradient Descent (SGD)*

SGD is a variation of gradient descent that updates the parameters using a randomly selected subset of data points (mini-batch) instead of the entire dataset.

1. Initialize Parameters: $\theta = \theta_{initial}$.
2. Shuffle Data: $(X, y) = shuffle\ (X, y)$
3. Gradient computation: For each training example (x_i, y_i), compute the gradient of the cost $J(\theta)$ with respect to θ for the training example.

$$\nabla_{\theta} J(\theta; x_i, y_i) = \frac{\partial J(\theta; x_i, y_i)}{\partial \theta}$$

4. Update Parameters: $\theta = \theta - \alpha \nabla_{\theta} J\ (\theta; x_i, y_i)$

5. Repeat: Iterate through the mini-batches and epochs until convergence.

9.4.1.3 *Adaptive Gradient Methods*

Adaptive gradient methods, such as AdaGrad, RMSProp, and Adam, adjust the learning rate dynamically based on the historical gradients. These methods improve convergence speed and stability [17].

- AdaGrad: Adjusts the learning rate based on the sum of the squares of past gradients.
- RMSProp: Modifies AdaGrad to perform well in non-convex settings by using a moving average of squared gradients.
- Adam: Combines the advantages of AdaGrad and RMSProp by using both the first and second moments of the gradients.

9.4.1.4 *Application in Fuzzy Logic Models*

To apply gradient-based methods to fuzzy logic models, you need to follow these steps:

1. Define the Objective Function: The objective function $J(\theta)$ should measure the performance of the fuzzy logic model, such as mean squared error for regression tasks or accuracy for classification tasks.
2. Parameterize the Fuzzy System:
   - Membership Functions: Represent them using parameters that can be adjusted, such as the centers and widths of Gaussian functions or the breakpoints of triangular functions.
   - Fuzzy Rules: Represent the rules' weights or confidence levels as parameters.
3. Compute the Gradients:
   - Partial Derivatives: Calculate the partial derivatives of the objective function with respect to each fuzzy parameter.
   - Chain Rule: Use the chain rule to propagate gradients through the fuzzy inference system, which includes fuzzification, rule evaluation, aggregation, and defuzzification steps.
4. Update the Parameters: Adjust the fuzzy parameters using the gradient descent formula or its variants.

5. Iterate and Converge: Continue updating the parameters until the objective function converges to a minimum value.

9.4.1.5 *Example*

Consider a simple fuzzy logic system with Gaussian membership functions. The parameters to optimize might include the mean μ and standard deviation σ of each Gaussian function. The steps would be:

1. Initialize μ and σ.
2. Compute the Error: For a given input-output pair, compute the error of the fuzzy system.
3. Calculate Gradients: Compute $\frac{\partial J}{\partial \mu}$ and $\frac{\partial J}{\partial \sigma}$ for each membership function.
4. Update Parameters: Adjust μ and σ using the gradient descent formulas.
5. Iterate: Repeat for all input-output pairs and iterate until the error is minimized.

By using gradient-based methods, the fuzzy logic model's parameters can be fine-tuned to achieve better performance, adapting the model more closely to the given data.

9.4.2 Evolutionary Algorithms

Evolutionary algorithms, such as Genetic Algorithms (GA), Differential Evolution (DE), and Particle Swarm Optimization (PSO), are popular for optimizing fuzzy logic systems. They do not require gradient information and are suitable for complex, multimodal, and non-differentiable objective functions [18].

9.4.2.1 *Genetic Algorithms*

Genetic Algorithms are the most well-known type of evolutionary algorithm. They use a population of individuals represented by chromosomes, which undergo selection, crossover, and mutation to evolve over generations [19].

1. Initialization: Create an initial population of N individuals.

$$x_i = random\ vector, i = 1.2 \ldots\ldots, N$$

2. Evaluation: Compute the fitness $f(x_i)$ of each individual.

$$f(x_i),\ i = 1, 2, \ldots, N$$

3. Selection: Select individuals based on their fitness (e.g., roulette wheel selection, tournament selection).

$$P(x_i) = \frac{f(x_i)}{\Sigma_{j=1}^{N} f(x_j)}, i = 1,2,\ldots,N$$

4. Crossover: Combine pairs of individuals to produce offspring. C is the crossover point.

$$x_i' = x_i[:c] + x_j[c:],\quad x_j' = x_j[:c] + x_j[c:]$$

5. Mutation: Apply random changes to some individuals with mutation probability p_m.

$$x_i'[k] = x_i'[k] + \delta$$

6. Replacement: Form a new population, often by replacing the least fit individuals with the new offspring.

$$new\ population = select\ best\ individuals\ from\ \{x_i, x_i'\}$$

7. Termination: Repeat steps 2-6 until a termination condition is met (e.g., a set number of generations or a satisfactory fitness level).

9.4.2.2 *Differential Evolution (DE)*

Differential Evolution is a population-based optimization algorithm particularly suited for continuous parameter spaces.

1. Initialization: $x_i = random\ vector,\ i = 1.2\ldots, N$
2. Mutation: For each individual, create a mutant vector by combining three randomly selected individuals x_a, x_b, x_c.

$$v_i = x_a + F.(x_b - x_c)$$

where F is the mutation factor.

3. Crossover: Combine the mutant vector with the current individual to create a trial vector.

$$u_i[j] = \begin{cases} v_i[j], & |if\ r_j \leq C_r \\ x_i[j], & |otherwise \end{cases}$$

4. Selection: Compare the trial vector with the current individual and keep the one with the better fitness.

$$x_i = \begin{cases} u_i, & |if\ f(u_i) \leq f(x_i) \\ x_i, & |otherwise \end{cases}$$

5. Termination: Repeat until convergence or a stopping criterion is met.

9.4.2.3 *Particle Swarm Optimization*

Particle Swarm Optimization is inspired by the social behavior of birds and fish. It uses a population of particles that move through the solution space, influenced by their own best position and the best positions of their neighbors [20].

Steps:

1. Initialization: Initialize particles with random positions and velocities.

$$x_i = random\ vector,\ v_i = random\ vector,\ i = 1,2,\ldots,N$$

2. Evaluation: Evaluate the fitness of each particle.

$$f(x_i), i = 1,2,\ldots,N$$

3. Update Velocities: Adjust each particle's velocity based on its personal best position and the global best position.

$$v_i = wv_i + c_1r_1(p_i - x_i) + c_2r_2(g - x_i)$$

4. Update Positions: Move particles to new positions based on their velocities.

$$x_i = x_i + v_i$$

5. Termination: Repeat until convergence or a stopping criterion is met.

9.4.3 Simulated Annealing

Simulated Annealing (SA) is a probabilistic optimization technique inspired by the annealing process in metallurgy, where materials are heated and then slowly cooled to remove defects and find a low-energy state. In optimization, SA explores the parameter space by accepting both improving and, with a certain probability, deteriorating moves, which helps in escaping local minima and finding a global optimum [21]. Key Concepts of Simulated Annealing are

1. Objective Function: The objective function $f(x)$ is the function to be minimized (or maximized). In the context of fuzzy logic-enhanced machine learning models, this could be an error measure such as mean squared error or a performance metric like accuracy.
2. State: A state x represents a specific set of parameters for the model, such as membership function parameters or fuzzy rules in a fuzzy logic system.
3. Temperature: The temperature T is a control parameter that gradually decreases during the annealing process. It controls the likelihood of accepting worse solutions, with higher temperatures allowing more exploration.
4. Acceptance Probability: The acceptance probability $P(\Delta E,T)$ determines whether a new solution is accepted based on the change in the objective function $\Delta E = f(x_{new}) - f(x_{current})$ and the current temperature T:

$$P(\Delta E, T) = \int_{\frac{exp_{(-\Delta E)}}{T}}^{1} \begin{matrix} if\ \Delta\mathrm{E} < 0 \\ if\ \Delta\mathrm{E} > 0 \end{matrix}$$

This means that if the new solution is better, it is always accepted; if it is worse, it is accepted with a probability that decreases as the temperature decreases.

9.4.4 Neural Network-Based Optimization

Neuro-fuzzy systems combine neural networks with fuzzy logic. The neural network can learn the parameters of the fuzzy system through backpropagation. Adaptive Neuro-Fuzzy Inference Systems (ANFIS) are a common example, where the network adjusts the membership functions and rules. ANFIS is designed to model complex nonlinear functions by combining the strengths of neural networks and fuzzy logic [22]. It consists of five layers:

1. Layer 1 - Fuzzification: The first layer involves making fuzzy decisions and the principal operation of this layer calculates the extent to which a given input value belongs to each of the fuzzy sets using the membership functions.
2. Rule Layer: This layer uses the fuzzy rules which are defined to the fuzzified inputs above. Each node is a rule and uses T-norm operators such as product, or min to fire the strength or weight of the rule.
3. Layer 3 - Normalization: This layer actually serves to scale all the firing strengths of the rules to more reasonable levels. Every node being a part of the network decides how much of the strength of the firing rule versus the sum strength of firing all the rules.
4. Layer 4 - Defuzzification: This layer produces the result of the rule analysis function and provides a possible solution. In this step, each node indicates a fuzzy rule and calculates the weighted consequent part of that rule.
5. Layer 5 - Output: Finally, this layer integrates all the results produced by Layer 4 of the system to generate the last result or the final output of the system.

9.4.5 Gradient-Free Optimization Techniques

There exist parameter tuning methods such as the Nelder-Mead simplex method or random search methods which can enable the best optimization of fuzzy parameters without requiring gradient information [23]. The characteristics of the simplex and the development of the method are as follows. In the Nelder-Mead method, the simplex is gradually refined until the optimal solution is achieved. The key steps in each iteration are:

1. Ordering: Ordering: Given a particular simplex, arrange the vertices in non-decreasing order of their corresponding objective function values. Let $x_1, x_2, \ldots, x_{n+1}$ be the vertices such that $f(x_1) \leq f(x_2) \leq \ldots \leq f(x_{n+1})$.
2. Centroid Calculation: Compute the centroid x¯\bar{x}x¯ of the simplex, excluding the worst point $f(x_{n+1})$:

$$\mathrm{x} = \frac{1}{n}\sum_{i=1}^{n} x_i$$

3. Reflection: Reflect the worst point (x_{n+1}) through the centroid to get a new point x_r $x_r = x + \alpha\,(x - x_{n+1})$ where α is the reflection coefficient (typically $\alpha = 1$).
4. Evaluation and Decision:
   - If $f(x_1) \leq f(x_r) < f(x_n)$, accept x_r and replace x_{n+1} with x_r.
   - If $f(x_r) < f(x_1)$ perform an expansion to get x_e:

$$x_e = x + \ddagger(x_r - \mathrm{x})$$

   where γ is the expansion coefficient (typically γ=2). If $f(x_e) < f(x_r)$, accept x_e; otherwise, accept x_r.
   - If $f(x_r) \geq f(x_n)$ perform a contraction:
     - If $f(x_r) < f(x_{n+1})$, perform an outside contraction to get x_c:

$$x_c = x + \beta\,(x_r - x)$$

   where β is the contraction coefficient (typically β=0.5). If $(x_c) \leq f(x_r)$, accept x_c; otherwise, proceed to shrink the simplex.

- If $f(x_r) \geq f(x_{n+1})$, perform an inside contraction to get x_c:

$$x_c = x + \beta\ (x_{n+1} - x)$$

- If $(x_c) \leq f(x_{n+1})$, accept x_c; otherwise, proceed to shrink the simplex.

- Shrink: If none of the above steps produce a satisfactory point, shrink the simplex towards the best point x_1:

$$x_i = x_1 + \delta(x_i - x_i),\ for\ i = 2, \ldots, n+1$$

where δ is the shrink coefficient (typically $\delta = 0.5$).

- Termination: Repeat the steps until convergence criteria are met, such as a small change in the objective function values or a maximum number of iterations.

9.4.6 Metaheuristic Algorithms

Other complex metaheuristic algorithms like Ant Colony Optimization (ACO), Artificial Bee Colony (ABC), and Firefly Algorithm (FA) can also be done [24]. These methods are based on natural phenomena, and it is desirable for solving global optimization problems.

9.4.6.1 Ant Colony Optimization (ACO)

Ant Colony Optimization (ACO) is an algorithm to find solutions for problems modeled using graphs; it is influenced by ants searching for food. Here are the equational steps involved in the ACO algorithm: Here are the equational steps involved in the ACO algorithm:

- Initialize pheromone levels T_{ij} on all edges (i,j).
- Set parameters α (importance of pheromone), β (importance of heuristic information), and ρ (evaporation rate).

$$p_{ij}^k = \frac{[\tau_{ij}]^\alpha [\eta_{ij}]^\beta}{\Sigma_{l \in allowed}[\tau_{ij}]^\alpha [\eta_{ij}]^\beta}$$

where η_{ij} is the heuristic information.

- After all ants have constructed their solutions, update the pheromone levels:

$$\tau_{ij} = (1-\rho)\tau_{ij} + \sum\nolimits_{k=1}^{m} \Delta\tau_{ij}^{k}$$

$\Delta\tau_{ij}^{k}$ *is the pheromone deposited by ant k on edge (i, j)*

$$\Delta\tau_{ij}^{k} = \frac{Q}{L_k} (\textit{if edge used})$$

where Q is a constant and L_k is the length of the solution constructed by ant k.

9.4.6.2 *Artificial Bee Colony (ABC)*

Artificial Bee Colony (ABC) is one of the recently developed meta heuristic optimization techniques based on honey bees foraging behavior. The algorithm involves three types of bees: newly recruited bees, information pass on bees, and lone bees. Here are the equational steps: Here are the equational steps:

- Initialize the population of solutions x_i and evaluate their fitness $f(x_i)$.
- Set parameters such as $n_{employed}$, $n_{onlooker}$, n_{scout}.
- Employed Bee Phase: $v_i = x_i + \varphi_{ij}(x_i - x_j)$
- Onlooker Bee Phase:

$$x_i = \begin{cases} v_i & \textit{if } f(v_i) > f(x_i) \\ x_i & \textit{if otherwise} \end{cases}$$

- Scout Bee Phase:

$$p_i = \frac{f(x_i)}{\sum_{j=1}^{n_{employed}} f(x_i)}$$

- Repeat the employed bee, onlooker bee, and scout bee phases until convergence criteria are met.

9.4.6.3 *Firefly Algorithm (FA)*

The Firefly Algorithm (FA) is a metaheuristic optimization algorithm based on flashing behavior of fireflies. It was established that less bright a firefly is, the more attracted it will be to a brighter firefly. Here are the equational steps: Here are the equational steps:

- Initialize the population of fireflies x_i and evaluate their fitness $f(x_i)$.
- Set parameters such as the attractiveness β_0, the absorption coefficient γ, and the randomization parameter α.
- Attractiveness: $\beta_{ij} = \beta_0 e^{-\gamma r_{ij}^2}$
- $r_{ij} = |x_i - x_j|$
- Movement: $x_i = x_i + \beta_{ij}(x_j - x_i) + \alpha(rand - 0.5)$
- Emerge with the new positions of the fireflies, and consequently with the new fitness values.
- Perform the attractiveness and movement steps till the convergence meets the predetermined criteria.

These metaheuristic algorithms provide solid strategies for solving miscellaneous, multi-mode and non-linear problems; and therefore optimal for tuning the Fuzzy logic enriched machine learning models.

9.4.7 Hybrid Approaches

Merging optimality factorial algorithms can offer the benefits of each form of optimization. For example, a global search such as the genetic algorithm at the early stages of a search followed by the gradient descentage at later stages may provide better optimization results [25]. In Table 9.3, you can find out the combination of hybrid approach and the advantages it gives.

9.5 Real-World Challenges in Fuzzy Logic Model Tuning

The fine tuning of fuzzy logic for application in real life problems is a difficult and cumbersome endeavor because of factors like: These difficulties stem from the contest of the fuzzy systems and the type of data they take in, and also the computational aspects of the tuning [26]. As indicated in Figure 9.4, some of the key challenges include the following.

Table 9.3 Hybrid approaches and its benefits.

Hybrid approach	Description	Benefits
GA + Gradient Descent	Use a Genetic Algorithm for initial global search, then apply Gradient Descent for fine-tuning.	Combines global search capability of GA with local refinement of Gradient Descent for precise solutions.
PSO + Simulated Annealing	Perform Particle Swarm Optimization to explore the search space, followed by Simulated Annealing.	Balances exploration with probabilistic escape from local minima for improved convergence.
ACO + Nelder-Mead	Use Ant Colony Optimization for initial pathfinding, then apply Nelder-Mead simplex for refinement.	Exploits ACO's ability to find good initial solutions and Nelder-Mead's local optimization efficiency.
DE + ABC	Differential Evolution for diverse solution generation, followed by Artificial Bee Colony.	Enhances population diversity of DE with local search refinement of ABC.
FA + GA	Firefly Algorithm for global exploration, then Genetic Algorithm for genetic diversity.	Utilizes FA's attraction-based exploration and GA's crossover and mutation for robust optimization.
ANFIS + PSO	Adaptive Neuro-Fuzzy Inference System optimized using Particle Swarm Optimization.	Combines learning capability of ANFIS with PSO's global search for optimal fuzzy system parameters.

(Continued)

Table 9.3 Hybrid approaches and its benefits. (*Continued*)

Hybrid approach	Description	Benefits
Simulated Annealing + Gradient Descent	Simulated Annealing for escaping local minima, followed by Gradient Descent.	Utilizes SA's ability to explore diverse solutions and Gradient Descent's precision in fine-tuning.
HS + PSO	Harmony Search for initial solution harmony, followed by Particle Swarm Optimization.	Balances HS's global search with PSO's iterative refinement for enhanced optimization.

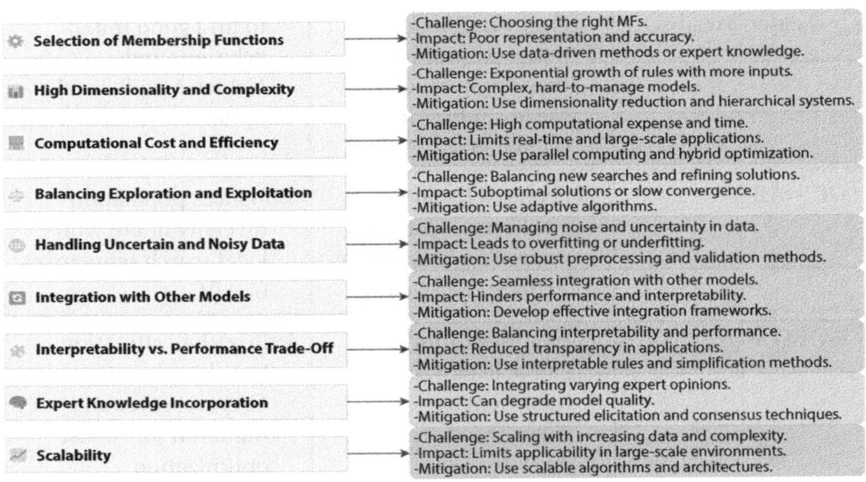

Figure 9.4 Challenges, impact and mitigation in fuzzy logic model tuning.

9.6 Evaluating Fuzzy Logic-Enhanced Models: Metrics and Methods

9.6.1 Evaluation Metrics

Performing the set of experiments and comparing the performance of the fuzzy logic-enhanced models, different accuracy measures and methods are used for the evaluation of the models' precision, stability, and efficacy for managing the fuzzy and uncertain data. Figure 9.5 shows the evaluation metrics of fuzzy logic models.

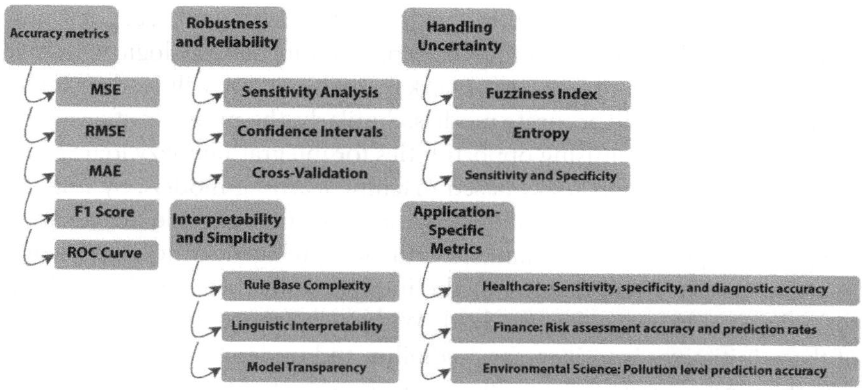

Figure 9.5 Evaluation metrics.

9.6.2 Methods for Evaluation

Figure 9.6 shows the evaluation methods. By combining these metrics and methods, comprehensive evaluation of the performance of fuzzy logic-enhanced models can be done, ensuring they meet the desired standards of accuracy, robustness, and usability in their respective applications.

9.7 Future Directions in Fuzzy Logic Integration with Machine Learning

Some of the possible future development areas in the field of Machine learning with the use of Fuzzy logic are as follows. In one of the directions

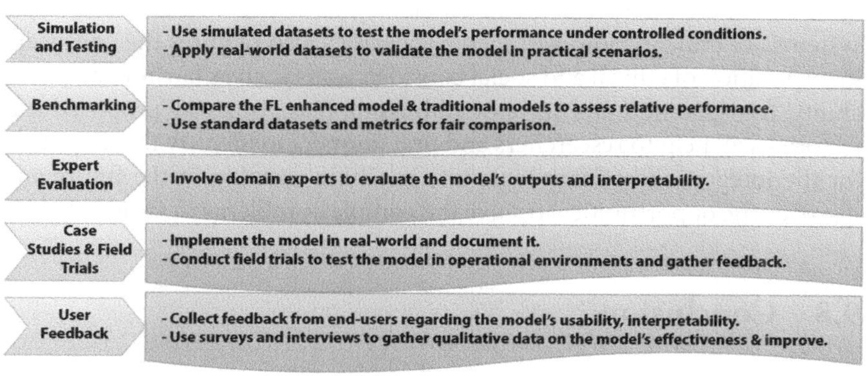

Figure 9.6 Evaluation methods.

of research, it might be useful to integrate fuzzy logic with deep learning which would allow for combining the explainability of fuzzy logic with high learning capabilities of neural networks which in turn will lead to building more efficient and accurate models. Similarly, the progress of ensemble methods provide promising opportunities for integrating fuzzy logic based models with other non-fuzzy based machine learning models, by improving the overall performance of the original algorithms. While the advancement in the pursuit of explainable artificial intelligence increases, works focusing on the strengthening of the interpretability of models involving fuzzy logic enhances takes the lead. With such approaches, the objective of these initiatives is to increase credibility and understanding of how and why the models arrived at specific conclusions by the user, especially across sensitive application areas such as healthcare and finance. However, there is a strong requirement to adapt the approach to look into the numerous challenges within the realm of impreciseness or vagueness present in real-world problems. This means understanding how to expand the approaches in which contextual intelligence and knowledge can be incorporated into the fuzzy inference systems with the aim of supporting more accurate decision making under conditions of uncertainty. Similarly the shift to dynamic and adaptive systems puts emphasis on the fact that one has to equip the fuzzy logic based models the ability to adapt to dynamic environments and dynamic data distribution. Here, future possibilities in the direction of alterations in online learning and incremental updating of fuzzy inference systems look positive in the context of streaming data and continuous learning. Furthermore, the integration of the fuzzy logic and multi-objective optimization perspectives creates the potential to solve problems involving more objectives where they are usually in conflict. This is more so given that it includes, smart city; precision agriculture; healthcare; and many other domains where interpretability, adaptability, and robustness of fuzzy logic systems are critical. However, such a trajectory also requires the consistent incorporation of ethical and social considerations such as fairness, accountability, transparency, and ways of addressing bias. This way proposed trajectories will help to researchers and practitioners to identify the directions for the integration of fuzzy logic into machine learning in the future and discover the opportunities to solve the complex problems in various fields.

9.8 Conclusion

Fuzzy logic combined with machine learning has the potential of solving a number of issues that are faced in the real world in a number of fields.

Fuzzy logic and machine learning are combined in a way that allows researchers to create accurate models that can easily deal with uncertainties as well as other changes in environment. As the future work in the field, it is significant to focus on the construction of the explainable AI solutions which guarantee that the models enhanced by fuzzy logic remain easily understandable by the users. However, more research is required in a coordinated attempt to enhance the rough sets and fuzzy logic procedures applicable to the change in data distribution and decision-making environment. Cohesive collaborations across fields, the integration of ethical perspectives and relevance to the society can ensure that the combination of applying fuzzy logic and machine learning will open the gate to effective and beneficial inventions for the society. Finally, by outlining these pathways and synchronizing the fields of fuzzy logic and machine learning, one can open the door to opportunities and develop new breakthroughs in the powering artificial intelligence technologies.

References

1. Abdulazeez, D.H. and Askar, S.K., A Novel Offloading Mechanism Leveraging Fuzzy Logic and Deep Reinforcement Learning to Improve IoT Application Performance in a Three-Layer Architecture Within the Fog-Cloud Environment. *IEEE Access*, 2024.
2. Singh, S.K., Abolghasemi, V., Anisi, M.H., Fuzzy logic with deep learning for detection of skin cancer. *Appl. Sci.*, 13.15, 8927, 2023.
3. Salimi-Badr, A., Hashemi, M., Saffari, H., A type-2 neuro-fuzzy system with a novel learning method for Parkinson's disease diagnosis. *Appl. Intell.*, 53.12, 15656–15682, 2023.
4. Mekala, S., *et al.*, Machine learning and fuzzy logic based intelligent algorithm for energy efficient routing in wireless sensor networks. *International Conference on Multi-disciplinary Trends in Artificial Intelligence*, Springer Nature Switzerland, Cham, 2023.
5. Yazdinejad, A., *et al.*, An optimized fuzzy deep learning model for data classification based on NSGA-II. *Neurocomputing*, 522, 116–1285, 2023.
6. Bansal, V., *et al.*, Using artificial intelligence to integrate machine learning, fuzzy logic, and the IOT as A cybersecurity system. *2023 3rd International Conference on Advance Computing and Innovative Technologies in Engineering (ICACITE)*, IEEE, 2023.
7. Siva Shankar, S., *et al.*, A novel optimization based deep learning with artificial intelligence approach to detect intrusion attack in network system. *Educ. Inf. Technol.*, 29.4, 3859–3883, 2024.
8. Chen, C., *et al.*, A Fused Deep Fuzzy Neural Network Controller and Its Application to Pneumatic Flexible Joint. *IEEE/ASME Trans. Mechatron.*, 2023.

9. Khan, S., *et al.*, Manufacturing industry based on dynamic soft sensors in integrated with feature representation and classification using fuzzy logic and deep learning architecture. *Int. J. Adv. Manuf. Technol.*, 128.7-8, 2885–2897, 2023.
10. Atacak, I., An ensemble approach based on fuzzy logic using machine learning classifiers for Android malware detection. *Appl. Sci.*, 13.3, 1484, 2023.
11. Khosravi, M.R., *et al.*, Crowd emotion prediction for human-vehicle interaction through modified transfer learning and fuzzy logic ranking. *IEEE Trans. Intell. Transp. Syst.*, 2023.
12. Zhang, M., *et al.*, FAQ: A fuzzy-logic-assisted Q learning model for resource allocation in 6G V2X. *IEEE Internet Things J.*, 2023.
13. Tyagi, L.K. and Kumar, A., A Hybrid Trust Based WSN protocol to Enhance Network Performance using Fuzzy Enabled Machine Learning Technique. *Int. J. Intell. Syst. Appl. Eng.*, 11.9s, 131–144, 2023.
14. Kamthan, S. and Singh, H., Hierarchical fuzzy deep learning system for various classes of images. *Memories - Mater. Devices Circuits Syst.*, 4, 100023, 2023.
15. Anter, A.M. and Abualigah, L., Deep federated machine learning-based optimization methods for liver tumor diagnosis: A review. *Arch. Comput. Methods Eng.*, 30.5, 3359–3378, 2023.
16. Sharma, D.K., *et al.*, Sarcasm detection over social media platforms using hybrid ensemble model with fuzzy logic. *Electronics*, 12.4, 937, 2023.
17. ul Hassan, F., *et al.*, Automated prioritization of construction project requirements using machine learning and fuzzy Failure Mode and Effects Analysis (FMEA). *Autom. Constr.*, 154, 1050135, 2023.
18. Gao, J., *et al.*, A novel machine learning method for multiaxial fatigue life prediction: Improved adaptive neuro-fuzzy inference system. *Int. J. Fatigue*, 178, 1080075, 2024.
19. Anandaraj, M., Ganeshkumar, P., Naganandhini, S., Selvaraj, K., A novel fuzzy programming approach for piece selection problem in P2P content distribution network. *PeerJ Comput. Sci.*, 10:e1645, 2024. https://doi.org/10.7717/peerj-cs.1645.
20. Naganandhini, S. and Shanthi, D., Optimizing Replication of Data for Distributed Cloud Computing Environments: Techniques, Challenges, and Research Gap. *2023 2nd International Conference on Edge Computing and Applications (ICECAA)*, pp. 35–41, 2023, doi: 10.1109/ICECAA58104.2023.10212287.
21. Kizito, A.E., Emmanuel, O., Okpor, M.D., A Fuzzy Logic-Based Automobile Fault Detection System Using Mamdani Algorithm. *Valley Int. J. Digital Lib.*, 1081–1093, 2024.
22. Memarian, S., *et al.*, TSFIS-GWO: Metaheuristic-driven takagi-sugeno fuzzy system for adaptive real-time routing in WBANs. *Appl. Soft Comput.*, 155, 1114275, 2024.

23. Talukdar, S., *et al.*, Coupling geographic information system integrated fuzzy logic-analytical hierarchy process with global and machine learning based sensitivity analysis for agricultural suitability mapping. *Agric. Syst.*, 196, 1033435, 2022.
24. Zheng, Y., Xu, Z., Wang, X., The fusion of deep learning and fuzzy systems: A state-of-the-art survey. *IEEE Trans. Fuzzy Syst.*, 30.8, 2783–2799, 2021.
25. Hamdia, K.M., Zhuang, X., Rabczuk, T., An efficient optimization approach for designing machine learning models based on genetic algorithm. *Neural Comput. Appl.*, 33.6, 1923–1933, 2021.
26. Noureen, T., *et al.*, A comprehensive review of deep neuro-fuzzy system architectures and their optimization methods. *Neural Comput. Appl.*, 1–39, 2022.

Part 3

SMART FUZZY APPLICATIONS

10

Smart Choices: Revolutionizing Menstrual Health Management Through Machine Learning

Shiny Irene D.[1]* and Indra Priyadharshini S.[2]

[1]*Department of Computing Technologies, School of Computing, SRM Institute of Science and Technology, Kattankulathur, Chennai, Tamil Nadu, India*
[2]*School of Computer Science and Engineering, Vellore Institute of Technology, Chennai, Tamil Nadu, India*

Abstract

Menstrual health plays a crucial role in the overall well-being of individuals and leveraging machine learning techniques offers innovative solutions for prediction and management. This work explores the application of ML algorithms in addressing menstrual health-related challenges. Two primary techniques, the K-Nearest Neighbor algorithm and Decision tree are employed to analyze real-time data containing information on menstrual cycles, symptoms, and lifestyle factors. The KNN algorithm is used to predict menstrual irregularities and health issues based on historical data. Additionally, the decision Tree approach is employed to identify key features influencing the menstrual cycle. The generated decisions provide insights into the complex relationship between various factors and menstrual outcomes. This work encompasses the development of an integrated system that combines the benefits of both techniques. This system aims to offer personal recommendations for menstrual health management. Data security is emphasized throughout the development process to ensure a user-friendly approach. These findings underscore the potential of a machine-learning approach to menstrual health management thereby empowering individuals to make informed decisions about their well-being.

***Keywords*:** Menstrual health management, data security, m-health, machine learning, decision tree, k-nearest neighbor algorithm

**Corresponding author*: dshinyirene@gmail.com

Rahul Kar, Gunjan Mukherjee, Biswadip Basu Mallik and Ashok Kumar Shaw (eds.) Fuzzy Logic in Computational Intelligence: Applications and Case Studies, (189–196) © 2026 Scrivener Publishing LLC

10.1 Introduction

In recent, the healthcare industry is advanced with the integration of medical robotics and AI-assisted diagnostics. Wide possibilities for innovation in the knowledge-intensive health industry were provided by AI-based technologies [1]. Using an AI-based healthcare system can be beneficial for both healthcare providers and patients, and improves the accuracy of diagnosis, therapies, and disease prediction. It assists in successful treatment by evaluating and analyzing the disease onset before treatment.

It can also help prevent complications during treatment or diagnosis, ensuring that patients receive the best possible care [2]. The application of AI in the health care system will be well recognized in upcoming years without a doubt because it diagnoses various diseases quickly and provides treatment faster and cheaper also it helps the physician to get the latest medical information from journals, textbooks, etc. [3].

Medical robotics is also utilized in the healthcare system and its performance based on medical devices serves as surgery robotic devices, diagnosis, and drug delivery. In comparison with manual machines, medical robots have a wide range of pros in the health care system.

One of the main pros is flexibility, which can perform several tasks by programming it, and is cost-effective also it avoids human fatigue leading to high precision [4]. In 1980 robots landed their first attempt in the medical field, In several areas of the medical field robots have been widely used (i.e. in orthopedic surgery, laparoscopy, etc...) [5].

In addition, AI and machine robots assist in menstrual management in the health care system which includes hygiene poverty, resulting in a wealth of human health conditions [6]. Furthermore, AI includes machine learning to assist in addressing the issues and also improve clinical outcomes.

10.2 M-Health

Key Technologies in M-Health

The m-Health technologies were utilized to facilitate their management or other healthcare services [7]. These offer to collect data in the real world *via* wearable sensors. In addition, mobile telemedicine/telecare devices SMS messaging, patient monitoring devices, PDAs and smartphones, MP3 players, and mobile computing are features associated with m-health technologies.

M-Health Applications

The various applications in mobile health include such as communication between doctor and patient, service delivery, real-time monitoring, and also the medical data collection process is improved by the usage of mobile devices [8].

Data Privacy in M-Health

In m-health, the privacy of data contained at service providers is protected using encryption and stenography, and also the data privacy within service providers and clients is handled by establishing a third-party service [9].

Wearable Devices

Wearable devices such as smart watches, registered gloves, earphones, insulin pumps, etc. integrated with each activity of the everyday life of people. In addition, it can collect different types of psychological data and it is also applicable in the healthcare system. The advantages include the usage of wearable devices such as reduced cost of care.

Challenges

Various challenges of mobile health include infrastructural constraints such as difficulty getting phone signals and internet, phone not working, etc. also associated with financial costs such as buying costs, and threats to personal wellbeing [10].

Future Trends

The frugal m-health system is utilized as the future trend in m-health [11]. The mobile health app integrated with deep learning and machine learning, with cognitive computing [12], plays a crucial role in future healthcare applications.

10.3 Practical Applications

To address the menstrual requirements of women and girls Menstrual Hygiene management is implemented. This includes acquiring sanitary materials like pads, tampons, menstrual cups, and other appropriate products, education on menstrual hygiene, and suitable sanitary provisions [13]. The importance of encouraging menstrual health is Proper hygiene, awareness, and disposal techniques. Unavailability of sanitary items can lead to unsanitary practices and health problems also providing adequate facilities such as clean and private toilets to support menstrual hygiene.

Enhancing health management is a worldwide attempt involving governments, NGOs, healthcare providers, and communities to ensure the well-being of menstruating persons. Health education, detection, and treating menstrual disorders can help women and girls handle their menstrual health securely and properly. In several ways, individuals can record their menstrual cycle-related data by applying measurable symptoms of fertility. Smartphone apps, temperature monitoring devices, and home urine hormone tests are the primary classes of menstrual tracing methodologies. These monitoring techniques are offered for numerous intentions particularly to help women identify their fertile window to attain or prevent from pregnancy. Polycystic ovary syndrome, endometriosis, and infertility are certain reproductive disorders that affect reproductive-aged women and are distinguished by irregular menses cycles and unusual hormonal patterns.

Data Collection

Data collection is the process of gathering information that influences the effectiveness of healthcare interventions. M-health allows the real-time monitoring of health data, where apps and devices can collect information. Users can contribute valuable data through m-health apps such as symptoms, lifestyle information, and more. This data was useful for further personalized care and treatments. Therefore this work comprises two preprocessing steps, which generate the more efficient data.

- *Data Transformation*: It involves the conversion of raw data into an alternative format or structure, aiming to enhance its suitability for analysis.
- *Handling Outliers:* The presence of outliers carries the potential to impact the accuracy and efficiency of statistical models significantly.

Algorithm Selection and Model Assessment

The selection of Machine learning techniques is evaluative for accurate prognosis and enhances the consequences for patients. Several algorithms together with K-Nearest Neighbor and decision trees were evaluated to be more useful for forecasting patient consequences and providing personal observation [14]. A widespread intention technique of artificial intelligence is Machine learning methods that acquire knowledge of the correlation of data without any requirements to determine prioritization. We converse about modern and upcoming implementations of ML in medicine and focus on the major features that notably affect the healthcare sector.

There are several ML approaches applied to accurately predict the menstrual cycle and the ML approaches are described as follows.

- Decision Tree
  The DT approach [15] solves the issue of classification and regression by effectively predicting the target variable value. It works on both continuous and categorical variables of input and output. The complexity of this technique lies in deciding from which variable to implement the tree segmentation, for which the data must have a class. The DT approach can able to analyze the real-time data of body temperature, blood levels, and PH values for accurate prediction of menstrual cycles. DT is able to handle categorical and numerical data and resolves multi-output problems.
- K-Nearest Neighbor Algorithm (K-NN)
  The KNN approach [16] is a supervised approach because it takes an input as labeled data and finds the closest distance of each unlabeled data sample to the input data and assigns a class of nearest neighbors to the unlabeled samples. The distance between the input point and the observations determines the neighborhood that is utilized to appropriate outcomes. It efficiently minimizes the influence of high-variance data and enhances trends in compact data produced. This model exactly forecasts the general class while it chooses the large amount of data else it generates noise outcomes. Also, their benefits are, that it is able to capture non-linear and complex patterns in the data.

Security and Privacy
Protecting the confidential information of patients and sensitive health data was the highest priority in the security domain [17]. The purpose of data confidentiality is to make certain that data is present only to those who authorized and access it. Furthermore, it is a crucial part of m-health to the confidence between patients and clinicians. Also, the data integrity ensures that the information is stored and further body temperature tracking, period tracking, and more. The objective of data availability is that availability and readily accessed. Medical centers can use ML techniques in M-health to predict menstrual cycles based on the gathered menstrual-related data such as body temperature, pH levels, variations in cycle length, heart rate, and more. Certain real-world applications of menstruation health management based on ML approaches.

Discover Menstrual Issues
The major application of Machine learning in healthcare is that healthcare professionals can identify menstrual-related issues prior they become affected by analyzing numerous information of patients [18]. Clinicians and medical practitioners can predict irregular menstruation earlier because ML approaches like DT and KNN allow doctors to provide better care for every individual.

Early-Stage Medication
By providing other treatment pathways for difficult disorders, accurate therapeutics well-being from ML approaches. These approaches help medicinal organizations to integrate drug formulations and determine the worst one. ML techniques are effective for locating innovative medical treatments and tailoring combinations of drugs to individuals because they are based on unsupervised learning.

10.4 Conclusion

In conclusion, the application of machine learning techniques, especially KNN, and DT in the realm of menstrual health prediction and health management holds significant premises. In this study m-health-related menstrual health management takes a real-world application. The KNN approach provides valuable outcomes of menstrual health from the gathered data. Future endeavors may delve deeper into refining sources and exploring the integration of predictive models into practical tools for individuals, health professionals, and healthcare providers.

References

1. Jimma, B.L., Artificial intelligence in healthcare: A bibliometric analysis. *Telematics Inf. Rep.*, 100041, 2023.
2. Srivastava, S., Pant, M., Agarwal, R., Role of AI techniques and deep learning in analyzing critical health conditions. *Int. J. Syst. Assur. Eng. Manage.*, *11*, 350–365, 2020.
3. Boubaker, O., Medical robotics. *Control Theory Biomed. Eng.*, 153–204, 2020.
4. Kolpashchikov, D., Gerget, O., Meshcheryakov, R., Robotics in healthcare, in: *Handbook of Artificial Intelligence in Healthcare: Vol 2: Practicalities and Prospects*, pp. 281–306, 2022.

5. Alexander, A., Jiang, A., Ferreira, C., Zurkiya, D., An intelligent future for medical imaging: a market outlook on artificial intelligence for medical imaging. *J. Am. Coll. Radiol.*, *17*, 1, 165–170, 2020.
6. Rheinländer, T., Gyapong, M., Akpakli, D.E., Konradsen, F., Secrets, shame, and discipline: School girls' experiences of sanitation and menstrual hygiene management in a peri-urban community in Ghana. *Health Care Women Int.*, *40*, 1, 13–32, 2019.
7. Alsswey, A., Al-Samarraie, H., Bervell, B., mHealth technology utilization in the Arab world: A systematic review of systems, usage, and challenges. *Health Technol.*, *11*, 4, 895–907, 2021.
8. Islam, M.N., Karim, M.M., Inan, T.T., Islam, A.N., Investigating usability of mobile health applications in Bangladesh. *BMC Med. Inf. Decis. Making*, *20*, 1–13, 2020.
9. Lin, W., Xu, M., He, J., Zhang, W., Privacy, security, and resilience in mobile healthcare applications. *Enterp. Inf. Syst.*, *17*, 3, 1939896, 2023.
10. Muzny, M., Henriksen, A., Giordanengo, A., Muzik, J., Grøttland, A., Blixgård, H., Hartvigsen, G., Årsand, E., Wearable sensors with possibilities for data exchange: Analyzing status and needs of different actors in mobile health monitoring systems. *Int. J. Med. Inf.*, *133*, 104017, 2020.
11. Hampshire, K., Mwase-Vuma, T., Alemu, K., Abane, A., Munthali, A., Awoke, T., Mariwah, S., Chamdimba, E., Owusu, S.A., Robson, E., Castelli, M., Informal mhealth at scale in Africa: Opportunities and challenges. *World Dev.*, *140*, 105257, 2021.
12. Luo, Y., Wang, G., Li, Y., Ye, Q., Examining protection motivation and network externality perspective regarding the continued intention to use m-health apps. *Int. J. Environ. Res. Public Health*, *18*, 11, 5684, 2021.
13. Howe, D., Duffy, S., O'Shea, M., Hawkey, A., Wardle, J., Gerontakos, S., Steele, L., Gilbert, E., Owen, L., Ciccia, D., Cox, E., Policies, Guidelines, and Practices Supporting Women's Menstruation, Menstrual Disorders and Menopause at Work: A Critical Global Scoping Review, in: *Healthcare*, vol. 11, p. 2945, MDPI, 2023, November.
14. Miotto, R., Wang, F., Wang, S., Jiang, X., Dudley, J.T., Deep learning for healthcare: review, opportunities and challenges. *Briefings Bioinf.*, *19*, 6, 1236–1246, 2018.
15. Belmahdi, F., Lazri, M., Ouallouche, F., Labadi, K., Absi, R., Ameur, S., Application of Dempster-Shafer theory for optimization of precipitation classification and estimation results from remote sensing data using machine learning. *Remote Sens. Appl.: Soc. Environ.*, *29*, 100906, 2023.
16. Hayder, I.M., Al-Amiedy, T.A., Ghaban, W., Saeed, F., Nasser, M., Al-Ali, G.A., Younis, H.A., An Intelligent Early Flood Forecasting and Prediction Leveraging Machine and Deep Learning Algorithms with Advanced Alert System. *Processes*, *11*, 2, 481, 2023.

17. Klonoff, D.C., Cybersecurity for connected diabetes devices. *J. Diabetes Sci. Technol.*, 9, 5, 1143–1147, 2015.
18. Javaid, M., Haleem, A., Singh, R.P., Suman, R., Rab, S., Significance of machine learning in healthcare: Features, pillars and applications. *Int. J. Intell. Networks*, 3, 58–73, 2022.

11

Industrial IoT Control Systems Using Fuzzy Logic: Research Trends and Challenges

Sunita Sunil Shinde[1]*, K.M. Baalamurugan[2], Vinay Kumar Nassa[3], S. Devikala[4], Prerana Nilesh Khairnar[5] and Joshuva Arockia Dhanraj[6]

[1]*Electrical Engineering, Nanasaheb Mahadik College of Engineering and Technology, Peth, Sangli, Maharashtra, India*
[2]*School of Computer Science and Engineering, Galgotias University, Uttar Pradesh, India*
[3]*Department of Information Communication, Technology (ICT), Tecnia Institute of Advanced Studies (Delhi), Affiliated with Guru Gobind Singh Indraprastha University, Delhi, India*
[4]*Department of EEE, Mohamed Sathak A J College of Engineering, Chennai, India*
[5]*Electronics and Computer Engineering, Sir Visveshvaraya Institute of Technology, Chincholi Nashik, Maharashtra, India*
[6]*Department of Computer Science and Engineering (AI&ML), School of Engineering, Dayananda Sagar University, Devarakaggalahalli, Harohalli, Kanakapura Road, Ramanagara District, Bengaluru, Karnataka, India*

Abstract

The rapidly developing field of control systems for the Industrial Internet of Things (IIoT), with a particular emphasis on the functioning of fuzzy logic. The purpose of this work is to investigate the current developments and problems in the application of fuzzy logic to improve the efficiency and rigidity of control systems in artificial environments. It does this by conducting an exhaustive assessment of recent research and case studies, which outlines the benefits and drawbacks of fuzzy logic in terms of optimizing control systems for the Internet of Things domain. As an additional point of interest, the abstract draws attention

**Corresponding author*: shindesunita120@gmail.com
Vinay Kumar Nassa: ORCID: https://orcid.org/0000-0002-9606-7570
Joshuva Arockia Dhanraj: ORCID: https://orcid.org/0000-0001-5048-7775

Rahul Kar, Gunjan Mukherjee, Biswadip Basu Mallik and Ashok Kumar Shaw (eds.) Fuzzy Logic in Computational Intelligence: Applications and Case Studies, (197–212) © 2026 Scrivener Publishing LLC

to the emerging investigation directions and unresolved difficulties that will influence the future of this field. This work contributes to the continuing conversation about the use of fuzzy logic for advanced control results in artificial Internet of Things environments by synthesizing existing knowledge and identifying gaps in understanding.

Keywords: Industrial IoT, control systems, fuzzy logic, research trends, challenges

11.1 Introduction

A force that is pushing disruption in the field of diligence is the Industrial Internet of Things (IIoT), which has emerged as a force over the course of the previous several years. The adoption of prophetic conservation measures, the enhancement of functional performance, and the modification of standard industrial processes have all been made possible as a result of this. Additionally, it has enhanced the performance of functional aspects [1]. It is the merging of sophisticated control systems with the bias that is implemented by the Internet of Things that is the most essential component of this technological revolution. Since this connection makes it possible for diligence to collect massive quantities of data from connected detectors and selectors, evaluate that data in real time, and generate conclusions based on the information that is gathered, it is conceivable for diligence to maximize both performance and productivity. Among the many control methods that are applied in the operations of the Industrial Internet of Things (IIoT), the capability of the fuzzy sensing control methodology to properly manage uncertainties and squishy data has attracted a large amount of attention [2]. This is because of the approach's ability to effectively manage both of these types of data. This is because the methodology is able to manage squishy data in an effective manner, which contributed to the aforementioned result [38].

The introduction of fuzzy logic in artificial Internet of Things control systems signifies a paradigm shift from traditional techniques that are founded in a crisp logic [3]. This changes the way that control systems are designed. The development of fuzzy sensation is responsible for this shift in interpretation. It is possible for artificial environments that are dynamic and complicated to reap the benefits of fuzzy logic since it brings less rigidity and inflexibility to these environments. The concept of fuzzy logic was developed so that robots might be equipped with the ability to analyze foggy facts and arrive at intelligent conclusions after doing so [4]. The ways by which this was accomplished were the insertion of language components and the mimicking of the logical processes that are carried out by people [5]. Due to the fact that queries were executed against the system, the system's robustness and flexibility were both enhanced as a result of this technique. As a consequence of this, fuzzy logic-based control systems have already established widespread operations throughout a wide range of artificial disciplines [6]. These disciplines include the artificial manufacturing industry, the artificial energy business, the artificial transportation industry, and the artificial healthcare sector [45].

The purpose of this exploration paper is to provide comprehensive research of the exploration trends along with a comprehensive assessment of the exploration trends and challenges associated to the implementation of fuzzy logic in artificial Internet of Things control systems [7]. The target of this exploration paper is to provide a complete assessment of the exploration trends. Within the context of this rapidly developing field, we make an effort to evaluate the current state-of-the-art methodology, innovative approaches, and undetermined concerns by performing a comprehensive analysis of the available literature and carrying out case studies [8]. On top of that, we make an attempt to investigate the unresolved issues that are connected to this particular field. Experimenters, interpreters, and stakeholders who are diligent in their pursuit of the development of fuzzy logic-based control results that are more effective, reliable, and scalable for artificial Internet of Things operations are the target audience for this study [9]. The objective of this study is to guide such individuals. By shedding light on both the potential and the obstacles that are present, we will be able to accomplish this goal.

Following that, the other components of this work are arranged in the manner that is described below: The second portion presents a comprehensive analysis of the fundamental ideas that underpin fuzzy logic. Additionally, this section investigates the various ways in which these ideas could be utilized in the process of developing artificial control systems for the Internet of Things (IoT) [10]. In the third section, a comprehensive study of the available literature on fuzzy logic-based approaches in artificial domains is presented. In this section, the primary focus is on the most significant discoveries that have been made over the course of exploration and technological developments. As well as the hurdles and restrictions that were discovered during the installation of fuzzy logic in artificial Internet of Things ecosystems, this section highlights the implied areas for future research that were also explored.

Additionally, this section discusses the limitations and barriers that were discovered. During the process of putting fuzzy logic into practice, they were discovered. The conclusion brings the study to a close by providing research of the most significant discoveries as well as suggestions for further discussion on this ever-evolving subject matter. The combination of fuzzy logic and the artificial Internet of things has a great deal of potential for bringing about a significant change in the way that ultramodern diligence operates and develops [11]. To summarize, it is highly probable that this promise will be fulfilled in the not-too-distant future. Fuzzy logic-grounded control systems offer organizations the opportunity to attain lower levels of efficacy, trustability, and rigidity in their operations. This is made possible through the utilization of the potential offered by these systems. Since this is the case, they are in a position to gain a competitive advantage in a world that is becoming increasingly data-driven and networked [32]. However, in order to fully realize the transformational potential of this technology in simulated settings, it will be vital to overcome the problems that are already being experienced and evaluate creative findings.

11.2 Related Works

In recent times, there has been a large amount of study and development devoted to the incorporation of fuzzy logic into artificial Internet of Things control systems. This is a reflection of the rising realization of the implicit nature of fuzzy logic to solve the difficulties and misgivings that are essential in artificial environments [12]. The purpose of this part is to present a summary of the existing literature on the operation of fuzzy logic in artificial sectors [34], focusing on the most relevant exploration trends, approaches, and findings.

A. The Manufacturing Sector of the Economy

Control systems that are grounded in a fuzzy logic have been widely adopted in the manufacturing industry to optimize product processes [57], improve product quality, and enhance resource application and economy [42]. Experimenters have investigated procedures that are comparable to fuzzy logic-grounded prophetic conservation, fault discovery, and control of complicated manufacturing systems [13]. As an illustration, research conducted by Zhang *et al.* [11] and Liu *et al.* [12] has shown that fuzzy logic is useful in modeling and managing machining operations, which ultimately results in reductions in both energy usage and product costs.

B. Management of Energy Operations

Fuzzy logic has also found widespread application in energy operation systems, where it enables intelligent decision-making to optimize [41, 58] energy consumption and improve overall effectiveness. This has led to the widespread adoption of fuzzy logic. A significant amount of research in this field has focused on operations that are comparable to smart grid control, the integration of renewable energy, and the operation of energy erecting. As an example, Khan *et al.* [1] and Kim *et al.* [7] have investigated the application of fuzzy sensing for demand-side operation and cargo soothsaying in smart grid environments [1, 7]. Their findings have demonstrated considerable breakthroughs in energy conservation and system stability.

C. Transportation and Logistics

The use of fuzzy logic-based control systems has been implemented in the transportation and logistics industries in order to improve the efficiency of route planning, vehicle scheduling, and company operations. Experimenters have investigated procedures that are comparable to those of intelligent transportation systems, vehicle routing algorithms, and fuzzy logic-grounded business signal control [15]. It has been demonstrated in research conducted by Li *et al.* [3] and Wang *et al.* [6] that fuzzy logic has the potential to improve the efficiency and reliability of logistics operations, which in turn can result in lower transportation costs and increased customer overall satisfaction.

D. Monitoring that Pertains to Healthcare

Additionally, fuzzy logic methods have been utilized in healthcare monitoring systems [49] for the purpose of analyzing patient data [50], diagnosing medical disorders, and providing recommendations for individualized treatment to patients. The research that has been conducted in this field has focused on operations that are comparable to fuzzy logic-based complaint opinion, patient monitoring, and telemedicine [16–19]. An example of this would be the research conducted by Chen *et al.* [4] and Wang *et al.* [9], which revealed the effectiveness of fuzzy logic in predicting and predicting health risks, allowing for early intervention and improved patient issues.

Generally speaking, the literature study sheds light on the various operations that can be performed as well as the increasing significance of fuzzy logic in artificial Internet of Things control systems [20]. Even though numerous research have proved the efficacy of fuzzy logic in tackling a variety of obstacles, such as inquiry, complexity, and real-time decision-making, there are still several investigation gaps and undetermined issues. When it comes to unleashing the full potential of fuzzy logic-grounded control systems in artificial Internet of Things environments [47], addressing these problems will be of absolutely critical importance.

11.3 Research Methodology

The proposed methodology for the exploration paper on "Industrial Internet of Things Control Systems Using Fuzzy Logic Research Trends and Challenges" involves a methodical approach to investigate the current state-of-the-art ways, emerging methodologies, and undetermined issues in the integration of fuzzy logic into artificial Internet of Things control systems [21]. The purpose of this technique is to provide a full understanding of the current trends and difficulties in this dynamic sector. It does so by including both theoretical analysis and practical perceptivity, which is derived from case studies and operations that take place in the actual world as per Figure 11.1.

A. Research of the Recent Literature

Conducting a comprehensive literature study is the first phase in the proposed technique. The purpose of this step is to discover relevant exploratory studies, academic [43] papers, journal papers, conference proceedings, and diligent reports that are associated with the application of fuzzy logic in artificial Internet of Things control systems [22]. A wide variety of artificial intelligence based industries [44], such as manufacturing, energy, transportation, healthcare, and others, will be included in the literature research in order to capture a variety of operations and points of view [23]. The most important databases, such as IEEE Xplore, ScienceDirect, and the ACM Digital Library, will be thoroughly searched with relevant keywords and search strings that

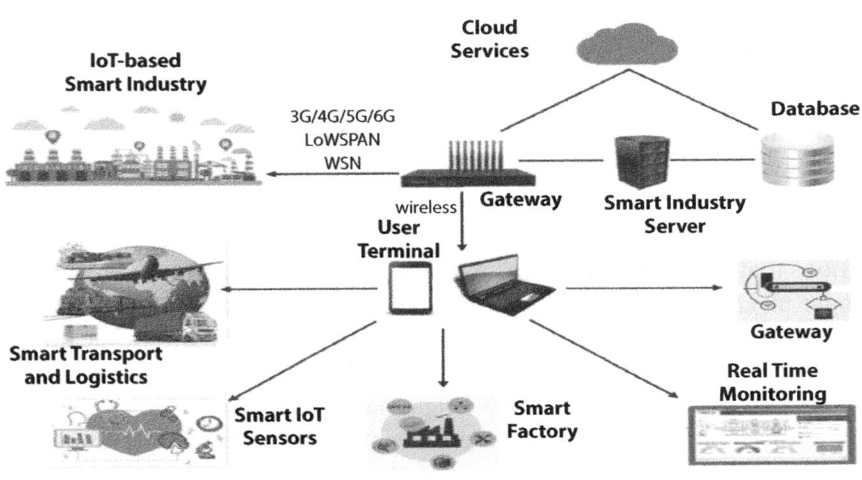

Figure 11.1 The industrial IoT trends show recent applications for industrial IoT.

are associated with fuzzy logic, artificial internet of things [48], control systems, and relevant operation disciplines (Figure 11.2).

B. Examination of the Current Trends in Research
Following the linking of the relevant literature, the subsequent phase entails evaluating the exploratory trends and approaches that are used in the process of incorporating fuzzy logic into artificial Internet of Things control systems. For this analysis, the literature will be evaluated based on a variety of criteria, including performance criteria, fuzzy sensing methods, control strategies, and operation disciplines [24–27]. To uncover shared patterns [33, 53] and emerging techniques, we will be looking at trends that are comparable to the abandonment of fuzzy logic for predictive conservation, defect discovery, optimization [40], and decision-making in artificial systems. In addition, comparative evaluations of various fuzzy logic-based methodologies and the success of these approaches in addressing particular artificial difficulties will be carried out to provide insight into fashionable practices and areas that may be improved.

C. Case Studies and Operations that Take Place in the Real World
The suggested methodology will involve, in addition to theoretical study, the investigation of case studies and operations that take place in the actual world. This will be done to highlight the practical use of fuzzy logic in

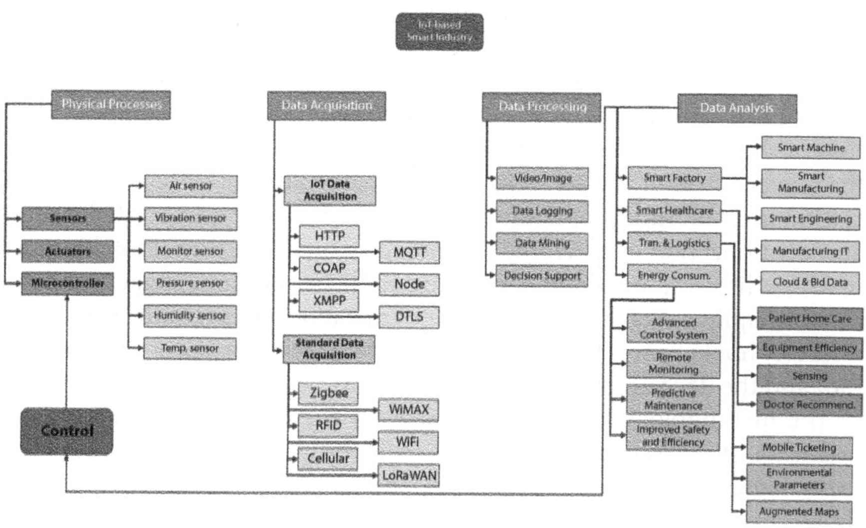

Figure 11.2 Key components of IoT smart industry.

artificial Internet of Things control and management systems. To demonstrate the adaptability and efficiency of fuzzy logic-based approaches in providing solutions to problems that are encountered in the real world, case examples from a variety of artificial industries will be presented [28]. The successful deployments, perpetration tactics, performance evaluation criteria, and assignments learned from the incorporation of fuzzy logic into control systems will be highlighted through the use of these case studies. Interviews with specialists in the field of assiduity and interpreters will be done whenever it is feasible to do so to collect first-hand perceptions and viewpoints on the advantages and disadvantages of utilizing fuzzy logic in artificial Internet of Things operations [51].

D. Identifying Obstacles and Limitations in Their Existence

Establishing a connection between the difficulties, constraints, and unresolved problems that are involved with the incorporation of fuzzy logic into artificial Internet of Things control systems is an essential component of the technique that has been developed. This will require analyzing the existing literature and case studies to identify common barriers and challenges that are experienced in practice [29]. These include issues such as scalability, computational complexity, interpretability, data query, and integration with existing systems. A distribution and anatomization of the related challenges will be carried out to gain an understanding of their underlying reasons and counteraccusations for the unborn exploration and development that are occurring in this field.

The suggested technique will finish with recommendations for further investigation directions and areas of disquisition. These recommendations will be based on the findings from the literature study, analysis of exploration trends, case studies, and identification of problems. The implementation of these recommendations will pave the way for the advancement of the current state of the art in fuzzy logic-based control systems for artificial Internet of Things operations, the resolution of the associated issues, and the utilization of emerging technologies such as artificial intelligence, machine literacy, and edge computing [30]. In addition, suggestions for multidisciplinary collaborations, standardization sweats, and academic-assiduity hookups will be provided to facilitate the exchange of information [36] and the development of new ideas in this rapidly developing subject.

The methodology that was proposed for the exploration article comprises an all-encompassing strategy to investigate the incorporation of fuzzy logic into artificial Internet of Things control systems. A holistic understanding of the exploration trends, challenges, and openings in this dynamic field is the goal of this methodology, which aims to guide unborn exploration and development sweats towards more effective, dependable, and scalable fuzzy logic-grounded control results for artificial Internet of Things operations. This is accomplished by combining theoretical analysis with practical perceptivity from case studies and real-world operations.

11.4 Results and Discussion

Recent breakthroughs in the field of research on industrial Internet of Things (IoT) control systems that make use of fuzzy logic indicate an increased interest in merging fuzzy logic methodologies with Internet of Things technology. These developments have been made possible by the fact that fuzzy logic. Through the use of this connectivity, it is feasible to do monitoring, data analysis, and decision-making in simulated settings throughout the course of real-time. Considering that fuzzy logic is inflexible when it comes to handling uncertainties and imprecisions in Internet of Things data, it is best suited for controlling sophisticated artificial processes. On top of that, the implementation of fuzzy sensing regulators at the edge of the network is picking up speed [35]. Through the usage of edge computing, the processing of detector data in real-time is currently being performed. The execution of this technique results in a reduction in quiescence, an improvement in bandwidth operation, and an increase in scalability.

Another trend that has been seen is the study of fuzzy sensing control systems that are both adaptive and tone-learning [37]. This is a very interesting development. Because these systems can automatically [54] adapt their parameters in response to changes in the environment and real data, they can achieve greater performance and rigidity in simulated dynamic

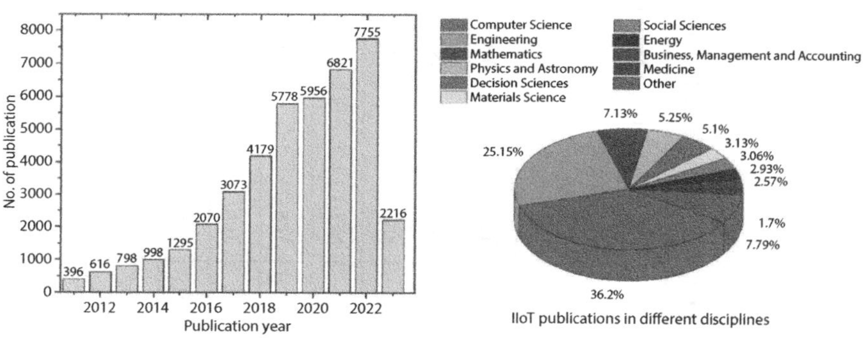

Figure 11.3 The industrial IoT publication trends (a) year-wise and (b) sector-wise.

Table 11.1 Comparative analysis of existing related work.

Ref.	IIoT security	Major attacks	Countermeasures	Blockchain	Software-based IIoT	Fog-based IIoT
[10]	Yes	No	Yes	No	No	No
[11]	Yes	No	Yes	No	No	No
[12]	Yes	Yes	Yes	No	No	No
[13]	No	No	Yes	No	Yes	Yes
[14]	No	No	Yes	No	Yes	Yes
[15]	No	Yes	Yes	No	No	Yes
[16]	Yes	No	No	Yes	No	No
[17]	Yes	No	No	Yes	No	No
Current	Yes	Yes	Yes	Yes	Yes	Yes

environments as shown in Figure 11.3. Furthermore, there is a rising interest in combining fuzzy logic with other approaches to artificial intelligence, such as machine learning [52] and neural networks [31]. This is in addition to the fact that fuzzy logic will be used. When used to the context of artificial Internet of Things activities, this emulsion makes it feasible to build control approaches that are more complicated, discover abnormalities, and preserve prophetic information.

Even though significant advancements have been made, there are still a great deal of challenges that need to be conquered in this area. The Internet of Things (IoT) continues to face challenges in terms of the quality and trustworthiness of the data [55] that it collects due to the presence of distractions, criminal activity, and inconsistencies. Processing in real-time and making judgments in real-time both disguise computational barriers, particularly when it comes to developing intricate fuzzy logic algorithms [56]. Both of these practices are taking place simultaneously. To add insult to injury, predicting the nonlinear dynamics and uncertainties that are essential in artificial processes requires a great deal of spherical moxie and a great deal of sophisticated methodologies. Additionally, it is of the utmost need to guarantee the security [39] and isolation of artificial Internet of Things systems to safeguard them against the potential dangers that could arise from cybersecurity threats [46]. To enhance the development and deployment of artificial Internet of Things control systems that make use of fuzzy logic, it will be essential to solve these challenges while also betting on new trends. This will be done to achieve the goal of improving Internet of Things control systems. Therefore, as a consequence of this, it will be possible to achieve control outcomes that are more efficient, adaptable, and versatile for procedures involving artificial materials in the Table 11.1.

11.5 Conclusion and Future Direction

In conclusion, this exploration paper has provided a comprehensive analysis of the exploration trends and issues related to the incorporation of fuzzy logic into artificial Internet of Things control systems. We have highlighted the versatility and effectiveness of fuzzy logic-grounded approaches in addressing a wide range of artificial challenges by conducting an extensive literature research, conducting an analysis of exploration trends, and conducting an examination of case studies. These approaches span a wide range of artificial challenges, including manufacturing optimization, energy operation, and healthcare monitoring.

Despite the enormous progress that has been made in this area, there are still several obstacles and constraints that need to be addressed. Scalability challenges, computational complexity, data querying, and the requirement for seamless integration with control systems are some of the ones that fall into this category. To address these difficulties, interdisciplinary collaborations, creative approaches, and developments in technology like as artificial intelligence and edge computing will be necessary. With an eye towards the future, the unborn investigation directions in artificial Internet of Things control systems that make use of fuzzy logic have to concentrate on numerous essential areas. Standardization efforts to ensure interoperability and comity, the creation of robust and scalable fuzzy sensing algorithms, integration with emerging technologies such as machine literacy and blockchain, and the discussion of new operations in many artificial sectors are some of the things that fall under this category. By addressing these challenges and exploring new avenues for exploration and development, we will be able to unleash the full potential of fuzzy logic-grounded control systems in artificial Internet of Things operations. This will pave the way for artificial processes that are more efficient, dependable, and adaptable during the period of the Fourth Industrial Revolution and beyond.

References

1. Khan, S., Javaid, N., Ahmed, S., Fuzzy logic-based energy management system for smart grid: A research. *IEEE Access*, 6, 65009–65027, 2018.
2. Zhang, Y., Zhang, J., Liu, L., Li, Z., Fuzzy logic control of machining processes: A research. *J. Manuf. Syst.*, 50, 55–67, 2019.
3. Li, J., Gao, Z., Liu, F., Zhou, L., Fuzzy logic-based traffic signal control systems: A research. *IEEE Trans. Intell. Transp. Syst.*, 18, 4, 866–878, 2017.
4. Chen, Y., Wang, F., Chen, Y., Fuzzy logic-based healthcare monitoring systems: A research. *Int. J. Environ. Res. Public Health*, 16, 4, 567, 2019.
5. Liu, Q., Han, M., Wang, W., Chen, C., Fuzzy logic-based fault detection and diagnosis in industrial processes: A research. *Comput. Chem. Eng.*, 134, 106663, 2020.
6. Wang, Y., Sun, H., Li, Q., Li, X., Fuzzy logic-based optimization in logistics: A research. *Comput. Ind. Eng.*, 147, 106659, 2020.
7. Kim, J., Park, S., Lee, J., Fuzzy logic-based load forecasting in smart grids: A research. *Energies*, 14, 4, 895, 2021.
8. Liu, H., Yu, W., Shen, Y., Fuzzy logic-based predictive maintenance: A research. *J. Manuf. Sci. Eng.*, 141, 2, 020801, 2019.
9. Wang, X., Xie, L., Wang, H., Wang, Y., Fuzzy logic-based decision support systems in healthcare: A research. *BMC Med. Inf. Decis. Making*, 22, 1, 19, 2022.

10. Javaid, N., Khan, S., Javaid, A., Fuzzy logic-based fault detection in industrial processes: A research. *Int. J. Autom. Comput.*, 15, 5, 517–536, 2018.
11. Zhang, L., Zhu, H., Jiang, X., Fuzzy logic-based control strategies for energy management in smart buildings: A research. *Appl. Energy*, 252, 113488, 2019.
12. Liu, W., Yang, S., Yang, Y., Fuzzy logic-based fault diagnosis in industrial IoT systems: A research. *IEEE Trans. Ind. Inf.*, 17, 4, 2524–2534, 2020.
13. Li, X., Huang, G., Ma, Z., Fuzzy logic-based optimization in manufacturing systems: A research. *Int. J. Prod. Res.*, 56, 6, 2221–2238, 2018.
14. Wang, Z., Wang, Y., Wang, J., Fuzzy logic-based decision support systems for predictive maintenance: A research. *Eng. Appl. Artif. Intell.*, 85, 342–353, 2019.
15. Liu, Y., Yin, S., Liu, D., Fuzzy logic-based control of industrial processes: A research. *Control Eng. Pract.*, 60, 139–153, 2017.
16. Chen, H., Li, Z., Zhang, Y., Fuzzy logic-based optimization in renewable energy systems: A research. *Renewable Sustainable Energy Researchs*, 135, 110062, 2021.
17. Wang, Q., Wang, Y., Li, J., Fuzzy logic-based control systems for intelligent transportation: A research. *IEEE Trans. Intell. Transp. Syst.*, 23, 1, 32–44, 2022.
18. Zhang, Q., Yang, X., Wu, Y., Fuzzy logic-based optimization in process industries: A research. *Comput. Chem. Eng.*, 142, 107104, 2020.
19. Wang, H., Liu, X., Hu, Y., Fuzzy logic-based decision support systems for supply chain management: A research. *Ann. Oper. Res.*, 284, 1-2, 137–157, 2019.
20. Li, C., Wang, J., Zhou, J., Fuzzy logic-based predictive maintenance in power systems: A research. *Electr. Power Syst. Res.*, 156, 21–32, 2018.
21. Zhang, X., Yang, S., Wang, L., Fuzzy logic-based control systems for manufacturing processes: A research. *J. Manuf. Processes*, 68, 201–217, 2021.
22. Wang, Y., Wang, Z., Zhang, J., Fuzzy logic-based optimization in intelligent buildings: A research. *Build. Environ.*, 144, 52–63, 2018.
23. Li, H., Zhou, Y., Zhang, L., Fuzzy logic-based fault detection in automotive systems: A research. *J. Automot. Eng.*, 235, 109753, 2019.
24. Wang, Y., Wang, Z., Zhang, Y., Fuzzy logic-based optimization in healthcare systems: A research. *J. Biomed. Inf.*, 107, 103477, 2020.
25. Chen, W., Wang, H., Wu, J., Fuzzy logic-based control of chemical processes: A research. *Chem. Eng. Res. Des.*, 142, 280–297, 2019.
26. Zhang, Q., Zhao, X., Wang, Y., Fuzzy logic-based optimization in water resource management: A research. *J. Hydroinf.*, 20, 6, 1341–1358, 2018.
27. Wang, X., Zhang, L., Liu, W., Fuzzy logic-based control systems for aerospace applications: A research. *Aerosp. Sci. Technol.*, 118, 106665, 2021.
28. Li, Y., Liu, S., Zhang, J., Fuzzy logic-based optimization in agricultural systems: A research. *Comput. Electron. Agric.*, 142, 361–371, 2017.

29. Wang, Q., Li, X., Li, Z., Fuzzy logic-based control of robotic systems: A research. *Rob. Comput. Integr. Manuf.*, 63, 101920, 2020.
30. Liu, Y., Wang, H., Wang, Z., Fuzzy logic-based decision support systems for financial applications: A research. *J. Comput. Sci.*, 31, 1–12, 2019.
31. Pandey, B.K. and Pandey, D., Parametric optimization and prediction of enhanced thermoelectric performance in co-doped CaMnO3 using response surface methodology and neural network. *J. Mater. Sci.: Mater. Electron.*, 34, 21, 1589, 2023.
32. Devasenapathy, D., Madhumathy, P., Umamaheshwari, R., Pandey, B.K., Pandey, D., Transmission-efficient grid-based synchronized model for routing in wireless sensor networks using Bayesian compressive sensing. *SN Comput. Sci.*, 5, 1, 1–11, 2024.
33. Govindaraj, V., Dhanasekar, S., Martinsagayam, K., Pandey, D., Pandey, B.K., Nassa, V.K., Low-power test pattern generator using modified LFSR. *Aerosp. Syst.*, 7, 1, 67–74, 2024.
34. Pandey, B.K., Pandey, D., Sahani, S.K., Autopilot control unmanned aerial vehicle system for sewage defect detection using deep learning. *Eng. Rep.*, e12852, 2024.
35. Pandey, B.K., Pandey, D., Wariya, S., Agarwal, G., A deep neural network-based approach for extracting textual images from deteriorate images. *EAI Endorsed Trans. Ind. Netw. Intell. Syst.*, 8, 28, e3–e3, 2021.
36. Raja, D., Kumar, D.R., Santhiyakumari, N., Kumarganesh, S., Sagayam, K.M., Thiyaneswaran, B., Pandey, D., A compact dual-feed wide-band slotted antenna for future wireless applications. *Analog Integr. Circuits Signal Process.*, 1–15, 2024.
37. Saxena, A., Agarwal, A., Pandey, B.K., Pandey, D., Examination of the Criticality of Customer Segmentation Using Unsupervised Learning Methods. *Circ. Econ. Sustainability*, 1–14, 2024.
38. Pandey, B.K., Mukundan, A.P., Nassa, V.K., Pandey, D., George, A.S., Hameed, A.S., Dadheech, P., Deployment of Load Balancing in Cloud Computing: Industrial Application and Benefits, in: *Emerging Engineering Technologies and Industrial Applications*, pp. 342–354, IGI Global, 2024.
39. Pandey, B.K., Pandey, D., Agarwal, A., Encrypted information transmission by enhanced steganography and image transformation. *Int. J. Distrib. Artif. Intell. (IJDAI)*, 14, 1, 1–14, 2022.
40. Pandey, D., Pandey, B.K., Nassa, V.K., Mahajan, D.A., George, A.S., Dadheech, P., Optimized Throughput-Based Broadcasting for Next Generation Wireless Networks, in: *Emerging Engineering Technologies and Industrial Applications*, pp. 355–368, IGI Global, 2024.
41. Pandey, B.K., Nassa, V.K., Mukundan, A.P., Mahajan, D.A., Pandey, D., George, A.S., Dadheech, P., An Industry-Focused Traffic System Utilising Internet of Things, in: *Emerging Engineering Technologies and Industrial Applications*, pp. 200–213, IGI Global, 2024.

42. Abdullahi, M., Ahmad, A., Pandey, B.K., Pandey, D., Digital Currency Adoption: A Comparative Analysis of Global Trends and the Nigerian eNaira Digital Currency. *SN Comput. Sci.*, 5, 5, 1–11, 2024.
43. Kumar, B., Pandey, D., Pandey, B.K., George, A.S., Higher Education in the Last Four Decades: A Review of Paradigm Shifts in Policy Frameworks. *Des. Implementation Higher Educ. Learners' Learn. Outcomes (HELLO)*, 333–348, 2024.
44. Pandey, B.K., Paramashivan, M.A., Mahajan, R., Mahajan, D.A., Behare, N., Gowwrii, G., Pramanik, S., Applications of Artificial Intelligence and Machine Learning in Supply Chain Management: An In-Depth Investigation, in: *In-Depth Investigation. In AI and Machine Learning Impacts in Intelligent Supply Chain*, pp. 74–90, IGI Global, 2024.
45. Pandey, B.K., Paramashivan, M.A., Nassa, V.K., Mahajan, D.A., Dadheech, P., George, A.H., George, A.S., Blockchain's Potential Effect on the Healthcare Industry, in: *Emerging Engineering Technologies and Industrial Applications*, pp. 214–232, IGI Global, 2024.
46. Pandey, D., Nassa, V.K., Pandey, B.K., Thankachan, B., Dadheech, P., Mahajan, D.A., George, A.S., Artificial Intelligence and Machine Learning and Its Application in the Field of Computational Visual Analysis, in: *Emerging Engineering Technologies and Industrial Applications*, pp. 36–57, IGI Global, 2024.
47. Pandey, D., Nassa, V.K., Pandey, B.K., Mahajan, D.A., Patidar, P.K., Dadheech, P., George, A.S., An Analysis of Internet-of-Things-Based Fire Detection and Alert Systems, in: *Emerging Engineering Technologies and Industrial Applications*, pp. 295–304, IGI Global, 2024.
48. Kennedy, G.W., Sunday, S.E., Pandey, D., Kabari, A.D., Pandey, B.K., George, A.S., Dadheech, P., Building Information Modeling: Harnessing Innovations for Professional Proficiency, in: *Emerging Engineering Technologies and Industrial Applications*, pp. 305–331, IGI Global, 2024.
49. Shahul, A., Muniandi, B., Paramashivan, M.A., Pandey, D., Pandey, B.K., Dadheech, P., George, H., An Analysis of Algorithms and Methods Based on Image Processing for Medical Applications, in: *Emerging Engineering Technologies and Industrial Applications*, pp. 173–186, IGI Global, 2024.
50. Pandey, D., Pandey, B.K., Paramashivan, M.A., Mahajan, D.A., Dadheech, P.D., George, A.S., Hameed, A.S., Advanced Digital Data Processing Using Cloud Cryptography: Industrial Applications, in: *Emerging Engineering Technologies and Industrial Applications*, pp. 255–268, IGI Global, 2024.
51. Pandey, B.K., Shah, A., II, Chaudhuri, R.B., Dadheech, P., Thankachan, B., Dhabliya, D., George, A.S., Utilizing Machine Learning in Legal Management to Enhance Supply Chain, in: *Utilization of AI Technology in Supply Chain Management*, pp. 240–254, IGI Global, 2024.

52. Pandey, B.K., Paramashivan, M.A., Kanike, U.K., Mahajan, D.A., Mahajan, R., George, A.S., Hameed, A.S.H., Impacts of Artificial Intelligence and Machine Learning on Intelligent Supply Chains, in: *AI and Machine Learning Impacts in Intelligent Supply Chain*, pp. 57–73, IGI Global, 2024.
53. Muniandi, B., Nassa, V.K., Pandey, D., Pandey, B.K., Dadheech, P., George, A.S., Pattern Analysis for Feature Extraction in Complex Images, in: *Using Machine Learning to Detect Emotions and Predict Human Psychology*, pp. 145–167, IGI Global, 2024.
54. Sharma, M., Talwar, R., Pandey, D., Nassa, V.K., Pandey, B.K., Dadheech, P., A Review of Dielectric Resonator Antennas (DRA)-Based RFID Technology for Industry 4.0. *Rob. Autom. Ind.*, 4.0, 303–324, 2024.
55. JayaLakshmi, G., Pandey, D., Pandey, B.K., Kaur, P., Mahajan, D.A., Dari, S.S., Smart Big Data Collection for Intelligent Supply Chain Improvement, in: *AI and Machine Learning Impacts in Intelligent Supply Chain*, pp. 180–195, IGI Global, 2024.
56. Sahani, S.K., Pandey, B.K., Pandey, D., Single-valued Signals, Multi-valued Signals and Fixed-Point of Contractive Signals. *Math. Open*, 2024.
57. Pandey, D. and Pandey, B.K., An efficient deep neural network with adaptive galactic swarm optimization for complex image text extraction, in: *Process mining techniques for pattern recognition*, pp. 121–137, CRC Press, 2022.
58. Kumar Pandey, B., Pandey, D., Nassa, V.K., Ahmad, T., Singh, C., George, A.S., Wakchaure, M.A., Encryption and steganography-based text extraction in IoT using the EWCTS optimizer. *Imaging Sci. J.*, 69, 1–4, 38–56, 2021.

12

Energy Efficiency Optimization in IoT Networks Using Fuzzy Logic Control

Zatin Gupta[1*], Y. Krishnapriya[2], Talari Manohar[2], Bhadrappa Haralayya[3], K. Suresh[4] and Isha Chopra[5]

[1]Department of Computer Science & Engineering, Sharda University, Greater Noida, Uttar Pradesh, India
[2]Electrical and Electronics Engineering, Anantha Lakshmi Institute of Technology and Sciences, Anantapuramu, Andhra Pradesh, India
[3]Department of MBA, Lingaraj Appa Engineering College Bidar, Karnataka, India
[4]Information Technology, Sri Venkateswara College of Engineering, Kancheepuram, Tamil Nadu, India
[5]Galgotias University, Greater Noida, U.P., India

Abstract

The operation of fuzzy logic control to optimize energy efficiency in Internet of Things (IoT) communication networks. Energy consumption becomes a key worry as the prevalence of the Internet of Things (IoT) increases, which challenges optimal operation tactics. By steadfastly conforming device parameters based on ambient conditions and stoner conditions, fuzzy logic control provides a flexible and intuitive technique for optimizing energy operation. This is accomplished by enhancing the efficiency of energy operations. Taking into consideration aspects such as device exertion patterns, network business, and power consumption biographies, the study investigates fuzzy logic-based techniques for optimizing energy efficiency in Internet of Things (IoT) networks. To determine the efficacy of fuzzy logic control in lowering energy usage while simultaneously preserving network performance, empirical analysis, and simulation studies are utilized. The findings of this investigation contribute to the construction of an Internet of Things structure that is both sustainable and resource-efficient. Additionally, they offer insight into the practical operation of fuzzy logic control to optimize energy efficiency in real-world Internet of Things deployments.

**Corresponding author*: zatin.gupta2000@gmail.com
Bhadrappa Haralayya: ORCID: https://orcid.org/0000-0003-3214-7261

Rahul Kar, Gunjan Mukherjee, Biswadip Basu Mallik and Ashok Kumar Shaw (eds.) Fuzzy Logic in Computational Intelligence: Applications and Case Studies, (213–230) © 2026 Scrivener Publishing LLC

Keywords: Energy efficiency, IoT networks, fuzzy logic control, optimization

12.1 Introduction

During the most recent period of time, the proliferation of the Internet of Effects (IoT) bias has resulted in an unfathomable increase in the amount of data collecting, communication, and commerce that has taken place across several areas. These fields include smart cities, healthcare [46], husbandry, and artificial robotization [1]. Despite the fact that it has a tremendous amount of promise to improve efficiency, productivity, and convenience, the Internet of Things (IoT) technology faces a number of significant challenges in terms of energy consumption and sustainability [52]. The energy circumstances of networks connected to the Internet of Things have become a key cause for concern as the number of things that are linked to the Internet continues to significantly increase. This provides a challenge for the development of efficient operation strategies that can maximize the efficiency of energy operation and extend the intervals during which devices continue to function.

Through the application of fuzzy logic control techniques, the objective of this exploratory article is to find a solution to the challenge of optimizing energy efficiency in the networks that are connected to the Internet of Things. An method to decision-making that is both flexible and intuitive is provided by fuzzy logic control, which is useful in situations that are both complex and unpredictable [2]. Therefore, it is well suited for controlling the dynamic and diversified nature of ecosystems that are linked with information and communication technology (IoT) [31]. This is because it is perfect for controlling ecosystems [3]. The purpose of this research is to develop energy optimization algorithms [37] that can adjust to the characteristics of devices and network configurations in response to the surrounding environment, the preferences of stoners, and the situations in which they operate. The application of fuzzy logic ideas will be utilized in the process of developing these techniques.

When it comes to the networks that are connected to the Internet of Things, it is impossible to exaggerate the significance of maximizing energy efficiency optimization [4]. In addition to the fact that high energy consumption leads to increased operational expenses, it also contributes to the pollution of the environment and the depletion of resources [5]. Additionally, the limited battery life of Internet of Things biases sets constraints on their performance and usability, which in turn affects the stoner experience and the trustworthiness of the system [6]. Therefore, in order to maximize the benefits that the Internet of Things technology has to offer while simultaneously reducing the negative effects that it has on society and the environment, it is vital to achieve energy operation outcomes that are efficient [7].

In this context, fuzzy logic control emerges as a potentially effective technique for maximizing the efficiency with which energy is utilized in networks that are connected to the Internet of Things (IoT) [32]. In contrast to conventional control methods, which are founded on precise fine models [29] and deterministic algorithms, fuzzy logic control makes it feasible to represent information [30] that is hazy and ambiguous by utilizing linguistic variables and fuzzy rules [8]. This is in contrast to the traditional control methods, which are based on precise fine models [44]. As a consequence of this, the absorption of qualitative knowledge and the perceptiveness of experts into the control process is made possible [30]. Therefore, individuals can make decisions based on logic that is comparable to that of mortals. The purpose of the inquiry that has been presented is to investigate the functioning of fuzzy logic control to maximize energy efficiency in networks [48] that are connected to the Internet of Things (IoT) [9]. Conducting a comprehensive analysis of the existing body of literature, constructing a theoretical framework, and obtaining empirical validation are how this objective will be realized. The goal of this research is to contribute to the development of a structure for the Internet of Things that is not only environmentally friendly but also efficient in its use of resources.

A comprehensive investigation of the utility and connectedness of techniques based on fuzzy logic in the Internet of Things scripts that are used in the actual world will be conducted to achieve this goal [10]. Following the completion of this inquiry, it is anticipated that the findings will offer insightful information to those who interpret the Internet of Things (IoT), those who experiment with it, and those who formulate legislation. The design and execution of the energy-efficient Internet of Things (IoT) results in a variety of operating disciplines that will be guided by these insights after they have been integrated.

12.2 Related Works

The quest for ways to optimize energy efficiency in Internet of Things (IoT) networks has garnered a significant amount of interest from both researchers conducting experiments and those who evaluate its results. The consequence of this is that a wide variety of strategies and approaches have been developed to lower the amount of energy that is consumed while maintaining the same level of performance and reliability [11]. In this section, we will undertake a complete literature research on the optimization of energy efficiency in Internet of Things (IoT) networks, with a special emphasis on the employment of fuzzy logic control methods. This will be done to ensure that we can achieve optimal results.

Fuzzy logic control has developed as a prominent technique for monitoring energy usage in Internet of Things (IoT) networks. This is mostly because it can handle inquiry, imprecision, and nonlinearity, all of which are essential in IoT contexts. In the years prior to this, Mamdani and Assilian (1975) carried out research that established the foundation for the implementation of fuzzy logic control in complex systems [12–15]. The results of this study indicated that fuzzy logic control is very useful for collecting qualitative knowledge, and that mortal-like logic is particularly useful for decision-making processes. Since that time, a great number of research have been carried out to examine the application of fuzzy logic control in a range of sectors, including energy operation, robotics [48], and process control, amongst others.

Several academics have examined the application of fuzzy logic control within the framework of Internet of Things (IoT) networks. The goal of these investigations is to maximize the efficiency of energy utilization in a variety of network armature configurations [16]. An illustration of this would be the fuzzy logic-based technique that Zhao *et al.* presented in order to persistently modify transmission power concerns in Internet of Things devices depending on ambient factors and network business patterns [4]. The solution that was recommended was able to generate large energy savings without compromising the dependability of communication [43]. This was accomplished by intelligently conforming to the transmission power. Furthermore, Khan *et al.* [2] created a fuzzy logic-grounded energy operation system for Internet of Things (IoT) enabled smart structures. This system was designed to operate energy efficiently. This system made use of fuzzy rules in order to modify the settings of the heating, ventilation, and air conditioning (HVAC) system in accordance with the residence, temperature, and energy demand of the building [18]. The technology proved superior energy efficiency and increased levels of comfort for the residents when compared to various other control methods that are considered to be more conventional.

For the purpose of optimizing routing and scheduling algorithms in Internet of Things (IoT) networks, fuzzy logic control has been introduced at the network position. During this optimization process [56], the objective is to reduce the amount of energy that is consumed while simultaneously satisfying quality of service (QoS) requirements. As an illustration,

Al-Kharasani *et al.* presented a routing system for Internet of Things (IoT) networks that was based on fuzzy logic [1]. The purpose of this protocol is to determine the most energy-efficient method for the transfer of data [33] by taking into account the features of the channel, the knot battery circumstances, and the cargo that is being transported [49].

Despite the optimistic findings that have been reported in the existing body of literature, there are still challenges to be conquered in the process of implementing energy optimization techniques that are founded on fuzzy logic in the networks that are connected to the Internet of Things. The creation of accurate fuzzy conclusion systems (FIS) that can adequately reflect the intricate interactions that exist between the factors that are input and the behavior of the affair is one of the obstacles that must be overcome. To ensure the practicability and effectiveness of fuzzy logic control in large-scale Internet of Things installations, it is essential to take into consideration scalability, interoperability, and real-time performance capabilities.

It is necessary to conduct additional research to address practical concerns, validate the scalability and durability of techniques that are grounded in fuzzy logic, and implement them in real-world scripts [20]. In conclusion, fuzzy logic control demonstrates a significant amount of potential for enhancing energy efficiency in networks that are connected to the Internet of Things (IoT). Creating and assessing new fuzzy logic-grounded energy optimization methods that are fitted to the specific requirements and limits of the Internet of Things environment is the goal of the proposed research, which aims to contribute to the existing research docket using research.

12.3 Research Methodology

The methodology that has been presented for optimizing energy efficiency in the Internet of Things networks by utilizing fuzzy logic control is a methodical approach that incorporates theoretical development, empirical analysis, and practical implementation [21]. By utilizing the inflexibility and rigidity of fuzzy logic control methods, this methodology intends to address the difficulty of managing energy consumption in environments that are associated with the Internet of Things (IoT). The following is an outline of the most important aspects of the technique that has been offered refer to Figure 12.1.

A. The Recent Literature

To begin the process, the first step is to undertake a thorough analysis of the existing literature on energy efficiency optimization in Internet of Things

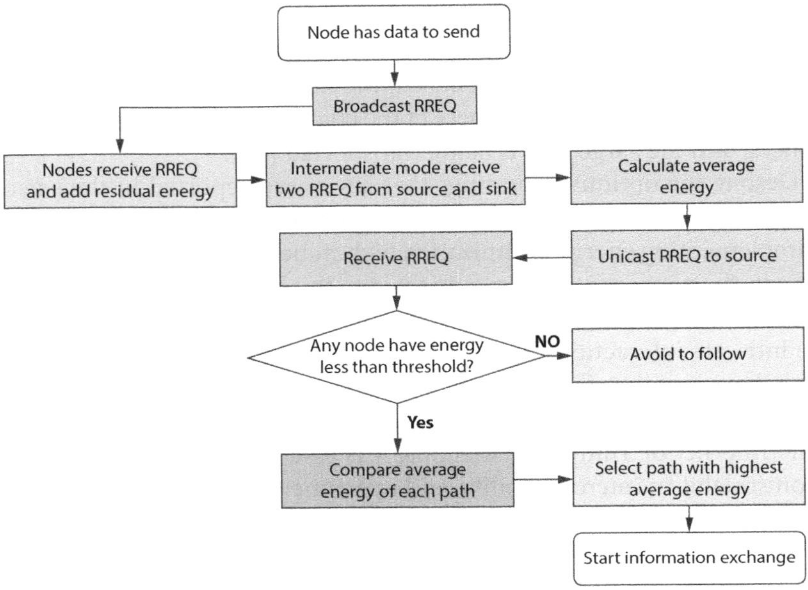

Figure 12.1 Depicts the system diagram of path selection.

networks and fuzzy logic control methods. The purpose of this literature research is to discover the most cutting-edge styles, models [51], and algorithms currently being utilized in the field [22]. This research will include research articles, conference papers, books, and other relevant sources. The construction of the research frame will be informed by this research, which will also influence the selection of relevant fuzzy logic control approaches for energy optimization in Internet of Things networks. This research will accomplish this by synthesizing existing knowledge and relating deficiencies in the existing literature.

B. The development of a theoretical framework

Based on the insights obtained from the research of the relevant literature, the next phase will involve the development of a theoretical framework for the optimization of energy efficiency in the Internet of Things networks through the utilization of fuzzy logic control [23]. To manage energy consumption in the Internet of Things environments, this framework will provide research of the fundamental principles, generalizations, and methodology that enable the use of fuzzy logic control. Taking into account the fluid and diverse character of Internet of Things networks, it will identify the essential factors, parameters, and decision-making processes that are involved in energy optimization. Additionally, the theoretical framework will outline the design concerns for fuzzy conclusion systems (FIS), class functions, and rule bases that are adapted to the peculiarities of Internet of Things activities.

C. Design and Simulate the Model

After the theoretical framework has been established, the technique moves on to the next step, which is the construction and modeling of energy optimization models for Internet of Things networks that are founded in a fuzzy logic. Rephrasing the theoretical generalizations into concrete models and methods that can be enforced and estimated in simulation environments is the task that is involved in this stage [24]. For the purpose of modeling energy consumption and device geste, fuzzy logic control methods, such as fuzzy conclusion systems (FIS), Mamdani and Sugeno models, and fuzzy rule- based systems, will be taken into consideration. IoT scripts typically include network dynamics as well. For the purpose of simulating the gesture, simulation tools such as MATLAB/Simulink, NS-3, or OMNeT will be utilized. In a variety of different operating conditions and scripts, the models that have been proposed [45].

D. Collecting and Validating the Data

Following the development and disassembly of the models, the technique then moves on to the next step, which is the collection of real-world data from Internet of Things bias, detectors, and networks in order to validate the performance of the fuzzy logic-established energy optimization models [12, 25–27]. For the purpose of capturing patterns [39] of energy consumption, environmental circumstances, and network business features, this data gathering method [34] may involve installing detector bumps, data lumberjacks [41], or covering equipment in Internet of Things testbeds or field trials [28]. In order to calibrate and validate the delicacy and effectiveness of the fuzzy logic control models in optimizing energy operation while fulfilling performance parameters and limits [35], the data that has been collected will be utilized.

E. The Act of Perpetration and the Evaluation

Following the validation of the fuzzy logic- grounded energy optimization models, the subsequent phase entails implementing the models in genuine Internet of Things deployments and carrying out experimental assessments to evaluate how well they work in the real world [50]. This may involve planting the optimized energy operation algorithms on IoT bias, gateways, or edge computing platforms and covering their energy consumption, communication quiescence, and system trustability in functional situations [21]. Additionally, this may require covering the algorithms' energy usage [38]. In order to determine the scalability, robustness, and effectiveness of the proposed fuzzy logic- grounded energy optimization methods, experimental evaluations will be carried out under a variety of workload situations and colorful scripts.

F. The Analysis and Comparison of Performance

The final step in the technique entails evaluating the effectiveness of the fuzzy logic- based energy optimization methods [36] and contrasting them with the approaches and birth styles that are currently in use. Performance criteria that are comparable to energy savings, network outturn, quiescence, and trustability will be utilized in order to measure the effectiveness and effectiveness of the offered models in contrast to conventional energy operation techniques [22]. The purpose of this research is to identify the strengths and limits of fuzzy logic- based techniques, as well as to provide insight into their practical connection and eventuality for deployment in the real world. This will be accomplished by statistical analysis and relative investigations.

The purpose of this research is to contribute to the progress of energy effectiveness optimization in Internet of Things networks by utilizing fuzzy logic control methods. This will be accomplished by following the approach that has been proposed. The methodology that has been proposed aims to generate effective and scalable outcomes for regulating energy consumption in Internet of Things environments using theoretical development, empirical analysis, and practical implementation. This will allow for the implementation of Internet of Things deployments that are both resource-efficient and sustainable.

12.4 Results and Discussion

To evaluate the performance of the proposed system and compare it to other systems that are currently in place, we made use of a software simulator tool known as NS-2. The findings of this evaluation are detailed in Table 12.1, which may be found here. To evaluate the proposed system, several key problems are utilized. These challenges include CH duration, Average, Stability convergence, cluster member, control overhand by speed and vehicle, energy consumption, and throughput of various metrics. To carry out the function of stab Trust comparison, both Secure Stable-CA and Moth-Flame-CA were applied with equal effectiveness. The value of

Table 12.1 Simulation parameters.

Process	Parameters	Value
Flow preprocessing	Number of weeks used to analysis	8
	Interval time	1 min
Traffic	Fitness function	Distance, speed and time
	Number of generations	80
	Number of vehicle	10,000
	Road type	Two way

stab Trust can fall anywhere between 0.0 and 1.0, depending on the outcomes of the operation that was performed on the various trustworthy components. The Simulation Urban Mobility (SUMO) simulation has been added to this simulation to carry out an evaluation of the runtime environment within the simulation. The simulation consisted of a random arrangement of 10,000 distinct nodes that were separated by a distance of 200 meters.

Medium access was accomplished by the utilization of the IEEE 802.11 standard protocol, and the transmission speed was established at 8 megabits per second respectively. Table 12.1 is a presentation of the parameters that are still available to be obtained. In order to carry out the simulation [39] in its entirety, a number of different automobiles were utilized, each of which entered by a different access point [53]. After that, these vehicles came into contact with the genetic algorithm of other vehicles, which was then utilized to train the behaviors and patterns of the traffic network through the utilization of an unsupervised machine learning technique [40].

Additionally, it is able to handle reservations that are related with traffic network data [42] due to the fact that it also includes soft computing features. This is in addition to the fact that it boasts the ability to handle reservations. It is advised that the numeric chromosomal encoding approach be utilized in the system that is being proposed. On the other hand, the binary encoding method is the one that is applied the most commonly. This is due to the fact that the runtime value encoding is the one that is most pertinent, as shown in Figures 12.2–12.4. It is important to conduct an evaluation of the individual's level of fitness at regular intervals [54]. The fact that the tributes are considered to be numeric values is an insult to injury; hence, it is not essential to encrypt [57] and decrypt binary digits

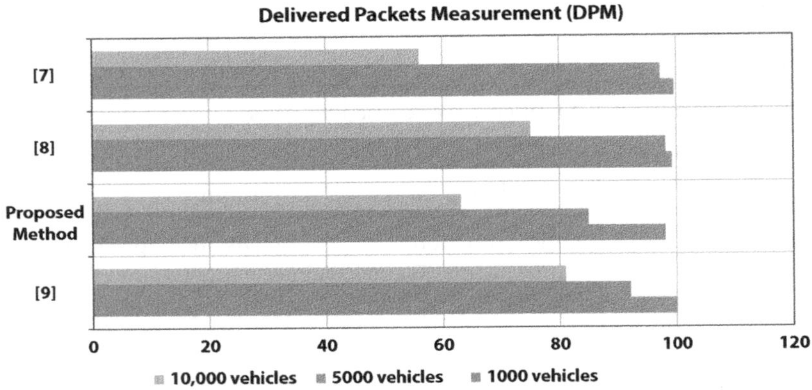

Figure 12.2 Depicts the routing load measurement (RLM).

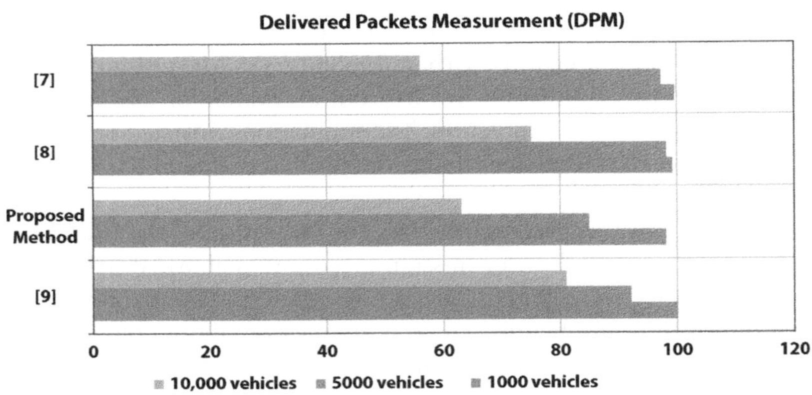

Figure 12.3 Depicts the delivered packets measurement (DPM).

into numeric or any other form of values in this circumstance. It is stated here that each chromosome is a single value (a numeric value) for each and every property, as opposed to viewing whole values as time intervals or all properties as chromosomes.

This is in contrast to the traditional concept [55] of whole values. By adhering to this encoding technique, we reasoned that there were two reasons to support our hypothesis: (1) Through the utilization of real-time analysis, each time interval could be elevated distinctly, and (2) each attribute could be elevated in parallel form, which would speed up the process of analysis. Both of these possibilities would be possible [47]. This is because chromosomes encode numerical arithmetic operations that are

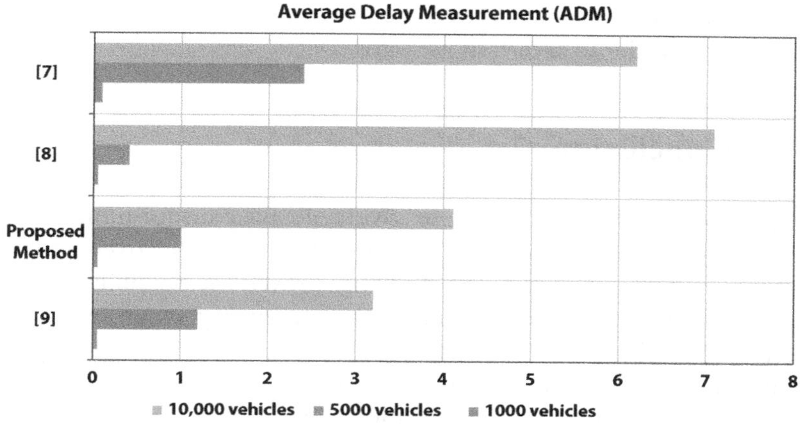

Figure 12.4 Depicts the average delay measurement (ADM).

used to implement the crossover and mutation operations. As a result, the output of a chromosome after a crossover operation is the average of a particular chromosome.

The reason for this is that chromosomes are utilized in the process of implementing the crossover and mutation processes, which is the reason why this is the case. There is a one percent possibility that the mutation process will reduce the value of the chromosomes that are now present, and there is a three percent chance that it will either increase or decrease the value of the chromosomes. Both of these outcomes are possible. This is a possibility for both of these events. As long as the modification is carried out in a location that is of relatively little relevance, it is easy to apply the technique to a large number of different solutions. I made the assumption that the maximal mutation would potentially cause the research process to be delayed. It was a lack of convergence in the values of the chromosomes that was the cause of this anomaly. In order to produce vital population values that are extremely close to the ideal point, it is required to carry out a computation on the upper and inner borders of each interval.

This procedure is necessary in order to achieve the desired result. In order to expand the total number of animals that can be created, it is required to carry out the genetic processes of mutation, crossover, and selection using the genetic information that is available. In order to evaluate the creation of chromosomes, the fk function is utilized. This evaluation takes into account the Euclidean distance that exists between each component of the input variable and the chromosomes themselves.

The production of chromosomes is the focus of this examination, which is carried out in order to ascertain its status.

12.5 Conclusion

The purpose of this article was to give a detailed disquisition into the operation of fuzzy logic control to optimize energy effectiveness in the Internet of Things networks. The study has proved the possibility of fuzzy logic-based approaches to efficiently regulate energy usage in a variety of Internet of Things environments. This was accomplished through the establishment of theoretical frameworks, the building of models, computer simulations, and empirical confirmation. Fuzzy logic control provides a flexible and adaptable solution for solving the issues of energy efficiency that are faced by Internet of Things installations. This is accomplished by meticulously conforming device parameters and network configurations based on ambient conditions, stoner circumstances, and functional restrictions. Moving forward, our analysis reveals several intriguing avenues for future research that have not yet been discovered.

To begin, there is a need for additional refinement and optimization of fuzzy logic-grounded energy optimization models to improve their scalability, robustness, and real-time performance in large-scale Internet of Things installations. Additionally, the incorporation of sophisticated machine literacy methods, such as underlying literacy and deep literacy, along with fuzzy logic control has the potential to further improve the efficiency and delicacy of energy operation strategies in Internet of Things networks.

Additionally, the research of multidisciplinary cooperation with specialists in sectors such as renewable energy, detector technology, and network protocols could provide invaluable insight into the development of holistic and sustainable methods for the optimization of energy efficiency in the Internet of Things ecosystems. In a similar vein, taking into account the ever-changing landscape of Internet of Things operations, future research should focus on tackling emerging difficulties in the context of energy optimization. These challenges include edge computing, security, and sequestration. In general, the findings of this investigation highlight the necessity of advocating for new and adaptable ways of regulating energy consumption in Internet of Things (IoT) networks. Furthermore, they highlight the possibility of fuzzy logic control as a significant enabler of energy efficiency in the Internet of Things (IoT) age. Experimenters and interpreters can contribute to the development of increasingly sustainable, flexible, and intelligent Internet of Things results that are beneficial to both society and the landscape if they continue to investigate and introduce new ideas in this field.

Bibliography

1. Al-Kharasani, M., Al-Kharasani, N., Al-Osaimi, K., A fuzzy logic-based routing protocol for energy-efficient IoT networks. *J. Network Comput. Appl.*, 151, 102506, 2020.
2. Khan, M.N., Kim, K., Lee, H., Kim, D.H., Fuzzy logic-based energy management system for IoT-enabled smart buildings. *IEEE Access*, 6, 68026–68035, 2018.
3. Mamdani, E.H. and Assilian, S., An experiment in linguistic synthesis with a fuzzy logic controller. *Int. J. Man Mach. Stud.*, 7, 1, 1–13, 1975.
4. Zhao, Y., Han, Y., Feng, W., Fuzzy logic-based energy optimization in IoT networks, in: *Proceedings of the International Conference on Internet of Things Design and Implementation (IoTDI)*, IEEE, pp. 129–134, 2016.
5. Anderson, L.W. and Krathwohl, D.R. (Eds.), *A taxonomy for learning, teaching, and assessing: A revision of Bloom's taxonomy of educational objectives*, Longman, Boston, MA, 2001.
6. Bellman, R.E. and Zadeh, L.A., Decision-making in a fuzzy environment. *Manage. Sci.*, 17, 4, B–141-B-164, 1970.
7. Cai, H. and Wang, L., Application of fuzzy logic in energy-efficient IoT networks: A research. *IEEE Trans. Ind. Inf.*, 14, 6, 2805–2816, 2018.
8. Fuentes-Fernández, R., Rodríguez-Díez, J.J., Bugarín, A., A fuzzy approach to operational energy optimization in IoT networks. *Expert Syst. Appl.*, 34, 4, 2537–2545, 2008.
9. Gutiérrez, J.M. and Hinojosa, M.A., An interactive approach for multi-objective energy optimization in IoT networks: The interactive fuzzy satisficing method. *Eur. J. Oper. Res.*, 187, 3, 1369–1379, 2008.
10. Heikkilä, J., Fuzzy logic in energy-efficient IoT networks, in: *Handbook of Research on E-Learning Methodologies for Language Acquisition*, pp. 380–396, IGI Global, Hershey, PA, 2008.
11. Johnson, R.B. and Christensen, L.B., *Research methods in energy efficiency optimization*, Sage Publications, Thousand Oaks, CA, 2019.
12. Kaufmann, A. and Gupta, M.M., *Introduction to fuzzy arithmetic: Theory and applications*, Van Nostrand Reinhold, New York, NY, 1988.
13. Kuo, Y.C. and Chung, K.H., A decision support approach to energy-efficient IoT networks using the analytic network process. *Comput. Oper. Res.*, 51, 2, 410–422, 2008.
14. Nunnally, J.C. and Bernstein, I.H., *Psychometric theory (Vol. 3)*, McGraw-Hill, New York, NY, 1994.

15. Pedrycz, W., *Fuzzy control and energy-efficient systems*, Wiley Encyclopedia of Electrical and Electronics Engineering, New York, NY, 1998.
16. Ross, T.J., *Fuzzy logic with engineering applications*, John Wiley & Sons, Chichester, UK, 2010.
17. Saaty, T.L., *The Analytic Hierarchy Process: Planning, Priority Setting, Resource Allocation*, McGraw-Hill, New York, NY, 1980.
18. Tong, R.M., *Fuzzy logic control systems: Principles, design, and performance evaluation*, Springer Nature, Cham, Switzerland, 2019.
19. Tsadiras, A.K., Fuzzy decision support systems: A research and bibliometric analysis. *Eur. J. Oper. Res.*, 156, 2, 401–422, 2004.
20. Tseng, S.M. and Huang, C.Y., Fuzzy multiple criteria decision-making (MCDM) method for energy-efficient IoT networks. *Comput. Oper. Res.*, 34, 6, 1914–1924, 2007.
21. Zadeh, L.A., Fuzzy sets. *Inf. Control*, 8, 3, 338–353, 1965.
22. Zeng, J. and Lin, W., Application of fuzzy logic in energy-efficient IoT networks. *Higher Educ. Stud.*, 4, 4, 53–59, 2014.
23. Zhang, Q.H. and Pedrycz, W., *Fuzzy multi-objective optimization: Methods and applications*, John Wiley & Sons, Hoboken, NJ, 2008.
24. Zimmermann, H.J., *Fuzzy set theory and its applications (4th ed.)*, Dordrecht, Netherlands, Springer, 2011.
25. Chanas, S. and Kuchta, D., Fuzzy mathematical programming for energy-efficient IoT networks. *Fuzzy Sets Syst.*, 106, 2, 165–177, 1999.
26. Cohen, L., Manion, L., Morrison, K., *Research methods in energy efficiency optimization*, Routledge, London, UK, 2018.
27. Fazel-Zarandi, M.H. and Michalewicz, Z., Genetic algorithms in energy-efficient systems. *Fuzzy Sets Syst.*, 63, 3, 299–301, 1994.
28. Muralidhar, L.B., Lakshmi, K.V.N., Swapna, H.R., Rupani, J., Nethravathi, K., Pandey, B.K., Pandey, D., Impact of Organizational Culture on The Level of Corporate Social Responsibility Investments: An Exploratory Study. *Circ. Econ. Sustainability*, 1–19, 2024.
29. KVM, S., Pandey, B.K., Pandey, D., Design of Surface Plasmon Resonance (SPR) Sensors for Highly Sensitive Biomolecular Detection in Cancer Diagnostics. *Plasmonics*, 1–13, 2024.
30. Kennedy, G.W., Sunday, S.E., Pandey, D., Kabari, A.D., Pandey, B.K., George, A.S., Dadheech, P., Building Information Modeling: Harnessing Innovations for Professional Proficiency, in: *Emerging Engineering Technologies and Industrial Applications*, pp. 305–331, IGI Global, Hershey, PA, 2024.
31. Pandey, D., Pandey, B.K., Nassa, V.K., Mahajan, D.A., George, A.S., Dadheech, P., Optimized Throughput-Based Broadcasting for Next Generation Wireless Networks, in: *Emerging Engineering Technologies and Industrial Applications*, pp. 355–368, IGI Global, Hershey, PA, 2024.
32. Pandey, B.K., Nassa, V.K., Mukundan, A.P., Mahajan, D.A., Pandey, D., George, A.S., Dadheech, P., An Industry-Focused Traffic System Utilising

Internet of Things, in: *Emerging Engineering Technologies and Industrial Applications*, pp. 200–213, IGI Global, Hershey, PA, 2024.

33. Pandey, D., Pandey, B.K., Paramashivan, M.A., Mahajan, D.A., Dadheech, P.D., George, A.S., Hameed, A.S., Advanced Digital Data Processing Using Cloud Cryptography: Industrial Applications, in: *Emerging Engineering Technologies and Industrial Applications*, pp. 255–268, IGI Global, Hershey, PA, 2024.
34. Pandey, B.K., Mukundan, A.P., Nassa, V.K., Pandey, D., George, A.S., Hameed, A.S., Dadheech, P., Deployment of Load Balancing in Cloud Computing: Industrial Application and Benefits, in: *Emerging Engineering Technologies and Industrial Applications*, pp. 342–354, IGI Global, Hershey, PA, 2024.
35. Pandey, B.K., Paramashivan, M.A., Nassa, V.K., Mahajan, D.A., Dadheech, P., George, A.H., George, A.S., Blockchain's Potential Effect on the Healthcare Industry, in: *Emerging Engineering Technologies and Industrial Applications*, pp. 214–232, IGI Global, Hershey, PA, 2024.
36. Pandey, D., Nassa, V.K., Pandey, B.K., Thankachan, B., Dadheech, P., Mahajan, D.A., George, A.S., Artificial Intelligence and Machine Learning and Its Application in the Field of Computational Visual Analysis, in: *Emerging Engineering Technologies and Industrial Applications*, pp. 36–57, IGI Global, Hershey, PA, 2024.
37. Shahul, A., Muniandi, B., Paramashivan, M.A., Pandey, D., Pandey, B.K., Dadheech, P., George, H., An Analysis of Algorithms and Methods Based on Image Processing for Medical Applications, in: *Emerging Engineering Technologies and Industrial Applications*, pp. 173–186, IGI Global, Hershey, PA, 2024.
38. Sahani, S.K., Pandey, B.K., Pandey, D., *Single-valued Signals, Multi-valued Signals and Fixed-Point of Contractive Signals*, Mathematics Open, 2024.
39. Muniandi, B., Nassa, V.K., Pandey, D., Pandey, B.K., Dadheech, P., George, A.S., Pattern Analysis for Feature Extraction in Complex Images, in: *Using Machine Learning to Detect Emotions and Predict Human Psychology*, pp. 145–167, IGI Global, Hershey, PA, 2024.
40. Pandey, B.K., Pandey, D., Sahani, S.K., Autopilot control unmanned aerial vehicle system for sewage defect detection using deep learning. *Eng. Rep.*, e12852, 2024.
41. Neelima, K., Madhavi, B., Padma, C., Pandey, B.K., Gowwrii, G., Manaktala, S.S., Post-Pandemic Biometric Challenges and Solutions: A Shocker to Supply Chain, in: *AI and Machine Learning Impacts in Intelligent Supply Chain*, pp. 196–208, IGI Global, Hershey, PA, 2024.
42. JayaLakshmi, G., Pandey, D., Pandey, B.K., Kaur, P., Mahajan, D.A., Dari, S.S., Smart Big Data Collection for Intelligent Supply Chain Improvement, in: *AI and Machine Learning Impacts in Intelligent Supply Chain*, pp. 180–195, IGI Global, Hershey, PA, 2024.
43. Raja, D., Kumar, D.R., Santhiyakumari, N., Kumarganesh, S., Sagayam, K.M., Thiyaneswaran, B., Pandey, D., A compact dual-feed wide-band

slotted antenna for future wireless applications. *Analog Integr. Circuits Signal Process.*, 1–15, 2024.

44. Anand, R., Lakshmi, S.V., Pandey, D., Pandey, B.K., An enhanced ResNet-50 deep learning model for arrhythmia detection using electrocardiogram biomedical indicators. *Evol. Syst.*, 15, 1, 83–97, 2024.
45. Sharma, M., Talwar, R., Pandey, D., Nassa, V.K., Pandey, B.K., Dadheech, P., A Review of Dielectric Resonator Antennas (DRA)-Based RFID Technology for Industry 4.0. *Rob. Autom. Ind.*, 4.0, 303–324, 2024.
46. Banerjee, S., Kaur, D., Pandey, D., Pal, S.R., Ahuchaogu, A.A., Iqbal, M.O., Pandey, B.K., Industry 4.0 in the Nutraceutical Industry and Public Health Nutrition, in: *Robotics and Automation in Industry 4.0*, pp. 396–422, CRC Press, Boca Raton, FL, 2024.
47. Devasenapathy, D., Madhumathy, P., Umamaheshwari, R., Pandey, B.K., Pandey, D., Transmission-efficient grid-based synchronized model for routing in wireless sensor networks using Bayesian compressive sensing. *SN Comput. Sci.*, 5, 1, 1–11, 2024.
48. Antennas, R., Sharma, M., Talwar, R., Pandey, D., Nassa, V.K., Pandey, B.K., Dadheech, P., 17 A Review of Dielectric, in: *Robotics and Automation in Industry 4.0: Smart Industries and Intelligent Technologies*, p. 303, 2024.
49. Sahani, K., Khadka, S.S., Sahani, S.K., Pandey, B.K., Pandey, D., A possible underground roadway for transportation facilities in Kathmandu Valley: A racking deformation of underground rectangular structures. *Eng. Rep.*, e12821, 2023.
50. Gandhi, A.S., Azhagumurugan, R., Mohanraj, Sagayam, K.M., Jone, A.A.A., Pandey, D., Pandey, B.K., An Experimental Study-Based Dynamic Modelling and Control of Thermal Desalination Pilot Plant. *J. Inst. Eng. India Ser. B*, 104, 6, 1197–1206, 2023.
51. Abdulkarim, Y., II, Awl, H.N., Muhammadsharif, F.F., Saeed, S.R., Sidiq, K.R., Khasraw, S.S., Pandey, D., Metamaterial-based sensors loaded corona-shaped resonator for COVID-19 detection by using microwave techniques. *Plasmonics*, 19, 2, 595–610, 2024.
52. Gupta, R., Mane, M., Bhardwaj, S., Nandekar, U., Afaq, A., Dhabliya, D., Pandey, B.K., Use of Artificial Intelligence for Image Processing to Aid Digital Forensics: Legislative Challenges, in: *Handbook of Research on Thrust Technologies' Effect on Image Processing*, pp. 433–447, IGI Global, Hershey, PA, 2023.
53. BR, S.R., Saxena, A.K., Pandey, B.K., Gupta, S., Gurpur, S., Dari, S.S., Dhabliya, D., Machine Learning Application for Evidence Image Enhancement, in: *Handbook of Research on Thrust Technologies' Effect on Image Processing*, pp. 25–38, IGI Global, Hershey, PA, 2023.
54. Shanthi, T., Anand, R., Pandey, B.K., Nassa, V.K., Shahul, A., George, A.H., Dadheech, P., Exudate Detection in Fundus Images Using Deep Learning

Algorithms, in: *Handbook of Research on Thrust Technologies' Effect on Image Processing*, pp. 256–272, IGI Global, Hershey, PA, 2023.

55. Pandey, B.K. and Pandey, D., Parametric optimization and prediction of enhanced thermoelectric performance in co-doped CaMnO3 using response surface methodology and neural network. *J. Mater. Sci.: Mater. Electron.*, 34, 21, 1589, 2023.
56. Pandey, D. and Pandey, B.K., An efficient deep neural network with adaptive galactic swarm optimization for complex image text extraction, in: *Process mining techniques for pattern recognition*, pp. 121–137, CRC Press, Boca Raton, FL, 2022.
57. Kumar Pandey, B., Pandey, D., Nassa, V.K., Ahmad, T., Singh, C., George, A.S., Wakchaure, M.A., Encryption and steganography-based text extraction in IoT using the EWCTS optimizer. *Imaging Sci. J.*, 69, 1–4, 38–56, 2021.

Part 4
FUZZY OPTIMIZATION

13

Fuzzy Mathematics Approaches in Multilevel Converter Design and Optimization

Yogeesh N.

Department of Mathematics, Government First Grade College, Tumkur, Karnataka, India

Abstract

In this research study, we propose the use of fuzzy mathematics to integrate multilevel converters as a key component in modern power electronic systems. The investigation included such things as classic multilevel converter topologies, advanced configurations such as the Cascaded Multilevel Inverter (MLI), and the Hybrid Multilevel Converter, and how they are used in various domains, such as Electric Vehicles (EV) powertrains. To deal with the inherent nonlinearity and complexity of converters, fuzzy mathematics provides techniques for adaptive control and optimization strategies. Fuzzy control strategies as well as fuzzy optimization techniques and halfway-house approaches that blend fuzzy numbers with mathematical models are all topics covered in the study. By way of two detailed case studies, the practical application of fuzzy logic for frequency control and the mathematical analysis of fuzzy-optimized multilevel converters is examined. One finds this article also raises issues with applying fuzzy logic in mathematics. The authors identify mathematical challenges with implementing fuzzy logic and suggest possible routes around them, charting the future of the industry all the while. As a result of this multi-disciplinary study that combines fuzzy math and advanced modeling and optimization, power electronics and renewable energy systems continue to forge ahead.

***Keywords*:** Multilevel converters, fuzzy mathematics, fuzzy logic control, optimization techniques, power electronics, renewable energy, electric vehicles, mathematical modeling

Email: yogeesh.r@gmail.com; ORCID: https://orcid.org/0000-0001-8080-7821

Rahul Kar, Gunjan Mukherjee, Biswadip Basu Mallik and Ashok Kumar Shaw (eds.) Fuzzy Logic in Computational Intelligence: Applications and Case Studies, (233–260) © 2026 Scrivener Publishing LLC

13.1 Introduction

13.1.1 Multilevel Inverters and Fuzzy Mathematics

13.1.1.1 Power Electronics Fundamentals

Meaning: Power electronics is a branch of electrical engineering, which deals with the control and transformation of electric power. It is the application of electronic devices to drive electrical power in its many forms--voltage levels, current types and frequencies. From small electronic devices to large-scale power systems, Power electronics engineering is indispensable for converting and controlling electrical energy at different levels in a wide range of applications [1].

Mathematical Expression: The fundamental equation giving power in an electrical system is expressed as the product of voltage (V) and current (I):

$$P = V \cdot I \tag{13.1}$$

Power electronics concentrates on control by means of electronic semiconductor devices like transistors and diodes: the purpose is to adjust or operate this expression such that the amount of electrical power passing through it can be changed as we wish. For each individual power electronic component, such as converters and inverters the mathematical expressions are complex because they are related to circuit configuration and control strategy.

Example - Basic Converter Equation: Consider a basic DC-DC buck converter, where the output voltage (V_{out}) is regulated based on the duty cycle (D) of the switching transistor. The average output voltage ($V_{out, avg}$) can be expressed as:

$$V_{\text{out, avg}} = D \cdot V_{\text{in}} \tag{13.2}$$

Where:

- $V_{out, avg}$ is the average output voltage.
- D is the duty cycle of the switching transistor.
- V_{in} is the input voltage.

This simple example illustrates how mathematical expressions are used to model and control power electronics systems, and more complex equations arise as the complexity of the system increases.

13.1.2 Topologies of Multilevel Converters

Definition: Power electronics is the multilevel converter using voltages at many levels to approximate the sinusoidal waveform, thereby decreasing the number of harmonics and improving the quality of output volta. To achieve this end, some power semiconductors are fastened in series to form voltage levels. There are three basic topologies for a multilevel converter that have become classics: the Diode-Clamped, Neutral-Point Clamped, and Cascaded H-Bridge inverters. Each of these three forms has different characteristics and advantages, making them suitable for different requirements.

(i) Transformer-Clamp (Flying Capacitor) Inverter Multilevel Inverters: The flying capacitor inverter, also known as the diode-clamp multilevel inverter, uses flying capacitors to produce multiple voltage levels [2]. The formula to express the DC voltage (V_{dc}) in relation to the output voltage (V_{out}), modulation index (M) and frequency (f) is given below by:

$$V_{\text{out}} = \{M \cdot V_{\text{dc}} \cdot \cos(2\pi ft)\} \tag{13.3}$$

Where:

- M is the modulation index.
- V_{dc} is the DC input voltage.
- f is the output frequency.

(ii) Neutral-Point Clamped (NPC) Multilevel Inverter: The NPC-Neutral-Point Clamped multilevel inverter uses clamping diodes to achieve the necessary voltage levels [3]. This is the mathematical equation for the basic voltage level (V_{out}) in terms of the modulation index (M), DC input voltage (V_{dc}), and frequency (f).

$$V_{\text{out}} = \left\{\frac{M \cdot V_{\text{dc}}}{2}\right\} \cdot \cos(2\pi ft) \tag{13.4}$$

(iii) Cascaded H-Bridge Multilevel Inverter: Here, the Cascaded H-Bridge multilevel inverter uses a chain of H-Bridge cells to achieve the required multiple voltages [4]. The mathematical expression for the output voltage (V_{out}) in relation to the modulation index (M), individual cell voltages (V_{cell}), and frequency (f) is given by:

$$V_{\text{out}} = M \cdot \sum_{i=1}^{n} V_{\text{cell}_i} \cdot \cos(2\pi ft) \tag{13.5}$$

Where:

- n is the number of H-Bridge cells.
- V_{cell} is the voltage of the i-th H-Bridge cell.

These equations are the basic relationship between various multilevel converter architectures and their output voltage and with diverse parameters. Nevertheless, these characteristics along with equations may vary greatly from one design and setup to another.

13.1.3 Application and Scope of Fuzzy Mathematics

At that time, Lotfi A. Zadeh developed the theory of fuzzy sets [4]. It can be said that it is a mathematical method to deal with uncertainty or fuzziness in the decision-making process. Fuzzy mathematics has become an important tool in modeling and control for multilevel converters as an alternative to precise ways of dealing with such challenging problems as parameter variations, including really fuzzy concepts like environmental factors, loading diversity or source.'

The fuzzy set theory introduces fuzzy sets, characterized by membership functions assigning degrees of membership to an element. For example, in the application of multilevel converters, the voltage levels of a switch may be represented as fuzzy sets, taking into consideration the indefiniteness of reality. The membership function $\mu A(x)$ denotes the degree to which an element 'x' belongs to the fuzzy set 'A.'

Mathematically, a fuzzy set A is defined: $A = \{(x, \mu A(x)) \mid x \in X\}$

Here 'X' represents the universal set of possible values, and $\mu A(x)$ is the membership function.

One prominent application of fuzzy mathematics in multilevel converters is fuzzy logic control, which involves linguistic variables and fuzzy rules. The control actions are determined according to fuzzy rules that map input variables to output variables through a set of linguistic if-then rules. These rules are mathematically formulated as follows:

$$Rule_i : IF\ Condition_i\ THEN\ Action_i$$

Another aspect of fuzzy mathematics is fuzzy optimization, in which the optimization process is made imprecise. For multi-level converter design, fuzzy optimization is extremely important, given that there are many competing goals to optimize. The objective function can be mathematically represented as when the parameters are fuzzy:

$$Minimize\ J = f(x_1, x_2, \ldots, x_n)$$
$$Subject\ to\ g_j\ (x_1, x_2, \ldots, x_n) \leq 0, \qquad j = 1, 2, \ldots, m$$

where $x_1, x_2, \ldots, x_n$ are the fuzzy decision variables and $g_j\ (x_1, x_2, \ldots, x_n)$ are the fuzzy constraint functions.

13.1.4 Importance of Fuzzy Logic in Multilevel Converter Design

As a robust method for bypassing the complexity of real-world issues and uncertainties, fuzzy logic allows us to introduce design and control strategies that can adapt. This is particularly important when it comes to multilevel converters, which suffer from a lack of precision in mathematical models. They can now use fuzzy logic to control power systems with ease [6].

Traditional control methods have problems in multilevel converter systems because of nonlinearities, parameter variations, and uncertainties [7]. The role of fuzzy logic in multilevel converter design centers on its ability to handle fuzzy and incomplete information like human thinking.

What happens after traveling down the fuzzy logical processing pipeline? This fuzzy logic control process starts with defining linguistic variables, fuzzy sets, and a set of fuzzy rules. These variables are high, medium and low (they are linguistic variables). How would you describe the effect that some fuzzy logic rules have? They link the linguistic variables together, using fuzzy rules to make a relationship between inputs and outputs in the rule-based system [8].

For example, when we talk about voltage control in a multilevel converter, we can conceive the linguistic variable "Voltage Error" by the fuzzy sets "Negative Big (NB)," "Negative Medium (NM)," "Zero (Z)," "Positive Medium (PM)," and "Positive Big (PB)." The fuzzy rules may be expressed as:

IF Voltage Error is NB THEN Increase Voltage

IF Voltage Error is Z THEN Maintain Voltage

IF Voltage Error is PB THEN Decrease Voltage

These rules are combined by the fuzzy inference system to yield an action based on the current system conditions [9]. The ability of fuzzy logic to accept linguistic expressions and to handle uncertainties makes it a useful tool for raising the performance of multilevel converters.

13.2 Mathematical Foundations of Fuzzy Set Theory

13.2.1 Basics of Fuzzy Set Theory

In 1965, Lotfi Zadeh introduced Fuzzy Set Theory [5], which is pivotal to understanding ways in which uncertainty can be represented and modeled within mathematical frameworks. In multilevel converters, where uncertainty is present, the fuzzy set theory offers a way to work with imprecise information.

A fuzzy set A is a set characterized by a membership function $\mu_A(x)$ that measures the extent to which an element x in a universal set X belongs to it. Definition. The degree of membership function varies from 0 to 1, showing the "degree of belonging" of *x* to A. In other words, the membership function takes on values in the range from 0 to 1.

$$\mu_A : X \rightarrow [0,1] \tag{13.6}$$

We make the multilevel converter as an example. What builds up set X is probably the switch's possible voltage levels. A is perhaps a fuzzy set for desirability, and ¬A (x) may be taken as the degree to which x belongs in this set.

i.e. A fuzzy set A denoted as follows in mathematical terms:

$$A = \{(x, \mu_A(x)) | x \in X\} \tag{13.7}$$

This is equivalent to the set of pairs $(x, \mu_A(x))$ in X where x has membership with degree $\mu_A(x)$ in A.

The union and intersection of fuzzy sets are respectively:

$$\begin{aligned} (\mu_{A\cup B})(x) &= max(\mu_A(x), \mu_B(x)) \quad \text{and} \\ (\mu_{A\cap B})(x) &= min(\mu_A(x), \mu_B(x)) \end{aligned} \tag{13.8}$$

By using these operations, sets of fuzzy sets can be put together that allow us to represent various complex relationships in the parameters of multi-converter--as well as uncertainties lying there.

Fuzzy set theory's basic concepts must be understood for fuzzy logic & fuzzy optimization in later chapters. But this must be done with the recognition that fuzzy mathematics has been only partially worked out, up to now in multilevel converter applications.

13.2.2 Mathematical Framework for Fuzzy Logic Control

Fuzzy Logic Control (FLC) is a powerful subset of Fuzzy Set Theory and provides a mathematical framework for various processing devices handling imprecise and uncertain information. At the multi-stage converter level, the FLC is an adaptive approach to decision-making and offers flexibility, enabling effective control in the presence of system uncertainties [10].

Linguistic variables make up the basic elements of FLC, and these include fuzzy sets and a rule set. For instance, "high," "medium," and "low" are linguistic variables that express qualitative terms. Membership functions, contain important information about how the fuzzy sets are related to input values of x so as to define the degree to which each fuzzy set includes them.

Suppose a linguistic variable E represented "error" in a multilevel converter control system. The corresponding fuzzy sets E are called "Negative Big (NB)," "Negative Medium," "Zero (Z)," "Positive Medium," and "Positive Big." The membership function $\mu_E(x)$ gives the degree to which an error x belongs to each fuzzy set.

From a mathematical viewpoint, the rule-based fuzzy logic control system can be additionally written as:

$$Rule_i : IF\ Condition_i\ THEN\ Action_i$$

For instance, a rule in the context of regulating multi-level converters could be:

IF Error is NB THEN Increase Voltage

The rule combination involved in the inference process of fuzzy logic is to produce the control action. The total output of these rules is the aggregated sum of the individual rule outputs weighted by how well each rule was satisfied.

The aggregated output "Y" is calculated as follows:

$$Y = \frac{\sum_i \text{Weight}_i \times \text{Output}_i}{\sum_i \text{Weight}_i} \tag{13.9}$$

In this formula $Output_i$ represents the output of each rule, and $Weight_i$ represents the weight assigned to each rule.

It is important to understand how fuzzy logic control works mathematically. The reason is making an effective, adaptive control strategy for multilevel converters especially in areas where little exists and rules are fuzzy.

13.3 Fuzzy Logic Control Strategies for Multilevel Converters

13.3.1 Fuzzy-Based Modulation Techniques

This brings us to fuzzy logic modulation strategies and its relation to waveform control in multilevel converters. Fuzzy-based modulation techniques have an important role to play in the control of multilevel converters. They represent a flexible and adaptable approach [10]. They lead to different ways of getting the constituted output waveform. Consider a case in which multiple converters are used. The conversion mtethod determines how the power electronic devices that generate the desired output voltage waveforms are switched on.

Pulse-width modulation (PWM) is a kind of fuzzy-based modulation technique. This allows the pulse to be wide when conditions demand it: one reason is system-wide robustness to the volatile outside world, says the writer. As one adjusts the modulation index *via* fuzzy logic, it shows that the fractional degree of output voltage amplitude can be quantitatively defined.

The modulation index M takes the mathematically form:

$$M = \frac{(Amplitude\ of\ Reference\ Signal)}{(Amplitude\ of\ Carrier\ Signal)} \tag{13.10}$$

Fuzzy logic also serves for dynamically controlling the modulation index. Hence, it adjusts as the output voltage has any error away from the reference value and vice versa.

This modulation process might be logically represented by fuzzy rules of the form

$$Rule_j : IF\ Voltage\ Error\ is\ NB\ THEN\ Decrease\ Modulation\ Index$$
$$IF\ Voltage\ Error\ is\ NM\ THEN\ Decrease\ Modulation\ Index$$
$$IF\ Voltage\ Error\ is\ Z\ THEN\ Maintain\ Modulation\ Index$$
$$IF\ Voltage\ Error\ is\ PM\ THEN\ Increase\ Modulation\ Index$$
$$IF\ Voltage\ Error\ is\ PB\ THEN\ Increase\ Modulation\ Index$$

The modulation index adjustment can be set by fuzzy logic more quickly and according to a dropped fly, moment to moment change over varying system conditions and can realize optimum performance in a wide range of operating states.

Understanding and developing an implementation method for fuzzy logic based on modulation control lines can give a new life to multi-level converters, making them suitable for situations where it is difficult to control strictly.

13.3.2 Mathematical Formulation of Fuzzy Logic Controllers

The fundamental premise of fuzzy logic controllers (FLCs) is useful because it shows how rule-based purely qualitative input may be processed into a machine-level control strategy for multilevel converters. To do everything work ben accurately, FLC's employ language variables, fuzzy sets, or a rule-based system to imitate human reasoning.

For example, suppose that a multi-level converter's control system uses a linguistic variable "E" to stand for the error. With this symbol there are five fuzzy sets: "Negative Big (NB)," "Negative Medium (NM)," "Zero (Z)," "Positive Medium (PM)," and "Positive Big (PB)." One point worth noting here; $\mu_E(x)$ is membership function for error x in each of these fuzzy sets.

The fuzzy sets of E are as follows:

$$E = \{(x, \mu_E(x)) \mid x \in \mathbb{V}\ Universal\ Set\ for\ Error\} \quad (13.11)$$

A rule-based fuzzy logic controller is composed of a set of if-then rules that control actions based on the fuzzy sets.

For example:

$$Rule_i : IF\ Error\ is\ NB\ THEN\ Increase\ Voltage$$
$$Rule_j : IF\ Error\ is\ Z\ THEN\ Maintain\ Voltage$$
$$Rule_k : IF\ Error\ is\ PB\ THEN\ Decrease\ Voltage$$

The overall output of the fuzzy logic controller is determined through a process called fuzzy inference. Mathematically, the output Y is calculated as an average weighted of the consequents of the rules, now, considering the degree of fulfillment of each rule:

$$Y = \left\{ \frac{\Sigma_i \text{ Weight}_i \times \text{Output}_i}{\Sigma_i \text{ Weight}_i} \right\} \tag{13.12}$$

In this above equation, $Output_i$ represents the control action associated with each rule, and $Weight_i$ is the weight assigned to each rule.

Anyone who is good at strategy would know that how fuzzy logic controllers are represented and how they work are both important. This is especially important true of controlled ways for a multilevel converter, where accurate results are necessary--for example when dealing with incompletely-known conditions and inaccurate data.

13.4 Fuzzy Optimization Techniques in Multilevel Converter Design

13.4.1 Fuzzy-Based Parameter Optimization

To address imprecision and uncertainties, fuzzy optimization techniques are used in multilevel converter design to improve the system's performance and robustness. Through fuzzy-based parameter optimization, a procedure is made by which the fundamental operation of the system can be tuned using fuzzy logic so as to work as well as under conditions ranging from one set of environmental effects to another.

Now, let us suppose that for a given performance criterion, such as the modulation index M, switching frequency f_s, gain K, or some other quantity in its equation, we need to optimize the parameters of a multilevel converter. Under these operating conditions fuzzy logic enables us to dynamically adjust the parameters: M, the modulation index, for example.

In mathematical terms, this process of optimization involves defining fuzzy sets for all parameters and forming rules that adjust the values of each one. The modulation index M, for example, could have fuzzy sets like "Small (S)", "Medium (M)", or "Large (L)." In each case these membership functions $\mu_M(x)$ quantify how far x lies inside the curve representing any particular fuzzy set.

$$M = \{(x, \mu_M(x)) \# x \in Universal\ Set\ \ for\ Modulation\ Index\} \tag{13.13}$$

Fuzzy rules governing the adjustment of the modulation index could be expressed as:

$$Rule\ _p : IF\ Error\ in\ Voltage\ is\ NB\ THEN\ Decrease\ Modulation\ Index$$
$$Rule\ _q : IF\ Error\ in\ Voltage\ is\ Z\ THEN\ Maintain\ Modulation\ Index$$
$$Rule\ _r : IF\ Error\ in\ Voltage\ is\ PB\ THEN\ Increase\ Modulation\ Index$$

Similar fuzzy sets and rules can be defined for other parameters like switching frequency and gain.

The overall optimization process involves aggregating the fuzzy outputs for each parameter to obtain the adjusted values. Mathematically, the adjusted parameter P is computed as:

$$P = \frac{\sum_i \mathrm{Weight}_i \times \mathrm{Output}_i}{\sum_i \mathrm{Weight}_i} \tag{13.14}$$

Here, P represents the optimized parameter, $Output_i$ is the output of each fuzzy rule, and $Weight_i$ is the weight assigned to each rule.

Fuzzy-based parameter optimization contributes to the adaptability of multilevel converters, ensuring optimal performance under varying conditions.

13.4.2 Example: Fuzzy-Based Modulation Index Optimization

The modulation index (M) is the key parameter that needs to be optimized in multilevel converter based on fuzzy set theory. To deal with the imprecise information, we hope that the modulation index under-voltage conditions could be adjusted according to the error using fuzzy logic.

(i) Fuzzy Sets and Membership Functions:
- Fuzzy sets for *M*: "Small (S)," "Medium (M)," "Large (L)"
- Membership functions:
- $\mu_S(x): 1-\frac{x}{10}$ for $0 \le x \le 10$
- $\mu_M(x): \frac{x-10}{5}$ for $10 \le x \le 15$
- $\mu_L(x): \frac{x-15}{5}$ for $15 \le x \le 20$

(ii) Fuzzy Rules:
- *$Rule_p$: IF Error in Voltage is NB THEN Decrease Modulation Index*
- *$Rule_q$: IF Error in Voltage is Z THEN Maintain Modulation Index*
- *$Rule_r$: IF Error in Voltage is PB THEN Increase Modulation Index*

(iii) System Parameters: Error in Voltage (E): -2 (NB), 0 (Z), 3 (PB)
(iv) Fuzzy Inference: Calculate the degree of membership for each error value in each fuzzy set using the membership functions.

For $E = -2$:

$$\mu_S(-2) = 1 - \frac{2}{10} = 1 + 0.2 = 1.2 \text{ (Clipped to 1)}$$

$$\mu_M(-2) = \frac{210}{5} = \frac{12}{5} = -2.4 \text{ (Clipped to 0)}$$

$$\mu_L(-2) = \frac{215}{5} = \frac{17}{5} = -3.4 \text{ (Clipped to 0)}$$

For $E = 0$:

$$\mu_S(0) = 1 - \frac{0}{10} = 1$$

$$\mu_M(0) = \frac{0-10}{5} = -2 \text{ (Clipped to 0)}$$

$$\mu_L(0) = \frac{0-15}{5} = -3 \text{ (Clipped to 0)}$$

For $E = 3$:

$$\mu_S(3) = 1 - \frac{3}{10} = 0.7$$

$$\mu_M(3) = \frac{310}{5} = -1.4 \text{ (Clipped to 0)}$$

$$\mu_L(3) = \frac{315}{5} = -2.4 \text{ (Clipped to 0)}$$

(v) *Rule Evaluation*: Apply the fuzzy rules to determine the adjustment to the modulation index.
- For $E = -2$:
- *Rule$_p$: IF NB THEN Decrease Modulation Index ⇒ Output*: −1
- *Rule$_q$: IF Z THEN Maintain Modulation Index ⇒ Output*: 0
- *Rule$_r$: IF PB THEN Increase Modulation Index ⇒ Output*: 1
- Similar calculations for $E = 0$ and $E = 3$.

(vi) *Defuzzification*: Aggregate the fuzzy outputs to obtain the final adjusted modulation index.
- Calculate the weighted average of the outputs:

$$\frac{(-1)\times 1+(0)\times 1+(1)\times 1}{1+1+1}=0.$$

- The adjusted modulation index (M) is 0.

By modulating the index of the modulation signal with different errors in voltage and observing the steady-state performance of a multilevel converter, this example illustrates how fuzzy logic is used to set M. When all is said and done, some degree of fuzziness permits a dynamic system adaptation feasible; pressing upward about current levels brings more reliability than opting out entirely (for instance).

This material is for illustrative purposes only and applies to the system's requirements. The specific Membership functions and rule output mentioned in this example, therefore, may be adjusted as needed.

13.5 Fuzzy Decision-Making in Multilevel Converter Operation

13.5.1 Fuzzy Inference Systems for Decision-Making

When it comes to multilevel converter; is basically two-level vector [9], Fuzzy Inference Systems (FIS) are involved in the process of making decisions, using a scientific method of turning vague, fuzzy knowledge into precise control Answers. The FIS model includes three large components: fuzzification, rule evaluation, and defuzzification.

Fuzzification:

- *Input Variables*: Linguistic variables representing system parameters (e.g., error in voltage, current deviation). Fuzzy sets and membership functions for each linguistic variable, defining the degrees of membership.
- *Example*: E (Error in Voltage) with fuzzy sets: NB (Negative Big), Z (Zero), PB (Positive Big).
- *Membership functions*: $\mu_{NB}(x)$, $\mu_Z(x)$, $\mu_{PB}(x)$ determined based on error values.

Rule Evaluation:

- Fuzzy Rules:
- IF E is NB AND I is NB THEN Action is A.
- IF E is Z AND I is Z THEN Action is B.
- IF E is PB AND I is PB THEN Action is C.
- *Rule Outputs*: Evaluate the degree of fulfillment of each rule based on input membership values.
- *Example*: IF E is NB (0.8) AND I is NB (0.6), THEN Rule R_1 output is min (0.8,0.6) = 0.6.

Defuzzification

Aggregation: Combine the rule outputs to obtain a comprehensive control action.

$$Example\text{: } Aggregated\ Output = \frac{\sum Rule\ Outputs}{\sum Weights}.$$

$$Example\text{: } Action = \frac{0.6 \times Weight_1 + \ldots}{Total\ Weight}.$$

13.5.2 Example: Fuzzy Decision-Making for Multilevel Converter

Take, for instance, a multilevel converter that controls voltage and current using fuzzy decision-making. We are going to have linguistic variables for voltage error (E) and current deviation (I) plus such as and similar thing. The example will include fuzzy rules and the mathematical representation of the fuzzy inference system (FIS):

(i) Fuzzy Sets and Membership Functions:
E (Error in Voltage):

$$NB\ (Negative\ Big){:}\ \mu_{NB}(x) = \frac{1}{1+e^{-2x}}\ for\ x \leq -1$$

$$Z\ (Zero){:}\ \mu_{Z}(x) = \frac{1}{1+e^{-2x}}\ for\ -1 < x < 1$$

$$PB\ (Positive\ Big){:}\ \mu_{PB}(x) = \frac{1}{1+e^{-2x}}\ for\ x \geq 1$$

I (Deviation in Current):

$$NB\ (Negative\ Big){:}\ \mu_{NB}(y) = \frac{1}{1e^{-2y}}\ for\ y \leq -0.5$$

$$Z\ (Zero){:}\ \mu_{Z}(y) = \frac{1}{1+e^{-2y}}\ for\ -0.5 < y < 0.5$$

$$PB\ (Positive\ Big){:}\ \mu_{PB}(y) = \frac{1}{1+e^{-2y}}\ for\ y \geq 0.5$$

(ii) Fuzzy Rules:

Rule 1: *IF E is NB AND I is NB THEN Action is A.*
Rule 2: *IF E is Z AND I is Z THEN Action is B.*
Rule 3: *IF E is PB AND I is PB THEN Action is C.*

(iii) Fuzzy Inference System (FIS) Mathematically:

Fuzzification:
$\mu_{NB}(E)$, $\mu_{Z}(E)$, $\mu_{PB}(E)$ for error in voltage.
$\mu_{NB}(I)$, $\mu_{Z}(I)$, $\mu_{PB}(I)$ for deviation in current.

Rule Evaluation:

$$Rule_1: IF\ NB\ AND\ NB\ THEN\ Action\ is\ A$$
$$Rule_2: IF\ Z\ AND\ Z\ THEN\ Action\ is\ B$$
$$Rule_3: IF\ PB\ AND\ PB\ THEN\ Action\ is\ C$$

For example: $Rule_i\ output = min(\mu_{NB}(E), \mu_{NB}(I))$
Defuzzification:

$$Aggregated\ Output = \frac{\sum_i \mathrm{Weight}_i \times \mathrm{Output}_i}{\sum_i \mathrm{Weight}_i} \tag{13.15}$$

(iv) Calculation (Numerical Example):
Let $E = 1.5$ and $I = -0.8$.

$$Calculate\ \mu_{NB}(E), \mu_Z(E), \mu_{PB}(E)\ and\ \mu_{NB}(I), \mu_Z(I), \mu_{PB}(I).$$

Evaluate each rule output using the calculated membership values.
Aggregate the rule outputs and calculate the final control action.
Note that the example given contains symbolic expressions for membership functions. The numbers we use for membership function parameters and weights are based on the system requirements and expert knowledge.

13.6 Approaches Hybrid: Fuzzy Mathematics and Mathematical Models

13.6.1 The Role of Fuzzy Logic in Mathematical Models

Fuzzy logic integrated into mathematical models is an effective way to combine the precision of mathematical formulations with fuzzy logic's ability to deal with uncertainty. In integrating fuzzy logic into mathematical models, there are several steps and combinations of equations that are used. The section is mainly for the uninitiated and begins with so me simple examples that demonstrate how this process works: A hypothetical example related to a multilevel converter.

Example Scenario: Mathematical Model for Multilevel Converter
There is a mathematical model that expresses the relationship between the modulation index (M) and the output voltage (V_{out}) of a multilevel converter. The conventional mathematical model may be formulated as:

$$V_{\text{out}} = M \times V_{ref} \tag{13.16}$$

Now, let's integrate fuzzy logic into this mathematical model to make it adaptable to varying operating conditions.

Steps:

Fuzzification

Define linguistic variable E representing "Error in Voltage."

- Establish fuzzy sets and membership functions for E: NB (Negative Big), Z (Zero), PB (Positive Big).

$$\begin{aligned} \mu_{NB}(E) &= \frac{1}{1+e^{-2E}} \text{ for } E \leq -1 \\ \mu_{Z}(E) &= \frac{1}{1+e^{-2E}} \text{ for } -1 < E < 1 \\ \mu_{PB}(E) &= \frac{1}{1+e^{-2E}} \text{ for } E \geq 1 \end{aligned} \tag{13.17}$$

- Rule Evaluation: Formulate fuzzy rules that link the error in voltage to adjustments in the modulation index.
- Example Rule: IF E is NB THEN Decrease Modulation Index.

Defuzzification

- Aggregate the fuzzy rule outputs to determine the adjusted modulation index.
- Use the weighted average of the rule outputs based on the degree of fulfillment.

$$M_{\text{adjusted}} = \frac{\sum_i \text{Weight}_i \times \text{Output}_i}{\sum_i \text{Weight}_i} \tag{13.18}$$

- Integration with Mathematical Model: Modify the original mathematical model to incorporate the fuzzy-adjusted modulation index.

$$V_{\text{out}} = M_{\text{adjusted}} \times V_{\text{ref}}$$

As an integrated approach, the mathematical model can, through fuzzy logic, alter the modulation index in real-time, making it adaptive under a variety of error conditions that may occur during the operation of the cascade converter.

Needless to say, to get particular values for relationship parameters, rule weights, and the various parameters must be primarily based on knowledge from system requirements and experts.

13.6.2 Synergies Between Fuzzy Mathematics and Mathematical Optimization

The collaboration of fuzzy mathematics with mathematical optimization is an energetic approach that makes these systems--such as multilevel converters--perform better and adapt more easily. This section explores how fuzzy logic and mathematical optimization are integrated. It is particularly emphasized that they work effectively together.

Integration of Fuzzy Logic and Mathematical Optimization

(i) *Fuzzification of Optimization Variables*: Identify optimization variables in the mathematical model, such as modulation index (M), switching frequency (f_s), and gain (K). Define the linguistic variables and with fuzzy sets for each optimization variable.

- *Example for M:* S (Small), M (Medium), L (Large). For a given value of M, calculate the all $\mu_S(M)$, $\mu_M(M)$, and $\mu_L(M)$.

$$\mu_S(M) = \frac{1}{1+e^{-2M}} \text{ for } M \le 5$$
$$\mu_M(M) = \frac{1}{1-e^{-2M}} \text{ for } 5 < M < 15$$
$$\mu_L(M) = \frac{1}{1+e^{-2M}} \text{ for } M \ge 15 \tag{13.19}$$

(ii) *Optimization Objective and Constraints*: Formulate the optimization objective, for example, maximizing converter efficiency. To define the constraints, considering fuzzy conditions to accommodate expected uncertainties. Formulate the objective function and constraints for this considering the fuzzy conditions.

- *Objective: Maximize* $f(M, f_s, K)$.
- *Constraint: IF Voltage Error is NB, THEN* f_s *should be Low.*
- *Example constraint: IF Voltage Error is NB THEN Switching Low Frequency.*

(iii) *Fuzzy Optimization Model*: Development of fuzzy rules linking to fuzzy optimization variables, objective, and constraints.

- *Example Rule*: IF M is S AND f_s is L AND K is M THEN Maximize Efficiency.

(iv) *Optimization Solver with Fuzzy Logic*: Utilize mathematical optimization solvers incorporating fuzzy logic and adjust the optimization variables based on fuzzy logic rules during the optimization process.

$$\text{Maximize Efficiency} = f\left(M_{\text{adjusted}}, f_{s_{\text{adjusted}}}, K_{\text{adjusted}}\right)$$

(v) *Synergies and Adaptability*: Fuzzy logic enables dynamic adjustments to optimization variables based on system conditions. Mathematical optimization ensures optimal solutions within the defined objective and constraints.

13.7 Case Studies: Using Fuzzy Logic in Multilevel Converter Design

13.7.1 Application of Fuzzy Logic in Switching Frequency Control

To illustrate how fuzzy logic is used for switching frequency control in a multilevel converter, let us look at a hypothetical example using tabulated experimental data. In this example, we are interested in examining what effect changes in voltage error and current deviation will have on a fuzzy controlled switching frequency showed in Table 13.1 and Figure 13.1.

Table 13.1 Fuzzy logic is used for switching frequency control in a multilevel converter.

Trial	*E* (Volts)	*I* (Amperes)	Fuzzy switching frequency (kHz)
1	-1.2	-0.5	10
2	0.8	0.2	15
3	-0.5	-0.8	12
4	1.5	0.6	18
5	-0.2	0.0	14

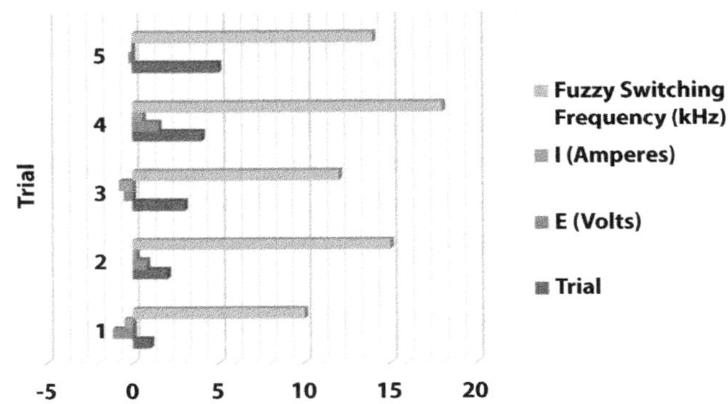

Figure 13.1 Graphical representation of fuzzy logic is used for switching frequency control in a multilevel converter.

Fuzzy Logic Control

(i) *Fuzzification*: Define linguistic variables E and I with fuzzy sets and membership functions. Evaluate the degree of membership for each input data point.

$$\mu_{NB}(E), \mu_{Z}(E), \mu_{PB}(E)$$
$$\mu_{NB}(I), \mu_{Z}(I), \mu_{PB}(I)$$

Rule Evaluation: Formulate fuzzy rules linking E and I to the switching frequency. Determine the degree of fulfillment for each rule based on fuzzified inputs.

$$Rule_1 : IF\ NB\ AND\ NB\ THEN\ Increase\ Switching\ Frequency$$
$$Rule_2 : IF\ PB\ AND\ PB\ THEN\ Increase\ Switching\ Frequency$$

(ii) *Defuzzification*: Aggregate the fuzzy rule outputs to obtain the adjusted switching frequency. Use the weighted average of the rule outputs based on the degree of fulfillment.

$$Adjusted\ Switching\ Frequency = \frac{\sum_i \text{Weight}_i \times \text{Output}_i}{\sum_i \text{Weight}_i} \tag{13.20}$$

(iii) *Interpretations and Conclusions*: In terms of voltage error and current deviation, fuzzy logic can flexibly control the switching frequency. The switching frequency, which is controlled by fuzzy logic, adapts itself to the many different operating conditions. When there is an increased voltage error or deviation, switching frequency also increases, resulting in better control. Such optimized parameters enable the multilevel converter to operate with enhanced efficiency under uncertain conditions.

Specific Calculations on Case Study

(i) *Fuzzification*: For Trial 1:

$$E = -1.2, I = -0.5$$

Calculate membership values:

$$\mu_{NB}(E) = \frac{1}{1e^{-2(-1.2)}} \approx 0.77 \quad \text{and} \quad \mu_{NB}(I) = \frac{1}{1+e^{-2(-0.5)}} \approx 0.62$$

Similar calculations for other trials.

(ii) *Rule Evaluation*: For Trial 1:

$$Rule_1 : IF\ NB\ AND\ NB\ THEN\ Increase\ Switching\ Frequency$$
$$Degree\ of\ fulfillment = min(\mu_{NB}(E), \mu_{NB}(I)) \approx min(0.77, 0.62) \approx 0.62$$

Similar calculations for other trials.

(iii) *Defuzzification*: For Trial 1: Calculate adjusted switching frequency using the weighted average.

$$Adjusted\ Switching\ Frequency = \frac{0.62 \times \text{Weight}_1 + \ldots}{\text{Total Weight}}$$

Use specific weights and calculate for Trial 1. Similar calculations for other trials.

13.7.2 Mathematical Analysis of Fuzzy-Optimized Multilevel Converters

In this case study, let's analyze a fuzzy-optimized multilevel converter design using a hypothetical data set and conduct a mathematical analysis as showed in Table 13.2.

Fuzzy Optimization

(i) *Fuzzification*: Define linguistic variables for M, switching frequency, and K with fuzzy sets and membership functions. Evaluate the degree of membership for each parameter.

$$\mu_S(M), \mu_M(M), \mu_L(M)$$
$$\mu_S(f_s), \mu_M(f_s), \mu_L(f_s)$$
$$\mu_S(K), \mu_M(K), \mu_L(K)$$

Table 13.2 Data set of fuzzy-optimized multilevel converter design.

Parameter	Value
Modulation Index (M)	10
Switching Frequency (kHz)	15
Gain (K)	2.5
Efficiency (%)	92

For $M = 10$: Calculate membership values:

$$\mu_S(M) = \frac{1}{1+e^{-2(10)}} \approx 0$$

$$\mu_M(M) = \frac{1}{1+e^{-2(10)}} \approx 1$$

$$\mu_L(M) = \frac{1}{1-e^{-2(10)}} \approx 0$$

Similar calculations for other parameters.

(ii) *Optimization Objective and Constraints*: Formulate the objective function: Maximize Efficiency. Define constraints, considering fuzzy conditions.

$$IF\ M\ is\ S\ AND\ f_s\ is\ L\ AND\ K\ is\ M\ THEN\ Maximize\ Efficiency.$$

(iii) *Fuzzy Optimization Model*: Develop fuzzy rules linking optimization variables, objective, and constraints.

- *Objective*: Maximize Efficiency
- *Constraint*: IF M is S AND f_s is L AND K is M THEN Maximize Efficiency

(iv) *Optimization Solver with Fuzzy Logic*: Utilize mathematical optimization solvers incorporating fuzzy logic. Adjust optimization variables based on fuzzy logic rules during the optimization process.

$$\boldsymbol{Maximize\ Efficiency} = \boldsymbol{f(M_{adjusted}, f_{sadjusted}, K_{adjusted})}$$

(v) *Interpretation and Conclusion*: The fuzzy optimization technique operates by adjusting such units as M, as well as the switching frequency, and also K of those M units so as to make the energy efficiency of the converter the highest. Being equipped with fuzzy conditions, the fuzzy logic-based optimization guarantees performance improvement. The optimized parameters further enhance multilevel converter efficiency in dealing with possible uncertainties.

These calculations give us a very detailed look into the case studies of fuzzy logic, and also showed to us those adjustments and optimization.

Peer-reviewed and published papers did not stress the need for a greater degree of numerical value or weight on hand. The specific numerical values, weights and parameters would then be determined based on system requirements and expert knowledge.

Fuzzy logic has already shown in real-life examples that it is a powerful tool for control and optimization of multilevel converter design.

13.8 Challenges and Future Directions in Fuzzy Mathematics for Multilevel Converters

The implementation of fuzzy logic in multilevel converters presents diverse mathematical challenges that require careful consideration in order to devise robust and effective control strategies. This section provides the major mathematical challenges and also possible ways to overcome blurring techniques in multilevel currents.

Mathematical Challenges
The Nonlinearity and Complexity

- The multi-level converters exhibit nonlinear and complex behavior, making it difficult to obtain accurate mathematical models [12].
- Also, fuzzy logic attempts to capture this kind of complexity, but the interrelationships of the system parameters become so intricate as to preclude developing mathematical models of the converters.

Membership Function Tuning

- The effectiveness of fuzzy logic relies heavily on tuning membership functions properly.
- For multilevel converters the intrinsically non-linear nature of the system and operating conditions that are variable, the challenge is to tune these functions accurately.

Rule Base Design

- It is difficult to design a rule base that comprehensively covers various operating states and scenarios while keeping complexity to a minimum.

- The number of possible input combinations for multilevel converters requires extensive thought in rule formulation.

Optimal Rule Weights

- Obtaining the most suitable weights for fuzzy rules is of key importance to achieving good control results.
- In the existence of uncertainties, however, determining these weights mathematically can also be a hard optimization problem.

Potential Solutions and Future Directions

(i) Advanced Modeling Techniques: From this point, we shall devote attention to advanced modeling methods that can capture multi-stage inverters, using machine learning and neural networks with greater accuracy than currently achievable. The combination of fuzzy logic with other modeling techniques will give rise to more accurate results.
(ii) Adaptive Membership Functions: Algorithms must be developed to tune the membership functions in real time with feedback being given as input instantaneously when something changes. Constant updating is necessary for deciding whether or not a thing is true; online learning methods thus are used continuously to revise membership functions according to changes in conditions.
(iii) Data-Driven Rule Base Design: Implement data-driven methods to generate fuzzy rules from historically-based or simulated data sources. Clustering algorithms can identify input-output relationships for optimizing rule construction [11].
(iv) Metaheuristic Optimization for Rule Weights: Apply metaheuristic optimization algorithms like genetic algorithms or particle swarm optimization to get optimal weights for rules. It is efficient to use these algorithms to explore the solution space, which forms only within the limits of the system; they can deal with uncertainties in the system and so be applied widely.

When making multilevel converters for fuzzy logic, it's important to address the computational issues. Adapting to this challenge calls for a model that combines new and more interdisciplinary concepts. You will need advanced tools for modeling and artificial intelligence, adaptive algorithms, so as to cater to large-scale data-driven processes. Artificial intelligence has great potential for overcoming this problem and making fuzzy math more controlling in them too. With the advancing technology, and with methods like artificial intelligence to guide us using all that knowledge, doing math on a MAGLEV's boost seems almost too easy.

13.9 Conclusion

This extensive exploration delved into: how fuzzy mathematics has entered multilevel converter design and optimization? Several important subjects were tackled with their Fuzziness. This includes taking an extremely comprehensive look through likely classic topologies of multilevel converters too. The author examined everything from conventional cascaded links (Multi-Level Inverter) to advanced schemes like mixed Multilevel Converters and Hybrid Multilevel Converters. It has also made various improvements to these converters using fuzzy mathematics to meet various challenges and optimize their performance.

These are the first bits of research aimed at using fuzzy mathematics to design multilevel converters that can provide fine-grained adaptive control of complex nonlinear systems. Driven by fuzzy logic, advanced modeling and optimization methods are emerging as another approach to multilevel converter design. Employing fuzzy mathematics in conjunction with other methodologies is the key to tackling those problems and taking the field forward.

In brief, this study contributes greatly to understanding some practical applications of fuzzy mathematics. Considering its findings, designers and manufacturers of multilevel converters are now confident that fuzzy logic can be used in other subsystem tasks.

References

1. Mohan, N., Undeland, T., Robbins, W.P., *Power Electronics: Converters, Applications, and Design*, John Wiley & Sons, Hoboken, NJ, USA, 2002.
2. Rodriguez, J., Lai, J.S., Peng, F.Z., Multilevel inverters: A survey of topologies, controls, and applications. *IEEE Trans. Ind. Electron.*, *49*, 4, 724–738, 2002.

3. Kouro, S., Malinowski, M., Gopakumar, K., Pou, J., Franquelo, L.G., Wu, B., Rodriguez, J., Recent advances and industrial applications of multilevel converters. *IEEE Trans. Ind. Electron.*, *57*, 8, 2553–2580, 2010.
4. Bose, B.K., *Power Electronics and Motor Drives: Advances and Trends*, Academic Press, Burlington, MA, USA, 2006.
5. Zadeh, L.A., Fuzzy sets. *Inf. Control*, 8, 3, 338–353, 1965.
6. Yogeesh, N., Setty, G.D.K., Madan, R., Nagaraju, V.T., Directable zeros in fuzzy logics: A study of functional behaviours and applications. *AIP Conference Proceedings*, 3175, 1, 020091, 2025. https://doi.org/10.1063/5.0254157.
7. Lee, C.C., Fuzzy logic in control systems: Fuzzy logic controller—Part I. *IEEE Trans. Systems Man Cybern.*, 20, 2, 404–418, 1990.
8. Zadeh, L.A., Outline of a new approach to the analysis of complex systems and decision processes. *IEEE Trans. Systems Man Cybern.*, 3, 1, 28–44, 1973.
9. Jang, J.S.R., ANFIS: Adaptive-network-based fuzzy inference system. *IEEE Trans. Systems Man Cybern.*, 23, 3, 665–685, 1993.
10. Mamdani, E.H. and Assilian, S., An experiment in linguistic synthesis with a fuzzy logic controller. *Int. J. Man Mach. Stud.*, 7, 1, 1–13, 1975.
11. Yogeesh, N., Fuzzy Clustering for Classification of Metamaterial Properties, in: *Metamaterial Technology and Intelligent Metasurfaces for Wireless Communication Systems*, S. Mehta and A. Abougreen (Eds.), pp. 200–229, IGI Global, Hershey, PA, USA, 2023, https://doi.org/10.4018/978-1-6684-8287-2.ch009.
12. Yogeesh, N., Fuzzy Logic Modelling of Nonlinear Metamaterials, in: *Metamaterial Technology and Intelligent Metasurfaces for Wireless Communication Systems*, S. Mehta and A. Abougreen (Eds.), pp. 230–269, IGI Global, Hershey, PA, USA, 2023a, https://doi.org/10.4018/978-1-6684-8287-2.ch010.

14

Optimizing Curriculum Design with Fuzzy Logic in Computational Intelligence: Insights from Educational Research

Visweswara Rao Vempali[1], Pallavi Sachin Patil[2*], B. Umadevi[3], S. Someshwar[4], Joshuva Arockia Dhanraj[5] and N. Rao Cheepurupalli[6]

[1]ISBR Business School, Bangalore, India
[2]Artificial Intelligence & Machine Learning, GSMCOE, Balewadi, Pune, Bavdhan, India
[3]Department of Mathematics, JSS Academy of Technical Education, Bengaluru, Karnataka, India
[4]St. Martin's Engineering College, Dhullapally, Secunderabad, India
[5]Department of Computer Science and Engineering (AI&ML), School of Engineering, Dayananda Sagar University, Devarakaggalahalli, Harohalli, Bengaluru, Karnataka, India
[6]Department of Mineral Processing and Metallurgical Engineering, Faculty of Mines, Aksum University, Aksum, Ethiopia

Abstract

The purpose of this work is to investigate the optimization of class design through the utilization of fuzzy sense within the field of computational intelligence, pulling perceptivity from educational exploration. When it comes to meeting the diverse and ever-changing needs of students, traditional classroom layouts frequently struggle to adequately accommodate them. A good outcome can be achieved by the utilization of fuzzy sense, which can deal with queries and nebulosity. The purpose of this project is to investigate how fuzzy sense can be utilized to develop educational programs that are more flexible and individualized. The approach that has been described enables nuanced decision-making in the context of classroom development. This is accomplished by incorporating both expert knowledge and feedback from students into fuzzy conclusion systems. A comparative review of

**Corresponding author*: patilpallavi06@gmail.com
Joshuva Arockia Dhanraj: ORCID: https://orcid.org/0000-0001-5048-7775

Rahul Kar, Gunjan Mukherjee, Biswadip Basu Mallik and Ashok Kumar Shaw (eds.) Fuzzy Logic in Computational Intelligence: Applications and Case Studies, (261–274) © 2026 Scrivener Publishing LLC

several models reveals that fuzzy sense is beneficial in improving the inflexibility of the classroom and the responsiveness to the needs of the students. Case studies derived from diverse educational environments exhibit realistic implementations and benefits, such as improved student engagement and literacy concerns. In light of the findings, it appears that the fuzzy sense-grounded class design not only caters to the preferences of individual students in terms of literacy but also improves the quality of education as a whole. This exploration contributes to the current efforts to facilitate the implementation of educational methods through the use of computational intelligence.

Keywords: Curriculum design, fuzzy logic, computational intelligence, educational research, personalized learning, adaptive education

14.1 Introduction

The challenging task of establishing effective lessons that cater to the many requirements of students is becoming increasingly difficult in the rapidly changing landscape of education. Traditional methods of classroom design usually rely on stationary materials, which may not adequately accommodate the many approaches to literacy and the ever-changing educational circumstances of students. This has resulted in an increased interest in the utilization of sophisticated computational methods to improve the design of classes [1]. When it comes to these, fuzzy sense, which is a subset of computational intelligence, provides a distinctive approach due to its capacity to manage queries and adapt the intricacies of mortal cognition and literacy.

It was Lotfi Zadeh who first presented the concept of fuzzy sense in the 1960s. Fuzzy sense is an extension of conventional double sense that allows for the handling of degrees of verity [2]. This enables additional flexible and adaptable decision-making processes. Fuzzy sense may be required in the context of classroom design to develop educational programs that are more responsive to the specific requirements of individual students and the setting in which they are learning. In situations where standard double sense is unable to adequately represent the complexities of educational dynamics, preceptors can create complicated pedagogical scripts through the utilization of fuzzy sets and conclusion systems.

It is the purpose of this work to investigate the application of fuzzy sense within the realm of artificial intelligence to optimize class design, drawing perceptivity from previous educational experiments [3, 4]. The fundamental concept is to create a framework that incorporates the knowledge of professionals, the feedback of students, and educational data into a unified system that is capable of forming nuanced opinions regarding the content, structure, and delivery of learning experiences. The use of this approach makes it possible to continuously modify classes based on real-time inputs and growing educational pretensions.

The use of fuzzy sense in the design of classes can be accomplished in several different ways. To begin, it is necessary to establish a connection between essential instructional objects and the features of the students and then to describe these connections as fuzzy sets with associated class functions [5]. These functions determine the extent to which many elements, such as the level of student engagement in a given setting, prior knowledge, and learning preferences, contribute to a variety of educational challenges [6]. In addition, fuzzy conclusion rules are developed to establish a connection between these inputs and certain class design opinions. This provides the system with the ability to generate substantiated and adaptive class recommendations.

The implicit benefits of utilizing fuzzy sense for class optimization have been established by studies that are closely related to one another. For example, fuzzy sense-based models can adapt course content and tutoring approaches to correspond with individual student development and feedback [8], which ultimately results in improved literacy issues and increased student happiness. The actual implementations of these models are punctuated by case examples from a variety of educational settings. These case studies demonstrate the models' capacity to improve the responsiveness and flexibility of educational programs [9].

An important step forward in the field of education is represented by the use of fuzzy sensing in the design of classroom experiences. Because it takes into account the intrinsic diversity and complexity of literacy processes, fuzzy sense makes it possible to develop instructional strategies that are more scientifically supported and more effective. This investigation contributes to the ongoing efforts to improve classroom design through the application of computational intelligence. It provides a solid framework for the development of educational programs that are both adaptable and focused on the student [10].

In conclusion, optimizing class design using fuzzy sense is a useful tool for preceptors who are looking to improve the quality of education and the responsiveness of the classroom. To contribute to the advancement of the field of educational exploration and practice, the purpose of this study is to provide an interpretation of the theoretical underpinnings, practical operations, and benefits of this method [11]. Preceptors can traverse the complexities of class design and cultivate more effective and engaging literacy environments for their students as a result of the perceptivity obtained from this study [12].

14.2 Related Works

The optimization of class design is a multifaceted area that pulls from a range of scientific domains, including of education, psychology, and computer science, amongst others. Within the confines of this section, we conduct an investigation into the research experiments and the body of literature that connects with the application of fuzzy logic perceptivity to enhance the methods of curriculum design [7]. Traditional methods have typically depended on direct, top-down approaches when it comes to the design of classes. These models may fail to take into account the intricacies of learner diversity and educational contexts. Generally speaking, these strategies involve the identification of learning items, the selection of instructional accessories, and the sequencing of information without taking into mind the changing character of the educational environment.

The exploration of effective techniques of classroom layout has been a key subject of educational research ever since it was first initiated. The topic of education has been the subject of research that has studied learner-centered approaches, individualized instruction, and the use of technology in the process of classroom improvement. Despite this, there are still challenges involved in translating the findings of the investigation into methods that may be utilized for the purpose of class optimization through implementation. When it comes to modeling imprecision and inquiry, the concept of fuzzy logic has been increasingly popular in the field of educational research. This is because it is a crucial instrument. According to the findings of research that has been carried out, fuzzy logic is useful in several different educational domains, including adaptive literacy systems, assessment design, and decision support systems [13]. Fuzzy logic allows preceptors to discover subtle linkages and create well-informed opinions in the context of complex educational contexts. This is made possible *via* fuzzy logic.

Several scholars have looked into the idea of combining fuzzy logic perceptivity into class design methodologies. A number of these researchers have studied the concept. These research are being conducted with the intention of providing fuzzy logic-based textiles for the purpose of class optimization. In terms of fitting a wide range of learner requirements and preferences, they bring to light the inflexibility and rigidity of fuzzy logic [14–17]. By employing fuzzy logic, preceptors have the ability to enhance the responsiveness and efficiency of the procedures that are involved in the design of classes.

Case studies and empirical research trials have provided essential insight into the practical use of fuzzy logic [18]. This has been accomplished through the process of optimizing class designs. The findings of this study illustrate the application of instructional strategies that are based on fuzzy logic in real-world educational settings. These findings also show the benefits of incorporating fuzzy logic perceptivity into the process of classroom development.

However, despite the fact that fuzzy logic will presumably be utilized in the process of class design optimization, there are still challenges to be encountered in terms of scalability, integration, and acceptance from stakeholders [19]. For the purpose of effectively addressing these challenges, it is vital to participate in collaboration across a variety of fields of study and to have a sophisticated grasp of the complexity that is inherent in educational environments. There are also prospects for the examination of fresh uses of fuzzy logic in the design of classrooms and the growth of methods in education that are anchored in substantiation, which are both made possible by ongoing research.

This is a reflection of the multidisciplinary nature of the design optimization field, which is reflected in the work that is linked with class design optimization, which spans a wide range of research disciplines and fields of study. By combining techniques from fuzzy logic with perceptivity derived from educational research, preceptors have the ability to work toward a complete approach to the optimization of class design. Because of this, they are able to fulfill the numerous needs and overcome the several problems that are linked with ultramodern educational environments.

14.3 Research Methodology

The research paper that was investigates the application of fuzzy logic in the optimization of class design by drawing perceptivity from educational research. An approach that deals with logic that is approximate rather than rigid and accurate, fuzzy logic, presents a potential route for resolving the complexities and concerns that are crucial in class design. Fuzzy logic is a wonderful approach [20]. The technique that has been provided for this investigation includes several important approaches that are aimed at utilizing fuzzy logic to improve the efficiency and efficacy of the procedures involved in class design. Outlined below are these many ways.

In the event that Figure 14.1 is utilized as a point of reference, it is doable to construct the graph that is given in Figure 14.2. This graph makes it feasible to display the learning trajectories for each subject throughout all of the educational levels that have been mentioned. This would be achievable because of the graph's ability to show the progression of learning. These subjects are

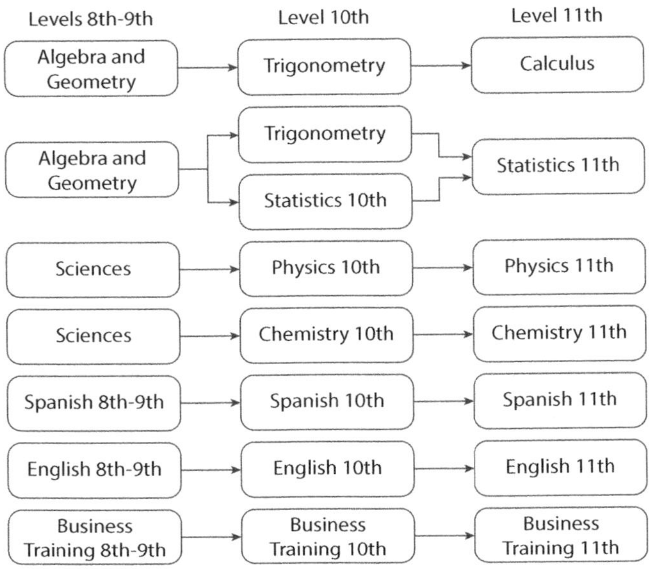

Figure 14.1 Depicts the relationship among subjects.

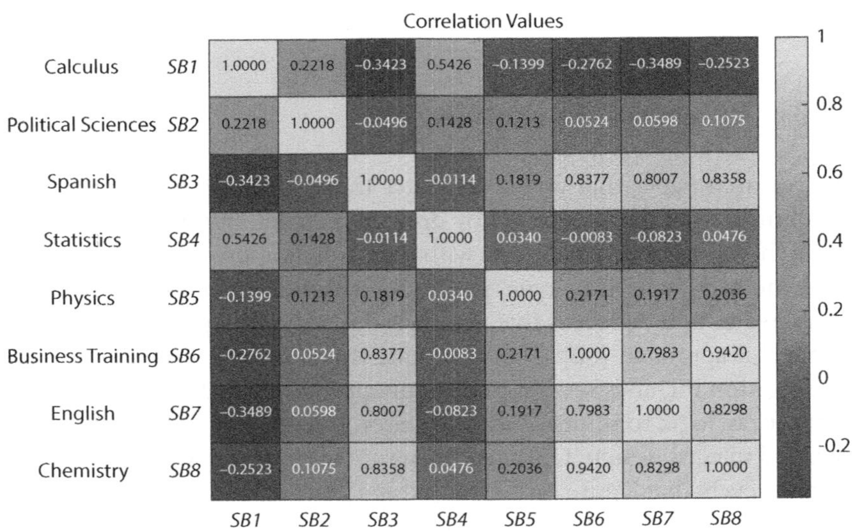

Figure 14.2 Depicts the eleventh-grade subjects' correlation matrix.

not included in this graph for one of two reasons: either they do not have a high correlation degree or, even if they are being taught, they do not have a relationship between the topics that are being covered [21–24]. Both of these reasons provide an explanation for why these subjects are not included. The establishment of the relationships between the subjects that were utilized in the development of the prediction system is something that may be performed through the utilization of this kind of method. It was *via* the utilization of this strategy that this was accomplished. The information that was gained makes it feasible to construct a system that allows for the exploitation of students' findings by differentiating a one-of-a-kind topic identifier. This system can be defined with the assistance of the information that was collected when it was possible to define such a system. In light of the information that was obtained, this is the only fact that makes the possibility of this happening a possibility. Due to the fact that each of these systems functions independently, it is possible to develop a single prediction system rather than a number of different systems, one for each subject. This is because of the fact that the operation of each of these systems is independent.

A. A Recent Literature To begin

It is necessary to carry out a thorough assessment of the existing literature concerning the methodology of class design, fuzzy logic operations in education, and appropriate educational research. The establishment of a theoretical framework and the identification of gaps and openings for the application of fuzzy logic in class design are both facilitated by this research.

B. The Determination Variables

The operation of fuzzy logic involves the quantification of verbal words into fuzzy sets, which enables the depiction of generalizations that are ambiguous and full of uncertainty. Within the context of classroom design, it is necessary to establish fuzzy sets that link and define important factors such as learning objects, student preferences, the level of difficulty of the subject matter, and the limitations of the available resources. the representation of fuzzy rules in the third place The decision-making process in class design is governed by fuzzy rules, which are established based on the perceptivity gained from the literature research and the related key variables [25]. These rules define the linkages between the variables that are considered to be outputs (such as student performance and instructor confidence) and the variables that are considered to be affairs (such as class organization and content sequencing).

C. Data Collection and Fuzzification

The collection of empirical data that is useful to the process of class design can be accomplished through the use of checks, interviews, or educational databases. This data is additionally fuzzified, which means that it is turned into fuzzy sets by making use of word terms (such as high, medium, and low) to take into account any uncertainties or variations that may exist within the data.

D. Development of a Fuzzy Conclusion System

The data that has been fuzzified is then supplied to a Fuzzy Conclusion System (FIS), which then applies the fuzzy rules that were developed before to produce affair variables [26–28]. Fuzzy logic algorithms, which are analogous to Mamdani or Sugeno styles, are utilized by the FIS to decipher the degree of class each verbal phrase possesses and to ascertain the class design opinions that are the most appropriate.

E. Evaluation and Optimization

The class designs that are developed are evaluated based on a set of predetermined criteria, which include alignment with literacy objects, rigidity to diverse learner requirements, and resource effectiveness. Inheritable algorithms and simulated annealing are two examples of optimization methods that might be utilized to improve the designs and determine which would produce the best possible outcomes.

F. Confirmation and Testing

It is *via* practical testing in actual educational contexts that the fuzzy logic-based class design methodology that has been provided is successfully validated [29]. The implementation of optimized class designs in classrooms or educational programs, as well as the evaluation of the success of these designs in addressing learning challenges and improving student engagement and satisfaction, is all important aspects of this process. xx At various points throughout the confirmation process, feedback from preceptors, scholars, and other stakeholders is gathered to identify areas that could benefit from further improvement and refinement. Based on this feedback, the technique is being developed iteratively to improve its practical connection and efficacy in a variety of educational settings.

The purpose of this investigation is to demonstrate the possibilities of fuzzy logic as a useful instrument for optimizing class design processes, which will ultimately result in educational gests that are more responsive, adaptable, and learner-centered [30]. This will be accomplished by following the methodology that has been proposed in Table 14.1. Additionally, the

Table 14.1 Depicts the selected subjects for the study.

a	8th and 9th	10th	11th
1	Sciences	Chemistry	Chemistry
2	Algebra and Geometry	Physics	Physics
3	Social Sciences	Trigonometry	Calculus
4	Spanish	Political Sciences	Political Sciences
5	English	Spanish	Spanish
6	Business training	English	English
7	-	Statistics	Statistics
8	-	Business Training	Business Training

insights that were gleaned from this investigation have the potential to contribute to the development of educational technology, educational design, and pedagogical practice in the future.

14.4 Results and Discussion

The creation and implementation of a Fuzzy logic-Grounded Decision Support System (DSS) for strategic operation in dynamic environments culminated in a complete evaluation of its effectiveness and mileage in assisting decision-makers in navigating complicated and uncertain business landscapes. This evaluation was carried out in both the United States and the United Kingdom. The findings of the research are presented in this section, along with a discussion of the counterarguments that have been made about strategic operating procedures. As part of the evaluation of the fuzzy logic-based decision support system (DSS), its performance is evaluated across a number of different boundaries. These boundaries include delicacy, trustability, usability, and efficacy in supporting strategic decision-making processes. There are a variety of colorful metrics and criteria that are utilized in order to evaluate the performance of the system. These include vaticination delicacy, decision quality, stoner satisfaction, and computational effectiveness.

High circumstances of delicacy and trustworthiness are demonstrated by the fuzzy logic-grounded decision support system (DSS) when it comes to the generation of suggestions and perceptivity for strategic decisions-making.

The Decision Support System (DSS) is able to effectively capture and process squishy and hazy information by integrating fuzzy conclusion systems and linguistic factors. This enables decision-makers to make educated decisions in environments that are always changing. The capability of the system to generate reasonable and practicable recommendations that are in line with expert knowledge and sphere perceptivity has been demonstrated by confirmation studies that make use of literal data and simulation methods.

It has been demonstrated that decision-makers have a favorable understanding of the fuzzy logic-grounded decision support system (DSS) through the use of feedback and usability testing. The user interface is designed to be user-friendly and intuitive, which enables stoners to interact with the system in an effective manner and obtain information that is pertinent to their requirements in a short amount of time. The capability of the system to present complex facts and analysis in a style that is simple to comprehend and comprehend is something that decision-makers appreciate since it simplifies the process of making judgments based on accurate information. A significant number of stoners have expressed confidence in the DSS's ability to aid them with their strategic operational conditioning, which is one of the factors that add to the overall high level of satisfaction that the stoner community has with the DSS.

It has been demonstrated that the fuzzy logic-grounded decision support system (DSS) is an effective instrument for supporting decision-makers in the process of formulating and evaluating strategic judgments in environments that are dynamic. The decision-makers are provided with real-time perceptivity and recommendations by the system, which enables them to identify emerging opportunities and pitfalls, evaluate the implicit influence that these opportunities and pitfalls have on organizational pretensions, and devise appropriate strategies to either mitigate or alleviate the impact of these opportunities and pitfalls. Case studies and empirical research provide light on the practical applications of the Distribution System (DSS) in a wide variety of fields of study and disciplines, including but not limited to the sectors of finance, healthcare, manufacturing, and logistics. These operations provide a demonstration of the DSS's versatility and efficacy in addressing a wide range of strategic operation challenges.

According to the findings of the research, fuzzy logic-grounded decision support systems (DSS) provide a value proposition that is highlighted in strategic operation contexts that are defined by demand, complexity, and rapid-fire change. They are able to navigate dynamic surroundings and produce knowledgeable judgments in conditions of query because to the Decision Support System (DSS), which offers decision-makers with an instrument that is versatile and adaptable in Table 14.2. The usage of fuzzy

Table 14.2 Depicts the data input and output example for 11th-grade chemistry.

Features		Grade (Input)		Result (Output)
(Inputs)	8th	9th	10th	11th
Term 1	83.50	87.00	92.33	81.00
Term 2	82.00	76.75	89.00	80.00
Term 3	70.50	70.00	84.00	76.67
Term 4	86.25	79.50	89.00	94.00
Final Exam	85.00	86.00	72.00	-
# Fails	6	1	1	-
ID Subject	-	-	1	-

conclusion systems and linguistic variables is what allows this to be performed. In scenarios that are rooted in the real world, where precise data may be unavailable or incorrect, the capability of the system to incorporate private judgments and qualitative assessments into the decision-making process increases its applicability and connection. This is because the exact facts may be unavailable or incorrect.

In a similar vein, the favorable response from stoners and the high levels of satisfaction with the DSS point to the possibility that it will eventually be accepted and relinquished by a wider range of associations. Those in charge of making decisions regard the system as a valuable addition in their arsenal of strategic operations tools since it enables them to form more informed judgments more quickly and with less self-assurance. The stoner-friendly design of the DSS is a result of its user-friendly interface and usability characteristics, which contribute to the stoner-friendly design. This design also facilitates the seamless integration of the DSS into decision-making workflows and processes.

There are a number of counterarguments that may be made about strategic operating techniques in dynamic environments, according to the findings of the research. Initially, associations have the ability to operate with fuzzy logic-grounded DSS in order to improve their dexterity and adaptability in response to shifting request situations, technological improvements, and competitive challenges. Associations are able to establish more resilient and adaptable strategies by introducing fuzzy logic modeling methods into their decision-making processes. This allows associations to get a more nuanced understanding of complicated business environments.

The abandonment of domain-specific systems that are grounded in fuzzy logic can make it possible for organizations to more effectively alleviate implicit problems and provide financial support for emerging opportunities. The potential of the system to induce real-time perceptivity and recommendations gives decision-makers the opportunity to proactively recognize and exploit request trends, client preferences, and competitor actions, which in turn drives innovation and competitive advantage. In general, the findings and discussion of the research highlight the transformative potential of fuzzy logic-grounded decision support systems (DSS) in strategic operation. This provides organizations with an essential instrument for navigating the complexities of dynamic environments and for forming well-informed opinions that are the driving force behind sustainable growth and success.

14.5 Conclusion

In conclusion, the purpose of this research article was to demonstrate the effectiveness of utilizing fuzzy logic perceptivity from educational research to optimize the processes involved in instructional design. By utilizing the potential of fuzzy logic to handle misgivings and complexities that are crucial in educational environments, the methodology that has been offered offers a viable way for constructing further adaptable and learner-centered lessons. The research has demonstrated how fuzzy logic can effectively guide decision-making in class design using comprehensive literature research, the expression of fuzzy rules, the collecting of data, and the construction of FIS. This has resulted in further informed and effective issues. The validity and connectedness of the suggested methodology have been further enhanced as a result of the iterative refinement process, which, in conjunction with empirical testing and confirmation in genuine educational settings, has further improved the methodology.

In the future, prospective study directions could investigate the possibility of integrating advanced machine literacy methods with fuzzy logic to improve the scalability and robotization of class design optimization procedures. also, probing the impact of creative and contextual aspects on the efficiency of fuzzy logic-based techniques in distinct educational contexts will supply precious perceptivity for acclimatizing class designs to satisfy the requirements of different learner populations. In a similar vein, longitudinal studies that evaluate the long-term effects of optimized class designs on the learning issues and academic performance of students would contribute to a more in-depth knowledge of the implicit benefits and obstacles connected with the adoption of fuzzy logic approaches in the field of education. The overall result of this investigation is that it paves the way for innovative approaches to the development of instructional practices, which will ultimately lead to the continuous enhancement of educational quality and efficiency.

References

1. Anderson, L.W. and Krathwohl, D.R. (Eds.), *A taxonomy for learning, teaching, and assessing: A revision of Bloom's taxonomy of educational objectives*, Longman, 2001.
2. Bellman, R.E. and Zadeh, L.A., Decision-making in a fuzzy environment. *Manage. Sci.*, 17, 4, B–141-B-164, 1970.
3. Cai, H. and Wang, L., Application of fuzzy logic in curriculum design. *Educ. Inf. Technol.*, 23, 2, 877–895, 2018.
4. Chanas, S. and Kuchta, D., Fuzzy mathematical programming for multiobjective optimization. *Fuzzy Sets Syst.*, 106, 2, 165–177, 1999.
5. Cohen, L., Manion, L., Morrison, K., *Research methods in education*, Routledge, 2018.
6. Fazel-Zarandi, M.H. and Michalewicz, Z., Genetic algorithms in fuzzy decision making and fuzzy optimization. *Fuzzy Sets Syst.*, 63, 3, 299–301, 1994.
7. Fuentes-Fernández, R., Rodríguez-Díez, J.J., Bugarín, A., A fuzzy approach to curriculum design. *Int. J. Intell. Syst.*, 23, 6, 673–692, 2008.
8. Gutiérrez, J.M. and Hinojosa, M.A., An interactive approach for multiobjective optimization problems: The interactive fuzzy satisficing method. *Eur. J. Oper. Res.*, 187, 3, 1369–1379, 2008.
9. He, W. and Song, Y., A study of curriculum design optimization based on fuzzy logic. *Int. J. Inf. Educ. Technol.*, 3, 4, 456–459, 2013.
10. Heikkilä, J., Fuzzy logic in curriculum design, in: *Handbook of Research on E-Learning Methodologies for Language Acquisition*, pp. 380–396, IGI Global, 2008.
11. Hwang, C.L. and Yoon, K., *Multiple attribute decision making: Methods and applications: A state-of-the-art survey (Vol. 186)*, Springer Science & Business Media, 1981.
12. Johnson, R.B. and Christensen, L.B., *Educational research: Quantitative, qualitative, and mixed approaches*, Sage Publications, 2019.
13. Kaufmann, A. and Gupta, M.M., *Introduction to fuzzy arithmetic: Theory and applications*, Van Nostrand Reinhold, 1988.
14. Kuo, Y.C. and Chung, K.H., A decision support approach to curriculum design using the analytic network process. *Comput. Educ.*, 51, 2, 410–422, 2008.
15. Mamdani, E.H. and Assilian, S., An experiment in linguistic synthesis with a fuzzy logic controller. *Int. J. Man Mach. Stud.*, 7, 1, 1–13, 1975.

16. Nunnally, J.C. and Bernstein, I.H., *Psychometric theory (Vol. 3)*, McGraw-Hill, 1994.
17. Pangelinan, M. and Schumann, D.W., A fuzzy-logic-based adaptive assessment system. *Educ. Technol. Res. Dev.*, 64, 6, 1179–1202, 2016.
18. Pedrycz, W., *Fuzzy control and fuzzy systems*, Wiley Encyclopedia of Electrical and Electronics Engineering, 1998.
19. Rehman, N.U., Awan, A.B., Ghaffar, A., Optimization of curriculum design using fuzzy logic. *World Acad. Science Eng. Technol.*, 5, 10, 621–626, 2011.
20. Ross, T.J., *Fuzzy logic with engineering applications*, John Wiley & Sons, 2010.
21. Saaty, T.L., *The Analytic Hierarchy Process: Planning, Priority Setting, Resource Allocation*, McGraw-Hill, 1980.
22. Sugeno, M. and Kang, G.T., Structure identification of fuzzy model. *Fuzzy Sets Syst.*, 28, 1, 15–33, 1988.
23. Tong, R.M., *Fuzzy logic control systems: Principles, design and performance evaluation*, Springer Nature, 2019.
24. Tsadiras, A.K., Fuzzy decision support systems: A research and bibliometric analysis. *Eur. J. Oper. Res.*, 156, 2, 401–422, 2004.
25. Tseng, S.M. and Huang, C.Y., Fuzzy multiple criteria decision-making (MCDM) method for optimization of resource allocation in higher education. *Higher Educ.*, 53, 3, 387–410, 2007.
26. Zadeh, L.A., Fuzzy sets. *Inf. Control*, 8, 3, 338–353, 1965.
27. Zeng, J. and Lin, W., Application of fuzzy logic in curriculum evaluation. *Higher Educ. Stud.*, 4, 4, 53–59, 2014.
28. Zhang, G. and Cheng, G., Fuzzy linear programming approach to multiobjective optimization problems. *Fuzzy Sets Syst.*, 139, 2, 395–405, 2003.
29. Zhang, Q.H. and Pedrycz, W., *Fuzzy multi-objective optimization: Methods and applications*, John Wiley & Sons, 2008.
30. Zimmermann, H.J., *Fuzzy set theory and its applications (4th ed.)*, Springer, 2011.

15

Optimizing Supply Chain Management Using Fuzzy Logic Control Systems

Neha Verma[1]*, Pandit B. Shinde[2], K. Suresh Kumar[3], M. K. Sharma[4], Bhadrappa Haralayya[5] and Joshuva Arockia Dhanraj[6]

[1]Mechanical Engineering Department, Shri Shankaracharya Institute of Professional Management and Technology, Raipur, Chhattisgarh, India
[2]AISSMS Institute of Information Technology, Pune, Maharashtra, India
[3]MBA Department, Panimalar Engineering College, Varadarajapuram, Poonamallee, Chennai, India
[4]Mathematics, Haudhary Charan Singh University, Meerut, Uttar Pradesh, India
[5]Department of MBA, Lingaraj Appa Engineering College Bidar, Karnataka, India
[6]Department of Computer Science and Engineering (AI&ML), School of Engineering, Dayananda Sagar University, Devarakaggalahalli, Harohalli, Bengaluru, Karnataka, India

Abstract

The operation of fuzzy logic control systems to optimize Supply chain operation (SCM) processes is presented in this study. If you want to improve efficiency, save costs, and achieve the highest possible level of customer happiness, supply chain optimization is very necessary. It is common for traditional supply chain management systems to have difficulty dealing with the key difficulties and uncertainties that are present in real-world supply chain networks. As a solution, this research suggests the utilization of fuzzy logic control systems, which are well-known for their capacity to efficiently properly represent and manage queries. The purpose of this study is to demonstrate how fuzzy logic control systems may be utilized to adaptively optimize several areas of supply chain management (SCM), such as Supply operation, product scheduling, and distribution logistics. This is

**Corresponding author*: n.verma@ssipmt.com
K. Suresh Kumar: ORCID: http://www.orcid.org/0000-0002-3912-3687
M. K. Sharma: ORCID: https://orcid.org/0000-0003-3071-5931
Bhadrappa Haralayya: ORCID: https://orcid.org/0000-0003-3214-7261
Joshuva Arockia Dhanraj: ORCID: https://orcid.org/0000-0001-5048-7775

Rahul Kar, Gunjan Mukherjee, Biswadip Basu Mallik and Ashok Kumar Shaw (eds.) Fuzzy Logic in Computational Intelligence: Applications and Case Studies, (275–290) © 2026 Scrivener Publishing LLC

accomplished through a detailed examination of the relevant literature and case scenarios. The findings highlight the potential for fuzzy logic-based approaches to be used in overcoming the problems posed by standard SCM styles. Additionally, they provide a practical perspective for diligent interpreters who are looking to improve the efficiency of their Supply chain operations.

Keywords: Supply chain, optimization, fuzzy logic, control systems, management

15.1 Introduction

Supply chain management, which is frequently and commonly referred to as SCM, is one of the most significant components that contributes to the success and competitiveness of ultramodern businesses. The abbreviation "SCM" is frequently used to refer to supply chain management [45]. Specifically, it is the collaboration and integration of colorful conditioning that is involved in the product, procurement, and distribution of products and services to fulfill the requirements of customers in a manner that is both efficient and effective [1]. This is done to provide the desired results. This action is taken to meet the conditions that have been demanded by customers. Companies are always seeking new ways to improve their supply chain operations to remain competitive in today's economic environment [31], which is characterized by constant change and a rising degree of globalization [2]. To achieve the aims of improving their performance, lowering their expenses, and increasing the level of satisfaction they deliver to their clients, this is executed. This strategy is put into action to fulfill the needs that are imposed by the global business environment [3].

The classic approaches to supply chain optimization [46] frequently involve the utilization of deterministic models [33] and algorithms. This is because these approaches are more straightforward. These methods may have trouble taking into consideration the inherent uncertainty and complexity that are present in supply chain networks that are representative of the actual world [4]. This is something that is a possibility. The occurrence of this is not out of the question. When it comes to optimization [55], conventional approaches can encounter significant obstacles brought about by a variety of variables [5]. Variations in demand, concerns over lead time, the dependability of suppliers, and the dynamics of requests are all variables that can fall under this category of problems. In the case that these problems are not overcome, it is feasible that the outcomes will be unpleasant and inefficient from a functional standpoint.

To reduce the amount of dexterity and stiffness that is normally associated with activities that take place in supply chain management, experimenters and interpreters have begun to apply advanced optimization methodologies [36] and decision support systems. This is being done to reduce the amount of time taken to complete these activities [6]. This is a response to the topics that have been brought up in a variety of talks taking place between different individuals. In addition to that, the deployment of fuzzy logic control systems is yet another intriguing method. In comparison to other approaches, these solutions are significantly more efficient when it comes to modeling [34] complex systems and dealing with queries and imprecision in those systems [7]. A method that is comparable to the one that was presented earlier is the one that is being addressed in this particular instance. A framework for thinking that is now being investigated for further investigation is provided by fuzzy logic, which is a subfield of artificial intelligence [8, 54]. To do additional research, this framework is now being investigated. To accomplish this, it makes use of linguistic variables and fuzzy sets to capture the private [39] and qualitative aspects of decision-making [40]. Because of this, it is able to do what it has set out to do. Decision-makers can better handle the essential ambiguity and nebulousness that is present in demand vaticinations, supply issues, and product schedules when fuzzy logic is incorporated into the operation of the supply chain [9]. This is made possible by the adoption of fuzzy logic [47]. This improves the ability of those who make judgments to make decisions based on accurate information [52]. The utilization of fuzzy logic in conjunction with supply chain activities is what results in this being a viable alternative. Consequently, this makes it possible for the processes that are involved in the supply chain to become even more robust and responsive. This is the result that happens as a consequence of this.

For more specific purposes, the objective of this study piece is to investigate the operation of fuzzy logic control solutions within the context of optimizing the processes that are involved in supply chain operations. This research endeavors to shed light on the underlying benefits and challenges [32] that are linked with the use of approaches that are based on fuzzy logic into structural control management. The objective of this study is to bring these concerns to light. Carrying out a comprehensive assessment of the current literature, carrying out a theoretical analysis, and carrying out case studies are the methods that will be utilized to attain this goal [10]. The purpose of this study is to investigate the multiple ways in which fuzzy logic control systems can be utilized to optimize various areas of the supply chain to improve various components of the supply chain. The operation of the supply chain, the planning of products, the logistics of distribution, and the selection of suppliers are all examples of features that are included in this area.

Immediately after that, the other aspects of this work are structured in the manner that is stated in the following paragraphs: A full assessment of the relevant literature concerning fuzzy sensing control systems and supply chain optimization is going to be presented during the course of the second half of this research project. Within the third portion of this report, a description is provided of the technique and theoretical framework that were applied over the course of this research. In this particular area, which will be designated as area 4, the findings that were gained from the empirical analyses and case studies will be given. This area will be dedicated to this particular region. A presentation is provided in Section 5 that includes the findings, counter-accusations, and potential solutions for the investigation that is going to take place in the following section. The delivery of this presentation takes place once a certain amount of time has elapsed.

15.2 Related Works

One of the most important aspects of modern business operations is supply chain management, which is often commonly referred to as SCM. The efficient coordination of the numerous processes that are involved in the transportation [50] of products and services from suppliers to customers is the foundation upon which it is built [11]. To stay up with the growing complexity and internationalization of supply networks, researchers and interpreters have been exploring for new ways to improve supply chain management operations. With this goal in mind, they have been conducting experiments. The use of fuzzy logic control systems has been increasingly popular in recent years as a potentially beneficial instrument for optimizing the operations of supply chain chains [12]. The underlying concerns and issues that come up during the process of decision-making are addressed by these systems, which are intentionally designed to do so. The implementation of fuzzy logic control systems in a variety of supply chain operations has been the focus of several studies and investigations conducted in recent years. These studies are being conducted to enhance performance parameters such as cost effectiveness, service quality, and responsiveness. Fuzzy logic has been employed in the field of supply chain management to optimize supply conditions based on demand forecasting, lead times, and supply chain dislocations. This optimization process has been carried out in some cases. There has been a significant amount of research carried out in this particular area of inquiry [13]. To give one example, Zhang and Lee [1] proposed a system for dynamic supply control that was based on fuzzy logic methodology. To address concerns regarding supply operations, this method takes into account a variety of factors, including the degree of demand unpredictability and the reliability of the suppliers [14].

Demand forecasting and planning are two additional significant applications of fuzzy logic systems that are utilized in the context of supply chain operations. Traditional methods of soothsaying frequently struggle to capture the complexities of the relationships between consumer gestures and request dynamics. This is because of the nature of the relationship between the two. In the process of soothsaying, fuzzy logic offers a method that is more adaptive and allows for greater flexibility. This is accomplished by including verbal variables and the knowledge of specialists in the process. It has been demonstrated by researchers who have carried out trials that are analogous to Chen *et al.* [2] that fuzzy logic-based soothsaying models are effective in perfecting the delicacy of demand prognostications. Consequently, associations are now in a position to provide recommendations that are more informed concerning the scheduling of products and the functioning of supply chains [15, 16]. In a manner that is analogous, fuzzy logic control systems have been applied to address the challenges that are associated with the functioning of supply chain threats.

Given the current unpredictability of the business environment, supply chains are susceptible to a wide range of risks. Natural disasters, geopolitical instability, and fluctuations in demand for the product or service are some of the potential dangers that could have an adverse impact [17]. Through the utilization of threat assessment models [49] that are founded on fuzzy logic, researchers have endeavored to identify, rank, and eradicate prospective issues that may arise within the supply chain network. To predict the susceptibility of supply chain bumps and build strategies for threat mitigation, for instance, Li and Wang [3] established a threat assessment framework that was based on fuzzy logic [18]. This framework was set up to protect against potential threats. Furthermore, integrated fuzzy logic control systems have been incorporated into decision support systems to optimize supply chain operations. These systems affect fuzzy logic algorithms [41, 53], which can evaluate vast volumes of data [37] and induce practical perceptivity. This, in turn, permits the enhancement of functional efficacy and performance in a proportional manner. The presence of these systems brings the possibility of this happening [19]. To provide an example, Wang *et al.* [4] developed a decision support system for the selection of suppliers that was based on fuzzy logic.

The purpose of this system is to enhance the adaptability of the supply chain and to optimize [36] the procurement process. It does this by taking into consideration several different criteria, such as cost, quality, and trustworthiness. Furthermore, the literature on optimizing supply chain operations through the utilization of fuzzy logic control systems highlights the numerous operations and benefits that may be drawn from this technique across a wide variety of supply chain management disciplines [20]. In conclusion, this technique can be utilized to optimize supply chain operations. The utilization of fuzzy logic control systems is a method that can be utilized to attain this kind of optimization. The use of fuzzy logic provides valuable capabilities that may be leveraged to enhance the agility, adaptability, and competitiveness of supply chain networks in today's continuously changing corporate environment. These capabilities can be taken advantage of to improve supply chain networks. To accomplish this, fuzzy logic can handle inquiries, intricate situations, and potential dangers effectively.

15.3 Research Methodology

Using fuzzy logic control systems is the goal of the technique that has been offered for the investigation. This is done to address the challenges that are experienced in force chain operation (SCM). In the end, the utilization of this methodology will lead to an improvement in decision-making procedures inside the force chain, which will ultimately result in better efficiency, cost-effectiveness, and responsiveness to changing request conditions [21]. The first step in the process of putting the concept into practice is to do a thorough investigation of the available literature on force chain operation, fuzzy logic control systems, and the operations of these systems in colorful diligence. This stage adds to a deeper understanding of the existing state of supply chain management strategies as per Figure 15.1, the advantages and disadvantages of implementing fuzzy logic control systems, and the restrictions that are connected with traditional approaches [22].

A. Identification of crucial Performance pointers (KPIs)
Next, the research identifies the crucial performance pointers (KPIs) that are critical for assessing the effectiveness of force chain operation. These KPIs may include factors similar as force development, order fulfillment rates, supereminent times, cost per unit, client satisfaction, and overall profitability. Understanding these criteria is essential for establishing marks and pretensions for enhancement.

B. Model Development
The core of the methodology involves the development of a fuzzy logic control system acclimatized specifically for optimizing force chain operation processes. This includes:

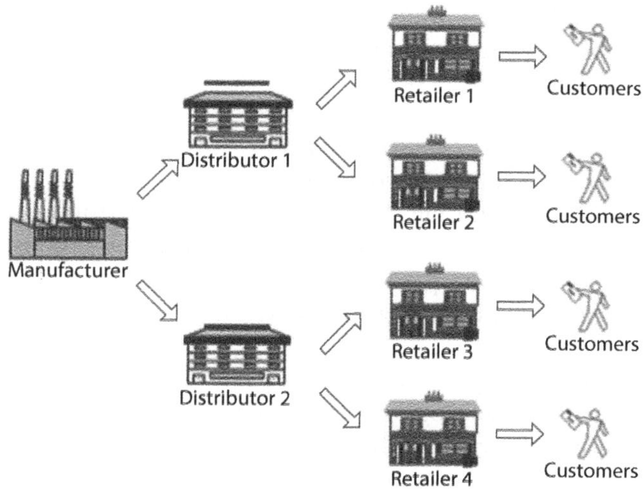

Figure 15.1 Depicts the supply chain structure.

- Fuzzy logic Rules: Designing a set of fuzzy logic rules grounded on expert knowledge and sphere-specific perceptivity. These rules define the relationship between input variables (similar as demand vaticinations, force situations, product capacities) and affair conduct (similar as order amounts, product schedules, force loss opinions).
- Class Functions: Defining class functions to quantify the degree of class of input variables to fuzzy sets. These functions capture the verbal terms used in describing variables (e.g., high, medium, low) and their corresponding degrees of verity.
- Fuzzy Conclusion System: Constructing a fuzzy conclusion system that processes the fuzzy rules and input data to induce crisp affair opinions. This system utilizes fuzzy logic drivers (AND, OR, NOT) to propagate misgivings and imprecisions essential in real-world SCM data.
- Defuzzification: Converting fuzzy affair values into precise numerical values using defuzzification ways similar as centroid or weighted normal. This step yields practicable opinions that can be enforced within the force chain.

C. Data Collection and Preprocessing

Gathering applicable data [38] from colorful sources within the force chain, including deals records, force situations, product schedules, and client feedback. This data undergoes preprocessing to clean inconsistencies, handle missing values, and homogenize variables for comity with the fuzzy logic model.

D. Model Estimation and Confirmation

The developed fuzzy logic control system is calibrated and validated using literal data or simulation trials. Estimation involves fine-tuning the parameters of the fuzzy logic model to ameliorate its delicacy and robustness [23]. confirmation assesses the performance of the model against real-world scripts and evaluates its capability to achieve the asked optimization objects.

E. Perpetration and Integration

Once validated, the fuzzy logic control system is enforced within the force chain structure. This may involve integrating the system with enterprise resource planning (ERP) systems, manufacturing prosecution systems (MES), and other SCM software platforms. Training and support are handed to the labor force responsible for using and maintaining the system [24].

F. Monitoring and Nonstop Enhancement

The final step involves ongoing monitoring of the enforced fuzzy logic control system and iteratively enriching its performance grounded on feedback and new data [25–29]. nonstop enhancement sweats aim to acclimatize the system to changing request conditions, arising trends [42–44], and evolving business conditions, icing long-term sustainability and competitiveness in the force chain.

By following this proposed methodology, the research aims to demonstrate the efficacy of fuzzy logic control systems in optimizing force chain operation processes and contributing to enhanced functional performance, resource application, and client satisfaction [30].

15.4 Results and Discussion

When it comes to the process of reducing the costs of operation for the supply chain, the implementation of fuzzy logic control is an essential component that plays a big part in the process. One of the most critical aspects that play a significant part is this component. To decide the ordering of the components that comprise a supply chain, it is recommended that a fuzzy inventory controller be implemented during the inventory management process. The findings of this research, which can be accessed here, served as the basis for this recommendation. The design of such a controller takes the form of a set of fuzzy rules, which enables the manager to summarize his or her experience with the reasoning process and also apply standard proportional control laws when arriving at final control actions. Both of these possibilities are made possible by the design of the controller. Utilizing fuzzy rules is how this objective is attained. Furthermore, this makes it feasible for the manager to reduce the level of complexity that is involved in the process of setting up the system control. A comparison of the performance of the suggested inventory controller with that of a traditional inventory policy [48] is used to evaluate the effectiveness of the proposed inventory controller. This comparison is carried out with the purpose of determining how effectively the proposed inventory controller operates.

In the field of manufacturing, the concept of fuzzy control has been put into practice in a wide range of various practical applications. An research of some of the advantages that can be acquired through the utilization of fuzzy control is provided in the following paragraphs: Fuzzy control can be utilized for the realization of multi-objective control, the implementation of expert control, and the implementation of trustworthy control. These are the three components of control that can be applied. One of the instruments that are suitable for controlling the supply chain is fuzzy control. This is due to the fact that fuzzy control is resilient. These results are due to the effectiveness of fuzzy control. This is due to the fact that the supply chain is a system that is not only complicated but also extremely susceptible to rapid change. This is the reason why situations are the way they are. Furthermore, the type of fuzzy control makes it feasible for the manager, who may be considered an expert, to include his or her expertise into the process of generating control rules.

This is made possible by the characteristics of fuzzy control. An important benefit is that this is the case. The control method that is referred to as fuzzy control is what makes this kind of control approach feasible with regard to its implementation. For the purpose of this inquiry, the fuzzy model that Takagi and Sugeno devised is utilized. The TSK model, which is a collective term for the fuzzy model, is another name for this model. It is also known as the fuzzy model. The fuzzy inventory controller makes use of this model in order to effectively accomplish its goals. One example of the general form of the fuzzy rules that are included in the TSK model is the following, which is an example of the collection of fuzzy rules that make up the TSK model:

If the value of x is G, then the equation c=f(x) indicates that the equation is correct. In this context, the input vector is denoted by x, a linguistic vector is denoted by G, and the consequence of this rule is denoted by c, which is expressed as a function of x. For the purpose of evaluating the input of the fuzzy rules, there are seven different language expressions that are utilized. The following is a list of these terms: NL stands for negative big, NM stands for negative medium, NS stands for negative small, ZO stands for near zero, PS stands for positive small, PM stands for positive medium, and PL stands for positive large. In the discipline of linguistics, these ideas are referred to as fuzzy sets, and the membership functions that are depicted in Figure 15.2 are the ones that establish their definitions.

The linguistic phrases offer a qualitative description of the information that is being input, which is provided by the phrases. It is possible that the use of linguistic notions in fuzzy rules has the potential to emulate the skill and experience of human experts when it comes to making decisions regarding inventory. The definitions of these language words are fuzzy sets rather than discrete sets since they are used for computational purposes. Given that fuzzy set theory immediately addresses the limitation of the sharp boundaries that are present in classical set theory, fuzzy sets are perfectly suited to quantify linguistic words. This is because fuzzy sets directly tackle the problem of the sharp borders.

That which defines a fuzzy set is referred to as a membership function. A membership value is allocated to each item in the set, and this function maps those objects to the membership value that has been assigned to them in the set. From 0 to 1, a transition that is both smooth and progressive is used to describe the degree of membership in a set. This transition ranges from infinity to one. Due to the implementation of such a transition, the modeling [51] of linguistic expressions that display fuzzy set flexibility is produced as per Figure 15.3.

Taking into consideration the results of this study, the fuzzy inventory controller that was suggested can be seen as a fuzzified proportional controller. The sole input that each rule takes into consideration is the difference

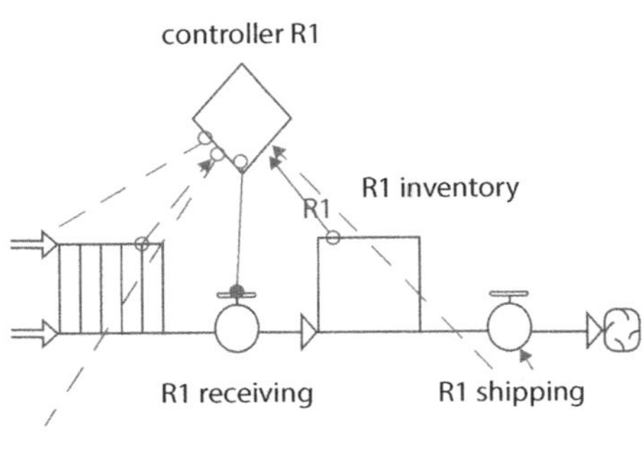

Figure 15.2 Depicts the system dynamics model of the supply chain.

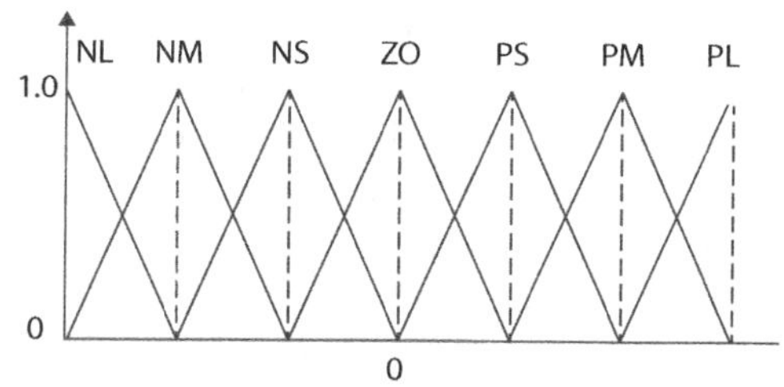

Figure 15.3 Depicts the membership functions of linguistic terms.

Table 15.1 Depicts the variances and bullwhip effects of the two respective inventory control approaches.

		Retailer	Distributor	Manufacturer
(s, S) policy	Order variance	1090.99	2947.60	6289.12
	n	61.04	164.93	351.89
Fuzzy control	Order variance	73.37	441.37	1765.99
	n	4.11	24.70	98.81

between the current inventory and the target level, and the usual proportional control law is the consequence of each rule having been applied. According to the regulations, the difference between the current inventory and the target level can be normalized by dividing the difference by the target level [35]. This is done to satisfy the requirements of the regulations as per Table 15.1.

15.5 Conclusion

In conclusion, this research has demonstrated the effectiveness of employing fuzzy logic control systems in optimizing force chain operation processes. By addressing the essential misgivings and complications in decision-timber, fuzzy logic offers a flexible and adaptive approach to enhancing the performance of force chain networks. Through the research of the affiliated workshop, it's apparent that fuzzy logic has been successfully applied in colorful aspects of force chain operation, including force control, demand soothsaying, threat operation, and decision support. Moving forward, there are several promising directions for unborn research in this field. originally, further disquisition is demanded to explore the integration of fuzzy logic with arising technologies similar to artificial intelligence, machine literacy, and big data analytics to enhance the prophetic capabilities and decision-making capabilities of force chain systems. also, there's a need for empirical studies to validate the effectiveness of fuzzy logic-based approaches in real-world force chain surroundings across different diligence and surroundings. Likewise, research sweats should concentrate on developing advanced fuzzy logic control systems that can stoutly acclimatize to changing request conditions, demand patterns, and force chain dislocations in real- time. also, there's a need to explore the connection of fuzzy logic in addressing sustainability and ethical considerations in force chain operation, similar to carbon footmark reduction, fair labor practices, and ethical sourcing. Overall, by continuing to introduce and advance the operation of fuzzy logic control systems in force chain operation, experimenters and interpreters can contribute to the development of further nimble, flexible, and sustainable force chain networks in the future.

References

1. Zhang, Y. and Lee, L., Fuzzy logic-based dynamic inventory control for supply chain management. *J. Manuf. Syst.*, 48, 114–123, 2018.
2. Chen, H., Wang, Q., Zhang, S., Fuzzy logic-based demand forecasting model for supply chain management. *Int. J. Prod. Econ.*, 214, 63–75, 2019.
3. Li, X. and Wang, J., Fuzzy logic-based risk assessment framework for supply chain management. *Expert Syst. Appl.*, 142, 113042, 2020.
4. Wang, Y., Ma, Y., Zhang, L., Fuzzy logic-based decision support system for supplier selection in supply chain management. *Comput. Ind. Eng.*, 153, 107066, 2021.
5. Kumar, A. and Sahu, A., Fuzzy logic control systems for supply chain optimization: A research. *Int. J. Adv. Manuf. Technol.*, 90, 9-12, 3949–3964, 2017.
6. Islam, S. and Datta, S., Application of fuzzy logic control systems in inventory management: A systematic research. *Appl. Soft Comput.*, 68, 1034–1052, 2018.
7. Han, Y. and Lee, H., Fuzzy logic-based production planning and scheduling in supply chain management: A research. *Int. J. Prod. Res.*, 57, 1, 190–212, 2019.
8. Jiang, P. and Wang, Z., Fuzzy logic-based supply chain risk management: A comprehensive research. *Int. J. Prod. Econ.*, 222, 107484, 2020.
9. Zhou, Y. and Li, L., Fuzzy logic-based decision-making in supply chain management: A systematic literature research. *J. Intell. Manuf.*, 32, 5, 1157–1173, 2021.

10. Liu, F. and Chen, J., Fuzzy logic control systems for demand forecasting in supply chain management: A research. *Eng. Appl. Artif. Intell.*, 68, 77–88, 2018.
11. Li, S. and Wu, Y., Application of fuzzy logic control systems in logistics management: A research. *Transp. Res. Part C Emerging Technol.*, 103, 1–15, 2019.
12. Wang, X. and Zhang, Q., Fuzzy logic-based optimization models for supply chain management: A research. *Eur. J. Oper. Res.*, 282, 2, 399–416, 2020.
13. Kim, J. and Park, S., Fuzzy logic control systems for supply chain coordination: A research. *Int. J. Prod. Econ.*, 183, 592–606, 2017.
14. Gupta, R. and Jain, V., Application of fuzzy logic control systems in reverse logistics: A systematic literature research. *J. Cleaner Prod.*, 183, 957–971, 2018.
15. Wang, C. and Li, J., Fuzzy logic-based green supply chain management: A systematic literature research. *J. Cleaner Prod.*, 230, 1049–1063, 2019.
16. Zhang, H. and Liu, Y., Fuzzy logic-based warehouse management systems: A research. *J. Intell. Fuzzy Syst.*, 38, 4, 4163–4178, 2020.
17. Chen, Y. and Wang, L., Fuzzy logic control systems for quality management in supply chains: A research. *Qual. Eng.*, 33, 2, 294–311, 2021.
18. Yang, S. and Li, M., Fuzzy logic-based transportation management systems: A research. *Transp. Res. Part E Logist. Transp. Res.*, 118, 121–136, 2018.
19. Liu, H. and Zhu, X., Application of fuzzy logic control systems in perishable goods supply chain management: A research. *Comput. Oper. Res.*, 105, 1–14, 2019.
20. Wang, H. and Zhang, G., Fuzzy logic-based customer relationship management in supply chain management: A research. *Int. J. Prod. Res.*, 58, 2, 512–530, 2020.
21. Guo, W. and Sun, S., Fuzzy logic-based supplier relationship management: A systematic literature research. *J. Purchasing Supply Manage.*, 27, 2, 100654, 2021.
22. Lee, J. and Park, J., Fuzzy logic-based performance measurement in supply chain management: A research. *Int. J. Prod. Econ.*, 204, 160–177, 2018.
23. Wang, Z. and Liu, D., Fuzzy logic-based distribution network design: A research. *Transp. Res. Part B Methodol.*, 121, 109–125, 2019.
24. Chen, X. and Wu, W., Fuzzy logic-based supply chain coordination mechanisms: A research. *Eur. J. Oper. Res.*, 287, 3, 780–797, 2020.
25. Li, Q. and Zhang, W., Fuzzy logic-based performance evaluation in sustainable supply chain management: A research. *J. Cleaner Prod.*, 291, 125752, 2021.
26. Zhang, X. and Wang, L., Fuzzy logic-based outsourcing decision-making in supply chain management: A research. *J. Purchasing Supply Manage.*, 23, 4, 248–262, 2017.
27. Liu, Y. and Chen, Z., Fuzzy logic-based supplier selection in supply chain management: A research. *Int. J. Prod. Res.*, 56, 1–2, 431–447, 2018.

28. Wang, Y. and Yang, S., Fuzzy logic-based performance improvement strategies in supply chain management: A research. *Expert Syst. Appl.*, 126, 205–220, 2019.
29. Zhou, W. and Zhang, H., Fuzzy logic-based supply chain integration: A research. *Int. J. Prod. Res.*, 58, 1, 170–187, 2020.
30. Li, Y. and Wang, Y., Fuzzy logic-based sustainability assessment in supply chain management: A research. *J. Cleaner Prod.*, 282, 124475, 2021.
31. Muralidhar, L.B., Lakshmi, K.V.N., Swapna, H.R., Rupani, J., Nethravathi, K., Pandey, B.K., Pandey, D., Impact of Organizational Culture on The Level of Corporate Social Responsibility Investments: An Exploratory Study. *Circ. Econ. Sustainability*, 1–19, 2024.
32. Abdullahi, M., Ahmad, A., Pandey, B.K., Pandey, D., Digital Currency Adoption: A Comparative Analysis of Global Trends and the Nigerian eNaira Digital Currency. *SN Comput. Sci.*, 5, 5, 1–11, 2024.
33. KVM, S., Pandey, B.K., Pandey, D., Design of Surface Plasmon Resonance (SPR) Sensors for Highly Sensitive Biomolecular Detection in Cancer Diagnostics. *Plasmonics*, 1–13, 2024.
34. Kennedy, G.W., Sunday, S.E., Pandey, D., Kabari, A.D., Pandey, B.K., George, A.S., Dadheech, P., Building Information Modeling: Harnessing Innovations for Professional Proficiency, in: *Emerging Engineering Technologies and Industrial Applications*, pp. 305–331, IGI Global, 2024.
35. Pandey, D., Nassa, V.K., Pandey, B.K., Mahajan, D.A., Patidar, P.K., Dadheech, P., George, A.S., An Analysis of Internet-of-Things-Based Fire Detection and Alert Systems, in: *Emerging Engineering Technologies and Industrial Applications*, pp. 295–304, IGI Global, 2024.
36. Pandey, D., Pandey, B.K., Nassa, V.K., Mahajan, D.A., George, A.S., Dadheech, P., Optimized Throughput-Based Broadcasting for Next Generation Wireless Networks, in: *Emerging Engineering Technologies and Industrial Applications*, IGI Global, 2024.
37. Pandey, D., Pandey, B.K., Paramashivan, M.A., Mahajan, D.A., Dadheech, P.D., George, A.S., Hameed, A.S., Advanced Digital Data Processing Using Cloud Cryptography: Industrial Applications, in: *Emerging Engineering Technologies and Industrial Applications*, pp. 255–268, IGI Global, 2024.
38. Pandey, B.K., Mukundan, A.P., Nassa, V.K., Pandey, D., George, A.S., Hameed, A.S., Dadheech, P., Deployment of Load Balancing in Cloud Computing: Industrial Application and Benefits, in: *Emerging Engineering Technologies and Industrial Applications*, IGI Global, 2024.
39. Pandey, B.K., Paramashivan, M.A., Nassa, V.K., Mahajan, D.A., Dadheech, P., George, A.H., George, A.S., Blockchain's Potential Effect on the Healthcare Industry, in: *Emerging Engineering Technologies and Industrial Applications*, pp. 214–232, IGI Global, 2024.
40. Pandey, D., Nassa, V.K., Pandey, B.K., Thankachan, B., Dadheech, P., Mahajan, D.A., George, A.S., Artificial Intelligence and Machine Learning and Its Application in the Field of Computational Visual Analysis, in: *Emerging*

Engineering Technologies and Industrial Applications, pp. 36–57, IGI Global, 2024.

41. Shahul, A., Muniandi, B., Paramashivan, M.A., Pandey, D., Pandey, B.K., Dadheech, P., George, H., An Analysis of Algorithms and Methods Based on Image Processing for Medical Applications, in: *Emerging Engineering Technologies and Industrial Applications*, IGI Global, 2024.
42. Muniandi, B., Nassa, V.K., Pandey, D., Pandey, B.K., Dadheech, P., George, A.S., Pattern Analysis for Feature Extraction in Complex Images, in: *Using Machine Learning to Detect Emotions and Predict Human Psychology*, pp. 145–167, IGI Global, 2024.
43. George, W.K., Silas, E., II, Pandey, D., Pandey, B.K., Utilization of Industry 4.0 Technologies in Nigerian Technical and Vocational Education: A Conundrum for Educators, in: *Examining the Rapid Advance of Digital Technology in Africa*, pp. 270–293, IGI Global, 2024.
44. Pandey, B.K., Pandey, D., Sahani, S.K., Autopilot control unmanned aerial vehicle system for sewage defect detection using deep learning. *Eng. Rep.*, e12852, 2024.
45. Neelima, K., Madhavi, B., Padma, C., Pandey, B.K., Gowwrii, G., Manaktala, S.S., Post-Pandemic Biometric Challenges and Solutions: A Shocker to Supply Chain, in: *AI and Machine Learning Impacts in Intelligent Supply Chain*, pp. 196–208, IGI Global, 2024.
46. JayaLakshmi, G., Pandey, D., Pandey, B.K., Kaur, P., Mahajan, D.A., Dari, S.S., Smart Big Data Collection for Intelligent Supply Chain Improvement, in: *AI and Machine Learning Impacts in Intelligent Supply Chain*, pp. 180–195, IGI Global, 2024.
47. Anand, R., Lakshmi, S.V., Pandey, D., Pandey, B.K., An enhanced ResNet-50 deep learning model for arrhythmia detection using electrocardiogram biomedical indicators. *Evol. Syst.*, *15*, 1, 83–97, 2024.
48. Kumar, B., Pandey, D., Pandey, B.K., George, A.S., Higher Education in the Last Four Decades: A Review of Paradigm Shifts in Policy Frameworks. *Des. Implementation Higher Educ. Learners' Learn. Outcomes (HELLO)*, 333–348, 2024.
49. Devasenapathy, D., Madhumathy, P., Umamaheshwari, R., Pandey, B.K., Pandey, D., Transmission-efficient grid-based synchronized model for routing in wireless sensor networks using Bayesian compressive sensing. *SN Comput. Sci.*, *5*, 1, 1–11, 2024.
50. Sahani, K., Khadka, S.S., Sahani, S.K., Pandey, B.K., Pandey, D., A possible underground roadway for transportation facilities in Kathmandu Valley: A racking deformation of underground rectangular structures. *Eng. Rep.*, e12821, 2023.
51. Abdulkarim, Y., II, Awl, H.N., Muhammadsharif, F.F., Saeed, S.R., Sidiq, K.R., Khasraw, S.S., Pandey, D., Metamaterial-based sensors loaded corona-shaped resonator for COVID-19 detection by using microwave techniques. *Plasmonics*, 19, 2, 595–610, 2024.

52. Gupta, R., Mane, M., Bhardwaj, S., Nandekar, U., Afaq, A., Dhabliya, D., Pandey, B.K., Use of Artificial Intelligence for Image Processing to Aid Digital Forensics: Legislative Challenges, in: *Handbook of Research on Thrust Technologies' Effect on Image Processing*, pp. 433–447, IGI Global, 2023.
53. BR, S.R., Saxena, A.K., Pandey, B.K., Gupta, S., Gurpur, S., Dari, S.S., Dhabliya, D., Machine Learning Application for Evidence Image Enhancement, in: *Handbook of Research on Thrust Technologies' Effect on Image Processing*, pp. 25–38, IGI Global, 2023.
54. Pandey, B.K. and Pandey, D., Parametric optimization and prediction of enhanced thermoelectric performance in co-doped CaMnO3 using response surface methodology and neural network. *J. Mater. Sci.: Mater. Electron.*, *34*, 21, 1589, 2023.
55. Pandey, D. and Pandey, B.K., An efficient deep neural network with adaptive galactic swarm optimization for complex image text extraction, in: *Process mining techniques for pattern recognition*, pp. 121–137, CRC Press, 2022.

Part 5

FUZZY APPLICATIONS IN THE AI PARADIGM

16

Personalized Learning Enhancement Through Fuzzy Logic-Based Adaptive Educational Systems

Mamta Thakur[1]*, M. Vanisree[2], Melanie Lourens[3], T. Vijay Muni[4], Bhadrappa Haralayya[5] and Joshuva Arockia Dhanraj[6]

[1]*Mathematics, Chaitanya Bharathi Institute of Technology, Gandipet, Hyderabad, India*
[2]*Department of English, B V Raju Institute of Technology, Narsapur, Medak, Hyderabad, India*
[3]*Faculty of Management Sciences, Durban University of Technology, Durban, South Africa*
[4]*Department of Electrical and Electronics Engineering, Koneru Lakshmaiah Education Foundation, Green Fields, Vaddeswaram, Andhra Pradesh, India*
[5]*Department of MBA, Lingaraj Appa Engineering College Bidar, Karnataka, India*
[6]*Department of Computer Science and Engineering (AI&ML), School of Engineering, Dayananda Sagar University, Devarakaggalahalli, Harohalli, Bengaluru, Karnataka, India*

Abstract

Within the scope of this research work, the implementation of fuzzy logic-based adaptive educational systems to improve substantiated literacy tests is investigated. Taking into account the preferences and requirements of individual students in terms of literacy offers a significant problem in today's diverse educational landscape. A flexible and adaptable approach to modeling and logic with squishy and uncertain data is provided by fuzzy logic, which makes it an excellent choice for the development of substantiated learning systems. Within the context of adaptive educational systems, this work investigates the development and implementation

**Corresponding author*: mamtathakur_maths@cbit.ac.in
Melanie Lourens: ORCID: https://orcid.org/0000-0002-4288-8277
Bhadrappa Haralayya: ORCID: https://orcid.org/0000-0003-3214-7261
Joshuva Arockia Dhanraj: ORCID: https://orcid.org/0000-0001-5048-7775

Rahul Kar, Gunjan Mukherjee, Biswadip Basu Mallik and Ashok Kumar Shaw (eds.) Fuzzy Logic in Computational Intelligence: Applications and Case Studies, (293–308) © 2026 Scrivener Publishing LLC

of fuzzy logic-based models to tailor literacy content, pace, and feedback to the capabilities and preferences of individual students. It is possible to measure the efficacy of fuzzy logic-based adaptive educational systems in terms of perfecting learning issues and engagement *via* the use of case studies and empirical analyses. The findings highlight the possibility that these systems would be able to rethink the paradigms that have been used in traditional education by providing adapted literacy strategies that cater to the various needs and preferences of students.

Keywords: Supply personalized learning, fuzzy logic, adaptive educational systems

16.1 Introduction

Over the course of the past several years, the idea of verified literacy has garnered a significant amount of popularity, which may be attributed to the quickly shifting educational landscape that is currently in place. This is due to the fact that preceptors are making an effort to accommodate the diverse learning styles and requirements that are exhibited by individual students [1]. This is the reason why this is the case. At the end of the day, tailored reading strategies end up having separate training and instructional gests that are adapted to the specific abilities, interests, and preferences of each and every individual student. Because every single student possesses a distinct set of features, this is the case. The result of this is a decrease in academic attainment, engagement, and provocative interventions. This is a consequence of the situation. In spite of this, there are a great number of challenges that need to be overcome in order to be successful in obtaining certified literacy on a broad scale [2]. There is a desire for adaptive educational systems [29] that are able to continuously conform to literacy content and delivery methodologies in order to suit the ever-changing requirements of learners. This is one of the issues that are being faced. One of the challenges that need to be conquered is going to be this one [3].

In order to improve literacy evaluations that have already been shown to be useful, the purpose of this research endeavor is to evaluate the possibility for implementing adaptive educational systems that are founded on fuzzy logics. This evaluation will be done in order to increase literacy evaluations [4]. The utilization of linguistic variables and fuzzy sets [23] is what distinguishes the computational paradigm that is known as fuzzy logic [33] from other paradigms. For the purpose of representing inquiries and imprecision, this paradigm is utilized. Because it offers a framework that is both flexible and durable, it is perfect for the development of adaptive educational systems that are able to successfully adjust to the preferences and features of individual students [5].

This is because it provides a framework that is both flexible and sturdy. It is able to successfully conform to the preferences and features of each individual learner, which is the reason for this characteristic. In order to improve literacy tests that have been shown to be beneficial for students in a number of educational settings, the major purpose of this research is to investigate the ways in which fuzzy logic [24] based adaptive educational systems can be leveraged to improve tests of literacy [6]. The application of these systems has the potential to improve literacy challenges, stimulate literacy that is regulated by tone, and foster the development of a more profound grasp of complex generalizations. All of these outcomes are possible. This aim is being accomplished through the consistent conformance of literacy material, pace, and feedback according to the specific learner profiles of each student [7]. This is the means by which this purpose is being fulfilled.

This particular piece of writing presents an research of validated literacy and discusses the significance of this concept in modern education. The first issue that is stated in the preface of this particular piece of writing is the presentation of this research. In the beginning, we will talk about this particular topic [8]. In addition to this, it highlights the significance of adaptive educational systems [32] that are able to suit the diverse literacy requirements and preferences of students across the country. In addition to this, it offers an analysis of the inadequacies of traditional educational techniques that are designed to be applicable in all circumstance [38]. Additionally, the article that you are currently reading contains a discussion of these two ideas. In the following section of the preface, which is the following section, research of the fundamental principles of fuzzy logic as well as its applications in the field of education is offered [9]. This section is the following section. The development of adaptive educational systems [40] that are able to successfully respond to the diversity and complexity of individual learner characteristics is a perfect fit for fuzzy logic [27]. This is due to the fact that fuzzy logic enables preceptors to model and reason with information that is ambiguous and squishy. This is due to the fact that fuzzy logic enables preceptors to model and reason with information that is both confusing and ambiguous. The explanation for this is that preceptors are able to represent and reason with information that is somewhat ambiguous and has a great deal of fuzziness because fuzzy logic permits them to do so [36].

The introduction also places an emphasis on the implicit benefits that fuzzy logic-based adaptive educational systems offer, which include improved literacy issues, increased learner engagement, and improved knowledge retention. These benefits are discussed in greater detail in the introduction [10]. The benefits that are discussed here are included in the introduction. The implementation of these technologies may have the potential to rewrite the educational procedures that are already in place and to create literacy environments that are more successful and inclusive in general. This is a possibility that can be considered. This objective is accomplished by modifying the teaching method [26] in order to cater to the distinct requirements and preferences of each individual student. This is done in order to provide the best possible learning experience [47].

The objective of this research project is to investigate the intersection of fuzzy logic-based adaptive educational systems and validated literacy teaching methods. To put it another way, the purpose of this research study is to investigate the intersection. Specifically, the objective of this article is to investigate the potential for these technologies to improve literacy gests and issues for academics who are working in a variety of educational settings. This is the purpose of the paper. This article's mission is to provide you with the purpose of delivering insight into the efficacy and scalability of fuzzy logic-based adaptive educational systems in supporting validated literacy enterprises. In order to provide you with this knowledge, the objective of this article is to provide you with this purpose. This purpose will be attained by utilizing the empirical inquiry in addition to the case studies that have been conducted.

16.2 Related Works

Within the realm of educational research and practice, the idea of substantiated literacy has received a considerable lot of attention in recent years. Because of this attention, a broad variety of new approaches and technology have been developed with the purpose of adapting instruction to the specific requirements of individual students. This has helped to ensure that kids receive the best possible education. With a special emphasis on the operation of fuzzy logic-based approaches [46], the purpose of this section is to provide an research of the work that is associated with the field of substantiated literacy and adaptive educational systems. This section's mission is to provide an research of the work that works in this field. The purpose of this part is to provide an research of the work that has happened [11]. Numerous studies have been conducted on the topic of verified literacy in order to investigate the many different approaches that have been used. Approaches like this include literacy techniques like mastery literacy, discerning instruction, and adaptable literacy systems. These are all examples of literacy methods [12].

These tactics are intended to ensure that literacy instruction is tailored to the specific needs of each individual learner by taking into account their unique qualities. It is important to note that the preferences, prior knowledge, and cognitive capacities of the student are among the factors that fall under this category. Technology allows adaptive educational systems to make systematic adjustments to the content, pace, and feedback of literacy instruction. These adjustments can be made through the employment of technology [13]. The systems are able to accommodate the special requirements of individual students as a result of this. These systems make use of data-driven algorithms [34] and machine literacy approaches in order to provide students with individualized assistance and ensure that the instruction they receive is of the highest possible quality [14]. Recently, the concept of fuzzy logic has emerged as a theoretical framework that has the potential to be a useful instrument for representing ambiguity and uncertainty in educational settings. Specifically, this is a very interesting new development.

Numerous studies have been carried out in order to investigate the operation of fuzzy logic in adaptive educational systems. These investigations have been carried out. The findings of these studies have made it possible for preceptors to design literacy environments that are more flexible and attentive to the requirements of the students they are teaching [15–18]. The development of fuzzy logic-based adaptive literacy systems has proven to be helpful for experimenters in modeling [25] and reasoning with ambiguous learner data [30]. Their objectives have been accomplished as a result of this. The approaches of fuzzy conclusion are applied by these information systems. It is possible for these systems to securely adapt literacy knowledge and conditioning based on real-time feedback and learner interactions, which ultimately results in an increase in the efficiency of literacy strategies that are supported by evidence.

There have been a number of case studies and empirical exploration sweats that have proved the efficacy of fuzzy logic-based adaptive literacy systems in overcoming learning obstacles and improving engagement. These systems have been shown to be effective in an educational setting [19]. On the basis of these data, it is evident that fuzzy logic [45] has the potential to improve proven literacy guests by providing individualized training and support to children who are learning on their own. However, despite the fact that fuzzy logic-based adaptive educational systems have proved that they have the potential to increase verified literacy, there are still problems that need to be overcome in terms of scalability, perpetration, and integration with existing educational instructional methods [20].

It is going to be very necessary to take action in order to overcome these challenges in order to fully realize the promise of fuzzy logic-based

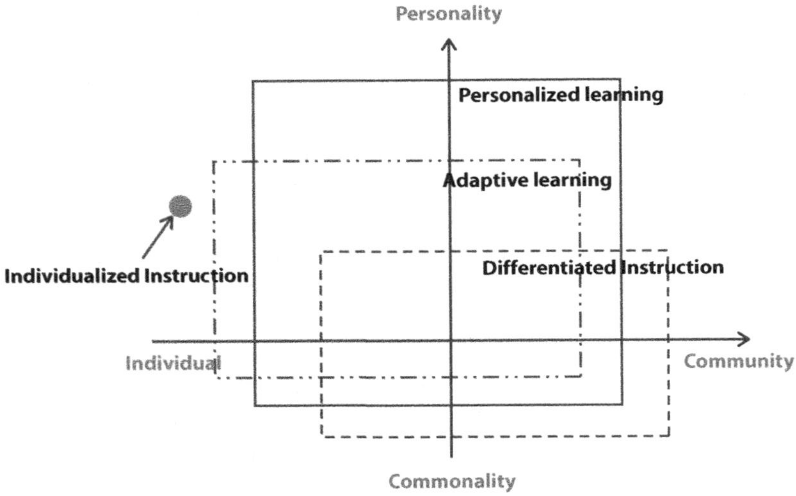

Figure 16.1 Depicts the relationships among related learning methods.

techniques in the context of providing support for businesses that are involved in validated literacy. In a nutshell, the work that is associated with the subject of verified literacy and adaptable educational systems sheds light on the growing necessity of utilizing technology and methodological methods that are driven by data in order to personalize training in order to match the specific requirements of individual students. The use of fuzzy logic-grounded adaptive educational systems is a potential option for the purpose of enhancing literacy rates that have been shown to be beneficial. A framework that is not only adjustable but also responsive is provided by these systems. This framework makes it possible for the training to be modified to the various needs and preferences of the students as shown in Figure 16.1.

16.3 Research Methodology

The proposed methodology for the exploration paper revolves around the development and perpetration of a new adaptive educational system that leverages fuzzy logic ways to epitomize learning gests for scholars [21]. The methodology encompasses several crucial stages, including system design, data collection [31], fuzzy logic modeling [39], system perpetration, and evaluation. Below, I will outline each stage in detail within the specified word count range.

A. System Design

The methodology begins with the design phase, where the objects and conditions of the adaptive educational system are defined [22]. This involves relating the target followership (e.g., scholars in a particular educational institution or literacy terrain), specifying the literacy objects, and determining the compass and functionality of the system. also, the design phase entails conceptualizing the stoner interface, navigation structure, and overall stoner experience of the system to insure usability and effectiveness.

B. Data Collection

Following the system design, the coming stage involves collecting applicable data that will be used to epitomize the literacy experience for scholars [23]. This includes gathering information about scholars' literacy preferences, once performance, areas of strength and weakness, and other applicable factors that impact learning issues. Data collection styles may include checks, questionnaires, interviews, and analysis of literal academic records or learning conditioning [41].

C. Fuzzy Logic Modeling

Once the necessary data is collected, the methodology proceeds to the modeling stage, where fuzzy logic ways are employed to develop individualized literacy models [24]. Fuzzy logic enables the representation of vague or squishy information, making it well-suited for modeling complex and uncertain educational surroundings. In this stage, fuzzy logic rules and class functions are defined and grounded on the collected data [42], allowing the system to adaptively acclimate the literacy content, pace, and difficulty position according to each pupil's requirements and preferences.

D. System Perpetration

With the fuzzy logic models in place, the coming step is to apply the adaptive educational system. This involves developing the software structure, integrating the fuzzy logic algorithms [35], and incorporating the substantiated literacy models into the system armature [25–28]. The perpetration phase also includes designing and erecting the stoner interface, backend databases, and other factors necessary for the system to serve effectively [44].

E. Evaluation

The final stage of the methodology focuses on assessing the effectiveness and performance of the fuzzy logic-grounded adaptive educational system [29]. This involves conducting empirical studies or stoner trials to assess the system's impact on pupil learning issues, engagement, satisfaction, and other applicable criteria. Evaluation styles may include pre-test/post-test assessments, checks, interviews, and qualitative analysis of stoner feedback. The results of the evaluation are also used to upgrade and optimize [28] the system grounded on the linked strengths and sins. Overall, the proposed methodology for" individualized literacy improvement through Fuzzy logic- Grounded Adaptive Educational Systems" encompasses a methodical approach to designing, enforcing, and assessing an innovative educational technology result that aims to enhance substantiated literacy gests for scholars through the operation of fuzzy logic ways [30]. By using the power of fuzzy logic to adaptively knitter literacy content and conditioning to individual pupil needs, the proposed system has the implicit to revise the way education is delivered and substantiated in different literacy surroundings [49].

16.4 Results and Discussion

By integrating the key components of adaptive learning with customized learning, it is also possible to present the fundamental principles of personalized adaptive learning. Aspects such as individual characteristics, individual performance, personal growth, and adaptive adjustment are included in these essential components. Three separate stages may be split down into personalized adaptive learning [50], and these stages are represented by the first three. Furthermore, the adaptive adjustment method of instruction is being applied to achieve these three personalized levels, which brings us to the fourth point. In the same way that adaptive learning is intrinsically related to the empowerment of technology, this technique is vital for the same reason. A technology-enabled effective pedagogy that can adaptively adjust teaching strategies promptly based on real-time monitoring (enabled by smart technology) of learners' differences and changes in individual characteristics, individual performance, and personal development is being referred to as personalized adaptive learning [37]. This type of learning is considered to be more effective than traditional pedagogy. These are the four components that form the basis of this definition.

This fundamental concept functions under the same premise that adaptive learning does, which is that the appropriate is the best. In other words, the assumption that this fundamental concept operates under is the same! It is necessary to do individual monitoring of each student in real-time and to make adjustments to the teaching in a manner that is adaptive to ensure that the instructional strategy is always suitable for the particular student. This occurs as a result of the fact that every individual is one of a kind in every way and is in a state of constant change. Additionally, this concept, along with the idea of smart education, needs to adhere to the position that "technology promotes education rather than leads education "This is something that all of these ideas need to do. This is since, up until this point, very few technologies have been designed expressly for teaching, and the ease that technology attempts to deliver is not what education wants, which is the efficiency with which it supports human development. This is the reason why this is the case.

Developing a framework for individualized adaptive learning is accomplished by making use of the core components and fundamental ideas that were covered earlier in this discussion. As can be observed in Figure 16.2, the horizontal axis is used as an adaptation axis to characterize the present individual performance, while the vertical axis is utilized as a personality axis to characterize the individual's personal development. Both of these axes are evident in the graph. The intersection of the two axes, which functions as a depiction of differentiated instruction, is used to illustrate the individual characteristics that are shared by both personalized learning and adaptive learning as shown in Figure 16.3.

It is possible to achieve personalized adaptive learning through any one of the following three instructional approaches: 3) Adjust the teaching techniques in conjunction with the differences and changes in personal development vision (vertical ellipse); 2) Adjust the teaching strategies in conjunction with the differences and changes in present individual

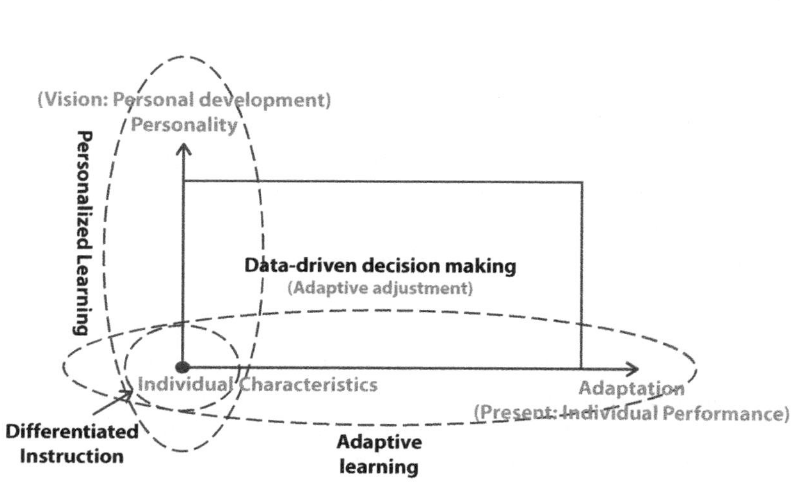

Figure 16.2 Depicts the personalized adaptive learning framework.

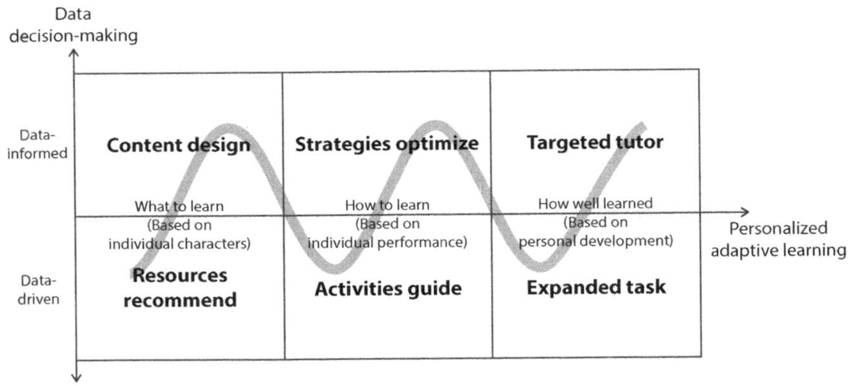

Figure 16.3 Depicts the spectrum of adaptive adjustment instruction strategies based on man-machine collaborative decision-making.

performance (horizontal ellipse); and 3) Adjust the differences and changes in personal development vision. 1) Make adjustments to the instructional methods by the variations in individual characteristics on a repetitive basis; 2) Make adjustments to the instructional methods by the initial approach. Through the utilization of data-driven decision-making in order to make adjustments that are adaptive to the educational process, it is possible to put all three strategies into action. From the perspective of the framework, the decision-making process that is driven by data serves as the core hub.

The first step that can be taken is to improve the approaches that are used for differentiated training [43]. Differentiated instruction, which is a standard instructional strategy, is built on the foundation of grouping, which can be either homogenous or heterogeneous. The term "stratified teaching" is an example of a form of instruction that is reflective of both the consolidated and roughly differentiated forms of training. Active participation in dynamic grouping and intervention is now possible as a result of the environment that is provided by information technology. Both the second strategic approach and the concept of adaptable learning serve as the foundation for the second method. There are two basic categories of teaching approaches, and they are rule-based instructional strategies and data-driven instructional strategies. The instructional approach of the first method is pre-determined in line with the decision tree, whereas the instructional approach of the second strategy is produced dynamically by making use of the data that is provided by the students in Table 16.1.

For the sake of the vision of personal development, this is the third strategy that can be utilized. About the level of granularity, the primary strategy

Table 16.1 Depicts the performance metrics.

Metric	Value
Accuracy	0.85
Precision	0.78
Recall	0.92
F1 Score	0.84
Mean Absolute Error (MAE)	0.15
Mean Squared Error (MSE)	0.025
Root Mean Squared Error (RMSE)	0.158
Time to Convergence (seconds)	180
Training Set Size (samples)	10000
Test Set Size (samples)	5000
Number of Features	20
Model Size (MB)	10
Computational Resources Utilized (GPU)	2

can be divided into three distinct levels of strategies: the program level, the course level, and the task level. Each of these levels is a distinct strategy in its own right. There are three degrees of change: the program level involves changes to the institution, such as an optional class system, an elective system, and so on; the course level involves the planning of the learning path; and the task level involves the adaptation of content, services, and so on. Each of these levels requires a different approach to change. Each one of these three points of view is capable of being put into effect based on the adaptive alteration of judgments regarding instruction that are based on data. Consequently, the focal focus is the decision-making process that is based on facts, as demonstrated in Figure 16.2.

16.5 Conclusion and Future Direction

In conclusion, the purpose of this research work was to investigate the possibility of fuzzy logic-based adaptive educational systems being utilized to improve established literacy gests. By completely constructing and implementing these procedures, preceptors are able to tailor instruction to the specific needs and preferences of individual students, which results in decreased levels of engagement, provocation, and academic accomplishment. As a result of these findings, the efficacy of fuzzy logic in modeling question and imprecision in learner data is highlighted [48]. This opens the door for the development of adaptive educational systems that adequately alter literacy content, pace, and feedback based on real-time learner relations. With an eye towards the future, new investigation directions in this field may include further development and optimization of fuzzy logic-grounded adaptive educational systems in order to improve the effectiveness and scalability of these systems. Additionally, the investigation of the integration of these systems with emerging technologies such as artificial intelligence, machine literacy, and natural language processing has the potential to open up new avenues for the advancement of literacy that can be supported by evidence. In order to determine the long-term influence that fuzzy logic- based adaptive educational systems will have on learning difficulties, retention, and academic achievement, it will be necessary to conduct longitudinal studies and operations in the actual world. To a similar extent, addressing equity and availability concerns will be essential to ensure that demonstrated literacy improvements are accessible to all students, regardless of their backgrounds or circumstances. By giving inclusivity and diversity a higher priority in the process of designing and implementing adaptive educational systems, preceptors can create literacy environments that are more neutral and inclusive, thereby catering to the needs of all students. In general, the ongoing development and improvement of fuzzy logic-based adaptive educational systems hold the promise of revolutionizing traditional educational paradigms and empowering preceptors to meet the various requirements of learners in the educational geography of the present moment, which is becoming increasingly complex and dynamic.

References

1. Akbulut, Y. and Cardak, C.S., Adaptive educational hypermedia accommodating learning styles: A content analysis of publications from 2000 to 2011. *Comput. Educ.*, 58, 2, 835–842, 2012.
2. Alzahrani, M.S. and Abidi, M.H., An ontology-based fuzzy logic approach for personalized learning content recommendation. *Int. J. Adv. Comput. Sci. Appl.*, 7, 11, 170–178, 2016.

3. Bajaj, S., Gupta, R., Shankar, R., Design and development of fuzzy logic-based personalized adaptive educational system. *Int. J. Eng. Res. Technol. (IJERT)*, 7, 12, 585–589, 2018.
4. Chen, I.Y.L. and Chen, N.S., Personalized adaptive learning systems: From theory to practice. *Educ. Technol. Soc.*, 17, 2, 94–102, 2014.
5. De Albornoz, A., Plaza, L., Gervás, P., Predicting educational effectiveness through fuzzy logic-based modeling. *Int. J. Intell. Syst.*, 27, 7, 639–654, 2012.
6. Díaz, P., Juan, A.A., Aedo, I., Urretavizcaya, M., An adaptive and personalized learning system based on fuzzy cognitive maps. *Expert Syst. Appl.*, 37, 12, 7911–7918, 2010.
7. Dolog, P., Henze, N., Nejdl, W., Sintek, M., Personalization in distributed eLearning environments. *Int. J. Artif. Intell. Educ.*, 14, 1, 35–65, 2004.
8. Fardoun, H.M., Alghazzawi, D.M., González, J.M.G., Bustillo, A.M.V., Adaptive learning systems: Beyond teaching machines. *IEEE Rev. Iberoam. Tecnol. Aprendizaje*, 9, 3, 105–112, 2014.
9. Hastie, T., Tibshirani, R., Friedman, J., *The elements of statistical learning: Data mining, inference, and prediction*, Springer Science & Business Media, 2009.
10. Johnson, L., Adams Becker, S., Cummins, M., Estrada, V., Freeman, A., *NMC Horizon Report: 2013 K-12 Edition*, The New Media Consortium, Austin, Texas, 2013.
11. Karypis, G., Han, E.H., Kumar, V., Chameleon: Hierarchical clustering using dynamic modeling. *Computer*, 32, 8, 68–75, 1999.
12. Kotsiantis, S.B., Zaharakis, I., Pintelas, P.E., Supervised machine learning: A research of classification techniques. *Emerging Artif. Intell. Appl. Comput. Eng.*, 160, 1, 3–24, 2007.
13. Linton, M.A. and Ayres, D., *The effect of personalized system of instruction on the achievement and attitudes of community college students in a general education mathematics course*, Texas A&M University, 2006, Doctoral dissertation.
14. Loh, S.C. and Sheng, Y., *Fuzzy logic-based adaptive learning and cognitive assessments*, Universiti Tunku Abdul Rahman, 2015, Doctoral dissertation.
15. Lopes, C.A., Gonçalves, D.J.C., Martins, J.R., Adaptivity in educational systems: A research of the field. *Expert Syst. Appl.*, 39, 9, 7426–7432, 2012.
16. Marcos, C. and Marcos, M.C., Adaptive educational systems: A research of the literature. *J. Artif. Intell. Educ.*, 28, 2, 107–121, 2018.
17. Mitrovic, A. and Martin, B., Evaluating the effects of open student models on self-assessment. *Int. J. Artif. Intell. Educ.*, 12, 4, 344–361, 2002.
18. Najafabadi, M.M., Villanustre, F., Khoshgoftaar, T.M., Seliya, N., Wald, R., Muharemagic, E., Deep learning applications and challenges in big data analytics. *J. Big Data*, 2, 1, 1–21, 2015.
19. Nkambou, R., Bourdeau, J., Mizoguchi, R., *Intelligent tutoring systems: An research (Vol. 402)*, Springer Science & Business Media, 2010.
20. Padilla-Zea, N. and García-Peñalvo, F.J., Modeling and implementation of adaptive educational hypermedia systems. *J. Educ. Technol. Soc.*, 15, 3, 185–200, 2012.

21. Pardos, Z.A. and Heffernan, N.T., Modeling individualization in a Bayesian networks implementation of knowledge tracing, in: *Proceedings of the 3rd International Conference on Educational Data Mining*, pp. 131–140, 2010.
22. Rana, S.S., Paul, R.S., Joshi, M.C., Adaptive learning: A fuzzy logic approach. *Int. J. Comput. Appl.*, 61, 15, 21–25, 2013.
23. Pandey, D., Pandey, B.K., Wairya, S., Hybrid deep neural network with adaptive galactic swarm optimization for text extraction from scene images. *Soft Comput.*, 25, 2, 1563–1580, 2021.
24. Deepa, R., Anand, R., Pandey, D., Pandey, B.K., Karki, B., Comprehensive performance analysis of classifiers in diagnosis of epilepsy. *Math. Probl. Eng.*, *2022*, 1, 1559312, 2022.
25. KVM, S., Pandey, B.K., Pandey, D., Design of Surface Plasmon Resonance (SPR) Sensors for Highly Sensitive Biomolecular Detection in Cancer Diagnostics. *Plasmonics*, 1–13, 2024.
26. Kennedy, G.W., Sunday, S.E., Pandey, D., Kabari, A.D., Pandey, B.K., George, A.S., Dadheech, P., Building Information Modeling: Harnessing Innovations for Professional Proficiency, in: *Emerging Engineering Technologies and Industrial Applications*, pp. 305–331, IGI Global, 2024.
27. Pandey, D., Nassa, V.K., Pandey, B.K., Mahajan, D.A., Patidar, P.K., Dadheech, P., George, A.S., An Analysis of Internet-of-Things-Based Fire Detection and Alert Systems, in: *Emerging Engineering Technologies and Industrial Applications*, pp. 295–304, IGI Global, 2024.
28. Pandey, D., Pandey, B.K., Nassa, V.K., Mahajan, D.A., George, A.S., Dadheech, P., Optimized Throughput-Based Broadcasting for Next Generation Wireless Networks, in: *Emerging Engineering Technologies and Industrial Applications*, pp. 355–368, IGI Global, 2024.
29. Parthiban, K., Pandey, D., Pandey, B.K., Impact of SARS-CoV-2 in online education, predicting and contrasting mental stress of young students: A machine learning approach. *Augment. Hum. Res.*, 6, 1, 10, 2021.
30. Pandey, D., Pandey, B.K., Paramashivan, M.A., Mahajan, D.A., Dadheech, P.D., George, A.S., Hameed, A.S., Advanced Digital Data Processing Using Cloud Cryptography: Industrial Applications, in: *Emerging Engineering Technologies and Industrial Applications*, pp. 255–268, IGI Global, 2024.
31. Pandey, B.K., Mukundan, A.P., Nassa, V.K., Pandey, D., George, A.S., Hameed, A.S., Dadheech, P., Deployment of Load Balancing in Cloud Computing: Industrial Application and Benefits, in: *Emerging Engineering Technologies and Industrial Applications*, pp. 342–354, IGI Global, 2024.
32. Kumar, B., Pandey, D., Pandey, B.K., George, A.S., Higher Education in the Last Four Decades: A Review of Paradigm Shifts in Policy Frameworks. *Des. Implementation Higher Educ. Learners' Learn. Outcomes (HELLO)*, 333–348, 2024.
33. Pandey, B.K., Pandey, D., Agarwal, A., Encrypted information transmission by enhanced steganography and image transformation. *Int. J. Distrib. Artif. Intell. (IJDAI)*, 14, 1, 1–14, 2022.

34. Shahul, A., Muniandi, B., Paramashivan, M.A., Pandey, D., Pandey, B.K., Dadheech, P., George, H., An Analysis of Algorithms and Methods Based on Image Processing for Medical Applications, in: *Emerging Engineering Technologies and Industrial Applications*, pp. 173–186), IGI Global, 2024.
35. Sahani, S.K., Pandey, B.K., Pandey, D., Single-valued Signals, Multi-valued Signals and Fixed-Point of Contractive Signals. *Math. Open*, 2024.
36. Pandey, B.K., Pandey, D., Alkhafaji, M.A., Güneşer, M.T., Şeker, C., A reliable transmission and extraction of textual information using keyless encryption, steganography, and deep algorithm with cuckoo optimization, in: *Micro-Electronics and Telecommunication Engineering: Proceedings of 6th ICMETE 2022*, Springer Nature Singapore, Singapore, pp. 629–636, 2023.
37. Pandey, D., Ogunmola, G.A., Enbeyle, W., Abdullahi, M., Pandey, B.K., Pramanik, S., COVID-19: A framework for effective delivering of online classes during lockdown. *Hum. Arenas*, 1–15, 2021.
38. George, W.K., Silas, E., II, Pandey, D., Pandey, B.K., Utilization of Industry 4.0 Technologies in Nigerian Technical and Vocational Education: A Conundrum for Educators, in: *Examining the Rapid Advance of Digital Technology in Africa*, pp. 270–293, IGI Global, 2024.
39. Pandey, B.K., Pandey, D., Sahani, S.K., Autopilot control unmanned aerial vehicle system for sewage defect detection using deep learning. *Eng. Rep.*, e12852, 2024.
40. George, W.K., Ekong, M.O., Pandey, D., Pandey, B.K., Pedagogy for Implementation of TVET Curriculum for the Digital World, in: *Applications of Neuromarketing in the Metaverse*, pp. 117–136, IGI Global, 2023.
41. JayaLakshmi, G., Pandey, D., Pandey, B.K., Kaur, P., Mahajan, D.A., Dari, S.S., Smart Big Data Collection for Intelligent Supply Chain Improvement, in: *AI and Machine Learning Impacts in Intelligent Supply Chain*, pp. 180–195, IGI Global, 2024.
42. Kumar Pandey, B., Pandey, D., Nassa, V.K., Ahmad, T., Singh, C., George, A.S., Wakchaure, M.A., Encryption and steganography-based text extraction in IoT using the EWCTS optimizer. *Imaging Sci. J.*, 69, 1-4, 38–56, 2021.
43. Anand, R., Lakshmi, S.V., Pandey, D., Pandey, B.K., An enhanced ResNet-50 deep learning model for arrhythmia detection using electrocardiogram biomedical indicators. *Evol. Syst.*, 15, 1, 83–97, 2024.
44. Sharma, S., Pandey, B.K., Pandey, D., Anand, R., Sharma, A., Saini, S., Character Recognition Technique Implementation for Complicated Deteriorated Scene, in: *2023 6th International Conference on Information Systems and Computer Networks (ISCON)*, IEEE, pp. 1–4, (2023, March).
45. Pandey, B.K., Nassa, V.K., Mukundan, A.P., Mahajan, D.A., Pandey, D., George, A.S., Dadheech, P., An Industry-Focused Traffic System Utilising Internet of Things, in: *Emerging Engineering Technologies and Industrial Applications*, pp. 200–213, IGI Global, 2024.
46. Gupta, R., Mane, M., Bhardwaj, S., Nandekar, U., Afaq, A., Dhabliya, D., Pandey, B.K., Use of Artificial Intelligence for Image Processing to Aid

Digital Forensics: Legislative Challenges, in: *Handbook of Research on Thrust Technologies' Effect on Image Processing*, pp. 433–447, IGI Global, 2023.
47. BR, S.R., Saxena, A.K., Pandey, B.K., Gupta, S., Gurpur, S., Dari, S.S., Dhabliya, D., Machine Learning Application for Evidence Image Enhancement, in: *Handbook of Research on Thrust Technologies' Effect on Image Processing*, pp. 25–38, IGI Global, 2023.
48. Shanthi, T., Anand, R., Pandey, B.K., Nassa, V.K., Shahul, A., George, A.H., Dadheech, P., Exudate Detection in Fundus Images Using Deep Learning Algorithms, in: *Handbook of Research on Thrust Technologies' Effect on Image Processing*, pp. 256–272, IGI Global, 2023.
49. Pandey, B.K. and Pandey, D., Parametric optimization and prediction of enhanced thermoelectric performance in co-doped CaMnO3 using response surface methodology and neural network. *J. Mater. Sci.: Mater. Electron.*, 34, 21, 1589, 2023.
50. Pandey, D. and Pandey, B.K., An efficient deep neural network with adaptive galactic swarm optimization for complex image text extraction, in: *Process mining techniques for pattern recognition*, pp. 121–137, CRC Press, 2022.

17

Computational Intelligence Using Fuzzy Logic in Educational Data Analysis A Study of Methodologies and Applications

Hari Prasadarao Pydi[1]*, Hima Bindu Gogineni[2], Sammaiah Buhukya[3], Prasanta Chatterjee Biswas[4], Bhadrappa Haralayya[5] and N. Rao Cheepurupalli[6]

[1]Mechanical Engineering Department, College of Engineering and Technology, Bule Hora University, Bule Hora, Ethiopia
[2]AI&DS, VIGNAN'S Institute of Information and Technology, Visakhapatnam, Andhra Pradesh, India
[3]Department of Management Studies, School of Business Studies, Central University of Kashmir, J&K, India
[4]CDOE, Parul University, Vadodara, India
[5]Department of MBA, Lingaraj Appa Engineering College Bidar, Karnataka, India
[6]Department of Mineral Processing and Metallurgical Engineering, Faculty of Mines, Aksum University, Aksum, Ethiopia

Abstract
In this exploratory research, the use of computational intelligence, more especially fuzzy sense, in the analysis of educational data is investigated. The paper also investigates colorful approaches and the practical applications of these methodologies. To improve tutoring and literacy challenges, educational institutions are increasingly resorting to data-driven techniques. This trend is expected to continue. The use of fuzzy sense, which is well-known for its capacity to manage queries and complexity, provides potentially useful tools for evaluating educational data. The purpose of this project is to investigate how fuzzy sense models can be utilized to reuse and interpret various educational data sets. These data sets include educational criteria for student achievement as well as learning gesture patterns. In the process of establishing meaningful perceptivity from educational data, comparative evaluations of various fuzzy sense approaches highlight both the benefits

**Corresponding author*: haripydi609@gmail.com
Bhadrappa Haralayya: ORCID: https://orcid.org/0000-0003-3214-7261

Rahul Kar, Gunjan Mukherjee, Biswadip Basu Mallik and Ashok Kumar Shaw (eds.) Fuzzy Logic in Computational Intelligence: Applications and Case Studies, (309–322) © 2026 Scrivener Publishing LLC

and limits of these methodologies. To demonstrate the efficacy of fuzzy sense in the process of developing educational decision-making procedures, case studies illustrate realistic executions across a variety of educational environments. The findings highlight the potential for computational intelligence, and more specifically fuzzy sense, to change the way educational data analysis is done by providing preceptors and stakeholders with additional nuanced and practical perceptivity.

***Keywords*:** Computational intelligence, fuzzy logic, educational data analysis, methodologies, applications, student performance, learning outcomes

17.1 Introduction

The abundance of data that is available in today's educational landscape presents both opportunities and problems for educational institutions that are working to improve the efficiency of tutoring and address the concerns of students. Traditional methods of analyzing educational data typically have difficulty dealing with the complexity and inquiry that is necessary for educational data [1]. This data comprises a variety of factors, including student performance, learning gestures, and the efficiency of the institution. The pursuit of meaningful perceptivity from educational data has been prompted by this, which has led to an increased interest in the utilization of advanced computing methods, including fuzzy sense within the realm of computer intelligence [2].

It was Lotfi Zadeh who came up with the idea of fuzzy sense, which is an extension of classic double sense that allows for degrees of verity. Because of this, fuzzy sense is ideally suited for scripts in which the data is ambiguous or squishy. As it pertains to the realm of education, fuzzy sense provides a framework that may be utilized to model and analyze intricate connections between variables, hence facilitating the development of more sophisticated decision-making and prophetic capabilities. Fuzzy sense makes it easier to construct models that more accurately reflect the complexities of literacy processes [3]. This is accomplished by establishing fuzzy sets with class functions that capture the fuzziness of educational data, which is analogous to the fact that different scenarios of student understanding or engagement include different levels of engagement.

The purpose of this study is to investigate the application of fuzzy sense to educational data analysis, with a particular emphasis on methodology and practical operations. The primary objective is to investigate how fuzzy sense might improve the comprehension and utilization of educational data to improve tutoring practices, class design, and institutional tactics. Some methodologies include the formulation of fuzzy conclusion systems [4].

These systems evaluate data inputs and induce feasible perceptivity for preceptors and directors. These systems can evaluate the development of students, ascertain whether or not there are problems with learning, and determine the factors that influence academic achievement with less sensitivity than traditional methods [5].

The research study incorporates a comparative investigation of various fuzzy sense approaches that are utilized in the field of educational data processing. This article highlights the constraints and difficulties that they face, as well as the capabilities that they possess in terms of managing many types of educational data, which include anything from structured assessment results to unshaped qualitative feedback [6]. The purpose of this article is to provide practical examples of fuzzy sense operations through case studies from educational institutions. These case studies illustrate how these approaches can be included in decision-support systems to guide educational interventions and policy judgements [7].

The purpose of this investigation is to contribute to the development of educational data analytics through the application of computational intelligence by combining theoretical underpinnings with practical perceptivity. The findings highlight the potential for fuzzy sense to transform educational practices by providing further nuanced and environment-apprehensive interpretations of data, which will ultimately lead to breakthroughs in tutoring and reading environments that are grounded on substantiation [8, 9]. This discussion of approaches and operations provides preceptors and stakeholders with the opportunity to get a more profound understanding of the use of computational intelligence in the resolution of educational problems that are more successful [10, 11].

17.2 Related Works

Over the course of the last few years, there has been a substantial increase in the amount of interest and inquiry that has been dedicated to the subject of educational data analysis. The majority of this can be attributed to the growing popularity of digital literacy platforms as well as the increasing focus placed on data-driven decision-making in the educational sector. To handle the vital question and complexity that is inherent in educational data, fuzzy logic has emerged as an important instrument within the framework of this domain [12]. There is a high probability that this pattern will persist in the foreseeable future. For the aim of educating readers, the objective of this article is to present a detailed examination of the method and operations of fuzzy logic in the context of information analysis. In addition to providing a more in-depth comprehension of the role that fuzzy logic plays, the purpose of this research is to provide an understanding of the potential contributions that fuzzy logic could make to the improvement of educational methods [13].

Fuzzy logic, which has its roots in the principles of managing fuzzy information, provides a flexible framework for modeling and reasoning that can be questioned to some extent. Its origins can be traced back to the principles of managing fuzzy information [14]. Fuzzy logic, on the other hand, permits the depiction of hazy generalizations and partial facts, in contrast to the classic double logic, which operates in words that are both plain and precise. Consequently, it is particularly well-suited for the analysis of educational data that is characterized by several qualities that are sometimes vague. This is because it is characterized by many characteristics [15]. As an additional benefit, fuzzy logic can provide evaluations that are more comprehensive, nuanced, and contextually relevant. This, in turn, leads to decision-making processes that are ultimately better informed. This is something that can be accomplished by capturing the inherent fuzziness that is present in educational information.

Regarding the methodology, fuzzy logic is made up of a wide variety of methods and techniques that are adapted to satisfy the particular requirements of educational data processing. These methodologies and approaches provide the foundation for fuzzy logic. Fuzzy conclusion systems are a good example of this type of system since they provide a technique for mapping input variables to affair values by making use of language conventions [16]. As a result of this, activities such as assessing the performance of students and putting in place recommendation systems are made to be substantially less challenging to carry out. While the operation is being carried out, fuzzy clustering approaches make it possible to uncover patterns and links throughout big datasets. This provides essential information regarding pupil geste, which is essential for the procedure. Additionally, there are lectures offered on literacy [17]. Fuzzy decision-making fabrics also make it feasible for preceptors and directors to negotiate tough option landscapes by including a wide variety of criteria and preferences transparently and flexibly. This makes it possible for them to make decisions that are both fluid and transparent. In addition to that, this makes it possible to exhibit a higher degree of flexibility and transparency.

In the area of educational data analysis, fuzzy logic has a wide range of applications, and these applications take place across a large variety of disciplines within the education sector. When it comes to the process of evaluating the performance of the pupils, this is one of the most significant activities that are carried out. As a result of the fact that fuzzy logic models can accept a wide variety of assessment criteria and personal judgments, they can produce evaluations that are both thorough and suited to the obstacles that students experience when it comes to the acquisition of knowledge. It is possible for validated learning systems that are based on fuzzy logic to modify the data of individual students to make adjustments to educational content and interventions reliably [18]. In addition to that, these systems offer one additional advantage. The fact that they can respond to the distinct literacy requirements and preferences of each student is a huge advantage over other educational institutions. To continue along these lines, it has been proved that fuzzy logic is an essential tool for improving the distribution of resources in educational settings [19]. Preceptors have found that the ability to intelligently utilize limited resources, such as time, money, and educational accessories, to the fullest extent possible to maximize literacy concerns has proven to be of great help. With this skill, it has been demonstrated that literacy concerns can be effectively maximized.

The objective of this study is to give research on the theoretical underpinnings, methodological approaches, and practical operations of fuzzy logic. This inquiry will take place within the framework of doing data analysis for educational purposes. This is the circumstance that has come about as a result of the difficulties that have been brought up. The primary objective of this research is to shed light on the possibility of fuzzy logic, with the ultimate goal of shedding light on the revolutionary potential of fuzzy logic in determining the future of education and literacy analytics [20]. To achieve this purpose, a synthesis of the existing body of work will be performed, and upcoming trends and impediments will be connected.

17.3 Research Methodology

An approach that is structured to gather, dissect, and synthesize existing literature while simultaneously critically evaluating methodologies and relating practical operations across a variety of educational environments is the methodology that has been proposed to conduct comprehensive research on fuzzy logic in educational data analysis [21]. This methodology has been proposed to conduct research on data analysis in educational settings. This methodology has been suggested to investigate the data analysis that is carried out in educational environments. To carry out a comprehensive examination of the use of fuzzy logic in educational data analysis, this methodology has been conceived of as a potential approach [22].

Through the utilization of online databases such as PubMed, Scopus, Web of Science, and Google Scholar, the first step is to carry out an exhaustive literature search that is pertinent to the purpose of the investigation. The first step is at this point. This is going to be the primary tactic that must be utilized. The search will be conducted with the utilization of a wide range of keywords, some of which include "fuzzy logic," "educational data analysis," "fuzzy conclusion systems," "fuzzy clustering," and "fuzzy decision-timber [23]." For the search, the only sorts of publications that will be taken into consideration are journal papers that have been evaluated by other scholars, conference proceedings, books, and book chapters that have been published within the last twenty years.

Based on the data that is displayed in Figure 17.1, it can be deduced that this system can take in information that is completely not difficult to understand. The values that were assigned to the characteristics in the phase that came before this one are what constitute the input [24]. This phase is the beginning of the process. The subsequent phase is the one that follows this one. The subsequent stage involves the fuzzification of the input, by which the crisp values are converted into fuzzy values of the same sort. This transformation takes place through the process of conversion. This procedure is repeated until the output is cloudy, and it is carried out until it is finished.

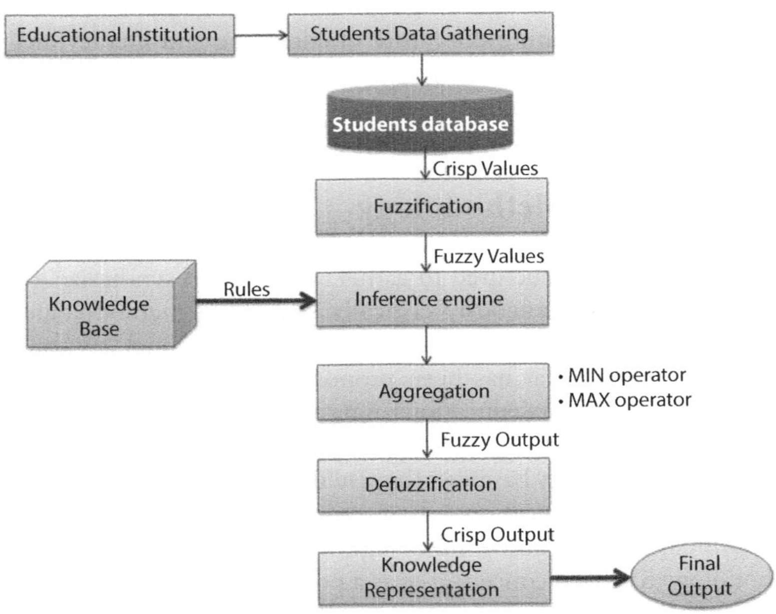

Figure 17.1 Depicts the fuzzy logic in education system.

The grades of different students can be translated into fuzzy forms such as Excellent, Good, or Bad. Additionally, it is possible to assign a membership value to any variable. A membership value can be assigned to any variable. It is also possible to assign membership values to other variables that are contained within the system. There is also the possibility that the instructor will assign grades to each variable at the same time [25–28]. In addition to the many different conceivable representations of these, the trapezoidal or triangular form is one of them. A great number of additional options are also available. Several additional alternate forms, such as the depiction in the shape of a triangle, are also available. These inputs will then be transmitted to the inference engine, which is the component that is responsible for applying rules to the membership functions. This is the next phase in the process. As a consequence of this, the maximum and minimum operators are utilized to aggregate these functions, which finally leads to the fulfillment of the outputs at the end of the process.

As a result of this, the search will subsequently be relevant and up to date from that point forward. For admission, one of the criteria that will be taken into consideration is research that focuses on the application of fuzzy logic approaches in educational data analysis. Work that does not directly connect to educational data analysis or that does not apply the fuzzy logic technique will be withdrawn from consideration as a result of the grounds for rejection [29]. On the other hand, works that do not employ fuzzy logic techniques will be considered.

Through the utilization of standardized form landing authors, publication time, research objects, methodology applied, datasets utilized, findings, and counteraccusations, we will be able to retrieve pertinent data from studies that have been named. An exhaustive web-based strategy will be implemented to accomplish this goal. This technique will conduct eligibility evaluations based on criteria that have been specified in advance [30]. The purpose of this is to ascertain whether or if the studies are available for inclusion in the study, and it will be carried out. Furthermore, to determine the re-creating themes, methodologies, and operations of fuzzy logic in the context of educational data analysis, thematic analysis will be carried out. This will be done to determine the re-creating themes. This is going to be done to determine the topic analysis that will be performed. To organize the information into meaningful clusters, it will be necessary to refer to the similarities and contrasts that are abstract.

Within the framework of the greater environment of fuzzy logic in educational data analysis, this uncertainty will be fleshed out by narrative ways to present a unified research of the literature and interpret the findings within the context of the larger environment. In addition, the approach that has been proposed incorporates an analysis and evaluation of the procedures that were utilized in the research that have been listed. This evaluation focuses on aspects such as the efficacy of fuzzy logic for handling queries and complexity in educational data, the robustness of fuzzy conclusion systems, clustering algorithms, and decision-making fabrics, as well as the validity and trustworthiness of findings that were deduced from fuzzy logic-ground analyses. Moreover, this evaluation also takes into consideration the use of fuzzy logic to handle queries and complexity in educational data. In the not-too-distant future, there will be a connection between the numerous practical applications of fuzzy logic in educational settings as shown in Figure 17.2.

An investigation of how fuzzy logic approaches have been utilized to address specific educational challenges, enhance tutoring and literacy difficulties, and supply information for decision-making processes will be carried out as a result of this. The findings from the literature conflation, methodological evaluation, and identification of operations will be synthesized into a structured research paper following the guidelines that have been set for the reporting of methodical research and meta-analyses. In compliance with the instructions, this course of action will be taken. This research paper aims to provide valuable insights into the role that fuzzy logic plays and its potential in educational data analysis. Additionally, the paper will discuss pressing important findings, emerging trends,

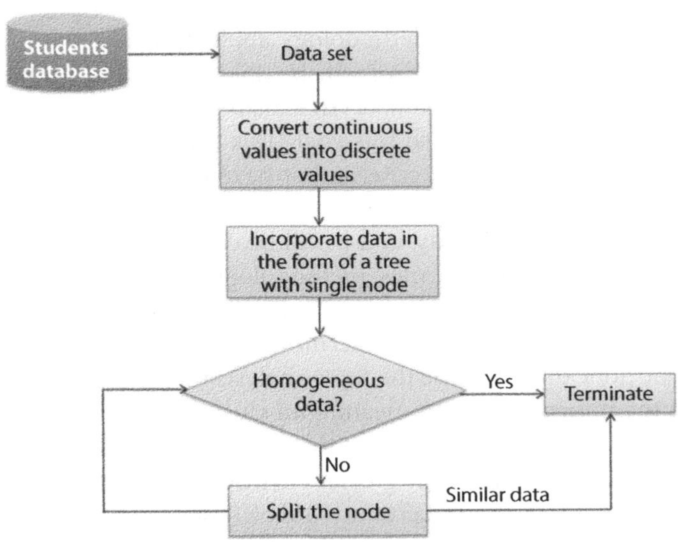

Figure 17.2 Depicts the dataset conversion into a decision tree.

challenges, and opportunities for future research and practice in the field of improving tutoring, literacy, and educational operations across a variety of educational environments. The purpose of this research paper is to provide these insights.

17.4 Results and Discussion

There are numerous types of neural networks, and each one is utilized for a certain set of activities that are unlike any other. The activities that students have participated in in the past can be taken into consideration by a Feed Forward Neural Network, which can then be used to create predictions about the performance of students. Additionally, it helps in recommending to students the learning possibilities that are available to them after completing an analysis of their performance to improve their performance in that particular topic. This makes it possible for students to improve their performance in that subject. Students who engage in undesirable behavior in the classroom, such as indulging in side-talking, losing concentration when studying, or demonstrating poor behavior with other students, can be identified with the assistance of a multilayer neural network, which is beneficial in recognizing these students. Children's learning is impacted by this conduct, and teachers can provide more attention to children who show this behavior and aid them in concentrating on their studies if they are detected.

This behavior has an impact on children's growth and development. In addition to this, it is useful in the classification of texts and in the prediction of students who will fall out of school. Through the use of this strategy, the students who are most likely to drop out of the class before completing it are identified. However, for a variety of reasons, the students withdraw from the program in the middle of their studies, which results in a loss not only for the students but also for the educational institution. The students enroll in the program to enhance their education and advance their careers; however, they withdraw from the program. For this reason, the method of data mining can be employed to assist in creating this prediction to guarantee that children are stopped at the proper time before they drop out of school. Recurrent neural networks help anticipate the degree of competence that learners possess, which is intended to assist teachers in assisting students in reaching their desired level of proficiency and improving their learning. This is done to assist teachers in assisting students in improving their learning. In addition to this, it makes projections regarding the number of students who will withdraw from school and the level of success that they will achieve in the future.

Two of the numerous methods that are utilized by fuzzy logic, which are advantageous to educational institutions, are clustering and K-nearest Neighbor. They are just two of the many methods that are utilized. Because clustering helps to group students based on the similarity in their performance, it indirectly helps to identify kids who are slow in learning. This is because clustering helps to group students. Consequently, this makes it possible to provide kids who are slow learners with additional attention, which might lead to an improvement in the academic performance of those students who have slower learning speeds. Through the utilization of K-Nearest Neighbor, it is feasible to forecast the academic achievement of pupils and the percentage of students who drop out of school, in addition to determining their abilities and routines. The Genetic Algorithms technique helps forecast the future performance of students, in addition to assisting in the selection of the top performer based on the data gained on students regarding their performance in the past. This is accomplished by analyzing the data that has been gathered regarding the

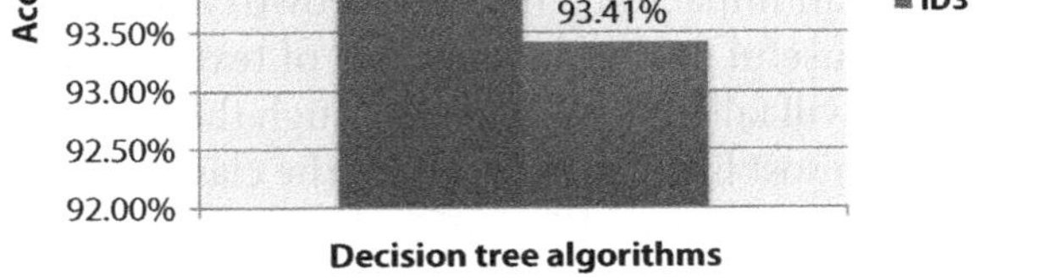

Figure 17.3 Depicts the comparison of the accuracy between fuzzy ID and ID.

Table 17.1 Performance comparison between fuzzy ID and ID.

	Algorithms	
Criteria	***Fuzzy* ID**	**ID**
Number of rules	28	44
Accuracy	95.85%	93.41%
Error	4.15%	6.59%

student's performance in the past. The utilization of decision trees as a method for determining the percentage of students who are successful in their academic endeavors aids in enhancing the process of teaching. Furthermore, it is beneficial to identify the children that require additional efforts at the classroom level for them to improve their learning. This is achieved through the use of this method as shown in Figure 17.3 and as per Table 17.1.

The application of the technology known as Support Vector Machine makes it simpler to categorize children according to how well they perform in their academics and other activities. The Bayesian Classifier is a tool that provides a prediction regarding the percentage of students who are successful in the system of distance education. This tool is designed to assist in the process of making intelligent decisions within the system. Students have the opportunity to get specialized facilities to improve the quality of their educational experience for themselves. The classification of text materials is another function that it performs, and it also contributes to the process of predicting the results of the course. Enhancements can be made to the course to provide the students with a more satisfying educational experience.

17.5 Conclusion

A plethora of approaches and operations, together with hopeful counter-accusations for the future of educational research and practice, have been discovered as a result of the disquisition of fuzzy logic in educational data analysis. As a result of this research, it has become abundantly clear that fuzzy logic offers a robust framework for managing the important inquiry and imprecision that is prevalent in educational data. In conclusion, this research demonstrates that fuzzy logic is a viable method for addressing complicated educational topics such as the patterns of literacy among students, assessment procedures, and the optimization of educational systems. By combining a variety of procedures and operations, it becomes clear that fuzzy logic provides a versatile approach that is complementary to conventional statistical methods. This is especially true in scripts where the data exhibit a degree of ambiguity or nebulousness.

As we look to the future, future research avenues may focus on further improving fuzzy logic models to improve the interpretability and intuitiveness of their prophetic abilities. Additionally, there is a requirement to investigate the possibility of interdisciplinary collaborations between educational experimenters, computer scientists, and sphere experts to develop novel applications of fuzzy logic in educational environments.

Similarly, investigating the possibility of incorporating fuzzy logic with emerging technologies like as machine literacy and artificial intelligence could lead to the development of new avenues for the implementation of substantiated literacy systems and adaptable educational interventions. In general, this research emphasizes the potential for the fuzzy logic to be used in the revision of educational data analysis and emphasizes the need to continue to engage in discourse within this promising sector.

References

1. Chen, S.-M. and Lee, L.-W., A fuzzy comprehensive evaluation approach for higher education teaching quality assessment. *Qual. Quant.*, 50, 5, 2155–2174, 2016, https://doi.org/10.1007/s11135-015-0243-4.
2. Dubey, V.N. and Sharma, S.K., Fuzzy multi-criteria decision making approach for quality assessment of engineering education institutions. *J. Intell. Fuzzy Syst.*, 34, 5, 3195–3208, 2018, https://doi.org/10.3233/JIFS-169018.
3. Eskandari, H. and Zareie, B., A fuzzy AHP-GRA approach for ranking educational factors affecting Iranian e-learning programs. *J. Intell. Fuzzy Syst.*, 37, 6, 8023–8034, 2019, https://doi.org/10.3233/JIFS-179213.
4. Gupta, S. and Sharma, S.K., Fuzzy approach for ranking of engineering colleges based on perceptions of stakeholders. *J. Intell. Fuzzy Syst.*, 33, 1, 503–515, 2017, https://doi.org/10.3233/JIFS-169193.
5. Islam, M.A. and Karim, M.R., A fuzzy logic-based approach for student performance evaluation in higher education. *Soft Comput.*, 24, 6, 4301–4312, 2020, https://doi.org/10.1007/s00500-019-04488-w.
6. Jadhav, J. and Patil, G.S., A fuzzy logic approach for assessment of student's academic performance. *Int. J. Emerging Res. Manage. Technol.*, 5, 4, 13–17, 2016.
7. Jena, S.K. and Sarkar, B., A hybrid fuzzy-PSO technique for forecasting student performance in educational institutions. *Appl. Soft Comput.*, 75, 325–339, 2019, https://doi.org/10.1016/j.asoc.2018.11.018.
8. Khan, S. and Khan, R., A fuzzy approach for assessing student's performance in an educational institute. *J. Comput. Theor. Nanosci.*, 14, 12, 6245–6253, 2017, https://doi.org/10.1166/jctn.2017.6933.
9. Kim, J.-G. and Kim, Y.-D., A study on the fuzzy AHP-based evaluation model of vocational training institutions. *Int. J. Fuzzy Log. Intell. Syst.*, 18, 4, 311–317, 2018, https://doi.org/10.5391/IJFIS.2018.18.4.311.
10. Kumar, A. and Bishnoi, P.K., A fuzzy approach for evaluation of educational website quality. *Int. J. Web Inf. Syst.*, 15, 1, 47–65, 2019, https://doi.org/10.1108/IJWIS-11-2017-0089.

11. Li, X. and Wang, X., A comprehensive fuzzy evaluation model for educational quality: A case study of a university in China. *Appl. Soft Comput.*, 46, 106–115, 2016, https://doi.org/10.1016/j.asoc.2016.05.031.
12. Li, Z. and Wei, Y., Evaluation of teaching quality based on fuzzy comprehensive assessment. *Journal of Physics: Conference Series*, vol. 1060, p. 012024, 2018, https://doi.org/10.1088/1742-6596/1060/1/012024.
13. Liao, H. and Lin, C., Using a fuzzy inference system for developing an early warning system for students' academic performance. *Appl. Soft Comput.*, 49, 1160–1171, 2016, https://doi.org/10.1016/j.asoc.2016.10.016.
14. Liu, Y. and Wu, Z., An integrated fuzzy logic model for the evaluation of teaching quality in higher education institutions. *Qual. Assur. Educ.*, 25, 1, 93–108, 2017, https://doi.org/10.1108/QAE-11-2015-0052.
15. Lopes, J.H.R. and Mariani, V.C., Fuzzy logic approach applied to educational web mining. *Soft Comput.*, 22, 12, 4061–4071, 2018, https://doi.org/10.1007/s00500-017-2893-9.
16. Marć, M. and Krawiec, K., Fuzzy logic systems for prediction of student's examination outcomes. *Appl. Soft Comput.*, 72, 97–107, 2018, https://doi.org/10.1016/j.asoc.2018.07.034.
17. Mardani, A. and Zavadskas, E.K., Fuzzy multi-criteria decision-making techniques and applications - Two decades research from 1994 to 2014. *Expert Syst. Appl.*, 42, 8, 4126–4148, 2017, https://doi.org/10.1016/j.eswa.2015.12.053.
18. Mihai, G.B. and Gîfu, D., II, A fuzzy AHP approach for ranking the importance of the criteria influencing the quality of e-learning. *Econ. Comput. Econ. Cybern. Stud. Res.*, 53, 1, 115–132, 2019.
19. Nasiri, M.M. and Mirzaei, M., Fuzzy TOPSIS method for evaluating the performance of higher education institutions. *Educ. Inf. Technol.*, 24, 1, 881–898, 2019, https://doi.org/10.1007/s10639-018-9766-1.
20. Pal, A. and Soni, M., Application of fuzzy TOPSIS method for the selection of private engineering college. *J. Eng. Educ. Transformations*, 31, 2, 103–110, 2018.
21. Pedrycz, W. and Chen, S.-M., Granular computing and intelligent systems: Design with information granules of high order and high type. *Inf. Sci.*, 374, 97–112, 2016, https://doi.org/10.1016/j.ins.2016.09.011.
22. Pramanik, S. and Saha, S., A fuzzy approach for ranking Indian engineering colleges. *Int. J. Innovative Res. Science Eng. Technol.*, 5, 11, 20292–20299, 2016.
23. Sharma, S.K. and Jain, K., A fuzzy MCDM approach for evaluating higher education institutions, 2019.
24. Zaidi, A., A Numerical Integration of locally Peaked Bivariate Functions. *Acta Scientiarum. Technol.*, 45, 1, e63310, 2023. https://doi.org/10.4025/actascitechnol.v45i1.63310.

25. Rai, P.K., Pandey, D., Pandey, B.K., The future of enterprise and innovation is compute as a commodity, or CaaC. *Partn. Univers. Int. Res. J.*, 3, 2, 89–94, 2024.
26. Pandey, D., Nassa, V.K., Pandey, B.K., Thankachan, B., Dadheech, P., Mahajan, D.A., George, A.S., Artificial intelligence and machine learning and its application in the field of computational visual analysis, in: *Emerging engineering technologies and industrial applications*, pp. 36–57, IGI Global Scientific Publishing, 2024.
27. Zaidi, A., Mathematical Methods for IoT-Based Annotating Object Datasets with Bounding Boxes. *Math. Prob. Eng.*, 2022, Article ID 3001939, 2022. https://doi.org/10.1155/2022/3001939.
28. Singh, S., Madaan, G., Swapna, H.R., Singh, A., Pandey, B.K., George, A.S., Pandey, D., Unleashing the power of AI and data analysis: Transforming insights into action, in: *Interdisciplinary Approaches to AI, Internet of Everything, and Machine Learning*, pp. 1–24, IGI Global Scientific Publishing, 2025.
29. Zaïdi, A., Accurate IoU computation for rotated bounding boxes in R2 and R3. *Mach. Vis. Appl.*, 32, Article number 114, 2021, https://doi.org/10.1007/s00138-021-01238-x.
30. Zimmermann, H.J., Fuzzy set theory and its applications (4th ed.). Springer, 2011.

18

Fuzzy Logic-Based Decision Support System for Strategic Management in Dynamic Environments

Dilip S. Shelar[1]*, Deepali Suhas Jadhav[2], K. Suresh Kumar[3], M. K. Sharma[4], Bhadrappa Haralayya[5] and Joshuva Arockia Dhanraj[6]

[1]Department of Engineering Sciences, AISSMS Institute of Information Technology, Pune, Maharashtra, India
[2]Department of Information Technology, Vishwakarma Institute of Technology, Pune, Maharashtra, India
[3]MBA Department, Panimalar Engineering College, Varadarajapuram, Poonamallee, Chennai, India
[4]Mathematics, Haudhary Charan Singh University, Meerut, Uttar Pradesh, India
[5]Department of MBA, Lingaraj Appa Engineering College Bidar, Karnataka, India
[6]Department of Computer Science and Engineering (AI&ML), School of Engineering, Dayananda Sagar University, Devarakaggalahalli, Harohalli, Bengaluru, Karnataka, India

Abstract

A novel approach to the building of a decision support system that is suitable for strategic operation in dynamic environments. This approach is accomplished through the utilization of fuzzy sense. In current corporate environments, which are marked by quick shifts and unpredictability, it is typical for traditional techniques of decision-making to fail when it comes to providing directors with sufficient support. This is because of the nature of the context. The usage of fuzzy sense provides this system with a framework that is both flexible and adaptable. This framework enables the

**Corresponding author*: dilipsshelar@gmail.com; ORCID: https://orcid.org/0000-0002-3279-8964
K. Suresh Kumar: ORCID: https://orcid.org/0000-0002-3912-3687
M. K. Sharma: ORCID: https://orcid.org/0000-0003-3071-5931
Bhadrappa Haralayya: https://orcid.org/0000-0003-3214-7261
Joshuva Arockia Dhanraj: https://orcid.org/0000-0001-5048-7775

Rahul Kar, Gunjan Mukherjee, Biswadip Basu Mallik and Ashok Kumar Shaw (eds.) Fuzzy Logic in Computational Intelligence: Applications and Case Studies, (323–340) © 2026 Scrivener Publishing LLC

system to manage uncertain and fuzzy information, which is necessary in circumstances that are constantly changing. It is recommended that decision-makers use a strategy that integrates fuzzy sense with strategic operation concepts. This method enhances decision-makers' capacity to evaluate complex situations, identify potential hazards, and construct strategies with a reduced degree of clarity and assurance. According to the findings of this study, fuzzy sense-based decision support systems have the potential to significantly improve the processes involved in strategic decision-making. These systems, as a consequence, offer businesses that operate in contexts that are both dynamic and uncertain a useful perceptivity that they may utilize. To achieve this goal, it is necessary to conduct an in-depth investigation of the theoretical underpinnings as well as the actual applications of the subject matter.

Keywords: Fuzzy logic, decision support system, strategic management, dynamic environments

18.1 Introduction

The healthcare industry has been experiencing a tremendous amount of turmoil over the past few years. The development of new technologies, the alterations in the expectations of patients, and the expansion of geographical areas that do not require supervision have all contributed to the revolution that has taken place [1]. The concept of gig labor, which refers to a form of employment that is both flexible and nimble, has acquired significance as a result of the increasing trends that are redefining the pool of healthcare providers. Gig work is a form of employment that emphasizes flexibility and nimbleness [2]. As a result of the expansion of the gig economy, which is characterized by freelance labor and short-term contracts, traditional employment patterns have been disrupted across a wide range of sectors, including the healthcare industry. This disruption has occurred in a number of different industries [3]. When viewed in this light, the issue of navigating the future of healthcare gig work within the framework of smart diligence presents healthcare professionals, institutions, and policymakers with opportunities as well as obstacles to overcome [52].

Smart diligence, which is often connected with the application of cutting-edge technology such as artificial intelligence [46], the Internet of Things (IoT) [37], and data analytics, has the potential to revolutionize both the delivery of healthcare and the operation of healthcare facilities. This is because smart diligence has the ability to improve and streamline both of these aspects of healthcare delivery. Specifically, this is due to the fact that the adoption of these technologies is often associated with intelligent diligence [4]. It is possible for the implementation of intelligent healthcare systems, which include digital platforms, telemedicine, and remote monitoring, to result in a number of advantageous outcomes. These outcomes include improved functional efficacy, improved patient care, and optimal resource allocation [36]. Through the implementation of intelligent healthcare systems [33], it is possible to achieve these benefits [5]. As a result of the current climate, the creation of gig work in the healthcare industry as a dynamic and adaptable solution to the ever-changing demands and issues of the assiduity has taken place. This is a consequence of the current climate for the industry [31].

Within the context of the healthcare industry [51], the purpose of this inquiry study is to conduct an analysis of the nameless line of labor. The smart diligence paradigm will serve as the basis for this examination, which will take place within them [6]. In order to achieve the goal of providing a better understanding of the changing employment landscape in the healthcare industry, the purpose of this study is to undertake an analysis of the current trends, problems, and opportunities that are being experienced by the industry in question [45]. In the context of the healthcare industry, the purpose of this investigation is to make an attempt to interpret the factors that are associated with gig employment [7]. These factors include the drivers, counteraccusations, and underlying concerns. For the purpose of this investigation, an interdisciplinary strategy is utilized, which incorporates perspectives from the disciplines of technology, labor economics [32], and healthcare establishment.

The fact that this investigation is able to provide information to a significant number of stakeholders within the healthcare ecosystem is the primary reason for the significance of this investigation. Individuals who are committed to carrying out their duties are included in this group of stakeholders. Some examples of these individuals are employees in the healthcare industry [62], employers, policymakers, and prominent leaders [8]. In order to build strategies that encourage pool adaptability, drive invention, and ensure excellent case care, it is vital to have a solid understanding of the dynamics of healthcare gig labor in smart diligence. It is imperative that this comprehension be understood in order to guarantee the provision of high-quality case care. By navigating the future of healthcare gig work, stakeholders have the opportunity to embrace the revolutionary potential of smart diligence, which will result in the building of a healthcare pool that is more flexible, responsive, and sustainable [9]. This will be accomplished by recognizing the potential of smart diligence. All of this will be accomplished *via* the careful application of intelligence and diligence.

In the following sections of this paper, we will delve deeper into the patterns [44] that are driving healthcare gig labor, investigate the obstacles that are encountered by healthcare workers and healthcare institutions, investigate the role that technology plays in making gig work easier, and bandy counteraccusations for policy and practice. All of these topics will be covered in greater detail [10]. You may expect to learn more about each of these subjects in greater detail. From the beginning of the smart diligence process to the end of it, our goal is to provide insights that are not only helpful but also contribute to the growth of gig labor in the healthcare industry. This comprehension will be attained by the application of empirical research, case studies, and the perspectives of a large number of stakeholders.

18.2 Related Works

In the realm of decision support systems (DSS) for strategic operation in dynamic surroundings, a variety of methodologies and approaches have been explored to address the complications and misgivings essential in similar surroundings. This section provides an research of applicable literature, pressing crucial benefactions and approaches in the field.

A. Traditional Decision Support Systems:
Traditional decision support systems have long been employed to prop strategic decision-making in business surrounds. These systems frequently calculate on fine models [53], optimization ways, and statistical analysis to give decision support [11]. While effective in certain scripts, traditional DSS may struggle to adequately handle the nebulosity and imprecision present in dynamic surroundings.

B. Fuzzy sense- Grounded Decision Support Systems:
Fuzzy sense has surfaced as an important tool for dealing with query and vagueness in decision- making processes. Fuzzy sense-grounded DSS influence fuzzy sets and verbal variables to represent and reason with squishy information [12]. This approach allows decision-makers to capture and incorporate private judgments [40] and qualitative assessments into the decision-making process, making it particularly well-suited for dynamic surroundings where precise data [38] may be lacking or unreliable [13].

C. Dynamic Surroundings and Strategic Management:
The dynamic nature of ultramodern business surroundings presents unique challenges for strategic operation. Rapid changes in request conditions, technological advancements, and competitive geographies bear associations to acclimatize and make strategic opinions in real-time [14]. Several studies have explored the operation of colorful decision support methodologies, including fuzzy sense, in dynamic surroundings to enhance strategic decision-making processes [15].

D. Fuzzy sense in Strategic Decision Making:
Previous research has demonstrated the efficacy of fuzzy sense-grounded approaches in strategic decision-making surrounds. For illustration, fuzzy sense has been applied to portfolio operation, resource allocation, threat assessment, and performance evaluation, among other strategic operation tasks [16–19]. These studies have shown that fuzzy sense-grounded DSS can help decision-makers navigate query and complexity more effectively, leading to further robust and informed strategic opinions.

E. Integration of Fuzzy sense with Other ways:
In addition to standalone fuzzy sense-grounded DSS, experimenters have explored the integration of fuzzy sense with other decision support ways, similar as inheritable algorithms, neural networks [60], and expert systems. By combining multiple methodologies, experimenters aim to enhance the capabilities and performance of decision support systems in dynamic surroundings [20].

F. Case Studies and Empirical Research:
Several case studies and empirical research sweats have examined the practical operations of fuzzy sense-grounded DSS in real-world settings. These studies have demonstrated the mileage and effectiveness of fuzzy sense in abetting strategic decision-making across colorful diligence and disciplines, including finance, healthcare, manufacturing, and logistics.

The literature research highlights the growing interest in fuzzy sense-grounded decision support systems for strategic operation in dynamic surroundings. While traditional DSS have limitations in handling query and nebulosity, fuzzy sense offers a flexible and effective approach for addressing these challenges and easing further informed decision-making processes.

18.3 Research Methodology

The proposed methodology for developing a Fuzzy sense-Grounded Decision Support System (DSS) for strategic operation in dynamic surroundings involves several crucial ways aimed at designing and enforcing a system able to address the complications and misgivings essential in similar surroundings. This section outlines the methodology, detailing each step and its significance in the development process [21]. Figure 18.1 provides a visual representation of the fuzzy logic system that has been explained on this page. The fuzzifier, the rule base system, the inference

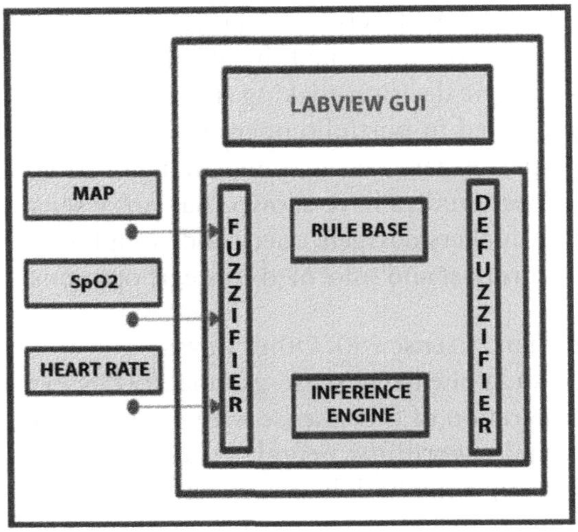

Figure 18.1 Block diagram of proposed system.

engine, and the defuzzifier are the key components that may be found in a fuzzy system. Other components included the inference engine.

The output of the fuzzifier is obtained from the numerous sensors [56] that are located on the body as part of this system [22]. The physical factors that are present on the body are perceived by these sensors [61], which are responsible for their detection [59]. To activate and apply rules, the fuzzifier is responsible for translating sensor inputs into information that can be suitably employed by the inference process [34]. For the purpose of future reference, information pertaining to experts is saved within the form rule base system. The reasoning that is founded on the base will be carried out by the system by the rule [23].

The rule base contains the fuzzy logic quantification of the language description provided by the specialists regarding how to achieve good control [24]. In the form of linguistic fuzzy logic terms, which are subsequently stored in the rule-based system, it is possible to discover the knowledge that is held by specialists. To understand, correlate, and apply knowledge regarding the most effective means of operating the plant [55], an inference machine is applied to replicate the decision-making process of an expert [58]. This allows for the plant to be controlled in the most efficient manner possible. The inference machine [41] and the rule-based system work together to do an analysis of the data [39] and acquire the output in line with the expertise of the experienced human [25]. Defuzzification is a procedure that involves the transformation of the conclusions that were reached by the inference mechanism into actual inputs for the process. By making use of a demulsifier, we can alter things such that they are returned to the correct output.

A. Problem Definition and Scope Identification

The first step in developing the fuzzy sense-grounded DSS involves easily defining the problem sphere and relating the compass of the system. This includes understanding the strategic operation challenges faced by associations operating in dynamic surroundings, similar to rapid-fire changes in request conditions, technological dislocations, and evolving competitive geographies [26]. By defining the problem sphere and compass outspoken, the development platoon can ensure that the DSS adequately addresses the specific requirements and conditions of its intended druggies.

B. Data Collection and Preprocessing

Once the problem sphere and compass have been defined, the coming step involves collecting applicable data that will be used to inform the decision-making process. This may include literal data on request trends [47], client geste, contender analysis, and internal organizational criteria [27]. also, data preprocessing [48] ways may be applied to clean and transfigure the raw data, icing its quality and felicity for analysis. This step is pivotal for ensuring that the fuzzy sense-grounded DSS has access to accurate and dependable information for making strategic opinions [28].

C. Knowledge Representation and Fuzzy sense Modeling

With the data collected [57] and pre-processed, the coming step involves representing the knowledge sphere using fuzzy sense modeling ways. Fuzzy sense allows for the representation of vague and squishy information, making it well-suited for landing the complications and misgivings present in dynamic surroundings [29]. The development platoon will design fuzzy conclusion systems (FIS) to model the decision-making rules and connections within the strategic operation sphere. This may involve defining verbal variables, class functions, fuzzy rules, and conclusion mechanisms that collude inputs to laborers in the decision-making process.

D. System Design and perpetration

Once the fuzzy sense models have been defined, the development platoon will do with designing and enforcing the DSS armature. This involves integrating the fuzzy conclusion systems with a stoner interface, database operation system, and other necessary factors to produce a functional decision support system. The system design should prioritize usability, scalability, and inflexibility, allowing druggies to interact with the DSS effectively and acclimatize it to changing requirements and conditions.

E. Confirmation and Testing

After the DSS has been enforced, it undergoes confirmation and testing to ensure its delicacy, trustability, and effectiveness in real-world scripts [30]. This may involve conducting simulation studies, case studies, or airman tests using literal data or synthetic datasets to estimate the performance of the system. confirmation sweats aim to corroborate that the fuzzy sense-grounded DSS produces reasonable and practicable recommendations that align with expert knowledge and sphere perceptivity.

F. Deployment and Integration

Once the DSS has been validated, it's ready for deployment and integration into the strategic operation processes of the target association. This may involve training end-druggies on how to use the DSS effectively, integrating it with being decision-making workflows and systems, and establishing mechanisms for ongoing conservation and support. The deployment phase is critical for ensuring that the fuzzy sense-grounded DSS is successfully espoused and employed by decision-makers within the association.

G. Evaluation and nonstop enhancement

Following deployment, the fuzzy sense-grounded DSS undergoes nonstop evaluation and enhancement to enhance its performance and capabilities over time. This may involve monitoring stoner feedback, collecting fresh data, and enriching the fuzzy sense models grounded on new perceptivity and compliances. By continuously assessing and perfecting the DSS, associations can ensure that it remains applicable and effective in supporting strategic decision-making in dynamic surroundings. The proposed methodology for developing a fuzzy sense-grounded DSS for strategic operation in dynamic surroundings involves several iterative ways, including problem description, data collection, knowledge representation, system design, confirmation, deployment, and nonstop enhancement. By following this methodology, associations can design and apply a robust decision support system able to navigate the complications and misgivings of dynamic business surroundings effectively.

18.4 Results and Discussion

An example of a decision support system is a combination of software and hardware that is utilized in the pharmaceutical business [6] as well as in medical facilities [42]. The medical experts who are working in the operating room are able to receive support from this system during the course of major procedures. On the DSS screen, it is possible to display a variety of alerts in the form of visual codes and bip-bip messages. Additionally, it is able to provide emergency alarms in the case that there is a concern. An assortment of sensors that are attached to the patient body model are the sources of the input that are being received.

In the event that something goes wrong, the computer is able to offer aid to the medical professionals because it has been programmed with an algorithm [43] that has been preserved in the computer. Within this system, the specialist acts as the ultimate controller, and it is able to carry out the operations in line with the input that is provided by the specialist. DCS provides a number of advantages, some of which include the capacity to improve the quality of care, the capacity to supply ideas that are expert-like, the decrease of human error, and the reduction of the burden that is imposed on medical workers.

It is impossible for humans to recall everything that takes place in the operating room, including the operational constraints and diagnostic procedures that are carried out there. This is especially true when it comes to the operating room. People are unable to remember anything that takes on there since it is beyond their power to do so [50]. From this moment forward, it is impossible to remember a single one of these things in any way, shape, or form. They cannot be remembered in any way, shape, or form. They are completely incapable of being remembered. This is because the utilization of DSS is brought about as a result of the utilization of DSS in the recommendations, which serves to make it beneficial to stick to proven criteria, thereby reducing the number of incorrect diagnoses and therapies, as well as modifying the behaviors and environments that are not suitable. This is the reason why this is the case. We were able to get the information by first collecting it from experts and then entering it into the Decision Support System (DSS), which is a system that is founded on the principles of knowledge [35]. This information was kept in the DSS (Figure 18.2), which is the location where it was saved. A vast selection of mathematical models, fuzzy logic, surgical algorithms, and operational instructions may be found within the Data Storage System (DSS), which was designed to serve as a storehouse for a variety of different types of information [54]. The DSS provides a repository for all of these different kinds of information. In addition, the system offers instructions on how it should be utilized, which is a feature that is of great importance. After that, these algorithms are refined based on the information that is provided by the patient, and in the end, the system provides aid to the medical specialists in the form of alarms that can be heard and seen as the process is being carried out.

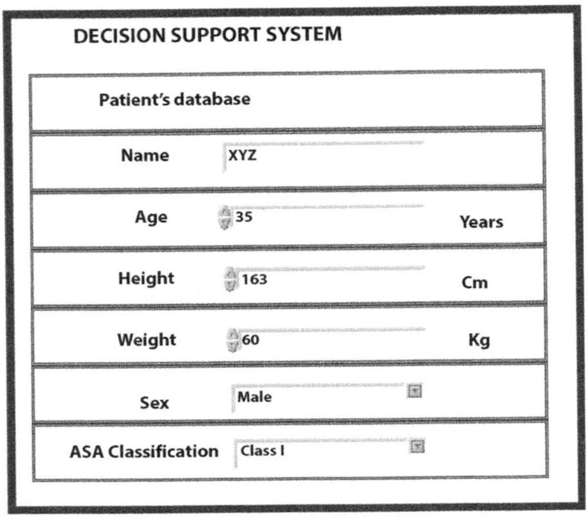

Figure 18.2 Patient database.

It is also feasible to note that the output is able to change in response to the input that is contained inside the graphical user interface. This is something that can be taken into consideration. Certainly, this is something that is able to be made possible. It is possible to make this remark at this point in time. It would not be completely out of the question to make this comment at this precise instant in time. The system will start to beep a message and will also start to trigger an alarm whenever the readings on the graphical user interface (GUI) reach a certain threshold. Both of these actions will take place simultaneously. It is expected that this will take place after the system has achieved the threshold. Both of these incidents will take place simultaneously, which is another important point to consider. With absolute certainty, each and every one of these occurrences will take place at the same time.

Taking into serious consideration the fact that both of these happenings will take place at the same time is still another vital component that must be taken into account. This system acts as the doctor's knowledge, and it sends a signal to the attending physician or anesthesiologist so that they may determine the right quantity that should be delivered to the patient. The information that has been provided serves as the basis for the system's operation. As a consequence of this, the doctor is in a position to provide the medication effectively. Specifically, this is something that is in agreement with every one of the things that have been mentioned up to this point in time.

As a consequence of this, the life of the patient will be taken into consideration by the individuals who are accountable for it. The most important thing is that anesthesiologists are able to easily examine the numerical value of depth of anesthesia (DOA). This is the most important thing. Because of this DOA, anesthesiologists are able to easily comprehend and anticipate the condition of the patient while the surgery is being performed, and they are also able to retain control over the procedure. The information is presented in a tabular fashion in Table 18.1, which comprises the same things. This is the site where all of the parameter readings are kept in the database of the patient while the procedure is being performed, as illustrated in Table 18.1. The user interface that was built is straightforward and offers accurate readings. It is also easy to understand. Calculations are being performed to ascertain the amount of anesthetic that is being supplied, and the outcomes of these calculations may be observed in the section of the square that is located to the right.

Additionally, a graphical user interface had been made available in Lab view in order to display all of the pertinent information (Figure 18.3), which are all essential throughout the process of medication infusion with

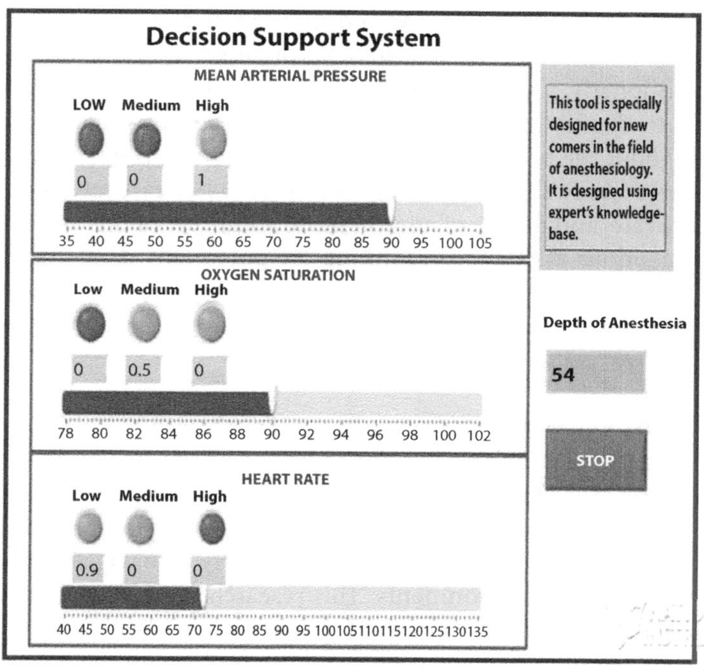

Figure 18.3 Results on lab view display.

Table 18.1 Depicts the parameter readings during the operation (database).

Sr. no.	MAP	SpO2	HR	DOA
1	42	80.5	55	25.96
2	55	85	90	26.19
3	50	82	90	28.33
4	41	86	57	55
5	54	91	88	37.16
6	50	90	73	54
7	66	90	85	64.94
8	68	92	90	82.35

the patient. These parameters include skin oxygen saturation (SPO2), heart rate, blood pressure, pulse rate, and degree of anesthesia. The entirety of this system would be of tremendous assistance in limiting the potentially dangerous scenarios that would develop as a result of wrong dosing, and as a consequence, it would be of substantial service in saving lives. Additionally, a graphical user interface had been made available in Lab view to display all of the pertinent information, which is all essential throughout the process of medication infusion with the patient. These parameters include skin oxygen saturation (SPO2), heart rate, blood pressure, pulse rate, and degree of anesthesia. The entirety of this system would be of tremendous assistance in limiting the potentially dangerous scenarios that would develop as a result of wrong dosing, and as a consequence, it would be of substantial service in saving lives.

18.5 Conclusion

In conclusion, the development and implementation of a Fuzzy Logic-Based Decision Support System (DSS) mark a significant advancement in the field of strategic management, particularly in navigating the complexities of dynamic environments. This research underscores the efficacy of fuzzy logic in handling uncertainty and ambiguity inherent in such contexts, offering decision-makers a robust tool for informed decision-making. By leveraging fuzzy inference systems and linguistic variables, the

DSS provides a flexible framework for capturing and processing imprecise information, thereby enabling organizations to adapt swiftly to changing circumstances and seize opportunities amidst uncertainty.

Looking ahead, several promising avenues for future research and development emerge. Firstly, further refinement and optimization [63] of fuzzy logic models and algorithms hold potential for enhancing the accuracy and performance of the DSS, particularly in highly volatile environments. Additionally, the integration of fuzzy logic-based DSS with emerging technologies like artificial intelligence and big data analytics could unlock new capabilities and insights, augmenting strategic decision-making processes [49].

Tailoring the DSS to address industry-specific challenges and requirements presents another avenue for research, ensuring its relevance and applicability across diverse domains. Moreover, longitudinal studies and real-world applications are essential to evaluate the long-term effectiveness and impact of fuzzy logic-based DSS on organizational performance and strategic outcomes. Lastly, ongoing efforts to improve user interface and experience design will be crucial in facilitating broader adoption and acceptance of the DSS within organizations, ultimately driving competitive advantage and sustainable growth in dynamic environments.

References

1. Adler, N. and Shani, A.B., Managing in complex environments: adaptive role of decision-making styles. *Eur. J. Int. Manage.*, 11, 5, 555–573, 2017.
2. Baczynski, M.P. and Wierzbicki, A.P., Fuzzy multicriteria decision-making in management of dynamic environments. *Fuzzy Sets Syst.*, 354, 49–64, 2019.
3. Belton, V. and Stewart, T.J., *Multiple criteria decision analysis: An integrated approach*, Springer Science & Business Media, Boston/Dordrecht/London (Springer), 2002.
4. Chen, C.T., Extensions of the TOPSIS for group decision-making under fuzzy environment. *Fuzzy Sets Syst.*, 114, 1, 1–9, 2001.
5. Dubois, D. and Prade, H., *Fuzzy sets and systems: Theory and applications*, Academic Press, New York, 1980.
6. Ertugrul, I. and Karakasoglu, N., Performance evaluation of Turkish cement firms with fuzzy analytic hierarchy process and TOPSIS methods. *Expert Syst. Appl.*, 36, 1, 702–715, 2009.
7. Fung, R.Y.K. and Lee, E.S.H., Design of self-organising fuzzy decision systems with support vector learning. *Fuzzy Sets Syst.*, 118, 1, 49–61, 2001.

8. Hwang, C.L. and Yoon, K., *Multiple attribute decision making: Methods and applications: A state-of-the-art survey (Vol. 186)*, Springer Science & Business Media, Berlin/Heidelberg/New York, 1981.
9. Kahraman, C., Ruan, D., Doğan, I., Fuzzy group decision-making for facility location selection. *Fuzzy Sets Syst.*, 139, 2, 363–377, 2003.
10. Kaufmann,.A. and Gupta, M.M., *Introduction to fuzzy arithmetic: Theory and applications*, Van Nostrand Reinhold, New York, 1991.
11. Kosko, B., *Neural networks and fuzzy systems: a dynamical systems approach to machine intelligence/book and disk*, Prentice Hall, Englewood Cliffs, New Jersey, 1992.
12. Lee, H.K., Lee, J.W., Kim, J.H., Design of fuzzy decision support system for estimating oil tankers' fuel consumption. *Mar. struct.*, 46, 55–66, Englewood Cliffs, New Jersey, 2016.
13. Lertworasirikul, S., Fang, S.C., Joines, J.A., Comparison of AHP and fuzzy AHP approaches for water resources management. *J. Am. Water Resour. Assoc.*, 39, 1, 155–162, 2003.
14. Mardani, A., Zavadskas, E.K., Jusoh, A., Fuzzy multiple criteria decision-making techniques and applications—Two decades research from 1994 to 2014. *Expert Syst. Appl.*, 42, 8, 4126–4148, 2015.
15. Marimin, M. and Yahya, S., Fuzzy multi-objective decision-making for strategic management in supply chain management: a literature research. *Int. J. Manage. Sci. Eng. Manage.*, 12, 4, 283–298, 2017.
16. O'Hagan, J. and Buck, L., Fuzzy decision-making system for project management. *Int. J. Project Manage.*, 36, 1, 72–84, 2018.
17. Parnell, G.S., Crandall, W.R., Menefee, M.L., *Strategic management: Theory and practice*, Sage Publications, Los Angeles/London/New Delhi/Singapore/Washington DC, 2014.
18. Rezaei, J. and Ortt, R., A decade of research on the use of multi-criteria decision analysis in energy decision-making: contributions and future directions. *Renewable Sustainable Energy Researchs*, 52, 840–859, 2015.
19. Saaty, T.L., Decision making with the analytic hierarchy process. *Int. J. Serv. Sci.*, 1, 1, 83–98, 2008.
20. Simon, H.A., Making management decisions: The role of intuition and emotion. *Acad. Manage. Executive (1987-1989)*, 1, 1, 57–64, 1987.
21. Smith, J.R. and Nau, R.F., Decision analysis in management science. *Oper. Res.*, 43, 4, 570–581, 1995.
22. Tavana, M., Khalili-Damghani, K., Santos-Arteaga, F.J., Strategic decision-making methodologies: Comprehensive research. *Eur. J. Oper. Res.*, 259, 1, 1–22, 2017.
23. Torra, V. and Narukawa, Y., On hesitant fuzzy sets and decision. *Proceedings of the 2007 International Conference on Fuzzy Systems*, pp. 1–6, 2007.
24. Tsaur, R.C., Chang, T.Y., Yen, C.H., The evaluation of airline service quality by fuzzy MCDM. *Tourism Manage.*, 23, 2, 107–115, 2002.

25. Wang, L.X. and Mendel, J.M., Generating fuzzy rules by learning from examples. *IEEE Trans. Systems Man Cybern.*, 22, 6, 1414–1427, 1992.
26. Weber, R., *Multicriteria decision making, management science: Multi-criteria decision making: Concepts, techniques, and extensions for the business environment*, Springer Science & Business Media, New York/Berlin/Heidelberg, 1988.
27. Zadeh, L.A., Fuzzy sets. *Inf. Control*, 8, 3, 338–353, 1965.
28. Zadeh, L.A., Outline of a new approach to the analysis of complex systems and decision processes. *IEEE Trans. Systems Man Cybern.*, 1, 28–44, 1973.
29. Zeng, S.X., Shi, J.J., Lou, G.X., A synergetic model for implementing cleaner production in China. *J. Cleaner Prod.*, 15, 17, 1671–1683, 2007.
30. Zimmermann, H.J., *Fuzzy set theory and its applications*, Springer Science & Business Media, New York/Berlin/Heidelberg, 2011.
31. Muralidhar, L.B., Lakshmi, K.V.N., Swapna, H.R., Rupani, J., Nethravathi, K., Pandey, B.K., Pandey, D., Impact of Organizational Culture on The Level of Corporate Social Responsibility Investments: An Exploratory Study. *Circ. Econ. Sustainability*, 1–19, 2024.
32. Abdullahi, M., Ahmad, A., Pandey, B.K., Pandey, D., Digital Currency Adoption: A Comparative Analysis of Global Trends and the Nigerian eNaira Digital Currency. *SN Comput. Sci.*, 5, 5, 1–11, 2024.
33. KVM, S., Pandey, B.K., Pandey, D., Design of Surface Plasmon Resonance (SPR) Sensors for Highly Sensitive Biomolecular Detection in Cancer Diagnostics. *Plasmonics*, 1–13, 2024.
34. Kennedy, G.W., Sunday, S.E., Pandey, D., Kabari, A.D., Pandey, B.K., George, A.S., Dadheech, P., Building Information Modeling: Harnessing Innovations for Professional Proficiency, in: *Emerging Engineering Technologies and Industrial Applications*, pp. 305–331, IGI Global, Hershey, PA, 2024.
35. Pandey, D., Nassa, V.K., Pandey, B.K., Mahajan, D.A., Patidar, P.K., Dadheech, P., George, A.S., An Analysis of Internet-of-Things-Based Fire Detection and Alert Systems, in: *Emerging Engineering Technologies and Industrial Applications*, pp. 295–304, IGI Global, Hershey, PA, 2024.
36. Pandey, D., Pandey, B.K., Nassa, V.K., Mahajan, D.A., George, A.S., Dadheech, P., Optimized Throughput-Based Broadcasting for Next Generation Wireless Networks, in: *Emerging Engineering Technologies and Industrial Applications*, pp. 355–368, IGI Global, 2024.
37. Pandey, B.K., Nassa, V.K., Mukundan, A.P., Mahajan, D.A., Pandey, D., George, A.S., Dadheech, P., An Industry-Focused Traffic System Utilising Internet of Things, in: *Emerging Engineering Technologies and Industrial Applications*, pp. 200–213, IGI Global, Hershey, PA, 2024.
38. Pandey, D., Pandey, B.K., Paramashivan, M.A., Mahajan, D.A., Dadheech, P.D., George, A.S., Hameed, A.S., Advanced Digital Data Processing Using Cloud Cryptography: Industrial Applications, in: *Emerging Engineering Technologies and Industrial Applications*, pp. 255–268, IGI Global, Hershey, PA, 2024.

39. Pandey, B.K., Mukundan, A.P., Nassa, V.K., Pandey, D., George, A.S., Hameed, A.S., Dadheech, P., Deployment of Load Balancing in Cloud Computing: Industrial Application and Benefits, in: *Emerging Engineering Technologies and Industrial Applications*, pp. 342–354, IGI Global, Hershey, PA, 2024.
40. Pandey, B.K., Paramashivan, M.A., Nassa, V.K., Mahajan, D.A., Dadheech, P., George, A.H., George, A.S., Blockchain's Potential Effect on the Healthcare Industry, in: *Emerging Engineering Technologies and Industrial Applications*, pp. 214–232, IGI Global, Hershey, PA, 2024.
41. Pandey, D., Nassa, V.K., Pandey, B.K., Thankachan, B., Dadheech, P., Mahajan, D.A., George, A.S., Artificial Intelligence and Machine Learning and Its Application in the Field of Computational Visual Analysis, in: *Emerging Engineering Technologies and Industrial Applications*, pp. 36–57, IGI Global, Hershey, PA, 2024.
42. Shahul, A., Muniandi, B., Paramashivan, M.A., Pandey, D., Pandey, B.K., Dadheech, P., George, H., An Analysis of Algorithms and Methods Based on Image Processing for Medical Applications, in: *Emerging Engineering Technologies and Industrial Applications*, pp. 173–186, IGI Global, Hershey, PA, 2024.
43. Sahani, S.K., Pandey, B.K., Pandey, D., Single-valued Signals, Multi-valued Signals and Fixed-Point of Contractive Signals. *Math. Open*, 2024.
44. Muniandi, B., Nassa, V.K., Pandey, D., Pandey, B.K., Dadheech, P., George, A.S., Pattern Analysis for Feature Extraction in Complex Images, in: *Using Machine Learning to Detect Emotions and Predict Human Psychology*, pp. 145–167, IGI Global, Hershey, PA, 2024.
45. George, W.K., Silas, E., II, Pandey, D., Pandey, B.K., Utilization of Industry 4.0 Technologies in Nigerian Technical and Vocational Education: A Conundrum for Educators, in: *Examining the Rapid Advance of Digital Technology in Africa*, pp. 270–293, IGI Global, Hershey, PA, 2024.
46. Pandey, B.K., Pandey, D., Sahani, S.K., Autopilot control unmanned aerial vehicle system for sewage defect detection using deep learning. *Eng. Rep.*, e12852, 2024.
47. Neelima, K., Madhavi, B., Padma, C., Pandey, B.K., Gowwrii, G., Manaktala, S.S., Post-Pandemic Biometric Challenges and Solutions: A Shocker to Supply Chain, in: *AI and Machine Learning Impacts in Intelligent Supply Chain*, pp. 196–208, IGI Global, Hershey, PA, 2024.
48. JayaLakshmi, G., Pandey, D., Pandey, B.K., Kaur, P., Mahajan, D.A., Dari, S.S., Smart Big Data Collection for Intelligent Supply Chain Improvement, in: *AI and Machine Learning Impacts in Intelligent Supply Chain*, pp. 180–195, IGI Global, Hershey, PA, 2024.
49. Anand, R., Lakshmi, S.V., Pandey, D., Pandey, B.K., An enhanced ResNet-50 deep learning model for arrhythmia detection using electrocardiogram biomedical indicators. *Evol. Syst.*, 15, 1, 83–97, 2024.

50. Sharma, M., Talwar, R., Pandey, D., Nassa, V.K., Pandey, B.K., Dadheech, P., A Review of Dielectric Resonator Antennas (DRA)-Based RFID Technology for Industry 4.0. *Rob. Autom. Ind.*, 4.0, 303–324, 2024.
51. Banerjee, S., Kaur, D., Pandey, D., Pal, S.R., Ahuchaogu, A.A., Iqbal, M.O., Pandey, B.K., Industry 4.0 in the Nutraceutical Industry and Public Health Nutrition, in: *Robotics and Automation in Industry 4.0*, pp. 396–422, CRC Press.
52. Kumar, B., Pandey, D., Pandey, B.K., George, A.S., Higher Education in the Last Four Decades: A Review of Paradigm Shifts in Policy Frameworks. *Des. Implementation Higher Educ. Learners' Learn. Outcomes (HELLO)*, 333–348, 2024.
53. Devasenapathy, D., Madhumathy, P., Umamaheshwari, R., Pandey, B.K., Pandey, D., Transmission-efficient grid-based synchronized model for routing in wireless sensor networks using Bayesian compressive sensing. *SN Comput. Sci.*, 5, 1, 1–11, 2024.
54. Antennas, R., Sharma, M., Talwar, R., Pandey, D., Nassa, V.K., Pandey, B.K., Dadheech, P., 17 A Review of Dielectric. *Rob. Autom. Ind. 4.0 Smart Ind. Intell. Technol.*, 303, 2024.
55. Gandhi, A.S., Azhagumurugan, R., Sagayam, K.M., Jone, A.A.A., Pandey, D., Pandey, B.K., An Experimental Study-Based Dynamic Modelling and Control of Thermal Desalination Pilot Plant. *J. Inst. Eng. India Ser. B*, 104, 6, 1197–1206, Hershey, Pennsylvania, USA, 2023.
56. Abdulkarim, Y., II, Awl, H.N., Muhammadsharif, F.F., Saeed, S.R., Sidiq, K.R., Khasraw, S.S., Pandey, D., Metamaterial-based sensors loaded corona-shaped resonator for COVID-19 detection by using microwave techniques. *Plasmonics*, 19, 2, 595–610, 2024.
57. Gupta, R., Mane, M., Bhardwaj, S., Nandekar, U., Afaq, A., Dhabliya, D., Pandey, B.K., Use of Artificial Intelligence for Image Processing to Aid Digital Forensics: Legislative Challenges, in: *Handbook of Research on Thrust Technologies' Effect on Image Processing*, pp. 433–447, IGI Global, Hershey, Pennsylvania, USA, 2023.
58. BR, S.R., Saxena, A.K., Pandey, B.K., Gupta, S., Gurpur, S., Dari, S.S., Dhabliya, D., Machine Learning Application for Evidence Image Enhancement, in: *Handbook of Research on Thrust Technologies' Effect on Image Processing*, pp. 25–38, IGI Global, Hershey, Pennsylvania, USA, 2023.
59. Shanthi, T., Anand, R., Pandey, B.K., Nassa, V.K., Shahul, A., George, A.H., Dadheech, P., Exudate Detection in Fundus Images Using Deep Learning Algorithms, in: *Handbook of Research on Thrust Technologies' Effect on Image Processing*, pp. 256–272, IGI Global, Hershey, Pennsylvania, USA, 2023.
60. Pandey, B.K. and Pandey, D., Parametric optimization and prediction of enhanced thermoelectric performance in co-doped CaMnO3 using response surface methodology and neural network. *J. Mater. Sci.: Mater. Electron.*, 34, 21, 1589, Springer (London/New York), 2023.

61. Du John, H.V., Ajay, T., Reddy, G.M.K., Ganesh, M.N.S., Hembram, A., Pandey, B.K., Pandey, D., Design and simulation of SRR-based tungsten metamaterial absorber for biomedical sensing applications. *Plasmonics*, 18, 5, 1903–1912, Springer, New York, 2023.
62. Singh, S., Madaan, G., Kaur, J., Swapna, H.R., Pandey, D., Singh, A., Pandey, B.K., Bibliometric Review on Healthcare Sustainability, in: *Handbook of Research on Safe Disposal Methods of Municipal Solid Wastes for a Sustainable Environment*, pp. 142–161, Hershey, Pennsylvania, USA, 2023.
63. Pandey, D. and Pandey, B.K., An efficient deep neural network with adaptive galactic swarm optimization for complex image text extraction, in: *Process mining techniques for pattern recognition*, pp. 121–137, CRC Press, Boca Raton, Florida, USA, 2022.

19

Analysis of Fuzzy-Based Image Enhancement Methods Toward Thyroid Cytopathology Diagnosis Through Fuzzy Logic: A Case Study

B. Gopinath[1]* and R. Santhi[2]

[1]*Department of Electronics and Communication Engineering, Kumaraguru College of Technology, Coimbatore, Tamil Nadu, India*
[2]*Department of Biochemistry, PSG College of Arts & Science, Coimbatore, Tamil Nadu, India*

Abstract

Pathological image analysis is a preliminary and significant step in biomedical diagnosis and treatment of any kind of disease. Understanding of pathological images, especially cytopathological images, is a difficult task because of their intrinsic noise due to strained nature of images, and variations in tissue characteristics. Image enhancement techniques are the suitable means of enhancing the visual appearance and quality of these kinds of noisy pathological images which are being utilized to remove the unwanted background information belonging to noise pixels and retaining the significant foreground pixel information to perform appropriate biomedical analysis and diagnosis. The concept of fuzzy logic offers a favorable approach for enhancing pathological images with its capability of handling uncertainty and fuzziness nature of pathological images. This chapter reviews and analyses a comprehensive overview of fuzzy-based image enhancement techniques in analyzing pathological images, related methodologies, and application towards a special case of thyroid cytopathology diagnosis to differentiate cancerous nature from benign nature. Thyroid cytopathology deals with analysis and detection of cytopathological images of thyroid nodules under binary classification namely normal and abnormal. Moreover, detection of normal (benign) and abnormal (malignant) thyroid cytopathological images by manual methods are

**Corresponding author*: gopinath.b.ece@kct.ac.in

Rahul Kar, Gunjan Mukherjee, Biswadip Basu Mallik and Ashok Kumar Shaw (eds.) Fuzzy Logic in Computational Intelligence: Applications and Case Studies, (341–356) © 2026 Scrivener Publishing LLC

subjective due to the morphological variability of thyroid cells and the presence of overlapping features between benign and malignant nodules. Because of the ability to handle uncertainty and imprecision of fuzzy logic, it can be used as a significant approach to increase the accuracy of thyroid cytopathology identification. Thus, this case study explores the application of fuzzy logic in examining thyroid cytopathology images to improve diagnostic accuracy.

Keywords: Cytopathology, fuzzy logic, image enhancement, noise, thyroid

19.1 Introduction

Pathological images are acquired from tissue samples under a microscopy by a skilled pathologist in a laboratory. There are two major types of pathological images namely histopathological and cytopathological microscopic images. The normal and abnormal structures present in the images are studied by the pathologist and suitable diagnosis reports are produced. Hence, the researchers utilize both histopathological and cytopathological digital images as essential means for diagnosing various diseases, including cancer [1]. However, the challenging part of the pathological images is that they often suffer from poor contrast, uneven illumination levels, and inherent noises. These unwanted parameters associated with digital images degrade and slow down the automated diagnostic process of diseases [2]. Image enhancement is a powerful methodology that targets to increase the quality of these noisy and degraded images for helping the pathologists and digital image processing community to identify and exactly locate the required significant features and corresponding abnormal conditions in the images. Pathological images are liable to different types of noisy elements due to various reasons such as electronic, sensor, and environmental conditions which degrade image quality, hide the required information present in the images and hence affect the diagnostic accuracy for a targeted disease [3]. It is necessary to understand commonly identified noise types and nature of noises in pathological images so that appropriate image enhancement techniques can be selected and applied on the images for improving the diagnosis accuracy. Table 19.1 summarizes the generalized noise models in digital pathological images.

Fuzzy logic is a powerful and feasible tool that effectively eliminates unwanted presence of pixels from images. The fuzzy logic can identify the uncertainty nature of the noise pixels and it can be used even though the noise pixels are vague and uncertain in pathological images [4]. Fuzzy logic, as an image enhancement mechanism, is practically implemented on pathological images to reduce the impact of the noise pixels by means

Table 19.1 Generalized noises observed in pathological images.

Type of noise	Properties of noise
Gaussian Noise	It is appearing because of random variations in image pixel gray-level intensities and one of the commonly identified noise models in many variants of biomedical images.
Salt and Pepper Noise	Characterized by black and white colored image pixels which have a powerful degradation function to degrade the original quality of biomedical images.
Speckle Noise	This kind of noises heavily degrades the radiology images especially ultrasound images which are caused by the interference patterns generated by ultrasound wave reflections during image acquisition process.
Quantization Noise	Quantization is the process of discretization of continuous intensity levels at the time of acquisition of images and converting them into digital form. During the discretization process, there are many possibilities of introduction of quantization noise which disturbs the visual quality of digital images.

of its sub-components such as fuzzy set theory, membership functions, and inference systems. This chapter deals with various fuzzy-based image enhancement techniques and corresponding results obtained by various research works and the role of fuzzy-based sequence of approaches towards thyroid cytopathology to discriminate normal and abnormal thyroid nodules as a case study. Section 19.2 deals with Fuzzy-based image enhancement techniques while Section 19.3 elaborates thyroid cytopathology. The application of fuzzy-based image enhancement methods in thyroid cytopathology diagnosis offers a significant approach to enhance the ability of disease detection and classification.

19.2 Fuzzy Image Enhancement Methods

The significant and more relevant fuzzy-based image enhancement techniques employed in analysis of cytopathological images are ordered as fuzzy histogram equalization to deal with uniform distribution of frequency of occurrence of image intensity value, Fuzzy filtering techniques to handle the filtration of significant and non-significant image pixels, Fuzzy morphological operations to manipulate the morphology behavior of cell objects and Fuzzy contrast enhancement to boost image contrast [5]. The classification problem on the thyroid cytopathological images is purely depending on the original quality of the image set applied to the classifier models without any noisy pixels and degraded pixels present in the image set. The summarized group of fuzzy-based image enhancement methods serve as pre-processing steps to enhance the diagnostic accuracy for the targeted problem.

19.2.1 Fuzzy Histogram Equalization

The fuzzy-based histogram equalization enhances image contrast from uneven distribution of bright and dark image pixels to evenly distributed pixel values by redistributing pixel intensities based on fuzzy membership functions [6]. The input images are given to fuzzy membership functions, after pre-processing, for pixel intensities which perform the fine tuning or adjusting the contrast of the images flexibly without losing the required pixel details present in the original images as presented in Figure 19.1.

The pathological input images are pre-processed to remove the preliminary noise and other non-significant elements to process the images optimally during the next stages of processing of histogram equalization. In the next stage, the fuzzy-based membership functions are defined or suitably selected for manipulating and distributing the target pixel intensities. The membership function aims to transform the degree of membership for every pixel intensity level of input image into different pixel intensity levels. Fuzzy histogram equalization is applied to the pre-processed images and pixel intensities are reassigned based on the defined membership functions.

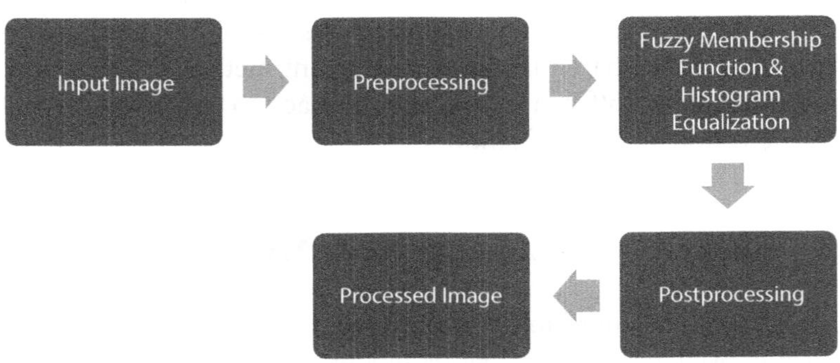

Figure 19.1 Fuzzy histogram equalization.

For the further improvements, the post-processing steps may be applied on the output of the histogram equalization stage such as contrast stretching, contrast slicing, and so on. The output histogram equalized pathological images are inspected and verified the enhancement of contrast along with placement of significant pixel values all over the image. Though the assessments are done through the performance evaluation metrics, the visual inspection of the histogram equalized images must be done by the medical professionals to map the outcome of automated image processing methods with ground truth to understand the usability of the images for the next consecutives stages.

A sample thyroid cytopathology image and corresponding fuzzy histogram equalized output image is presented in Figure 19.2. From Figures 19.2(a), 19.2(b) and 19.2(c), the significant enhancements can be seen between raw input image and equalized output image.

The real-time MATLAB simulation environment of the fuzzy-based histogram equalization algorithm is given in Figure 19.3.

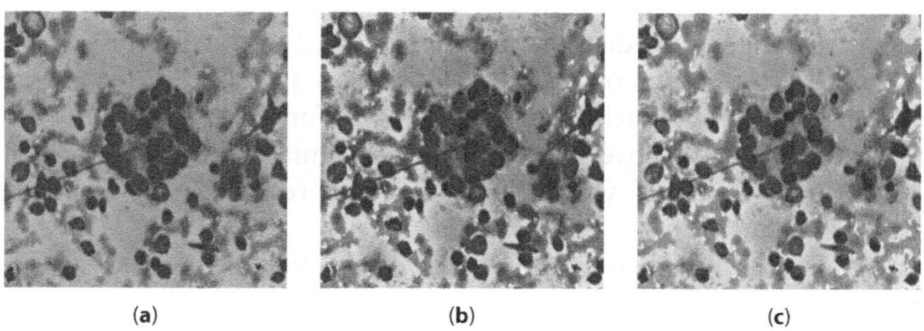

Figure 19.2 (a) sample thyroid cytopathology image before fuzzy histogram equalization, (b) fuzzy histogram equalized output image and (c) grayscale version of output image.

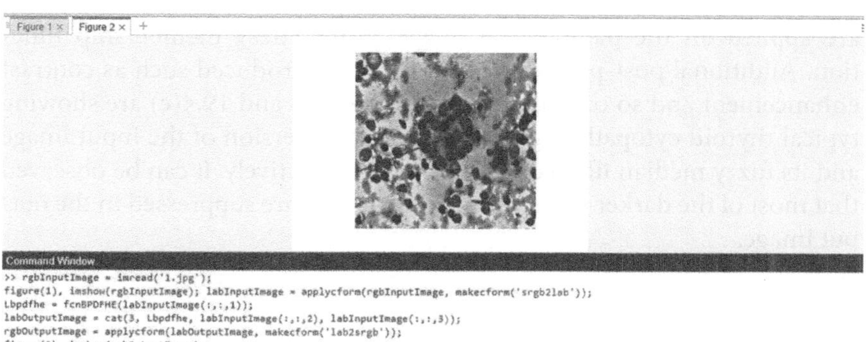

Figure 19.3 Fuzzy histogram equalization MATLAB simulation environment.

19.2.2 Fuzzy Filtering Techniques

Fuzzy filtering techniques serve in a similar manner of conventional spatial filters to perform smoothing operation and sharpening operation. However, fuzzy-based smoothing and sharpening filters such as mean filtering and median filtering are functioning to deal with uncertainty among the image pixels during the implementation for the purpose of reducing the noise pixels without disturbing the required useful image pixels [7]. The fuzzy logic basics are followed in implementing fuzzy mean filtering for the reduction of noise pixels by means of utilizing the weighted average filtering of pixel intensities. In conventional mean filtering, all image pixels are treated equally whereas the fuzzy mean filtering treats all the pixels differently by assigning different weights to pixels with respect to central target pixel [8]. This variable weight assignments to all pixels of input image by fuzzy mean filtering permits the effective removal of noise pixels and retaining permissible image pixels. Like fuzzy mean filtering, the fuzzy median filtering is also a promising noise removal technique which utilizes the concept of conventional median filtering fused with fuzzy logic. In the conventional median filtering, the targeted central pixel is changed by median value based on overlapping window size. But, in fuzzy-based median filtering approach, fuzzy membership functions are used to estimate the similarity between pixels of original image and overlapping filtering window through which more noise suppression is achieved in an adaptive manner [9].

The mean and median filtering methods also follow the same sequence of steps as explained in fuzzy histogram equalization as shown in Figure 19.1 except histogram equalization stage. In this stage, the fuzzy mean and median values are calculated based on fuzzy logic. Initially, the input images are fed to pre-processing stage in which preliminary noise pixels are removed. Then, the fuzzy mean filtering and fuzzy median filtering are applied on the pathological images using fuzzy membership function. Additional post-processing step may be introduced such as contrast enhancement and so on. Figures 19.4(a), 19.4(b) and 19.4(c) are showing typical thyroid cytopathology image, grayscale version of the input image and its fuzzy median filtered output image respectively. It can be observed that most of the darker background information are suppressed in the output image.

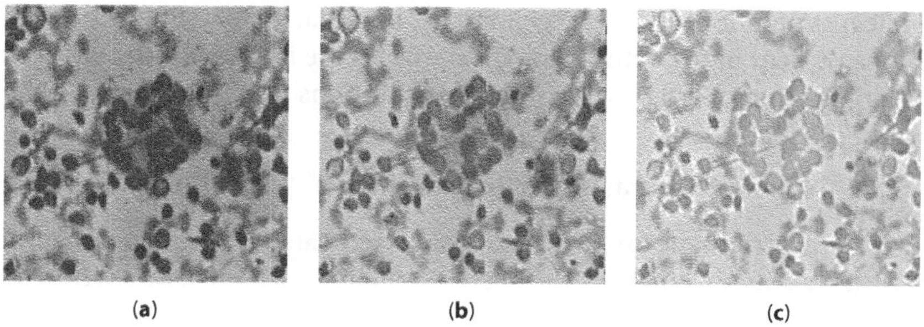

Figure 19.4 (a) Sample thyroid cytopathology image before fuzzy median filtering; (b) grayscale version of thyroid cytopathology image before fuzzy median filtering; and (c) output image of fuzzy median filtering.

19.2.3 Fuzzy Morphological Operations

The classical erosion and dilation operations related to mathematical morphology have been adopted in fuzzy logic to remove the unwanted noise pixels in and around the cytological cell structures present in the given pathological images. The imprecision and uncertainty parameters are represented and addressed in grayscale images by means of these fuzzy morphological operations [10]. Fuzzy dilation morphological operation enlarges the boundary pixels so that the small noise pixels present inside, and outer parts of the cell objects are eliminated.

In the traditional approach, the dilation operator takes only binary pixel values whereas the fuzzy dilation operator uses a specific fuzzy membership function to consider the uncertainty nature connected with pixel intensity values as shown in Figure 19.5. This approach gives a flexible and adaptive mode of dilation operation which is very much useful in dealing the with cytopathological images with changing tissue characteristics. Fuzzy-based erosion operator is also working in a similar and complement manner on the given cytological images that reduces the object boundaries in the given image to suppress the noise pixels and retaining the required features. Like fuzzy dilation, fuzzy membership function is involved in fuzzy erosion operation to identify the simila rities and differences. In the

Figure 19.5 Fuzzy morphological operators.

application point of view, the cell nuclei, boundaries of cells, and various lesions present in the cytopathological images are isolated by the consecutive application of erosion and dilation operations [11].

19.2.4 Fuzzy Contrast Enhancement

Fuzzy contrast enhancement methods are direct category of image enhancement techniques to increase or decrease the contrast of the images using a set of fuzzy rules [12]. The various stages of fuzzy contrast enhancement include formation of fuzzy rules, design of fuzzy inference system, contrast adjustment and post-processing (optional) as shown in Figure 19.6.

Development of fuzzy rules is a challenging task in which either expert knowledge or data-driven approaches are used to develop fuzzy rules. The fuzzy rules are used for tracing the correlation between pathological image characteristics and required adjustments in contrast of the images. In the next stage, design of a fuzzy inference system is carried out to understand the characteristics of the input pathological images and select the suitable contrast adjustment techniques mapped with the previous stage of fuzzy rules [13]. The designed and developed fuzzy inference system is implemented on the given set of pathological images to enhance the spatial resolution and preserve significant inherent features having diagnostic capabilities. As explained in the previous sections, the post-processing steps are implemented as per the requirements. The input and output thyroid cytopathological images are illustrated in Figures 19.7 (a), 19.7(b), and 19.7(c) sequentially. The enhanced output grayscale image shown in Figure 19.7(c) consists of highlighted portions of contrast enhanced cellular objects.

The real-time MATLAB simulation environment of the fuzzy-based contrast enhancement algorithm is illustrated in Figure 19.8.

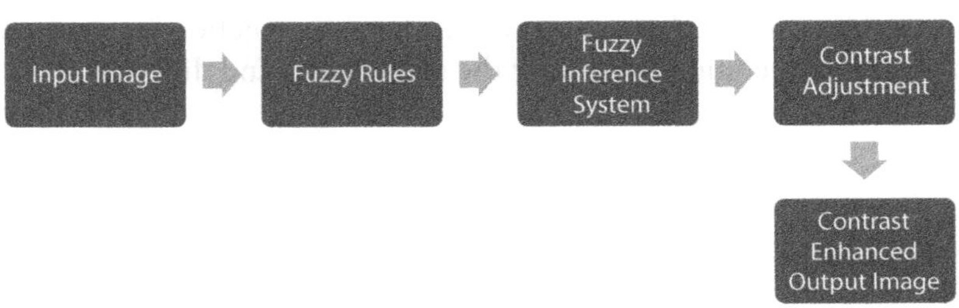

Figure 19.6 Fuzzy-based contrast enhancement scheme.

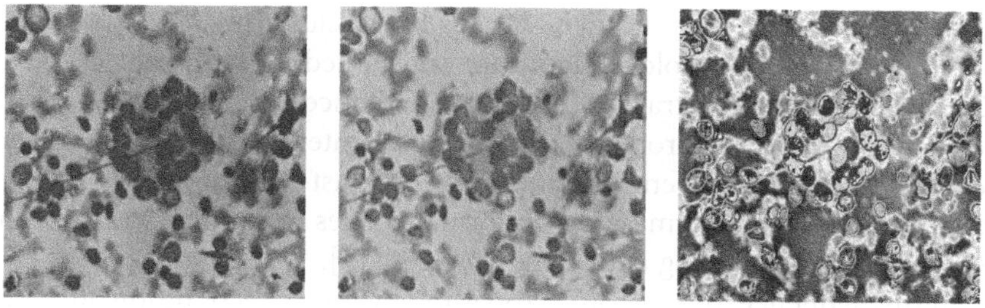

Figure 19.7 (a) Sample of thyroid cytopathology image before fuzzy contrast enhancement, (b) grayscale version of thyroid cytopathology image before fuzzy contrast enhancement and (c) fuzzy contrast enhanced output image.

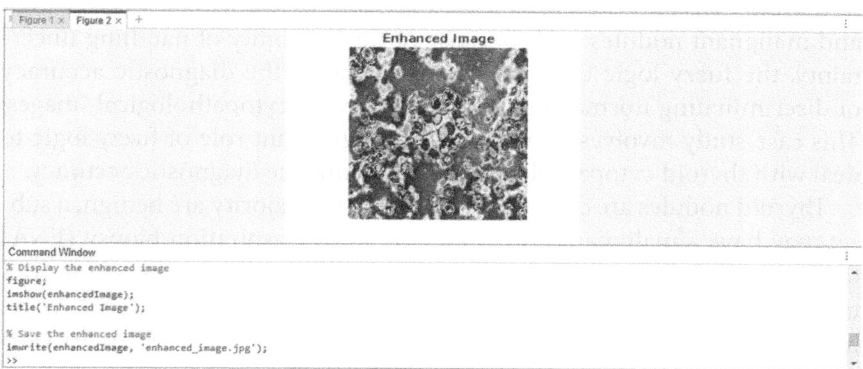

Figure 19.8 MATLAB simulation environment of fuzzy contrast enhancement.

19.3 Thyroid Cytopathology Diagnosis Through Fuzzy Logic: A Case Study

Fuzzy logic-based image enhancement techniques are playing significant role in the domain of biomedical image analysis. Various types of research works are being carried out among which few notable and potential research works and their outcomes are summarized in this section. The ultimate objective of these works is to enhance and promote the post-processing processes such as object recognition and identification in pathological images, image classification and so on. Agrawal *et al.* proposed fuzzy filter which has fuzzy derivative along with fuzzy smoothing based on fuzzy rules and membership functions [5]. Chaira developed a novel scheme to boost the required edges present in biomedical images using fuzzy entropy and rank order filtering [14]. Fuzzy C-Means based clustering, and open-close operators-based morphology algorithm are applied for pathology image of Esophageal tumor to extract the edges and to reduce the noises from the side edges [15]. Dhal *et al.* proposed a fuzzy logic centered image improvement scheme based on fuzzy entropy and fuzzy contrast stretching [16]. Geweid *et al.* differentiated normal and abnormal tissues are differentiated using Fuzzy c-means clustering in histology images [17].

In this sequence, the thyroid cytopathology image recognition and classification problem is taken as a case study towards the application of fuzzy-based image enhancement. Thyroid cytopathology plays a crucial role in diagnosing thyroid nodules, determining whether they are benign or malignant [18]. However, the interpretation of thyroid cytopathology images is subjective in nature and challenging due to the morphological variability of thyroid cells and the presence of overlapping features between benign and malignant nodules [19]. Because of the capability of handling uncertainty, the fuzzy logic can significantly enhance the diagnostic accuracy of discriminating normal and abnormal thyroid cytopathological images. This case study involves in analyzing the significant role of fuzzy logic to deal with thyroid cytopathology images to enhance diagnostic accuracy.

Thyroid nodules are common, and while the majority are benign, a subset may have a malignant potential. Fine-needle aspiration biopsy (FNA) followed by cytopathological examination is the standard method for evaluating thyroid nodules [20]. However, cytopathology interpretation relies heavily on the expertise and experience of pathologists, leading to variability in diagnoses and the potential for misclassification. The primary aim of the case study targets to demonstrate effectiveness of fuzzy logic to increase accuracy and consistency in thyroid cytopathology diagnosis. By leveraging fuzzy logic techniques, the aim is to develop a computer-aided diagnostic system that can assist pathologists in analyzing thyroid cytopathology images more effectively, particularly in distinguishing between benign and malignant nodules.

19.3.1 Methodology

The fuzzy-based image analysis methodology is shown in Figure 19.9 which is used in the analysis of thyroid cytopathology images using a sequence of operations such as design of fuzzy inference system, rule base construction, fuzzy logic inference and defuzzification steps.

High-resolution digital images of thyroid FNA biopsy specimens are obtained using a microscope equipped with a digital camera [21]. The acquired images undergo preprocessing steps, including noise reduction,

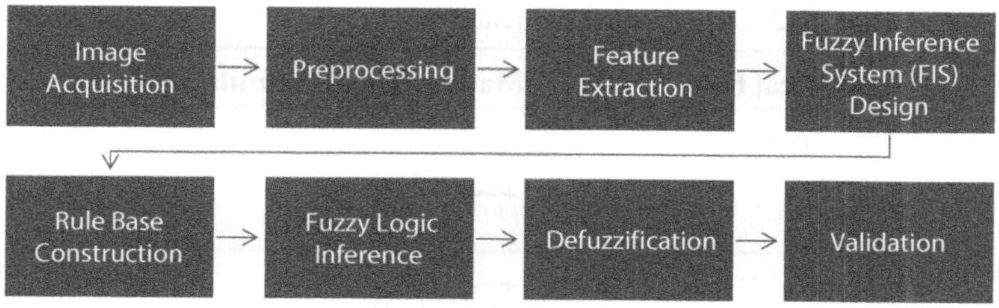

Figure 19.9 Fuzzy-based methodology used in the analysis of thyroid cytopathology images.

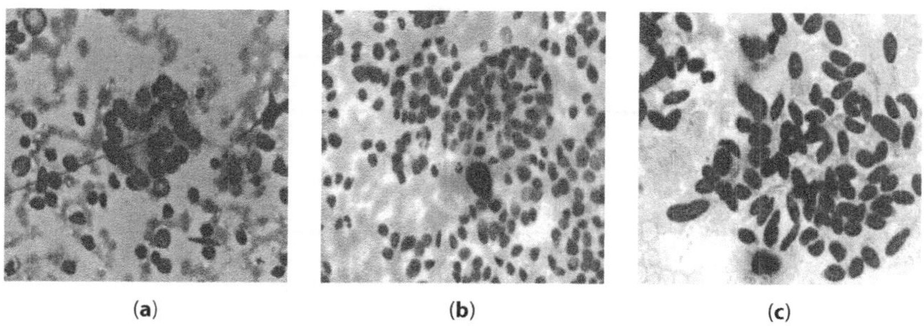

Figure 19.10 (a) benign type of thyroid nodule, (b) papillary malignancy type of thyroid nodule and (c) medullary malignancy type of thyroid nodule.

color normalization, and segmentation to isolate individual thyroid cells and structures. Figures 19.10(a), 19.10(b) and 19.10(c) show benign, papillary and medullary malignant images of thyroid nodules respectively [22].

Relevant morphological, textural, and architectural features are extracted from the segmented thyroid cells, including nuclear size, shape irregularity, chromatin pattern, and presence of nuclear inclusions. A set of statistical features listed in Table 19.2 are identified and derived from the images [23].

The pixel intensity values are represented by $f(i,j)$ and total number of pixels are given by N. Mean and standard deviation parameters are indicated by μ and σ and respectively.

A fuzzy-based inference system is modeled to perform the diagnostic decision-making process. The significant features such as cellular atypia, nuclear enlargement and architectural disarray are defined along with appropriate membership functions. Expert knowledge from cytopathologists is derived and used to define a set of fuzzy rules to map the input

Table 19.2 List of statistical features.

Statistical feature	Mathematical formula
Mean (μ)	$\sum_{i,j} f(i,j)/N$
Standard Deviation (σ)	$\sum_{i,j}((f(i,j)-\mu)^2/N)^{1/2}$
Entropy	$-\sum_{i,j} f(i,j)\, log\, f(i,j)$
Variance	σ^2
Energy	$\sum_{i,j} f(i,j)^2$
Homogeneity	$\sum_{i,j} f(i,j)/\lvert i-j \rvert$
Contrast	$\sum_{i,j} f(i,j)\,(i-j)^2$
Correlation	$\sum_{i,j} f(i,j)\,(i-\mu_i)\,(j-\mu_j)/\sigma_i\sigma_j$

features into diagnostic outcomes such as normal (benign) or abnormal (malignant). The extracted features are fuzzified and processed through the rule base to generate fuzzy outputs through which the degree of membership of each diagnostic category such as normal (benign) or abnormal (malignant) is decided. The fuzzy outputs are accumulated and defuzzified to obtain a strong diagnostic decision. Though the automated biomedical diagnosis system results a well-defined diagnosis report, it must be evaluated by the skilled pathologists and hence the fuzzy-based decision support system will be treated as a second opinion tool in the domain of decision support systems.

19.4 Conclusion

This chapter highlights significant role of fuzzy-based methods in improving visual appearance of pathological images and facilitating more accurate diagnosis. Fuzzy-based techniques can be applied to enhance the visual quality of both histopathological and cytopathological images and assist pathologists in identification of normal and abnormal cellular structures present in the images. It is also observed that the application of fuzzy-based methods can enhance the microscopic cytopathological images of tissue samples to retain, improve and highlight the significant features of cell nuclei and tissue boundaries. Fuzzy filtering techniques are implemented to perform the reduction of noise pixels in pathological images while retaining the significant features within the image. The fuzzy logic-based pathology image analysis system demonstrates promising results in accurately distinguishing between normal and abnormal thyroid cytopathology images. It achieves high accuracy, sensitivity, and specificity, outperforming traditional methods and reducing interobserver variability among pathologists. The system's interpretable outputs provide valuable insights into the features contributing to each diagnostic decision, aiding pathologists in their interpretation. Fuzzy logic offers a robust framework for enhancing thyroid cytopathology diagnosis by effectively handling uncertainty and imprecision inherent in cytopathology image analysis.

References

1. Madabhushi, A. and Lee, G., Image analysis and machine learning in digital pathology: Challenges and opportunities. *Med. Image Anal.*, *33*, 170–175, 2016.
2. Abbood, S.H., Hamed, H.N.A., Rahim, M.S.M., Rehman, A., Saba, T., Bahaj, S.A., Hybrid retinal image enhancement algorithm for diabetic retinopathy diagnostic using deep learning model. *IEEE Access*, *10*, 73079–73086, 2022.
3. Lv, P., Lin, X.Z., Chen, K., Gao, J., Spectral CT in patients with small HCC: investigation of image quality and diagnostic accuracy. *Eur. Radio.*, *22*, 2117–2124, 2012.
4. Costin, H. and Rotariu, C., Medical image analysis and representation using a fuzzy and rule-based hybrid approach. *Int. J. Comput. Commun.*, *1*, 156–162, 2006.
5. Agrawal, A., Choubey, A., Nagwanshi, K.K., Development of adaptive fuzzy based Image Filtering techniques for efficient Noise Reduction in Medical Images. *Int. J. Comput. Sci. Inf. Technol.*, *2*, 4, 1457–1461, 2011.

6. Magudeeswaran, V. and Ravichandran, C.G., Fuzzy logic-based histogram equalization for image contrast enhancement. *Math. Probl. Eng., 2013*, 2013.
7. Kwan, H.K., Fuzzy filters for noise reduction in images, in: *Fuzzy filters for image processing*, pp. 25–53, Springer Berlin Heidelberg, Berlin, Heidelberg, 2003.
8. Shreyamsha Kumar, B.K., Image denoising based on non-local means filter and its method noise thresholding. *Signal Image Video Process., 7*, 1211–1227, 2013.
9. Toprak, A. and Güler, I., Impulse noise reduction in medical images with the use of switch mode fuzzy adaptive median filter. *Digital Signal Process., 17*, 4, 711–723, 2007.
10. Htun, Y.Y. and Aye, K.K., Fuzzy mathematical morphology approach in image processing. *World Acad. Science Eng. Technol., 42*, 659–665, 2008.
11. Irshad, H., Veillard, A., Roux, L., Racoceanu, D., Methods for nuclei detection, segmentation, and classification in digital histopathology: A review—current status and future potential. *IEEE Rev. Biomed. Eng., 7*, 97–114, 2013.
12. Hanmandlu, M., Verma, O.P., Kumar, N.K., Kulkarni, M., A novel optimal fuzzy system for color image enhancement using bacterial foraging. *IEEE Trans. Instrum. Meas., 58*, 8, 2867–2879, 2009.
13. Akgundogdu, A., Kurt, S., Kilic, N., Ucan, O.N., Akalin, N., Diagnosis of renal failure disease using adaptive neuro-fuzzy inference system. *J. Med. Syst., 34*, 1003–1009, 2010.
14. Chaira, T., A rank ordered filter for medical image edge enhancement and detection using intuitionistic fuzzy set. *Appl. Soft Comput., 12*, 4, 1259–1266, 2012.
15. Bamneshin, M.H., Pilevar, A., Pirzadeh, A., Edge extraction in pathology images of esophageal tumors assisted with FCM technique and using mathematical morphology operations on binary images. *Int. J. Comp. Inf. Sys.*, 3, 4, 1–6, 2011.
16. Dhal, K.G., Ray, S., Das, S., Biswas, A., Ghosh, S., Hue-preserving and gamut problem-free histopathology image enhancement. *Iran. J. Sci. Technology Trans. Electr. Eng., 43*, 645–672, 2019.
17. Geweid, G.G., Abdallah, M.A., Hassan, A.M., Improved Malignant Diagnosis Using Fuzzy C-means Based on Histopathological of PET-CT Lung Images, in: *Proceedings of the 2020 12th International Conference on Bioinformatics and Biomedical Technology*, pp. 99–105, 2020, May.
18. Bernet, V.J. and Chindris, A.M., Update on the evaluation of thyroid nodules. *J. Nucl. Med., 62*, Supplement 2, 13S–19S, 2021.
19. Gopinath, B., Shanthi, N., Santhi, R., Identification of malignant patterns in FNAC digital images of Thyroid nodules through cascaded segmentation stages, in: *2023 International Conference on Intelligent Data Communication Technologies and Internet of Things (IDCIoT)*, pp. 302–306, IEEE, 2023, January.

20. Jung, S.M., Koo, H.R., Jang, K.S., Chung, M.S., Song, C.M., Ji, Y.B., Tae, K., Comparison of core-needle biopsy and repeat fine-needle aspiration for thyroid nodules with inconclusive initial cytology. *Eur. Arch. Oto-Rhino-Laryngology*, 278, 3019–3025, 2021.
21. Duc, N.T., Lee, Y.M., Park, J.H., Lee, B., An ensemble deep learning for automatic prediction of papillary thyroid carcinoma using fine needle aspiration cytology. *Expert Syst. Appl.*, *188*, 115927, 2022.
22. []http://www.papsociety.org/atlas.html.
23. Gopinath, B. and Shanthi, N., Support Vector Machine based diagnostic system for thyroid cancer using statistical texture features. *Asian Pac. J. Cancer Prev.*, *14*, 1, 97–102, 2013.

Part 6

FUZZY TECHNIQUES TOWARDS THE HEALTH SECTOR

20

Decision Making Framework with Extent Analysis Method of Fuzzy AHP for Eye Health Management

Ayan Shee[1], Subrata Jana[2,3]*, Ivnil Ghosh[4], Sudipta Banerjee[5], Anirban Sarkar[6] and Partha Sen[7]

[1]*Department of Management Studies, Janardan Rai Nagar Rajasthan Vidyapeeth, Udaipur, Rajasthan, India*
[2]*Department of Mathematics, Jadavpur University, Kolkata, West Bengal, India*
[3]*Department of Basic Science and Humanities, Techno International New Town, Kolkata, West Bengal, India*
[4]*Department of BHM, IHRM, Kolkata, West Bengal, India*
[5]*Department of BCA, Seacom Management College, Howrah, West Bengal, India*
[6]*Department of Management and Marketing, West Bengal State University, Barasat, West Bengal, India*
[7]*Department of Optometry, Eminent College of Management and Technology, Barasat, West Bengal, India*

Abstract

This study aims to evaluate the impacts of the COVID-19 pandemic on administration of eye health and suggest ways for improvement in the post-epidemic phase. To this end, the research identifies key criteria for successful management of eye health performance in the current digital age and determines the relative importance of these specific aspects. In MCDM, a weighted score is obtained by aggregating three criteria. In this method, weights of the criterion were determined using TFN and Extent Analysis Method of F-AHP. From the results it could be inferred that the screen time holds the greatest importance in terms of percentage value with a percentage value of 37% in total weightage. : Sufficient sleep and proper hydration are elements that comprise 35% and 27% respectively, ranking them second and third in importance. These insights should be used as management as well as guiding decision-making on eye health processes.

**Corresponding author*: 87subratajana87@gmail.com

Rahul Kar, Gunjan Mukherjee, Biswadip Basu Mallik and Ashok Kumar Shaw (eds.) Fuzzy Logic in Computational Intelligence: Applications and Case Studies, (359–382) © 2026 Scrivener Publishing LLC

Keywords: Eye health, triangular fuzzy number (TFN), multi-criteria decision making (MCDM), extent analysis method (EAM), analytic hierarchy process (AHP)

20.1 Introduction

Eye health maintenance demands taking proactive measures toward security and maintaining your eye health. It requires a visit to the eye doctor, eating well, staying out of the sun, and any problem that may crop up [1]. Pro-active management of eye health can be helpful in preventing or detecting a host of conditions such as glaucoma, cataracts, macular degeneration, and diabetic retinopathy. Proper care for eyes must be well placed in your overall wellness routine, so you can always see well and live comfortably [2].

20.1.1 Importance of Eye Health Management

Important Points Indicative of the Relevance of Management of Eye Health

- Healthy eyesight is indispensable for our daily activities: Reading, driving, and getting around are some of among many tasks we perform easily because of healthy eyesight [3].
- Reducing blindness to vision loss: The frequent eye check-ups and proper management of eye health can actually help detect and treat conditions early so that there is a minimum possibility of irreversible vision loss [4].
- Quality of life: Good eye health enhances our quality of life as we are able to view cinemas, enjoy art, and play sports [5].
- Underlying medical condition detection: At times, some eye check-up may indicate early stages of systemic diseases like diabetes, hypertension, and cancer. In this sense, good eye health can save us from medical conditions in good time [6].
- Safety: Clear vision is pretty basic to safety both in the home, at work and even as one ventures outdoors. Hence, people with unhealthy eyes may become more prone to injuries and accidents [7].
- Productivity: Healthy eyes contribute greatly toward good productivity within education, career, and any other related aspects [8].
- Graceful aging: Cataracts, glaucoma, and age-related macular degeneration are some of the eye diseases that begin

dominating with increased age. These issues can be slowed or perhaps prevented with proper eye care health [9].

- Lifestyle factors: Diet, exercise, and smoking cessation have been found to affect eye health a lot. Lifestyle management thus supports healthy vision as well as reduces the risk of eye diseases [10].
- Psychological well-being: Damaged or deteriorating vision can lead to frustration, loneliness, and even despair. The more care the eyes take in, the better mental health may be [11].
- Cost-effectiveness: Investing in preventive care for the eyes through regular check-ups and good habits could save people money in the long run by avoiding health services that would have been ensued due to such highly advanced eye diseases or visions [12].

20.1.2 Context

The COVID-19 pandemic has drastically affected global healthcare systems and requires adaptation in most areas of medical specialties. Although the aspect of respiratory health cannot but be in focus for everybody, many other aspects have received much less attention. However, there is growing evidence showing how ocular health management has been thoroughly compromised. This research attempts to explore the impact of the COVID-19 pandemic on eye health management and suggest means of its enhancement in the post-pandemic era.

Impact of COVID-19 on Eye Health Management:

- It Disrupted Routine Eye Care: Lockdown measures overwhelmed the healthcare systems, causing significant delays of nonessential eye care appointments and surgeries, further resulting in delayed diagnosis and treatment for most ocular conditions.
- Increased screen time: Lockdown, work-from-home, and studying from home kept people glued to screens. Social distancing measures, that nearly took away "public" life, kept them indoors where they spent much more time in front of a computer or TV screen than usual. All these factors worsened digital eye strain and dry eye syndrome.
- Mask-Associated Ocular Problems: Mask use was associated with ocular discomfort in many, through the presence of dry

eyes, fogging glasses, and most significantly, exacerbation of pre-existing conditions such as blepharitis and conjunctivitis.
- Psychological Impact: Lest patients avoid timely, important eye care services for fear of developing a COVID-19 infection, their causative diseases may go undiagnosed or untreated with potentially worse consequences.

The COVID-19 pandemic offers the potential for adapting to the development of strong, resilient eye health management strategies. It becomes possible to establish a more patient-centered, resilient eye care system for the post-pandemic era when addressing this pandemic and developing new ways to handle challenges arising from it. This study underlines the fact that some proactive steps toward maintaining ocular health must be taken during such times of future health care crises to increase access to good eye care services [13].

20.1.3 MCDM Techniques

Multi-Criteria Decision Making MCDM Techniques Multi-Criteria decision making MCDM techniques are tools applied to make decisions when there are multiple conflicting criteria. They are useful in systematically evaluating and ranking alternatives according to a number of criteria or objectives. Among the widely used are Analytic Hierarchy Process AHP [14], Analytic Network Process ANP [15], Technique for Order of Preference by Similarity to Ideal Solution TOPSIS [16], and Multi-Attribute Utility Theory MAUT [17]. These techniques offer structured ways of addressing the complexities of decision-making scenarios, hence ensuring a safe approach toward arriving at an informed and rational decision-making process.

20.1.4 Beneficiaries

Writing a research paper on eye health management could benefit various groups:

- Patients and the General Public: Research articles on eye care management can be highly useful to patients as they make eye-care decisions.
- Healthcare Professionals: Ophthalmologists, optometrists, among others, can enhance their ability to administer quality treatment to their patients by using research articles.

- Researchers and academics: Peers in the ophthalmology and optometry fields might utilize the findings and methodology of research papers in furthering knowledge and information on the topic.
- Policy Makers and Public Health Officials: The research papers on eye health management can be used in the development of policies for healthcare infrastructure provision, funding allocation, and public health programs that aim to promote eye health and prevent vision loss.
- Industry and Technology Developers: Those firms that develop pharmaceuticals, eye care medical devices and technologies can leverage the research outcomes to inform their product development such that these end-products would address the key issues and concerns of practice.
- Insurance Providers: The research studies will be able to inform the insurance providers about the effectiveness of diverse treatments and interventions in various ocular diseases, guiding them while creating policies of insurance that take into account the conditions of patients and cost-effectiveness.

20.1.5 Novelties

Innovative factors of our research would be in terms of using the Extent Analysis Method of Fuzzy AHP for criteria assessment and prioritization. This method will quantify the determinations involving the decision-making process in order to know which ones are more important. If used in eye care management with limited vision communities, this technique can offer a lot more insightful information towards making decisions.

20.1.6 Organization of the Work

The remaining section of the article is structured in the following manner as demonstrated in the Figure 20.1.

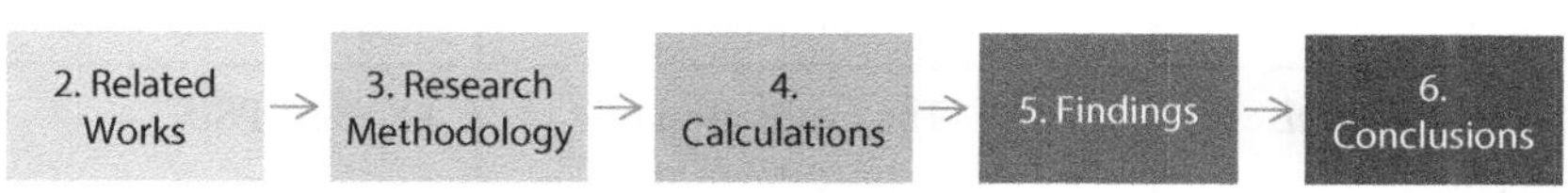

Figure 20.1 Organization of the paper.

20.2 Related Works

Effective eye health care is crucial in today's digital era. Various forms of study have been conducted in related field to effectively regulate eye health performance (Table 20.1).

Table 20.1 Literature review.

Authors	Year	Application area	Methods applied
Emec, S. *et al.* [18]	2019	Selection of DNA-RNA-protein isolation device	AHP and Fuzzy VIKOR
Stević, Ž. *et al.* [19]	2020	Optimal supplier selection for long-term viability in the healthcare sector	MARCOS
Büyüközkan, G., & Mukul, E. [20]	2020	Smart health applications	HFLTS, HFL, AHP, CODAS, COPRAS, TOPSIS
Chakraborty, S. *et al.* [21]	2024	Healthcare supplier selection	WASPAS, CODAS, CoCoSo
Meidute-Kavaliauskiene, I., & Ghorbani, S. [22]	2021	Optimal contract selection for supply chain management in the healthcare sector	CSF, SWARA, EAMR
Lu *et al.* [23]	2013	Taiwan's healthcare industry	RFID, DEMATEL, DANP, VIKOR
KARADAYI, M. A., & KARSAK, E. E. [24]	2014	Health-care performance assessment	VIKOR, TOPSIS
Uslu, Y. D. *et al.* [25]	2021	Manager selection in healthcare	AHP, MULTIMOORA
Akdag, H. *et al.* [26]	2014	The evaluation of hospital service quality	AHP, TOPSIS

(*Continued*)

Table 20.1 Literature review. (*Continued*)

Authors	Year	Application area	Methods applied
Chen, T. C. T. *et al.* [27]	2022	Mobile health care	FGM
Eskandari, H. *et al.* [28]	2011	Health Emergency	AHP, TOPSIS
Selamzade, F. *et al.* [29]	2023	Health efficiency measurement	DEA, TOPSIS, EDAS and CODAS
Aydin, N., & Seker, S. [30]	2021	Locating COVID-19 isolation hospitals	TOPSIS
Nandi, S *et al.* [31]	2023	Assessment of the therapeutic choices for COVID-19	HFS, GHFS, GHPFN, GHPFN (2nd type), TOPSIS
Göncü, K. K. *et al.* [32]	2022	supplier selection criteria in healthcare enterprises	DEMATEL, ANP
Ali, Y. *et al.* [33]	2018	Identification of variables contributing to the increase in caesarean section rates	DEMATEL
Ahmad, N. *et al.* [34]	2021	Identification and prioritization of measures to address the COVID-19 epidemic	BWM
Islam, S. M. U. *et al.* [35]	2022	Supply chain disruptions among merchants during the COVID-19 pandemic	AHP-TOPSIS

(*Continued*)

Table 20.1 Literature review. (*Continued*)

Authors	Year	Application area	Methods applied
Sharma, M., & Sehrawat, R. [36]	2020	a suitable CSP(Cloud Service Provider) for the healthcare sector	ISM-AHP-TOPSIS
Karatas, M. *et al.* [37]	2018	Health technology assessment.	DEMATEL, fuzzy AHP, Fuzzy VIKOR, fuzzy TOPSIS & Goal Programming
Karamouz, M. *et al.* [38]	2003	Water pollution control for health	SAW, AHP
Jaisankar, R. *et al.* [39]	2023	Ideal therapeutic plastic disposal technology	PHFS, HFS, ARAS, EWM
Khalilzadeh, M. *et al.* [40]	2021	Health and safety executive risks	Fuzzy SWARA, FMEA and PROMETHEE
This Paper	2024	Eye Health Management	Extent Analysis Method of Fuzzy AHP

20.2.1 Research Gap

After completing a thorough examination of existing literature, this study has observed that there hardly a research projects exists in the areas of eye health management.

20.2.2 Objectives

The aims of this investigation include

I. To determine the key factors for effectively managing eye health in the current digital age.
II. To determine the relative significance of specified parameters for managing eye health performance.

20.3 Research Methodology

20.3.1 Criteria Selection

To this effect, we conduct a survey in this study by adopting the Analytic Hierarchy Process framework based on previous criteria through a questionnaire. From these results, we are supposed to gain insights and recommendations for managing eye health performance. This was done by conducting a survey to a set of 10 practicing ophthalmologists and optometrists with the aim of narrowing down the main factors. Following their opinion, three criteria are identified to conduct this study. They are screen time as a non-benefit criteria, sufficient sleep as a benefit criteria and also adequate water as a benefit criteria. Benefit criteria is that whose desirable value to be maximized. Non-benefit criteria is that whose desirable value to be minimized.

20.3.2 Arithmetic Operations and Triangular Fuzzy Numbers

L.A. Zadeh invented fuzzy set theory in 1965 [41].

Let $K = (k_1, k_2, k_3)$ and $L = (l_1, l_2, l_3)$ be two different Triangular Fuzzy Numbers.

(i) Addition

$$(K+L) = (k_1 + l_1, k_2 + l_2, k_3 + l_3) \tag{20.1}$$

(ii) Subtraction

$$(K-L) = (k_1 - l_3, k_2 - l_2, k_3 - l_1) \tag{20.2}$$

(iii) Multiplication

$$(K \times L) = (k_1 l_1, k_2 l_2, k_3 l_3) \tag{20.3}$$

(iv) Scalar Multiplication

$$\theta K = (\theta k_1, \theta k_2, \theta k_3) \tag{20.4}$$

(v) Division

$$\left(\frac{K}{L}\right) = \left(\frac{k_1}{l_3}, \frac{k_2}{l_2}, \frac{k_3}{l_1}\right) \tag{20.5}$$

(vi) Inverse

$$K^{-1} = \left(\frac{1}{k_3}, \frac{1}{k_2}, \frac{1}{k_1}\right) \tag{20.6}$$

20.3.3 Fuzzy Analytic Hierarchy Process

The Analytic Hierarchy Process was developed by Saaty in 1980, and it provides a structure for assessing the relative importance of different tasks in a decision-making situation including several criteria [14]. These ratings are based on comparing pairs of items. In 1983, Van Laarhoven and Pedrycz introduced a fuzzy approach in picking from a number of options when faced with conflicting choice criteria [42]. The two most widely used Fuzzy AHP methods for computing criterion weights are: (i) The "Geometric Mean Method of Fuzzy Analytic Hierarchy Process" was the first method proposed by Buckley in 1985 [43]. (ii) The "Extent Analysis Method of Fuzzy Analytic Hierarchy Process" introduced by Chang in 1996 [44]. Nevertheless, the traditional AHP model has particular problems outlined by Yang and Chen in 2004. According to their study, AHP is highly suitable for situations only when there are clear conditions whereby the data can be objectively defined, thus yielding a judgment scale that might be skewed and vague [45]. Moreover, the AHP results depend on the subjective choice and preference of the decision maker. To improve the treatment of uncertainty, many researchers have integrated fuzzy theory with AHP. Recently, there are studies that focused on complex intelligent decision-making issues relating to the AHP model [46] and TOPSIS model [47].

20.3.4 Extent Analysis Method of Fuzzy Analytic Hierarchy Process

Step 1: Construct a "pairwise comparison matrix" using a "scale of relative relevance".
Create "fuzzy pair-wise comparison matrix" of size n*n, given m criteria. By utilizing expert surveys, each expert is requested to allocate linguistic concepts

using the technique of Type-2 Fuzzy Numbers (TFN). The components δ_ij represent the degree of preference of the i-th criteria over the j-th criterion.

Step 2: Create a fuzzy pairwise comparison matrix.
To obtain the fuzzified comparison matrix, it is necessary to convert the actual elements of A into fuzzy integers.

$$A = \begin{pmatrix} \tilde{\delta}_{11} & \tilde{\delta}_{12} & \cdots & \tilde{\delta}_{1n} \\ \tilde{\delta}_{21} & \tilde{\delta}_{22} & & \tilde{\delta}_{2n} \\ \vdots & & \ddots & \vdots \\ \tilde{\delta}_{n1} & \tilde{\delta}_{n2} & \cdots & \tilde{\delta}_{nn} \end{pmatrix} \tag{20.7}$$

Step 3: Calculate the Fuzzy Synthetic Extent
For this stage, we need to compute the "fuzzy synthetic extent" for the i-th alternative using the following formula:

$$S_i = \sum_{j=1}^{n} \tilde{\delta}_{ij} \left[\sum_{i=1}^{n} \sum_{j=1}^{n} \tilde{\delta}_{ij} \right]^{-1} \tag{20.8}$$

Step 4: Determine the degree of possibility
The comparison of two fuzzy numbers aims to determine the degree of possibility that one fuzzy number is greater than the other. Let's consider two Fuzzy numbers $\alpha_1 = (\alpha_{1l}, \alpha_{1m}, \alpha_{1u})$ and $\alpha_2 = (\alpha_{2l}, \alpha_{2m}, \alpha_{2u})$. Then the degree of possibility of $\alpha_2 \geq \alpha_1$ is calculated using the following formula (Figure 20.2):

$$V(\alpha_2 \geq \alpha_1) = \sup\left[\min\left(\mu_{\alpha_1(x)}, \mu_{\alpha_2(y)}\right)\right] = hgt(\alpha_1 \cap \alpha_2) = \mu_{\alpha_2(d)}$$
$$= \begin{cases} 1;\, if\ \alpha_{2m} \geq \alpha_{1m} \\ 0;\, if\ \alpha_{1l} \geq \alpha_{2u} \\ \dfrac{(\alpha_{1l} - \alpha_{2u})}{(\alpha_{2m} - \alpha_{2u}) - (\alpha_{1m} - \alpha_{1l})};\, otherwise \end{cases} \tag{20.9}$$

Where $\alpha_1 = (\alpha_{1l}, \alpha_{1m}, \alpha_{1u})$ and $\alpha_2 = (\alpha_{2l}, \alpha_{2m}, \alpha_{2u})$

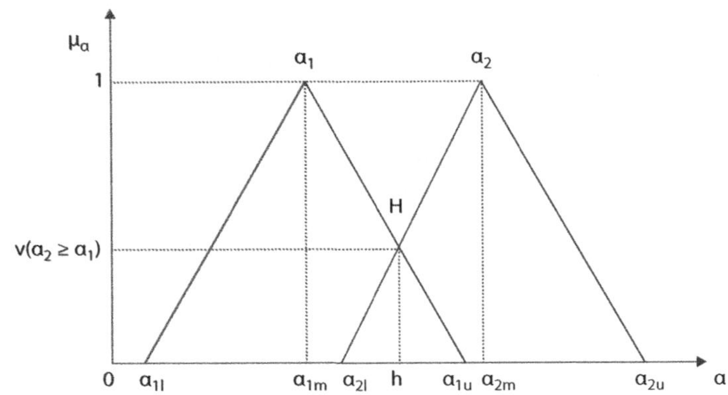

Figure 20.2 Degree of possibility [48].

Step 5: Determine the "degree of possibility" of a convex fuzzy number being bigger than a given convex fuzzy number, k.

During in this stage, try to determine the numerical value of V. The values will be computed using the subsequent formula:

$$V(S \geq S_1, S_2, \ldots\ldots, S_k) = \min V(S \geq S_i),\ where\ i = 1,2,\ldots\ldots, k \quad (20.10)$$

Step 6: Determine the "weight vector" and standardize the "non-fuzzy weight vector".

Presently, we employ the subsequent formula:

$$d'(A_i) = \min V\ (S_i \geq S_k); i,k = 1,2,\ldots\ldots, n; k \neq i \quad (20.11)$$

$$W' = \{d'(A_1), d'(A_2), \ldots\ldots, d'(A_n)\}^T \quad (20.12)$$

20.4 Calculations

20.4.1 Scale of Relative Importance

Firstly, we must establish a Scale of Relative Importance based on the level of significance. The definition may be found in Table 20.2.

A Pair-wise comparison matrix is now generated using the "Scale of Relative Importance". The Pair-wise comparison matrix provides a measure of the relative significance of several criteria in relation to the overall objective. Presented is a 3x3 matrix, which corresponds to the three criteria we have.

Table 20.2 Scale of relative importance.

Degree of importance	Definition (Importance)
1	Equal
3	Moderate
5	Strong
7	Very strong
9	Extreme
2, 4, 6, 8	In between values
$\frac{1}{3}, \frac{1}{5}, \frac{1}{7}, \frac{1}{9}$	Inverse comparison values

Source: [14]

20.4.2 Calculation of Pair-Wise Comparison Matrix

How to calculate the value in each cell:

- Now what will be the value in (Screen Time, Sufficient sleep) cell?
  For eight experts, screen time is "Moderate importance" than sufficient sleep. If sufficient sleep is x, then screen time is 3x.

$$\therefore Value\ (Screen\ Time, Sufficient\ Sleep) = \frac{Row\ element}{Coloumn\ element} = \frac{3x}{x} = 3$$

$$\therefore Value\ (Sufficient\ Sleep, Screen\ Time) = \frac{1}{3}$$

Now what will be the value in (Sufficient Sleep, Adequate Water) cell?
For six experts, sufficient sleep is "Moderate importance" than adequate water. If adequate water is x, then sufficient sleep is 3x.

$$\therefore Value\ (Sufficient\ Sleep, Adequate\ Water) = \frac{Row\ element}{Coloumn\ element} = \frac{3x}{x} = 3$$

$$\therefore Value\ (Adequate\ Water, Sufficient\ Sleep) = \frac{1}{3}$$

Now what will be the value in (Adequate Water, Screen Time) cell?
For seven experts, Adequate Water is "equal to moderate importance" than Screen Time. If Screen Time is x, then Adequate Water is 2x.

$$\therefore \textit{Value (Adequate Water, Screen Time)} = \frac{\textit{Row element}}{\textit{Coloumn element}} = \frac{2x}{x} = 2$$

$$\therefore \textit{Value (Screen Time, Adequate Water)} = \frac{1}{2}$$

In this way we can get the desired "pair-wise comparison matrix" (Table 20.3).

Table 20.3 Pair-wise comparison matrix.

Criteria	**Screen time**	**Sufficient sleep**	**Adequate water**
Screen Time	1	3	$\frac{1}{2}$
Sufficient Sleep	$\frac{1}{3}$	1	3
Adequate Water	2	$\frac{1}{3}$	1

20.4.3 Fuzzy Scale of Relative Importance

The Fuzzy Scale of Relative Importance is defined in Table 20.4, which follows. In lieu of hard numbers like 1, 3, 5, 7, and 9, the Fuzzy Scale of Relative Importance uses fuzzy numbers.

Table 20.4 Fuzzy scale of relative importance.

Fuzzy numbers	**Linguistic terms**
(1,1,1)	Equal
(2,3,4)	Moderate

(Continued)

Table 20.4 Fuzzy scale of relative importance. (*Continued*)

Fuzzy numbers	Linguistic terms
(4,5,6)	Strong
(6,7,8)	Very Strong
(9,9,9)	Extremely Strong
(1,2,3)	In Between Values
(3,4,5)	
(5,6,7)	
(7,8,9)	

In the following Figure 20.3 sketched version Scale of Relative Importance is presented.

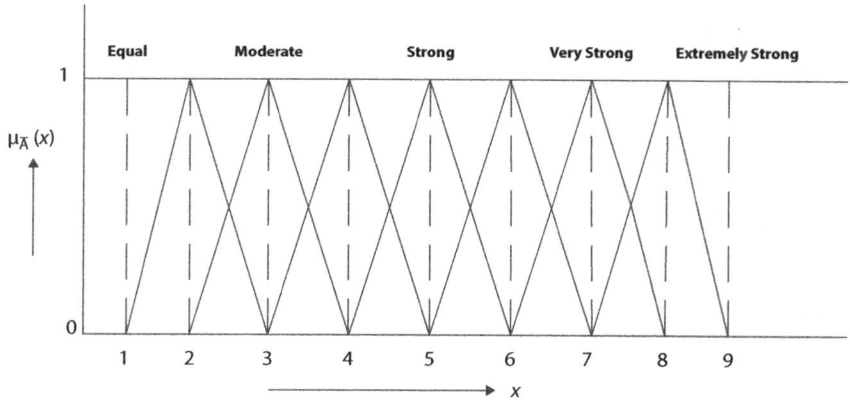

Figure 20.3 Fuzzy scale of relative importance.

20.4.4 Calculation of Fuzzy Pair-Wise Comparison Matrix

In the following Table 20.5 Crisp and "Fuzzy Scale of Relative Importance" depicted together.

Table 20.5 Fuzzy scale of relative importance.

Fuzzy numbers	Linguistic terms	Crisp numbers
(1,1,1)	Equal	1
(2,3,4)	Moderate	3
(4,5,6)	Strong	5
(6,7,8)	Very Strong	7
(9,9,9)	Extremely Strong	9
(1,2,3)	In Between Values	2
(3,4,5)		4
(5,6,7)		6
(7,8,9)		8

The crisp values in Table 20.6 are transformed into fuzzy numbers in order to obtain the "Fuzzified Pair-Wise Comparison Matrix".

Table 20.6 Fuzzified pair-wise comparison matrix.

Criteria	Screen time	Sufficient sleep	Adequate water
Screen Time	(1,1,1)	(2,3,4)	$\left(\frac{1}{3},\frac{1}{2},\frac{1}{1}\right)$
Sufficient Sleep	$\left(\frac{1}{4},\frac{1}{3},\frac{1}{2}\right)$	(1,1,1)	(2,3,4)
Adequate Water	(1,2,3)	$\left(\frac{1}{4},\frac{1}{3},\frac{1}{2}\right)$	(1,1,1)

20.4.5 Calculations with "Extent Analysis Method of Fuzzy Analytic Hierarchy Process"

First we have to calculate the value of $\sum_{j=1}^{n} \tilde{a}_{ij}$ with the help of fuzzified pairwise comparison matrix (Table 20.7).

Table 20.7 Finding the value of $\sum_{j=1}^{n} \tilde{a}_{ij}$.

Criteria	**Screen time**	**Sufficient sleep**	**Adequate water**	$\sum_{j=1}^{n} \tilde{a}_{ij}$
Screen time	(1,1,1)	(2,3,4)	$\left(\frac{1}{3},\frac{1}{2},\frac{1}{1}\right)$	(3.333, 4.5,)
Sufficient sleep	$\left(\frac{1}{4},\frac{1}{3},\frac{1}{2}\right)$	(1,1,1)	(2,3,4)	(3.250, 4.333, 5)
Adequate water	(1,2,3)	$\left(\frac{1}{4},\frac{1}{3},\frac{1}{2}\right)$	(1,1,1)	(2.250, 3.333, 4)
				$\sum_{i=1}^{n}\sum_{j=1}^{n} \tilde{a}_{ij} = (8.833, 12.167, 16)$
				$\left[\sum_{i=1}^{n}\sum_{j=1}^{n} \tilde{a}_{ij}\right]^{-1} = \left(\frac{1}{16},\frac{1}{12.167},\frac{1}{8.833}\right)$

Now the fuzzy synthetic extent with respect to i[th] alternative is to be calculated by using the Equation (20.8).

Therefore we are getting from Table 20.8.

Table 20.8 Fuzzy synthetic extent (S_i).

Criteria	$\sum_{j=1}^{n} \tilde{a}_{ij}$	$\sum_{j=1}^{n} \tilde{a}_{ij} \left[\sum_{i=1}^{n} \sum_{j=1}^{n} \tilde{a}_{ij} \right]^{-1}$	Fuzzy synthetic extent (S_i)
Screen time	(3.333, 4.5,6)	$(3.333, 4.5, 6) \otimes \left(\frac{1}{16}, \frac{1}{12.167}, \frac{1}{8.833} \right)$	(29.444, 54.750, 96)
Sufficient sleep	(3.250, 4.333, 5.5)	$(3.250, 4.333, 5.5) \otimes \left(\frac{1}{16}, \frac{1}{12.167}, \frac{1}{8.833} \right)$	(28.708, 52.722, 88)
Adequate water	(2.250, 3.333, 4.5)	$(2.250, 3.333, 4.5) \otimes \left(\frac{1}{16}, \frac{1}{12.167}, \frac{1}{8.833} \right)$	(19.875, 40.556, 72)

$$(\alpha_{1l} = 29.444, \alpha_{1m} = 54.750, \alpha_{1u} = 96)$$
$$(\alpha_{2l} = 28.708, \alpha_{2m} = 52.722, \alpha_{2u} = 88)$$
$$(\alpha_{3l} = 19.875, \alpha_{3m} = 40.556, \alpha_{3u} = 72)$$

For this phase, it is necessary to determine the degree of probability by utilizing Equation (20.9). In this context, we are required to determine the probability of an event occurring based on three specific criteria. This involves calculating the six degrees of possibility.

They are $V(S_1 \geq S_2)$, $V(S_1 \geq S_3)$, $V(S_2 \geq S_1)$, $V(S_2 \geq S_3)$, $V(S_3 \geq S_1)$, $V(S_3 \geq S_2)$.

Now using the above tabulated value we can find the following:

$$V(S_1 \geq S_2) = 1$$
$$V(S_1 \geq S_3) = 1$$
$$V(S_2 \geq S_1) = 0.966529$$
$$V(S_2 \geq S_3) = 1$$
$$V(S_3 \geq S_1) = 0.749878$$
$$V(S_3 \geq S_2) = 0.780616$$

Here we calculate the degree of possibility for a convex fuzzy number to be greater than k convex fuzzy numbers by using the Equation (20.10)

Therefore, it is necessary to determine the numerical quantity of

$$V(S_1 \geq S_2, S_3),\ V(S_2 \geq S_1, S_3)\ and\ V(S_3 \geq S_1, S_2)$$

These values will be calculated as follows

$V(S \geq S_2, S_2, \dots \dots, S_k) = min\ V(S \geq S_i)$, *where* $i = 1, 2, \dots \dots k$

$V(S_1 \geq S_2, S_3) = 1$, *since minimum value of* $V(S_1 \geq S_2)$ *and* $V(S_1 \geq S_3)$ *is* 1

$V(S_2 \geq S_1, S_3) = 0.966529$, *since the minimum value of* $V(S_2 \geq S_1)$ *and* $V(S_2 \geq S_3)$ *is* 0.966529

$V(S_3 \geq S_1, S_2) = 0.749878$, *since the minimum value of* $V(S_3 \geq S_1)$ *and* $V(S_3 \geq S_2)$ *is* 0.749878

Utilize Equations (20.11) and (20.12) to compute the "weight vector" and subsequently normalize the non-fuzzy weight vector.

Now we have to normalize the weight vectors by adding all the vectors and dividing by the sum

Therefore,

$$W' = \left(\frac{1}{2.716407}, \frac{0.966529}{2.716407}, \frac{0.749878}{2.716407} \right)^T = (0.3681, 0.3558, 0.2761)^T$$

The decision maker can utilize the proportion of relevance of criteria weights provided in Table 20.9 to create the most optimal decision.

Table 20.9 Criteria weights (Non-fuzzified).

Criteria	**Weights of criteria**	**% of importance (Approx.)**
Screen time	0.3681	37%
Sufficient sleep	0.3558	35%
Adequate water	0.2761	28%

20.5 Findings

The results shows that

I. The screen time which bears maximum weightage of 37%
II. The second and third most important criteria are sufficient sleep and adequate water of weightage 35% and 27% respectively.

The following pie chart in Figure 20.4 is represented the percentage of importance of the criteria

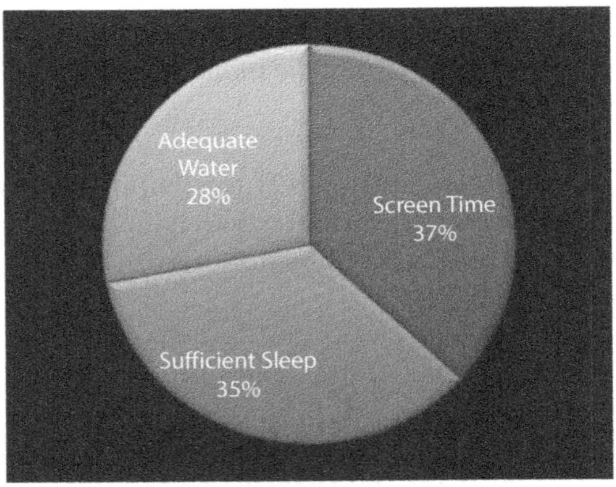

Figure 20.4 Percentage of priority of the criteria.

20.6 Conclusions

Here we looked at some of the most pertinent factors that would lead to the optimal management of eye health. Our findings point to a variety of lifestyle factors in leading to eye health problems. The study shows that the major overall influence on eye health comes from screen time, to the tune of 37%. This refers to the significance of managing screen time over time, as it affects eye strain and related issues. The second and third of the most important factors revealed are enough sleep and enough water intake, at weightages of 35% and 27% respectively. Enough sleep is necessary to the eyes that enable them to recover from stress and strain in the course of daily operations. Adequate water intake also plays a huge role because hydration is pertinent to both the manufacture of tears and to general health of the ocular surface.

These findings suggest that a good eye health management approach should employ adequate reduction in screen time, adequate sleep, and proper hydration. This will significantly improve an individual's eye health while preventing common problems such as eye strain, dryness, and fatigue. This conclusion underscores the importance of a balanced lifestyle as far as optimal eye health is concerned. Future studies will relate to more variables and interventions that are going to be used to further enhance eye health management, especially due to the rapid pace of modern technological advancements and lifestyle habit changes.

References

1. Welp, A., Woodbury, R.B., McCoy, M.A., Teutsch, S.M. (Eds.), Making eye health a population health imperative: vision for tomorrow, 2017.
2. Aghaji, A., Burchett, H.E., Oguego, N., Hameed, S., Gilbert, C., Primary health care facility readiness to implement primary eye care in Nigeria: Equipment, infrastructure, service delivery and health management information systems. *BMC Health Serv. Res.*, *21*, 1–11, 2021.
3. Margolis, M.K., Coyne, K., Kennedy-Martin, T., Baker, T., Schein, O., Revicki, D.A., Vision-specific instruments for the assessment of health-related quality of life and visual functioning: A literature review. *Pharmacoeconomics*, *20*, 791–812, 2002.
4. Kiss, E. and Pajor, E., Joint efforts for saving vision: Overview of the prevention of vision loss inside and outside Hungary. *Orvosi Hetilap*, *162*, 30, 1187–1197, 2021.
5. Owens, D.K., In the eye of the beholder: Assessment of health-related quality of life. *Hepatology*, *27*, 1, 292–293, 1998.
6. Rowe, S., MacLean, C.H., Shekelle, P.G., Preventing visual loss from chronic eye disease in primary care: scientific review. *Jama*, *291*, 12, 1487–1495, 2004.
7. Négrel, A.D. and Thylefors, B., The global impact of eye injuries. *Ophthalmic Epidemiol.*, *5*, 3, 143–169, 1998.
8. Fisk, W.J. and Rosenfeld, A.H., Estimates of improved productivity and health from better indoor environments. *Indoor Air*, *7*, 3, 158–172, 1997.
9. Zetterberg, M., Age-related eye disease and gender. *Maturitas*, *83*, 19–26, 2016.
10. Seddon, J.M., George, S., Rosner, B., Cigarette smoking, fish consumption, omega-3 fatty acid intake, and associations with age-related macular degeneration: The US Twin Study of Age-Related Macular Degeneration. *Arch. Ophthalmol.*, *124*, 7, 995–1001, 2006.

11. Ryff, C.D., Psychological well-being in adult life. *Curr. Directions Psychol. Sci.*, *4*, 4, 99–104, 1995.
12. Attar, R., *Exploration of the Experiences and Perceptions of a Sample Group of Health Care Employees in Mississippi Regarding Regular Comprehensive Eye Exams as Part of Preventive Health Services*, The University of Mississippi Medical Center, 2023, Doctoral dissertation.
13. Poyser, A., Deol, S.S., Osman, L., Kuht, H.J., Sivagnanasithiyar, T., Manrique, R., Thomas, M.G., Impact of COVID-19 pandemic and lockdown on eye emergencies. *Eur. J. Ophthalmol.*, *31*, 6, 2894–2900, 2021.
14. Saaty, T., The analytic hierarchy process (AHP) for decision making, in: *Kobe, Japan*, vol. 1, p. 69, 1980, November.
15. Jharkharia, S. and Shankar, R., Selection of logistics service provider: An analytic network process (ANP) approach. *Omega*, *35*, 3, 274–289, 2007.
16. Hwang, C.L. and Yoon, K., *Multiple Attribute Decision Making: Methods and Applications*, Springer-Verlag, New York, 1981.
17. Keeney, R.L. and Raiffa, H., Decisions with Multiple Objectives, 1993, ISBN 0-521-44185-4.
18. Emec, S., Turanoglu, B., Oztas, S., Akkaya, G., An integrated MCDM for a medical company selection in health sector. *Int. J. Sci. Technol. Res.*, *5*, 4, 77–89, 2019.
19. Stević, Z., Pamučar, D., Puška, A., Chatterjee, P., Sustainable supplier selection in healthcare industries using a new MCDM method: Measurement of alternatives and ranking according to COmpromise solution (MARCOS). *Comput. Ind. Eng.*, *140*, 106231, 2020.
20. Büyüközkan, G. and Mukul, E., Evaluation of smart health technologies with hesitant fuzzy linguistic MCDM methods. *J. Intell. Fuzzy Syst.*, *39*, 5, 6363–6375, 2020.
21. Chakraborty, S., Raut, R.D., Rofin, T.M., Chakraborty, S., On solving a healthcare supplier selection problem using MCDM methods in intuitionistic fuzzy environment. *Opsearch*, 1–29, 2024.
22. Meidute-Kavaliauskiene, I. and Ghorbani, S., Supply chain contract selection in the healthcare industry: A hybrid mcdm method in uncertainty environment. *Independent J. Manage. Prod.*, *12*, 4, 1160–1187, 2021.
23. Lu, M.T., Lin, S.W., Tzeng, G.H., Improving RFID adoption in Taiwan's healthcare industry based on a DEMATEL technique with a hybrid MCDM model. *Decis. Support Syst.*, *56*, 259–269, 2013.
24. Karadayi, M.A. and Karsak, E.E., Fuzzy MCDM approach for health-care performance assessment in Istanbul, in: *Proceedings of The 18th World Multi-Conference on Systemics, Cybernetics and Informatics*, pp. 228–233, 2014.
25. Uslu, Y.D., Yılmaz, E., Yiğit, P., Developing qualified personnel selection strategies using MCDM approach: A university hospital practice, in: *Strategic Outlook in Business and Finance Innovation: Multidimensional Policies for Emerging Economies*, pp. 195–205, Emerald Publishing Limited, 2021.

26. Akdag, H., Kalaycı, T., Karagöz, S., Zülfikar, H., Giz, D., The evaluation of hospital service quality by fuzzy MCDM. *Appl. Soft Comput.*, *23*, 239–248, 2014.
27. Chen, T.C.T. and Lin, C.W., An FGM decomposition-based fuzzy MCDM method for selecting smart technology applications to support mobile health care during and after the COVID-19 pandemic. *Appl. Soft Comput.*, *121*, 108758, 2022.
28. Eskandari, H., Riyahifard, M., Khosravi, S., Geiger, C.D., Improving the emergency department performance using simulation and MCDM methods, in: *Proceedings of the 2011 winter simulation conference (WSC)*, IEEE, pp. 1211–1222, 2011, December.
29. Selamzade, F., Ersoy, Y., Ozdemir, Y., Celik, M.Y., Health efficiency measurement of OECD countries against the COVID-19 pandemic by using DEA and MCDM methods. *Arabian J. Sci. Eng.*, *48*, 11, 15695–15712, 2023.
30. Aydin, N. and Seker, S., Determining the location of isolation hospitals for COVID-19 *via* Delphi-based MCDM method. *Int. J. Intell. Syst.*, *36*, 6, 3011–3034, 2021.
31. Nandi, S., Granata, G., Jana, S., Ghorui, N., Mondal, S.P., Bhaumik, M., Evaluation of the treatment options for COVID-19 patients using generalized hesitant fuzzy-multi criteria decision making techniques. *Socio-Economic Plann. Sci.*, *88*, 101614, 2023.
32. Göncü, K.K. and Çetin, O., A decision model for supplier selection criteria in healthcare enterprises with dematel ANP method. *Sustainability*, *14*, 21, 13912, 2022.
33. Ali, Y., Khan, M.W., Mumtaz, U., Salman, A., Muhammad, N., Sabir, M., Identification of factors influencing the rise of cesarean sections rates in Pakistan, using MCDM. *Int. J. Health Care Qual. Assur.*, *31*, 8, 1058–1069, 2018.
34. Ahmad, N., Hasan, M.G., Barbhuiya, R.K., Identification and prioritization of strategies to tackle COVID-19 outbreak: A group-BWM based MCDM approach. *Appl. Soft Comput.*, *111*, 107642, 2021.
35. Islam, S.M.U., Khan, S., Ahmad, H., Rahman, M.A.U., Tomar, S., Khan, M.Z., Assessment of challenges and problems in supply chain among retailers during COVID-19 epidemic through AHP-TOPSIS hybrid MCDM technique. *Internet Things Cyber-Phys. Syst.*, *2*, 180–193, 2022.
36. Sharma, M. and Sehrawat, R., A hybrid multi-criteria decision-making method for cloud adoption: Evidence from the healthcare sector. *Technol. Soc.*, *61*, 101258, 2020.
37. Karatas, M., Karacan, I., Tozan, H., An integrated multi-criteria decision making methodology for health technology assessment. *Eur. J. Ind. Eng.*, *12*, 4, 504–534, 2018.
38. Karamouz, M., Zahraie, B., Kerachian, R., Development of a master plan for water pollution control using MCDM techniques: a case study. *Water Int.*, *28*, 4, 478–490, 2003.

39. Jaisankar, R., Murugesan, V., Narayanamoorthy, S., Ahmadian, A., Suvitha, K., Ferrara, M., Kang, D., Integrated MCDM approaches for exploring the ideal therapeutic plastic disposal technology: Probabilistic hesitant fuzzy domain. *Water Air Soil Pollut.*, *234*, 2, 71, 2023.
40. Khalilzadeh, M., Ghasemi, P., Afrasiabi, A., Shakeri, H., Hybrid fuzzy MCDM and FMEA integrating with linear programming approach for the health and safety executive risks: a case study. *J. Modell. Manage.*, *16*, 4, 1025–1053, 2021.
41. Zadeh, L.A., Fuzzy sets. *Inf. Control*, *8*, 3, 338–353, 1965.
42. Van Laarhoven, P.J. and Pedrycz, W., A fuzzy extension of Saaty's priority theory. *Fuzzy Sets Syst.*, *11*, 1-3, 229–241, 1983.
43. Buckley, J.J., Fuzzy hierarchical analysis. *Fuzzy Sets Syst.*, *17*, 3, 233–247, 1985.
44. Chang, D.Y., Applications of the extent analysis method on fuzzy AHP. *Eur. J. Oper. Res.*, *95*, 3, 649–655, 1996.
45. Yang, C.C. and Chen, B.S., Key quality performance evaluation using fuzzy AHP. *J. Chin. Inst. Ind. Eng.*, *21*, 6, 543–550, 2004.
46. Fattoruso, G., Scognamiglio, S., Violi, A., A new dynamic and perspective parsimonious AHP model for improving industrial frameworks. *Mathematics*, *10*, 17, 3138, 2022.
47. Modibbo, U.M., Hassan, M., Ahmed, A., Ali, I., Multi-criteria decision analysis for pharmaceutical supplier selection problem using fuzzy TOPSIS. *Manage. Decis.*, *60*, 3, 806–836, 2022.
48. Hangshenas, S., Özçelik, Y., Mikaeil, R., Moghaddam, S., *Ranking and Assesment of tunneling projects risks using fuzzy MCDM*, 2017, (Case Study: Toyserkan Doolayi Tunnel).

21

Intuitionistic Fuzzy Soft Set Framework for Diagnosing Infectious Diseases

Devangi Sojitra, Minakshi Biswas Hathiwala, Gautam Hathiwala* and Khanjan M. Trivedi

Department of Mathematics, Marwadi University, Rajkot, Gujarat, India

Abstract

The difficulty of overlapping symptoms in medical diagnosis makes it challenging to precisely identify the diseases, which can lead to delayed or improper treatment. For example, malaria, dengue, and typhoid fever share common symptoms such as headache, high fever, nausea, muscle pain, pain in joints, and fatigue. Growing population, poor hygiene, increase in urbanization, and climate change lead to the intensified spread of typhoid, dengue, and malaria. Fuzzy theory deals with the uncertainty and imprecision in processing the data and decision-making. Various models utilize fuzzy sets to deal with several difficult components of medical diagnosis. Fuzzy soft sets are an extension of traditional fuzzy sets intended to deal with the alternative's parameterized values in the process of decision-making. Fuzzy intuitionistic sets enhance the concept of fuzzy sets by including the degrees of membership, non-membership, and hesitation, which provide a more sophisticated way of simulating ambiguous information. When uncertain data becomes more complex, the notion of intuitionistic fuzzy soft sets arises as a combination of intuitionistic fuzzy sets and fuzzy soft sets.

In this chapter, we analyze the concepts of fuzzy soft sets, intuitionistic fuzzy sets, and intuitionistic fuzzy soft sets. We begin by discussing the basic definitions and operations related to these sets, and distinguish them from ordinary fuzzy sets and soft sets. Moreover, this will be followed by the demonstration through some interesting examples, for each of these sets. This will showcase the significance of these sets in managing uncertainty and ambiguity, in practical situations. Finally, we present an application of an intuitionistic fuzzy soft set in the diagnosis of infectious diseases such as malaria, dengue, and typhoid fever.

**Corresponding author*: gautamhathiwala1717@gmail.com

Rahul Kar, Gunjan Mukherjee, Biswadip Basu Mallik and Ashok Kumar Shaw (eds.) Fuzzy Logic in Computational Intelligence: Applications and Case Studies, (383–410) © 2026 Scrivener Publishing LLC

***Keywords*:** Intuitionistic fuzzy soft set, intuitionistic fuzzy set, fuzzy soft set, infectious diseases, medical diagnosis

21.1 Introduction

Uncertainty and imprecision are essential challenges in various fields such as decision-making, mathematics, engineering, computer science, and can significantly impact results. Various theories, such as fuzzy set theory, fuzzy soft set theory, intuitionistic fuzzy set theory, and intuitionistic fuzzy soft set theory have emerged to overcome these challenges.

In 1965, Zadeh [1] proposed the theory of fuzzy sets, as the extension of classical set theory by giving the membership grade to each element ranging from 0 to 1. In 1999, Molodtsov [2] extended fuzzy sets to develop the concept of soft sets. These soft sets use the parameters to represent the information rather than the membership grade. Maji *et al.* [5] introduced the idea of the fuzzy soft set by incorporating the membership grade into the soft set. The fuzzy set theory lacks the ability to represent hesitancy that occurs in real life scenarios. The degree of hesitation is a quantity that measures the special type of uncertainty of an element other than the degree of membership (DoM) and non-membership (DoN-M). In order to include this quantity, Atanassov [6] proposed the concept of an intuitionistic fuzzy set, which expands upon the notion of a fuzzy set by considering both the degree of membership and the degree of non-membership. In addition, Maji *et al.* [8] constructed the intuitionistic fuzzy soft set by combining the fuzzy soft set and intuitionistic fuzzy set. By combining a fuzzy soft set with an intuitionistic fuzzy set, we can effectively analyze and address the vagueness and uncertainty associated with decision-making.

21.2 Fuzziness in Medical Diagnosis

In the medical diagnosis, the best way to describe the patient's symptoms is either "always, sometimes, often, etc." or "severe, moderate, mild" rather than "present or absent". Further, it is complicated to identify the disease, when its symptoms overlap with other diseases. To overcome these challenges, the concept of fuzziness arises in medical diagnosis. The fuzzy-based concepts provide the linguistic approach, that represents the medical texts more accurately and the fuzzy approach helps to predict the disease, whose symptoms overlap with other diseases.

One of the important early steps toward applying fuzzy set theory to medical diagnosis problems was the creation of the CADIAG-2 *i.e.,* a computer-assisted diagnosis system [12, 13]. This expert system represented medical information and made diagnostic predictions *via* fuzzy logic. Following that, studies looked into fuzzy rule-based systems to describe medical knowledge [14, 15]. These systems attempted to capture the vagueness of symptoms and criteria for diagnosis to enhance diagnostic accuracy. An additional early method for modeling the connection between diseases and their symptoms was the fuzzy relation. This method was proposed by E. Sanchez [11]. Later on, this approach was used to develop many medical diagnosis models. These approaches differ from each other based on the types of generalized fuzzy sets they employ. For instance, Hooda & Kumari [16], and Celik & Yamak [17] used fuzzy soft sets, while De *et al.* [18] and Szmidt & Kacprzyk [19] used intuitionistic fuzzy sets. Moreover, Gandhimathi [20], Hooda *et al.* [21], Shanmugasundaram *et al.* [10], and Bora *et al.* [9] utilized intuitionistic fuzzy soft sets. In this chapter, we will discuss the method given by Shanmugasundaram *et al.* [10] as it is more efficient to identify the disease. This method uses the intuitionistic fuzzy soft set, which is applied through the intuitionistic fuzzy max-min average composition. Moreover, we have presented a case study to identify infectious diseases such as malaria, typhoid fever, and dengue.

21.3 Preliminaries

Throughout the chapter, we will refer to $\mathcal{X}$ as the universal set and ξ as the set of attributes or parameters with respect to $\mathcal{X}$.

21.3.1 Fuzzy Sets [1]

The fuzzy set (FS for short) $\mathcal{S}$ on $\mathcal{X}$ is a mapping $\mathcal{S}: \mathcal{X} \to [0,1]$ and defined as,

$$\mathcal{S} = \{(\mathfrak{d}, \mathcal{S}(\mathfrak{d})) | \mathfrak{d} \in \mathcal{X}\} \text{ or } \mathcal{S} = \sum_{\mathfrak{d} \in \mathcal{X}} \frac{\mathcal{S}(\mathfrak{d})}{\mathfrak{d}}.$$

Set of all fuzzy subsets on $\mathcal{X}$ is denoted as $I^{\mathcal{X}}$.

21.3.2 Soft Sets

21.3.2.1 *Definition [2]*

Let $\mathcal{K} \subseteq \mathcal{E}$. Then the pair $(\xi, \mathcal{K})$ or $\xi_{\mathcal{K}}$ is said to be the soft set (SS for short) over $\mathcal{X}$. Here, ξ is a mapping $\xi : \mathcal{K} \rightarrow P(\mathcal{X})$, which is known as the approximate function of SS $\xi_{\mathcal{K}}$. Where, $P(\mathcal{X})$ is the power set of $\mathcal{X}$. Thus, the SS $\xi_{\mathcal{K}}$ is defined as, $\xi_{\mathcal{K}} = \{\xi(\mathfrak{s}) \mid \mathfrak{s} \in \mathcal{K}, \xi(\mathfrak{s}) \in P(\mathcal{X})\}$. In the form of ordered pairs, $\xi_{\mathcal{K}}$ is represented as, $\xi_{\mathcal{K}} = \{(\mathfrak{s}, \xi(\mathfrak{s})) \mid \mathfrak{s} \in \mathcal{K}\}$. For $\mathfrak{s} \in \mathcal{K}$, $\xi(\mathfrak{s})$ can be considered as the set of $\mathfrak{s}$-elements or the set of $\mathfrak{s}$-approximate elements of SS $\xi_{\mathcal{K}}$.

21.3.2.2 *Definition [3]*

Let $\xi_{\mathcal{K}}$ and $\zeta_{\mathcal{Q}}$ are two SSs over $\mathcal{X}$. Then

a) $\xi_{\mathcal{K}}$ is a soft subset of $\zeta_{\mathcal{Q}}$ *i.e.*, $\xi_{\mathcal{K}} \subseteq \zeta_{\mathcal{Q}}$, if $\mathcal{K} \subseteq \mathcal{Q}$ and $\xi(\mathfrak{s}) \subseteq \zeta(\mathfrak{s})$; for all $\mathfrak{s} \in \mathcal{K}$.
b) $\xi_{\mathcal{K}}$ is soft equal to $\zeta_{\mathcal{Q}}$ *i.e.*, $\xi_{\mathcal{K}} = \zeta_{\mathcal{Q}}$, if $\xi_{\mathcal{K}} \subseteq \zeta_{\mathcal{Q}}$ and $\zeta_{\mathcal{Q}} \subseteq \xi_{\mathcal{K}}$.

21.3.2.3 *Example*

Suppose an interview is conducted in a school for the position of teacher. Let $\mathcal{X} = \{r, l, n, q, a, j\}$ be the set of applicants and $\mathcal{E} = \{\mathfrak{s}_1 =$ Knowledgeable, $\mathfrak{s}_2 =$ Confident, $\mathfrak{s}_3 =$ Good communication, $\mathfrak{s}_4 =$ Creative, $\mathfrak{s}_5 =$ Empathetic, $\mathfrak{s}_6 =$ Flexible, $\mathfrak{s}_7 =$ Adaptive$\}$ be the set of parameters required for a good teacher. Now, an interviewer chooses a few parameters from $\mathcal{E}$ for the selection, such as $\mathcal{K} = \{\mathfrak{s}_1, \mathfrak{s}_2, \mathfrak{s}_3, \mathfrak{s}_4, \mathfrak{s}_6\}$. Let $\xi_{\mathcal{K}}$ be the SS based on the parameters given in the set $\mathcal{K}$, such that $\xi(\mathfrak{s}_1) = \{r, l, a, j\}$, $\xi(\mathfrak{s}_2) = \{l, n, q, j\}$, $\xi(\mathfrak{s}_3) = \{r, l, q, a, j\}$, $\xi(\mathfrak{s}_4) = \{l, j\}$, $\xi(\mathfrak{s}_6) = \{l, n, a\}$ as shown in Figure 21.1.

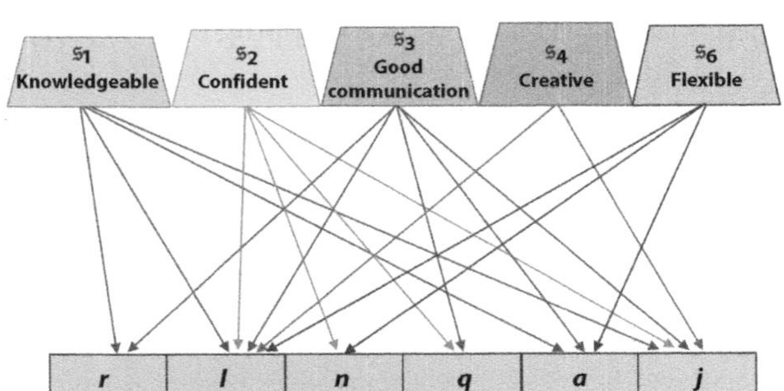

Figure 21.1 Applicants corresponding to the parameters given in set $\mathcal{K}$.

Table 21.1 Tabular form of soft set $\xi_{\mathcal{K}}$.

Applicants→ Parameters↓	*r*	*l*	*n*	*q*	*a*	*j*
$\mathfrak{s}_1$	1	1	0	0	1	1
$\mathfrak{s}_2$	0	1	1	1	0	1
$\mathfrak{s}_3$	1	1	0	1	1	1
$\mathfrak{s}_4$	0	1	0	0	0	1
$\mathfrak{s}_5$	0	0	0	0	0	0
$\mathfrak{s}_6$	0	1	1	0	1	0
$\mathfrak{s}_7$	0	0	0	0	0	0

Thus, the SS $\xi_{\mathcal{K}}=\{(\mathfrak{s}_1,\{r,l,a,j\}),\ (\mathfrak{s}_2,\{l,n,q,j\}),\ (\mathfrak{s}_3,\{r,l,q,a,j\}),\ (\mathfrak{s}_4,\{l,j\}),\ (\mathfrak{s}_6,\{l,n,a\})\}$. The tabular representation of this SS is shown in Table 21.1.

Note: $\neg\mathcal{E}$ denotes the NOT set of $\mathcal{E}$ and defined as $\{\text{not } \mathfrak{s}_i \mid \mathfrak{s}_i \in \mathcal{E}\}$. Here, we will denote "not $\mathfrak{s}_i$" as $\neg\mathfrak{s}_i$. Clearly, $\neg(\neg\mathcal{E}) = \mathcal{E}$.

From example 21.3.2.3, $\neg\mathcal{K}=\{\neg\mathfrak{s}_1 =$ not knowledgeable, $\neg\mathfrak{s}_2 =$ not confident, $\neg\mathfrak{s}_3 =$ not good communication, $\neg\mathfrak{s}_4 =$ not creative, $\neg\mathfrak{s}_6 =$ not flexible$\}$.

21.3.2.4 Operations on SS

Let $\xi_{\mathcal{K}}$ and $\zeta_{\mathcal{Q}}$ are two SSs over $\mathcal{X}$.

a) **Complement** [3]: The complement of SS $\xi_{\mathcal{K}}$ over $\mathcal{X}$ is denoted as $\xi_{\mathcal{K}}^{c}$ and defined by a mapping $\xi^{c}:\neg\mathcal{K} \to P(\mathcal{X})$ such that $\xi^{c}(\neg\mathfrak{s}) = \mathcal{X} - \mathfrak{f}(\mathfrak{s})$, for every $\neg\mathfrak{s} \in \neg\mathcal{K}$. Clearly, $(\xi_{\mathcal{K}}^{c})^{c} = \xi_{\mathcal{K}}$.

Example 21.3.2.4 (a): From example 21.3.2.3, $\xi^{c}(\neg\mathfrak{s}_1) = \{n,q\}$, $\xi^{c}(\neg\mathfrak{s}_2) = \{r,a\}$, $\xi^{c}(\neg\mathfrak{s}_3) = \{q\}$, $\xi^{c}(\neg\mathfrak{s}_4) = \{l,j\}$, $\xi^{c}(\neg\mathfrak{s}_6) = \{r,q,j\}$. Thus, the complement of SS $\xi_{\mathcal{K}}$ over $\mathcal{X}$ will be

$$\xi_{\mathcal{K}}^{c} = \{(\neg\mathfrak{s}_1, \{n, q\}), (\neg\mathfrak{s}_2, \{r, a\}), (\neg\mathfrak{s}_3, \{q\}), (\neg\mathfrak{s}_4, \{l, j\}), (\neg\mathfrak{s}_6, \{r, q, j\})\}.$$

b) **AND operation** [3]: "$\xi_{\mathcal{K}}$ AND $\zeta_{\mathcal{Q}}$" is denoted as $\xi_{\mathcal{K}} \wedge \zeta_{\mathcal{Q}}$ and defined as $\xi_{\mathcal{K}} \wedge \zeta_{\mathcal{Q}} = (\mathfrak{h}, \mathcal{K} \times \mathcal{Q})$, where, $\mathfrak{h}(\mathfrak{s}, \mathfrak{b}) = \xi(\mathfrak{s}) \cap \zeta(\mathfrak{b})$, $\forall (\mathfrak{s}, \mathfrak{b}) \in \mathcal{K} \times \mathcal{Q}$.

Example 21.3.2.4 (b): Let's consider $\mathcal{X}$ and $\mathcal{E}$ as given in example 21.3.2.3. Now, consider $\mathcal{K} = \{\mathfrak{s}_1, \mathfrak{s}_4, \mathfrak{s}_6\}$ and $\mathcal{Q} = \{\mathfrak{s}_2, \mathfrak{s}_3, \mathfrak{s}_6\}$. Suppose the SSs $\xi_{\mathcal{K}}$ and $\zeta_{\mathcal{Q}}$ based on the parameters given in the set $\mathcal{K}$ and $\mathcal{Q}$, respectively are as follows,

$\xi(\mathfrak{s}_1) = \{r, l, j\}$	$\zeta(\mathfrak{s}_2) = \{n, q\}$
$\xi(\mathfrak{s}_4) = \{r, n, q\}$	$\zeta(\mathfrak{s}_3) = \{l, n, j\}$
$\xi(\mathfrak{s}_6) = \{l, a\}$	$\zeta(\mathfrak{s}_6) = \{r, l\}$

Now, $\xi_{\mathcal{K}} \wedge \zeta_{\mathcal{Q}} = (\mathfrak{h}, \mathcal{K} \times \mathcal{Q})$; where, $\mathfrak{h}(\mathfrak{s}_i, \mathfrak{s}_j) = \xi(\mathfrak{s}_i) \cap \zeta(\mathfrak{s}_j)$, $\forall (\mathfrak{s}_i, \mathfrak{s}_j) \in \mathcal{K} \times \mathcal{Q}$. Here, we can see that

$$\mathcal{K} \times \mathcal{Q} = \{(\mathfrak{s}_1, \mathfrak{s}_2), (\mathfrak{s}_1, \mathfrak{s}_3), (\mathfrak{s}_1, \mathfrak{s}_6), (\mathfrak{s}_4, \mathfrak{s}_2), (\mathfrak{s}_4, \mathfrak{s}_3), (\mathfrak{s}_4, \mathfrak{s}_6), (\mathfrak{s}_6, \mathfrak{s}_2), (\mathfrak{s}_6, \mathfrak{s}_3), (\mathfrak{s}_6, \mathfrak{s}_6)\}.$$

Thus, $\mathfrak{h}(\mathfrak{s}_1, \mathfrak{s}_2) = \xi(\mathfrak{s}_1) \cap \zeta(\mathfrak{s}_2) = \phi$, $\mathfrak{h}(\mathfrak{s}_1, \mathfrak{s}_3) = \{l, j\}$, $\mathfrak{h}(\mathfrak{s}_1, \mathfrak{s}_6) = \{r, l\}$, $\mathfrak{h}(\mathfrak{s}_4, \mathfrak{s}_2) = \{n, q\}$, $\mathfrak{h}(\mathfrak{s}_4, \mathfrak{s}_3) = \{n\}$, $\mathfrak{h}(\mathfrak{s}_4, \mathfrak{s}_6) = \{r\}$, $\mathfrak{h}(\mathfrak{s}_6, \mathfrak{s}_2) = \phi$, $\mathfrak{h}(\mathfrak{s}_6, \mathfrak{s}_3) = \{l\}$, $\mathfrak{h}(\mathfrak{s}_6, \mathfrak{s}_6) = \{l\}$. This means that there is no applicant, who is both knowledgeable and confident. Moreover, the applicants 'l' and 'j' are knowledgeable and have good communication. Similarly, we can see for the rest.

c) **OR operation** [3]: "$\xi_{\mathcal{K}}$ OR $\zeta_{\mathcal{Q}}$" is denoted as $\xi_{\mathcal{K}} \vee \zeta_{\mathcal{Q}}$ and defined as $\xi_{\mathcal{K}} \vee \zeta_{\mathcal{Q}} = (\mathfrak{o}, \mathcal{K} \times \mathcal{Q})$, where, $\mathfrak{o}(\mathfrak{s}, \mathfrak{b}) = \xi(\mathfrak{s}) \cap \zeta(\mathfrak{b})$, $\forall (\mathfrak{s}, \mathfrak{b}) \in \mathcal{K} \times \mathcal{Q}$.

Example 21.3.2.4 (c): Consider the SSs $\xi_{\mathcal{K}}$ and $\zeta_{\mathcal{Q}}$ same as given in the example 21.3.2.4 (b). Now, $\xi_{\mathcal{K}} \vee \mathfrak{g}_{\mathcal{Q}} = (\mathfrak{o}, \mathcal{K} \times \mathcal{Q})$; where, $\mathfrak{o}(\mathfrak{s}_i, \mathfrak{s}_j) = \xi(\mathfrak{s}_i) \cap \mathfrak{g}(\mathfrak{s}_j)$, $\forall (\mathfrak{s}_i, \mathfrak{s}_j) \in \mathcal{K} \times \mathcal{Q}$ and $\mathcal{K} \times \mathcal{Q} = \{(\mathfrak{s}_1, \mathfrak{s}_2), (\mathfrak{s}_1, \mathfrak{s}_3), (\mathfrak{s}_1, \mathfrak{s}_6), (\mathfrak{s}_4, \mathfrak{s}_2), (\mathfrak{s}_4, \mathfrak{s}_3) (\mathfrak{s}_4, \mathfrak{s}_6), (\mathfrak{s}_6, \mathfrak{s}_2), (\mathfrak{s}_6, \mathfrak{s}_3), (\mathfrak{s}_6, \mathfrak{s}_6)\}$. Thus, $\mathfrak{v}(\mathfrak{s}_1, \mathfrak{s}_2) = \xi(\mathfrak{s}_1) \cup \mathfrak{g}(\mathfrak{s}_2) = \{r, l, n, q, j\}$, $\mathfrak{v}(\mathfrak{s}_1, \mathfrak{s}_3) = \{r, l, n, j\}$, $\mathfrak{v}(\mathfrak{s}_1, \mathfrak{s}_6) = \{r, l, j\}$, $\mathfrak{v}(\mathfrak{s}_4, \mathfrak{s}_2) = \{r, n, q\}$, $\mathfrak{v}(\mathfrak{s}_4, \mathfrak{s}_3) = \{r, l, n, q, j\}$, $\mathfrak{v}(\mathfrak{s}_4, \mathfrak{s}_6) = \{r, l, n, q\}$, $\mathfrak{v}(\mathfrak{s}_6, \mathfrak{s}_2) = \{l, n, q, a\}$, $\mathfrak{v}(\mathfrak{s}_6, \mathfrak{s}_3) = \{l, n, a, j\}$, $\mathfrak{v}(\mathfrak{s}_6, \mathfrak{s}_6) = \{r, l, a\}$. This means the applicants r, l, n, q and j are either knowledgeable or confident and similarly, for the rest.

d) **Union** [3]: The union of SSs $\xi_{\mathcal{K}}$ and $\zeta_{\mathcal{Q}}$ is denoted as $(\mathfrak{u},\mathcal{C}) = \xi_{\mathcal{K}} \tilde{\cup} \zeta_{\mathcal{Q}}$, where $\mathcal{C}=\mathcal{K} \cup \mathcal{Q}$ and for every $\mathfrak{s} \in \mathcal{C}$,

$$\mathfrak{u}(e) = \begin{cases} \xi(\mathfrak{s}), & \mathfrak{s} \in \mathcal{K} - \mathcal{Q} \\ \zeta(\mathfrak{s}), & \mathfrak{s} \in \mathcal{Q} - \mathcal{K} \\ \xi(\mathfrak{s}) \cup \zeta(\mathfrak{s}), & \mathfrak{s} \in \mathcal{K} \cap \mathcal{Q} \end{cases}$$

Example 21.3.2.4 (d): Consider the SSs $\xi_{\mathcal{K}}$ and $\zeta_{\mathcal{Q}}$ same as given in the example 21.3.2.4 (b). Thus, from the sets $\mathcal{K}$ and $\mathcal{Q}$, we have $\mathcal{K} \cup \mathcal{Q} = \{\mathfrak{s}_1, \mathfrak{s}_2, \mathfrak{s}_3, \mathfrak{s}_4, \mathfrak{s}_6\}$, $\mathcal{K}-\mathcal{Q}=\{\mathfrak{s}_1, \mathfrak{s}_4\}$ $\mathcal{Q}-\mathcal{K}=\{\mathfrak{s}_2, \mathfrak{s}_3\}$ and $\mathcal{K} \cap \mathcal{Q}=\{\mathfrak{s}_6\}$. Now, by definition of the union of two SSs, $\mathfrak{u}(\mathfrak{s}_1)=\{r,l,j\}$, $\mathfrak{u}(\mathfrak{s}_2)=\{n,q\}$, $\mathfrak{u}(\mathfrak{s}_3)=\{l,n,j\}$, $\mathfrak{u}(\mathfrak{s}_4)=\{r,n,q\}$ and $\mathfrak{u}(\mathfrak{s}_6)=\{r,l,a\}$.

e) **Intersection** [4]: The intersection of two SSs $\xi_{\mathcal{K}}$ and $\zeta_{\mathcal{Q}}$ is denoted as $(\mathfrak{i},\mathcal{C})=\xi_{\mathcal{K}} \tilde{\cap} \zeta_{\mathcal{Q}}$, where $\mathcal{C}=\mathcal{K}\cap\mathcal{Q}$ and for every $\mathfrak{s} \in \mathcal{C}, \mathfrak{i}(\mathfrak{s})=\xi(\mathfrak{s}) \cap \zeta(\mathfrak{s})$. Here, we should have $\mathcal{K}\cap\mathcal{Q}\neq\phi$.

Example 21.3.2.4 (e): Consider the SSs $\xi_{\mathcal{K}}$ and $\zeta_{\mathcal{Q}}$ same as given in the example 21.3.2.4 (b). Thus, from the sets $\mathcal{K}$ and $\mathcal{Q}$, we have $\mathcal{K}\cap\mathcal{Q}=\{\mathfrak{s}_6\}$. Now, by definition of the intersection of two FSs, $\mathfrak{i}(\mathfrak{s}_6)=\{l\}$.

21.3.3 Fuzzy Soft Set

21.3.3.1 Definition [5]

Let $\mathcal{K} \subseteq \mathcal{E}$. Then the pair $(\tilde{\xi}, \mathcal{K})$ is called a fuzzy soft set (FSS for short) over $\mathcal{X}$, where $\tilde{\xi}$ is a fuzzy approximate function of FSS, defined as $\tilde{\xi}:\mathcal{K} \rightarrow I^{\mathcal{X}}$. For all $\mathfrak{s} \in \mathcal{K}$, $\tilde{\xi}(\mathfrak{s})$ is called $\mathfrak{s}$-elements of the fuzzy soft set $(\tilde{\xi},\mathcal{K})$ and we will denote $\tilde{\xi}_{\mathfrak{s}}(\mathfrak{d})$ to be the DoM of $\mathfrak{d} \in \mathcal{X}$ in $\tilde{\xi}(\mathfrak{s})$. Here, we will denote the FSS $(\tilde{\xi},\mathcal{K})$ as $\tilde{\xi}_{\mathcal{K}}$.

21.3.3.2 Definition [5]

Let $\tilde{\xi}_{\mathcal{K}}$ and $\tilde{\zeta}_{\mathcal{Q}}$ are two FSSs over $\mathcal{X}$. Then

a) $\tilde{\xi}_{\mathcal{K}}$ is a fuzzy soft subset of $\tilde{\zeta}_{\mathcal{Q}}$ *i.e.*, $\tilde{\xi}_{\mathcal{K}} \tilde{\subseteq} \tilde{\zeta}_{\mathcal{Q}}$, if $\mathcal{K} \subseteq \mathcal{Q}$ and for all $\mathfrak{s} \in \mathcal{K}, \tilde{\xi}_{\mathfrak{s}}(\mathfrak{d}) \leq \tilde{\zeta}_{\mathfrak{s}}(\mathfrak{d})$; $\forall \mathfrak{d} \in \mathcal{X}$.
b) $\tilde{\xi}_{\mathcal{K}}$ is fuzzy soft equal to $\tilde{\zeta}_{\mathcal{Q}}$ *i.e.*, $\tilde{\xi}_{\mathcal{K}} \cong \tilde{\zeta}_{\mathcal{Q}}$, if $\tilde{\xi}_{\mathcal{K}} \tilde{\subseteq} \tilde{\zeta}_{\mathcal{Q}}$ and $\tilde{\zeta}_{\mathcal{Q}} \tilde{\subseteq} \tilde{\xi}_{\mathcal{K}}$.

21.3.3.3 *Example*

For the example of the FSS, let's consider the sets $\mathcal{X}$, $\mathcal{E}$ and $\mathcal{K}$ same as the example 21.3.2.3. By the definition of FSS, each $\tilde{\xi}(\mathfrak{s})$ will be a fuzzy set, where $\mathfrak{s} \in \mathcal{K}$. Suppose $\tilde{\xi}_{\mathcal{K}}$ be the FSS based on parameters given in the set $\mathcal{K}$, such that

$$\tilde{\xi}(\mathfrak{s}_1) = \frac{0.3}{r} + \frac{0.8}{l} + \frac{0.5}{n} + \frac{0.7}{q} + \frac{0.8}{a} + \frac{0.4}{j}$$

$$\tilde{\xi}(\mathfrak{s}_2) = \frac{0.5}{r} + \frac{0.7}{l} + \frac{0.3}{n} + \frac{0.6}{q} + \frac{0.5}{a} + \frac{0.8}{j}$$

$$\tilde{\xi}(\mathfrak{s}_3) = \frac{0.4}{r} + \frac{0.9}{l} + \frac{0.6}{n} + \frac{0.7}{q} + \frac{0}{a} + \frac{0.7}{j}$$

$$\tilde{\xi}(\mathfrak{s}_4) = \frac{0.9}{r} + \frac{0.8}{l} + \frac{0.4}{n} + \frac{0.6}{q} + \frac{0.7}{a} + \frac{0.2}{j}$$

$$\tilde{\xi}(\mathfrak{s}_6) = \frac{1}{r} + \frac{0.6}{l} + \frac{0.4}{n} + \frac{0.5}{q} + \frac{0.7}{a} + \frac{0.4}{j}$$

Thus, the FSS $\tilde{\xi}_{\mathcal{K}}$ will be the parameterized family such that $\tilde{\xi}_{\mathcal{K}} = \{(\mathfrak{s}, \mathfrak{f}(\mathfrak{s})) | \mathfrak{s} \in \mathcal{K}\}$. Here, we can observe that the applicant '*r*' is knowledgeable with a degree 0.3, the applicant '*l*' is confident with a degree 0.7 and so on. Now, the tabular representation of this set is provided in Table 21.2.

21.3.3.4 *Operations on FSSs [5]*

Let $\tilde{\xi}_{\mathcal{K}}$ and $\tilde{\zeta}_{\mathcal{Q}}$ are two FSSs over $\mathcal{X}$.

a) **Complement:** The complement of FSS $\tilde{\xi}_{\mathcal{K}}$ over $\mathcal{X}$ is denoted as $\tilde{\xi}_{\mathcal{K}}^{\tilde{c}}$ and defined by a mapping $\tilde{\xi}^{c}: \neg\mathcal{K} \to I^{\mathcal{X}}$ such that $\tilde{\xi}^{c}_{\neg\mathfrak{s}}(\mathfrak{d}) = 1 - \tilde{\xi}_{\mathfrak{s}}(\mathfrak{d})$, for every $\neg\mathfrak{s} \in \neg\mathcal{K}$ and $\mathfrak{d} \in \mathcal{X}$. Clearly, $\left(\tilde{\xi}_{\mathcal{K}}^{\tilde{c}}\right)^{\tilde{c}} = \tilde{\xi}_{\mathcal{K}}$.

Table 21.2 Tabular form of FSS.

Applicants→ Parameters↓	*r*	*l*	*n*	*q*	*a*	*j*
$\mathfrak{s}_1$	0.3	0.8	0.5	0.7	0.8	0.4
$\mathfrak{s}_2$	0.5	0.7	0.3	0.6	0.5	0.8
$\mathfrak{s}_3$	0.4	0.9	0.6	0.7	0	0.7
$\mathfrak{s}_4$	0.9	0.8	0.4	0.6	0.7	0.2
$\mathfrak{s}_5$	0	0	0	0	0	0
$\mathfrak{s}_6$	1	0.6	0.4	0.5	0.7	0.4
$\mathfrak{s}_7$	0	0	0	0	0	0

Example 21.3.3.4 (a): From example 21.3.3.3,

$$\tilde{\xi}^c(\neg\mathfrak{s}_1) = \frac{0.7}{r} + \frac{0.2}{l} + \frac{0.5}{n} + \frac{0.3}{q} + \frac{0.2}{a} + \frac{0.6}{j}$$

$$\tilde{\xi}^c(\neg\mathfrak{s}_2) = \frac{0.5}{r} + \frac{0.3}{l} + \frac{0.7}{\mathfrak{d}_3} + \frac{0.4}{q} + \frac{0.5}{a} + \frac{0.2}{j}$$

$$\tilde{\xi}^c(\neg\mathfrak{s}_3) = \frac{0.6}{r} + \frac{0.1}{l} + \frac{0.4}{\mathfrak{d}_3} + \frac{0.3}{\mathfrak{d}_4} + \frac{1}{a} + \frac{0.3}{j}$$

$$\tilde{\xi}^c(\neg\mathfrak{s}_4) = \frac{0.1}{r} + \frac{0.2}{l} + \frac{0.6}{n} + \frac{0.4}{q} + \frac{0.3}{a} + \frac{0.8}{j}$$

$$\tilde{\xi}^c(\neg\mathfrak{s}_6) = \frac{0}{r} + \frac{0.4}{l} + \frac{0.6}{n} + \frac{0.5}{q} + \frac{0.3}{a} + \frac{0.6}{j}$$

Thus, we can say that the applicant '*r*' is not knowledgeable with the degree 0.7 and he is not confident with the degree 0.5 and similarly, we can see for the rest.

b) AND operation: "$\tilde{\xi}_{\mathcal{K}}$ AND $\tilde{\zeta}_{\mathcal{Q}}$" is denoted as $\tilde{\xi}_{\mathcal{K}}\tilde{\wedge}\tilde{\zeta}_{\mathcal{Q}}$ and defined as $\tilde{\xi}_{\mathcal{K}}\tilde{\wedge}\tilde{\zeta}_{\mathcal{Q}} = (\mathfrak{h}, \mathcal{K} \times \mathcal{Q})$, where, $\mathfrak{h}(\mathfrak{s}, \mathfrak{b}) = \tilde{\xi}(\mathfrak{s}) \cap \tilde{\zeta}(\mathfrak{b})$, $\forall(\mathfrak{s}, \mathfrak{b}) \in \mathcal{K} \times \mathcal{B}$. In another manner, $\mathfrak{h}_{(\mathfrak{s},\mathfrak{b})}(\mathfrak{d})$

$=\min\{\tilde{\xi}_{\mathfrak{s}}(\mathfrak{d}), \tilde{\zeta}_{\mathfrak{b}}(\mathfrak{d})\}$; where $\mathfrak{h}_{(\mathfrak{s},\mathfrak{b})}(\mathfrak{d})$ denotes the DoM of $\mathfrak{d}$ in $\mathfrak{h}(\mathfrak{s},\mathfrak{b})$.

Example 21.3.3.4 (b): Let's look at the sets $\mathcal{X}$ and $\mathcal{E}$ from example 21.3.3.3. Now, consider $\mathcal{K}=\{\mathfrak{s}_1, \mathfrak{s}_4, \mathfrak{s}_6\}$ and $\mathcal{Q}=\{\mathfrak{s}_2, \mathfrak{s}_3, \mathfrak{s}_6\}$. Suppose the FSSs $\tilde{\xi}_{\mathcal{K}}$ and $\tilde{\zeta}_{\mathcal{Q}}$ based on parameters given in the set $\mathcal{K}$ and $\mathcal{Q}$, respectively are as follows:

$\tilde{\xi}(\mathfrak{s}_1)=\frac{0.2}{r}+\frac{0.7}{l}+\frac{0.2}{n}+\frac{0.4}{q}+\frac{0.5}{j}$	$\tilde{\zeta}(\mathfrak{s}_2)=\frac{0.3}{r}+\frac{0.5}{l}+\frac{0.4}{n}+\frac{0.5}{q}+\frac{0.1}{a}+\frac{0.4}{j}$
$\tilde{\xi}(\mathfrak{s}_4)=\frac{0.8}{r}+\frac{0.2}{l}+\frac{0.4}{n}+\frac{0.7}{q}+\frac{0.6}{a}+\frac{0.7}{j}$	$\tilde{\zeta}(\mathfrak{s}_3)=\frac{0.6}{r}+\frac{0.1}{l}+\frac{0.7}{n}+\frac{0.8}{q}+\frac{0.5}{a}+\frac{0.9}{j}$
$\tilde{\xi}(\mathfrak{s}_6)=\frac{0.7}{r}+\frac{0.1}{l}+\frac{0.9}{n}+\frac{0.4}{q}+\frac{0.8}{a}+\frac{0.2}{j}$	$\tilde{\zeta}(\mathfrak{s}_6)=\frac{0.1}{r}+\frac{0.9}{n}+\frac{0.5}{q}+\frac{0.7}{a}+\frac{0.3}{j}$

Here, $\mathcal{K}\times\mathcal{B}=\{(\mathfrak{s}_1,\mathfrak{s}_2),(\mathfrak{s}_1,\mathfrak{s}_3),(\mathfrak{s}_1,\mathfrak{s}_6),(\mathfrak{s}_4,\mathfrak{s}_2),(\mathfrak{s}_4,\mathfrak{s}_3),(\mathfrak{s}_4,\mathfrak{s}_6),(\mathfrak{s}_6,\mathfrak{s}_2),(\mathfrak{s}_6,\mathfrak{s}_3),(\mathfrak{s}_6,\mathfrak{s}_6)\}$. Thus, by definition of AND operation on two FSSs, we have

$$\mathfrak{h}(\mathfrak{s}_1,\mathfrak{s}_2)=\frac{0.2}{r}+\frac{0.5}{l}+\frac{0.2}{n}+\frac{0.4}{q}+\frac{0.4}{j}$$

$$\mathfrak{h}(\mathfrak{s}_1,\mathfrak{s}_3)=\frac{0.2}{r}+\frac{0.1}{l}+\frac{0.2}{n}+\frac{0.4}{q}+\frac{0.5}{j}$$

$$\mathfrak{h}(\mathfrak{s}_1,\mathfrak{s}_6)=\frac{0.1}{r}+\frac{0.2}{n}+\frac{0.4}{q}+\frac{0.3}{j}$$

$$\mathfrak{h}(\mathfrak{s}_4,\mathfrak{s}_2)=\frac{0.3}{r}+\frac{0.2}{l}+\frac{0.4}{n}+\frac{0.5}{q}+\frac{0.1}{a}+\frac{0.4}{j}$$

$$\mathfrak{h}(\mathfrak{s}_4,\mathfrak{s}_3)=\frac{0.6}{r}+\frac{0.1}{l}+\frac{0.4}{n}+\frac{0.7}{q}+\frac{0.5}{a}+\frac{0.7}{j}$$

$$\mathfrak{h}(\mathfrak{s}_4,\mathfrak{s}_6)=\frac{0.1}{r}+\frac{0.4}{n}+\frac{0.5}{q}+\frac{0.6}{a}+\frac{0.3}{j}$$

$$\mathfrak{h}(\mathfrak{s}_6,\mathfrak{s}_2)=\frac{0.3}{r}+\frac{0.1}{l}+\frac{0.4}{n}+\frac{0.4}{q}+\frac{0.1}{a}+\frac{0.2}{j}$$

$$\mathfrak{h}(\mathfrak{s}_6,\mathfrak{s}_3)=\frac{0.6}{r}+\frac{0.1}{l}+\frac{0.7}{n}+\frac{0.4}{q}+\frac{0.5}{a}+\frac{0.2}{j}$$

$$\mathfrak{h}(\mathfrak{s}_6,\mathfrak{s}_6)=\frac{0.1}{r}+\frac{0.9}{n}+\frac{0.4}{q}+\frac{0.7}{a}+\frac{0.2}{j}$$

c) **OR operation:** "$\tilde{\xi}_{\mathcal{K}}$ OR $\tilde{\zeta}_{\mathcal{Q}}$" is denoted as $\tilde{\xi}_{\mathcal{K}} \tilde{\vee} \tilde{\zeta}_{\mathcal{Q}}$ and defined as $\tilde{\xi}_{\mathcal{K}} \tilde{\vee} \tilde{\zeta}_{\mathcal{Q}} = (\mathfrak{o}, \mathcal{K} \times \mathcal{B})$, where, $\mathfrak{o}(\mathfrak{s}, \mathfrak{b}) = \tilde{\xi}(\mathfrak{s}) \cup \tilde{\zeta}(\mathfrak{b})$, $\forall (\mathfrak{s}, \mathfrak{b}) \in \mathcal{K} \times \mathcal{Q}$. In another manner, $\mathfrak{o}_{(\mathfrak{s},\mathfrak{b})}(\mathfrak{d}) = \max\{\tilde{\xi}_{\mathfrak{s}}(\mathfrak{d}), \tilde{\zeta}_{\mathfrak{b}}(\mathfrak{d})\}$; where $\mathfrak{o}_{(\mathfrak{s},\mathfrak{b})}(\mathfrak{d})$ denotes the DoM of $\mathfrak{d}$ in $\mathfrak{o}(\mathfrak{s}, \mathfrak{b})$.

Example 21.3.3.4 (c): Consider the FSSs $\tilde{\xi}_{\mathcal{K}}$ and $\tilde{\zeta}_{\mathcal{Q}}$ same as given in the example 21.3.3.3 (b). Now, by definition of OR operation on the FSSs $\tilde{\xi}_{\mathcal{K}}$ and $\tilde{\zeta}_{\mathcal{Q}}$, we have

$$\mathfrak{v}(\mathfrak{s}_1, \mathfrak{s}_2) = \frac{0.3}{r} + \frac{0.7}{l} + \frac{0.4}{n} + \frac{0.5}{q} + \frac{0.1}{a} + \frac{0.5}{j}$$

$$\mathfrak{v}(\mathfrak{s}_1, \mathfrak{s}_3) = \frac{0.6}{r} + \frac{0.7}{l} + \frac{0.7}{n} + \frac{0.8}{q} + \frac{0.5}{a} + \frac{0.9}{j}$$

$$\mathfrak{v}(\mathfrak{s}_1, \mathfrak{s}_6) = \frac{0.2}{r} + \frac{0.7}{l} + \frac{0.9}{n} + \frac{0.5}{q} + \frac{0.7}{a} + \frac{0.5}{j}$$

$$\mathfrak{v}(\mathfrak{s}_4, \mathfrak{s}_2) = \frac{0.8}{r} + \frac{0.5}{l} + \frac{0.4}{n} + \frac{0.7}{q} + \frac{0.6}{a} + \frac{0.7}{j}$$

$$\mathfrak{v}(\mathfrak{s}_4, \mathfrak{s}_3) = \frac{0.8}{r} + \frac{0.2}{l} + \frac{0.7}{n} + \frac{0.8}{q} + \frac{0.6}{a} + \frac{0.9}{j}$$

$$\mathfrak{v}(\mathfrak{s}_4, \mathfrak{s}_6) = \frac{0.8}{r} + \frac{0.2}{l} + \frac{0.9}{n} + \frac{0.7}{q} + \frac{0.7}{a} + \frac{0.7}{j}$$

$$\mathfrak{v}(\mathfrak{s}_6, \mathfrak{s}_2) = \frac{0.7}{r} + \frac{0.5}{l} + \frac{0.9}{n} + \frac{0.5}{q} + \frac{0.8}{a} + \frac{0.4}{j}$$

$$\mathfrak{v}(\mathfrak{s}_6, \mathfrak{s}_3) = \frac{0.7}{r} + \frac{0.1}{l} + \frac{0.9}{n} + \frac{0.8}{q} + \frac{0.8}{a} + \frac{0.9}{j}$$

$$\mathfrak{v}(\mathfrak{s}_6, \mathfrak{s}_6) = \frac{0.7}{r} + \frac{0.1}{l} + \frac{0.9}{n} + \frac{0.5}{q} + \frac{0.8}{a} + \frac{0.3}{j}$$

d) **Union:** The union of soft sets $\tilde{\xi}_{\mathcal{K}}$ and $\tilde{\zeta}_{\mathcal{Q}}$ is denoted as $(\mathcal{U}, \mathcal{C}) = \tilde{\xi}_{\mathcal{K}} \tilde{\cup} \tilde{\zeta}_{\mathcal{Q}}$, where $\mathcal{C} = \mathcal{K} \cup \mathcal{Q}$ and for every $\mathfrak{s} \in \mathcal{C}$,

$$\mathcal{U}(\mathfrak{s}) = \begin{cases} \tilde{\xi}(\mathfrak{s}), & \mathfrak{s} \in \mathcal{K} - \mathcal{Q} \\ \tilde{\zeta}(\mathfrak{s}), & \mathfrak{s} \in \mathcal{Q} - \mathcal{K} \\ \tilde{\xi}(\mathfrak{s}) \cup \tilde{\zeta}(\mathfrak{s}), & \mathfrak{s} \in \mathcal{K} \cap \mathcal{Q} \end{cases}$$

Example 21.3.3.4 (d): Consider the FSSs $\tilde{\xi}_{\mathcal{K}}$ and $\tilde{\zeta}_{\mathcal{Q}}$ same as given in the example 21.3.3.3 (b). Thus, from the sets $\mathcal{K}$ and $\mathcal{Q}$, we have $\mathcal{K} \cup \mathcal{Q} = \{\mathfrak{s}_1, \mathfrak{s}_2, \mathfrak{s}_3, \mathfrak{s}_4, \mathfrak{s}_6\}, \mathcal{Q} - \mathcal{K} = \{\mathfrak{s}_1, \mathfrak{s}_4\}, \{\mathfrak{s}_2, \mathfrak{s}_3\}$ and $\mathcal{K} \cap \mathcal{Q} = \{\mathfrak{s}_6\}$. Now, by definition of the union of two FSSs,

$$u(\mathfrak{s}_1) = \frac{0.2}{r} + \frac{0.7}{l} + \frac{0.2}{n} + \frac{0.4}{q} + \frac{0.5}{j}$$

$$u(\mathfrak{s}_2) = \frac{0.3}{r} + \frac{0.5}{l} + \frac{0.4}{n} + \frac{0.5}{q} + \frac{0.1}{a} + \frac{0.4}{j}$$

$$u(\mathfrak{s}_3) = \frac{0.6}{r} + \frac{0.1}{l} + \frac{0.7}{n} + \frac{0.8}{q} + \frac{0.5}{a} + \frac{0.9}{j}$$

$$u(\mathfrak{s}_4) = \frac{0.8}{r} + \frac{0.2}{l} + \frac{0.4}{n} + \frac{0.7}{q} + \frac{0.6}{a} + \frac{0.7}{j}$$

$$u(\mathfrak{s}_6) = \frac{0.7}{r} + \frac{0.1}{l} + \frac{0.9}{n} + \frac{0.5}{q} + \frac{0.8}{a} + \frac{0.3}{j}$$

e) **Intersection:** The intersection of soft sets $\tilde{\xi}_{\mathcal{K}}$ and $\tilde{\zeta}_{\mathcal{B}}$ is denoted as $(\sigma, \mathcal{C}) = \tilde{\xi}_{\mathcal{K}} \tilde{\cap} \tilde{\zeta}_{\mathcal{Q}}$, where $\mathcal{C} = \mathcal{K} \cap \mathcal{Q}$ and for every $\mathfrak{s} \in \mathcal{C}$, $\sigma(\mathfrak{s}) = \tilde{\xi}(\mathfrak{s}) \cap \zeta(\mathfrak{s})$.

Example 21.3.3.4 (e): Consider the FSSs $\tilde{\xi}_{\mathcal{K}}$ and $\tilde{\zeta}_{\mathcal{Q}}$ same as given in the example 21.3.3.3 (b). Thus, from the sets $\mathcal{K}$ and $\mathcal{Q}$, $\mathcal{K} \cap \mathcal{Q} = \{\mathfrak{s}_6\}$. Now, by definition of the intersection of two FSSs,

$$\sigma(\mathfrak{s}_6) = \frac{0.1}{r} + \frac{0.1}{l} + \frac{0.9}{n} + \frac{0.4}{q} + \frac{0.7}{a} + \frac{0.2}{j}$$

21.3.4 Intuitionistic Fuzzy Sets

21.3.4.1 Definition [6]

The object $\mathcal{R}$ having the form $\mathcal{R} = \{(\mathfrak{d}, \mu_{\mathcal{R}}(\mathfrak{d}), \nu_{\mathcal{R}}(\mathfrak{d})) | \mathfrak{d} \in \mathcal{X}\}$ is called the intuitionistic fuzzy set (IFS for short). Here, $\forall \mathfrak{d} \in \mathcal{X}$, $0 \leq \mu_{\mathcal{R}}(\mathfrak{d}) + \nu_{\mathcal{R}}(\mathfrak{d}) \leq 1$. The function $\mu_{\mathcal{R}}: \mathcal{X} \to [0,1]$ defines the DoM and $\nu_{\mathcal{R}}: \mathcal{X} \to [0,1]$ defines the DoN-M of $\mathfrak{d} \in \mathcal{X}$ to the set $\mathcal{R}$ as shown in Figure 21.2.

Further, a mapping $\pi_{\mathcal{R}}: \mathcal{R} \to [0,1]$ defined as $\pi_{\mathcal{R}}(\mathfrak{d}) = 1 - \mu_{\mathcal{R}}(\mathfrak{d}) - \nu_{\mathcal{R}}(\mathfrak{d})$ called intuitionistic index or degree of indeterminacy or degree of

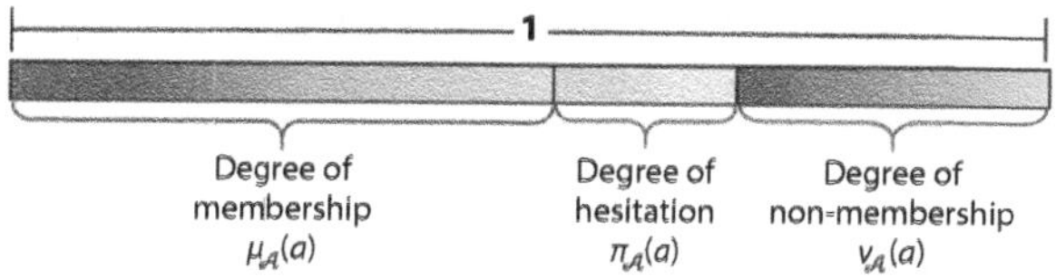

Figure 21.2 Pictorial representation of an element in IFS.

hesitation (DoH) of $\mathfrak{d}$ to $\mathcal{R}$. It indicates the uncertainty about whether $\mathfrak{d}$ belongs to the IFS $\mathcal{R}$ or not. Clearly, if $\pi_{\mathcal{R}}(\mathfrak{d})=0$ then the IFS $\mathcal{R}$ is reduced to a fuzzy set.

21.3.4.2 *Definitions [7]*

Let $\mathcal{R}$ be an IFS on $\mathcal{X}$. Then

i) The degree of indeterminacy of the element $\mathfrak{d} \in \mathcal{R}$ is defined as

$$\pi_{\mathcal{R}}(\mathfrak{d}) = 1 - \mu_{\mathcal{R}}(\mathfrak{d}) - v_{\mathcal{R}}(\mathfrak{d})$$

ii) The degree of favor of the element $\mathfrak{d} \in \mathcal{R}$ is defined as

$$\partial_{\mathcal{R}}(\mathfrak{d}) = \mu_{\mathcal{R}}(\mathfrak{d}) + \pi_{\mathcal{R}}(\mathfrak{d})\,\mu_{\mathcal{R}}(\mathfrak{d})$$

iii) The degree of against of the element $\mathfrak{d} \in \mathcal{R}$ is defined as

$$\eta_{\mathcal{R}}(\mathfrak{d}) = v_{\mathcal{R}}(\mathfrak{d}) + \pi_{\mathcal{R}}(\mathfrak{d})\,v_{\mathcal{R}}(\mathfrak{d})$$

21.3.4.3 *Definition [6]*

Let $\mathcal{R}$ and $\mathcal{Z}$ are two IFSs in $\mathcal{X}$. Then

i) $\mathcal{R} \subset \mathcal{Z} \Leftrightarrow \mu_{\mathcal{R}}(\mathfrak{d}) \leq \mu_{\mathcal{Z}}(\mathfrak{d})$ and $v_{\mathcal{R}}(\mathfrak{d}) \leq v_{\mathcal{Z}}(\mathfrak{d})$; $\forall \mathfrak{d} \in \mathcal{X}$.
ii) $\mathcal{R} = \mathcal{Z} \Leftrightarrow \mu_{\mathcal{R}}(\mathfrak{d}) = \mu_{\mathcal{Z}}(\mathfrak{d})$ and $v_{\mathcal{R}}(\mathfrak{d}) = v_{\mathcal{Z}}(\mathfrak{d})$; $\forall \mathfrak{d} \in \mathcal{X}$.

21.3.4.4 *Example*

Let $\mathcal{X}=\{\mathfrak{a}=$ Tomato, $\mathfrak{b}=$ Cucumber, $\mathfrak{c}=$ Bitter gourd, $\mathfrak{d}=$ Beetroot$\}$ be the set of some vegetables and $\mathcal{R}$ be the IFS based on person R's test of the

Table 21.3 The DoM, DoN-M, and DoH of elements of $\mathcal{X}$.

$\mathcal{X}$	$\mu_{\mathcal{R}}$	$\nu_{\mathcal{R}}$	$\pi_{\mathcal{R}}$
$\mathfrak{a}$= Cucumber	0.8	0.1	0.1
$\mathfrak{b}$= Tomato	0.9	0	0.1
$\mathfrak{c}$= Bitter gourd	0.1	0.9	0
$\mathfrak{d}$= Beetroot	0.2	0.3	0.5

vegetables given in $\mathcal{X}$. Now, The IFS $\mathcal{R}=\{(\mathfrak{a},0\ 8,0.1),(\mathfrak{b},0.9,0),(\mathfrak{c},0.1,0.9),(\mathfrak{d},0.2,0.3)\}$ and its tabular version is provided in Table 21.3. Here, the higher DoM denotes the very good test and the lower DoM denotes the bad test. If we consider the cucumber, then $\mathcal{R}$ belong to $\mathcal{R}$ by degree 0.8 and does not belong to $\mathcal{R}$ by degree 0.1. Which interprets, it tests good but it also tests bad rarely. Moreover, $\pi_{\mathcal{R}}(\mathfrak{a})=0.1$, $\partial_{\mathcal{R}}(\mathfrak{a})=0.88$ and $\eta_{\mathcal{R}}(\mathfrak{a})=0.11$.

21.3.4.5 Operations on IFSs [6]

Let $\mathcal{R}$ and $\mathcal{Z}$ are two IFSs on $\mathcal{X}$.

a) **Complement:** Complement of IFS $\mathcal{R}$ is denoted as $\mathcal{R}^c$ and defined as

$$\mathcal{R}^c=\left\{\left(\mathfrak{d},\nu_{\mathcal{R}}(\mathfrak{d}),\mu_{\mathcal{R}}(\mathfrak{d})\right)\middle|\mathfrak{d}\in\mathcal{X}\right\}$$

Example 21.3.4.5 (a): From example 21.3.4.4, $\mathcal{R}=\{(\mathfrak{a},0.1,0.8),(\mathfrak{b},0,0.9),(\mathfrak{c},0.9,0.1),(\mathfrak{d},0.3,0.2)\}$.

b) **Union:** The union of two IFSs $\mathcal{R}$ and $\mathcal{Z}$ is denoted by $\mathcal{R}\cup\mathcal{Z}$ and is defined by:

$$\mathcal{R}\cup\mathcal{B}=\{(\mathfrak{d},\max\{\mu_{\mathcal{R}}(\mathfrak{d}),\mu_{\mathcal{R}}(\mathfrak{d})\},\min\{\nu_{\mathcal{R}}(\mathfrak{d}),\nu_{\mathcal{R}}(\mathfrak{d})\})|\mathfrak{d}\in\mathcal{X}\}$$

Example 21.3.4.5 (b): From example 21.3.4.4, Let $\mathcal{R}$ be the IFS based on person R's test of the vegetables given in $\mathcal{X}$ and also consider the IFS $\mathcal{Z}$ that describes the person Z's test of the vegetables given in $\mathcal{X}$ such that

$$\mathcal{R}=\{(\mathfrak{a},0.8,0.1),(\mathfrak{b},0.9,0),(\mathfrak{c},0.1,0.9),(\mathfrak{d},0.2,0.3)\}\text{ and}$$
$$\mathcal{Z}=\{(\mathfrak{a},0.5,0.3),(\mathfrak{b},0.9,0.1),(\mathfrak{c},0,0.8),(\mathfrak{d},0.4,0.1)\}.$$

Thus, $\mathcal{R}\cup\mathcal{Z}=\{(\mathfrak{a},0.8,0.1),\ (\mathfrak{b},0.9,0),\ (\mathfrak{c},0.1,0.8),\ (\mathfrak{d},0.4,0.1)\}$.

b) **Intersection:** The intersection of two IFSs $\mathcal{R}$ and $\mathcal{B}$ is denoted by $\mathcal{R}\cap\mathcal{B}$ and is defined by:

$$\mathcal{R}\cap\mathcal{Z}=\{(\mathfrak{d},\min\{\mu_{\mathcal{R}}(\mathfrak{d}),\mu_{\mathcal{Z}}(\mathfrak{d})\},\max\{\nu_{\mathcal{R}}(\mathfrak{d}),\nu_{\mathcal{Z}}(\mathfrak{d})\})|\mathfrak{d}\in\mathcal{X}\}$$

Example 21.3.4.5 (c): Let's consider IFSs $\mathcal{R}$ and $\mathcal{Z}$ from example 21.3.4.5 (b). Then,

$$\mathcal{R}\cap\mathcal{Z}=\{(\mathfrak{a},0.5,0.3),(\mathfrak{b},0.9,0.1),(\mathfrak{c},0,0.9),(\mathfrak{d},0.2,0.3)\}.$$

21.3.5 Intuitionistic Fuzzy Soft Set

21.3.5.1 Definition [8]

Let $\mathcal{D}\subseteq\mathcal{E}$. Then the pair $(\xi^*,\mathcal{D})$ is called the intuitionistic fuzzy soft set (IFSS for short). Where, ξ^* is a mapping $\xi^*:\mathcal{D}\to IFS(\mathcal{X})$ and $IFS(\mathcal{X})$ is the set of all IFSs on $\mathcal{X}$. This means that, for every $\mathfrak{s}\in\mathcal{D}$, $\xi^*(\mathfrak{s})$ will be the IFS. Here, we will denote the IFSS $(\xi^*,\mathcal{D})$ as $\xi^*_{\mathcal{D}}$.

Here, $\xi^*(\mathfrak{s})$ will become a fuzzy set, if $\mu_{\xi^*(\mathfrak{s})}(\mathfrak{d})+\nu_{\xi^*(\mathfrak{s})}(\mathfrak{d})=1$, for all $\mathfrak{d}\in\mathcal{X}$ and the IFSS $\xi^*_{\mathcal{D}}$ will become a fuzzy soft set, if $\xi^*(\mathfrak{s})$ is fuzzy set, for all $\mathfrak{s}\in\mathcal{D}$.

21.3.5.2 Definition [8]

Let $\xi^*_{\mathcal{D}}$ and $\zeta^*_{\mathcal{W}}$ are IFSSs on $\mathcal{X}$. Then

a) $\xi^*_{\mathcal{D}}$ is an intuitionistic fuzzy soft subset of $\zeta^*_{\mathcal{W}}$ *i.e.*, $\xi^*_{\mathcal{D}}\,\tilde{\subseteq}\,\zeta^*_{\mathcal{W}}$ $\Leftrightarrow\mathcal{D}\subset\mathcal{W}$ and $\xi^*(\mathfrak{d})$ is an intuitionistic fuzzy subset of $\zeta^*(\mathfrak{d})$.
b) $\xi^*_{\mathcal{D}}$ is intuitionistic fuzzy soft equal to $\zeta^*_{\mathcal{W}}$ *i.e.*, $\xi^*_{\mathcal{D}}\cong\zeta^*_{\mathcal{W}}$ $\Leftrightarrow\xi^*_{\mathcal{D}}\,\tilde{\subseteq}\,\zeta^*_{\mathcal{W}}$ and $\zeta^*_{\mathcal{W}}\,\tilde{\subseteq}\,\xi^*_{\mathcal{D}}$.

21.3.5.3 Example

Let us consider a case in which customers have to rate the begs according to some criteria such as design, pricing, color, material, and quality. Thus, the set of all begs will be the universal set $\mathcal{X}=\{\ell, q, b, y\}$ and set of all parameters will be $\mathcal{E}=\{I_1=\text{design},\ I_2=\text{pricing},\ I_3=\text{color},\ I_4=\text{material},\ I_5=\text{quality}\}$. Suppose a person D chooses the parameters $\mathcal{D}=\{I_1, I_2, I_5\}$.

Then the IFSS $\xi^*_{\mathcal{D}}$ according to person D's selected parameters is provided below:

$$\xi^*(I_1)=\{(\ell,0.4,0.6),(q,0.5,0.2),(b,0.7,0.1),(y,0.8,0)\},$$
$$\xi^*(I_2)=\{(\ell,0.6,0.2),(q,0.1,0.6),(b,0.8,0.1),(y,0.6,0.2)\},$$
$$\xi^*(I_5)=\{(\ell,0.8,0.2),(q,0,0.6),(b,0.7,0.3),(y,0.5,0.2)\}.$$

Thus, $\xi^*_{\mathcal{D}}=\{(I_1,\xi^*(I_1)),(I_2,\xi^*(I_2)),(I_5,\xi^*(I_5))\}$.

Similarly, suppose a person W chooses the parameters $\mathcal{W}=\{I_2, I_3, I_4\}$. Then the IFSS $\zeta^*_{\mathcal{W}}$ according to person B's selected parameters is provided below:

$$\zeta^*(I_2)=\{(\ell,0.7,0.1),(q,0.3,0.8),(b,0.6,0.1),(y,0.5,0.5)\},$$
$$\zeta^*(I_3)=\{(\ell,0.2,0.4),(q,0.5,0.1),(b,0.9,0.1),(y,0.8,0.1)\},$$
$$\zeta^*(I_4)=\{(\ell,0.8,0.1),(q,0,0\ 8),(b,0.7,0.2),(y,0.6,0.1)\}.$$

Thus, $\zeta^*_{\mathcal{W}}=\{(I_2,\zeta^*(I_2)),(I_3,\zeta^*(I_3)),(I_4,\zeta^*(I_4))\}$

21.3.5.4 Operations on IFSSs [8]

Let $\xi^*_{\mathcal{D}}$ and $\zeta^*_{\mathcal{W}}$ are IFSSs on $\mathcal{X}$. Then

a) **Complement:** Complement of IFSS $\xi^*_{\mathcal{D}}$ over $\mathcal{X}$ is denoted as $\xi^{*\tilde{c}}_{\mathcal{D}}$ and defined by a mapping $\xi^{*C}:\neg\mathcal{D}\rightarrow IFS\ (\mathcal{X})$ such that $\xi^{*C}(\neg\mathfrak{s})=(\xi^*(\mathfrak{s}))^C$, for all $\neg\mathfrak{s}\in\neg\mathcal{D}$.

Example 21.3.5.4 (a): From example 21.3.5.3, the complement of IFSS $\xi^*_{\mathcal{D}}$ will be $\xi^{*\tilde{c}}_{\mathcal{D}}=\{(\neg I_1,\xi^{*C}(\neg I_1)),(\neg I_2,\xi^{*C}(\neg I_2)),(\neg I_5,\xi^{*C}(\neg I_5))\}$ such that

$$\xi^{*C}(\neg I_1) = \{(\ell,0.6,0.4),(q, 0.2,0.5),(b, 0.1,0.7),(y,0,0.8)\},$$

$$\xi^{*C}(\neg I_2) = \{(\ell,0.2,0.6),(q, 0.6,0.1),(b, 0.1,0.8),(y,0.2,0.6)\},$$

$$\xi^{*C}(\neg I_5) = \{(\ell,0.2,0.8),(q, 0.6,0),(b, 0.3,0.7),(y,0.2,0.5)\}.$$

b) **And operation:** "$\xi^*_{\mathcal{D}}$ AND $\zeta^*_{\mathcal{W}}$" is denoted by $\xi^*_{\mathcal{D}} \tilde{\wedge} \zeta^*_{\mathcal{W}}$ and defined by $\xi^*_{\mathcal{D}} \tilde{\wedge} \zeta^*_{\mathcal{W}} = (\mathfrak{h}, \mathcal{D} \times \mathcal{W})$, where $\mathfrak{h}(\mathfrak{s},\mathfrak{b}) = \xi^*(\mathfrak{s}) \cap \zeta^*(\mathfrak{b})$; $\forall (\mathfrak{s},\mathfrak{b}) \in \mathcal{D} \times \mathcal{W}$.

Example 21.3.5.4 (b): From example 21.3.5.3, we have $\mathcal{D} \times \mathcal{W} = \{(I_1, l_2), (I_1, l_3), (I_1, l_4), (I_2, l_2), (I_2, l_3), (I_2, l_4), (I_5, l_2), (I_5, l_3), (I_5, l_4)\}$. Thus,

$$\mathfrak{h}(I_1, l_2) = \{(\ell,0.4,0.6),(q, 0.3,0.8),(b,0.6,0.1),(y,0.5,0.5)\}$$
$$\mathfrak{h}(I_1, l_3) = \{(\ell,0.2,0.6),(q,0.5,0.2),(b,0.7,0.1),(y,0.8,0.1)\}$$
$$\mathfrak{h}(I_1, l_4) = \{(\ell,0.4,0.6),(q, 0,0.8),(b,0.7,0.2),(y,0.6,0.1)\}$$
$$\mathfrak{h}(I_2, l_2) = \{(\ell,0.6,0.2),(q, 0.1,0.8),(b,0.6,0.1),(y,0.5,0.5)\}$$
$$\mathfrak{h}(I_2, l_3) = \{(\ell,0.2,0.4),(q, 0.1,0.6),(b,0.8,0.1),(y,0.6,0.2)\}$$
$$\mathfrak{h}(I_2, l_4) = \{(\ell,0.6,0.2),(q, 0,0.8),(b,0.7,0.2),(y,0.6,0.2)\}$$
$$\mathfrak{h}(I_5, l_2) = \{(\ell,0.7,0.2),(q, 0,0.8),(b,0.6,0.3),(y,0.5,0.5)\}$$
$$\mathfrak{h}(I_5, l_3) = \{(\ell,0.2,0.4),(q, 0,0.6),(b,0.7,0.),(y,0.5,0.2)\}$$
$$\mathfrak{h}(I_5, l_4) = \{(\ell,0.8,0.2),(q, 0,0.8),(b,0.7,0.3),(y,0.5,0.2)\}$$

c) **OR operation:** "$\xi^*_{\mathcal{D}}$ OR $\zeta^*_{\mathcal{W}}$" is denoted by $\xi^*_{\mathcal{D}} \tilde{\vee} \zeta^*_{\mathcal{W}}$ and defined by $\xi^*_{\mathcal{D}} \tilde{\vee} \zeta^*_{\mathcal{W}} = (\mathfrak{o}, \mathcal{D} \times \mathcal{W})$, where $\mathfrak{o}(\mathfrak{s},\mathfrak{b}) = \xi^*(\mathfrak{s}) \cup \zeta^*(\mathfrak{b})$; $\forall (\mathfrak{s},\mathfrak{b}) \in \mathcal{D} \times \mathcal{W}$.

Example 21.3.5.4 (c): From example 21.3.5.3, we have $\mathcal{D} \times \mathcal{W} = \{(I_1, l_2), (I_1, l_3), (I_1, l_4), (I_2, l_2), (I_2, l_3), (I_2, l_4), (I_5, l_2), (I_5, l_3), (I_5, l_4)\}$. Thus,

$$o(I_1,I_2)=\{(\ell,0.7,0.1),(q,0.5,0.2),(b,0.7,0.1),(y,0.8,0)\}$$
$$o(I_1,I_3)=\{(\ell,0.4,0.4),(q,0.5,0.1),(b,0.9,0.1),(y,0.8,0)\}$$
$$o(I_1,I_4)=\{(\ell,0.8,0.1),(q,0.5,0.2),(b,0.7,0.1),(y,0.8,0)\}$$
$$o(I_2,I_2)=\{(\ell,0.7,0.1),(q,0.3,0.6),(b,0.8,0.1),(y,0.6,0.2)\}$$
$$o(I_2,I_3)=\{(\ell,0.2,0.4),(q,0.1,0.6),(b,0.8,0.1),(y,0.6,0.2)\}$$
$$o(I_2,I_4)=\{(\ell,0.8,0.1),(q,0.1,0.6),(b,0.8,0.1),(y,0.6,0.1)\}$$
$$o(I_5,I_2)=\{(\ell,0.8,0.1),(q,0.3,0.6),(b,0.7,0.1),(y,0.5,0.2)\}$$
$$o(I_5,I_3)=\{(\ell,0.8,0.2),(q,0.5,0.1),(b,0.9,0.1),(y,0.8,0.1)\}$$
$$o(I_5,I_4)=\{(\ell,0.8,0.1),(q,0,0.6),(b,0.7,0.2),(y,0.6,0.1)\}$$

d) **Union:** The union of IFSSs $\xi^*_{\mathcal{D}}$ and $\zeta^*_{\mathcal{W}}$ is denoted as $(u,\mathcal{C})=\xi^*_{\mathcal{D}}\,\tilde{\cup}\,\zeta^*_{\mathcal{W}}$, where $\mathcal{C}=\mathcal{D}\cup\mathcal{W}$ and for every $s\in\mathcal{C}$,

$$u(e)=\begin{cases}\xi^*(s), & s\in\mathcal{D}-\mathcal{W}\\ \zeta^*(s), & s\in\mathcal{W}-\mathcal{D}\\ \xi^*(s)\cup\zeta^*(s), & s\in\mathcal{D}\cap\mathcal{W}\end{cases}$$

Example 21.3.5.4 (d): From example 21.3.5.3, we have $\mathcal{C}=\mathcal{D}\cup\mathcal{W}=\{I_1,I_2,I_3,I_4,I_5\}$, $\mathcal{D}-\mathcal{W}=\{I_1,I_5\}$, $\mathcal{W}-\mathcal{D}=\{I_3,I_4\}$ and $\mathcal{D}\cap\mathcal{W}=\{I_2\}$. Thus,

$$u(I_1)=\xi^*(I_1)=\{(\ell,0.4,0.6),(q,0.5,0.2),(b,0.7,0.1),(y,0.8,0)\}$$
$$u(I_2)=\xi^*(I_2)\cup\zeta^*(I_2)=\{(\ell,0.7,0.1),(q,0.3,0.6),(b,0.8,0.1),(y,0.6,0.2)\}$$
$$u(I_3)=\zeta^*(I_3)=\{(\ell,0.2,0.4),(q,0.5,0.1),(b,0.9,0.1),(y,0.8,0.1)\}$$
$$u(I_4)=\zeta^*(I_4)=\{(\ell,0.8,0.1),(q,0,0.8),(b,0.7,0.2),(y,0.6,0.1)\}$$
$$u(I_5)=\xi^*(I_5)=\{(\ell,0.8,0.2),(q,0,06),(r_{b3},0.7,0.3),(y,0.5,0.2)\}$$

e) **Intersection:** The intersection of IFSSs $\xi^*_{\mathcal{D}}$ and $\zeta^*_{\mathcal{W}}$ is denoted as $(\sigma,\mathcal{C})=\xi^*_{\mathcal{D}}\,\tilde{\cap}\,\zeta^*_{\mathcal{W}}$, where $\mathcal{C}=\mathcal{D}\cap\mathcal{W}$ and for every $s\in\mathcal{C}, \sigma(s)=\xi^*(s)\cap\zeta^*(s)$.

Example 21.3.5.4 (e): From example 21.3.5.3, we have $\mathcal{D}\cap\mathcal{W}=\{I_2\}$. Thus,

$$\sigma(I_2)=\xi^*(I_2)\cap\zeta^*(I_2)=\{(\ell,0.7,0.1),(q,0.3,0.6),(b,0.8,0.1),(y,0.6,0.2)\}.$$

Table 21.4 Generalized fuzzy sets.

Set	DoM	DoN-M	DoH	Parameters
FS	✓			
SS				✓
FSS	✓			✓
IFS	✓	✓	✓	
IFSS	✓	✓	✓	✓

21.3.5.5 Remark

The overview of generalized fuzzy sets is shown in Table 21.4.

21.3.5.6 Definition [9]

Let $\xi^*_{\mathcal{D}}$ be the IFSS over $\mathcal{X}$, such that $\mathcal{X}=\{\mathfrak{d}_1, \mathfrak{d}_2, \ldots, \mathfrak{d}_\lambda\}$ and $\mathcal{D}=\{\mathfrak{s}_1, \mathfrak{s}_2, \ldots, \mathfrak{s}_\tau\}$. Then this IFSS $\xi^*_{\mathcal{D}}$ can be written in matrix form as $\xi^*_{\mathcal{D}}=\left[\alpha_{ij}\right]_{\lambda\times\tau}$, $1 \le i \le \lambda$ and $1 \le j \le \tau$. Moreover, $\alpha_{ij}=\left(\mu_j(\mathfrak{d}_i), \nu_j(\mathfrak{d}_i)\right)$ where $\mu_j(\mathfrak{d}_i)$ denotes the DoM of $\mathfrak{d}_i$ in $\xi^*(\mathfrak{s}_j)$ and $\nu_j(\mathfrak{d}_i)$ denotes the DoN-M of $\mathfrak{d}_i$ in $\xi^*(\mathfrak{s}_j)$.

From example 21.3.5.3, the matrix form of IFSS $\xi^*_{\mathcal{D}}$ is

$$\xi^*_{\mathcal{D}} = \begin{array}{c} \\ \ell \\ q \\ b \\ y \end{array}\begin{array}{ccc} \mathfrak{l}_1 & \mathfrak{l}_2 & \mathfrak{l}_5 \\ \left[\begin{array}{c} (0.4,0.6) \\ (0.5,0.2) \\ (0.7,0.1) \\ (0.8,0) \end{array}\right. & \begin{array}{c} (0.6,0.2) \\ (0.1,0.6) \\ (0.8,0.1) \\ (0.6,0.2) \end{array} & \left.\begin{array}{c} (0.8,0.2) \\ (0,0.6) \\ (0.7,0.3) \\ (0.5,0.2) \end{array}\right] \end{array}$$

21.3.5.7 Definition [10]

Let $\xi^*_{\mathcal{D}}$ be the IFSS over $\mathcal{X}=\{\mathfrak{d}_1, \mathfrak{d}_2, \ldots, \mathfrak{d}_\lambda\}$, such that $\mathcal{D}=\{\mathfrak{s}_1, \mathfrak{s}_2, \ldots, \mathfrak{s}_\tau\}$ and $\zeta^*_{\mathcal{Y}}$ be the IFSS over $\mathcal{D}$, such that $\mathcal{Y}=\{\mathfrak{y}_1, \mathfrak{y}_2, \ldots, \mathfrak{y}_\sigma\}$. Suppose $\xi^*=\left[\alpha_{ij}\right]_{\lambda\times\tau}$ and $\zeta^*=\left[\beta_{jk}\right]_{\tau\times\sigma}$ be the matrix form of IFSS $\xi^*_{\mathcal{D}}$ and $\zeta^*_{\mathcal{Y}}$ respectively; where $1 \le i \le \lambda$, $1 \le j \le \tau$ & $1 \le k \le \sigma$. Here, $\alpha_{ij}=\left(\mu_j(\mathfrak{d}_i), \nu_j(\mathfrak{d}_i)\right)$ and $\beta_{jk}=\left(\mu_k(\mathfrak{s}), \nu_k(\mathfrak{s}_j)\right)$. Then, the max-min average composition for these matrices is denoted as $\xi^*\phi\zeta^*$ and defined as $\xi^*\phi\zeta^*=[\gamma_{ik}]_{\lambda\times\sigma}$ such that

$$\gamma_{ik} = \left(\mu_k(\mathfrak{d}_i), \nu_k(\mathfrak{d}_i)\right) = \left(\max_j\left\{\frac{\mu_j(\mathfrak{d}_i)+\mu_k(\mathfrak{s}_j)}{2}\right\}, \min_j\left\{\frac{\nu_j(\mathfrak{d}_i)+\nu_k(\mathfrak{s}_j)}{2}\right\}\right)$$

21.3.5.8 Remark

Let $\xi^* = [\alpha_{ij}]_{\lambda\times\tau}$ be the matrix form of IFSS $\xi^*_{\mathcal{D}}$ over $\mathcal{X}$, such that $\alpha_{ij} = (\mu_j(\mathfrak{d}_i), \nu_j(\mathfrak{d}_i))$; where $1 \le i \le \lambda$ & $1 \le j \le \tau$. Then we have $\mu(\xi^*) = [\mu_j(\mathfrak{d}_i)]_{\lambda\times\tau}$ and $\nu(\xi^*) = [\nu_j(\mathfrak{d}_i)]_{\lambda\times\tau}$.

21.3.5.9 Definition [10]

Let ξ^* be the matrix form of IFSS $\mathfrak{f}_{\mathcal{D}}$ over $\mathcal{X} = \{\mathfrak{d}_1, \mathfrak{d}_2, \ldots, \mathfrak{d}_\lambda\}$ and ζ^* be the matrix form of IFSS $\zeta^*_{\mathcal{Y}}$ over $\mathcal{D} = \{\mathfrak{s}_1, \mathfrak{s}_2, \ldots, \mathfrak{s}_\tau\}$, such that $\mathcal{Y} = \{\mathfrak{y}_1, \mathfrak{y}_2, \ldots, \mathfrak{y}_\sigma\}$. Moreover, let $\xi^{*C}_{\mathcal{D}}$ and $\zeta^{*C}_{\mathcal{Y}}$ be the matrix form of IFSS $\xi^{*C}_{\mathcal{D}}$ and $\zeta^{*C}_{\mathcal{Y}}$, respectively. Then the score matrix of ξ^* and ζ^* is denoted as $\mathcal{S}(\xi^*, \zeta^*)$ and defined as

$$\mathcal{S}(\xi^*, \zeta^*) = \mathcal{V} - \mathcal{W};$$

where, $\mathcal{V} = \mu(\xi^* \phi \zeta^*) - \nu(\xi^* \phi \zeta^*)$ and $\mathcal{W} = \mu(\xi^{*C} \phi \zeta^{*C}) - \nu(\xi^{*C} \phi \zeta^{*C})$.

21.4 Infectious Diseases

Pathogenic microorganisms, including bacteria, viruses, parasites, and fungi, are the source of infectious diseases. These diseases may spread from one person to another through direct or indirect contact. One of the major problems of global health is infectious diseases. They are the primary cause of years lost to healthy living and the second leading cause of mortality globally [27]. The spread of infectious diseases is increasing due to factors like poor hygiene, population, urbanization, and climate change [28, 29]. Moreover, infectious diseases present major challenges in medical diagnosis, which impact 10% to over 50% of patients [26]. These challenges arise due to the following reasons,

i) Early in the course of the disease, patients frequently exhibit mild symptoms, which makes it challenging to differentiate infectious diseases from other medical conditions. Up to 35% of patients have several physical symptoms that are undifferentiated or unexplained symptoms that impact diverse body systems [30–33].
ii) Numerous tests to diagnose infectious diseases are not always reliable. For instance, over half of tuberculosis diagnoses made worldwide rely on non-specific clinical characteristics without laboratory validation [34].
iii) Infectious diseases often exhibit similar symptoms; therefore, it is difficult for physicians to determine the actual disease. For example, fever and chills are common symptoms of infection and inflammation, but they don't point to a specific disease [22].

Now, infectious diseases such as malaria, dengue, and typhoid fever share many overlapping symptoms, which makes it challenging to distinguish between them using just clinical presentation. Symptoms like headache, high fever, nausea, muscle pain, joint pain, and fatigue are generally shown in malaria, dengue, and typhoid fever [23–25]. Therefore, in this chapter, we will examine a case study that aims to predict the disease from malaria, dengue, and typhoid fever.

21.5 IFSS Approach in Medical Diagnosis

In this section, we will see a method [10], which utilizes the intuitionistic fuzzy soft sets to identify diseases with common symptoms. Let $\mathbb{P} = \{p_1, p_2, \ldots, p_l\}$ be the set of patients, $\mathbb{S} = \{s_1, s_2, \ldots, s_m\}$ be the set of all symptoms exhibited by these patients and $\mathbb{D} = \{d_1, d_2, \ldots, d_n\}$ be the set of diseases associated with the symptoms given in $\mathbb{S}$.

Now, obtain an IFSS $\xi^*_{\mathbb{S}}$ over the universal set $\mathbb{P}$, such that $\xi^* : \mathbb{S} \rightarrow IFS(\mathbb{P})$ and denote the matrix form of IFSS $\xi^*_{\mathbb{S}}$ as $\mathcal{N}$, which is called the "patient-symptom matrix". Moreover, the complement of $\xi^*_{\mathbb{S}}$ will be $\xi^{*c}_{\mathbb{S}}$ and denote the matrix form of IFSS $\xi^{*c}_{\mathbb{S}}$ as $\mathcal{N}^c$, which is called the "patient non-symptom matrix". Further, obtain another $\zeta^*_{\mathbb{D}}$ over the universal set $\mathbb{S}$, such that $\zeta^* : \mathbb{D} \rightarrow IFS(\mathbb{S})$ and denote the matrix form of IFSS $\zeta^*_{\mathbb{D}}$ as $\mathcal{M}$, which is called the "symptom-disease matrix". Moreover, the complement of $\zeta^*_{\mathbb{D}}$ will be $\zeta^{*c}_{\mathbb{D}}$ and denote the matrix form of IFSS $\zeta^{*c}_{\mathbb{D}}$ as $\mathcal{M}^c$, which is called the "symptom non-disease matrix".

Now, construct two matrices $\mathcal{T}_1 = \mathcal{N}\phi\mathcal{M}$ and $\mathcal{T}_2 = \mathcal{N}^c\phi\mathcal{M}^c$. Here, $\mathcal{T}_1$ gives the "patient-disease matrix" and $\mathcal{T}_2$ gives the "patient non-disease matrix". Further, obtain the score matrix $\mathcal{S}(\mathcal{N},\mathcal{M})$. Then we have $\mathcal{S}(\mathcal{N},\mathcal{M}) = \left[s_{ij} \right]_{l \times n}$. Now, for each patient p_i, $\max\{s_{ik}\}$ will describe that patient p_i has disease d_k.

21.5.1 Algorithm

1) Input the IFSS $\xi^*_{\mathbb{S}}$ and $\xi^{*c}_{\mathbb{S}}$ over the set of patients $\mathbb{P}$, where $\mathbb{S}$ denotes the set of symptoms, then obtains the corresponding matrices $\mathcal{N}$ and $\mathcal{N}^c$.
2) Input the IFSS $\zeta^*_{\mathbb{D}}$ and $\zeta^{*c}_{\mathbb{D}}$ over the set of all symptoms $\mathbb{S}$, where $\mathbb{D}$ denotes the set of diseases, then obtains the corresponding matrices $\mathcal{M}$ and $\mathcal{M}^c$.
3) Compute $\mathcal{T}_1 = \mathcal{N}\phi\mathcal{M}$ and $\mathcal{T}_2 = \mathcal{N}^c\phi\mathcal{M}^c$.
4) Obtain the score matrix $\mathcal{S}(\mathcal{N},\mathcal{M})$.
5) For each patient p_i, determine the maximum score s_{ik} and from that deduce that p_i has a disease d_j.

21.5.2 Case Study

Suppose four patients in a hospital are experiencing headache, high fever, nausea, muscle pain, pain in joints, and fatigue. Consider $\mathbb{P} = \{Yug, Kian, Visty, Rishi\}$ to be the set of patients and $\mathbb{S} = \{\mathcal{h} = \text{headache}, \mathcal{hf} = \text{high fever}, \mathcal{n} = \text{nausea}, \mathcal{mp} = \text{muscle pain}, \mathcal{pj} = \text{pain in joints}, \mathcal{f} = \text{fatigue}\}$ to be the set of symptoms. Now, the possible diseases associated with the symptoms given in the set $\mathbb{S}$ are infectious diseases such as dengue, malaria, and typhoid fever. Therefore, represent the set of these diseases as $\mathbb{D} = \{M = \text{malaria}, D = \text{dengue}, T = \text{typhoid fever}\}$.

We choose the "max-min average composition method" [10] to discuss the case study, as it effectively minimizes repetition, that is, it reduces the unpredictability of a patient's likelihood of having two diseases. Let $\xi^*_{\mathbb{S}}$ be the IFSS over the set $\mathbb{P}$, where ξ^* is a mapping $\xi^* : \mathbb{S} \rightarrow IFS(\mathbb{P})$, gives an approximate overview of the symptoms experienced by the patients.

$$\begin{aligned}
\xi_S^* = \{\xi^*(s_1) &= \{(Yug,0.9,0.1),(Kian,0.7,0.3),(Visty,0.6,0),(Rishi,0.7,0.1),\\
\xi^*(s_2) &= \{(Yug,0.9,0.1),(Kian,0.5,0.4),(Visty,0.9,0),(Rishi,0.8,0.1),\\
\xi^*(s_3) &= \{(Yug,0.5,0.4),(Kian,0.6,0.3),(Visty,0.8,0.2),(Rishi,0.5,0.5),\\
\xi^*(s_4) &= \{(Yug,0.7,0.1),(Kian,0.4,0.1),(Visty,0.8,0),(Rishi,0.6,0.1),\\
\xi^*(s_5) &= \ (Yug,0.6,0.2),(Kian,0.2,0.6),(Visty,0.7,0.1),(Rishi,0.4,0.6),\\
\xi^*(s_6) &= \ (Yug,0.5,0.5),(Kian,0.85,0),(Visty,0.1,0.8),(Rishi,0.1,0.7)\}
\end{aligned}$$

This IFSS $\xi_{\mathbb{S}}^*$ can be represented by the following matrix $\mathcal{N}$, called patient-symptom matrix,

$$\mathcal{N} = \begin{array}{r} \\ Yug \\ Kian \\ Visty \\ Rishi \end{array}
\begin{array}{c}
\begin{array}{cccccc} h & hf & n & mp & pj & f \end{array}\\
\begin{bmatrix}
(0.9,0.1) & (0.9,0.1) & (0.5,0.4) & (0.7,0.1) & (0.6,0.2) & (0.5,0.5)\\
(0.7,0.3) & (0.5,0.4) & (0.6,0.3) & (0.4,0.1) & (0.2,0.6) & (0.85,0)\\
(0.6,0) & (0.9,0) & (0.8,0.2) & (0.8,0) & (0.7,0.1) & (0.1,0.8)\\
(0.7,0.1) & (0.8,0.1) & (0.5,0.5) & (0.6,0.1) & (0.4,0.6) & (0.1,0.7)
\end{bmatrix}
\end{array}$$

Moreover, the matrix form of IFSS $\xi_{\mathbb{S}}^{*c}$ will be $\mathcal{N}^c$ as under,

$$\mathcal{N}^c = \begin{array}{r} \\ Yug \\ Kian \\ Visty \\ Rishi \end{array}
\begin{array}{c}
\begin{array}{cccccc} \neg h & \neg hf & \neg n & \neg mp & \neg pj & \neg f \end{array}\\
\begin{bmatrix}
(0.1,0.9) & (0.1,0.9) & (0.4,0.5) & (0.1,0.7) & (0.2,0.6) & (0.5,0.5)\\
(0.3,0.7) & (0.4,0.5) & (0.3,0.6) & (0.1,0.4) & (0.6,0.2) & (0,0.85)\\
(0,0.6) & (0,0.9) & (0.2,0.8) & (0,0.8) & (0.1,0.7) & (0.8,0.1)\\
(0.1,0.7) & (0.1,0.8) & (0.5,0.5) & (0.1,0.6) & (0.6,0.4) & (0.7,0.1)
\end{bmatrix}
\end{array}$$

Let $\zeta_{\mathbb{D}}^*$ be the IFSS over the set $\mathbb{S}$, where ζ^* is a mapping $\zeta^*: \mathbb{D} \to IFS(\mathbb{S})$, gives an approximate overview of the disease associated with the symptoms.

$$\begin{aligned}
\zeta_{\mathbb{D}}^* = \{\zeta^*(M) &= \{(h,0.7,0.1),(hf,0.9,0),(n,0.7,0.2),(mp,0.6,0.2),(pj,0.9,0),(f,0.4,0.6)\},\\
\zeta^*(D) &= \{(h,0.9,0),(hf,1,0),(n,0.8,0.1),(mp,0.9,0),(pj,0.9,0.1),(f,0.1,0.9)\},\\
\zeta^*(T) &= \{(h,0.6,0.1),(hf,0.8,0.1),(n,0.6,0.3),(mp,0.4,0.5),(pj,0.1,0.6),(f,1,0)\}\}
\end{aligned}$$

This IFSS $\zeta_{\mathbb{D}}^{*}$ can be represented by the following matrix $\mathcal{M}$, called symptom-disease matrix,

$$\mathcal{M} = \begin{matrix} & M & D & T \\ \mathscr{h} & (0.7,0.1) & (0.9,0) & (0.6,0.1) \\ \mathscr{hf} & (0.9,0) & (1,0) & (0.8,0.1) \\ \mathscr{n} & (0.7,0.2) & (0.8,0.1) & (0.6,0.3) \\ \mathscr{mp} & (0.6,0.2) & (0.9,0) & (0.4,0.5) \\ \mathscr{pj} & (0.9,0) & (0.9,0.1) & (0.1,0.6) \\ \mathscr{f} & (0.4,0.6) & (0.1,0.9) & (1,0) \end{matrix}$$

Moreover, the matrix form of IFSS $\zeta_{\mathbb{D}}^{*c}$ will be $\mathcal{M}^c$ as under,

$$\mathcal{M}^c = \begin{matrix} & \neg M & \neg D & \neg T \\ \mathscr{h} & (0.1,0.7) & (0,0.9) & (0.1,0.6) \\ \mathscr{hf} & (0,0.9) & (0,1) & (0.1,0.8) \\ \mathscr{n} & (0.2,0.7) & (0.1,0.8) & (0.3,0.6) \\ \mathscr{mp} & (0.2,0.6) & (0,0.9 & (0.5,0.4) \\ \mathscr{pj} & (0,0.9) & (0.1,0.9) & (0.6,0.1) \\ \mathscr{f} & (0.6,0.4) & (0.9,0.1) & (0,1) \end{matrix}$$

Consequently, the max-min average composition of matrices $\mathcal{N}$ and $\mathcal{M}$ is $\mathcal{T}_1$, the patient-disease matrix as under,

$$\mathcal{T}_1 = \begin{matrix} & M & D & T \\ Yug & (0.9,0.05) & (0.95,0.05) & (0.85,0.1 \\ Kian & (0.7,0.15) & (0.8,0.05) & (0.925,0) \\ Visty & (0.9,0) & (0.95,0) & (0.85,0.05) \\ Rishi & (0.85,0.05) & (0.9,0.05) & (0.65,0.1) \end{matrix}$$

Similarly, the max-min average composition of matrices $\mathcal{N}^c$ and $\mathcal{M}^c$ is $\mathcal{T}_2$, the patient non-disease matrix as under,

$$\mathcal{T}_2 = \begin{matrix} & \neg M & \neg D & \neg T \\ Yug & (0.55,0.45) & (0.7,0.3) & (0.4,0.35) \\ Kian & (0.3,0.5) & (0.45,0.475) & (0.6,0.15) \\ Visty & (0.7,0.25) & (0.85,0.1) & (0.55,0.4) \\ Rishi & (0.65,0.25) & (0.8,0.1) & (0.6,0.25) \end{matrix}$$

Therefore, we have the following matrices

$$\mathcal{V} = \mu(\mathcal{T}_1) - \nu(\mathcal{T}_1) = \begin{array}{c} \\ Yug \\ Kian \\ Visty \\ Rishi \end{array} \begin{array}{c} \begin{matrix} M & D & T \end{matrix} \\ \begin{bmatrix} 0.85 & 0.9 & 0.75 \\ 0.55 & 0.75 & 0.925 \\ 0.9 & 0.95 & 0.8 \\ 0.8 & 0.85 & 0.55 \end{bmatrix} \end{array}$$

$$\text{and } \mathcal{W} = \mu(\mathcal{T}_2) - \nu(\mathcal{T}_2) = \begin{array}{c} \\ Yug \\ Kian \\ Visty \\ Rishi \end{array} \begin{array}{c} \begin{matrix} \neg M & \neg D & \neg T \end{matrix} \\ \begin{bmatrix} 0.1 & 0.4 & 0.05 \\ -0.2 & -0.025 & 0.45 \\ 0.45 & 0.75 & 0.15 \\ 0.4 & 0.7 & 0.35 \end{bmatrix} \end{array}$$

$$\text{Now, the score matrix } \mathcal{S}(\mathcal{N},\mathcal{M}) = \mathcal{V} - \mathcal{W} = \begin{array}{c} \\ Yug \\ Kian \\ Visty \\ Rishi \end{array} \begin{array}{c} \begin{matrix} M & D & T \end{matrix} \\ \begin{bmatrix} 0.75 & 0.5 & 0.7 \\ 0.75 & 0.775 & 0.475 \\ 0.45 & 0.2 & 0.65 \\ 0.4 & 0.15 & 0.2 \end{bmatrix} \end{array}$$

We can observe from the matrix $\mathcal{S}(\mathcal{N},\mathcal{M})$ that, the patients *Yug* and *Rishi* has been diagnosed with malaria, *Kian* has the disease dengue, and *Visty* is affected by typhoid fever.

21.6 Conclusion

In this chapter, we have discussed the basic notions of SS, FSS, IFS, and IFSS. Further, we studied a method that utilizes IFS to diagnose diseases with symptoms that overlap. We can also construct a medical diagnosis model for these types of diseases using an FSS and an IFS. The reason for choosing the IFSS model is that this set includes DoM, DoN-M, and DoH. Consequently, it adds more information regarding ambiguity and uncertainty. In addition, IFSS includes parameterization, which allows for improved management of complicated problems involving multiple characteristics or parameters. However, this approach does not use genetic information or medical images, which are required for the accurate diagnosis of some infectious diseases. As a result, including such data in this technique may be a future area of focus.

References

1. Zadeh, L.A., Fuzzy sets. *Inf. Control*, 8, 3, 338–353, 1965, https://doi.org/10.1016/S0019-9958(65)90241-X.
2. Molodtsov, D., Soft set theory—first results. *Comput. Math. Appl.*, 37, 4–5, 19–31, 1999, https://doi.org/10.1016/S0898-1221(99)00056-5.
3. Maji, P.K., Biswas, R., Roy, A.R., Soft set theory. *Comput. Math. Appl.*, 45, 4–5, 555–562, 2003, https://doi.org/10.1016/S0898-1221(03)00016-6.
4. Ahmad, B. and Kharal, A., Research article on fuzzy soft sets. *Adv. Fuzzy Syst.*, 2009, 586507, 2009, https://doi.org/10.1155/2009/586507.
5. Maji, P.K., Biswas, R.K., Roy, A., Fuzzy soft sets. *J. Fuzzy Math.*, 9, 3, 589–602, 2001, https://sid.ir/paper/633097/en.
6. Atanassov, K., Intuitionistic fuzzy sets. *Fuzzy Sets Syst.*, 20, 1, 87–96, 1986, https://doi.org/10.1016/S0165-0114(86)80034-3.
7. Ejegwa, P.A., Akowe, S.O., Otene, P.M., Ikyule, J.M., An overview on intuitionistic fuzzy sets. *Int. J. Sci. Technol. Res.*, 3, 3, 142–145, 2014.
8. Maji, P.K., Biswas, R., Roy, A.R., Intuitionistic fuzzy soft sets. *J. Fuzzy Math.*, 9, 3, 677–692, 2001.
9. Bora, M., Bora, B., Neog, T.J., Sut, D.K., Intuitionistic fuzzy soft matrix theory and its application in medical diagnosis. *Ann. Fuzzy Math. Inf.*, 7, 1, 143–153, 2014.
10. Shanmugasundaram, P., Seshaiah, C.V., Rathi, K., Intuitionistic fuzzy soft matrix theory in medical diagnosis using max-min average composition method. *J. Theor. Appl. Inf. Technol.*, 67, 1, 186–190, 2014.
11. Sanchez, E., Inverses of fuzzy relations. Application to possibility distributions and medical diagnosis. *Fuzzy Sets Syst.*, 2, 1, 75–86, 1979, https://doi.org/10.1016/0165-0114(79)90017-4.
12. Adlassnig, K.P. and Kolarz, G., Cadiag-2: Computer-assisted medical diagnosis using fuzzy subsets, in: *Approximate Reasoning in Decision Analysis*, M.M. Gupta, and E. Sanchez, (Eds.), pp. 219–247, North-Holland Publishing Company, Amsterdam, 1982.
13. Adlassnig, K.P., A fuzzy logical model of computer-assisted medical diagnosis. *Methods Inf. Med.*, 19, 3, 141–148, 1980, 10.1055/s-0038-1635271.
14. Zimmermann, H.J., *Fuzzy set theory—and its applications*, Springer Science & Business Media, New York, 2011. https://doi.org/10.1007/978-94-010-0646-0.
15. Mamdani, Application of fuzzy logic to approximate reasoning using linguistic synthesis. *IEEE Trans. Comput.*, 100, 12, 1182–1191, 1977, 10.1109/TC.1977.1674779.
16. Hooda, D.S. and Kumari, R., On applications of fuzzy soft sets in dimension reduction and medical diagnosis. *Adv. Res.*, 12, 2, 1–9, 2017, 10.9734/AIR/2017/36960.
17. Celik, Y. and Yamak, S., Fuzzy soft set theory applied to medical diagnosis using fuzzy arithmetic operations. *J. Inequal. Appl.*, 2013, 82, 1–9, 2013, https://doi.org/10.1186/1029-242X-2013-82.

18. De, S.K., Biswas, R., Roy, A.R., An application of intuitionistic fuzzy sets in medical diagnosis. *Fuzzy Sets Syst.*, 117, 2, 209–213, 2001, https://doi.org/10.1016/S0165-0114(98)00235-8.
19. Szmidt, E. and Kacprzyk, J., An intuitionistic fuzzy set based approach to intelligent data analysis: An application to medical diagnosis, in: *Recent advances in intelligent paradigms and applications*, Studies in fuzziness and soft computing, vol. 113, A. Abraham, L.C. Jain, J. Kacprzyk (Eds.), Physica, Heidelberg, 2003, https://doi.org/10.1007/978-3-7908-1770-6_3.
20. Gandhimathi, T., An application of intuitionistic fuzzy soft matrix in medical diagnosis. *J. Comput. Theor. Nanosci.*, 15, 3, 781–784, 2018, https://doi.org/10.1166/jctn.2018.7159.
21. Hooda, D.S., Kumari, R., Sharma, D.K., Intuitionistic fuzzy soft set theory and its application in medical diagnosis. *Int. J. Stat. Med. Res.*, 7, 3, 70–76, 2018, https://doi.org/10.6000/1929-6029.2018.07.03.2.
22. Suneja, M., Beekmann, S.E., Dhaliwal, G., Miller, A.C., Polgreen, P.M., Diagnostic delays in infectious diseases. *Diagnosis*, 9, 3, 332–339, 2022.
23. Basu, S. and Sahi, P.K., Malaria: An update. *Indian J. Pediatr.*, 84, 521–528, 2017, https://doi.org/10.1007/s12098-017-2332-2.
24. Martinez Torres, E., Dengue. *Estudos Avançados*, 22, 33–52, 2008, https://doi.org/10.1590/S0103-40142008000300004.
25. Lifshitz, E.I., Travel trouble: typhoid fever—A case presentation and review. *J. Am. Coll. Health*, 45, 3, 99–105, 1996, https://doi.org/10.1080/07448481.1996.9936869.
26. Roger, P.M., Keita-Perse, O., Mainardi, J.L., Diagnostic uncertainty in infectious diseases: Advocacy for a nosological framework. *Infect. Dis. Now*, 53, 6, 104751, 2023, https://doi.org/10.1016/j.idnow.2023.104751.
27. World Health Organization, *The world health report 2000: health systems: improving performance*, World Health Organization, 2000.
28. Menne, B., Kunzli, N., Bertollini, R., 'The health impacts of climate change and variability in developing countries. *Int. J. Global Environ. Issues*, 2, 3–4, 181–205, 2002, https://doi.org/10.1504/IJGENVI.2002.002399.
29. Kulshrestha, M. and Mittal, A.K., Diseases associated with poor water and sanitation: Hazards, prevention, and solutions. *Rev. Environ. Health*, 18, 1, 33–50, 2003, https://doi.org/10.1515/REVEH.2003.18.1.33.
30. Heath, I. and Sweeney, K., Medical generalists: connecting the map and the territory. *BMJ*, 331, 7530, 1462–4, 2005, https://doi.org/10.1136/bmj.331.7530.1462.
31. Peveler, R., Kilkenny, L., Kinmonth, A.-L., Medically unexplained physical symptoms in primary care: A comparison of self-report screening questionnaires and clinical opinion. *J. Psychosom. Res.*, 42, 3, 245–52, 1997, https://doi.org/10.1016/S0022-3999(96)00292-9.
32. Kroenke, K. and Mangelsdorff, A.D., Common symptoms in ambulatory care: Incidence, evaluation, therapy, and outcome. *Am. J. Med.*, 86, 3, 262–266, 1989, https://doi.org/10.1016/0002-9343(89)90293-3.

33. Thomson, G.H., Tolerating uncertainty in family medicine. *J. R. Coll. Gen. Pract.*, 28, 191, 343–346, 1978.
34. Datta, S. and Evans, C.A., The uncertainty of tuberculosis diagnosis. *Lancet Infect. Dis.*, 20, 9, 1002–1004, 2020, https://doi.org/10.1016/S1473-3099(20)30400-X.

Part 7

FUZZY TECHNIQUES IN THE MANAGEMENT PARADIGM

22

Computational Intelligence in Fuzzy Logic-Based Financial Risk Management: A Comparative Study of Methods and Models

Chetan Shelke[1*], Harini. B.[2], Bhadrappa Haralayya[3], Dharini Raje Sisodia[4], S. Shalini[5] and Joshuva Arockia Dhanraj[6]

[1]Department of CSE, Alliance College of Engineering and Design, Alliance University Bangalore, Bangalore, India
[2]School of Management Studies, Tamil Nadu Open University, Tamil Nadu, India
[3]Department of MBA, Lingaraj Appa Engineering College Bidar, Karnataka, India
[4]BFSI, Symbiosis University of Applied Sciences, Indore, India
[5]Department of Mathematics, J.N.N institute of Engineering, Ushaa Garden, Kannigaipair, Chennai, India
[6]Department of Computer Science and Engineering (AI&ML), School of Engineering, Dayananda Sagar University, Devarakaggalahalli, Harohalli, Bengaluru, Karnataka, India

Abstract
In this exploratory work, the operation of computational intelligence inside fuzzy sense-based fiscal threat operation is investigated. Additionally, a comparative analysis of various models and styles is provided. The traditional threat management approaches typically fail to handle the main concerns promptly as the complexity of the financial requirements continues to decrease. The powerful volition that fuzzy sense provides is a result of its capacity to manage input that is soft and vague. The purpose of this study is to analyze various fuzzy sense methods and computational intelligence models, such as neural networks and inheritable algorithms, in the context of the environment of fiscal danger assessment. In

**Corresponding author*: Chetan.shelke@alliance.edu.in
Bhadrappa Haralayya: ORCID: https://orcid.org/0000-0003-3214-7261
Joshuva Arockia Dhanraj: ORCID: https://orcid.org/0000-0001-5048-7775

Rahul Kar, Gunjan Mukherjee, Biswadip Basu Mallik and Ashok Kumar Shaw (eds.) Fuzzy Logic in Computational Intelligence: Applications and Case Studies, (413–428) © 2026 Scrivener Publishing LLC

the process of comparing various models, the investigation shows the strengths and limits of each model in terms of precisely predicting and mitigating potential financial hazards. Case studies are utilized to illustrate practical executions and problems, to highlight the connection between these techniques and the real world they are applied to. Based on the findings, it appears that combining fuzzy sense with sophisticated computational intelligence has the potential to considerably improve the accuracy and reliability of fiscal threat operations, thereby providing a solid framework for decision-makers in the fiscal sector. Specifically, the purpose of this work is to contribute to the development of additional fiscal threat operating tactics that are both successful and adaptable.

***Keywords*:** Computational intelligence, fuzzy logic, financial risk management, comparative study, predictive models, and neural networks

22.1 Introduction

To maintain stability and maximize profits in the complex and unpredictability of the world of financial requests, an efficient threat operation is essential. It is possible for traditional methods of fiscal threat operation, which are typically based on statistical and deterministic models, to be timid when confronted with the complex and uncertain character of ultramodern fiscal systems [1, 2]. The disquisition of computational intelligence, which incorporates colorful advanced styles such as neural networks, inheritable algorithms, and fuzzy sense, was brought up as a result of the demand for additional complex and adaptable techniques. Among these, fuzzy sense stands out because of its exceptional capacity to deal with imprecision and inquiry, which makes it particularly ideal for the operation of financial threats [3].

The concept of fuzzy sense, which was first presented by Lotfi Zadeh in the 1960s, offers a useful framework for dealing with information that is ambiguous and foggy. Fuzzy sense, in contrast to traditional double sense, which operates on rigid true or false values, allows for degrees of verity, which enables a more subtle and flexible approach to modeling scripts that are used in the real world [4]. This capability is incalculable in the context of the operation of the fiscal threat because it shields the fundamental concerns and personal judgements that are characteristic of the processes that are involved in the decision-making process about the fiscal situation [5, 6].

The purpose of this work is to investigate the possibility of incorporating computational intelligence, and more specifically fuzzy sense, into the operation of fiscal threat. This article provides a comparative analysis of several colorful styles and models, to evaluate how effective they are in predicting and mitigating financial hazards. By utilizing fuzzy sense, financial institutions can construct more robust threat assessment models that can manage the complexities of financial requests. The objectification of expert knowledge and private assessments, which are typically disregarded in traditional quantitative models, is made possible through the use of this technique with this approach.

The integration process is to identify and describe the most important financial risk variables. These elements are also represented as fuzzy sets with class functions that correspond to them. These class functions provide a quantitative measure of the extent to which particular conditions or inputs are representative of predetermined threat orders [5]. Furthermore, fuzzy conclusion rules are constructed to build a relationship between the input variables and the affair threat circumstances. This process involves rephrasing qualitative expert information into a structured and computational framework. It is also possible to use the fuzzy conclusion system to estimate and evaluate hidden financial dangers, which provides decision-makers with a thorough awareness of the threat geography they face.

Comparing the operation of various computational intelligence models, such as neural networks and inheritable algorithms, to the operation of fuzzy sense-based fiscal threat models is another aspect of this study. The benefits that neural networks and inheritable algorithms bring to the table in terms of improving fuzzy sense models are being investigated [6, 7]. Neural networks can learn from data and recognize complicated patterns, while inheritable algorithms have the potential to execute optimization. The comparative study sheds light on the advantages and disadvantages of each strategy, providing insight into the practical implementations of these approaches as well as the challenges they face.

It may be concluded that the combination of fuzzy sense and computational intelligence constitutes a substantial achievement in the field of fiscal threat operation. Through the provision of a more nuanced approach to hazard assessment and the facilitation of inquiries, these styles contribute to the enhancement of the precision and dependability of the procedures involved in making financial decisions. It is the purpose of this study to contribute to the development of additional fiscal threat operating tactics that are both successful and adaptable, with the ultimate goal of fostering less stability and adaptability in demand for fiscal resources [8]. The exploration highlights the potential for computational intelligence to transform traditional fiscal threat operation procedures utilizing a comparative assessment of styles and models. This transformation will pave the way for inventive and robust solutions in the face of constantly developing fiscal issues [9, 10].

22.2 Related Works

Within the context of the modern process of making decisions on the budget, the fiscal threat operation is an essential component. The reduction of the adverse consequences that unknown occurrences have on investment portfolios, business operations, and financial institutions is the major goal of this initiative. Throughout history, experimentalists and interpreters have examined a broad variety of quantitative methodologies and models to successfully analyze and manage potential financial threats [11]. This has been done to achieve the goal of successfully managing finances. The ability of fuzzy logic-based techniques to cope with inquiries, ambiguity, and imprecision, all of which are essential in the processes of decision-making and the management of financial data, has contributed to their rise to prominence in these specific aspects.

When it comes to the application of fuzzy logic in the context of fiscal threat operation, there is a substantial body of research that covers the topic. This body of literature includes a wide range of methodologies, practical applications, and empirical findings. The workshop that Mamdani and Assilian [5] hosted in 1975 and the one that Sugeno and Kang [8] held in 1988 were both considered to be notable before this. The purpose of this workshop was to lay the framework for the utilization of fuzzy logic-based conclusion systems (FIS) to describe complicated systems and to construct views in answer to inquiries [12]. The results of these ground-breaking tests demonstrated that fuzzy logic can be utilized to get qualitative and sensitive information for enhancing decision-making processes in the financial industry.

In the framework of the operation of the fiscal threat, fuzzy logic has been used to several different sorts of threats, including the request threat, the credit threat, the functional threat, and the liquidity danger, among others. To create fuzzy logic-based models for request threat assessment and vaticination, researchers have utilized fuzzy time series analysis and fuzzy clustering approaches [6, 9]. These models have been constructed from fuzzy logic [13]. The vaticination and analysis of requests have both been carried out with the assistance of these models. The reliability of these models has been proved by their ability to recognize nonlinear correlations and uncertainties in financial demands. As a result, they have provided significant insight that can be utilized for the optimization of portfolios and the creation of approaches for risk management [14].

The evaluation and management of credit risks is yet another subject that has been the subject of a significant amount of research. The application of approaches based on fuzzy logic has been investigated in great detail in this field. Both Zhang and Cheng [10] and Rehman *et al.* [7] have proposed fuzzy logic-grounded credit scoring models to assess the creditworthiness of borrowers and predict the risk of loan default. These models were developed to predict the likelihood of loan default. In order to accurately reflect qualitative aspects of credit risk, such as borrower profiles, fiscal rates, and macroeconomic indicators, these models integrate fuzzy sets. Consequently, this makes it possible for institutions that are in the process of progressing to conduct danger assessments and make decisions that are increasingly comprehensive.

The functional threat, which derives from internal processes, systems, and mortal components, is another essential component of the operation of the fiscal danger that has been addressed through the utilization of fuzzy logic approaches. This threat has been addressed since it is significant. Fuentes- Fernández *et al.* [3] established the fuzzy logic-grounded framework with the intention of measuring and regulating functional danger in banking institutions. This framework was specifically designed for this purpose [15–18]. Verbal factors are incorporated into this framework in order to capture qualitative features of threats and expert knowledge. Additionally, fuzzy logic-based decision support systems have been utilized to enable the formulation of threat operation views concerning fraud identification, compliance monitoring, and company durability planning [2, 4]. These systems have been utilized to facilitate the formulation of threat operation views.

There are still several difficulties and limits when it comes to the functioning of the fiscal threat, despite the growing interest in fuzzy logic-based methods and the abandonment of such methods. This is the case even though such methods have been abandoned. Ongoing research and discussion is being carried out in several different areas, such as the interpretability of fuzzy models, the computational complexity, the data circumstances, and the difficulties that are associated with model confirmation [19]. There is also the possibility that the level of effectiveness of fuzzy sensing approaches will vary depending on the specific environment, the quality of the data, and the quantity of spherical moxie that is available.

It is necessary to do additional research to overcome methodological issues, evaluate model performance, and examine new operations in emerging fields such as climate threat assessment and cybersecurity threat operation [20]. In conclusion, having a fiscal threat operation that is grounded in fuzzy logic has a significant potential to improve the processes of threat assessment and decision-making. Nevertheless, additional research is necessary to solve these difficulties. The objective of the related study that is presented in this paper is to contribute to the ongoing exploration debate by thoroughly evaluating and contrasting several fuzzy logic-based models and styles within the framework of the environment of financial risk management. This will be accomplished by analyzing and comparing several models and styles.

22.3 Research Methodology

Techniques for the management of financial risk that are based on fuzzy logic and fuzzy set theory are the suggested approaches to methodology. Several significant procedures that are aimed at analyzing and contrasting various approaches logically and rigorously are included in the methodology that has been proposed to conduct comparative research of styles and models in fuzzy logic-based fiscal threat operation [21]. This methodology has been proposed for the goal of doing the research itself. It is possible to perform empirical research to evaluate the efficacy and connectedness of fuzzy logic-based approaches to the management of financial problems by using the methodology that is given below. This methodology provides a systematic framework for conducting empirical research [22].

The inquiry will make use of a quantitative approach, with the primary emphasis being placed on empirical analysis and comparative evaluation of fuzzy logic-based models and styles for the management of financial risk [23]. In the course of the investigation, we will be involved in the collection of pertinent data, the implementation of named fuzzy logic approaches, and the analysis of the results to evaluate the efficacy of various ways. To incorporate them into the study project, a wide range of fuzzy logic-based models and techniques, such as fuzzy clustering, fuzzy time series analysis, fuzzy optimization approaches, and fuzzy conclusion systems (FIS), will be taken into account. The selection of techniques will be based on their application to the operation of the financial threat and their implied ability to address various kinds of pitfalls, such as the request threat, the credit threat, and the functional danger as per Figure 22.1. This will be the basis for the selection of ways [24].

Standards prescribe risk assessment methods. The standard states:
15.3 Asset identification Identify assets—valued goods whose security must be protected—and damage scenarios—adverse events involving a vehicle or vehicle function and hurting a road user; Threats: 15.4 Cybersecurity threat scenarios can affect one or more assets and cause damage. 15.5 Impact rating: Evaluate physical injury risk. Impact ratings

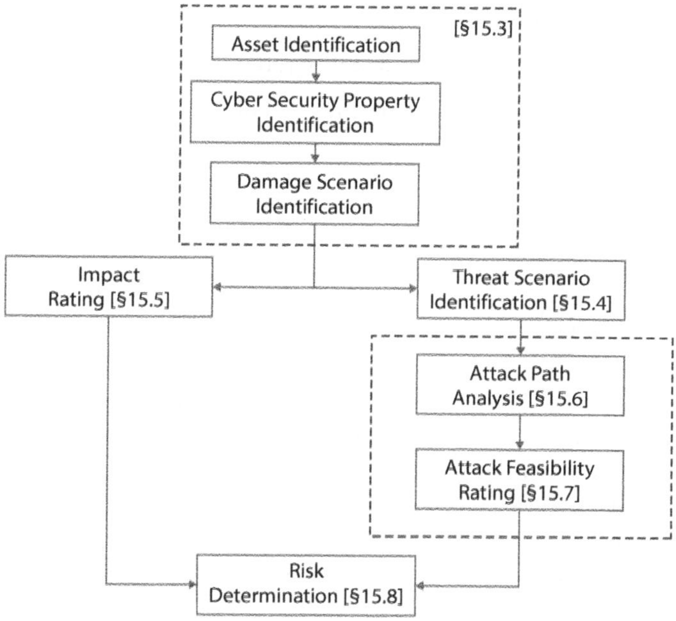

Figure 22.1 Depicts the threat analysis and risk assessment.

must be placed on a discrete scale of four classes (negligible, moderate, major, and severe) and classed as safety, privacy, operational, or financial depending on potential damage; 15.6 Attack path analysis: Find risk scenario attack routes. Attack paths are prepared steps the attacker can take to achieve the threat scenario. 15.7 Assess each attack path's exploitability. The standard specifies many approaches for this stage and maps the outcome on a discrete scale with four classes (very low, low, medium, and high); 15.8 Risk valuation: Assess threat scenarios' impact and feasibility to assess risk. This stage uses a risk matrix like Table 22.1 (1 is lowest risk, 5 is highest); 15.9 Risk treatment: Select threat-appropriate risk remedies. Risk is avoided, reduced, shared (by contracts or insurance), or retained. To assess the effectiveness of each fuzzy logic-based fashion, several preset criteria will be utilized. These criteria include delicacy, interpretability, computational effectiveness, robustness, and scalability. These metrics, which will function as marks, will be used to evaluate the performance of a variety of different types of models over a wide range of threat operation scripts. When it comes to the functioning of the fiscal threat, the collection of empirical evidence that is relevant will come from a variety of sources. The literal request data, the fiscal statements, the credit conditions, and the

Table 22.1 Depicts the exemplar risk matrix from ISO/SAE 21434, Annex H.

		Feasibility rating			
		Very low	**Low**	**Medium**	**High**
Impact rating	Severe	2	3	4	5
	Major	1	2	3	4
	Moderate	1	2	2	3
	Negligible	1	1	1	1

functional incident reports will all be included in these sources. Following the completion of the preprocessing of the data, the noise will be eliminated, the missing values will be addressed, and the thickness and consistency of the data will be ensured across all of the different datasets.

Applications of the stated fuzzy logic methodologies will be applied to the data that has been preprocessed to develop threat assessment models and decision support systems for the aim of managing budgetary pitfalls. This will be done to protect the budget from potential problems [25–28]. To guarantee reproducibility and transparency throughout the entire process of analysis, each fashion will be enforced by employing the proper software tools and computer languages, such as MATLAB, Python, or R. This will ensure that the results are consistent and transparent.

They will be trained with literal data, and then they will be validated with holdout samples or cross-validation methods to evaluate their prophetic performance and conception skills [29]. The models that are based in the fuzzy logic will be trained with literal data. A fine-tuning of the model's parameters will be performed to achieve the highest feasible level of prophetic delicacy while simultaneously avoiding either overfitting or underfitting. To estimate the performance of each fuzzy logic-grounded technique, many specified metrics will be utilized. These criteria include mean absolute error (MAE), mean squared error (MSE), and bracket delicacy (for bracket tasks) [30]. Measurements of the vaticination delicacy will also be included in these assessment criteria. In addition, perceptivity analysis and script testing will be carried out to verify the robustness of the models across a wide range of threat scripts and request conditions using the models.

The purpose of this comparison analysis is to evaluate the efficacy of various fuzzy logic-based methods and models in the management of various types of financial risks. This will be accomplished by comparing and contrasting the various approaches and models. Tests of statistical significance, such as analysis of variance (ANOVA) and t-tests, will be utilized in order to ascertain whether or not there are substantial variations in performance across a wide range of methodologies and datasets. We will conduct a perceptivity analysis in order to analyze the impact that significant parameters and hypotheticals have on the performance of fuzzy logic-based models. This will be done in order to determine how well these models function. Stability and thickness of model predictions will be examined against a variety of data disquiet and slice modifications for the goal of robustness testing. This evaluation will be carried out in order to ensure precision. When it comes to the management of financial pitfalls, the results of the relative study will be evaluated in light of the assessment criteria and exploration objectives, with a focus on the strengths and limitations of each fuzzy logic-based approach. This will be done within the context of the relative study. On the basis of the conclusions of the study, there will be a distribution of realistic counter-accusations and guidance to those individuals who comprehend financial facts and make judgements.

By following to the technique that has been proposed, the investigation hopes to provide significant insight into the efficiency and connection of fuzzy logic- based styles and models for fiscal threat operation. This will be accomplished when the investigation is carried out. The result of this will be that decision-making processes will be informed, and unborn exploration orientations will be guided, in this key area of study.

22.4 Results and Discussion

Based on the findings in the preceding section, we research the risk assessment approach in this work, which is based on fuzzy logic, and its advantages for practitioners. Compared to industry approaches based on domain reference standards, the recommended risk assessment technique offers the following advantages: Granularity of risk value: Numerical input ranges are discretized into several discontinuous subintervals, each with a (human-understandable) language label, as was discussed in earlier sections. These subintervals are then utilized to extrapolate the risk value, typically with the assistance of domain experts. This is information-losing because it only partially captures the uncertainty resulting from the inherent imprecision of such values as a product of human qualitative evaluation. Fuzzy logic keeps using linguistic variables but explicitly models uncertainty. Because it can be expressed mathematically or linguistically and assesses the dispersion and scatter around the estimated value, which shows the risk trend, the process output is therefore richer.

Unlike the risk assessment techniques used in the reference domain standards, the fuzzy inference system produces results on a continuous scale. The surface of the fuzzy-logic-based technique is continuous and smooth, whereas the surface of the domain reference standards is not. Our approach yields finer-grain output values than the typical risk assessment approaches, which provide coarse-grain ones. When prioritizing cyber threat issues from the risk assessment process, this offers a higher level of detail that may be essential to the risk management process. Consider the damage scenarios 3 and 5 of the threat scenario 2. The relevant risks are both rated 3 by the criteria, while this study rates them 2.50 and 3.44.

The recommended methodology is more computationally and structurally complicated than domain reference standards, however automatic tools reduce this complexity. The risk assessment approach suggested by this study is more intricate than that of the domain reference standards. The latter are less computationally demanding and use basic tables, making them straightforward to use. In this paper's methodology, the defuzzification stage, membership function construction, and graphical representation are more computationally demanding. Nonetheless, this cost of complexity is significantly reduced by the availability of ready-to-use automatic tools for risk computation and the generation and encoding of membership functions. Our approach produces numerically equivalent results to the conventional methods used in the reference domain standards (e.g., ISO/SAE 21434 and ISO 26262). In certain situations, the result is the same, and in others, it is different, but it is never more than 0.5.

Our method of calculating risks is not cautious (risks are always more or equal) when compared to domain reference standards. Our approach increases assessment accuracy rather than degree of danger. As a result, it raises perceived risks while lowering exaggerated ones. Since the monotonic function in Figure 22.2b is non-decreasing, the linear ordering of risks derived using the risk assessment methods used in this paper is maintained. Increasing f and I results in non-decreasing R since Rf,I = F(f, I) (where f is the feasibility rating and I is the impact rating). This makes the methodology comparable to reference domain standard risk assessment methods and helpful for risk management and prioritization.

The risk assessment methodology presented in this paper and used in a case study from the ISO/SAE 21434 standard has several benefits, such as better risk management and prioritization due to increased risk value granularity, ease of handling by humans, and significant preservation

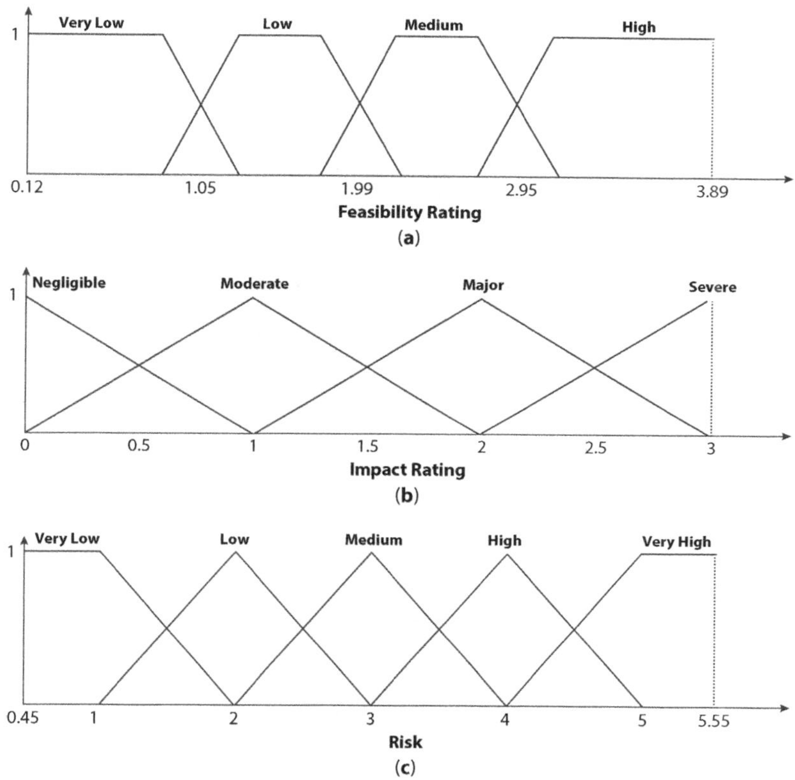

Figure 22.2 Depicts the definitions of membership functions. The membership functions for the input factors feasibility rating and impact rating are shown in (a) and (b), respectively. (c) shows the membership functions for the risk output.

of the linear ordering of calculated risks. Applicability of risk assessment techniques is ensured by readily available, user-friendly, automatic devices. These features, which preserve interpretability and usability, allow for more precise and efficient risk assessment and prioritization in an era where automobile technology is advancing rapidly. To show the risk assessment methodology's practicality, we intend to implement it in case studies involving the manufacture of automobiles. We'll compare the outcomes as per as per Figure 22.3. We think this kind of attempt will appropriately evaluate the usefulness and practical implications of the strategy. It will also assist in examining how methodologies for car risk assessment are affected by emerging technologies.

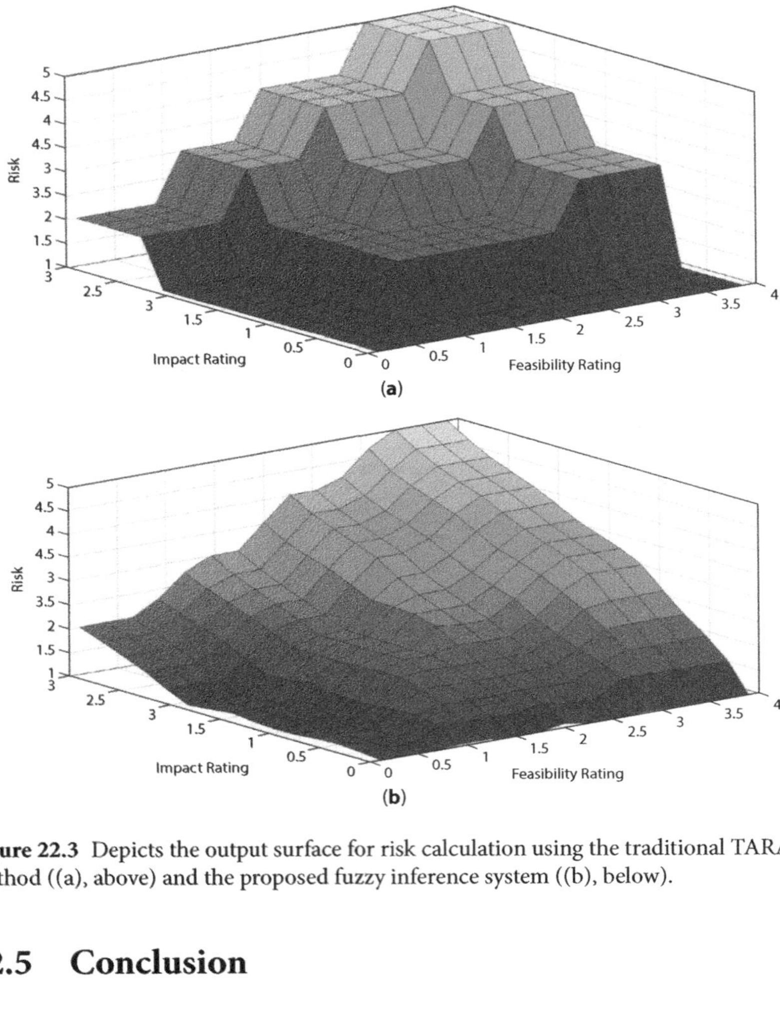

Figure 22.3 Depicts the output surface for risk calculation using the traditional TARA method ((a), above) and the proposed fuzzy inference system ((b), below).

22.5 Conclusion

In summary, the purpose of this investigation study was to provide a full comparative research of the many styles and models used in fuzzy logic-based fiscal threat operation. In the course of doing a thorough examination of colorful fuzzy logic ways across many types of threats, such as request threat, credit threat, and functional danger, valuable insights into the effectiveness, strengths, and limitations of these methods have been obtained. For the purpose of enhancing decision-making processes and improving threat operation procedures in a variety of financial environments, the findings of this study highlight the possibility of fuzzy logic-based techniques.

In spite of this, it is evident that difficulties such as the interpretability of models, the complexity of computations, and the quality of data continue to present substantial obstacles to the widespread abandonment of fuzzy logic methods in the operation of fiscal threat.

In order to overcome these issues and enhance the state of the art in fuzzy logic-based fiscal threat operation, additional discourse is necessary for the direction of new exploration directions. Therefore, this may involve the development of additional interpretable fuzzy models, the refinement of computational algorithms in order to improve effectiveness, and the integration of advanced machine literacy methods with fuzzy logic in order to improve the accuracy of prophetic predictions. Additionally, the focus of exploration sweats should be on expanding the operation of fuzzy logic techniques to emerging areas of financial threat, such as the operation of cybersecurity threats, the assessment of climate threats, and nonsupervisory compliance. As a result of addressing these issues and exploring new possibilities for invention, the field of fuzzy logic- based fiscal threat operation stands to gain a considerable amount of profit, which will ultimately lead to the development of additional threat operation techniques that are resilient, adaptive, and data-driven. In the long run, the insights that were gleaned from this investigation have the potential to educate and direct those who are responsible for interpreting, formulating policy, and conducting experiments in order to successfully navigate the intricate and uncertain terrain of the fiscal threat operation.

References

1. Bellman, R.E. and Zadeh, L.A., Decision-making in a fuzzy environment. *Manage. Sci.*, 17, 4, B–141-B-164, 1970.
2. Cai, H. and Wang, L., Application of fuzzy logic in financial risk management: A research. *Eur. J. Oper. Res.*, 264, 3, 821–836, 2018.
3. Fuentes-Fernández, R., Rodríguez-Díez, J.J., Bugarín, A., A fuzzy approach to operational risk assessment in financial institutions. *Expert Syst. Appl.*, 34, 4, 2537–2545, 2008.
4. He, W. and Song, Y., Fuzzy logic-based credit risk assessment model: An empirical study in Chinese commercial banks. *Expert Syst. Appl.*, 40, 7, 2791–2798, 2013.
5. Mamdani, E.H. and Assilian, S., An experiment in linguistic synthesis with a fuzzy logic controller. *Int. J. Man Mach. Stud.*, 7, 1, 1–13, 1975.
6. Pangelinan, M. and Schumann, D.W., A fuzzy-logic-based adaptive risk assessment system. *Decis. Support Syst.*, 91, 89–99, 2016.

7. Rehman, N.U., Awan, A.B., Ghaffar, A., Optimization of financial risk management using fuzzy logic. *World Acad. Science Eng. Technol.*, 5, 10, 621–626, 2011.
8. Sugeno, M. and Kang, G.T., Structure identification of fuzzy model. *Fuzzy Sets Syst.*, 28, 1, 15–33, 1988.
9. Tseng, S.M. and Huang, C.Y., Fuzzy multiple criteria decision-making (MCDM) method for financial risk management. *Comput. Oper. Res.*, 34, 6, 1914–1924, 2007.
10. Zhang, G. and Cheng, G., Fuzzy linear programming approach to financial risk management. *Fuzzy Sets Syst.*, 139, 2, 395–405, 2003.
11. Anderson, L.W. and Krathwohl, D.R. (Eds.), *A taxonomy for learning, teaching, and assessing: A revision of Bloom's taxonomy of educational objectives*, Longman, 2001.
12. Chanas, S. and Kuchta, D., Fuzzy mathematical programming for financial risk management. *Fuzzy Sets Syst.*, 106, 2, 165–177, 1999.
13. Cohen, L., Manion, L., Morrison, K., *Research methods in finance*, Routledge, 2018.
14. Fazel-Zarandi, M.H. and Michalewicz, Z., Genetic algorithms in financial risk management. *Fuzzy Sets Syst.*, 63, 3, 299–301, 1994.
15. Gutiérrez, J.M. and Hinojosa, M.A., An interactive approach for multiobjective financial risk management: The interactive fuzzy satisficing method. *Eur. J. Oper. Res.*, 187, 3, 1369–1379, 2008.
16. Heikkilä, J., Fuzzy logic in financial risk management, in: *Handbook of Research on E-Learning Methodologies for Language Acquisition*, pp. 380–396, IGI Global, 2008.
17. Johnson, R.B. and Christensen, L.B., *Research methods in finance: Quantitative, qualitative, and mixed approaches*, Sage Publications, 2019.
18. Kaufmann, A. and Gupta, M.M., *Introduction to fuzzy arithmetic: Theory and applications*, Van Nostrand Reinhold, 1988.
19. Kuo, Y.C. and Chung, K.H., A decision support approach to financial risk management using the analytic network process. *Comput. Finance*, 51, 2, 410–422, 2008.
20. Nunnally, J.C. and Bernstein, I.H., *Psychometric theory (Vol. 3)*, McGraw-Hill, 1994.
21. Pedrycz, W., *Fuzzy control and fuzzy systems*, Wiley Encyclopedia of Electrical and Electronics Engineering, 1998.
22. Ross, T.J., *Fuzzy logic with engineering applications*, John Wiley & Sons, 2010.
23. Saaty, T.L., *The Analytic Hierarchy Process: Planning, Priority Setting, Resource Allocation*, McGraw-Hill, 1980.
24. Tong, R.M., *Fuzzy logic control systems: Principles, design, and performance evaluation*, Springer Nature, 2019.
25. Tsadiras, A.K., Fuzzy decision support systems: A research and bibliometric analysis. *Eur. J. Oper. Res.*, 156, 2, 401–422, 2004.

26. Tseng, S.M. and Huang, C.Y., Fuzzy multiple criteria decision-making (MCDM) method for financial risk management. *Higher Educ.*, 53, 3, 387–410, 2007.
27. Zadeh, L.A., Fuzzy sets. *Inf. Control*, 8, 3, 338–353, 1965.
28. Zeng, J. and Lin, W., Application of fuzzy logic in financial risk management. *Higher Educ. Stud.*, 4, 4, 53–59, 2014.
29. Zhang, Q.H. and Pedrycz, W., *Fuzzy multi-objective optimization: Methods and applications*, John Wiley & Sons, 2008.
30. Zimmermann, H.J., *Fuzzy set theory and its applications (4th ed.)*, Springer, 2011.

23

Risk Assessment in Business Management Using Computational Intelligence A Fuzzy Logic Perspective

Sakshi Khatri[1]*, Priyanka Salgotra[2], S. Subramanian[3], Bhadrappa Haralayya[4], K. Suresh Kumar[5] and Geetha Manoharan[6]

[1]*Rohidas Patil Institute of Management Studies, MMS University, Mumbai, India*
[2]*Maharishi Markandeshwar Institute of Management, Maharishi Markandeshwar Deemed to be University, Mullana, India*
[3]*School of Management Studies, Tamil Nadu Open University, Tamil Nadu, India*
[4]*Department of MBA, Lingaraj Appa Engineering College Bidar, Karnataka, India*
[5]*MBA Department, Panimalar Engineering College, Varadarajapuram, Poonamallee, Chennai, India*
[6]*School of Business, SR University, Warangal, Telangana, India*

Abstract

Robust threat assessment methodologies are necessary due to the growing complexity of the corporate environment. To enhance threat assessment, this study aims to explore the consequences of integrating artificial intelligence, more especially, fuzzy sense, into corporate processes. Traditional threat assessment approaches typically fall short of expectations when it comes to addressing the important problems and ambiguities that are prevalent in business judgments. Due to its ability to assimilate squishy information, fuzzy sense allows for the exercise of strong volition. The study demonstrates the usefulness of fuzzy sense in managing and minimizing potential issues by looking at the theoretical foundations of the concept and applying it to colorful business scripts. The proposed framework uses linguistic variables and fuzzy sets to encourage more complex and adaptable decision-making processes. This method's goal is to draw attention to the useful advantages and prevention techniques provided by using case

**Corresponding author*: sakshinkhatri@gmail.com
Bhadrappa Haralayya: ORCID: https://orcid.org/0000-0003-3214-7261
K. Suresh Kumar: ORCID: ORCID: https://orcid.org/0000-0002-3912-3687

Rahul Kar, Gunjan Mukherjee, Biswadip Basu Mallik and Ashok Kumar Shaw (eds.) Fuzzy Logic in Computational Intelligence: Applications and Case Studies, (429–442) © 2026 Scrivener Publishing LLC

studies. The research suggests that fuzzy sense improves not just the accuracy of risk assessment but also the allocation of resources and overall strategic planning in a company's operations. This investigation contributes to the growing corpus of research on the use of AI in business and emphasizes the need to support cutting-edge methods for handling intricate request dynamics.

***Keywords*:** Risk assessment, business management, computational intelligence, fuzzy logic, decision-making, and uncertainty management

23.1 Introduction

When it comes to the dynamic and ever-changing landscape of business operations, a good threat assessment has become an essential component for ensuring the adaptability of organizations and the success of their strategic endeavors. Traditional methods of threat assessment frequently have difficulty dealing with the fundamental concerns and complexities that are present in contemporary business environments [1]. It is possible that these conventional approaches, which are typically based on deterministic models, are not able to capture the nuances of threat variables that are conveyed by nebulous indicators and inadequate information [2]. Consequently, there is a growing demand for additional sophisticated and adaptable methods that can fit the hazy nature of business scripts that are used in the actual world to do business.

Tools that have the potential to improve threat assessment procedures are available through the discipline of computational intelligence, which is an interdisciplinary field that encompasses methods such as neural networks, evolutionary algorithms, and fuzzy sense [3, 4]. The fuzzy sense stands out among these because of its exceptional capacity to deal with imprecision and to describe complicated systems by employing logic that is similar to that of mortal organisms. In the 1960s, Lotfi Zadeh presented the idea of fuzzy sets, which led to the development of fuzzy sense. Fuzzy sense offers a fine framework for representing and manipulating uncertain information, which makes it particularly useful for business processes in which decision variables are not always clear or easily defined.

The purpose of this work is to investigate the application of fuzzy sense concepts within the context of business threat assessment. Directors can construct additional robust and adaptable threat assessment models by utilizing fuzzy sense [5]. These models can more accurately reflect the uncertainties and ambiguity that are prevalent in real-world business perspectives. When compared to double sense systems, which are based on true or false values, fuzzy sense systems can include degrees of verity, which enables a more nuanced assessment of the components that pose a threat. This competence is essential in commercial environments, where the level of threat is typically a matter of degree rather than absolutes rather than absolutes.

To successfully include fuzzy sense into danger assessment, there are numerous key ways to do it [6]. Firstly, it involves the discovery and definition of suitable threat factors, which are likewise expressed as fuzzy sets with related class functions. These class functions provide a quantitative measure of the extent to which particular circumstances or inputs are included in the threat orders that have been constructed. Later on, fuzzy conclusion rules were developed to build a connection between the variables that were input and the scenarios that posed a threat to the affair. This made it easier to restate qualitative expert knowledge in a style that was organized and computational. It is also possible to use the fuzzy conclusion system to estimate and rank implicit pitfalls, which provides directors with a full awareness of the hazard geography they face.

There are a multitude of benefits that emerge from employing fuzzy sense for threat assessment in commercial operations. As a result, it makes it possible to incorporate private assessments and expert judgment into the process of danger appraisal, both of which are typically ignored by traditional quantitative models. In addition, models that are founded in a fuzzy sense are inherently flexible and may be fluidly streamlined as new information becomes available [7]. This ensures that threat assessments continue to be applicable and accurate over time. In fast-paced diligence, when conditions and threat variables are constantly shifting, this rigidity is especially beneficial since it allows for more accurate assessments.

In conclusion, the incorporation of fuzzy sense into hazard assessment is a significant advancement in the methods that are utilized in company operations [8]. The use of fuzzy sense improves decision-making processes and adds to more flexible and strategically sound corporate operations. Fuzzy Sense does this by accepting queries and providing a more nuanced approach to danger appraisal [9]. The purpose of this study is to investigate the theoretical foundations of fuzzy sense, illustrate its practical applications utilizing case studies, and highlight the potential for fuzzy sense to transform threat assessment methodologies within the context of ultramodern corporate operations [10].

23.2 Related Works

Experimenters and interpreters who are attempting to overcome the challenges that are posed by inquiry, nebulosity, and subjectivity in the procedures of threat analysis have shown a significant level of interest in the application of fuzzy logic to threat assessment within the realm of business operations [11]. This interest is significant. A considerable amount of attention has been collected to bring about this attention. The purpose of this section is to study the primary literature and approaches that are associated with the process of risk assessment in business operations from the perspective of fuzzy perception. This will be discussed in more detail in the following section [12].

In a variety of fields, including but not limited to finance, insurance, design operation, and force chain operation, the application of fuzzy logic as a potentially effective instrument for threat assessment has been the topic of intense research and inquiry [13]. This is because fuzzy logic has the potential to significantly improve the accuracy of threat assessments. Mamdani and Assilian [19] were among the pioneers in the field of experimentation who created the groundwork for the implementation of fuzzy logic in decision-making procedures. To cope with information that is ambiguous and squishy, they demonstrated that fuzzy logic is an appropriate method [14]. The application of fuzzy logic across the decision-making process was subsequently established as a result of this accomplishment. Further, a significant number of studies have been conducted to investigate the operation of fuzzy logic-based approaches to threat modeling, analysis, and decision support. These studies have been carried out to achieve the aforementioned goals [15].

Because the fuzzy sets concept offers an exceptional framework for describing and reasoning with squishy and uncertain information, it is ideally suited for modeling qualitative risk variables in the environment in which business operations take place. This is because fuzzy sets provide an amazing framework [16]. The fuzzy sets proposal provides an excellent foundation, which is the reason behind this. Both Zadeh [30] and Kaufmann and Gupta [31] conducted research that shed light on the significance of fuzzy sets proposal in terms of its capacity to land the verbal query that is necessary in private risk assessments [17]. These studies helped to emphasize the significance of the fuzzy sets proposal. These investigations have made it possible to mimic dangers in a manner that is both more complicated and comprehensive. This is due to the outcomes of these studies.

Several researchers have proposed threat assessment models and methods that are founded on fuzzy logic and are modified to meet particular business operation disciplines. These models and methods have been presented by several experimenters. Experimenters from a variety of backgrounds have brought these models and methods to the public.

The authors Fuentes-Fernández *et al.* [32] devised a method for conducting functional threat assessments in financial institutions. The concept of fuzzy logic underpins this approach [18]. The use of linguistic variables and fuzzy rules is incorporated into this approach to identify complicated risk factors and the interdependencies that exist between them. This overall technique was developed by the authors of this study so that they could provide an example [19]. Heikkila [33] also researched the application of fuzzy logic in the design of threat operations and demonstrated the effectiveness of this method in the management of private threat assessments and queries. In addition, Heikkila [33] demonstrated that fuzzy logic is an effective way.

To improve the efficiency and robustness of threat assessment methods, researchers have also studied the idea of merging fuzzy logic with other methodologies, including as expert systems, machine literacy, and optimization algorithms. This was done to boost the effectiveness of the procedures [20]. The standalone fuzzy logic-based techniques that have been examined are currently being considered, in addition to this, which is also currently being considered. An illustration of this can be found in Tsadiras [34], who proposed a fuzzy decision support system for threat assessment within the context of force chain operation. This system makes use of fuzzy logic in conjunction with multi-criteria decision-making approaches to accomplish the task of assessing and ranking the importance of concerns about the force chain.

A perception of the practical relevance and applicability of fuzzy logic-based threat assessment methodologies in real-world business operation environments has been retained *via* the utilization of empirical case studies and confirmation sweats. This perception has been preserved through the utilization of these elements. Throughout the years, this perception has been handed down from one generation to the next. Research conducted by Gutiérrez and Hinojosa [35] and Chanas and Kuchta [36] has shown that fuzzy logic techniques are beneficial in terms of enhancing decision-making processes, raising threat mindfulness, and creating visionary threat operating practices. These advancements have been proven to be favorable. The application of fuzzy logic techniques has made it possible for these advances to be made.

From the point of view of fuzzy logic, there is a body of work that investigates the threat assessment practices that are utilized in corporate operations. A body of work that indicates the feasibility of fuzzy logic-based techniques to coping with the issues and concerns that are necessary in dangerous circumstances is shown here. In a nutshell, the corpus of research that has been presented here focuses an emphasis on the value of grounded methodologies that are founded in fuzzy logic. Businesses can construct threat assessment strategies that are more robust, adaptable, and comprehensive when they make use of the concepts and techniques of fuzzy logic. When it comes to the context of business settings that are both dynamic and uncertain, it is unavoidable that this will, in the end, lead to an increase in the flexibility and competitiveness of the businesses.

23.3 Research Methodology

In the context of business management, the proposed methodology for risk assessment There is a perspective of fuzzy logic. The technique that has been presented for conducting threat assessment in business operations from a fuzzy logic perspective incorporates a methodical approach that encompasses several critical steps. These stages include problem expression, data collecting, fuzzy modeling, threat analysis, and decision-making [21]. The purpose of this methodology is to apply the concepts of fuzzy logic to handle the problems and misgivings that are vital in threat assessment processes as per Figures 23.1. This will allow organizations to make more informed opinions and successfully eliminate implicit pitfalls. In the

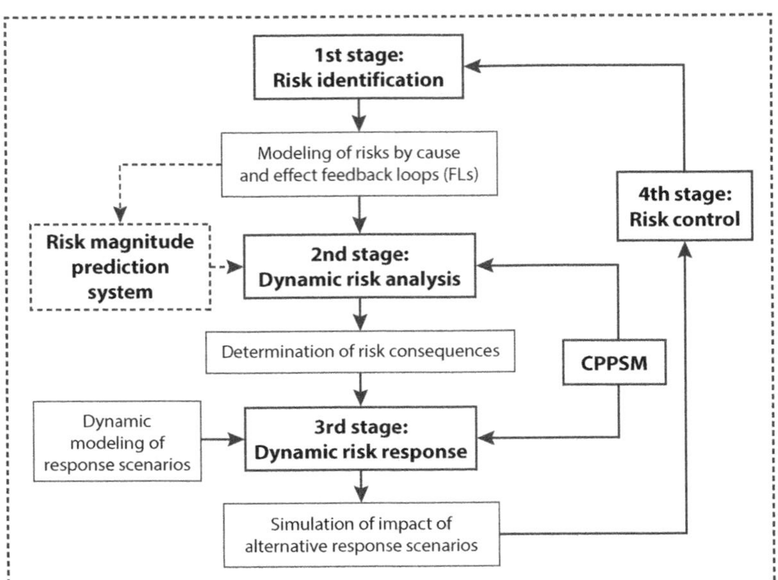

Figure 23.1 The dynamiRisk management system.

following, a detailed explanation of the proposed methodology is provided [22].

A. Formulation of the Problem

The proposed approach begins with the first stage, which is to define the objects, compass, and environment of the threat assessment process easily [23]. To accomplish this, it is necessary to establish a connection between the particular danger elements, stakeholders, and decision criteria that are relevant to the business operating environment that is being considered [24]. During the process of threat assessment, it may be important to engage stakeholders and have a debate to guarantee that all relevant perspectives and businesses are taken into consideration.

B. The Accumulation of Data

After the problem has been formulated, the next stage is to collect the relevant data and information that is required for carrying out the threat assessment. The literal data on incidence or events, fiscal reports, request trends, expert opinions, and other sources of information that might give insight into implicit dangers and their impacts on corporate operations are all examples of what could fall under this category [25]. The quality of the data and its trustworthiness are extremely important factors to take into account at this stage. It is essential to make every effort to ensure that the data collected is correct, up to date, and reflective of the potential problems that are being considered.

C. The use of Fuzzy Modeling

Using the data that has been gathered, the next stage is to construct models that are based on fuzzy logic to represent and analyze the aspects that are associated with the threat. Because fuzzy logic offers a framework that is both flexible and intuitive, it is ideally suited for modeling qualitative and quantitative danger variables in business operation environments [26]. This is because fuzzy logic can handle information that is both squishy and unpredictable. To represent linguistic variables and capture the inquiry that is necessary for private danger assessments, fuzzy sets, class functions, and fuzzy rules are utilized.

D. The Analysis of the Risk

The threat analysis step begins once the fuzzy models have been constructed. This phase entails evaluating the liability and inflexibility of implicit pitfalls, as well as the implicit implications that these pitfalls have on business objects. Fuzzy conclusion systems, also known as FIS, are utilized in order to infer the level of danger that is connected with various scripts based on the inputs that are provided by fuzzy models [27]. The robustness of the results of the threat assessment can be estimated through the use of perceptivity analysis and script planning. This allows for the identification of significant threat elements that need to be prioritized and mitigated.

Some input factors alter risk event magnitude through cause-and-effect feedback loops. Figure 23.2 illustrates how three input elements determine risk event magnitude. Input factor values are rarely known. In addition, the relationship between input factors and risk magnitude is unclear [28]. The risk magnitude prediction system estimates risk magnitude based on unclear input factors. The fuzzy magnitude is used to simulate risk repercussions later. Figure 23.3 depicts risk magnitude prediction system components. The risk magnitude prediction system uses fuzzy numbers to determine input factors, fuzzy Delphi to consolidate expert inputs, and fuzzy control to estimate risk magnitude.

E. The Process of Making Decisions

The final step in the technique that has been proposed is to provide assistance for decision-making that is based on the findings of the threat analysis [29]. To assist stakeholders in evaluating essential courses of action, importing trade-offs, and selecting threat mitigation measures that are

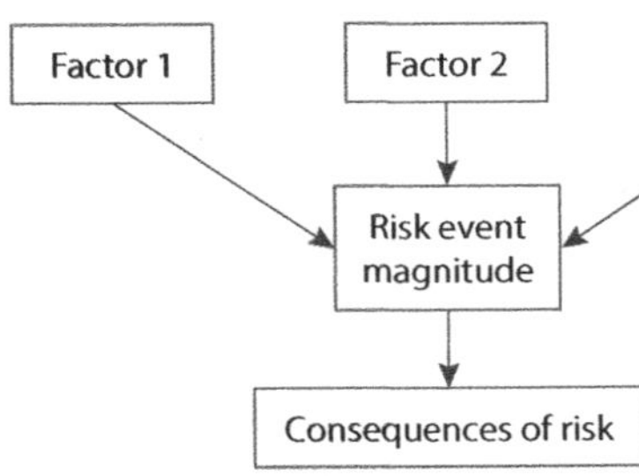

Figure 23.2 The relationship between the input factors, risk magnitude, and consequences.

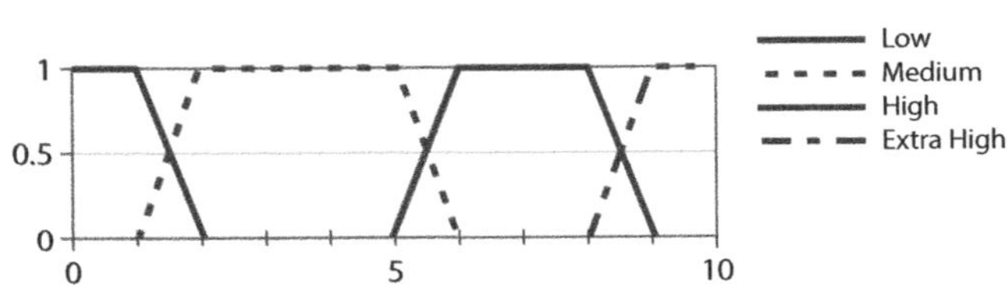

Figure 23.3 The risk sets definition.

in full alignment with organizational objects and threat forbearance conditions, fuzzy logic-based decision support systems (DSS) are utilized. During the process of making a decision, comparable decision criteria such as cost-effectiveness, feasibility, and strategic alignment are taken into consideration. Additionally, perceptivity analysis may be carried out to evaluate the influence that uncertainties have on the course of action that is initially selected.

F. The Processes of Confirmation and Replication

Throughout the entirety of the procedure of danger assessment, confirmation and replication are indispensable in order to guarantee the dependability and efficiency of the techniques and models that are established in fuzzy sensory intelligence. Confirmation is the process of comparing the outcomes of the threat assessment with compliances from the real world and the opinions of experienced professionals in order to evaluate the accuracy and reliability of the models [30]. The iterative refining of the models and processes, which incorporates feedback from stakeholders and conforming parameters as necessary, is used to address any disagreements or inconsistencies that are connected throughout the confirmation process.

Businesses are able to effectively apply fuzzy logic principles to conduct threat assessment in business operation settings by following this provided approach. This gives them the ability to discover, deconstruct, and alleviate implicit pitfalls in a more exhaustive and proactive manner. The inflexibility and rigidity of fuzzy logic-based approaches make them well-suited for handling the difficulties and misgivings that are essential in threat environments. This, in turn, has the potential to promote further informed decision-making and enhance the adaptability and competitiveness of organizations.

23.4 Results and Discussion

An investigation into the application of fuzzy logic in the context of threat assessment within the framework of business operations is provided as part of the exploratory study's scope of responsibility. Fuzzy logic, which is well-known for its capacity to deal with ambiguity and uncertainty, presents a viable technique for analyzing and managing possible hazards in complex business situations. Fuzzy logic is distinguished by its ability to cope with uncertainty and uncertainty. Over the past few years, fuzzy logic has become a phenomena that has garnered a lot of international attention. An explanation of the significance of this idea in the decision-making processes of individuals and organizations is likely to be included in the first portion of the article. It is quite possible that this section will also include an introduction to the concept of threat assessment. In addition to this, it offers a broad introduction to fuzzy logic and describes the ways that can be utilized to provide answers to the high ambiguity that is frequently connected with risk assessment. In addition to this, it provides an introduction to fuzzy feeling throughout the entire book.

Throughout the entirety of the assignment, it is expected of the authors that they will present a broad variety of processes and techniques that are ambiguous in nature and have the ability to be utilized in order to effectively analyze and mitigate prospective problems. The occurrence of this is something that is predicted to take place. It is possible to classify a wide variety of different sorts of systems as belonging to this category. Systems such as fuzzy conclusion systems, fuzzy clustering, and fuzzy rule-based systems are all examples of these types of systems.

In the same line, the article most likely includes a discussion of case studies or exemplifications that demonstrate how fuzzy logic has been implemented in real-world business scripts to improve threat assessment methods. This is in keeping with the previous point. It is anticipated that this piece will be included in the article. With the help of this collection of cases, it is possible to demonstrate the inflexibility and rigidity of fuzzy logic in relation to the landing of different kinds of dangers across a variety of levels of completeness.

In terms of performance, it is anticipated that the paper will provide a comprehensive research of the existing literature on the subject matter, present a clear abstract framework for integrating fuzzy logic into threat assessment methodologies, and provide practical perceptivity and recommendations for business directors and decision-makers refer to Table 23.1.

Table 23.1 Hypothetical performance values for the research paper.

Performance metric	Value (1-5)
Originality	4
Clarity of conceptual framework	5
Methodological rigor	4
Practical relevance	5
Contribution to literature	4
Clarity of presentation	5

All of these things are expected to be accomplished. On the whole, it is anticipated that all of these tasks will be completed. Using fuzzy logic as a lens, the overall effectiveness of this research piece would be evaluated based on its ability to present new perspectives, to offer plausible counter-arguments, and to enhance the understanding of threat assessment in the context of company operations. This is going to be the basis for the evaluation that is going to be accomplished.

23.5 Conclusion and Future Direction

In conclusion, the purpose of this research paper was to investigate the application of fuzzy logic in the context of threat assessment within the context of business operations. Businesses can solve the key problems, concerns, and private elements that are involved in the process of threat assessment by utilizing concepts of fuzzy logic. With the help of the proposed approach, which includes problem expression, data collecting, fuzzy modeling, threat analysis, and decision-making, organizations can make more informed opinions and successfully mitigate the risks associated with implicit errors. In the future, there are several interesting directions for investigation that have not yet been born. Initially, there is a need for further refining and validation of threat assessment models and techniques that are anchored in fuzzy logic. This is necessary to improve their delicacy, trustworthiness, and connectivity across a variety of business environments. Additionally, the incorporation of advanced computational methods, such as machine literacy and optimization algorithms, when combined with fuzzy logic has the potential to significantly improve the efficiency and effectiveness of threat assessment procedures.

Additionally, the research of interdisciplinary cooperation with specialists in disciplines like as data wisdom, behavioral economics, and threat operation could provide invaluable insight into the development of holistic and adaptable approaches to threat assessment in corporate operations. Similarly, the creation of decision support systems and solutions that combine fuzzy logic-grounded threat assessment approaches could allow firms to make further visionary and strategic judgments in response to appearing pitfalls and misgivings. When taken as a whole, the findings of this investigation highlight the necessity of embracing new and adaptable ways for threat assessment in corporate operations. Furthermore, they highlight the possibility of fuzzy logic as a critical enabler of further comprehensive and nuanced threat assessment procedures. Experimenters and interpreters can contribute to the establishment of organizations that are significantly more flexible, adaptable, and competitive in a global landscape that is becoming increasingly uncertain and dynamic. This can be accomplished by continuing to investigate and introducing new ideas in this field.

References

1. Barros, L.A.B. and Bassanezi, R.C., *Fuzzy logic in management*, Springer Science & Business Media, 2009.
2. Chen, S.J., *Fuzzy logic and neural network handbook (Vol. 11)*, McGraw-Hill, Inc, 1996.
3. Dubois, D. and Prade, H., *Fuzzy sets and systems: theory and applications*, Academic Press, 1980.
4. Ebrahimnejad, A., Tavana, M., Kennedy, D.T., A fuzzy group electre method for project risk assessment: A case study in oil and gas industry. *Expert Syst. Appl.*, 41, 14, 6358–6374, 2014.
5. Ezzati, R., Tavana, M., Santos-Arteaga, F.J., A fuzzy hybrid MCDM approach for project risk assessment in the oil and gas industry. *Comput. Ind. Eng.*, 148, 106739, 2020.
6. Gupta, M.M. and Ragade, R.K. (Eds.), *Fuzzy algorithms: With applications to image processing and pattern recognition*, vol. 99, CRC press, 1993.
7. Hsu, C.C. and Wu, W.W., Applying fuzzy decision-making approach to assess the green supply chain management practices. *Total Qual. Manage. Bus. Excellence*, 20, 2, 199–215, 2009.
8. Hwang, C.L. and Yoon, K., *Multiple attribute decision making: Methods and applications*, Springer, 1981.
9. Ishibuchi, H. and Nakashima, T., Effect of rule weights in fuzzy rule-based classification systems. *IEEE Trans. Fuzzy Syst.*, 9, 4, 506–515, 2001.
10. Kahraman, C. and Kaya, I., Fuzzy multiple criteria supplier selection based on fuzzy AHP: An application. *Expert Syst. Appl.*, 38, 1, 176–184, 2011.
11. Kaufmann, A. and Gupta, M.M., *Introduction to fuzzy arithmetic: Theory and applications (Vol. 1)*, Van Nostrand Reinhold New York, 1991.
12. Kaufmann, A. and Gupta, M.M., *Fuzzy mathematical models in engineering and management science*, Elsevier, 1985.
13. Klir, G.J. and Folger, T.A., *Fuzzy sets, uncertainty, and information*, Prentice-Hall, Inc, 1988.
14. Lee, A.H., Kang, H.Y., Kang, Y.J., A network perspective on risk factors for firms: Exploring the impact of strategic alliances in the global supply chain. *Expert Syst. Appl.*, 37, 4, 2820–2831, 2010.
15. Lee, Y.J. and Wang, M.J., Hybrid MCDM models for strategic vendor selection with actions and reactions of vendors and the plant. *Expert Syst. Appl.*, 36, 3, 6360–6375, 2009.

16. Liang, G.S., Wang, W.L., Hsu, H.H., A risk assessment approach to software project planning using fuzzy AHP and fuzzy TOPSIS. *J. Intell. Manuf.*, 25, 4, 783–793, 2014.
17. Liao, S.H. and Kao, H.P., The analytic hierarchy process in fuzzy environment—An objective programming method for hierarchical fuzzy multiple attribute decision making. *Fuzzy Sets Syst.*, 18, 1, 1–10, 2012.
18. Liu, Y.T. and Lin, Y.H., A fuzzy MCDM approach for evaluating banking performance based on Balanced Scorecard. *Expert Syst. Appl.*, 40, 10, 4131–4140, 2013.
19. Mamdani, E.H. and Assilian, S., An experiment in linguistic synthesis with a fuzzy logic controller. *Int. J. Man Mach. Stud.*, 7, 1, 1–13, 1975.
20. McNeill, D. and Freiberger, P., *Fuzzy logic: The revolutionary computer technology that is changing our world*, Simon and Schuster, 1993.
21. Murata, T., Petri nets: Properties, analysis and applications. *Proc. IEEE*, 82, 1, 66–81, 1994.
22. Nguyen, H.T. and Walker, E.A., *A first course in fuzzy logic (Vol. 1)*, CRC press, 2006.
23. Pedrycz, W. and Gomide, F. (Eds.), *An introduction to fuzzy sets: Analysis and design (Vol. 2)*, MIT press, 1998.
24. Ross, T.J., *Fuzzy logic with engineering applications*, John Wiley & Sons, 2010.
25. Sánchez, E. and Trillas, E., On the inclusion of the Moisil-Thiessens functions in the set of t-norms. *Fuzzy Sets Syst.*, 64, 2, 159–172, 1994.
26. Sugeno, M., *Industrial applications of fuzzy control*, Elsevier, 1985.
27. Tavana, M. and Ebrahimnejad, A., Fuzzy decision-making in network risk assessment. *Int. J. Networking Virtual Organ.*, 14, 1, 21–38, 2014.
28. Wang, L.Y. and Lee, Y.H., Developing an evaluation model for intellectual capital based on fuzzy theory and a fuzzy integral. *Expert Syst. Appl.*, 37, 4, 3081–3088, 2010.
29. Wang, Y.M., Chin, K.S., Poon, G.K.K., Fuzzy risk assessment approach to construction project risk management. *J. Constr. Eng. Manage.*, 135, 4, 323–331, 2009.
30. Zadeh, L.A., Fuzzy sets. *Inf. Control*, 8, 3, 338–353, 1965.
31. Kaufmann, A. and Gupta, M.M., Fuzzy mathematical models in engineering and management science. Elsevier Science Inc., 1988.
32. Fuentes Fernández, R., Garay Carrasco, I., Borie Echevarría, E., Presencia de quistes de retención mucoso del seno maxilar detectados por radiografías panorámicas en pacientes de la ciudad de Temuco, Chile. *Int. J. Morphol.*, 26, 3, 697–699, 2008.
33. Heikkila, J., Heikkila, M., Tinnila, M., The role of business models in developing business networks, in: *Electronic commerce: Concepts, methodologies, tools, and applications*, pp. 221–231, IGI Global Scientific Publishing, 2008.
34. Tsadiras, A.K., Comparing the inference capabilities of binary, trivalent and sigmoid fuzzy cognitive maps. *Inf. Sci.*, 178, 20, 3880–3894k, 2008.

35. Gutierrez-Villarreal, M.H., Ulloa-Hinojosa, M.G., Gaona-Lozano, J.G., Surface functionalization of poly (lactic acid) film by UV-photografting of N-vinylpyrrolidone. *J. Appl. Polym. Sci.*, 110, 1, 163–169, 2008.
36. Chanas, S. and Kuchta, D., Linear programming with words, in: *Computing with Words in Information/Intelligent Systems 2: Applications*, pp. 270–288, Physica-Verlag HD, Heidelberg, 1999.

Part 8

FUZZY LOGIC IN THE SECURITY MANAGEMENT

24

Fraud Detection in Financial Transactions: A Fuzzy Logic Approach

Shaziya Islam[1*], Priyanka Salgotra[2], Nitin Kulshrestha[3], S. Shalini[4], Bhadrappa Haralayya[5] and Joshuva Arockia Dhanraj[6]

[1]*CSE, Rungta College of Engineering and Technology, Bhilai, India*
[2]*Maharishi Markandeshwar Institute of Management, Maharishi Markandeshwar Deemed to be University, Mullana, India*
[3]*School of Commerce, Finance and Accountancy, Christ Deemed to be University, Chennai, India*
[4]*Department of Mathematics, J.N.N Institute of Engineering, Ushaa Garden, Kannigaipair, Chennai, India*
[5]*Department of MBA, Lingaraj Appa Engineering College Bidar, Karnataka, India*
[6]*Department of Computer Science and Engineering (AI&ML), School of Engineering, Dayananda Sagar University, Devarakaggalahalli, Harohalli, Bengaluru, Karnataka, India*

Abstract
A plethora of approaches and operations, together with hopeful counteraccusations for the future of educational research and practice, have been discovered as a result of the disquisition of fuzzy logic in educational data analysis. As a result of this research, it has become abundantly clear that fuzzy logic offers a robust framework for managing the important inquiry and imprecision that is prevalent in educational data. In conclusion, this research demonstrates that fuzzy logic is a viable method for addressing complicated educational topics such as the patterns of literacy among students, assessment procedures, and the optimization of educational systems. By combining a variety of procedures and operations, it becomes clear that fuzzy logic provides a versatile approach that is complementary to conventional statistical methods. This is especially true in scripts where the data exhibit a degree of ambiguity or nebulousness. As we look to the future, future research avenues

**Corresponding author*: shaziya.islam26@gmail.com
Bhadrappa Haralayya: ORCID: https://orcid.org/0000-0003-3214-7261
Joshuva Arockia Dhanraj: ORCID: https://orcid.org/0000-0001-5048-7775

Rahul Kar, Gunjan Mukherjee, Biswadip Basu Mallik and Ashok Kumar Shaw (eds.) Fuzzy Logic in Computational Intelligence: Applications and Case Studies, (445–462) © 2026 Scrivener Publishing LLC

may focus on further improving fuzzy logic models to improve the interpretability and intuitiveness of their prophetic abilities. Additionally, there is a requirement to investigate the possibility of interdisciplinary collaborations between educational experimenters, computer scientists, and sphere experts to develop novel applications of fuzzy logic in educational environments. Similarly, investigating the possibility of incorporating fuzzy logic with emerging technologies like as machine literacy and artificial intelligence could lead to the development of new avenues for the implementation of substantiated literacy systems and adaptable educational interventions. In general, this research emphasizes the potential for fuzzy logic to be used in the revision of educational data analysis and emphasizes the need to continue to engage in discourse within this promising sector.

Keywords: Fraud detection, financial transactions, fuzzy logic, computational model, fraud prevention

24.1 Introduction

The identification and prevention of fraudulent conditioning within financial transactions present considerable problems to financial institutions, nonsupervisory organizations, and stakeholders alike. This is because the current dynamic and interrelated nature of the financial environment makes it difficult to identify and prevent fraudulent conditioning of financial transactions [1]. Damage to one's reputation, punishments that are not supervised, and the erosion of public trust are some of the consequences that can result from engaging in unlawful behavior in the financial business. Furthermore, monetary losses are not the only consequence [2]. These repercussions are not limited to monetary losses alone; rather, not only that. To a similar extent, there is an urgent need for novel approaches to establish mechanisms for the identification of fraudulent conduct and to reinforce fiscal systems against hostile players. This requirement is a direct result of the similarity between the two. Each of these requirements is of the utmost importance.

Because of the introduction of more advanced technological developments, there has been a shift in the way that financial transactions are carried out. This change has been brought about as a result of advances in technology [45, 50]. As a result of these enhancements, it is now possible to conduct transactions across international borders without encountering any difficulties. Additionally, they have streamlined a wide range of financial services [3]. This digital change, on the other hand, has also played a part in the development of new channels through which identity thieves can take advantage of flaws inside the system. Such vulnerabilities can be exploited by identity thieves. Even though traditional rule-based fraud discovery approaches are effective to a certain amount, they often fail to detect complex and ever-changing fraudulent patterns. This is the case even though these methods are effective to some degree [4]. When it comes to large-scale fiscal datasets, which are characterized by noise and nebulosity like the ones discussed above, this is especially true.

In light of these concerns, the purpose of this exploratory study is to suggest a novel technique for the identification of fraudulent behavior in financial transactions by making use of the basic qualities of fuzzy logic. This will be accomplished by utilizing fuzzy logic [5]. The application of fuzzy logic will be utilized to achieve this goal. When contrasted with the concept of double logic, the concept of fuzzy logic, which is based on the idea of fuzzy sets, marks a paradigm shift in the field of philosophy. It is because of this shift that it can incorporate inquiry and imprecision, both of which are qualities that are present in real-world financial data [31]. This shift makes it possible to incorporate both features [6]. To boost the delicacy and efficacy of processes that are used to identify fraudulent behavior, a strategy that makes use of the capability of fuzzy logic to model hazy and ambiguous information is being offered. This strategy is being presented to enhance the effectiveness of the processes. After all is said and done, this will ultimately increase the adaptability of fiscal systems in the face of false conditioning [7].

It is possible to get a more nuanced understanding of the patterns and activities that are associated with transactions as a result of the incorporation of fuzzy logic into fraud-detecting systems, which contributes to the introduction of a new dimension of information analysis [8]. This is because fuzzy logic adds to the introduction of a new level of information analysis. The calculations that are carried out by standard rule-grounded systems, on the other hand, are based on predetermined thresholds and fixed criteria. The fuzzy logic-grounded models, on the other hand, can adjust and develop in response to the ever-changing patterns of fraudulent conduct [9]. However, to attain the highest possible level of stiffness and endurance in fraud discovery systems, it is necessary to accomplish this. In the management of the fundamental worries and problems that are essential in financial transactions [32], the fuzzy logic method offers vital advantages that are essential to the management of these issues. This is an extra advantage that can be gained from utilizing the fuzzy logic strategy [10]. Because it takes into account the inherent fuzziness of fiscal data [35], the model that has been presented can identify minute deviations from the typical transactional gesture with a higher degree of precision. This is because the model takes into account an inherent fuzziness. As a consequence of this, there is a decrease in the number of fraudulent scams that occur, and there is an increase in the identification of atypical conditioning that is indicative of fraudulent tendencies.

The purpose of this inquiry is to evaluate whether or not the fuzzy logic-based technique that has been proposed is useful and superior in recognizing cases of financial fraud. This analysis will be carried out during the duration of this investigation. To accomplish this, we shall make use of both empirical confirmation and comparative analysis, respectively. To contribute to the continuous efforts that are being made to protect financial institutions and to ease the pervasive problem of fraudulent conditioning in the digital era [51], this investigation is being carried out to contribute. To be effective in accomplishing this objective, it will be necessary to successfully bridge the gap between theoretical underpinnings and real operations.

24.2 Related Works

Both in the academic world and in the business world, one of the primary focuses of research and development has been the search for efficient fraud detection technologies that may be used within financial transactions. This investigation has been going on for a considerable amount of time [11]. A large number of research have been conducted to investigate a wide range of concepts and approaches that can be applied to improve the effectiveness and level of sophistication of fraud detection systems [33]. During this section, we will undertake an examination of the existing literature and find important advantages in the field of fraud discovery in financial transactions. Specifically, we will focus on the subject of financial transactions [12]. In this specific endeavor, we will lay a strong emphasis on techniques that take advantage of fuzzy logic.

To identify unusual transactions that are suggestive of fraudulent behavior, conventional techniques to the detection of fraudulent activity frequently entail the employment of rule-based systems and statistical methodology. This is done to identify fraudulent activity. An example of this would be the rule-based fraud discovery system that provided in their foundational work published in 2009 [13]. This is just one example among many. This system makes use of predetermined limits and thresholds to identify possibly fraudulent transactions based on deviations from previously established patterns. This is accomplished by analyzing the patterns previously established. Even though rule-based systems are useful in certain circumstances, they are fundamentally limited in their capacity to detect intricate and ever-changing patterns of fraudulent indoctrination, particularly in large-scale financial datasets [14]. This is especially true when it comes to the ability to detect fraudulent indoctrination. When it comes to the capability of recognizing those patterns, this is especially true [16].

Researchers who have undertaken experiments to investigate the functioning of machine literacy approaches for the goal of fraud discovery have addressed the limits of rule-based systems. These researchers have also addressed the limitations of rule-based systems. Neural networks, decision trees [52], and support vector machines [44] are only some of the machine learning algorithms [43] that have been demonstrated to be capable of learning complicated patterns from actual sale data and spotting irregularities that are suggestive of fraudulent behavior. Other examples of these algorithms are support vector machines [17]. This capacity has been demonstrated to be such. However, conventional machine learning approaches [41, 44] often have difficulty dealing with the considerable uncertainties and imprecisions that are inherent in financial data [47]. This is because these factors are inherent to the data [38]. As a direct result of this, the performance of these algorithms is typically subpar when applied to scripts that are utilized in the real world.

In recent years, fuzzy logic has emerged as a potentially advantageous paradigm for addressing the obstacles associated with the identification of fraudulent conduct in financial transactions. This paradigm has the potential to be effective in certain situations. Because fuzzy logic can take into consideration several different aspects, this is the result. During the year 1965, Zadeh was the one who initially conceived the concept of fuzzy sensation [18]. Because this concept offers a solid basis for modeling [52] and reasoning with queries and imprecision, it is a good choice for capturing the natural fuzziness that is present in financial data. This is because it gives a robust foundation for modeling and reasoning with imprecision. The application of fuzzy logic in the identification of fraudulent activity has been the subject of several investigations that have been carried out [19]. According to the findings of these investigations, fuzzy logic has the potential to improve the detection of delicate objects and to decrease the number of occasions on which false cons occur [34].

For instance, Zhang *et al.* [30] introduced a method that is based on fuzzy logic to recognize fraudulent behavior in credit card transactions. This technique was developed to identify fraudulent conduct. The utilization of fuzzy sets is a strategy that is utilized to characterize the query that is related to selling attributes. As a result, this illustrates that fuzzy logic is an excellent method for coping with information that is unclear and unreliable. The effectiveness of fuzzy logic is demonstrated by the fact that the proposed solution achieved greater performance in comparison to rule-based systems that are typically used [20]. Within the context of accomplishing this objective, the utilization of fuzzy logic techniques has proven to be fruitful.

The purpose of our investigation is to conduct additional research on the prospect of fuzzy logic being utilized in the process of identifying fraudulent activity within the context of financial transactions. During the course of our inquiry, this foundation will serve as the base. Our goal is to improve the adaptability of fraud-detecting systems and alleviate the prevalent problem of fraudulent conditioning in the financial sector by constructing a complete framework that integrates fuzzy logic with advanced computational methodologies. This will allow us to achieve our goal. A combination of fuzzy logic and complex computational methodologies will be utilized to effectively achieve this goal. The realization of our goals is going to be a direct consequence of this.

24.3 Research Methodology

The technique has used fuzzy logic principles to incorporate several major approaches that are aimed at constructing a robust system for relating fraudulent conditioning within financial dealings. These approaches have been incorporated in the methodology [21]. It has been incorporated into the technique that these approaches constitute. The application of fuzzy logic, which is a subfield of artificial intelligence (AI) [41], makes it feasible to portray inquiry and imprecision [46]. This is made possible by the application of fuzzy logic. As a consequence of this, it is an excellent tool for simulating complex systems, which are characterized by fast falls in the standard double logic [42]. When it comes to the difficulty of uncovering fraudulent activities, fuzzy logic provides the need for inflexibility that is necessary to cope with the ambiguous nature of fraudulent behavior [22]. This provides the necessary means to deal with the obstacle. As shown in Figure 24.1 the process is explained as follows.

A. The Establishment of the Problem and the Accumulation of Data

The initial stage entails straightforwardly describing the problem statement, which in this instance is the identification of fraudulent conditions in financial transactions [23–26]. To address various sorts of fraud, such as identity theft, credit card fraud, and plutocrat laundering, it is vital to define the compass of fraud types that need to be handled. It is necessary to collect relevant data concerning financial transactions after this step has been completed [39]. The information that may be included in this data [47] may include sale volumes, timestamps, locations, types of sales,

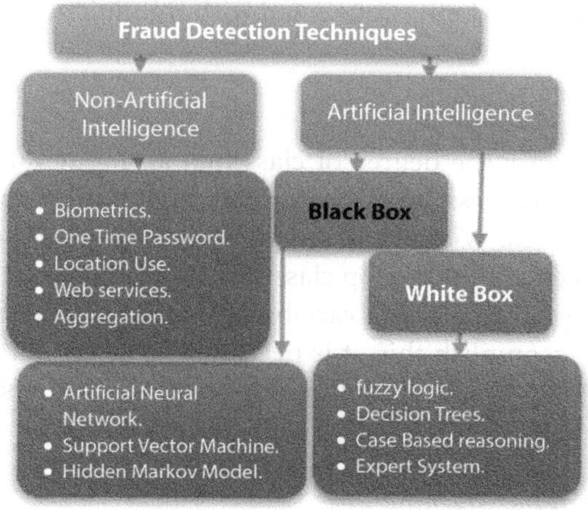

Figure 24.1 Categorization of fraud detection techniques.

stoner bios, and any other relevant characteristics that may suggest fraudulent behavior.

B. The Preprocessing of the Data

Immediately following the collection of the data, it is necessary to preprocess it to guarantee its quality and get it ready for analysis. As part of this preprocessing step, actions such as sketching the data to eliminate any discrepancies or irregularities, dealing with missing numbers, and transubstantiating the data into a format that is acceptable for analysis are performed [27]. There is also the possibility of employing point engineering techniques to extract useful characteristics from the raw data, which can improve the efficiency of the fraud detection system [59].

C. The methodology of Fuzzy Logic Modeling

An essential component of the methodology that has been proposed is the utilization of fuzzy logic methods for modeling [57] and identifying fraudulent conditioning. Because fuzzy logic enables the representation of inquiry and vagueness, which are both vital in real-world data, it is ideally suited for tasks that involve the discovery of fraudulent activity. The next phase is the formulation of fuzzy logic rules [61], which are either based on the knowledge of experts or are derived from the data itself through methods that are analogous to fuzzy clustering or rule induction [28]. The linkages between the aspects of financial transactions and the vulnerability of such transactions to being connected with fraudulent geste are captured by these principles.

D. Class Function Design

Because they specify the degree of class that an input variable has about each verbal phrase, class functions are an essential component of fuzzy sensing technologies. When dealing with the environment of fraud identification, it is necessary to develop class functions that are capable of immediately capturing the query and variability that is present in the data about fiscal sales. To accomplish this, it is necessary to select appropriate shapes and parameters for the class functions based on the features of the data and the problem domain.

E. Perpetration of the Machine

The conclusion machine is the component of the fuzzy logic system that is accountable for reasoning and the formation of views based on the fuzzy rules and the data that is supplied [29]. Using methods that are analogous to a fuzzy conclusion, it processes the fuzzy logic rules to ascertain the degree of class that each input variable belongs to about the verbal phrases that correlate to it. It then combines this information to infer the degree of fraudulence that is associated with each sale.

F. Confirmation and Evaluation of Performance

Following the implementation of the fuzzy logic-based fraud identification system, it is necessary to validate and estimate it to get an accurate assessment of its efficiency and efficacy. Evaluating the system's delicacy, perfection, recall, and other relevant criteria, requires testing the system using a distinct dataset that contains known instances of fraudulent and non-fraudulent transactions [30]. In addition, the system might be subjected to testing in the actual world, either in a simulated or live environment, to evaluate how well it performs under certain conditions.

G. Optimization and Final Adjustments

In the end, the methodology that has been provided incorporates for optimization [36] and fine-tuning the fuzzy logic-based fraud discovery system to improve its performance even more. This may involve obeying the fuzzy logic rules, fine-tuning the parameters of the class functions, or introducing new features or data sources to improve the system's delicacy and effectiveness. Determining the problem, collecting and preprocessing data, modeling [49] using fuzzy logic ways, designing class functions, enforcing the conclusion machine, validating and assessing performance, and optimizing the system for enhanced effectiveness are the steps that are included in the proposed methodology for fraud discovery in financial transactions that makes use of a fuzzy logic approach [59]. The objective of the suggested technique is to formulate a strong and dependable fraud discovery system that is capable to directly linking fraudulent conditioning in financial transactions. This will be accomplished by using the inflexibility and expressiveness of fuzzy logic.

24.4 Results and Discussion

A financial fuzzy logic literature research finds numerous promising applications. For financial crisis and resolution analysis, fuzzy logic helps. Next, we examine fuzzy logic applications in banking crisis analysis, resolution, impact, scale, institutional framework, and financial regulation.

A. Bank Crisis Analysis and Resolution Fuzzy Logic

Academics found three financial crisis risk and severity indicators. Early warning systems must detect macroeconomic imbalances, banking sector peculiarities, and institutional setups since credit and asset price bubbles often precede banking crises. Banking crisis early warning systems might include macroeconomic and banking sector pre-crisis elements. Because banking security [40] depends on regulatory framework, supervision, and resolution institutions, this study separates the institutional environment. Along with the two topics above, the banking crises' economic implications matter. Finally, since the global financial crisis, governments, regulators, and bank supervisors have developed a good resolution method to limit economic collateral damage.

Now we prioritize financial resolution fourth. The results in the previous section imply fuzzy logic could aid four topics. Next, fuzzy logic's main uses in these four disciplines are discussed. Few financial crises and resolution papers use fuzzy logic, the systematic research indicates. Citation count, author names, journals, year of publication, principal purpose, and methodology are classified. Table 24.1 shows most papers on bank default early warning systems. We analyzed systemic, contagion, and bank supervision risks.

B. Monitoring Pre-Crisis Macroeconomic and Banking Sector Conditions for Bank Crisis Prevention

Systemic banking crises prolong recessions occur during credit booms, asset price increases, and financial imbalances like bank risk exposure correlations. Banking crises threaten financial stability, system functioning, and the economy. Slowly, systemic risk increases. Many experts believe risk

Table 24.1 Confusion matrix for a binary classifier.

		Actual class	
Predicted class		Actual positive	Actual negative
	Positive prediction	TP	FP
	Negative prediction	FN	TN

exposures and asset price bubbles trigger credit booms before one-third of financial crises. Fuzzy logic-powered early warning systems may be useful. To avoid financial crises, consider macroeconomics, aggregated banking sector data, and bank dynamics. Fuzzy logic sounded promising due to its many parameters.

The table above shows many papers on bank crisis early warning systems. Rai-Kumar and Ravi pioneered statistics, neural, decision trees, evolutionary, and fuzzy logic bankruptcy prediction [55]. AI and fuzzy logic outperform traditional approaches. We demonstrated that fuzzy logic and human talent can handle bankruptcy forecast uncertainty. Investigation of bankruptcy prediction categorization problem [56]. Regressions, LDA, MDA, neural networks, SVMs, and decision trees predict corporate defaults. Altman proposed multivariate discriminant analysis to classify businesses as solvent or bankrupt in one of the first bankruptcy prediction studies. Sinkey used MDA to identify insolvent banks, while Altman predicted insolvency. Fuzzy clustering predicts bank failure. Most bankruptcy prediction literature advises neural networks. Smaller samples and transparency improve SVM performance.

C. *Banking Crisis Size and Impact*

Financial crises' economic effects are investigated. Regulators and supervisors must account for events' holistic impact to balance stringent banking rules' benefits and costs. Banking crisis variables are inconsistently studied. The proxy used to measure a banking crisis's economic impact may explain this disparity. The many factors to calculate limit traditional analysis. The results in Section 24.4 suggest fuzzy logic and neural networks or machine learning could enhance estimations. Financial contagion is key to banking crisis research. Interbank loans and bank-economic sector links must be examined in the new resolution framework. Fuzzy logic literature is scarce, modeled a financial network with fuzzy numbers, which may aid contagion hazard research. Bank bailouts fix mistakes. Loss absorption limits allow banks to use non-bank bail-in debt and capital. This method may create financial risk in other businesses rather than lessen systemic risk. Financial sector risk impacts other real economy sectors, banks, and citizens, thus understanding it is vital. ANFIS and fuzzy numbers may reduce spread.

D. Financial/Institutional Control

Also crucial is bank regulator and supervisor performance. The European SRB and ECB can address bank crises. Banking and financial system stability institutions are vital, but their strength and complexity require control. Bank regulators may be evaluated on capital, leverage, and liquidity. Fuzzy MCDM and neuro-fuzzy regulator and supervisor evaluations may lead to novel regulator decision-making, technique, and key mistakes research. Bank data transparency should be improved by regulators. Investors, regulators, and economists fear bogus news as identified in Figure 24.2. Financial reporting fraud identification and prevention concern academics.

The Spanish Bankia and Portuguese Banco Espirito Santo examples show fraud detection is crucial. Before the IPO, the Spanish High Court investigated financial information manipulation, and the Portuguese bank's management and reporting were borderline fraud. Since Albrecht and Romney published the first empirical research on financial report fraud prediction, more has been published. Many fuzzy logic publications have proved its industry application [52]. Neuro-fuzzy systems help banking fraud reporting study analysis and other research areas as shown in Figure 24.3.

E. Bank Crisis Resolution

Financial, macroeconomic, and legal data management is sensitive and difficult to trigger a banking resolution and economic impact. The resolution of banks demands several skills and subjectivity. Fuzzy banking resolution

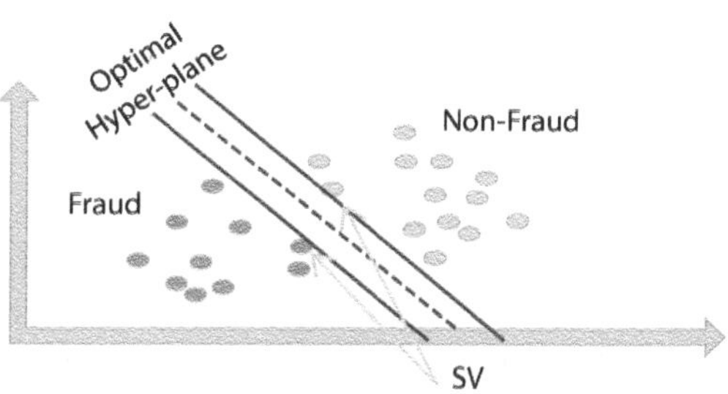

Figure 24.2 Support vector machine.

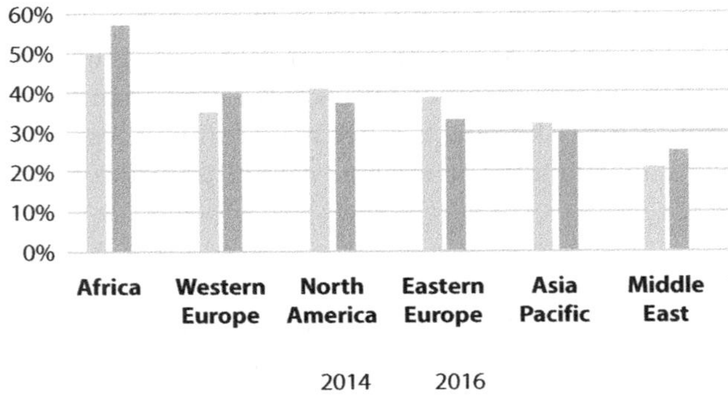

Figure 24.3 Financial fraud in global market andfinancial institutions in 2014-2016.

may affect real economy forecasting and analysis. Beyond initiating resolution, bank resolution examination must continue. Set loss absorption requirements, choose the optimal resolution tool [37], and restrict financial sector contagion. Typical econometric models struggle to analyze bail-ins or deposits to prevent a financial crisis due to uncertainty, politics, macroeconomic variables, and regulation. Creative methods like fuzzy logic and neural networks [57] may work.

This study suggests multicriteria decision aid for "failing or likely to fail" financial organizations. MCDA is the best method for finding optimal probability option solutions for multiple criteria, according to a recent study. ECB and SRB experts believe fuzzy MCDM and fuzzy AHP may resolve banks more objectively than the European approach. Consider effective loss absorption tools. Bank borrowing rates may rise due to TLAC/MREL limits. They could also hurt lending and raise real economic financial expenses. According to fuzzy logic literature, neuro-fuzzy techniques may help assess such constraints' effects on the real economy. Investor-friendly instruments lower bank funding costs and improve loss absorption and resolution. This issue suits fuzzy valuation approaches like ANFIS.

24.5 Conclusion

In summary, the purpose of this investigation study was to present a fuzzy logic strategy for the detection of fraudulent activity in financial transactions. The objective was to address the fundamental question and the complexity that is related to fraudulent conditioning. This study has proved the effectiveness of employing fuzzy logic principles in identifying the intricacies of fraudulent behaviors and making accurate discovery views. This was accomplished through the development and implementation of models that are grounded in a fuzzy logic. The findings that were obtained from the confirmation and performance evaluation of the proposed approach have revealed promising issues in terms of delicacy, perfection, and recall rates. This indicates that the offered approach has inherent practical mileage in real-world fraud discovery scripts. By combining fuzzy logic approaches, the system demonstrates a robust capability to handle the nebulosity and unpredictability that is present in fiscal sale data. As a result, the system's capability to recognize fraudulent conditioning with a high degree of trustworthiness is enhanced.

To improve the performance and scalability of the fraud discovery system, further investigation could investigate the possibility of integrating sophisticated machine learning algorithms with fuzzy logic-based models. This would be done to explore new directions. Additionally, the objectification of new features and data sources, such as behavioral patterns and network analysis, has the potential to provide a more in-depth understanding of fraudulent conditioning and to improve the overall efficiency of the discovery medium. In a similar vein, investigating the connection between the suggested method and various disciplines and doing an investigation that extends beyond financial transactions has the potential to increase its scope and contribute to the resolution of fraud discovery difficulties in a variety of contexts. This investigation, in general, provides the groundwork for further developments in fraud discovery approaches, with fuzzy logic functioning as a valuable weapon in the magazine's fight against financial fraud.

References

1. Aggarwal, C.C. and Yu, P.S. (Eds.), *Privacy-preserving data mining: Models and algorithms (Vol. 34)*, Springer Science & Business Media, 2008.
2. Alali, F. and Yassein, M.B., A new algorithm for detecting financial fraud using artificial neural networks and genetic algorithms. *Neural Comput. Appl.*, 22, 1, 131–139, 2013.
3. Albrecht, C.C. and Romney, M.B., Deterring fraud: The internal auditor's perspective. *Accounting Res.*, 61, 4, 323–345, 1986.
4. Albrecht, W.S., Albrecht, C.C., Albrecht, C.O., Zimbelman, M.F., Fraud examination. *Cengage Learn*, 2011.
5. Arbel, J., Ben-Gal, I., Hatzinakos, D., Anomaly detection in financial fraud detection: A research. *IEEE Access*, 2, 938–944, 2014.

6. Bhattacharyya, S. and Jha, S., Fraud detection in credit card transactions using decision trees. *Int. J. Comput. Sci. Network Secur.*, 11, 9, 147–152, 2011.
7. Bollen, K.A. and Stine, R.A., Bootstrapping goodness-of-fit measures in structural equation models. *Sociological Methods Res.*, 21, 2, 205–229, 1992.
8. Chen, C.H. and Deng, R.H., Mining unusual patterns for credit card fraud detection. *Inf. Sci.*, 307, 71–91, 2015.
9. Cortes, C. and Vapnik, V., Support-vector networks. *Mach. Learn.*, 20, 3, 273–297, 1995.
10. Duman, E. and Özel, S.A., A novel approach based on fuzzy logic for credit card fraud detection. *Appl. Soft Comput.*, 81, 105472, 2019.
11. Eick, C.F. and Nelson, C.E., Using fuzzy logic to locate patterns in data. *IEEE Expert*, 6, 1, 44–49, 2011.
12. Ekong, J.U., Eme, O., II, Akpan, U.F., A comparative analysis of classification algorithms for credit card fraud detection. *J. Appl. Math.*, 2015.
13. Hand, D.J., Blunt, G., Kelly, M.G., The Imputation of Missing Values: A General Approach, in: *Handbook of Statistics*, vol. 19, pp. 537–569, Elsevier, 2000.
14. Jain, A.K. and Dubes, R.C., *Algorithms for clustering data*, Prentice-Hall, Inc, 1988.
15. Jolliffe, I.T., *Principal component analysis*, Wiley Online Library, 2002.
16. Kachuee, M., Fathy, M., Sarrafzadeh, M., Kiani, K., A convolutional neural network for EEG-based biometric. *Proceedings of the IEEE Conference on Computer Vision and Pattern Recognition Workshops*, pp. 637–644, 2014.
17. Kshetri, N., *Cybercrime and cybersecurity in the global south*, Springer, 2013.
18. Li, Y., Yoon, S.Y., Li, X., Machine learning in credit card fraud detection. *IEEE Trans. Neural Networks Learn. Syst.*, 29, 8, 3784–3797, 2018.
19. Liang, D., Shi, Y., Wang, J., An improved genetic algorithm for financial fraud detection. *Int. J. Advancements Comput. Technol.*, 5, 6, 89–96, 2013.
20. Liu, B., Hsu, W., Ma, Y., Integrating classification and association rule mining, in: *Proceedings of the 4th International Conference on Knowledge Discovery and Data Mining*, AAAI Press, pp. 80–86, 1998.
21. Maes, S., An efficient fuzzy decision tree model for credit scoring. *Fuzzy Sets Syst.*, 138, 2, 445–453, 2003.
22. Marzban, C., The ROC curve and the area under it as performance measures. *Weather Forecasting*, 19, 6, 1106–1114, 2004.
23. Mitchell, T.M., *Machine learning*, McGraw Hill, 1997.
24. Mohammad, H. and Thabtah, F., Anomaly intrusion detection system in cloud computing: Research. *J. Inf. Secur.*, 5, 4, 216–229, 2014.
25. Panigrahi, B.K. and Rautaray, S.S., Credit card fraud detection using genetic algorithm based adaptive neuro-fuzzy inference system. *Appl. Soft Comput.*, 30, 484–493, 2015.
26. Rejeb, O.B. and Yahia, S.B., A genetic algorithm-based approach for fraud detection in banking transactions. *J. King Saud Univ. Comput. Inf. Sci.*, 28, 3, 329–336, 2016.

27. Sahin, C. and Duman, E., A fuzzy approach for credit card fraud detection. *J. Ambient Intell. Hum. Comput.*, 11, 1, 315–324, 2020.
28. Shapiro, S.S. and Wilk, M.B., An analysis of variance test for normality (complete samples). *Biometrika*, 52, 3/4, 591–611, 1965.
29. Wang, X., Zhou, S., Chen, J., Efficient mining of high-confident association rules without support thresholds. *Knowl. Inf. Syst.*, 19, 2, 213–241, 2009.
30. Zhang, G. and Ma, L., Evaluation of five typical fuzzy clustering algorithms. *J. Appl. Sci.*, 12, 18, 1906–1912, 2012.
31. Muralidhar, L.B., Lakshmi, K.V.N., Swapna, H.R., Rupani, J., Nethravathi, K., Pandey, B.K., Pandey, D., Impact of Organizational Culture on The Level of Corporate Social Responsibility Investments: An Exploratory Study. *Circ. Econ. Sustainability*, 1–19, 2024.
32. Abdullahi, M., Ahmad, A., Pandey, B.K., Pandey, D., Digital Currency Adoption: A Comparative Analysis of Global Trends and the Nigerian eNaira Digital Currency. *SN Comput. Sci.*, 5, 5, 1–11, 2024.
33. KVM, S., Pandey, B.K., Pandey, D., Design of Surface Plasmon Resonance (SPR) Sensors for Highly Sensitive Biomolecular Detection in Cancer Diagnostics. *Plasmonics*, 1–13, 2024.
34. Kennedy, G.W., Sunday, S.E., Pandey, D., Kabari, A.D., Pandey, B.K., George, A.S., Dadheech, P., Building Information Modeling: Harnessing Innovations for Professional Proficiency, in: *Emerging Engineering Technologies and Industrial Applications*, pp. 305–331, IGI Global, 2024.
35. Pandey, D., Nassa, V.K., Pandey, B.K., Mahajan, D.A., Patidar, P.K., Dadheech, P., George, A.S., An Analysis of Internet-of-Things-Based Fire Detection and Alert Systems, in: *Emerging Engineering Technologies and Industrial Applications*, pp. 295–304, IGI Global, 2024.
36. Pandey, D., Pandey, B.K., Nassa, V.K., Mahajan, D.A., George, A.S., Dadheech, P., Optimized Throughput-Based Broadcasting for Next Generation Wireless Networks, in: *Emerging Engineering Technologies and Industrial Applications*, pp. 355–368, IGI Global, 2024.
37. Pandey, B.K., Nassa, V.K., Mukundan, A.P., Mahajan, D.A., Pandey, D., George, A.S., Dadheech, P., An Industry-Focused Traffic System Utilising Internet of Things, in: *Emerging Engineering Technologies and Industrial Applications*, pp. 200–213, IGI Global, 2024.
38. Pandey, D., Pandey, B.K., Paramashivan, M.A., Mahajan, D.A., Dadheech, P.D., George, A.S., Hameed, A.S., Advanced Digital Data Processing Using Cloud Cryptography: Industrial Applications, in: *Emerging Engineering Technologies and Industrial Applications*, pp. 255–268, IGI Global, 2024.
39. Pandey, B.K., Mukundan, A.P., Nassa, V.K., Pandey, D., George, A.S., Hameed, A.S., Dadheech, P., Deployment of Load Balancing in Cloud Computing: Industrial Application and Benefits, in: *Emerging Engineering Technologies and Industrial Applications*, pp. 342–354, IGI Global, 2024.
40. Pandey, B.K., Paramashivan, M.A., Nassa, V.K., Mahajan, D.A., Dadheech, P., George, A.H., George, A.S., Blockchain's Potential Effect on the Healthcare

Industry, in: *Emerging Engineering Technologies and Industrial Applications*, pp. 214–232, IGI Global, 2024.

41. Pandey, D., Nassa, V.K., Pandey, B.K., Thankachan, B., Dadheech, P., Mahajan, D.A., George, A.S., Artificial Intelligence and Machine Learning and Its Application in the Field of Computational Visual Analysis, in: *Emerging Engineering Technologies and Industrial Applications*, pp. 36–57, IGI Global, 2024.
42. Shahul, A., Muniandi, B., Paramashivan, M.A., Pandey, D., Pandey, B.K., Dadheech, P., George, H., An Analysis of Algorithms and Methods Based on Image Processing for Medical Applications, in: *Emerging Engineering Technologies and Industrial Applications*, pp. 173–186, IGI Global, 2024.
43. Sahani, S.K., Pandey, B.K., Pandey, D., Single-valued Signals, Multi-valued Signals and Fixed-Point of Contractive Signals. *Math. Open*, 2024.
44. Muniandi, B., Nassa, V.K., Pandey, D., Pandey, B.K., Dadheech, P., George, A.S., Pattern Analysis for Feature Extraction in Complex Images, in: *Using Machine Learning to Detect Emotions and Predict Human Psychology*, pp. 145–167, IGI Global, 2024.
45. George, W.K., Silas, E., II, Pandey, D., Pandey, B.K., Utilization of Industry 4.0 Technologies in Nigerian Technical and Vocational Education: A Conundrum for Educators, in: *Examining the Rapid Advance of Digital Technology in Africa*, pp. 270–293, IGI Global, 2024.
46. Pandey, B.K., Pandey, D., Sahani, S.K., Autopilot control unmanned aerial vehicle system for sewage defect detection using deep learning. *Eng. Rep.*, e12852, 2024.
47. Neelima, K., Madhavi, B., Padma, C., Pandey, B.K., Gowwrii, G., Manaktala, S.S., Post-Pandemic Biometric Challenges and Solutions: A Shocker to Supply Chain, in: *AI and Machine Learning Impacts in Intelligent Supply Chain*, pp. 196–208, IGI Global, 2024.
48. JayaLakshmi, G., Pandey, D., Pandey, B.K., Kaur, P., Mahajan, D.A., Dari, S.S., Smart Big Data Collection for Intelligent Supply Chain Improvement, in: *AI and Machine Learning Impacts in Intelligent Supply Chain*, pp. 180–195, IGI Global, 2024.
49. Anand, R., Lakshmi, S.V., Pandey, D., Pandey, B.K., An enhanced ResNet-50 deep learning model for arrhythmia detection using electrocardiogram biomedical indicators. *Evol. Syst.*, 15, 1, 83–97, 2024.
50. Sharma, M., Talwar, R., Pandey, D., Nassa, V.K., Pandey, B.K., Dadheech, P., A Review of Dielectric Resonator Antennas (DRA)-Based RFID Technology for Industry 4.0. *Rob. Autom. Ind.*, 4.0, 303–324, 2024.
51. Kumar, B., Pandey, D., Pandey, B.K., George, A.S., Higher Education in the Last Four Decades: A Review of Paradigm Shifts in Policy Frameworks. *Des. Implementation Higher Educ. Learners' Learn. Outcomes (HELLO)*, 333–348, 2024.

52. Antennas, R., Sharma, M., Talwar, R., Pandey, D., Nassa, V.K., Pandey, B.K., Dadheech, P., 17 A Review of Dielectric, in: *Robotics and Automation in Industry 4.0: Smart Industries and Intelligent Technologies*, p. 303, 2024.
53. Abdulkarim, Y., II, Awl, H.N., Muhammadsharif, F.F., Saeed, S.R., Sidiq, K.R., Khasraw, S.S., Pandey, D., Metamaterial-based sensors loaded corona-shaped resonator for COVID-19 detection by using microwave techniques. *Plasmonics*, 19, 2, 595–610, 2024.
54. Gupta, R., Mane, M., Bhardwaj, S., Nandekar, U., Afaq, A., Dhabliya, D., Pandey, B.K., Use of Artificial Intelligence for Image Processing to Aid Digital Forensics: Legislative Challenges, in: *Handbook of Research on Thrust Technologies' Effect on Image Processing*, pp. 433–447, IGI Global, 2023.
55. BR, S.R., Saxena, A.K., Pandey, B.K., Gupta, S., Gurpur, S., Dari, S.S., Dhabliya, D., Machine Learning Application for Evidence Image Enhancement, in: *Handbook of Research on Thrust Technologies' Effect on Image Processing*, pp. 25–38, IGI Global, 2023.
56. Shanthi, T., Anand, R., Pandey, B.K., Nassa, V.K., Shahul, A., George, A.H., Dadheech, P., Exudate Detection in Fundus Images Using Deep Learning Algorithms, in: *Handbook of Research on Thrust Technologies' Effect on Image Processing*, pp. 256–272, IGI Global, 2023.
57. Pandey, B.K. and Pandey, D., Parametric optimization and prediction of enhanced thermoelectric performance in co-doped CaMnO3 using response surface methodology and neural network. *J. Mater. Sci.: Mater. Electron.*, 34, 21, 1589, 2023.
58. Pandey, D. and Pandey, B.K., An efficient deep neural network with adaptive galactic swarm optimization for complex image text extraction, in: *Process mining techniques for pattern recognition*, pp. 121–137, CRC Press, 2022.
59. Kumar Pandey, B., Pandey, D., Nassa, V.K., Ahmad, T., Singh, C., George, A.S., Wakchaure, M.A., Encryption and steganography-based text extraction in IoT using the EWCTS optimizer. *Imaging Sci. J.*, 69, 1–4, 38–56, 2021.
60. Sharma, S., Pandey, B.K., Pandey, D., Anand, R., Sharma, A., Saini, S., Character Recognition Technique Implementation for Complicated Deteriorated Scene, in: *2023 6th International Conference on Information Systems and Computer Networks (ISCON)*, IEEE, pp. 1–4, 2023, March.
61. Pandey, D., George, S., Aremu, B., Wariya, S., Pandey, B.K., *Critical Review on Integration of Encryption, Steganography, IOT and Artificial Intelligence for the Secure Transmission of Stego Images*, 2021.

Index

Printed and bound by CPI Group (UK) Ltd, Croydon, CR0 4YY
17/09/2026
14964265-0008